CJ[5]

CRIMINAL JUSTICE

Larry K. Gaines
California State University, San Bernardino

Roger LeRoy Miller
Institute for University Studies, Arlington, Texas

CENGAGE

Australia • Brazil • Mexico • Singapore • United Kingdom • United States

CENGAGE

CJ5
Larry Gaines, Roger LeRoy Miller

Senior Vice President, Higher Ed Product, Content, and Market Development: Erin Joyner

Product Team Manager: Carolyn Henderson-Meier

Content Developer: Jessica Alderman

Product Assistant: Megan Nauer

Senior Marketing Manager: Mark Linton

Marketing Coordinator: Alex Rainford

Senior Content Project Manager: Martha Conway

Senior Art Director: Bethany Bourgeois

Text Designer: Tippy McIntosh

Cover Designer: Lisa Kuhn, Curio Press, LLC / Chris Miller, Cmiller Design

Cover Image: YAY Media AS / Alamy Stock Photo

Design Images: icons, bearsky23/Shutterstock.com; scale and balance icon, bearsky23/Shutterstock.com; highlighter elements, schab/Shutterstock.com

Intellectual Property Analyst: Alexandra Ricciardi

Intellectual Property Project Manager: Nick Barrows

Production Service: SPi Global

Library of Congress Control Number: 2017956989

Student Edition ISBN: 978-1-337-40248-4
Student Edition with MindTap ISBN: 978-1-337-40247-7

Cengage
20 Channel Center Street
Boston, MA 02210
USA

Printed in the United States of America
Print Number: 01 Print Year: 2018

GAINES / MILLER

CJ5

BRIEF CONTENTS

YAY Media AS / Alamy Stock Photo

CONTENTS

Part 1
THE CRIMINAL JUSTICE SYSTEM

ArtOlympic/Shutterstock.com

Part 2 THE POLICE AND LAW ENFORCEMENT

Eduardo Munoz Alvarez/Getty Images News/Getty Images

Part 3
CRIMINAL COURTS

trekandshoot/Shutterstock.com

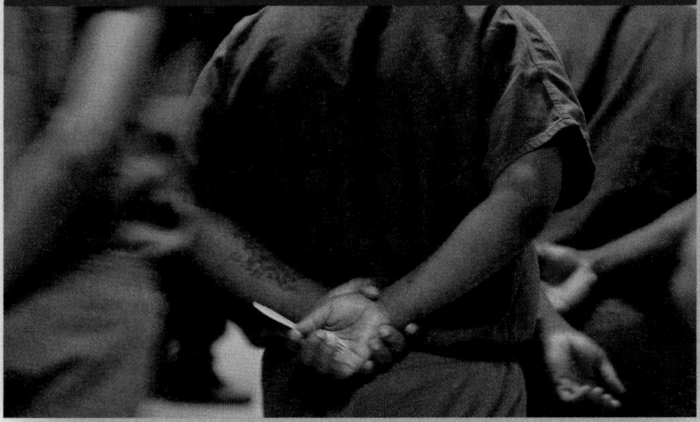
AP Images/Julie Jacobson

Creativa/Shutterstock.com

SKILL PREP

A Study Skills Module

Welcome!

With this course and this textbook, you've begun what we hope will be a fun, stimulating, and thought-provoking journey into the world of criminal justice.

In this course, you will learn all the basics about crime, law enforcement, the court system, corrections, and other special issues like justice for juveniles, homeland security, and cyber crime. Knowledge of these basics will get you well on your way to a great future in criminal justice.

We have developed this study skills module to help you gain the most from this course and this textbook. Whether you are a recent high school graduate or an adult returning to the classroom after a few years, you want RESULTS when you study. You want to be able to understand the issues and ideas presented in the textbook, talk about them intelligently during class discussions, and remember them as you prepare for exams and papers.

This module is designed to help you develop the skills and habits you'll need to succeed in this course. With tips on how to be more engaged when you study, how to get the most out of your textbook, how to prepare for exams, and how to write papers, this guide will help you become the best learner you can be!

Monkey Business Images/Shutterstock.com

STUDY PREP

What does it take to be a successful student? Although you may think success depends on how naturally smart you are, the truth is that successful students aren't born, they're made. Even if you don't consider yourself "book smart," you can do well in this course by developing study skills that will help you understand, remember, and apply key concepts.

Reading for Learning

Your textbook is the foundation for information in a course. It contains key concepts and terms that are important to your understanding of the subject. For this reason, it is essential that you develop good reading skills. As you read your textbook with the goal of learning as much of the information as possible, work on establishing the following habits:

FOCUS

Make an effort to focus on the book and tune out other distractions so that you can understand and remember the information it presents.

TAKE TIME

To learn the key concepts presented in each chapter, you need to read slowly, carefully, and with great attention.

REPEAT

To read for learning, you have to read your textbook a number of times. Follow a preview-read-review process:

1. **PREVIEW: Look over the chapter title, section headings, and highlighted or bold words. This will give you a good preview of important ideas in the chapter.** Notice that each major section heading in this textbook has one or more corresponding **Learning Objectives.** By turning headings or subheadings in all of your textbooks into questions—and then answering them—you will increase your understanding of the material. Note graphs, pictures, and other visual illustrations of important concepts.

2. **READ: During this phase, it is important to read with a few questions in mind:** What is the main point of this paragraph or section? What does the author want me to learn from this? How does this relate to what I read before? Keeping these questions in mind will help you be an attentive reader who is actively focusing on the main ideas of the passage.

   It is helpful to take notes while reading in detail. You can mark your text or write an outline, as explained next. Taking notes will help you read actively, identify important concepts, and remember them. Then when it comes time to review for the exam, the notes you've made will make your studying more efficient.

3. **REVIEW: Review each section of the text and the notes you made, asking this question: What was this section about?** You'll want to answer the question in some detail, readily identifying the important points. Use the Learning Objectives in the text to help focus your review.

QUICK TIP! Tear out the Chapter Review cards in the back of the textbook for on-the-go review!

A reading group is a great way to review the chapter. After completing the reading individually, group members should meet and take turns sharing what they learned. Explaining the material to others will reinforce and clarify what you already know. Getting a different perspective on a passage will increase your knowledge, since different people will find different things important during a reading.

Diego Cervo/Shutterstock.com

Take Notes

Being *engaged* means listening to discover (and remember) something. One way to make sure that you are listening attentively is to take notes. Doing so will help you focus on the professor's words and will help you identify the most important parts of the lecture.

The physical act of writing makes you a more efficient learner. In addition, your notes provide a guide to what your instructor thinks is important. That means you will have a better idea of what to study before the next exam if you have a set of notes that you took during class.

Make an Outline

As you read through each chapter of your textbook, you might want to make an outline—a simple method for organizing information. You can create an outline as part of your reading or at the end of your reading. Or you can make an outline when you reread a section before moving on to the next one. The act of physically writing an outline for a chapter will help you retain the material in this text and master it.

To make an effective outline, you have to be selective. Your objectives in outlining are, first, to identify the main concepts and, then, to add the details that support those main concepts.

Your outline should consist of several levels written in a standard format. The most important concepts are assigned Roman numerals; the second most important, capital letters; and the third most important, numbers. Here is a quick example:

I. What Is the Criminal Justice System?
   A. The Purpose of the Criminal Justice System
      1. Controlling and Preventing Crime
      2. Maintaining Justice
   B. The Structure of the Criminal Justice System
      1. Law Enforcement
      2. The Courts
      3. Corrections
   C. The Criminal Justice Process
      1. The Assembly Line
      2. The Formal Criminal Justice Process
      3. The Informal Criminal Justice Process

Mark Your Text

If you own your own textbook for this course, you can greatly improve your learning by marking your text. By doing so, you will identify the most important concepts of each chapter, and at the same time, you'll be making a handy study guide for reviewing material at a later time. Marking allows you to become an active participant in the mastery of the material. Researchers have shown that the physical act of marking, just like the physical acts of note-taking during class and outlining, increases concentration and helps you better retain the material.

WAYS OF MARKING

The most common form of marking is to underline important points. The second most commonly used method is to use a felt-tipped highlighter, or marker, in yellow or some other transparent color. Put a check mark next to material that you do not understand. Work on better comprehension of the checkmarked material after you've finished the chapter. Marking also includes circling, numbering, using arrows, jotting brief notes, or any other method that allows you to remember things when you go back to skim the pages in your textbook prior to an exam.

> Researchers have shown that the physical act of marking, just like the physical acts of note-taking during class and outlining, increases concentration and helps you better retain the material.

TWO POINTS TO REMEMBER WHEN MARKING

- **Read one section at a time before you do any extensive marking.** You can't mark a section until you know what is important, and you can't know what is important until you read the whole section.
- **Don't overmark.** Don't fool yourself into thinking that you have done a good job just because each page is filled up with arrows, circles, and underlines. The key to marking is selective activity. Mark each page in a way that allows you to see the most important points at a glance. You can follow up your marking by writing out more in your subject outline.

Try These Tips

Here are a few more hints that will help you develop effective study skills.

- **Do schoolwork as soon as possible after class.** The longer you wait, the more likely you will be distracted by television, video games, texts from friends, or social networking.
- **Set aside time and a quiet, comfortable space where you can focus on reading.** Your school library is often the best place to work. Set aside several hours a week of "library time" to study in peace and quiet. A neat, organized study space is also important. The only work items that should be on your desk are those that you are working on that day.
- **Reward yourself for studying!** Rest your eyes and your mind by taking a short break every twenty to thirty minutes. From time to time, allow yourself a break for doing something else that you enjoy. These interludes will refresh your mind, give you more energy required for concentration, and enable you to study longer and more efficiently.
- **To memorize terms or facts, create flash (or note) cards.** On one side of the card, write the question or term. On the other side, write the answer or definition. Then, use the cards to test yourself or have a friend quiz you on the material.
- **Mnemonic (pronounced ne-mon-ik) devices are tricks that increase our ability to memorize.** A well-known mnemonic device is the phrase ROY G BIV, which helps people remember the colors of the rainbow—Red, Orange, Yellow, Green, Blue, Indigo, Violet. You can create your own for whatever you need to memorize. The more fun you have coming up with mnemonics for yourself, the more useful they will be.
- **Take notes twice.** First, take notes in class. Writing down your instructor's key points will help you be a more active, engaged listener. Taking notes will also give you a record of what your instructor thinks is important. Later, when you have a chance, rewrite your notes. The rewrite will act as a study session by forcing you to think about the material again.

Vladyslav Danilin/Shutterstock.com

bikeriderlondon/Shutterstock.com

TEST PREP

You have worked hard throughout the term, reading the book, paying close attention in class, and taking good notes. Now it's test time, and you want to show mastery of the material you have studied. To be well prepared, you should know which reading materials and lectures will be covered. You should also know whether the exam will contain essays, objective questions, or both. Finally, you should know how much time will be allowed. By taking these steps, you will reduce any anxiety you feel, and you can approach the test with confidence.

Follow Directions

Students are often in a hurry to start an exam, so they take little time to read the instructions. The instructions can be critical, however. In a multiple-choice exam, for example, if there is no indication that there is a penalty for guessing, then you should never leave a question unanswered. Even if only a few minutes are left at the end of an exam, you should guess on the questions that you remain uncertain about.

Additionally, you need to know the weight given to each section of an exam. In a typical multiple-choice exam, all questions have equal weight. In other types of exams, particularly those with essay questions, different parts of the exam carry different weights. You should use these weights to apportion your time. If the essay portion of an exam accounts for 20 percent of the total points on the exam, you should not spend 60 percent of your time on the essays.

Finally, you need to make sure you are marking the answers correctly. Some exams require a No. 2 pencil to fill in the dots on a machine-graded answer sheet. Other exams require underlining or circling. In short, you have to read and follow the instructions carefully.

Objective Exams

An objective exam consists of multiple-choice, true/false, fill-in-the-blank, or matching questions that have only one correct answer. Students usually commit one of two errors when they read objective exam questions: (1) they read things into the questions that do not exist, or (2) they skip over words or phrases. Most test questions include key words such as:

>ALL >NEVER
>ALWAYS >ONLY

If you miss any of these key words, you may answer the question wrong even if you know the information.

Whenever the answer to an objective question is not obvious, start with the process of elimination. Throw out the answers that are clearly incorrect. Typically, the easiest way to eliminate incorrect answers is to look for those that are meaningless, illogical, or inconsistent. Often, test authors put in choices that make perfect sense and are indeed true, but they are not the answer to the question under study.

Here are a few more tips that will help you become an efficient, results-oriented student.

- **Review your notes thoroughly** as part of your exam preparation. Instructors usually lecture on subjects they think are important, so those same subjects are also likely to be on the exam.

- **Create a study schedule** to reduce stress and give yourself the best chance for success. At times, you will find yourself studying for several exams at once. When this happens, make a list of each study topic and the amount of time needed to review that topic.
- **Form a small group for a study session.** Discussing a topic out loud can improve your understanding of that topic and will help you remember the key points that often come up on exams.
- **Study from old exams.** Some professors make old exams available, either by posting them online or by putting them on file in the library. Old tests can give you an idea of the kinds of questions the professor likes to ask.
- **Avoid cramming just before an exam.** Cramming tires the brain unnecessarily and adds to stress, which can severely hamper your testing performance. If you've studied wisely, have confidence that you will be able to recall the information when you need it.
- **Be sure to eat** before taking a test so you will have the energy you need to concentrate.
- **Be prepared.** Make sure you have everything you will need for the exam, such as a pen or pencil. Arrive at the exam early to avoid having to rush, which will only add to your stress. Good preparation helps you focus on the task at hand.
- **When you first receive your exam, make sure that you have all the pages.** If you are uncertain, ask your professor or exam proctor. This initial scan may uncover other problems as well, such as illegible print or unclear instructions.
- **With essay questions, look for key words** such as "compare," "contrast," and "explain." These will guide your answer. Most important, get to the point without wasting your time (or your professor's) with statements such as "There are many possible reasons for . . . ."
- **Review your answers** when you finish a test early. You may find a mistake or an area where some extra writing will improve your grade.
- **Keep exams in perspective.** Worrying too much about a single exam can have a negative effect on your performance. If you do poorly on one test, it's not the end of the world. Rather, it should motivate you to do better on the next one.

Diego Cervo/Shutterstock.com

WRITE PREP

A key part of succeeding as a student is learning how to write well. Whether writing papers, presentations, essays, or even e-mails to your instructor, you have to be able to put your thoughts into words and do so with force, clarity, and precision. In this section, we outline a three-phase process that you can use to write almost anything.

Phase 1: Getting Ready to Write

First, make a list. Divide the ultimate goal—a finished paper—into smaller steps that you can tackle right away. Estimate how long it will take to complete each step. Start with the date your paper is due and work backward to the present: For example, if the due date is December 1, and you have about three months to write the paper, give yourself a cushion and schedule November 20 as your targeted completion date. Then, list what you need to get done by October 1 and November 1.

PICK A TOPIC

To generate ideas for a topic, any of the following approaches work well:

- **Brainstorm with a group.** There is no need to create in isolation. You can harness the energy and the natural creative power of a group to assist you.

- **Speak it.** To get ideas flowing, start talking. Admit your confusion or lack of clear ideas. Then just speak. By putting your thoughts into words, you'll start thinking more clearly.

- **Use free writing.** Free writing, a technique championed by writing teacher Peter Elbow, is also very effective when trying to come up with a topic. There's only one rule in free writing: Write without stopping. Set a time limit—say, ten minutes—and keep your fingers dancing across the keyboard the whole time. Ignore the urge to stop and rewrite. There is no need to worry about spelling, punctuation, or grammar during this process.

There is no need to create in isolation. Brainstorm ideas for a topic with a group. Ask for feedback from your instructor or a friend as you prepare an outline and revise your first draft.

REFINE YOUR IDEA

After you've come up with some initial ideas, it's time to refine them:

- **Select a topic and working title.** Using your instructor's guidelines for the paper, write down a list of topics that interest you. Write down all of the ideas you think of in two minutes. Then choose one topic. The most common pitfall is selecting a topic that is too broad. "Terrorism" is probably not a useful topic for your paper. Instead, consider "The Financing of Terrorist Activities."

- **Write a thesis statement.** Clarify what you want to say by summarizing it in one concise sentence. This sentence, called a *thesis statement,* refines your working title. A thesis is the main point of the paper—it is a declaration of some sort. You might write a thesis statement such as "Drug trafficking and other criminal activities are often used to finance terrorism."

SET GOALS

Effective writing flows from a purpose. Think about how you'd like your reader or listener to respond after considering your ideas.

- If you want to persuade someone, make your writing clear and logical. Support your assertions with evidence.

- If your purpose is to move the reader into action, explain exactly what steps to take, and offer solid benefits for doing so.

To clarify your purpose, state it in one sentence—for example, "The purpose of this paper is to discuss and analyze the role of women and minorities in law enforcement."

BEGIN RESEARCH

At the initial stage, the objective of your research is not to uncover specific facts about your topic. That comes later. First, you want to gain an overview of the subject. Say you want to advocate for indeterminate sentencing. You must first learn enough about determinate and indeterminate sentencing to describe the pros and cons of each one.

MAKE AN OUTLINE

An outline is a kind of map. When you follow a map, you avoid getting lost. Likewise, an outline keeps you from wandering off topic. To create your outline, follow these steps:

1. **REVIEW YOUR THESIS STATEMENT** and identify the three to five main points you need to address in your paper to support or prove your thesis.

wavebreakmedia/Shutterstock.com

2. **NEXT, FOCUS ON THE THREE TO FIVE MAJOR POINTS** that support your argument and think about what minor points or subtopics you want to cover in your paper. Your major points are your big ideas. Your minor points are the details you need to fill in under each of those ideas.
3. **ASK FOR FEEDBACK.** Have your instructor or a classmate review your outline and offer suggestions for improvement. Did you choose the right points to support your thesis? Do you need more detail anywhere? Does the flow from idea to idea make sense?

DO IN-DEPTH RESEARCH

Dig in and start reading. Keep a notebook, tablet, or laptop handy and make notes as you read. It can help to organize your research into three main categories:

1. **SOURCES** (bibliographical information for a source),
2. **INFORMATION** (nuggets of information from a correctly quoted source), and
3. **IDEAS** (thoughts and observations that occur to you as you research, written in your own words).

You might want to use these categories to create three separate documents as you work. This will make it easy to find what you need when you write your first draft.

When taking research notes, be sure to:

- Copy all of the information correctly.
- Always include the source and page number while gathering information. With Internet searches, you must also record the date a site was accessed.
- Stay organized; refer to your outline as you work.

Jacob Lund/Shutterstock.com

> If you get stuck, ask for help. Most schools have writing resource centers where you can go for assistance and guidance.

Phase 2: Writing a First Draft

To create your draft, gather your notes and your outline (which often undergoes revision during the research process). Then write about the ideas in your notes. It's that simple. Just start writing. Write in paragraphs, with one idea per paragraph. As you complete this task, keep the following suggestions in mind:

- **Remember that the first draft is not for keeps.** You can worry about quality later. Your goal at this point is simply to generate words and ideas.
- **Write freely.** Many writers prefer to get their first draft down quickly and would advise you to keep writing, much as in free writing. You may pause to glance at your notes and outline, but avoid stopping to edit your work.
- **Be yourself.** Let go of the urge to sound "scholarly" and avoid using unnecessary big words or phrases. Instead, write in a natural voice.
- **Avoid procrastination.** If you are having trouble getting started, skip over your introduction and just begin writing about some of your findings. You can go back later and organize your paragraphs.
- **Get physical.** While working on the first draft, take breaks. Go for a walk. From time to time, practice relaxation techniques and breathe deeply.
- **Put the draft away for a day.** Schedule time for rewrites, and schedule at least one day between revisions so that you can let the material sit. After a break, problems with the paper or ideas for improvement will become more evident.

Phase 3: Revising Your Draft

During this phase, keep in mind the saying, "Write in haste; revise at leisure." When you are working on your first draft, the goal is to produce ideas and write them down. During the revision phase, however, you need to slow down and take a close look at your work. One guideline is to allow 50 percent of writing time for planning, researching, and writing the first draft. Then use the remaining 50 percent for revising.

Here are some good ways to revise your paper:

1. **READ IT OUT LOUD.** The combination of voice and ears forces us to pay attention to the details. Is the thesis statement clear and supported by enough evidence? Does the introduction tell your reader what's coming? Do you end with a strong conclusion that expands on your introduction rather than just restating it?

2. **HAVE A FRIEND LOOK OVER YOUR PAPER.** This is never a substitute for your own review, but a friend can often see mistakes you miss. With a little practice, you will learn to welcome feedback because it provides one of the fastest ways to approach the revision process.

3. **CUT.** Look for excess baggage. Also, look for places where two (or more) sentences could be rewritten as one. By cutting text you are actually gaining a clearer, more polished product. For maximum efficiency, make the larger cuts first—sections, chapters, pages. Then go for the smaller cuts—paragraphs, sentences, phrases, words.

4. **PASTE.** The next task is to rearrange what's left of your paper so that it flows logically. Look for consistency within paragraphs and for transitions from paragraph to paragraph and section to section.

5. **FIX.** Now it's time to look at individual words and phrases. Define any terms that the reader might not know. In general, focus on nouns and verbs. Too many adjectives and adverbs weaken your message and add unnecessary bulk to your writing. Write about the details, and be specific. Also, check your writing to ensure that you:
   - **Use the active voice.** Write *"The research team began the project"* rather than (passively) *"A project was initiated."*
   - **Write concisely.** Instead of *"After making a timely arrival and observing the unfolding events, I emerged totally and gloriously victorious,"* be concise with *"I came, I saw, I conquered."*
   - **Communicate clearly.** Instead of *"The speaker made effective use of the television medium, asking in no uncertain terms that we change our belief systems,"* you can write specifically, *"The reformed criminal stared straight into the television camera and said, 'Take a good look at what you are doing! Will it get you what you really want?'"*

iStock.com/Izabela Habur

6. **PREPARE.** Format your paper following accepted standards for margin widths, endnotes, title pages, and other details. Ask your instructor for specific instructions on how to cite the sources used in writing your paper. You can find useful guidelines in the *MLA Handbook for Writers of Research Papers.* If you are submitting a hard copy (rather than turning it in online), use quality paper for the final version. For an even more professional appearance, bind your paper with a plastic or paper cover.

7. **PROOFREAD.** As you ease down the home stretch, read your revised paper one more time, and look for the following:
   - A clear thesis statement.
   - Sentences that introduce your topic, guide the reader through the major sections of your paper, and summarize your conclusions.
   - Details—such as quotations, examples, and statistics—that support your conclusions.
   - Lean sentences that have been purged of needless words.
   - Plenty of action verbs and concrete, specific nouns.
   - Spelling and grammar mistakes. Use contractions sparingly, if at all. Use spell-check by all means, but do not rely on it completely, as it will not catch everything.

Academic Integrity: Avoiding Plagiarism

Using another person's words, images, or other original creations without giving proper credit is called *plagiarism.* Plagiarism amounts to taking someone else's work and presenting it as your own—the equivalent of cheating on a test. The consequences of plagiarism can range from a failing grade to expulsion from school.

To avoid plagiarism, ask an instructor where you can find your school's written policy on this issue. Don't assume that you can resubmit a paper you wrote for another class for a current class. Many schools will regard this as plagiarism even though you wrote the paper. The basic guidelines for preventing plagiarism are to cite a source for each phrase, sequence of ideas, or visual image created by another person. While ideas cannot be copyrighted, the specific way that an idea is *expressed* can be. You also need to list a source for any idea that is closely identified with a particular person. The goal is to clearly distinguish your own work from the work of others. There are several ways to ensure that you do this consistently:

- **Identify direct quotes.** If you use a direct quote from another source, put those words in quotation marks. If you do research online, you might copy text from a Web page and paste it directly into your notes. This is the same as taking direct quotes from your source. Always identify such passages in an obvious way.
- **Paraphrase carefully.** Paraphrasing means restating the original passage in your own words, usually making it shorter and simpler. Students who copy a passage word for word and then just rearrange or delete a few phrases are running a serious risk of plagiarism. Remember to cite a source for paraphrases, just as you do for direct quotes. When you use the same sequence of ideas as one of your sources—even if you have not paraphrased or directly quoted—cite that source.
- **Note details about each source.** For books, include the author, title, publisher, publication date, location of publisher, and page number. For articles from print sources, record the author, date, article title, and the name of the magazine or journal as well. If you found the article in an academic or technical journal, also include the volume and number of the publication. A librarian can help identify these details.
- **Most professors don't regard Wikipedia as a legitimate source.** If your source is a Web page, record as many identifying details as you can find—author, title, sponsoring organization, URL, publication date, and revision date. In addition, list the date that you accessed the page. Be careful when using Web resources, as not all Web sites are considered legitimate sources.
- **Cite your sources as endnotes or footnotes to your paper.** Ask your instructor for examples of the format to use. You do not need to credit wording that is wholly your own. Nor do you need to credit general ideas, such as the suggestion that people use a to-do list to plan their time. But if you borrow someone else's words or images to explain the idea, do give credit.
- **When in doubt, don't.** Sometimes you will find yourself working against a deadline for a paper, and in a panic, you might be tempted to take "shortcuts." You'll find a source that expressed your idea perfectly, but you must cite it or completely rephrase the idea in your own words. Professors are experts at noticing a change in tone or vocabulary that signals plagiarism. Often, they can simply Google a phrase to find its source online. Do not let a moment's temptation cause you to fail the course or face an academic integrity hearing.

Dragon Images/Shutterstock.com

DEDICATION

This book is dedicated to my good friend and colleague, Lawrence Walsh, of the Lexington, Kentucky Police Department. When I was a rookie, he taught me about policing. When I became a researcher, he taught me about the practical applications of knowledge. He is truly an inspiring professional in our field.

L.K.G.

To Larry Mayle,

The mind is
everything.

R.L.M.

1 Criminal Justice Today

ArtOlympic/Shutterstock.com

LEARNING OBJECTIVES

After studying this chapter, you will be able to . . .

- **1-1** Define *crime*.
- **1-2** Outline the three levels of law enforcement.
- **1-3** List the essential elements of the corrections system.
- **1-4** Define *ethics*, and describe the role that it plays in discretionary decision making.
- **1-5** Describe the defining aspects of a terrorist act, and identify one common misperception concerning domestic terrorism.

After finishing this chapter, go to **PAGE 20** for **STUDY TOOLS**

Trolling Trouble

On March 17, 2017, law enforcement agents arrested John Rivello for sending a tweet. Several months earlier, journalist Kurt Eichenwald, seeing that someone using the account @jew_goldstein had replied to one of his Twitter posts with a moving image tweet known as a GIF, clicked on the file. The message, "You deserve a seizure for your posts," appeared, along with a blinding strobe light. Eichenwald, who suffers from a brain disorder called epilepsy, immediately fell to the ground and became unresponsive. He lost feeling in his left hand and had trouble speaking for several weeks following the episode.

Searching the suspect's Twitter account, agents from the Federal Bureau of Investigation found a great deal of evidence that Rivello intended to injure Eichenwald. Rivello had sent numerous messages to other Twitter users about his victim, including one that said, "I know that he has epilepsy," and another expressing the hope that the strobe light GIF "sends [Eichenwald] into a seizure."

Rivello was charged with criminal cyberstalking with intent to kill or cause bodily harm—a rare instance in which an online violent threat triggered a response from the criminal justice system. Millions of such threats are made each year via social media, the difference being that most of these tweets are intended to cause emotional distress rather than the physical damage done to Eichenwald.

Under certain circumstances, however, the practice known as "trolling" can lead to prosecution. Earlier in 2017, Kyler Schmitz, outraged over what he saw as this country's lax attitude toward firearm ownership, sent a number of angry tweets to pro-gun politicians. "I am literally going to buy a gun shoot you in the face I watch your brains splat [sic]," he tweeted at Senator Roy Blount, a Republican from Missouri. Schmitz was eventually charged with making threatening interstate communications and spent two weeks in jail. "I wanted to get a rise," Schmitz said, defending his actions. "I wanted to make a point that I thought was civil disobedience and nonviolent, because I wasn't [planning to hurt anyone]."

Although a significant number of violent threats are made on Twitter and other social media platforms, these threats rarely result in criminal charges. *Under what circumstances, if any, do you believe that those who threaten others on social media should be arrested and charged with a crime?*

PiXXart/Shutterstock.com

1-1 WHAT IS CRIME?

Generally speaking, the criminal justice system does not punish Internet speech, no matter how violent, threatening, or distasteful. "People have a right to say what they want. No matter how bad it is and how hurtful it is to other people," says a detective with the Los Angeles Sheriff's Department who investigates bias-related crimes.[1] That right is protected by the First Amendment of the United States Constitution, which gives Americans the freedom to express themselves—even in a hateful or violent manner—without having to worry about being censored by the government.

This right does, however, have a limitation. If speech reasonably causes a person to fear that she or he is in imminent danger from the speaker, that speech is not constitutionally protected.[2] This "true threat" exception allowed law enforcement officials to arrest Kyler Schmitz, whose tweets crossed the line between protected and unprotected speech. As this example shows, a *crime* is not simply an act that seems dishonest or dangerous or taboo. A **crime** is a wrong against society that is *proclaimed by law* and that, if committed under specific circumstances, is punishable by the criminal justice system.

Crime An act that violates criminal law and is punishable by criminal sanctions.

One problem with the definition of crime just provided is that it obscures the complex nature of societies. A society is not static—it evolves and changes, and its concept of criminality evolves and changes as well. Several years ago, for example, the United States Supreme Court ruled that, in "true threat" cases, courts must take into account the motive of the person making the alleged threat.[3] This decision suggests that Kyler Schmitz may not have committed a crime if he could have proven that he never intended to harm the recipients of his tweets.

International examples also show how different societies can have different concepts of criminality. India's Supreme Court recently ordered the country's movie theaters to play the national anthem, accompanied by images of the Indian flag, before films to instill "a sense of committed patriotism and nationalism."[4] Within two weeks of the ruling, Indian authorities had arrested at least twenty moviegoers for failing to stand during the anthem, another requirement of the decision. It is highly unlikely that American courts, bound by our traditions of freedom of speech, would allow any similar police action.

To more fully understand the concept of crime, it will help to examine the two most common models of how society "decides" which acts are criminal: the consensus model and the conflict model.

1-1a The Consensus Model

The term *consensus* refers to general agreement among the majority of any particular group. Thus, the **consensus model** rests on the assumption that as people gather together to form a society, its members will naturally share similar norms and values. Those individuals whose actions deviate from the established norms and values are considered to pose a threat to the well-being of society as a whole and must be sanctioned (punished). The society passes laws to control and prevent unacceptable behavior, thereby setting the boundaries for acceptable behavior within the group.[5]

The consensus model, to a certain extent, assumes that a diverse group of people can have similar **morals.** In other words, they share an ideal of what is "right" and "wrong." Consequently, as public attitudes toward morality change, so do laws. In seventeenth-century America, a person found guilty of *adultery* (having sexual relations with someone other than one's spouse) could expect to be publicly whipped, branded, or even executed. Furthermore, a century ago, one could walk into a pharmacy and purchase heroin. Today, social attitudes have shifted to consider adultery a personal issue, beyond the reach of the state, and to consider the sale of heroin a criminal act.

Consensus Model A criminal justice model in which the majority of citizens in a society share the same values and beliefs.

Morals Principles of right and wrong behavior, as practiced by individuals or by society.

Conflict Model A criminal justice model in which the content of criminal law is determined by the groups that hold economic, political, and social power in a community.

1-1b The Conflict Model

Some people reject the consensus model on the ground that moral attitudes are not constant or even consistent. In large, democratic societies such as the United States, different groups of citizens have widely varying opinions on controversial issues of morality and criminality such as abortion, the war on drugs, immigration, and assisted suicide. These groups and their elected representatives are constantly coming into conflict with one another. According to the **conflict model,** then, the most politically powerful segments of society—based on class, income, age, and race—have the most influence on criminal laws and are therefore able to impose their values on the rest of the community.

Consequently, what is deemed criminal activity is determined by whichever group happens to be holding power at any given time. Because certain groups do not have access to political power, their interests are not served by the criminal justice system. For instance, nearly eight of every ten elected prosecutors in the United States are white men, while only 5 percent of these posts are held by members of minority groups.[6] Given the authority of prosecutors to decide which criminal charges will be brought against defendants, this lack of diversity can contribute to the mistrust of law enforcement felt in many minority communities.

1-1c An Integrated Definition of Crime

LO1-1 Define *crime*.

Considering both the consensus and conflict models, we can construct a definition of crime that will be useful throughout this textbook. For our purposes, crime is an action or activity that is:

1. Punishable under criminal law, as determined by the majority or, in some instances, by a powerful minority.
2. Considered an *offense against society as a whole* and prosecuted by public officials, not by victims and their relatives or friends.
3. Punishable by sanctions based on laws that bring about the loss of personal freedom or life.

Ehab Edward/Shutterstock.com

Forty-one states and the District of Columbia have local laws that ban cigarette smoking in workplaces, restaurants, and/or bars. **Based on the definition in the text, is smoking considered *deviant* behavior in our society? Do *you* consider it deviant behavior? Explain your answers.**

At this point, it is important to understand the difference between crime and **deviance,** or behavior that does not conform to the norms of a given community or society. Deviance is a subjective concept. For example, some segments of society may think that smoking marijuana or killing animals for clothing and food is deviant behavior. Deviant acts become crimes only when society as a whole, through its legislatures, determines that those acts should be punished—as is the situation today in the United States with using certain drugs but not with eating meat. Furthermore, not all crimes are considered particularly deviant—little social disapproval is attached to those who fail to follow the letter of parking laws. In essence, criminal law reflects those acts that we, as a society, agree are so unacceptable that steps must be taken to prevent them from occurring.

1-1d Types of Crime

How crimes are classified depends on their seriousness. Federal, state, and local legislation has provided for the classification and punishment of hundreds of thousands of different criminal acts, ranging from jaywalking to first degree murder. For general purposes, we can group criminal behavior into five categories: violent crime, property crime, public order crime, white-collar crime, and cyber crime.

VIOLENT CRIME Crimes against persons, or *violent crimes*, have come to dominate our perspectives on crime. There are four major categories of violent crime:

- **Murder,** or the unlawful killing of a human being.
- **Sexual assault,** or *rape*, which refers to coerced actions of a sexual nature against an unwilling participant.
- **Assault** and **battery,** two separate acts that cover situations in which one person physically attacks another (battery) or, through threats, intentionally leads another to believe that he or she will be physically harmed (assault).
- **Robbery,** or the taking of funds, personal property, or any other article of value from a person by means of force or fear.

As you will see in Chapter 3, these violent crimes are further classified by *degree*, depending on the circumstances surrounding the criminal act. These circumstances include the intent of the person committing the crime, whether a weapon was used, and (in cases other than murder) the level of pain and suffering experienced by the victim.

CAREER TIP Universities and community colleges, hospitals, mental health clinics, and social service agencies often hire *rape crisis counselors* to help victims of sexual assault cope with the physical, emotional, and legal consequences of sexual violence.

PROPERTY CRIME The most common form of criminal activity is *property crime*, or those crimes in which the goal of the offender is some form of economic gain or the damaging of property. There are three major forms of property crime:

1. Pocket-picking, shoplifting, and the stealing of any property without the use of force are covered by laws against **larceny,** also known as theft.
2. **Burglary** refers to the unlawful entry of a structure with the intention of committing a serious crime, such as theft.
3. *Motor vehicle theft* describes the theft or attempted theft of a motor vehicle. Motor vehicles include any vehicle commonly used

Deviance Behavior that is considered to go against the norms established by society.

Murder The unlawful killing of one human being by another.

Sexual Assault Forced or coerced sexual intercourse (or other sexual acts).

Assault A threat or an attempt to do violence to another person that causes that person to fear immediate physical harm.

Battery The act of physically contacting another person with the intent to do harm, even if the resulting injury is insubstantial.

Robbery The act of taking property from another person through force, threat of force, or intimidation.

Larceny The act of taking property from another person without the use of force with the intent of keeping that property.

Burglary The act of breaking into or entering a structure (such as a home or office) without permission for the purpose of committing a felony.

for transportation, such as a motorcycle or motor scooter, but not farm equipment or watercraft.

Arson is also a property crime. It involves the willful and malicious burning of a home, automobile, commercial building, or any other construction.

PUBLIC ORDER CRIME The concept of **public order crime** is linked to the consensus model discussed earlier. Historically, societies have always outlawed activities that are considered contrary to public values and morals. Today, the most common public order crimes include public drunkenness, prostitution, gambling, and illicit drug use. These crimes are sometimes referred to as *victimless crimes* because they often harm only the offender. As you will see throughout this textbook, however, that term is rather misleading. Public order crimes may create an environment that gives rise to property and violent crimes.

Joe Raedle/Getty Images News/Getty Images

In 2017, three executives at the Takata Corporation were criminally charged for fabricating airbag test data, a coverup that has been linked to at least eleven deaths. **If found guilty of this white-collar crime, should these executives be punished the same as someone who commits a violent crime? Why or why not?**

WHITE-COLLAR CRIME Business-related crimes are popularly referred to as **white-collar crimes.** The term *white-collar crime* is broadly used to describe an illegal act or series of acts committed by an individual or business entity using some nonviolent means to obtain a personal or business advantage.

As you will see in Chapter 14, where we consider the topic in much greater detail, white-collar crimes involve the use of legal business facilities and legitimate employees to commit illegal acts. For example, a bank teller can't embezzle (steal funds from the bank) unless she or he is an authorized bank employee. This characteristic distinguishes white-collar crime from *organized crime*, which refers to acts by illegal organizations. The traditional preferred illicit markets for organized crime operations include gambling, prostitution, illegal narcotics, and loan sharking (lending funds at higher-than-legal interest rates), along with more recent ventures into counterfeiting and credit-card scams.

Public Order Crime Behavior that has been labeled criminal because it is contrary to shared social values, customs, and norms.

White-Collar Crimes Nonviolent crimes committed by business entities or individuals to gain a personal or business advantage.

CYBER CRIME The newest variation on crime is directly related to the increased presence of computers in everyday life. The Internet, with approximately 3.6 billion users worldwide, is the site of numerous *cyber* crimes—defined simply as crimes that occur in the virtual community of the Internet. The dependence of businesses on computer operations has left corporations especially vulnerable to sabotage, fraud, and embezzlement. Earlier in this decade, two separate incidents of "hacking," or unauthorized access to computer systems, exposed approximately 1.5 billion Yahoo user accounts. The information in these accounts, including names, dates of birth, telephone numbers, and passwords, was eventually offered for sale on the "dark web," a hidden, lawless corner of the Internet that can only be accessed by special software.[7]

Shifting and expanding with each new technological advance, cyber crime poses particular challenges to the criminal justice system. During the past few years, for example, explosive growth in the "Internet of Things" has raised new security concerns. The term refers to the wireless interconnections linking tiny computers in automobiles, security cameras, kitchen appliances, and other objects of everyday use via the Internet. These "smart" devices, which number about fifteen billion worldwide, often lack proper security protections and have proved easy prey for hackers. In addition, terrorists increasingly are using "end-to-end" encryption technology available on the Signal, Telegram, and Wickr apps (among others) to hide their communications from authorities.[8] We will cover this particular criminal activity in much greater detail in Chapter 14.

CAREER PREP

Crime Scene Photographer

Job Description:

- Photograph physical evidence and crime scenes related to criminal investigations.
- Be able to compose reports, testify in court, and operate digital and fluorescent camera equipment.

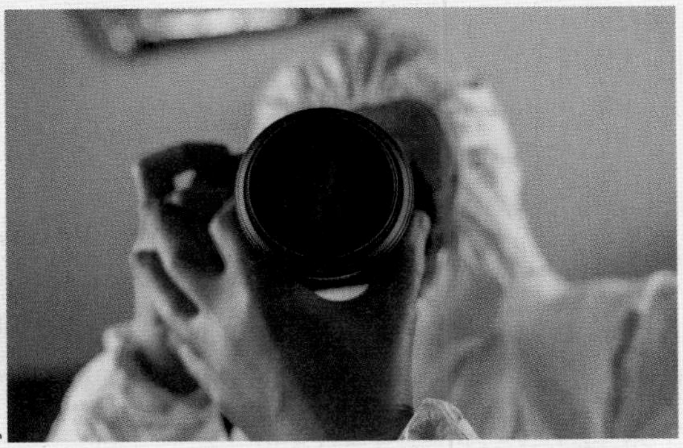

igorstevanovic/Shutterstock.com

What Kind of Training Is Required?

- One year in law enforcement or commercial photography OR a degree or certificate in photography OR some combination of the above training or experience totaling one year.
- Must be willing to work irregular hours, weekends, holidays, and evenings.

Annual Salary Range?

- $40,000–$75,000

SOCIAL MEDIA CAREER TIP
When you are posting on Facebook, assume that your post will be published in your local newspaper and read by a potential employer. If you think the post might reflect poorly on you as a potential employee, keep it offline.

ETHICS CHALLENGE

Earlier in this section, we used the example of killing animals for clothing and food as behavior that, although deviant to some, is generally accepted by the majority. What is a widespread activity that, although considered "normal" in modern American society, goes against your personal values or morals? What is the likelihood that this activity eventually will become illegal in the United States?

1-2 WHAT IS THE PURPOSE OF CRIMINAL JUSTICE?

Defining which actions are to be labeled "crimes" is only the first step in safeguarding society from criminal behavior. Institutions must be created to apprehend alleged wrongdoers, to determine whether these persons have indeed committed crimes, and to punish those who are found guilty according to society's wishes. These institutions combine to form the **criminal justice system.** As we begin our examination of the American criminal justice system in this introductory chapter, it is important to have an idea of its purpose.

1-2a Maintaining Justice

As its name implies, the explicit goal of the criminal justice system is to provide *justice* to all members of society. Because **justice** is a difficult concept to define, this goal can be challenging, if not impossible, to meet. Broadly stated, justice means that all individuals are equal before the law and that they are free from arbitrary arrest or seizure as defined by the law. In other words, the idea of

Criminal Justice System The interlocking network of law enforcement agencies, courts, and corrections institutions designed to enforce criminal laws and protect society from criminal behavior.

Justice The quality of fairness that must exist in the processes designed to determine whether individuals are guilty of criminal wrongdoing.

justice is linked with the idea of fairness. Above all, we want our laws and the means by which they are carried out to be fair.

Justice and fairness are subjective terms, which is to say that people may have different concepts of what is just and fair. If a woman who has been beaten by her husband retaliates by killing him, what is her just punishment? Reasonable persons could disagree. Some might think that the homicide was justified and that she should be treated leniently. Others might insist that she should not have taken the law into her own hands. Police officers, judges, prosecutors, prison administrators, and other employees of the criminal justice system must decide what is "fair." Sometimes, their course of action is obvious, but often, as we shall see, it is not.

1-2b Protecting Society

Within the broad mandate of "maintaining justice," Megan Kurlychek of the University at Albany, New York, has identified four specific goals of our criminal justice system:

1. To protect society from potential future crimes of the most dangerous or "risky" offenders.
2. To determine when an offense has been committed and provide the appropriate punishment for that offense.
3. To rehabilitate those offenders who have been punished so that it is safe to return them to the community.
4. To support crime victims and, to the extent possible, return them to their precrime status.[9]

Again, though these goals may seem straightforward, they often are difficult to achieve. After nearly four decades of steady declines, for example, highway fatalities have skyrocketed in recent years.[10] Although no direct link has been proved, many experts blame this trend on the high incidence of *distracted driving*, which occurs when a driver engages in any sort of activity that could distract him or her from safely operating a vehicle. Indeed, a recent poll found that seven out of ten Americans admit to texting, accessing social media, or taking selfies while behind the wheel.[11]

The criminal justice system has fashioned a response to this threat. Fourteen states specifically prohibit the use of hand-held electronic devices by drivers, and forty-six ban texting behind the wheel.[12] Rarely, however, does the punishment for distracted driving rise above a monetary fine, causing one observer to complain that "right now, we have a reed, not a stick" to deter the practice.[13]

Furthermore, it is difficult for law enforcement officers to detect distracted driving or for prosecutors to prove that an accident was caused by a texting driver. Technology does exist that would enable police to determine whether a suspected driver had recently been using a smartphone. Privacy advocates worry, however, that such methods would lead to improper searches of constitutionally protected information, an issue we will address in Chapter 6.[14] Thus, the question of how best to protect society from distracted drivers is, like so many questions relating to criminal justice, complex and difficult to answer.

Federalism A form of government in which a written constitution provides for a division of powers between a central government and several regional governments.

1-3 HOW DOES THE CRIMINAL JUSTICE SYSTEM WORK?

To understand the structure of the criminal justice system, you must understand the concept of **federalism,** a form of government in which powers are shared by the national (federal) government and the states. The framers of the U.S. Constitution, fearful of tyranny and a too-powerful central government, chose the system of federalism as a compromise.

1-3a Federalism in Action

The appeal of federalism is that it establishes a strong national government capable of handling large-scale problems while allowing for state powers and local traditions. For example, in 2016, California became the fifth state—after Montana, Oregon, Vermont, and Washington—to legalize physician-assisted suicide for certain terminally ill patients. About a decade ago, the federal government challenged the decision made by voters in Oregon and Washington to allow the practice. With its ruling in *Gonzales v. Oregon* (2006), the United States Supreme Court sided with the states, ruling that the principle of federalism supported their freedom to differ from the majority viewpoint in this instance.[15]

FEDERAL CRIMINAL LAW The Constitution gave the national government certain express powers, such as the power to coin money, raise an army, and regulate interstate commerce. All other powers were left to the states, including police power, which allows the states to enact whatever laws are necessary to protect the health, morals, safety, and welfare of their citizens. As the American criminal justice system has evolved, the ideals of federalism have ebbed somewhat. Specifically, the powers of the national government have expanded significantly. In the early 1900s, only about one hundred specific activities were illegal under federal criminal law. Today, there are nearly five thousand federal criminal statutes, meaning that Americans are increasingly likely to come in contact with the federal criminal justice system.[16]

MARIJUANA AND THE STATES Today, issues relating to federalism are an important part of the ongoing clash between federal and state marijuana laws. Under federal law, any use of marijuana is illegal. Indeed, the Drug Enforcement Administration (DEA) recently reaffirmed marijuana's status as a Schedule 1 drug—in the same category as heroin—because of its "high potential for abuse."[17] At the same time, the recreational use of small amounts of marijuana is legal in eight states plus Washington, D.C. Twenty-eight states allow marijuana consumption for medicinal purposes, and the drug has been decriminalized in thirteen states, meaning that its use is treated as an infraction similar to a traffic violation rather than as a crime. (See Figure 1.1.)

In *Gonzales v. Raich* (2005), the United States Supreme Court ruled that, when it comes to marijuana regulation, "if there is any conflict between federal and state law, federal law shall prevail."[18] How, then, have numerous states been able to pass laws that clearly are incompatible with federal marijuana prohibitions? In recent years, based on policy decisions in the administrative branch, the federal government has chosen generally to ignore recreational and medicinal marijuana use in those states with liberalized marijuana laws.[19] The DEA has still conducted raids of large-scale marijuana-growing operations in "pot-friendly" states, however, and recreational marijuana use has remained a crime in federal parks located in those states. Furthermore, depending on the political views of the current presidential administration, the federal government's *laissez-faire* attitude toward marijuana could change in the future.

FIGURE 1.1 MARIJUANA AND CRIMINAL LAW

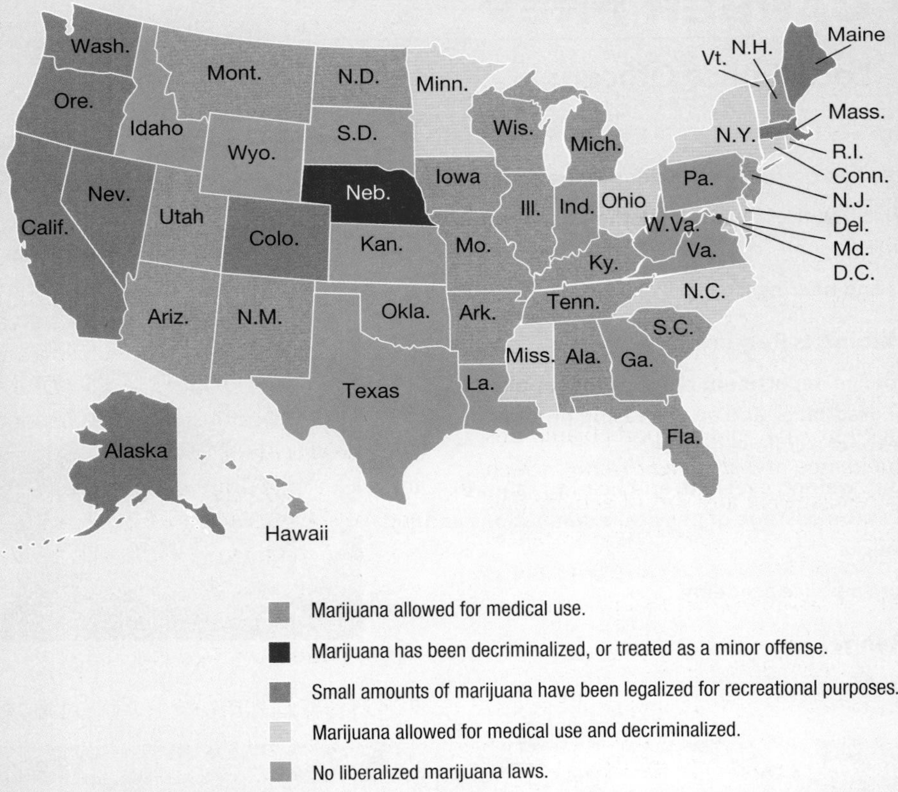

As this map shows, at the beginning of 2017 most states—representing about three-fourths of the population of the United States—allow for the use of marijuana under certain circumstances. Remember that *any* use of the drug is outlawed under federal law.

1-3b Law Enforcement

The ideals of federalism can be clearly seen in the local, state, and federal levels of law enforcement. Though agencies from the different levels cooperate if the need arises, they have their own organizational structures and tend to operate independently of one another. We briefly introduce each level of law enforcement here and cover them in more detail in Chapters 4, 5, and 6.

LO1-2 Outline the three levels of law enforcement.

LOCAL LAW ENFORCEMENT On the local level, the duties of law enforcement agencies are split between counties and municipalities. The chief law enforcement officer of most counties is the county sheriff. Those who hold the position of sheriff are typically elected, often for a two- or four-year term. In some areas, where city and county governments have merged, there is a county police force, headed by a chief of police. The bulk of all police officers in the United States are employed on a local level. The majority of these work in departments that consist of fewer than 10 officers, but a large city such as New York may have a police force of about 34,500.

Local police are responsible for the "nuts and bolts" of law enforcement work. They investigate most crimes and attempt to deter crime through patrol activities. They apprehend criminals and participate in trial proceedings, if necessary. Local police are also charged with "keeping the peace," a broad set of duties that includes crowd and traffic control and the resolution of minor conflicts between citizens. In many areas, local police have the added obligation of providing social services such as dealing with domestic violence and child abuse.

CAREER PREP

Local Police Officer

Job Description:

- Protect the lives and property of citizens in the community.
- Maintain order, catch those who break the law, and strive to prevent crimes.
- Testify at trials and hearings.

What Kind of Training Is Required?

- Almost every police department requires that applicants be high school graduates, and an increasing number of departments expect a college degree.
- Minimum height, weight, eyesight, and hearing requirements, as well as the passage of physical examinations and background checks.
- Graduation from a police academy.

Annual Salary Range?

- $44,000–$90,000

John Roman Images/Shutterstock.com

GETTING LINKEDIN

A recent job posting by the City of Farmington, New Mexico, noted that all its police officers are required to work "days, evenings, and nights, including weekends and holidays." Irregular hours are one of the most challenging aspects of a career in law enforcement.

STATE LAW ENFORCEMENT Hawaii is the only state that does not have a state law enforcement agency. Generally, there are two types of state law enforcement agencies, those designated simply as "state police" and those designated as "highway patrols." State highway patrols concern themselves mainly with infractions on public highways and freeways. Other state law enforcers include fire marshals, who investigate suspicious fires and educate the public on fire prevention. State fish, game, and watercraft wardens police a state's natural resources and often oversee its firearms laws. Some states also have alcoholic beverage control officers, as well as agents who investigate welfare and food stamp fraud.

FEDERAL LAW ENFORCEMENT The enactment of new national laws over the past forty years has led to an expansion in the size and scope of the federal government's participation in the criminal justice system. Among other things, these laws have dealt with terrorism, guns, drugs, and violent crime. The Department of Homeland Security, which we will examine in detail in Chapter 4, combines the police powers of twenty-four federal agencies to protect the United States from terrorist attacks. Other federal agencies with police powers include the Federal Bureau of Investigation (FBI), the Drug Enforcement Administration (DEA), the U.S. Secret Service, and the Bureau of Alcohol, Tobacco, Firearms and Explosives (ATF). In fact, almost every federal agency, including the postal and forest services, has some kind of police power.

Federal law enforcement agencies operate throughout the United States and often work in cooperation with their local and state counterparts. There can be tension between the different branches of law enforcement, however, when state criminal law and federal criminal law are incompatible. For example, as noted earlier, even though a number of states have legalized the sale and possession of small amounts of marijuana, the drug is still illegal under federal law. Consequently, federal officers are authorized to make marijuana arrests in those states, regardless of the content of those states' criminal codes.

1-3c The Courts

The United States has a *dual court system*, which means that we have two independent judicial systems, one at the federal level and one at the state level. In practice, this translates into fifty-two different court systems: one federal court system and fifty different state court systems, plus that of the District of Columbia. In general, defendants charged with violating federal criminal law will face trial in federal court, while defendants charged with violating state law will appear in state court.

The *criminal court* and its work group—the judge, prosecutors, and defense attorneys—are charged with the weighty responsibility of determining the innocence or guilt of criminal suspects. We will cover these important participants, their roles in the criminal trial, and the court system as a whole in Chapters 7, 8, and 9.

1-3d Corrections

Once the court system convicts and sentences an offender, she or he is delegated to the corrections system. (Those convicted in a state court will be under the control of that state's corrections system, and those convicted of a federal crime will find themselves under the control of the federal corrections system.) Depending on the seriousness of the crime and their individual needs, offenders are placed on probation, incarcerated, or transferred to community-based correctional facilities.

LO1-3 List the essential elements of the corrections system.

- *Probation*, the most common correctional treatment, allows the offender to return to the community and remain under the supervision of an agent of the court known as a probation officer. While on probation, the offender must follow certain rules of conduct. When probationers fail to follow these rules, they may be incarcerated.
- If the offender's sentence includes a period of *incarceration*, he or she will be remanded to a correctional facility for a certain amount of time. *Jails* hold those convicted of minor crimes with relatively short sentences, as well as those awaiting trial or involved in certain court proceedings. *Prisons* house those convicted of more serious crimes with longer sentences. Generally speaking, counties and municipalities administer jails, while prisons are the domain of federal and state governments.
- *Community-based corrections* have increased in popularity as jails and prisons have been plagued with problems of funding and overcrowding. Community-based correctional facilities include halfway houses, residential centers, and work-release centers. They operate on the assumption that not all convicts need or benefit from incarceration in jail or prison.

The majority of inmates released from incarceration are not finished with the corrections system. The most frequent type of release from a jail or prison is *parole*, in which an inmate, after serving part of his or her sentence in a correctional facility, is allowed to serve the rest of the term in the community. Like someone on probation, a

View Apart/Shutterstock.com

America's state and federal prisons hold just over 1.5 million inmates, while, on any given day, about 740,000 inmates are locked up in the nation's jails. **What are the basic differences between prisons and jails?**

parolee must conform to certain conditions of freedom, with the same consequences if these conditions are not followed. Issues of probation, incarceration, community-based corrections, and parole will be covered in Chapters 10, 11, and 12.

1-3e The Criminal Justice Process

Some liken the criminal justice system to a sports team, which is the sum of an indeterminable number of decisions, relationships, conflicts, and adjustments.[20] Such a volatile mix is not what we generally associate with a "system." For most, the word **system** indicates a certain degree of order and discipline. That we refer to our law enforcement agencies, courts, and correctional facilities as part of a "system" may reflect our hopes rather than reality. Still, it will be helpful to familiarize yourself with the basic steps of the *criminal justice process*, or the procedures through which the criminal justice system meets the expectations of society. These basic steps are outlined in Figure 1.2.

In his classic study of the criminal justice system, Herbert Packer, a professor at Stanford University, compared the ideal criminal justice process to an assembly line "down which moves an endless stream of cases, never stopping."[21] In Packer's image of assembly-line justice, each step of the **formal criminal justice process** involves a series of "routinized operations" with the end goal of getting the criminal defendant from point A (his or her arrest by law enforcement) to point B (the criminal trial) to point C (if guilty, her or his punishment).[22]

As Packer himself was wont to point out, the daily operations of criminal justice rarely operate so smoothly. In this textbook, the criminal justice process will be examined as the end product of many different decisions made by many different criminal justice professionals in law enforcement, the courts, and corrections.

System A set of interacting parts that, when functioning properly, achieve a desired result.

Formal Criminal Justice Process The model of the criminal justice process in which participants follow formal rules to create a smoothly functioning disposition of cases from arrest to punishment.

Discretion The ability of individuals in the criminal justice system to make operational decisions based on personal judgment instead of formal rules or official information.

Informal Criminal Justice Process A model of the criminal justice system that recognizes the informal authority exercised by individuals at each step of the criminal justice process.

1-4 HOW DO CRIMINAL JUSTICE PROFESSIONALS MAKE DECISIONS?

Practically, the formal criminal justice process suffers from a serious drawback: it is unrealistic. Law enforcement agencies do not have the staff or funds to investigate every crime, so they must decide where to direct their limited resources. Increasing caseloads and a limited amount of time in which to dispose of them constrict many of our nation's courts. Overcrowding in prisons and jails affects both law enforcement agencies and the courts—there is simply not enough room for all convicts.

The criminal justice system relies on *discretion* to alleviate these pressures. By **discretion,** we mean the authority to choose between and among alternative courses of action, based on individual judgment and conscience. Collectively, the discretionary decisions made by criminal justice professionals are said to produce an **informal criminal justice process** that does not operate within the rigid confines of formal rules and laws.

1-4a Informal Decision Making

By its nature, the informal criminal justice system relies on the discretion of individuals to offset the rigidity of criminal statutes and procedural rules. For example, even if a prosecutor believes that a suspect is guilty, she or he may decide not to bring charges against the suspect if the case is weak or the police erred during the investigative process. In many instances, prosecutors will not squander the scarce resource of court time on

FIGURE 1.2 THE CRIMINAL JUSTICE PROCESS

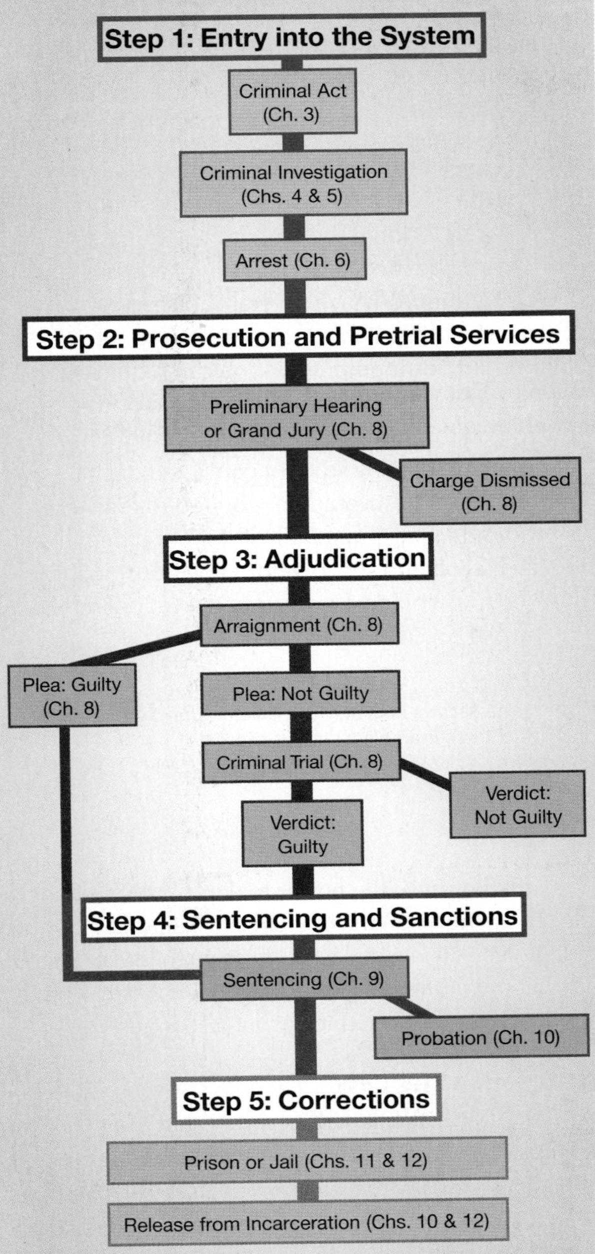

This diagram provides a simplified overview of the basic steps of the criminal justice process, from criminal act to release from incarceration. Below each step, you will find the chapter of this textbook in which the event is covered.

a case they might not win. Some argue that the informal process has made our system more just. Given the immense pressure of limited resources, the argument goes, only rarely will an innocent person end up before a judge and jury.[23]

INTERPRETING THE LAW In many instances, criminal justice professionals must use their discretion to interpret laws that are overly broad, vague, or even obsolete. For example, although twenty-one states still ban adultery, such laws are routinely ignored by authorities.[24] Consider, too, an issue mentioned earlier—state distracted-driving legislation. Georgia's law prohibits drivers from engaging in "any actions which shall distract such driver from the safe operation of [her or his] vehicle."[25] This statute could be interpreted to cover a wide range of behavior, from texting or using a smartphone to listening to music while driving. In fact, several years ago an Atlanta police officer came under criticism for using his discretion to ticket a driver who was eating a hamburger while behind the wheel.[26]

In later chapters, we will examine many other circumstances that call for discretionary decision making by law enforcement officers. We will also cover discretion on the part of judges, who must interpret the law when overseeing criminal trials and sentencing guilty defendants, and corrections officials, who have a great deal of discretion in determining how to control prison and jail inmates. (See the feature *Discretion in Action—The "Sexting" Scandal* for insight into how the informal criminal justice process applies to a distinct form of child pornography.)

THE PITFALLS OF DISCRETION Unfortunately, the informal criminal justice system does not always benefit from measured, rational decision making. Individual judgment can be tainted by personal bias, erroneous or irrational thinking, and plain ill will. When this occurs, discretion becomes "the power to *get away* with alternative decisions [emphasis added]."[27] Indeed, many of the rules of the formal criminal justice process are designed to keep its employees from substituting their own judgment for that of the general public, as expressed by the law.

One of the primary arguments for easing marijuana laws, a subject discussed earlier in the chapter, is that those laws are often selectively (and unfairly) enforced. According to a recent Human Rights Watch survey of thirty-nine states, for example, African American adults were four times more likely to be arrested for marijuana possession than white adults, even though usage rates are similar between the two races.[28] In Chapter 6, you will learn more about *racial profiling*, which is the police practice of improperly targeting members of minority groups based on personal characteristics such as race or ethnicity.

Discretion in the courts has also come under criticism. Associate Supreme Court justice Antonin Scalia (1936–2016) believed that discretion in the courts tends to cause discriminatory and disparate criminal sentences,

DISCRETION IN ACTION

The "Sexting" Scandal

THE SITUATION The first hint of a serious problem came from an anonymous tip on the high school's Safe2Tell hotline. According to the tipster, numerous students were using a photo vault app to share inappropriate images of themselves. Following a lengthy investigation by school officials and local law enforcement, the full extent of the "sexting" activity was revealed: more than one hundred students, both male and female, had contributed photos of themselves posing nude or in their underwear. As far as the investigators could determine, none of these images had been posted on the Internet or shown to adults, and no coercion or bullying was involved.

THE LAW Under state law, any person who takes, receives, or shares a photo of a "naked body part" of someone under the age of eighteen has committed a Class C felony child pornography offense. Under the law, the fact that such activity is consensual is irrelevant. A conviction for a Class C felony is punishable by four to twelve years in a state prison and a fine of up to $750,000.

WHAT WOULD YOU DO? You are the prosecutor responsible for deciding the fate of the students involved in this "sexting" scandal. With nearly unlimited discretion, you have several choices: (1) you can charge the students with committing crimes involving child pornography; (2) you can require that they undergo counseling; or (3) you can do nothing, relying on the students' parents to "straighten them out." Note that any student convicted of child pornography charges would be required to register as a sex offender, making it difficult for her or him to find or keep a job and secure affordable housing in the future. How would you use your discretion in this situation?

To see how a prosecutor in Cañon City, Colorado, reacted in similar circumstances, go to Example 1.1 in Appendix A.

a subject we will discuss in Chapter 9. According to Scalia, the need for fairness and certainty in the criminal justice system outweighs the practical benefits of widespread and unpredictable discretionary decision making.[29]

1-4b Ethics and Justice

> LO1-4 Define *ethics*, and describe the role that it plays in discretionary decision making.

How can we reconcile the need for some sort of discretion in criminal justice with the ever-present potential for abuse? Part of the answer lies in our initial definition of discretion, which mentions not only individual judgment but also *conscience*. Ideally, actors in the criminal justice system will make moral choices about what is right and wrong based on the norms that have been established by society. In other words, they will behave *ethically*.

> **Ethics** The moral principles that govern a person's perception of right and wrong.

Ethics in criminal justice is closely related to the concept of justice. Because criminal justice professionals are representatives of the state, they have the power to determine whether the state is treating its citizens fairly. If some law enforcement officers in fact make the decision to issue a jaywalking citation on the basis of the offender's race, then they are acting not only unethically but also unjustly.

ETHICS AND THE LAW The line between ethics and justice is often difficult to discern, as ethical standards are usually not written into criminal statutes. Consequently, individuals must often "fill in" the ethical blanks. To make this point, ethics expert John Kleinig uses the real-life example of a police officer who refused to arrest a homeless person for sleeping in a private parking garage. A local ordinance clearly prohibited such behavior. The officer, however, felt it would be unethical to arrest a homeless person under those circumstances unless he or she was acting in a disorderly manner. The officer's supervisors were unsympathetic to this ethical stance, and he was suspended from duty without pay.[30]

ETHICS AND CRITICAL THINKING Did the police officer in the preceding example behave ethically by inserting his own beliefs into the letter of the criminal law? Would an officer who arrested peaceful homeless trespassers be acting unethically? In some cases, the ethical decision will be *intuitive*, reflecting an automatic response determined by a person's background and experiences. In other cases, however, intuition is not enough. *Critical thinking* is needed for an ethical response. Throughout this textbook, we will use the principle of critical thinking—which involves developing analytical skills and reasoning—to address the many ethical challenges inherent in the criminal justice system.

ETHICS CHALLENGE

Refer back to this section's discussion of the police officer who refused to arrest the nonviolent homeless person for ethical reasons. Did the officer act properly in this situation, or should he have carried out the law regardless of his personal beliefs? Explain your answer.

1-5 WHAT'S HAPPENING IN CRIMINAL JUSTICE TODAY?

In describing the general direction of the criminal justice system as a whole, many observers point to two models introduced by Professor Herbert Packer: the *crime control model* and the *due process model*.[31] The underlying value of the **crime control model** is that the most important function of the criminal justice process is to punish and repress criminal conduct. The system must be quick and efficient, placing as few restrictions as possible on the ability of law enforcement officers to make discretionary decisions in apprehending criminals.

Although not in direct conflict with crime control, the underlying values of the **due process model** focus more on protecting the rights of the accused through formal, legal restraints on the police, courts, and corrections. That is, the due process model relies on the courts to make it more difficult to prove guilt. It rests on the belief that it is more desirable for society that ninety-nine guilty suspects go free than that a single innocent person be condemned.[32]

1-5a Crime and Law Enforcement: The Bottom Line

It is difficult to say which of Packer's two models has the upper hand today. As we will see throughout the textbook, homeland security concerns have brought much of the criminal justice system in line with crime control values. At the same time, decreasing arrest and imprisonment rates suggest that due process values are strong, as well. Indeed, most measurements of criminal activity are at historically low levels. Federal crime statistics do indicate one worrisome trend, however: in 2015, the murder rate rose by nearly 11 percent, the largest such jump since the 1960s.[33] In Chapter 2, we will discuss some of the reasons for this development, including why violent crime appears to be clustering in the nation's largest cities.

SMARTER POLICING Just as law enforcement inevitably gets a great deal of the blame when crime rates are high, American police forces have received much credit for the apparent decline in criminality. The consensus is that the police have become smarter and more disciplined over the past several decades, relying, like many other criminal justice institutions, on **evidence-based practices,** or strategies that demonstrably result in positive outcomes.

For example, *predictive policing*, sometimes also known as intelligence-led policing, employs statistical models to anticipate which locations are at the highest risk for criminal activity. Once these high-risk locations, or *hot spots*, are identified, law enforcement agencies can direct resources toward preventing crime in the area. A more controversial strategy called *proactive policing* promotes rigorous enforcement of minor offenses—such as drunkenness and public disorder—with an eye toward preventing more serious wrongdoing. We will explore these innovative policing strategies, along with many others, more fully in Chapter 5.

IDENTIFYING CRIMINALS Technology has also played a significant role in improving law enforcement efficiency. Police investigators are enjoying the benefits of perhaps the most effective new crime-fighting tool since fingerprint identification: DNA profiling. This technology allows law enforcement agents to identify a suspect from body fluid evidence (such as blood, saliva, or semen) or biological evidence (such as hair strands or fingernail clippings). As we will also see in Chapter 5, by collecting DNA from convicts and storing the information in databases,

Crime Control Model A criminal justice model that places primary emphasis on the right of society to be protected from crime and violent criminals.

Due Process Model A criminal justice model that places primacy on the right of the individual to be protected from the power of the government.

Evidence-Based Practices Approaches or strategies that have been extensively researched and shown consistently to produce the desired outcomes.

CJ and TECHNOLOGY

Facial Recognition Software

Recently developed facial recognition software makes even the most technologically advanced fingerprint-matching systems seem sluggish by comparison. This software distinguishes 16,000 points on a person's face—such as the shape of the lips and the distance between the eyes—and conducts point comparisons with photos in law enforcement databases at a rate of more than one million faces a second. Designed by the U.S. military to identify potential terrorists in Iraq and Afghanistan, this technology is linked to surveillance cameras in cities like Chicago and New York for purposes of fighting street crime. It was also used more than 20,000 times from 2011 to 2015 by San Diego patrol officers hoping to establish the identity of suspects in the field.

For all its speed, this technology does have its limitations. The error rate is as high as 20 percent, which suggests the possibility of regular misidentifications. In San Diego, the software succeeded in finding a criminal record match only a quarter of the time, meaning that police officers were, for the most part, photographing noncriminals. Boston recently decided not to link the software to surveillance cameras because, in the words of its police commissioner, "I don't want people to think we're always spying on them."

Thinking about Facial Recognition Software

Suppose a convenience store manager was able to use her smartphone to take a picture of someone robbing the store. How could facial recognition software help solve the crime? What are some of the potential drawbacks of allowing citizens with smartphone cameras to help identify criminal suspects?

investigators have been able to reach across hundreds of miles and back in time to catch wrongdoers.

Law enforcement's ability to identify criminal suspects is set to receive another boost with the increased use of **biometrics.** The term refers to the measurement and analysis of a person's unique physical characteristics, especially as a way to establish identity. The use of biometrics gives law enforcement personnel the technological ability to identify whether a person is a criminal suspect.

Perhaps the best-known biometric is the fingerprint, which has been used for decades to establish and authenticate the identity of suspects. Today, police officers in the field can use handheld mobile devices to match a suspect's fingerprints against those stored in state and federal databases. This mobile ID technology enables officers to accomplish a task that used to take hours or even days in as little as forty-five seconds.

1-5b The Changing Landscape of American Policing

Biometrics Methods to identify a person based on unique physical characteristics, such as fingerprints or facial configuration.

Over the course of three tumultuous days in the summer of 2016, American law enforcement found itself under the national spotlight because of three separate, though linked, incidents. On July 5, police officers in Baton Rouge, Louisiana, fatally shot Alton Sterling four times as he was being restrained on the ground. On July 6, a St. Anthony, Minnesota, police officer shot and killed Philando Castile, who was apparently in the process of reaching for his driver's license. Then, on July 7, during a march in Dallas to protest these two deaths, a lone sniper opened fire on the law enforcement officers assembled for the event, killing five and wounding nine others.

The shootings crystallized many of the controversies that plague modern American policing. Both Sterling and Castile were African American, the latest in a series of black men to die at the hands of law enforcement. Their deaths were caught on videotape, and each involved a questionable use of police force. Micah Xavier Johnson, the Dallas sniper, was a black man motivated by "recent police shootings" to "kill white people, especially white [police] officers."[34] According to James Comey, former director of the FBI, it seems clear that "something in policing has changed."[35]

Every year, about 44 million face-to-face contacts between police and civilians take place.[36] The vast majority of these interactions are routine and fail to generate any public interest. On the rare occasions when police-civilian contact does involve force, it has become increasingly likely that the incident will be caught on bystanders' smartphones, surveillance systems, or officers' body cameras. "The video camera has become omnipresent," says Richard Aborn, president of the Citizens Crime Commission of New York City, "and it has become an absolute check on police credibility."[37]

Although videos may shed light on a given incident, law enforcement experts caution that the footage is rarely complete. "Everything happens so quickly and you have just a moment to [think about] living or not getting up tomorrow, or your partner being dead," says one New York City detective.[38] In any case, however, public scrutiny and criticism create pressure. And this pressure has added to the already considerable stresses that come with life as a police officer, a topic we will discuss in Chapter 5.

1-5c Homeland Security and Domestic Terrorism

Without question, the attacks of September 11, 2001—when terrorists hijacked four commercial airlines and used them to kill nearly three thousand people in New York City, northern Virginia, and rural Pennsylvania—were the most significant events of the first decade of the 2000s as far as crime fighting is concerned. As we will see throughout this textbook, the resulting **homeland security** movement has touched nearly every aspect of criminal justice. This movement has the ultimate goal of protecting America from **terrorism,** which can be broadly defined as the random use of staged violence to achieve political goals.

LO**1-5** Describe the defining aspects of a terrorist act, and identify one common misperception concerning domestic terrorism.

PROTECTING THE HOMELAND Immediately following 9/11, homeland security in the United States concentrated on preventing large-scale assaults by foreign terrorist operatives. More recently, however, the terrorist threat has shifted to homegrown, self-radicalized individuals who attempt to operate undetected on U.S. soil. Consequently, counterterrorism efforts now focus primarily on **domestic terrorism,** generally defined as acts of terror that are carried out within one's own country and against one's own people.

Despite public perception, domestic terrorism does *not* refer only to extremist acts by radical Muslims in the United States. In fact, a recent survey of local law enforcement agency administrators found that 74 percent identified antigovernment zealots as one of the primary terrorist threats in their jurisdictions, compared with 39 percent who singled out Muslim extremists as a significant danger.[39]

One threat posed by domestic terrorists is that they often behave like ordinary criminals. Compared with preventing traditional large-scale acts of terrorism,

Pool/Getty Images News/Getty Images

In January 2017, Dylann Roof, center, was sentenced to death for fatally shooting nine African American worshippers at a church in Charleston, South Carolina. A self-described white supremacist, Roof chose his victims because they were black. **Should Roof be considered a domestic terrorist? Why or why not?**

Homeland Security A concerted national effort to prevent terrorist attacks within the United States and reduce the country's vulnerability to terrorism.

Terrorism The use or threat of violence to achieve political objectives.

Domestic Terrorism Acts of terrorism that take place on U.S. soil without direct foreign involvement.

stopping them is more like stopping a shooting at a mall or the robbery of a liquor store. These "lone wolves" have little terrorist expertise and little outside support from or contact with known terrorist organizations. Instead of directly managing American-based extremists, Middle East–based groups such as the Islamic State (ISIS) and al Qaeda seek to "crowdsource" their goals with general statements of encouragement. "Determination! Determination!" Abu Mohammed al-Adanani, a senior military leader of ISIS, urged followers before his death in 2016. "The smallest act that you do in [your] lands is more beloved to us than the biggest act done here."[40]

Crowdsourcing efforts take place mostly on social media sites such as Twitter and Instagram, as well as other Internet platforms. ISIS, for example, produces thousands of Internet videos designed to recruit foreign adherents. The terrorist group also maintains a twenty-four-hour online recruiting operation. "By assimilating into the Internet world instead of the real world, I became absorbed in a 'virtual' struggle while disconnecting from what was real," said a Virginia teenager who was arrested several years ago for driving a friend to the airport so the friend could join ISIS in Syria.[41]

SECURITY VERSUS PRIVACY "We've created the world's most powerful terrorism hindsight machine," insists one critic of U.S. counterterrorism efforts.[42] To develop more foresight in this area, homeland security officials have relied on various electronic methods of gathering information on possible terrorist plots. In particular, over the past decade the federal government has conducted surveillance operations in which the phone records of Americans are collected in bulk and analyzed to uncover any links with suspected terrorists. The surveillance does not record the contents of the calls, but rather the metadata, which includes the time of the call, the number of the caller, and the number of the phone that was called.

As we will discuss in Chapter 14, when details of the metadata surveillance program came to light in 2013, it raised the ire not only of American Muslims, who felt they were unfairly targeted, but also of *civil liberties* groups. The term **civil liberties** refers to the personal freedoms guaranteed by the U.S. Constitution, particularly the first ten amendments, called the Bill of Rights. Concerns about balancing personal freedoms and personal safety permeate our criminal justice system. In fact, an entire chapter of this textbook—Chapter 6—is needed to properly examine the rules that law enforcement must follow to protect the civil liberties of crime suspects.

Civil Liberties The basic rights and freedoms for American citizens guaranteed by the U.S. Constitution, particularly in the Bill of Rights.

Justice Reinvestment A corrections policy that promotes (a) a reduction in spending on prisons and jails and (b) reinvestment of the resulting savings in programs that decrease crime and reduce reoffending.

CAREER TIP If you are interested in ensuring that all Americans are treated equally by federal, state, and local governments, you should consider becoming a *civil liberties lawyer.*

1-5d Prison Population Trends

After increasing by 500 percent from 1980 to 2008, the prison population in the United States decreased in five of the six following years.[43] To be sure, these decreases were comparatively modest (an average of about 0.9 percent per year),[44] and the American corrections system remains immense. More than 2.1 million offenders are in prison or jail in this country, and another 4.65 million are under community supervision.[45] Still, the trend reflects a series of crucial changes in the American criminal justice system.

THE "DEINCARCERATION" MOVEMENT There is no question that economic considerations have played a role in the nation's shrinking inmate population. Federal, state, and local governments spend $80 billion a year on prisons and jails, and many corrections officials are under pressure to decrease costs.[46] Many state officials have also embraced the concept of **justice reinvestment,** an umbrella term for policies that redirect funds saved by lowering a state's prison population into programs aimed at improving community safety. For instance, policymakers in Alabama hope to reduce that state's inmate rolls by nearly five thousand over the next decade, freeing up $26 million to hire additional parole officers and increase behavioral health treatment services for ex-offenders.[47]

In addition to economic concerns, downsizing efforts increasingly reflect "the message that locking up a lot of people doesn't necessarily bring public safety," says Joan Petersilia, co-director of Stanford University's Criminal Justice Center.[48] To reduce prison populations, therefore,

FIGURE 1.3 FEDERAL PRISONS: ADMISSIONS AND RELEASES

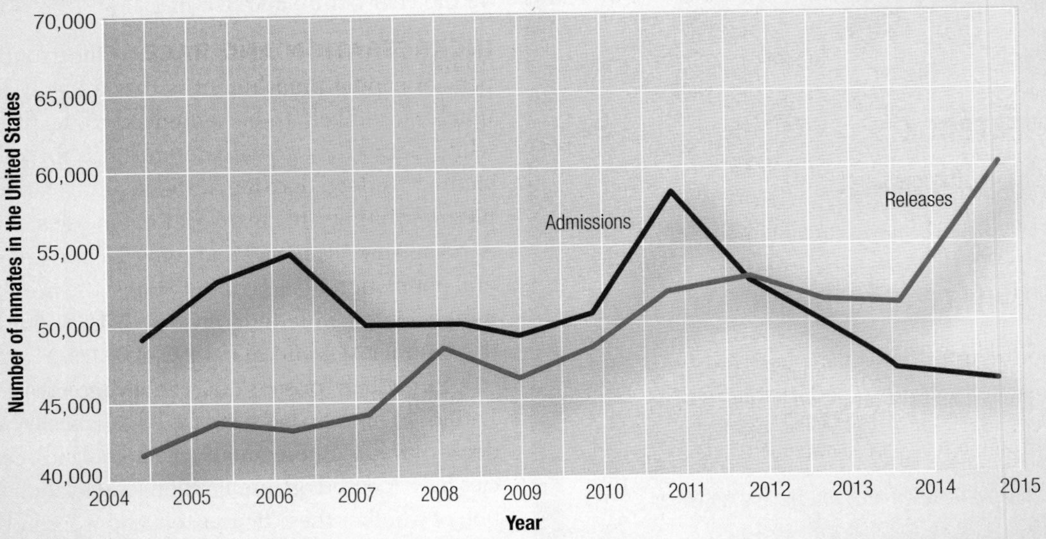

From 2012 to 2015, the number of inmates released from federal prisons has been greater than the number of inmates admitted to federal prisons, an important factor in the overall reduction of federal inmates in the United States.

Source: Bureau of Justice Statistics, *Prisoners in 2014* (Washington, D.C.: U.S. Department of Justice, September 2015), Appendix table 2, page 29; and Bureau of Justice Statistics, *Prisoners in 2015* (Washington, D.C.: U.S. Department of Justice, December 2016), Table 7, page 11.

federal and state correctional officials are implementing programs designed to curtail the *recidivism* rate of ex-convicts. **Recidivism** refers to the act of committing another crime (and possibly returning to incarceration) after having been punished for previous criminal behavior. To further promote deincarceration, federal and state corrections systems are making efforts to release qualified inmates from prison before their terms end.

RELEASE AND REENTRY Under pressure from federal courts to reduce prison overcrowding, California decreased the number of inmates in its state prisons by 51,000—over 30 percent—between 2006 and 2016.[49] Nationwide, similar actions have focused on early release for offenders that Stanford's Joan Petersilia characterizes as "triple-nons": nonserious, nonviolent, and nonsexual. For example, over the past several years, the U.S. Justice Department released more than six thousand nonviolent drug offenders from federal prisons. Indeed, as Figure 1.3 highlights, releases are now consistently surpassing admissions in federal prisons, resulting in an overall decline in the number of federal inmates in the United States.

Some observers feel that this aspect of the deincarceration movement inevitably will lead to increased crime rates as the newly freed prisoners revert to their "old ways." To lessen this possibility, the corrections system has embraced *reentry programs* that provide ex-offenders with treatment for drug and alcohol addictions and mental illness, as well as help in finding housing and employment. We will examine the deincarceration movement, including policies that promote reentry, in much more detail in Chapters 10, 11, and 12.

DECLINING USE OF THE DEATH PENALTY Another interesting corrections trend involves death row inmates, who are in prison awaiting execution after having been found guilty of committing a **capital crime.** Near the end of 2016, the death row population in American prisons stood at about 2,900, down from 3,653 in 2000.[50] During that same time period, the number of annual executions in this country dropped from 85 to 20, a twenty-five year low. In addition, it seems that judges and juries have become less willing to

Recidivism The act of committing a new crime after having been punished for a previous crime by being convicted and sent to jail or prison.

Capital Crime A criminal act that makes the offender eligible to receive the death penalty.

STUDY TOOLS 1

LOCATED IN TEXTBOOK

- ☐ Rip out the Chapter Review Card.
- ☐ Review with the Chapter Quiz following this chapter.

LOCATED AT WWW.CENGAGEBRAIN.COM

- ☐ Review key terms flash cards.
- ☐ Read the chapter on all your favorite devices.
- ☐ Complete an Exam to test your knowledge.
- ☐ Check out Visual Summaries and You Decide activities to explore chapter concepts.

sentence the "worst of the worst" criminals to death. In 2016, 30 offenders were sentenced to death, down from 49 the year before and 315 in 1996.[51]

INCARCERATION AND RACE One troublesome aspect of capital punishment is that a black defendant is much more likely to be sentenced to death for killing a white victim than a white defendant is for killing a black victim.[52] Indeed, looking at the general statistics, a bleak picture of minority incarceration emerges. Even though African Americans make up only 13 percent of the general population in the United States, the number of black men in state and federal prisons (523,000) is larger than the number of white men (499,400).[53]

In federal prisons, one in every three inmates is Latino.[54] This ratio has increased dramatically over the past decade as law enforcement and homeland security agencies have focused on immigration law violations. The question of whether these figures reflect purposeful bias on the part of certain members of the criminal justice community will be addressed at various points in this textbook.

Quiz

1. Murder, assault, and robbery are labeled ________________ crimes because they are committed against persons.
2. The category of crime that includes larceny, motor vehicle theft, and arson is called ________________ crime.
3. To protect against a too-powerful central government, the framers of the U.S. Constitution relied on the principle of ________________ to balance power between the national government and the states.
4. The United States has a dual court system, with parallel court systems at the federal level and at the ________________ level.
5. At every level, the criminal justice system relies on the ________________ of its employees to keep it from being bogged down by formal rules.
6. Ideally, criminal justice professionals rely on a strong sense of ________________ to make moral and just decisions as part of their daily routines.
7. The ________________ model of criminal justice places great importance on high rates of apprehension and conviction of criminal suspects.
8. The ________________ model emphasizes the rights of individual criminal defendants over the powers of the government.
9. America's homeland security system has been designed to protect the country from violent acts committed to further political goals, otherwise known as ________________.
10. To reduce inmate populations, corrections officials are implementing programs aimed at reducing the ________________ rate, or the rate at which ex-inmates are rearrested and returned to jail or prison.

Answers for Chapter 1 Quiz can be found in the Answers section in the back of the book.

2 The Crime Picture: Theories and Trends

The Washington Post/Getty Images

LEARNING OBJECTIVES

After studying this chapter, you will be able to . . .

2-1 Discuss the difference between a hypothesis and a theory in the context of criminology.

2-2 Contrast the medical model of addiction with the criminal model of addiction.

2-3 Identify the publication in which the FBI reports crime data and list the two main ways in which the data are reported.

2-4 Describe the three ways that victims' rights legislation increases the ability of crime victims to participate in the criminal justice system.

2-5 Explain why income level appears to be more important than race when it comes to crime trends.

After finishing this chapter, go to **PAGE 44** for **STUDY TOOLS**

Excess Baggage

For his long flight from Anchorage, Alaska, to South Florida, Esteban Santiago checked only a single piece of luggage. When he arrived at the Ft. Lauderdale–Hollywood Airport, at about 1 p.m. on January 6, 2017, Santiago retrieved his bag and went into a bathroom. There, he unpacked and loaded a Walther 9-millimeter handgun. Then, he emerged into the baggage claim area and started shooting. After killing five victims and wounding eight more, Santiago—out of ammunition—lay spread-eagled on the floor, quietly surrendering.

In the days that followed, a number of disturbing details about Santiago's past emerged. A year earlier, he had been arrested and charged with assault for breaking down a bathroom door to get at his girlfriend. In November 2016, Santiago walked into the Federal Bureau of Investigation (FBI) field office in Anchorage to report that his mind was being controlled by a U.S. spy agency. FBI agents eventually turned him over to local authorities, who briefly held him for a psychiatric evaluation. According to his brother, Santiago had become "furious" since serving in Iraq from April 2010 to February 2011 with the Puerto Rico National Guard. He had recently complained about hearing voices and hallucinating.

For the most part, Santiago fit the profile for those who commit random multiple shootings in public places. He was male, single, and had a history of mental illness. Like a number of other mass shooters, he had previously been charged with crimes involving domestic violence. This accumulation of "red flags" does little, however, to answer the basic questions that always arise after outbreaks of seemingly senseless bloodshed. Why did it happen? Can we stop it from happening again? Unfortunately, the evidence suggests that potential killers such as Santiago are unremarkable until, suddenly, they're not. "He was a walk-in complaint," said an FBI spokesperson, defending the agency's handling of the case in Anchorage. "This is something that happens at [our] offices around the country every day."

AP Images/Lynne Sladky

Esteban Santiago is taken to federal court in Broward County, Florida, after being charged with fatally shooting five people at the Fort Lauderdale–Hollywood International Airport. *Should law enforcement in Alaska have focused more attention on Santiago because he fit the profile of a mass shooter? What are some of the drawbacks of this crime prevention strategy?*

2-1 WHAT IS A THEORY?

The study of crime, or **criminology,** is rich with different explanations for why people commit crimes. At the same time, *criminologists*, or those who study the causes of crime, warn against using models or profiles to predict violent behavior. To be sure, the risk factors exhibited by a "furious" Esteban Santiago, with his history of mental illness and domestic violence, seem obvious in retrospect. Such characteristics are also found in scores of people who will not become multiple-victim shooters, however. "You can't go out and round up all the alienated angry young men," points out Jeffrey Swanson, a professor of psychiatry and behavioral sciences at the Duke University School of Medicine.[1]

Still, in the case of Santiago, there did seem to be some connection between his characteristics and his violent outburst, particularly when one considers that he had briefly been held in an Anchorage psychiatric hospital unit. That is, there may have been a *correlation* between his behavior and his crimes, a concept that is crucial to criminology.

Criminology The scientific study of crime and the causes of criminal behavior.

2-1a Correlation and Cause

Correlation between two variables means that they tend to vary together. **Causation,** in contrast, means that one variable is responsible for the change in the other. As we will see later in the chapter, there is a correlation between drug abuse and criminal behavior: statistically, many criminals are also drug abusers. But drug abuse does not cause crime: not everyone who abuses drugs is a criminal.

To give another example, a study led by Scott Wolfe, a criminologist at the University of South Carolina, looked at crime rates in counties where the megastore Walmart added new stores during the 1990s. Wolfe and his co-author found that crime rates in those counties were significantly higher than those in neighboring counties with no Walmart expansion.[2] Despite these results, no criminologist would assert that new Walmart stores *caused* the higher crime rates. Other factors, such as unemployment, poverty, and zoning patterns, must also be taken into account to get a fuller understanding of the crime picture in the studied areas.

So, correlation does not equal cause. Such is the quandary for criminologists. We can say that there is a correlation between many factors and criminal behavior, but it is quite difficult to prove that the factors directly cause criminal behavior. Consequently, the question that is the underpinning of criminology—What causes crime?—has yet to be definitively answered.

Correlation The relationship between two measurements or behaviors that tend to move in the same direction.

Causation The relationship in which a change in one measurement or behavior creates a recognizable change in another measurement or behavior.

Theory An explanation of a happening or circumstance that is based on observation, experimentation, and reasoning.

Hypothesis A possible explanation for an observed occurrence that can be tested by further investigation.

Rational Choice Theory A school of criminology that holds that wrongdoers act as if they weigh the possible benefits of criminal or delinquent activity against the expected costs of being apprehended.

2-1b The Role of Theory

Criminologists have, however, uncovered a wealth of information concerning a different, and more practically applicable, inquiry: Given a certain set of circumstances, why do individuals commit criminal acts? This information has allowed criminologists to develop a number of *theories* concerning the causes of crime.

LO2-1 Discuss the difference between a hypothesis and a theory in the context of criminology.

THE SCIENTIFIC METHOD Many of us tend to think of a *theory* as some sort of guess or a statement that is lacking in credibility. In the academic world, and therefore for our purposes, a **theory** is an explanation of a happening or circumstance that is based on observation, experimentation, and reasoning. Scientific and academic researchers observe facts and their consequences to develop *hypotheses* about what will occur when a similar fact pattern is present in the future. A **hypothesis** is a proposition that can be tested by researchers or observers to determine if it is valid. If enough authorities do find the hypothesis valid, it will be accepted as a theory. See Figure 2.1 for an example of this process, known as the *scientific method*, in action.

THEORY IN ACTION Criminological theories are primarily concerned with attempting to determine the reasons for criminal behavior. For example, two criminologists from Arizona State University, Matthew Larson and Gary Sweeten, wanted to test their hypothesis that young people involved in romantic breakups are at high risk for destructive behavior.

Relying on a survey of high school and college students who were asked about issues in their personal lives, Larson and Sweeten found some support for their hypothesis. According to the data, breakups do indeed correlate with higher rates of criminal offending and substance abuse among young men and higher rates of substance abuse among young women.[3]

2-2 WHICH THEORIES OF CRIME ARE MOST WIDELY ACCEPTED?

As you read this chapter, keep in mind that theories are not the same as facts, and most, if not all, of the criminological theories described in these pages have their detractors. Over the past century, however, a number of theories of crime have gained wide, if not total, acceptance. We now turn our attention to these theories, starting with those that focus on the psychological and physical aspects of criminal behavior.

2-2a The Brain and the Body

For the purposes of the American criminal justice system, the answer to why a person commits a crime is rather straightforward: because that person chooses to do so. This is the underpinning of the **rational choice theory**

FIGURE 2.1 THE SCIENTIFIC METHOD

The scientific method is a process through which researchers test the accuracy of a hypothesis. This simple example should provide an idea of how the scientific method works.

Observation: I left my home at 7:00 this morning, and I was on time for class.

Hypothesis: If I leave home at 7:00 every morning, then I will never be late for class. (Hypotheses are often presented in this "If . . . , then . . ." format.)

Test: For three straight weeks, I left home at 7:00 every morning. Not one time was I late for class.

Verification: Four of my neighbors have the same morning class. They agree that they are never late if they leave by 7:00 A.M.

Theory: As long as I leave home at 7:00 A.M., I don't have to worry about being late for class.

Prediction: Tomorrow morning I'll leave at 7:00, and I will be on time for my class.

Note that even a sound theory supported by the scientific method, such as this one, does not *prove* that the prediction will be correct. Other factors not accounted for in the test and verification stages, such as an unexpected traffic accident, may disprove the theory. Predictions based on complex theories, such as the criminological ones we will be discussing in this chapter, are often challenged in such a manner.

of crime, summed up by criminologist James Q. Wilson (1931–2012) as follows:

> At any given moment, a person can choose between committing a crime and not committing it. The consequences of committing a crime consist of rewards (what psychologists call "reinforcers") and punishments; the consequences of not committing the crime also entail gains and losses. The larger the ratio of the net rewards of crime to the net rewards of [not committing a crime], the greater the tendency to commit a crime.[4]

In other words, a person, before committing a crime, acts as if she or he is weighing the benefits (which may be money, in the case of a robbery) against the costs (the possibility of being caught and going to prison or jail). If the perceived benefits are greater than the potential costs, the person is more likely to commit the crime.

RATIONAL CHOICE THEORY AND PUBLIC POLICY The theory that wrongdoers choose to commit crimes is a cornerstone of the American criminal justice system. Because crime is seen as the end result of a series of rational choices, policymakers have reasoned that severe punishment can deter criminal activity by adding another variable to the decision-making process. Supporters of the death penalty—now used by thirty-one states and the federal government—emphasize its deterrent effects, and legislators have used harsh mandatory sentences to control illegal drug use and trafficking.

TRAIT THEORIES OF CRIME If society is willing to punish crimes that are the result of a rational decision-making process, what should be its response to criminal behavior that is irrational or even unintentional? What if, for example, a schoolteacher who made sexual advances to young girls, including his stepdaughter, could prove that his wrongdoing was actually caused by an egg-sized tumor in his brain? Somewhat in contrast to rational choice theory, *trait theories* suggest that certain *biological* or *psychological* traits in individuals could incline them toward criminal behavior, given a certain set of circumstances.

Biology is a very broad term that refers to the scientific study of living organisms, while **psychology** pertains more specifically to the study of the mind and its processes. "All behavior is biological," pointed out geneticist David C. Rowe. "All behavior is represented in the brain, in its biochemistry, electrical activity, structure, and growth and decline."[5]

Genetics and Crime Criminologists who study biological theories of crime often focus on the effect that *genes* have on human behavior. Genes are coded sequences of DNA that control every aspect of our biology, from the color of our eyes and hair to the type of emotions we have. Every person's genetic makeup is determined by genes inherited from his or her parents. Consequently, when scientists study ancestral or evolutionary developments, they are engaging in **genetics,** a branch of biology that deals with traits that are passed from one generation to another through genes.

Genetics is at the heart of criminology's "nurture versus nature" debate. In other words, are traits such as aggressiveness and antisocial behavior, both of which often lead to criminality, a result of a person's environment (nurture) or her or his genes (nature)? To tip the balance toward "nature," a criminologist must be able to prove that, all other things being equal, the offspring of aggressive or antisocial parents are at

Biology The science of living organisms, including their structure, function, growth, and origin.

Psychology The scientific study of mental processes and behavior.

Genetics The study of how certain traits or qualities are transmitted from parents to their offspring.

CJ and TECHNOLOGY

Neurocriminology

What can someone's brain activity tell us about her or his potential criminality? Neurocriminology uses brain-scanning technology to help scientists answer that question—at least in part. A technique known as functional magnetic resonance imaging (fMRI) measures the flow of blood in the brain as a subject carries out certain tasks. With the help of fMRI, criminologists have been able to pinpoint areas of the brain that control behavior such as impulsiveness, emotions, and decision making, all of which are associated with antisocial and criminal behavior.

Recently, specialists with the Mind Research Network used a mobile fMRI device to scan the brains of inmates in a New Mexico prison who were soon to be released. The researchers focused on an area of the brain that regulates impulsive behavior, called the anterior cingulate cortex (ACC). These experts predicted, correctly, that inmates with low activity in the ACC were more likely to be rearrested after release than those with normal ACC activity. Another study shows that men with a smaller amygdala—a part of the brain's frontal lobe that controls anger and fear reactions to outside stimuli—are as much as three times more likely to commit violence than those with an average-sized amygdala.

Thinking about Neurocriminology

At present, brain scans cannot come close to predicting future criminal offending. They can only indicate a possibility of future criminal offending. With this limitation in mind, what use should the criminal justice system make of brain-mapping technology, if any?

greater risk to exhibit those traits than are the offspring of parents who are not aggressive or antisocial.

Hormones and Aggression Chemical messengers known as **hormones** have also been the subject of much criminological study. Criminal activity in males has been linked to elevated levels of hormones—specifically, **testosterone,** which controls secondary sex characteristics and has been associated with traits of aggression. Testing of inmate populations shows that those incarcerated for violent crimes exhibit higher testosterone levels than other prisoners.[6] Elevated testosterone levels have also been used to explain a lessening in criminal behavior with age, as the average testosterone level of men under twenty-eight is double that of men between thirty-one and sixty-six years old.[7]

Hormone A chemical substance, produced in tissue and conveyed in the bloodstream, that controls certain cellular and body functions, such as growth and reproduction.

Testosterone The hormone primarily responsible for the production of sperm and the development of male secondary sex characteristics.

A very specific form of female violent behavior is believed to stem from hormones. In 2016, a judge sentenced Carol Coronado to three consecutive life terms in prison for fatally stabbing her three young daughters at their home near Carson, California. Coronado's defense attorney had claimed his client was suffering from *postpartum psychosis* at the time of her alleged crime. This temporary illness, thought to be caused partly by the hormonal changes that women experience after childbirth, triggers abnormal behavior in a small percentage of new mothers.[8]

The Brain and Crime Dr. Margaret Spinelli, a women's health expert at New York City's Columbia University, explains that during pregnancy, a pregnant woman's hormones increase "more than a hundredfold." Then, following birth, hormone levels plummet. This roller coaster of hormonal activity can "disrupt brain chemistry," contributing to postpartum psychosis.[9] The study of how genetics and brain activity influence criminal behavior is called *neurocriminology*. Its practitioners have contributed a great deal to the understanding of what predisposes humans to violent behavior.

Mental Illness and Crime According to the federal government, more than half of all prison and jail inmates in the United States have mental health problems, with smaller percentages suffering from severe brain disorders.[10] In recent years, thanks to several high-profile murders, violent crime has been linked to *schizophrenia*, a chronic brain disorder that can lead to erratic, uncontrollable behavior. Persons suffering from this disease are at an unusually high risk for committing suicide or harming others. Culling data from 160 cases of public mass killings, Grant Duwe, a criminologist with the Minnesota Department of Corrections, found that 61 percent of those responsible showed evidence of mental illness, with the two most common ailments being schizophrenia and depression.[11]

Some criminologists reject any explicit connections between mental illness and violent crime, however. One recent study estimates that eliminating the effects of mental illness would reduce overall gun violence in the United States by only 4 percent.[12] Additional research shows that only about 5 percent of all gun homicides in this country are committed by people who have been diagnosed with a mental illness.[13] Consequently, there may be a correlation between mental conditions such as schizophrenia and violence, but such conditions cannot be said to cause violent behavior.

AP Images/Ben Margot

In February 2017, to protest a public appearance by a controversial political figure, demonstrators at the University of California, Berkeley, set bonfires and hurled smoke bombs, causing $100,000 worth of damage. **How does social psychology explain acts of violence or disorder by large groups of people?**

PSYCHOLOGY AND CRIME Like biological theories of crime, psychological theories of crime operate under the assumption that individuals have traits that make them more or less predisposed to criminal activity. To a certain extent, however, psychology rests more heavily on abstract ideas than does biology. Even Sigmund Freud (1856–1939), perhaps the most influential of all psychologists, considered the operations of the mind to be, like an iceberg, mostly hidden.

One influential branch of psychology—social psychology—focuses on human behavior in the context of how human beings relate to and influence one another. **Social psychology** rests on the assumption that the way we view ourselves is shaped to a large degree by how we think others view us. Generally, we act in the same manner as those we like or admire because we want them to like or admire us. Thus, to a certain extent, social psychology tries to explain the influence of crowds on individual behavior.

In the early 1970s, psychologist Philip Zimbardo highlighted the power of group behavior in dramatic fashion. Zimbardo randomly selected some Stanford University undergraduate students to act as "guards" and other students to act as "inmates" in an artificial prison environment. Before long, the students began to act as if these designations were real, with the "guards" physically mistreating the "inmates," who rebelled with equal violence. Within six days, Zimbardo was forced to discontinue the experiment out of fear for its participants' safety.[14] One of the basic assumptions of social psychology is that people are able to justify improper or even criminal behavior by convincing themselves that it is actually acceptable behavior. As Zimbardo's experiment showed, they find it much easier to do this when they are acting in groups where others are behaving in the same manner than when they are acting alone.[15]

2-2b Bad Neighborhoods and Other Economic Disadvantages

From 1995 to 1998, the Chicago Housing Authority demolished a number of buildings in that city's public housing projects because of substandard living conditions. In a recently completed study, Eric Chyn, an economist at the University of Michigan, found that the children of families who moved to other neighborhoods because of this demolition benefited from the forced relocation. Those children were 9 percent more likely to be employed than children who remained in the housing projects and had annual earnings that were 19 percent higher.[16] Indeed, criminologists focusing on **sociology** have long argued that

Social Psychology The study of how individual behavior is influenced by the behavior of groups in social situations.

Sociology The study of the development and functioning of groups of people who live together within a society.

neighborhood conditions are perhaps the most important variable in predicting criminal behavior.

SOCIAL DISORGANIZATION THEORY In the early twentieth century, juvenile crime researchers Clifford Shaw and Henry McKay popularized sociological explanations for crime with their **social disorganization theory.**

Shaw and McKay studied various high-crime neighborhoods in Chicago and discovered certain "zones" that exhibited high rates of crime. These zones were characterized by "disorganization," or a breakdown of the traditional institutions of social control such as family, school systems, and local businesses. In contrast, in the city's "organized" communities, residents had developed certain agreements about fundamental values and norms.

Social Disorganization Theory The theory that deviant behavior is more likely in communities where social institutions such as the family, schools, and the criminal justice system fail to exert control over the population.

Strain Theory The assumption that crime is the result of frustration felt by individuals who cannot reach their financial and personal goals through legitimate means.

Shaw and McKay found that residents in high-crime neighborhoods had to a large degree abandoned these fundamental values and norms. Also, a lack of social controls had led to increased levels of antisocial, or criminal, behavior.[17] According to social disorganization theory, factors that lead to crime in these neighborhoods are:

1. High levels of high school dropouts
2. Chronic unemployment
3. Deteriorating buildings and other infrastructures
4. Concentrations of single-parent families

(See Figure 2.2 to better understand social disorganization theory.)

STRAIN THEORY Another self-perpetuating aspect of disorganized neighborhoods is that once residents gain the financial means to leave a high-crime community, they usually do so. This desire to escape the inner city is related to the second branch of social structure theory: **strain theory.** Most Americans have similar life goals, which include gaining a certain measure of wealth and financial freedom. The means of attaining these goals,

FIGURE 2.2 THE STAGES OF SOCIAL DISORGANIZATION

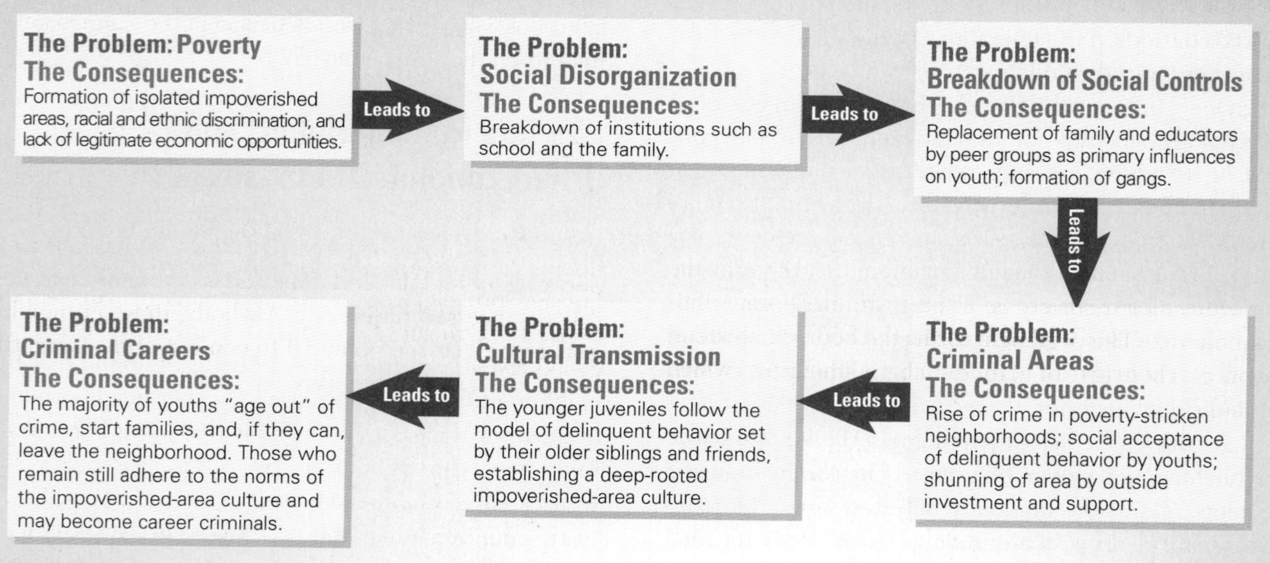

Social disorganization theory holds that crime is related to the environmental pressures that exist in certain communities or neighborhoods. These areas are marked by the desire of many of their inhabitants to "get out" at the first possible opportunity. Consequently, residents tend to ignore the important institutions in the community, such as businesses and schools, causing further erosion and an increase in the conditions that lead to crime.

Source: Adapted from Larry J. Siegel, *Criminology*, 10th ed. (Belmont, CA: Thomson/Wadsworth, 2009), 180.

however, are not universally available. Many citizens do not have access to the education or training necessary for financial success. This often results in frustration and anger, or *strain*.

Strain theory has its roots in the works of French sociologist Emile Durkheim (1858–1917) and his concept of ***anomie*** (derived from the Greek word for "without norms"). Durkheim believed that *anomie* resulted when social change threw behavioral norms into a flux, leading to a weakening of social controls and an increase in deviant behavior.[18] Another sociologist, American Robert K. Merton, expanded on Durkheim's ideas in his own theory of strain. Merton believed that *anomie* was caused by a social structure in which all citizens have similar goals without equal means to achieve them.[19] One way to alleviate this strain is to gain wealth by the means that are available to the residents of disorganized communities: drug trafficking, burglary, and other criminal activities.

Spencer Platt/Getty Images News/Getty Images

Two law enforcement officers investigate a burglary in Camden, New Jersey—one of the poorest cities in the United States. **How would a criminologist who advocates social conflict theories of criminal behavior explain high crime rates in low-income communities such as Camden?**

CAREER TIP A *sociologist* is someone who studies human social behavior. Because crime is such an important–and interesting–facet of human behavior, sociologists often study criminality.

SOCIAL CONFLICT THEORIES Strain theory and the concept of *anomie* seem to suggest that the unequal structure of our society is, in part, to blame for criminal behavior. This argument forms the bedrock of **social conflict theories** of crime. These theories, which entered mainstream criminology in the 1960s, hold capitalism responsible for high levels of violence and crime because of the disparity of income that it encourages.

According to social conflict theory, the poor commit property crimes for reasons of need and because, as members of a capitalist society, they desire the same financial rewards as everybody else. They commit violent crimes because of the frustration and rage they feel when these rewards seem unattainable. Laws, instead of reflecting the values of society as a whole, reflect only the values of the segment of society that has achieved power and is willing to use the criminal justice system as a tool to keep that power.[20] Thus, the harsh penalties for "lower-class" crimes such as burglary can be seen as a means of protecting the privileges of the "haves" from the aspirations of the "have-nots."

2-2c Life Lessons and Criminal Behavior

Some criminologists find class theories of crime overly narrow. Surveys that ask people directly about their criminal behavior have shown that the criminal instinct is pervasive in middle- and upper-class communities, even if it is expressed differently. Anybody, these criminologists argue, has the potential to commit crimes, regardless of class, race, or gender.

THE ABANDONED CAR EXPERIMENT Philip Zimbardo conducted a well-known, if rather unscientific, experiment to show the broad potential for misbehavior. The psychologist placed an abandoned automobile with its hood up on the campus of Stanford University. The car remained in place, untouched, for a week.

Anomie A condition in which the individual feels a disconnect from society due to the breakdown or absence of social norms.

Social Conflict Theories Theories that view criminal behavior as the result of class conflict.

Then, Zimbardo smashed the car's window with a sledgehammer. Within minutes, passersby had joined in the destruction of the automobile, eventually stripping its valuable parts.[21]

Social process theories function on the same basis as Zimbardo's "interdependence of decisions experiment": the potential for criminal behavior exists in everyone and will be realized depending on an individual's interaction with various institutions and processes of society. Two major branches of social process theory are (1) learning theory and (2) control theory.

LEARNING THEORY Popularized by Edwin Sutherland in the 1940s, **learning theory** contends that criminal activity is a learned behavior. In other words, a criminal is taught both the practical methods of crime (such as how to pick a lock) and the psychological aspects of crime (how to deal with the guilt of wrongdoing).

Sutherland's *theory of differential association* held that individuals are exposed to the values of family and peers such as school friends or co-workers. If the dominant values a person is exposed to favor criminal behavior, then that person is more likely to mimic such behavior.[22] Sutherland's focus on the importance of family relations in this area is underscored by research showing that sons of fathers who have been incarcerated are at an increased risk of delinquency and arrest.[23]

More recently, learning theory has been expanded to include the growing influence of the media. In the latest in a long series of studies, researchers released data in 2013 showing that children and adolescents who watched "excessive" amounts of violent television content faced an elevated risk of exhibiting antisocial behavior such as criminality in early adulthood.[24] In 2011, the United States Supreme Court ruled, however, that because violent video games have not been proved to *cause* aggressive behavior in children, the government cannot prohibit the sale or rental of such entertainment to juveniles.[25]

Social Process Theories Theories that consider criminal behavior to be the predictable result of a person's interaction with his or her environment.

Learning Theory The theory that delinquents and criminals must be taught both the practical and the emotional skills necessary to participate in illegal activity.

Control Theory A series of theories that assume that all individuals have the potential for criminal behavior, but are restrained by the damage that such actions would do to their relationships with family, friends, and members of the community.

Life Course Criminology The study of crime based on the belief that behavioral patterns developed in childhood can predict delinquent and criminal behavior later in life.

CONTROL THEORY Criminologist Travis Hirschi focuses on the reasons why individuals do not engage in criminal acts, rather than why they do. According to Hirschi, social bonds promote conformity to social norms. The stronger these social bonds—which include attachment to, commitment to, involvement with, and belief in societal values—the less likely that any individual will commit a crime.[26]

Control theory holds that although we all have the potential to commit crimes, most of us are dissuaded from doing so because we care about the opinions of our family and peers. James Q. Wilson and George Kelling described control theory in terms of the " broken windows" effect. Neighborhoods in poor condition are filled with cues of lack of social control (for example, broken windows) that invite further vandalism and other deviant behavior.[27] If these cues are removed, according to Wilson and Kelling, so is the implied acceptance of crime within a community.

LIFE COURSE THEORIES OF CRIME If crime is indeed learned behavior, some criminologists are asking, shouldn't we be focusing on early childhood—the time when humans do the most learning? Many of the other theories we have studied in this chapter tend to attribute criminal behavior to factors—such as unemployment or poor educational performance—that take place long after an individual's personality has been established. Practitioners of **life course criminology** believe that risk factors that exist in early childhood are the strongest predictors of future criminal behavior and have been seriously undervalued in the examination of why crime occurs.[28]

Self-Control Theory Focusing on childhood behavior raises the question of whether conduct problems established at a young age can be changed over time. Michael Gottfredson and Travis Hirschi, whose 1990 publication *A General Theory of Crime* is one of the foundations of life course criminology, think not.[29] Gottfredson and Hirschi believe that criminal behavior is linked to "low self-control," a personality trait that is formed before a child reaches the age of ten and can usually be attributed to poor parenting.[30]

In general, someone who has low self-control is:

1. Impulsive,
2. Thrill-seeking, and
3. Likely to solve problems with violence rather than intellect.

Gottfredson and Hirschi think that once low self-control has been established, it will persist. In other words, childhood behavioral problems are not "solved" by positive developments later in life, such as healthy personal relationships or a good job.[31] Thus, these two criminologists subscribe to what has been called the

CAREER PREP

Criminologist

Job Description:

- Analyze criminal and delinquent behavior, and provide theoretical explanations for such behavior.
- Work with and for law enforcement agencies to prevent crime by offering profiles of criminal behavior and scrutinizing crime statistics.

What Kind of Training Is Required?

- Research skills, computer proficiency, and expertise in statistics.
- An undergraduate degree in a field relating to criminal justice with, preferably, a minor in psychology or sociology. A postgraduate degree is necessary for an academic career in criminology.

Annual Salary Range?

- $73,000–$140,000

igorstevanovic/Shutterstock.com

SOCIAL MEDIA CAREER TIP

Social media technologies are about connecting and sharing information—which means privacy is an important issue. Make sure you understand who can see the material you post and how you can control it. Facebook has numerous privacy settings, for example, as does Instagram.

continuity theory of crime, which essentially says that once negative behavior patterns have been established, they cannot be changed.

The Possibility of Change Not all of those who practice life course criminology follow the continuity theory. Terrie Moffitt, for example, notes that youthful offenders can be divided into two groups. The first group are life-course-persistent offenders: they are biting playmates at age five, skipping school at ten, stealing cars at sixteen, committing violent crimes at twenty, and perpetrating fraud and child abuse at thirty.[32] The second group are adolescent-limited offenders: as the name suggests, their "life of crime" is limited to the teenage years.[33] So, according to Moffitt, change is possible, if not for the life-course-persistent offenders (who are saddled with psychological problems that lead to continued social failure and misconduct), then for the adolescent-limited offenders. (See Figure 2.3) for a review of theories discussed so far in this chapter.)

2-3 WHAT IS THE CONNECTION BETWEEN DRUG USE AND CRIME?

Criminologists have long studied the link between crime and *drugs*. In general, offenders who use greater amounts of alcohol and illegal drugs have significantly higher crime rates than those who are less involved with these substances. Actually, alcohol falls under the broadest possible definition of a drug, which is any substance that modifies biological, psychological, or social behavior.

Drug Any substance that modifies biological, psychological, or social behavior; in particular, an illegal substance with those properties.

In popular usage, however, the word **drug** has a more specific connotation. When people speak of the

FIGURE 2.3 THE CAUSES OF CRIME

Choice Theories	
Key Concept:	Crime is the result of rational choices made by those who decide to engage in criminal activity for the rewards—financial and otherwise—that it offers.
Example:	Over a six-month period, LaTroy Staglin intentionally caused a series of car accidents in Oklahoma City so that he could file false insurance claims for damages worth thousands of dollars. Staglin was sentenced to eighteen years behind bars.
Biological and Psychological Trait Theories	
Key Concept:	Criminal behavior is explained by the biological and psychological attributes of an individual.
Example:	A sixty-three-year-old physician from Southern California who illegally distributed a massive amount of prescription drugs was found to be afflicted with a form of brain damage called frontotemporal dementia (FTLD). Research shows that about one-third of FTLD sufferers exhibit criminal behavior.
Sociological Theories	
Key Concept:	Crime is not something a person is "born to do." Rather, crime is the result of the social conditions such as poverty, poor schools, unemployment, and discrimination with which a person lives.
Example:	Five large cities with significant recent murder rate increases (Chicago, Dallas, Las Vegas, San Diego, and San Jose) have experienced higher-than-average rates of poverty and unemployment since the mid-2000s.
Social Conflict Theories	
Key Concept:	Through criminal laws, the dominant members of society control the minority members, using institutions such as the police, courts, and prisons as tools of oppression.
Example:	Between July 2006 and June 2007, law enforcement officers from the Arizona Department of Public Safety stopped and searched African American and Latino drivers 2.5 times more often than white drivers. These higher search rates were not justified by evidence that African American or Latino drivers were more likely to be carrying illegal contraband.
Social Process Theories	
Key Concept:	Family, friends, and peers have the greatest impact on an individual's behavior, and it is the interactions with these groups that ultimately determine whether a person will become involved in criminal behavior.
Example:	According to the Pittsburgh Youth Study, having a close relative—particularly a father—convicted of a crime significantly increases the chances that a young male subject will eventually be convicted of a crime.
Life Course Theories	
Key Concept:	Criminal and antisocial behavior is evident at each stage of a person's life. By focusing on such behavior in early childhood, criminologists may be able to better understand and predict offending patterns that emerge as a person grows older.
Example:	Children who suffer from issues such as lack of concentration, a tendency to daydream, and restlessness at the age of five are more likely than their peers to engage in delinquency at the age of fourteen.

drug problem, or the war on drugs, or drug abuse, they are referring specifically to illegal **psychoactive drugs**, which affect the brain and alter consciousness or perception. Almost all of the drugs that we will be discussing in this textbook, such as marijuana, cocaine, heroin, and amphetamines, are illegal and psychoactive.

About 27.1 million Americans regularly use illegal drugs such as marijuana (illegal at the federal level and in most states) and cocaine, with another 200 million using legal drugs such as alcohol and nicotine. For criminologists, these data raise two questions. First, why do people use drugs? Second, what are the consequences for the criminal justice system?

Psychoactive Drug
A chemical that affects the brain, causing changes in emotions, perceptions, and behavior.

2-3a The Criminology of Drug Use

At first glance, the reason people use drugs, including legal drugs such as alcohol, is obvious: such drugs give users pleasure and provide a temporary escape for those who may feel tension or anxiety. Ultimately, though, such explanations are unsatisfactory because they fail to explain why some people use drugs while others do not.

DRUGS AND THE "LEARNING PROCESS" Focusing on the question of why first-time drug users become habitual users, sociologist Howard Becker sees three factors in the "learning process." He believes first-time users:

1. Learn the techniques of drug use.
2. Learn to perceive the pleasurable effects of drug use.
3. Learn to enjoy the social experience of drug use.[34]

Becker's assumptions are evident in the widespread belief that positive images of drug use in popular culture "teach" adolescents that such behavior is not only acceptable but desirable. The entertainment industry, in particular, has been criticized for glamorizing various forms of drug use.

DRUG USE AND DRUG ABUSE Another theory rests on the assumption that some people possess overly sensitive drug receptors in their brains and are therefore biologically disposed toward drug use.[35] Though there is little conclusive evidence that biological factors can explain initial drug experimentation, scientific research has provided a great deal of insight into patterns of long-term drug use.

Cheryl Senter/The New York Times/Redux

A young woman prepares to use heroin under a bridge in Portland, Maine. **Do you think that drug abusers should be treated as criminals to be punished or as ill people in need of treatment? Explain your answer.**

In particular, science has aided in understanding the difference between drug *use* and drug *abuse*. **Drug abuse** can be defined as the use of any drug—licit or illicit—that causes either psychological or bodily harm to the abuser or to third parties. Just as most people who drink beer or wine avoid abusing alcohol, most users of illegal substances are not abusers. Indeed, more than 90 percent of first-time users do not become dependent on illicit drugs, though the number drops sharply among those who continue to use the drug for more than one year.[36]

Despite their relatively small numbers, drug abusers have a disparate impact on the drug market. The 20 percent of Americans, for example, who drink the most consume more than 80 percent of all alcoholic beverages sold in the United States. The data are similar for illicit substance abusers, leading to the conclusion that, to a large extent, abusers and addicts sustain the market for illegal drugs.

2-3b The Drug-Crime Relationship

Studies that connect drug use to criminality can be problematic, mainly because such activity is likely one risk factor among many in a criminal user's life. Still, drugs and crime are related in three general ways:[37]

1. *Drug-defined offenses,* or violation of laws prohibiting the possession, use, distribution, or manufacture of illegal drugs. Examples include possession of marijuana and methamphetamine production.
2. *Drug-related offenses,* such as crimes motivated by drug abuse or committed to further the illegal drug trade. Examples include gang violence between rival drug dealers and theft to get money to buy illegal drugs.
3. *The drug-using lifestyle,* experienced by many drug abusers who do not participate in the legitimate economy and thus rely on crime for the means of survival. These users often support short-term goals with illegal activities such as prostitution and welfare fraud.

According to the federal government, at least two-thirds of all persons arrested in this country have illegal drugs in their systems when apprehended.[38] Legal drugs also play a role in the crime picture of the United States. About 37 percent of state prisoners and 33 percent of jail inmates incarcerated for a violent crime were under the influence of alcohol at the time of their arrest.[39] Richard Friedman, who studies the effect of drugs on behavior, estimates that abusing alcohol and other drugs increases the likelihood of violence by a factor of seven.[40]

MODELS OF ADDICTION What is the best way for society to deal with addicts? According to the **medical model of addiction,** addicts are not criminals,

Drug Abuse The use of drugs that results in physical or psychological problems for the user, as well as disruption of personal relationships and employment.

Medical Model of Addiction An approach to drug addiction that treats drug abuse as a mental illness, and focuses on treating and rehabilitating offenders rather than punishing them.

but mentally or physically ill individuals who are forced into acts of petty crime to "feed their habit." Those who believe in the *enslavement theory of addiction* advocate treating addiction as a disease and hold that society should not punish addicts but rather attempt to rehabilitate them, as would be done for any other unhealthy person.[41]

> **LO2-2** Contrast the medical model of addiction with the criminal model of addiction.

Although a number of organizations, including the American Medical Association, recognize alcoholism and other forms of drug dependence as diseases, the criminal justice system tends to favor the **criminal model of addiction** over the medical model. The criminal model holds that illegal drug abusers and addicts endanger society with their behavior and should be punished the same as persons who commit non-drug-related crimes.

MARIJUANA LAW TRENDS How would the link between certain illegal drugs and crime change if those drugs were legalized? That is, what if a particular illegal drug was treated in the same manner as alcohol and tobacco—heavily regulated, but available to persons over the age of twenty-one? While these questions are not being asked with regard to "hard" drugs such as heroin and cocaine, the **legalization** of marijuana—America's most-used illicit drug—has become an important policy issue. Indeed, as we noted in Chapter 1, in 2016, four states voted to legalize the possession and sale of small amounts of marijuana for recreational use, bringing to eight the total number of states where the once unlawful drug is now part of the legal mainstream.

Those in favor of marijuana legalization generally rely on the following arguments to support their position:

1. Nationwide legalization would put the black market for marijuana—estimated at about $41 billion year[42]—out of business, ending violent crime associated with the pot trade and depriving scores of criminals of their livelihood.
2. It would remove the stigma of recreational marijuana use for millions of people who are otherwise unconnected with criminal activity and keep millions of nonviolent offenders out of prison.
3. It would provide a double "peace dividend" by saving our criminal justice system the costs associated with the approximately 640,000 marijuana arrests that occur each year,[43] while at the same time providing governmental agencies with millions of dollars in tax receipts.

> **Criminal Model of Addiction** An approach to drug abuse that holds that drug offenders harm society by their actions to the same extent as other criminals and should face the same punitive sanctions.
>
> **Legalization** Making a formerly illegal product or action lawful. In the context of marijuana, the process includes strict regulation, including a ban on sale to or use by minors.
>
> **Uniform Crime Reports (UCR)** A set of annual reports compiled by the FBI to give an indication of criminal activity in the United States.

Proponents also insist that casual marijuana use by adults is relatively benign,[44] a claim that the opponents of marijuana legalization argue is only marginally relevant. These detractors point out that, more crucially, in the first year that recreational marijuana use was legal in Washington State, "drugged driving" arrests, marijuana-related fatal car crashes, and hospitalizations for overdoses all increased.[45]

> **ETHICS CHALLENGE**
>
> **In fiscal year 2015, the Colorado Department of Revenue brought in $70 million in taxes related to the sale of legal marijuana. Do you think there are any ethical issues with collecting taxes on a product that may have harmful health effects for users? Why or why not? (Note that Colorado also collected $42 million in taxes on alcohol that year.)**

2-4 HOW IS CRIME MEASURED?

So far in this textbook, you have been exposed to a number of studies relating to the criminal justice system. For the most part, these analyses have dealt with narrow topics such as the racial makeup of marijuana arrestees and the impact of Walmart expansion on offending. The best-known annual survey of criminal behavior, however, tries to answer the broadest of questions: How much crime is there in the United States?

2-4a The Uniform Crime Reports

The nation's most far-reaching and oft-cited set of national crime statistics is known as the **Uniform Crime Reports (UCR).** The UCR is a compilation of data prepared by the Federal Bureau of Investigation (FBI). Since its inception in 1930, the UCR has attempted to measure the overall rate of crime in the United States by collecting data on "offenses known to law enforcement."[46] To produce the UCR, the FBI relies on the voluntary participation of local law enforcement agencies. These agencies—approximately 18,000 in total, covering most of the population—base their information on three measurements:

1. The number of persons arrested.
2. The number of crimes reported by victims, witnesses, or the police themselves.
3. Police employee data.[47]

Once this information has been sent to the FBI, the agency presents the crime data in two important ways:

1. As a *rate* per 100,000 people. For example, suppose the crime rate in a given year is 3,000. This means that, for every 100,000 inhabitants of the United States, 3,000 *Part I offenses* were reported to the FBI by local police departments. The crime rate is often cited by media sources when discussing the level of crime in the United States.
2. As a percentage change from the previous year or other time periods. From 2006 to 2015, there was a 22.2 percent decrease in violent crime and a 25 percent decrease in property crime. Thus, according to the UCR, that decade saw a significant reduction in criminal behavior in the United States.[48]

LO2-3 Identify the publication in which the FBI reports crime data and list the two main ways in which the data are reported.

The FBI publishes its data annually in *Crime in the United States*. Along with the basic statistics, this publication offers an exhaustive array of crime information, including breakdowns of crimes committed by city, county, and other geographic designations, and by the demographics (gender, race, age) of the individuals who have been arrested for crimes.

PART I OFFENSES The UCR divides the criminal offenses it measures into two major categories: Part I and Part II offenses. **Part I offenses** are those crimes that, due to their seriousness and frequency, are recorded by the FBI to give a general idea of the "crime picture" in the United States in any given year. For a description of the seven Part I offenses, see Figure 2.4.

Part I violent offenses are those most likely to be covered by the media and, consequently, most likely to inspire fear in the population. These crimes have come to dominate crime coverage to such an extent that, for most Americans, the first image that comes to mind at the mention of "crime" is one person physically attacking another person or a robbery taking place with the use or threat of force. Furthermore, in the stereotypical crime, the offender and the victim do not know each other.

Given the trauma of violent crimes, this perception is understandable, but it is not accurate. According to UCR statistics, almost half of the homicides in the United States are committed by a relative or other acquaintance of the victim.[49] Furthermore, as is evident from Figure 2.4, the majority of Part I offenses committed are property crimes. Notice that 62 percent of all reported Part I offenses are larceny/thefts, and another 17 percent are burglaries.[50]

PART II OFFENSES Not only do violent crimes represent the minority of Part I offenses, but Part I offenses are far outweighed by **Part II offenses,** which include all crimes recorded by the FBI that do not fall into the category of Part I offenses. While Part I offenses are almost always felonies, Part II offenses include crimes that may be classified as misdemeanors. Of the nineteen categories that make up Part II offenses, the most common are drug abuse violations, simple assaults (in which no weapons are used and no serious harm is done to the victim), driving under the influence, and disorderly conduct.[51]

Information gathered on Part I offenses reflects those offenses "known," or reported to the FBI by local agencies. Part II offenses, in contrast, are measured only by arrest data. In 2015, the FBI recorded about 2 million arrests for Part I offenses in the United States. That same year, about 8.8 million arrests for Part II offenses took place.[52] In other words, Part II offenses were four and one-half times more common than Part I offenses. Such statistics have prompted Marcus Felson, a professor at Rutgers University School of Criminal Justice, to comment that "most crime is very ordinary."[53]

CAREER TIP With their expert knowledge of statistics and their ability to organize numerical data, ***statisticians*** are crucial employees for the FBI and other federal and state law enforcement agencies that regularly publish crime reports.

2-4b The National Incident-Based Reporting System

In the 1980s, well aware of the various criticisms of the UCR, the Department of Justice began seeking ways to revise its data-collecting system. The result was the National Incident-Based Reporting

Part I Offenses The most serious crimes recorded by the FBI in its Uniform Crime Reports.

Part II Offenses All crimes recorded by the FBI that do not fall into the category of Part I offenses.

FIGURE 2.4 PART I OFFENSES

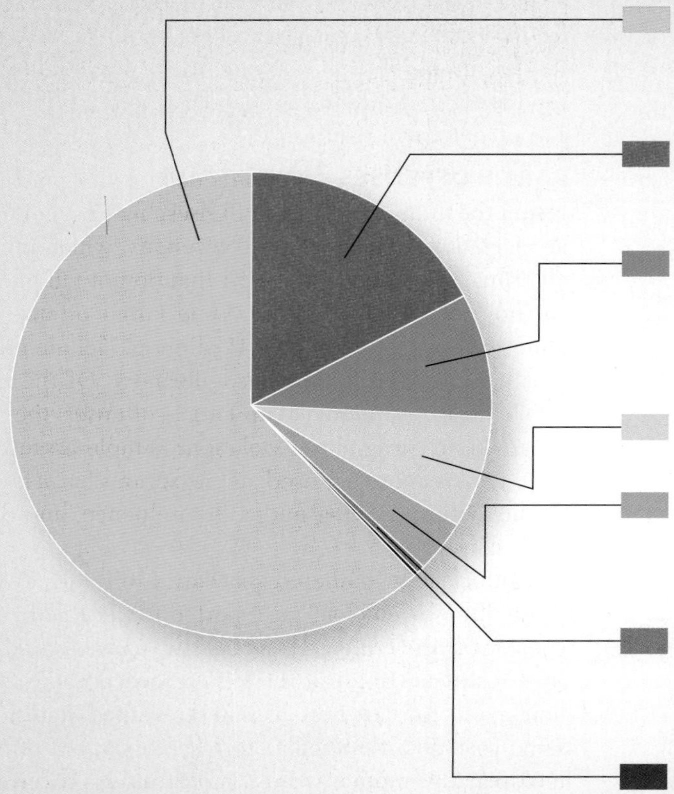

Larceny/Theft 62.1%
(Except motor vehicle theft) The unlawful taking, carrying, leading, or riding away of property from the possession or constructive possession of another.

Burglary—breaking and entering 17.3%
The unlawful entry of a structure to commit a felony or a theft. Attempted forcible entry is included.

Aggravated Assault 8.4%
An unlawful attack by one person on another for the purpose of inflicting severe or aggravated bodily injury. This type of assault is usually accompanied by the use of a weapon or by means likely to produce death or great bodily harm.

Motor Vehicle Theft 7.8%
The theft or attempted theft of a motor vehicle.

Robbery 3.6%
The taking or attempting to take of anything of value from the care, custody, or control of a person or persons by force or threat of force or violence and/or by putting the victim in fear.

Rape 0.7%
The penetration, no matter how slight, of the vagina or anus with any body part or object, or oral penetration by a sex organ of another person, without the consent of the victim.

Murder 0.1%
The willful (nonnegligent) killing of one human being by another.

Arson
Any willful or malicious burning or attempt to burn, with or without intent to defraud, a dwelling house, public building, motor vehicle or aircraft, personal property of another, and the like.

Every month, local law enforcement agencies voluntarily provide information on serious offenses in their jurisdiction to the FBI. These serious offenses, known as Part I offenses, are defined here. (Arson is not included in the national crime report data, but it is sometimes considered a Part I offense nonetheless, so its definition is included here.) As the graph shows, most Part I offenses reported by local police departments in any given year are property crimes.

Source: Federal Bureau of Investigation, *Crime in the United States, 2015,* Offense Definitions. *www.ucr.fbi.gov.* U.S. Department of Justice: 2016, Web; and Federal Bureau of Investigation, *Crime in the United States, 2015,* Table 1. *www.ucr.fbi.gov.* U.S. Department of Justice: 2016, Web.

System (NIBRS). In the NIBRS, local agencies collect data on each single crime occurrence within twenty-three offense categories made up of forty-nine specific crimes called Group A offenses. These data are recorded on computerized record systems provided—though not completely financed—by the federal government.

The NIBRS became available to local agencies in 1989. Twenty-six years later, 36 percent of all law enforcement agencies that participate in the UCR program were submitting data to the NIBRS, and NIBRS is slated to replace the UCR in 2021.[54] Criminologists are responding enthusiastically to the NIBRS because the system provides information about four "data sets"—offenses, victims, offenders, and arrestees—unavailable through the UCR.

The NIBRS also presents a more complete picture of crime by monitoring all criminal "incidents" reported to the police, not just those that lead to an arrest. For example, the 2015 NIBRS, which recorded about 4.9 million criminal incidents, found that sex offenses were most likely to take place between midnight and 12:59 a.m. and that 4 percent of all aggravated assaults resulted from "lover's quarrels."[55]

2-4c Victim Surveys

One alternative method of data collecting attempts to avoid the distorting influence of the "intermediary," or the local police agencies. In **victim surveys,** criminologists or other researchers ask the victims of crime directly about their experiences, using techniques such as interviews or e-mail and phone surveys. The most comprehensive such project in the United States is the National Crime Victimization Survey (NCVS), which started in 1972. Conducted by the U.S. Bureau of the Census in cooperation with the Bureau of Justice Statistics of the Justice Department, the NCVS conducts an annual survey of approximately 90,000 households with about 169,000 occupants over twelve years of age. Participants are interviewed twice a year concerning their experiences with crimes in the prior six months. As you can see in Figure 2.5, NCVS questions are quite detailed.

Proponents of the NCVS highlight a number of ways in which the victim survey is superior to the UCR:

1. It measures both reported and unreported crime.
2. It is unaffected by police bias and distortions in reporting crime to the FBI.
3. It does not rely on victims directly reporting crime to the police.[56]

Because of these factors, victim surveys such as the NCVS can provide criminologists with a better understanding of the **dark figure of crime**, or the actual—rather than reported—amount of crime that takes places in the United States.

FIGURE 2.5 SAMPLE QUESTIONS FROM THE NCVS (NATIONAL CRIME VICTIMIZATION SURVEY)

36a Was something belonging to YOU stolen, such as

(a) Things that you carry, like luggage, a wallet, purse, briefcase, book
(b) Clothing, jewelry, or cell phone
(c) Bicycle or sports equipment
(d) Things in your home—like a TV, stereo, or tools
(e) Things outside your home, such as a garden hose or lawn furniture
(f) Things belonging to children in the household
(g) Things from a vehicle, such as a package, groceries, camera, or CDs?

41a Has anyone attacked or threatened you in any of these ways?

(a) With any weapon, for instance, a gun or knife
(b) With anything like a baseball bat, frying pan, scissors, or stick
(c) By something thrown, such as a rock or a bottle
(d) Include any grabbing, punching, or choking
(e) Any rape, attempted rape, or other type of sexual attack
(f) Any face to face threats OR
(g) Any attack or threat or use of force by anyone at all? Please mention it even if you are not certain it was a crime.

43a Incidents involving forced or unwanted sexual acts are often difficult to talk about. Have you been forced or coerced to engage in unwanted sexual activity by

(a) Someone you didn't know
(b) A casual acquaintance OR
(c) Someone you know well?

45 During the last six months, did anything you thought was a crime happen to YOU, but you did NOT report it to the police?

(a) Yes
(b) No

Source: Adapted from U.S. Department of Justice, *National Crime Victimization Survey 2009* (Washington, D.C.: Bureau of Justice Statistics, 2013).

2-4d Self-Reported Surveys

Based on many of the same principles as victim surveys, but focusing instead on offenders, **self-reported surveys** are a third source of information for criminologists. In this form of data collection, persons are asked directly—through personal interviews or questionnaires, or over the telephone—about specific criminal activity to which they may have been a party.

Self-reported surveys are most useful in situations in which the group to be studied is already gathered in an institutional setting, such as a juvenile facility or a prison. One of the most widespread self-reported surveys in the United States, the Drug Use Forecasting Program, collects information on narcotics use from arrestees who have been brought into booking facilities.

Because there is no penalty for admitting to criminal activity in a self-reported survey, subjects tend to be more forthcoming in discussing their behavior. Researchers often use self-reported studies to get a better idea of the actual amount of

Victim Survey A method of gathering crime data that directly surveys participants to determine their experiences as victims of crime.

Dark Figure of Crime A term used to describe the actual amount of crime that takes place. The "figure" is "dark," or impossible to detect, because a great number of crimes are never reported to the police.

Self-Reported Surveys Methods of gathering crime data that rely on participants to reveal and detail their own criminal or delinquent behavior.

sexual assault that takes place in our society. These studies invariably show that many more rapes take place than are reported to the police.[57] Such conclusions underscore the most striking finding of self-reported surveys: the dark figure of crime, referred to earlier as the actual *amount* of crime that takes place, appears to be much larger than the UCR or NCVS would suggest.

Boston Globe/Getty Images

Andrea Volcy addresses a criminal court in Boston during the sentencing of Shabazz Augustine for murdering her niece. **What aspect of the American criminal justice system contributes to the frustration often experienced by crime victims?**

2-5 WHAT ROLE DO VICTIMS PLAY IN CRIMINAL JUSTICE?

Thirty-five years ago, a presidential task force invited federal and state legislatures to "address the needs of the millions of Americans and their families who are victimized by crime every year and who often carry its scars into the years to come."[58] This call to action was, in large part, a consequence of the rather peculiar position of **victims** in our criminal justice system. That is, once a crime has occurred, the victim is relegated to a single role: being a witness against the suspect in court. Legally, he or she has no say in the prosecution of the offender, or even whether such a prosecution is to take place. Such powerlessness can be extremely frustrating, particularly in the wake of a traumatic, life-changing event.

2-5a Legal Rights of Crime Victims

LO2-4 Describe the three ways that victims' rights legislation increases the ability of crime victims to participate in the criminal justice system.

To remedy this situation, all states have passed legislation creating certain rights for victims. On a federal level, such protections are encoded in the Crime Victims' Rights Act of 2004 (CVRA), which gives victims "the right to participate in the system."[59] This participation primarily focuses on three categories of rights:

Victim Any person who suffers physical, emotional, or financial harm as the result of a criminal act.

1. The right to be *informed*. This includes receiving information about victims' rights in general, as well as specific information such as the dates and times of court proceedings relating to the relevant crime.
2. The right to be *present*. This includes the right to be present at court hearings involving the case at hand, so long as the victim's presence does not interfere with the rights of the accused.
3. The right to be *heard*. This includes the ability to consult with prosecutorial officials before the criminal trial (addressed in Chapter 8), to speak during the sentencing phase of the trial (Chapter 9), and to offer an opinion when the offender is scheduled to be released from incarceration (Chapter 10).[60]

Some jurisdictions also provide victims with the right of law enforcement protection from the offender during the time period before a criminal trial. In addition, most states require *restitution*, or monetary payment, from offenders to help victims repay any costs associated with the crime and rebuild their lives. In 2016, for instance, a circuit court judge ordered Krystal Gonzalez to pay $1.2 million to the residents of an apartment complex in D'Iberville, Mississippi, that she accidentally burned down after intentionally setting fire to her boyfriend's T-shirt.

2-5b The Risks of Victimization

Anybody can be a victim of crime. This does not mean, however, that everybody is at an equal risk of being victimized. (See Figure 2.6 for an overview of how this risk is distributed among different demographic groups.) For instance, residents of neighborhoods with heavy concentrations of payday lending businesses are targeted by criminals at unusually high rates.[61] To better explain the circumstances surrounding this type of victimization, criminologists Larry Cohen and Marcus Felson devised the *routine activities theory*. According to Cohen and Felson, most criminal acts require the following:

1. A likely offender.
2. A suitable target (a person or an object).
3. The absence of a capable guardian—that is, any person (not necessarily a law enforcement agent) whose presence or proximity prevents a crime from happening.[62]

When these three factors are present, the likelihood of crime rises.

Cohen and Felson cite routine activities theory in explaining the link between payday lenders and crime. People who use payday lenders often leave those establishments with large sums of cash, late at night or during weekends when there is less street traffic. Consequently, they act as suitable targets, attracting likely offenders to neighborhoods where the payday lenders are located.[63]

FIGURE 2.6 CRIME VICTIMS IN THE UNITED STATES

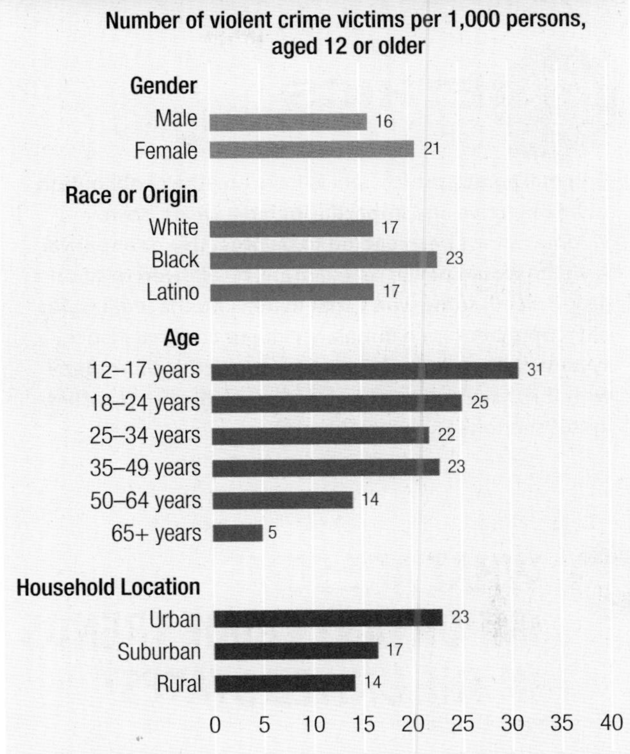

According to the U.S. Department of Justice, minorities, residents of urban areas, and young people are most likely to be victims of violent crime in this country.

Source: Bureau of Justice Statistics, *Criminal Victimization, 2015* (Washington, D.C.: U.S. Department of Justice, December 2016), 9, 10.

REPEAT VICTIMIZATION Cohen and Felson also hypothesize that offenders attach "values" to suitable targets. The higher the value, the more likely that target is going to be the subject of a crime.[64] A gold watch, for example, would obviously have a higher value for a thief than a plastic watch and therefore is more likely to be stolen. Similarly, people who are perceived to be weak or unprotected can have high value for criminals. Some research, for example, shows that undocumented Latino immigrants have elevated victimization rates because criminals know that these noncitizens are afraid to report crimes to authorities for fear of being removed from the country.[65]

Resources such as the National Crime Victimization Survey provide criminologists with an important tool for determining which types of people are most valued as potential victims. Statistics clearly show that a relatively small number of victims are involved in a disproportionate number of crimes. These findings support an approach to crime analysis known as **repeat victimization.** This theory is based on the premise that certain populations—mostly low-income residents of urban areas—are more likely to be victims of crimes than others and, therefore, past victimization is a strong predictor of future victimization.[66] Further criminological research shows that factors such as drug and alcohol use and depression also increase the possibility that a crime victim will be revictimized.[67]

THE VICTIM-OFFENDER CONNECTION Not only does past victimization seem to increase the risk of future victimization, but so does past criminal behavior. For example, the Chicago Police Department keeps a list of those known offenders who are most likely to be violent offenders or victims of violent crime. A primary factor on the list is a previous arrest on a firearms charge. About 70 percent of those Chicago residents victimized by gun violence are on this list.[68] "The notion that [violent crimes] are random bolts of lightning, which is the commonly

Repeat Victimization The theory that certain people and places are more likely to be subject to repeated criminal activity and that past victimization is a strong indicator of future victimization.

held image, is not the reality at all," says David Kennedy, a professor at New York's John Jay College of Criminal Justice.[69]

ETHICS CHALLENGE

Criminal justice professionals have an ethical obligation to be objective and impartial. In most cases, however, victims cannot be expected to be objective or impartial. A victim would never, for example, be allowed to sit on a jury. Indeed, some worry that increasing the legal rights of victims creates an imbalance in our criminal justice system. Do you agree? Do you see any ethical problems with the three categories of victim's rights listed earlier in this section? Explain your answers.

2-6 WHAT ARE SOME IMPORTANT CRIME TRENDS IN THE UNITED STATES?

The UCR, NCVS, and other statistical measures we have discussed so far in this chapter, though important, represent only the tip of the iceberg of crime data. Thanks to the efforts of law enforcement agencies, educational institutions, and private individuals, more information on crime is available today than at any time in the nation's history.

When interpreting and predicting general crime trends, experts tend to rely on what University of California at Berkeley law professor Franklin Zimring calls the three "usual suspects" of crime fluctuation:

1. *Imprisonment,* based on the principle that (a) an offender in prison or jail is unable to commit a crime on the street, and (b) a potential offender on the street may be deterred from committing a crime by the fear of winding up behind bars.
2. *Youth populations,* because those under the age of twenty-four commit the majority of crimes in the United States.
3. *The economy,* because when legitimate opportunities to earn income become scarce, some people will turn to illegitimate methods such as crime.[70]

Pure statistics do not always tell the whole story, however, and crime rates often fail to behave in the ways that the experts predict.

2-6a Looking Good: Crime in the 1990s and 2000s

In 1995, eminent crime expert James Q. Wilson, noting that the number of young males in the United States was set to increase dramatically over the next decade, predicted that "30,000 more young muggers, killers, and thieves" would be on the streets by 2000. "Get ready," he warned.[71] Other criminologists offered their own dire projections. John DiIulio foresaw a swarm of "juvenile super-predators" on the streets,[72] and James A. Fox prophesied a "blood bath" by 2005.[73]

Given previous data, these experts could be fairly confident in their predictions. Fortunately for the country, they were wrong. As is evident from Figure 2.7, starting in 1994 the United States experienced a steep crime decline that, despite a few upticks, we are still enjoying today.

THE GREAT CRIME DECLINE The crime statistics of the 1990s are startling. Even with the upswing at the beginning of the decade, from 1990 to 2000 the homicide rate dropped 39 percent, the robbery rate 44 percent, the burglary rate 41 percent, and the auto theft rate 37 percent. By most measures, this decline was the longest and deepest of the twentieth century.[74]

In retrospect, the 1990s seem to have encompassed a "golden era" for the leading indicators of low crime rates. The economy was robust. The incarceration rate was skyrocketing. Plus, despite the misgivings of James Q. Wilson and many of his colleagues, the percentage of the population in the high-risk age bracket in 1995 was actually lower than it had been in 1980.[75]

CONTINUING DECREASES According to the UCR and the NCVS, the two most extensive measurements of national crime rates, the United States is presently enjoying historically low levels of crime. Since the early 1990s, both the violent crime rate (see Figure 2.7 again) and the property crime rate have declined by about 50 percent.[76]

Amid this general good news, the 2015 UCR—released in the fall of 2016—delivered something of a shock: the national murder rate rose 11 percent (the largest one-year increase in nearly half a century), and violent crime in general rose about 4 percent.[77] A number of explanations have been given for this violent crime surge, including gang violence, the heroin epidemic, and the economy. Some experts have also pointed to a reluctance among police officers to confront criminal suspects for fear of being accused of using excessive force or displaying institutional racism.[78]

On closer inspection, however, the data from 2015 were more ambiguous. Notably, the nation's overall

FIGURE 2.7 VIOLENT CRIME IN THE UNITED STATES, 1990–2015

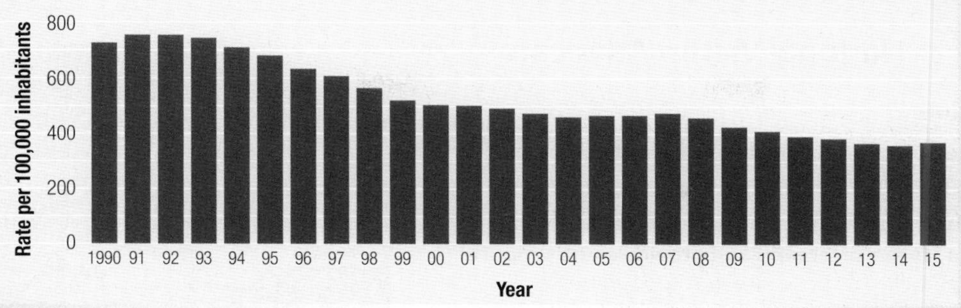

According to statistics gathered each year by the FBI, American violent crime rates dropped steadily in the second half of the 1990s, leveled off for several years, and then decreased steadily until a slight rise in 2015.

Source: Federal Bureau of Investigation.

crime rate dropped for the fourteenth consecutive year. The NCVS, which does not record murders, saw no increase in violent crime.[79] Furthermore, only four urban areas—Baltimore, Chicago, Milwaukee, and Washington, D.C.—accounted for about 20 percent of the year's murder increase.[80] According to Richard Berk, a criminology professor at the University of Pennsylvania, "It isn't a national trend, it's a city trend, and it's not even a city trend, but a problem in certain neighborhoods."[81]

Thus, most criminologists are taking a "wait and see" attitude toward the possibility of continued rising crime rates, while police chiefs and residents of many major American cities are hoping that 2015 was a "one-year blip."[82]

2-6b Crime, Race, and Poverty

Although crime and victimization rates have decreased across racial lines over the past twenty years, the trends have been less positive for African Americans than for whites. For example, blacks are considerably more likely to be both homicide victims and homicide offenders than are whites.[83] African Americans are particularly susceptible to gun violence, with firearm murder rates of 14.6 per 100,000 adults, compared with 1.9 for whites and 4.0 for Latinos.[84] Chicago's West Garfield Park neighborhood, which is 96 percent black, has a homicide rate of 116 per 100,000 people. By comparison, Honduras, the worldwide leader in murders, has a homicide rate of 90 per 100,000.[85]

RACE AND CRIME Homicide rates are not the only area in which there is a divergence in crime trends between the races. Official crime data seem to indicate a strong correlation between minority status and crime: African Americans—who make up 13 percent of the population—constitute 36 percent of those arrested for violent crimes and 28 percent of those arrested for property crimes.[86] Even as overall marijuana arrests plummeted in Colorado and Washington State after the drug was legalized, African Americans were still twice as likely as whites to be arrested for using the drug.[87] Furthermore, a black juvenile in the United States is more than twice as likely as a white juvenile to wind up in delinquency court and 30 percent more likely to have his or her case transferred to adult criminal court.[88]

CLASS AND CRIME The racial differences in the crime rate are one of the most controversial areas of the criminal justice system. At first glance, crime statistics seem to support the idea that the subculture of African Americans in the United States is disposed toward criminal behavior. Not all of the data, however, support that assertion.

A recent research project led by sociologist Ruth D. Peterson of Ohio State University gathered information on nearly 150 neighborhoods in Columbus, Ohio. Peterson and her colleagues separated the neighborhoods based on race and on levels of disadvantage such as poverty, joblessness, lack of college graduates, and high levels of female-headed families. She found that whether the neighborhoods were predominantly white or predominantly black had little impact on violent crime rates. Those neighborhoods with higher levels of disadvantage, however, had uniformly higher violent crime rates.[89]

INCOME LEVEL AND CRIME Peterson's research suggests that, regardless of race, a person is at a much

CAREER PREP

National Victim Advocate

Job Description:

- Provide direct support, advocacy, and short-term crisis counseling to crime victims.
- Act as a liaison between victims or witnesses and district attorneys or law enforcement, and provide court support for victims.

What Kind of Training Is Required?

- A bachelor's degree in criminal justice, social work/psychology, or a related field.
- A minimum of two years' experience in the criminal justice system, one year of which should have involved direct services with victims.

Annual Salary Range?

- $30,000–$42,000

John Roman Images/Shutterstock.com

Getting LinkedIn

Victim advocates must be comfortable working with a wide range of victims. For example, the University of Colorado at Boulder's posting for this position referenced an applicant's ability to respond to "hazing, bias motivated incidents, death, discrimination and harassment."

higher risk of being a violent offender or a victim of violence if he or she lives in a disadvantaged neighborhood. Given that African Americans are two times more likely than whites to live in poverty and hold low-wage-earning jobs, they are, as a group, more susceptible to the factors that contribute to criminality.[90]

LO2-5 Explain why income level appears to be more important than race when it comes to crime trends.

Indeed, a considerable amount of information suggests that income level is more important than skin color when it comes to crime trends. A 2002 study of nearly 900 African American children (400 boys and 467 girls) from neighborhoods with varying income levels showed that family earning power had the only significant correlation with violent behavior.[91]

More recent research conducted by William A. Pridemore of Indiana University found a "positive and significant association" between poverty and homicide.[92] Lack of education, another handicap most often faced by low-income citizens, also seems to correlate with criminal behavior. About one in every ten male high school dropouts winds up in juvenile detention or as an adult inmate, compared with about one in thirty-three male high school graduates.[93]

2-6c Women and Crime

To put it bluntly, crime is an overwhelmingly male activity. Sixty-three percent of all murders involve a male victim and a male perpetrator, and in only 2.5 percent of homicides are both the offender and the victim female.[94] Only about 9 percent of the national prison and jail population are female, and in 2015 only 24 percent of all arrests involved women.[95]

A GROWING PRESENCE The statistics just cited fail to convey the startling rate at which the female presence in the criminal justice system has been increasing.

DISCRETION IN ACTION

Prosecuting Domestic Violence

THE SITUATION According to the arrest warrant, during an argument at their home, Greg threw Nicole to the floor and into a bathtub, slammed her against a futon, and "strangled" her. Greg also threatened to kill Nicole "in a manner and under circumstances which would cause a reasonable person to believe that the threat was likely to be carried out."

Soon after the alleged assault, however, Nicole told prosecutors that she did not want Greg to be charged with a crime, and she left the state so that she wouldn't have to act as a witness against him in court.

THE LAW Legally, crime victims are not the clients of public prosecutors. That is, as you will see in Chapter 8, prosecutors have the ultimate authority to decide when to bring a case to court, regardless of the victim's wishes.

In practice, domestic violence cases unfold somewhat differently. Because the victim is usually the only witness to the violence, if she or he refuses to participate, such cases can be very difficult to prosecute successfully.

WHAT WOULD YOU DO? For a number of reasons, domestic violence victims frequently choose not to side with law enforcement against their abusers. These motivations include fear of retaliation, financial dependence on the offender, issues of custody and child support, and complex emotional ties. Indeed, if a domestic violence victim chooses to cooperate with law enforcement officials, she or he often becomes more vulnerable to retaliatory attacks by the abuser.

At the same time, many observers believe that the public benefits when prosecutors ignore the wishes of domestic violence victims in these instances. Arguably, aggressively prosecuting domestic violence offenses will deter others from committing similar wrongdoing and send the message that domestic violence is a serious crime. Taking both sides of the issue into account, if you were a prosecutor, would you file charges against Greg despite Nicole's opposition? Explain your answer.

To see how a similar case in Mecklenburg County, North Carolina, was resolved, go to Example 2.1 in Appendix A.

Between 1991 and 2015, the number of men arrested each year declined about 18 percent. Over that time period, annual arrests for women increased by 31 percent.[96] In 1970, there were about 6,000 women in federal and state prisons, but today, there are about 11,500.[97] Two possible explanations have been offered to explain these increases. Either (1) the life circumstances and behavior of women have changed dramatically in the past forty years, or (2) the criminal justice system's attitude toward women has changed over that time period.[98]

In the 1970s, when female crime rates started surging upward, many observers accepted the former explanation. "You can't get involved in a bar fight if you're not allowed in the bar," said feminist theorist Freda Adler in 1975.[99] It has become clear, however, that a significant percentage of women arrested are involved in a narrow band of wrongdoing, mostly drug- and alcohol-related offenses or minor property crimes such as shoplifting.[100] Research shows that as recently as the 1980s, many of the women now in prison would not have been arrested or would have received lighter sentences for their crimes.[101] Consequently, more scholars are convinced that rising female criminality is the result of a criminal justice system that is "more willing to incarcerate women."[102]

WOMEN AS CRIME VICTIMS Although males dominate criminal violent offender statistics, women are victims of violent crime at a higher rate than men, as shown in Figure 2.6 earlier in the chapter.[103] The most striking aspect of women as victims of crime is the extent to which such victimization involves a prior relationship.

Prior Ties According to the National Crime Victimization Survey, a male is twice as likely as a female to experience violence at the hands of a stranger.[104] With regard to intimate partner violence—involving a spouse, ex-spouse, boyfriend, girlfriend, ex-boyfriend, or ex-girlfriend—the gender difference is even more pronounced. Nearly one in ten women in the United States has been raped by

Domestic Violence An act of willful neglect or physical violence that occurs within a familial or other intimate relationship.

Stalking The criminal act of causing fear in a person by repeatedly subjecting that person to unwanted or threatening attention.

an intimate partner, compared with one in forty-five men, and over their lifetimes, women are at significantly more risk for intimate partner violence than are men (24 percent versus 14 percent).[105]

STUDY TOOLS 2

LOCATED IN TEXTBOOK

- ☐ Rip out the Chapter Review Card.
- ☐ Review with the Chapter Quiz following this chapter.

LOCATED AT WWW.CENGAGE BRAIN.COM

- ☐ Review key terms flash cards.
- ☐ Read the chapter on all your favorite devices.
- ☐ Complete an Exam to test your knowledge.
- ☐ Check out Visual Summaries and You Decide activities to explore chapter concepts.

Statistically, women are also at greater risk of being victims of **domestic violence.** This umbrella term covers a wide variety of maltreatment, including physical violence and psychological abuse, inflicted among family members and others in close relationships. Though data show that women are significantly more likely to be victims of domestic violence than men,[106] these findings are not unquestioned. Men, many observers assume, are less likely to report abuse because of the social stigma surrounding female-on-male violence.[107] Domestic violence presents a number of problems for the criminal justice system, as you can see in the feature *Discretion in Action—Prosecuting Domestic Violence*.

Causing Fear A third crime that appears to mainly involve female victims is **stalking,** or a course of conduct directed at a person that would reasonably cause that person to feel fear. Such behavior includes unwanted phone calls, following or spying, and a wide range of online activity that we will address in Chapter 14. Stalkers target women at about three times the rate they target men, and seven out of ten stalking victims have had some prior relationship with their stalkers.[108]

Quiz

1. Researchers who study the causes of crime are called ________________________.

2. If a hypothesis proves valid, it can be used to support a ________________________ that explains a possible cause of crime.

3. ________________________ ________________________ theory holds that criminals make a deliberate decision to commit a crime after weighing the possible rewards or punishments involved.

4. Social ________________________ focuses on how individuals justify their own antisocial or criminal behavior by patterning it after similar behavior by others.

5. Social ________________________ theory examines living conditions to explain the crime rate in any given neighborhood or community.

6. Among social process theories, ________________________ theory could be used to explain why the younger sibling of a gang member would be at a particular risk to join a gang him- or herself.

7. Drug ________________________ is defined as the use of any drug that causes harm to the user or a third party.

8. To produce its annual ________________________ ________________________ ________________________, the Federal Bureau of Investigation relies on the cooperation of local law enforcement agencies.

9. ________________________ surveys rely on those who have been the subjects of criminal activity to discuss the incidents with researchers.

10. ________________________-________________________ surveys ask participants to detail their own criminal behavior.

Answers to the Chapter 2 Quiz can be found in the Answers section in the back of the book.

3 Inside Criminal Law

Photo By Chris Maddaloni/CQ Roll Call/

LEARNING OBJECTIVES

After studying this chapter, you will be able to . . .

3-1 List the four written sources of American criminal law.

3-2 Discuss the primary goals of civil law and criminal law and explain how these goals are realized.

3-3 List and briefly define the most important excuse defenses for crimes.

3-4 Describe the four most important justification criminal defenses.

3-5 Explain the importance of the due process clause in the criminal justice system.

After finishing this chapter, go to **PAGE 68** for STUDY TOOLS

"Death by Dealer"

The night before he died, twenty-three-year-old Christian Hernandez chatted via video from Palm Beach County, Florida, with his former fiancée, who was in Maine. As he took "hit after hit" on-screen of what he thought was heroin, he told her that it "tasted funny." In fact, Hernandez was ingesting fentanyl, which is much more potent than heroin, and it killed him. Following clues on Hernandez's cell phone, law enforcement traced the fentanyl to Christopher Massena, a local dealer. Massena was eventually charged with homicide under a federal law that holds a person who sells drugs criminally responsible if those drugs cause a fatal overdose. In December 2016, a jury convicted Massena, and he was sentenced to thirty years in federal prison.

For the most part, criminal law treats fatal drug overdoses as accidents, not crimes. In response to a wave of drug-related deaths that have plagued the country in recent years, however, the federal government and a number of states have enacted or revised laws designed to punish dealers for the overdose deaths of their clients. By law, then, the fact that Massena had not meant for Hernandez to die was irrelevant. Prosecutors needed only prove that he had sold Hernandez the fentanyl that led to the overdose.

Such "death by dealer" prosecutions are controversial within the legal community. "Where's the intent to cause death?" asks one former prosecutor. "And how can it be proved that dealer sold the exact drugs that caused someone's death?" Indeed, as you will see later in the chapter, criminal law usually requires *intent* and *causation* to convict someone of a crime, particularly a homicide. Supporters of these laws counter that drug dealers should be held responsible for the damage that results from their illegal activity. Furthermore, Frank Hernandez—Christian's father—is not alone in praising the deterrent impact of harsh sentences for those who contribute to overdoses. "[Drug dealers will] think twice now before they pick this as a career path," he said after Massena's trial.

Robert Nickelsberg/Archive Photos/Getty Images

Numerous states and the federal government are enforcing laws designed to punish the person who sells the illegal drugs, such as this heroin confiscated by the Burlington (Vermont) Police Department, that are used in a fatal overdose. *Who deserves more blame in the aftermath of such situations: the drug dealer or the drug abuser? Why?*

3-1 WHAT ARE THE WRITTEN SOURCES OF AMERICAN CRIMINAL LAW?

In any society that is, like our own, governed by the **rule of law,** all persons and institutions, including the government itself, must abide by the law. Furthermore, the law must be applied equally and enforced fairly, and must not be altered arbitrarily by any individual or group, no matter how powerful. As the rule of law has evolved over the course of U.S. history, Americans and their government have come to rely on several written sources of criminal law, also known as "substantive" criminal law.

LO3-1 List the four written sources of American criminal law.

These sources include:

1. The U.S. Constitution and the constitutions of the various states.
2. Statutes, or laws, passed by Congress and by state legislatures, plus local ordinances.
3. Regulations, created by regulatory agencies, such as the federal Food and Drug Administration.
4. Case law (court decisions).

Rule of Law The principle that the rules of a legal system apply equally to all persons, institutions, and entities—public or private—that make up a society.

We describe each of these important written sources of law in the remainder of this section. (For a preview, see Figure 3.1.)

3-1a Constitutional Law

The federal government and the states have separate written constitutions that set forth the general organization and powers of, and the limits on, their respective governments. **Constitutional law** is the law as expressed in these constitutions.

The U.S. Constitution is the supreme law of the land. As such, it is the basis of all law in the United States. Any law that violates the Constitution, as ultimately determined by the United States Supreme Court, will be declared unconstitutional and will not be enforced.

The Tenth Amendment, which defines the powers and limitations of the federal government, reserves to the states all powers not granted to the federal government. Under our system of federalism (see Chapter 1), each state also has its own constitution. Unless they conflict with the U.S. Constitution or a federal law, state constitutions are supreme within their respective borders. (You will learn more about how constitutional law applies to our criminal justice system throughout this textbook.)

Constitutional Law Law based on the U.S. Constitution and the constitutions of the various states.

Statutory Law The body of law enacted by legislative bodies.

Supremacy Clause A clause in the U.S. Constitution establishing that federal law is the "supreme law of the land" and shall prevail when in conflict with state constitutions or statutes.

3-1b Statutory Law

Statutes enacted by legislative bodies at any level of government make up another source of law, which is generally referred to as **statutory law.** *Federal statutes* are laws that are enacted by the U.S. Congress. *State statutes* are laws enacted by state legislatures, and statutory law also includes the *ordinances* passed by cities and counties. A federal statute, of course, applies to all states. A state statute, in contrast, applies only within that state's borders. City or county ordinances apply only to those jurisdictions where they are enacted.

LEGAL SUPREMACY It is important to keep in mind that there are essentially fifty-two different criminal codes in this country—one for each state, the District of Columbia, and the federal government. Originally, the federal criminal code was quite small. The U.S. Constitution mentions only three federal crimes: treason, piracy, and counterfeiting. Today, according to a recent study, federal law includes nearly 5,000 offenses that carry criminal penalties.[1] Inevitably, these federal criminal statutes are bound to overlap or even contradict state statutes. In such cases, thanks to the **supremacy clause** of the Constitution, federal law will almost always prevail. Simply put, the supremacy clause holds that federal law is the "supreme law of the land."

So, for example, hundreds of individuals have been charged with violating federal law for possessing or selling medical marijuana in states where such actions are legal under state law.[2] As we discussed earlier in the textbook, marijuana use—for medicinal purposes or otherwise—remains illegal under federal law, and, in the words of one federal judge, "we are all bound by federal law, like it or not."[3]

Along the same lines, any statutory law—federal or state—that violates the Constitution will be overturned. Therefore, in the late 1980s, the United States Supreme Court ruled that state laws banning the burning of the American flag were unconstitutional because they impinged on the individual's right to freedom of expression.[4]

FIGURE 3.1 SOURCES OF AMERICAN LAW

Constitutional Law	**Definition:** The law as expressed in the U.S. Constitution and the various state constitutions.	**Example:** The Fifth Amendment to the U.S. Constitution states that no person shall "be compelled in any criminal case to be a witness" against himself or herself.
Statutory law	**Definition:** Laws or ordinances created by federal, state, and local legislatures and governing bodies.	**Example:** Texas state law considers the theft of cattle, horses, or exotic livestock or fowl a felony.
Administrative law	**Definition:** The rules, orders, and decisions of federal or state government administrative agencies.	**Example:** The federal Environmental Protection Agency's rules criminalize the use of lead-based paint in a manner that causes health risks to the community.
Case law	**Definition:** Judge-made law, including judicial interpretations of the other three sources of law.	**Example:** A federal judge overturns a Nebraska state law making it a crime for sex offenders to use social networking sites on the ground that the statue violates the constitutional right of freedom of speech.

BALLOT INITIATIVES On a state and local level, voters can write or rewrite criminal statutes through the **ballot initiative.** In this process, a group of citizens draft a proposed law and then gather a certain number of signatures to get the proposal on that year's ballot. If a majority of the voters approve the measure, it is enacted into law.

Currently, twenty-four states and the District of Columbia accept ballot initiatives, and these special elections have played a crucial role in shaping criminal law in those jurisdictions. Changes in state laws regarding assisted suicide, marijuana legalization, and victims' rights, discussed earlier in this text, resulted from ballot initiatives.

Like other state laws, laws generated by ballot initiatives are not immune from review by state and federal courts. In 2015, for example, a federal judge invalidated the results of a ballot initiative that would have banned the farming of genetically modified crops in Maui County, Hawaii. According to the judge, decisions concerning agricultural policy could be made only at the federal or state level, and thus the county had overstepped the boundaries of its legislative power.[5]

Csehak Szabolcs/Shutterstock.com

In Washington State, because of a ballot initiative, the trafficking of products made from endangered species such as tigers could result in a maximum of five years in prison and a $10,000 fine. **What are some of the pros and cons of using ballot initiatives to create criminal law?**

3-1c Administrative Law

A third source of American criminal law consists of **administrative law**—the rules, regulations, orders, and decisions of *regulatory agencies*. A regulatory agency is a federal, state, or local government agency established to perform a specific function. The Occupational Safety and Health Administration (OSHA), for example, oversees the safety and health of American workers. The Environmental Protection Agency (EPA) is concerned with protecting the natural environment, and the Food and Drug Administration (FDA) regulates food and drugs produced in the United States.

Breaking an administrative rule can be a criminal violation. For example, the Food, Drug, and Cosmetic Act authorizes the FDA to enforce regulations to which criminal sanctions are attached. In an ongoing inquiry, the FDA's Office of Criminal Investigations found that ConAgra Grocery Products had caused an outbreak of salmonella poisoning several years ago by shipping contaminated peanut butter to stores around the country. In December 2016, the company agreed to pay an $8 million criminal fine and forfeit $3.2 million in assets—the largest penalty ever paid in a food safety case.[6]

CAREER TIP The federal government employs law enforcement agents called *consumer safety officers* to investigate reports of injury, illness, or death caused by certain consumer products.

3-1d Case Law

Another basic source of American law consists of the rules of law announced in court decisions, or **precedents.** These rules of law include interpretations of constitutional provisions, of statutes enacted by legislatures, and of regulations created by administrative agencies. Today, this body of law is referred to variously as the common law, judge-made law, or **case law.**

Ballot Initiative A procedure in which the citizens of a state, by collecting enough signatures, can force a public vote on a proposed change to state law.

Administrative Law The body of law created by administrative agencies (in the form of rules, regulations, orders, and decisions) in order to carry out their duties and responsibilities.

Precedent A court decision that furnishes an example or authority for deciding subsequent cases involving similar facts.

Case Law The rules of law announced in court decisions.

CJ and TECHNOLOGY

Unmanned Aerial Vehicles (UAVs)

An estimated one million unmanned aerial vehicles (UAVs), commonly referred to as drones, are operating in the United States. Most of them weigh only a few pounds and are "virtually toys," according to one enthusiast. These "toys" have, however, caused a multitude of problems. They have interfered with firefighters, crashed into buildings, and been used to smuggle contraband into prisons. Most seriously, pilots of passenger planes and other aircraft are reporting about one hundred sightings or close calls with UAVs each month.

The law is now trying to catch up with this emerging technology. The Federal Aviation Administration recently announced that recreational UAV owners must register their drones with the government. Any registered operator who interferes with air traffic will be subject to a fine. In addition, twenty states have passed criminal legislation related to UAVs. For example, New Hampshire prohibits the use of drones for hunting, fishing, or trapping. In Texas, it is, for the most part, a crime to take photographs of people or real estate with the aid of UAVs.

Thinking about UAVs
Should it be against the law to fly a camera-equipped drone onto or over another person's private property? Should the law punish someone who damages a drone that is flying over her or his property without permission or is flying unreasonably close to her or his family? Explain your answers.

Case law is the basis for a doctrine called ***stare decisis*** ("to stand on decided cases"). Under this doctrine, judges are obligated to follow the precedents established within their jurisdiction. For example, any decision of a particular state's highest court will control the outcome of future cases on that issue brought before all the lower courts within that state. Under the supremacy clause, discussed earlier, all U.S. Supreme Court decisions involving the U.S. Constitution are binding on *all* courts, because the U.S. Constitution is the supreme law of the land.

The doctrine of *stare decisis* does not require the U.S. Supreme Court *always* to follow its own precedent, though the Court often does so. At times, a change in society's values will make an older ruling seem obsolete, at least in the eyes of the Supreme Court justices. In *Bowers v. Hardwick* (1986), for example, the Court upheld a state law that banned certain homosexual acts that were lawful when performed by a man and a woman.[7]

Seventeen years later, in *Lawrence v. Texas* (2003), the Court overturned that decision, ruling that the government cannot treat one class of citizens differently from the rest of society when it comes to sexual practices between consenting adults. The original case "was not correct when it was decided, and it is not correct today," wrote Justice Anthony Kennedy.[8]

Stare Decisis (pronounced ster-ay dih-*si*-*ses*). A legal doctrine under which judges are obligated to follow the precedents established in prior decisions.

3-2 WHY DO SOCIETIES NEED LAWS?

Many criminologists believe that criminal law has two basic functions: one relates to the legal aspects of a society, and the other pertains to the society's need to maintain and promote social values.

3-2a Protect and Punish: The Legal Function of the Law

The primary legal function of the law is to maintain social order by protecting citizens from *criminal harm*. This term refers to a variety of harms that can be generalized to fit into two categories:

1. Harms to individual citizens' physical safety and property, such as the harm caused by murder, theft, or arson.
2. Harms to society's interests collectively, such as the harm caused by unsafe foods or consumer products, a polluted environment, or poorly constructed buildings.[9]

The first category is self-evident, although even murder, as you shall soon see, involves different degrees, or grades, of offense to which different punishments are assigned. The second category, however, has proved more problematic, for it is difficult to measure society's "collective" interests.

3-2b Maintain and Teach: The Social Function of the Law

If criminal laws against acts that cause harm or injury to others are almost universally accepted, the same cannot be said for laws that criminalize "morally" wrongful activities that may do no obvious, physical harm outside the families of those involved. Why criminalize gambling or prostitution, for instance, if the participants are consenting?

EXPRESSING PUBLIC MORALITY The answer lies in the social function of criminal law. Many observers believe that the main purpose of criminal law is to reflect the values and norms of society, or at least of those segments of society that hold power. Legal scholar Henry Hart has stated that the only justification for criminal law and punishment is "the judgment of community condemnation."[10]

Take, for example, the misdemeanor of bigamy, which occurs when someone knowingly marries a second person without terminating her or his first marriage. Apart from moral considerations, there would appear to be no victims in a bigamous relationship, and indeed many societies have allowed and continue to allow bigamy to exist. In the American social tradition, however, as John L. Diamond of the University of California's Hastings College of the Law points out:

> Marriage is an institution encouraged and supported by society. The structural importance of the integrity of the family and a monogamous marriage requires unflinching enforcement of the criminal laws against bigamy. The immorality is not in choosing to do wrong, but in transgressing . . . a fundamental social boundary that lies at the core of social order.[11]

Of course, public morals are not uniform across the entire nation, and a state's criminal code often reflects the values of its residents. In Kentucky, for example, someone who uses a reptile as part of a religious service is subject to up to $100 in fines, and New Hampshire prohibits any person or agency from introducing a wolf into the state's wilds.[12]

Sometimes, local values and federal law will conflict with one another. Nine states, mostly in the western half of the country, have passed "nullification" laws that seek to void federal gun legislation within their borders. For example, in Idaho, state law enforcement officers can be charged with a misdemeanor and fined up to $1,000 dollars for enforcing a federal gun law.[13] (No state has, as of yet, attempted to enforce this form of "nullification," which probably would violate the supremacy clause, discussed earlier in the chapter.)

Mark Van Scyoc/Shutterstock.com

Many gun activists support state "nullification" laws that aim to void federal gun legislation. **Why does the supremacy clause, discussed earlier in the chapter, make it unlikely that such state laws would withstand a court challenge?**

TEACHING SOCIETAL BOUNDARIES Some scholars believe that criminal laws not only express the expectations of society, but "teach" them as well. Professor Lawrence M. Friedman of Stanford University thinks that just as parents teach children behavioral norms through punishment, criminal justice " 'teaches a lesson' to the people it punishes, and to society at large." Making burglary a crime, arresting burglars, putting them in jail—each step in the criminal justice process reinforces the idea that burglary is unacceptable and is deserving of punishment.[14]

This teaching function can also be seen in traffic laws. There is nothing "natural" about most traffic laws: Americans drive on the right side of the street, the British on the left side, with no obvious difference in the results. These laws do, however, lead to a more orderly flow of traffic and fewer accidents—certainly socially desirable goals.

The laws can also be updated when needed. For instance, California recently banned the use of handheld cell phones while driving. Various forms of punishment for breaking traffic laws teach drivers the social order of the road.

ETHICS CHALLENGE

For a variety of reasons, many parents in this country are refusing to have their infant children vaccinated against measles and other infectious diseases. By doing so, according to the medical community, these parents are putting not only their own children but also other children at a much greater risk of contracting a wide range of diseases, some of which are fatal. Would it be ethical for the government to pass a law forcing parents to have their children vaccinated for the good of society as whole? Why or why not?

3-3 WHAT IS THE DIFFERENCE BETWEEN CIVIL AND CRIMINAL LAW?

All law can be divided into two categories: civil law and criminal law. These two strands of law are distinguished by their primary goals. The criminal justice system is concerned with protecting society from harm by preventing and prosecuting crimes. A crime is an act so reprehensible that it is considered a wrong against society as a whole, as well as against the individual victim. Therefore, the state prosecutes a person who commits a criminal act. If the state is able to prove that a person is guilty of a crime, the government will punish her or him with imprisonment or fines, or both.

LO3-2 Discuss the primary goals of civil law and criminal law and explain how these goals are realized.

Civil law, which includes all types of law other than criminal law, is concerned with disputes between private individuals and between entities. Proceedings in civil lawsuits are normally initiated by an individual or a corporation (in contrast to criminal proceedings, which are initiated by public prosecutors). Such disputes may involve, for example, the terms of a contract, the ownership of property, or an automobile accident.

Civil Law The branch of law dealing with the definition and enforcement of all private or public rights, as opposed to criminal matters.

Plaintiff The person or institution that initiates a lawsuit in civil court proceedings by filing a complaint.

Defendant In a civil court, the person or institution against whom an action is brought. In a criminal court, the person or entity who has been formally accused of violating a criminal law.

Liable In a civil court, legal responsibility for one's own or another's actions.

Under civil law, the government provides a forum for the resolution of *torts*—or private wrongs—in which the injured party, called the **plaintiff,** tries to prove that a wrong has been committed by the accused party, or the **defendant.** (Note that the accused party in both criminal and civil cases is known as the *defendant*.)

3-3a Guilt and Responsibility

A criminal court is convened to determine whether the defendant is *guilty*—that is, whether the defendant has, in fact, committed the offense charged. In contrast, civil law is concerned with responsibility, a much more flexible concept.

For example, in 2012 Ruth Kurka lost control of the motorized shopping cart she was piloting in a Cleveland area Giant Eagle supermarket and struck seventy-one-year-old Barbara Rieger. The impact caused Rieger to suffer significant neck and head injuries. The incident was certainly an accident, and local authorities never considered charging Kurka with any crime. At the same time, in 2016 a civil jury decided that Giant Eagle was **liable,** or legally responsible, for Rieger's injuries because the corporation failed to properly instruct Kurka how to use the motorized shopping cart.

Most civil cases involve a request for monetary damages to compensate for the wrong that has been committed. Thus, the civil court ordered Giant Eagle to pay Barbara Rieger $1.3 million as compensation for her pain and suffering and as punishment for the corporation's carelessness.

3-3b The Burden of Proof

Although criminal law proceedings are completely separate from civil law proceedings in the modern legal system, the two systems do have some similarities. Both attempt to control behavior by imposing sanctions on those who violate society's definition of acceptable behavior. Furthermore, criminal and civil law often supplement each other. In certain instances, a victim may file a civil suit against an individual who is also the target of a criminal prosecution by the government.

Because the burden of proof is much greater in criminal trials than civil ones, it is almost always easier to win monetary damages than a criminal conviction. The most famous (or infamous) example of such a situation in recent memory occurred about twenty years ago. After former professional football player O. J. Simpson was acquitted of murder charges in the deaths of his ex-wife, Nicole, and Ronald Goldman, the families of the two victims sued Simpson. In 1997, a civil court jury found

Simpson liable for the wrongful deaths of his ex-wife and Goldman, and ordered him to pay their families $33.5 million in damages.

During the criminal trial, the jury did not find enough evidence to prove **beyond a reasonable doubt** (the burden of proof in criminal cases) that Simpson was guilty of any crime. In contrast, the civil trial established by a **preponderance of the evidence** (the burden of proof in civil cases) that Simpson had killed his victims in a fit of jealous rage. (See Figure 3.2 for a comparison of civil and criminal law.)

3-4 WHAT ARE THE DIFFERENT CATEGORIES OF CRIMES?

Depending on their degree of seriousness, crimes are classified as *felonies* or *misdemeanors*. **Felonies** are crimes punishable by death or by imprisonment in a federal or state prison for one year or longer (though some states, such as North Carolina, consider felonies to be punishable by at least two years' incarceration). For the most part, felonies involve crimes of violence, such as armed robbery or sexual assault, or other "serious" crimes, such as stealing a large amount of money or selling illegal drugs.

3-4a Types of Misdemeanors

Under federal law and in most states, any crime that is not a felony is considered a **misdemeanor.** Misdemeanors are crimes punishable by a fine or by confinement for up to a year. If imprisoned, the guilty party goes to a local jail instead of a prison. Disorderly conduct and trespassing are common misdemeanors.

Most states distinguish between *gross misdemeanors*, which are offenses punishable by thirty days to a year in jail, and *petty misdemeanors*, which are offenses punishable by fewer than thirty days in jail. Probation and community service are often imposed on those who commit misdemeanors, especially juveniles. As you will see in Chapter 7, whether a crime is a felony or misdemeanor can also determine in which criminal court the case will be tried.

3-4b Infractions

The least serious form of wrongdoing is often called an **infraction** and is punishable only by a fine. Even though infractions such as parking tickets and traffic violations technically represent illegal activity, they generally are not considered "crimes." Therefore, infractions rarely lead to jury trials and are deemed to be so minor that they do not appear on the offender's criminal record.

In some jurisdictions, the terms *infraction* and *petty offense* are interchangeable. In others, however, they are different. Under federal guidelines, for example, an infraction can be punished by up to five days behind bars, while a petty offender is liable only for a fine.[15] Finally, those who string together a series of infractions (or fail to pay

Beyond a Reasonable Doubt The degree of proof required to find the defendant in a criminal trial guilty of committing the crime. The defendant's guilt must be the only reasonable explanation for the criminal act before the court.

Preponderance of the Evidence The degree of proof required in a civil case. In general, this requirement is met when a plaintiff proves that a fact more likely than not is true.

Felony A serious crime, usually punishable by death or imprisonment for a year or longer.

Misdemeanor A criminal offense that is not a felony; usually punishable by a fine and/or a jail term of less than one year.

Infraction In most jurisdictions, a noncriminal offense for which the penalty is a fine rather than incarceration.

FIGURE 3.2 CIVIL LAW VERSUS CRIMINAL LAW

Issue	Civil Law	Criminal Law
Area of Concern	Rights and duties between individuals	Offenses against society as a whole
Wrongful act	Harm to a person or business entity	Violation of a statute that prohibits some type of activity
Party who brings suit	Person who suffered harm (plainfiff)	The state (prosecutor)
Party who responds	Person who supposedly caused harm (defendant)	Person who allegedly committed a crime (defendant)
Standard of proof	Preponderance of the evidence	Beyond a reasonable doubt
Remedy	Damages to compensate for the harm	Punishment (fine or incarceration)

the fines that come with such offenses) are in danger of being criminally charged. In Illinois, having three or more speeding violations in one year is considered criminal behavior.[16]

3-4c *Mala in Se* and *Mala Prohibita*

Criminologists often express the social function of criminal law in terms of *mala in se* or *mala prohibita* crimes. A criminal act is referred to as ***mala in se*** if it would be considered wrong even if there were no law prohibiting it. *Mala in se* crimes are said to go against "natural laws"—that is, against the "natural, moral, and public" principles of a society. Murder, rape, and theft are examples of *mala in se* crimes. These crimes are generally the same from country to country and culture to culture.

In contrast, the term ***mala prohibita*** refers to acts that are considered crimes only because they have been codified as such through statute—"human-made" laws. A *mala prohibita* crime is considered wrong only because it has been prohibited. It is not inherently wrong, though it may reflect the moral standards of a society at a given time. Thus, the definition of a *mala prohibita* crime can vary from country to country and even from state to state. Bigamy, or the offense of having two legal spouses, could be considered a *mala prohibita* crime.

Some observers question the distinction between *mala in se* and *mala prohibita*. In many instances, it is difficult to define a "pure" *mala in se* crime. That is, it is difficult to separate a crime from the culture that has deemed it a crime.[17] Even murder, under certain cultural circumstances, is not considered a criminal act. In a number of poor, traditional areas of the Middle East and Asia, the law excuses "honor killings," in which men kill female family members suspected of sexual indiscretion.

Our own legal system excuses homicide in extreme situations, such as self-defense or when a law enforcement agent kills in the course of upholding the law. Therefore, "natural" laws can be seen as culturally specific. Similar difficulties occur in trying to define a "pure" *mala prohibita* crime because different cultures have different ways of looking at similar behavior. More than 150 countries, including most members of the European Union, have legalized prostitution. With the exception of seven rural counties of Nevada, prostitution is illegal in the United States.

Mala In Se A descriptive term for acts that are inherently wrong, regardless of whether they are prohibited by law.

Mala Prohibita A descriptive term for acts that are made illegal by criminal statute and are not necessarily wrong in and of themselves.

Corpus Delicti The body of circumstances that must exist for a criminal act to have occurred.

3-5 WHAT ARE THE ELEMENTS OF A CRIME?

In fictional accounts of police work, the admission of guilt is often portrayed as the crucial element of a criminal investigation. Although an admission is certainly useful to police and prosecutors, it alone cannot establish the innocence or guilt of a suspect. Criminal law normally requires that the ***corpus delicti,*** a Latin phrase for "the body of the crime," be proved before a person can be convicted of wrongdoing.[18]

Corpus delicti can be defined as "proof that a specific crime has actually been committed by someone."[19] It consists of the following:

1. The *actus reus,* or guilty act
2. The *mens rea,* or guilty intent
3. Concurrence, or the coming together of the criminal act or the guilty mind
4. A link between the act and the legal definition of the crime
5. Any attendant, or accompanying, circumstances
6. The harm done by the crime

3-5a Criminal Act: *Actus Reus*

Suppose Mr. Smith walks into a police department and announces that he just killed his wife. In and of itself, the confession is insufficient for conviction unless the police find Mrs. Smith's corpse, for example, with a bullet in her brain and establish through evidence that Mr. Smith fired the gun. (This does not mean that an actual dead body has to be found in every homicide case. Rather, it is the fact of the death that must be established in such cases.)

Most crimes require an act of *commission*, meaning that a person must *do* something in order to be accused of a crime. The prohibited act is referred to as the *actus reus*, or guilty act. Furthermore, the act of commission must be voluntary. For example, if Mr. Smith had an epileptic seizure while holding a hunting rifle and accidentally shot his wife, he normally would not be held criminally liable for her death.

A LEGAL DUTY In some cases, an act of *omission* can be a crime, but only when a person has a legal duty to perform the omitted act. One such legal duty is assumed to arise in "special relationships," such as those between parents and their children, adult children and their aged parents, and spouses.[20]

CAREER PREP

Paralegal/Legal Assistant

Job Description:

- Assist lawyers in many aspects of legal work, including preparing for trial, researching legal documents, drafting contracts, and investigating cases.
- In addition to criminal law, work includes civil law, corporate law, intellectual property, bankruptcy, immigration, family law, and real estate.

What Kind of Training Is Required?

- A community college–level paralegal program that leads to an associate degree.
- For those who already have a college degree, a certificate in paralegal studies.

Annual Salary Range?

- $41,000–$65,000

JHDT Stock Images LLC/Shutterstock.com

GETTING LINKEDIN
In one posting, a Houston law firm noted that potential paralegal candidates must be able to "research, analyze, and summarize relevant legal precedents for applicability to assigned cases." Precedents, discussed earlier in this chapter, are crucial judicial decisions that criminal lawyers often must either rely on or overcome to best serve their clients.

Certain persons involved in contractual relationships with others, such as physicians and lifeguards, must also perform legal duties to avoid criminal penalty. A number of states have even passed "duty to aid" statutes requiring their citizens to report criminal conduct and help victims of such conduct if possible.[21] Another example of a criminal act of omission is failure to file a federal income tax return when required by law to do so.

A PLAN OR ATTEMPT The guilty act requirement is based on one of the premises of criminal law—that a person is punished for harm done to society. Planning to kill someone or to steal a car may be wrong, but the thoughts do no harm and are therefore not criminal until they are translated into action.

Of course, a person can be punished for *attempting* murder or robbery, but normally only if he or she took substantial steps toward the criminal objective and the prosecution can prove that the desire to commit the crime was present. Furthermore, the punishment for an **attempt** normally is less severe than the punishment for a completed act.

3-5b Mental State: *Mens Rea*

A wrongful mental state—***mens rea***—is usually as necessary as a wrongful act in determining guilt. The mental state, or requisite intent, required to establish guilt of a crime is indicated in the applicable statute or law. For theft, the wrongful act is the taking of another person's property, and the required mental state involves both the awareness that the property belongs to another and the desire to deprive the owner of it.

Attempt The act of taking substantial steps toward committing a crime while having the ability and the intent to commit the crime, even if the crime never takes place.

Mens Rea (pronounced mehns *ray*-uh). Mental state, or intent. A wrongful mental state is usually as necessary as a wrongful act to establish criminal liability.

THE CATEGORIES OF *MENS REA* A guilty mental state includes elements of purpose, knowledge, negligence, and recklessness.[22] A defendant is said to have *purposefully* committed a criminal act when he or she intended to engage in certain criminal

EdwinAC/Shutterstock.com

Suppose a seventeen-year-old babysitter falls asleep while smoking a cigarette, accidentally starting a fire that burns down the clients' home. (Nobody is harmed in the blaze.) **Has the babysitter acted negligently or recklessly, or neither? Would your answer change if she had sneaked into the clients' liquor cabinet and was drunk at the time of the accident? Why or why not?**

conduct or to cause a certain criminal result. For a defendant to have *knowingly* committed an illegal act, he or she must be aware of the illegality, must believe that the illegality exists, or must correctly suspect that the illegality exists but fail to do anything to dispel (or confirm) his or her belief.

Negligence A failure to exercise the standard of care that a reasonable person would exercise in similar circumstances.

Recklessness The state of being aware that a risk does or will exist and nevertheless acting in a way that consciously disregards this risk.

Negligence Criminal **negligence** involves the mental state in which the defendant grossly deviates from the standard of care that a reasonable person would use under the same circumstances. The defendant is accused of taking an unjustified, substantial, and foreseeable risk that resulted in harm.

In 2016, for example, authorities charged Michael Pekarek with negligent homicide as the result of a bow-hunting accident. Pekarek and Jeffrey Cummings were sighting a mule deer near the side of a road in Deschutes County, Oregon. After losing sight of the deer, Pekarek turned with his bow pointed toward Cummings and mistakenly shot an arrow into his friend's stomach. Pekarek obviously had no intention of killing Cummings. At the same time, there is a foreseeable risk in handling a deadly weapon so carelessly.

Recklessness A defendant who commits an act recklessly is more blameworthy than one who is criminally negligent. The standard definition of criminal **recklessness** involves "consciously disregard[ing] a substantial and unjustifiable risk.[23] So, in 2016, a Milwaukee jury convicted Carl Barrett, Jr., of first degree reckless homicide for fatally shooting a five-year-old girl who was sitting on her grandfather's lap inside their home. Barrett mistakenly thought he was firing at the house of a different target, someone against whom he had a grudge. Although Barrett—like Michael Pekarek in the previous example—had no intention of killing his victim, the substantial risk of serious harm to bystanders in carrying out a "revenge shooting" is evident.

DEGREES OF CRIME Crimes are graded by degree. Generally speaking, the degree of a crime is a reflection of the seriousness of that crime and is used to determine the severity of any subsequent punishment.

With many crimes, degree is a function of the criminal act itself, as determined by statute. For example, most criminal codes consider a burglary that involves a nighttime forced entry into a home to be a burglary in the first degree. If the same act takes place during the day and involves a nonresidential building, then it is burglary in the second degree. As you might expect, burglary in the first degree carries a harsher penalty than burglary in the second degree.

First Degree Murder With murder, the degree of the crime is, to a large extent, determined by the mental state of the offender. Murder is generally defined as the willful killing of a human being. It is important to emphasize the word *willful*, which means that murder does not include homicides caused by accident or negligence. A death that results from negligence or accident generally is considered a private wrong and therefore a matter for civil law.

In addition, criminal law punishes those who plan and intend to do harm more harshly than it does those who act wrongfully because of strong emotions or other extreme circumstances. First degree murder—usually punishable by life in prison or the death penalty—occurs under two circumstances:

1. When the crime is premeditated, or contemplated beforehand by the offender, instead of being a spontaneous act of violence.
2. When the crime is deliberate, meaning that it was planned and decided on after a process of decision making. Deliberation does not require a lengthy planning process. A person can be found guilty of first degree murder even if she or he made the decision to kill only seconds before committing the crime.

Second Degree Murder Usually punishable by a minimum of fifteen to twenty-five years in prison, second degree murder does not involve premeditation or deliberation. It does, however, involve an offender's wanton disregard for the consequences of his or her actions. Both these conditions—the premeditation and deliberation of first degree murder and the wanton disregard of second degree murder—fall under the classification of *malice aforethought*.

The difference between first and second degree murder is illustrated by the case of Thu Hong Nguyen, a Kansas City woman who, several years ago, intentionally set fire to a business that she owned. This alleged act of arson turned deadly when a wall of the burning building collapsed, killing two firefighters who were battling the blaze.

Although Nguyen may have intentionally committed arson, there was no evidence that she planned to kill either of the two men. At the same time, she certainly acted with wanton disregard for her victims' safety. Therefore, local authorities charged Nguyen with second degree murder, which carries a maximum penalty of life in prison in Missouri, rather than first degree murder, which is punishable by death.

CAREER TIP *Certified arson investigators* are trained to read the clues left by suspicious fires and determine their causes. In the words of one arson specialist, "Fire does not destroy evidence–it creates it."

Types of Manslaughter A homicide committed without malice toward the victim is known as *manslaughter* and is commonly punishable by up to fifteen years in prison. **Voluntary manslaughter** occurs when the intent to kill may be present, but malice is lacking. Voluntary manslaughter covers crimes of passion, in which the emotion of an argument between two friends leads to homicide. Voluntary manslaughter can also occur when the victim provoked the offender to act violently.

Involuntary manslaughter covers incidents in which the offender's acts may have been careless, but he or she had no intent to kill. For example, Maria Hyrnenko and three associates knowingly installed illegal gas lines in a building she owned in New York City and conspired to hide the faulty system from inspectors. A malfunction in the gas lines caused an explosion that burned down the building and set fire to several adjoining businesses, killing two people who were eating at a nearby restaurant. In 2016, prosecutors charged Maria Hyrnenko and her co-conspirators with involuntary manslaughter. Although Hyrnenko did not intend to kill anybody, local authorities believed her to be criminally responsible for the two deaths.

Comparing Hyrnenko's case with that of Thu Hong Nguyen on the previous page, you can see that the distinction between malice aforethought and carelessness is not always clear. The feature *Discretion in Action—Murder or Manslaughter?* provides further insight into the differences between various homicide charges, with an emphasis on the importance of ascertaining the offender's intent.

STRICT LIABILITY For certain crimes, criminal law holds the defendant to be guilty even if intent to commit the offense is lacking. These acts are known as **strict liability crimes** and generally involve endangering the public welfare in some way.[24] Drug control statutes, health and safety regulations, and traffic laws are all strict liability laws.

Protecting the Public In some ways, the concept of strict liability is inconsistent with the traditional principles of criminal law, which hold that *mens rea* is required for an act to be criminal. The goal of strict liability laws is to protect the public by eliminating the possibility that wrongdoers could claim ignorance or mistake to

Voluntary Manslaughter
A homicide in which the intent to kill was present in the mind of the offender, but malice was lacking.

Involuntary Manslaughter
A homicide in which the offender had no intent to kill the victim.

Strict Liability Crimes
Certain crimes, such as traffic violations, in which the defendant is guilty regardless of her or his state of mind at the time of the act.

DISCRETION IN ACTION

Murder or Manslaughter?

THE SITUATION It is after midnight, and George, drunk and angry, decides to pay a visit to Yeardley, his ex-girlfriend. When Yeardley refuses to let George in her apartment, he kicks the door down, grabs Yeardley by the neck, and wrestles her to the floor before leaving. Several hours later, Yeardley's roommate finds her dead, lying face down on a pillow soaked with blood.

THE LAW George can be charged with one of three possible crimes: (1) first degree murder, which is premeditated and deliberate; (2) second degree murder, which means he acted with wanton disregard for the consequences of his actions; or (3) involuntary manslaughter, which involves extreme carelessness but no intent to kill.

WHAT WOULD YOU DO? Further investigation shows that, two years prior to Yeardley's death, a jealous George put her in a chokehold in public. Furthermore, just days before breaking into her apartment, George sent Yeardley an e-mail in which he reacted to news that she was dating someone else by threatening, "I should have killed you."

In his defense, George says that although he did have a physical confrontation with Yeardley, she did not seem injured when he left the apartment. George's lawyer claims that Yeardley died from suffocation, not from any wound caused by George.

If it were your decision, would you charge George with first degree murder, second degree murder, or involuntary manslaughter? Why?

To see how a Charlottesville, Virginia, jury responded to a similar situation, see Example 3.1 in Appendix A.

absolve themselves of criminal responsibility.[25] Thus, a person caught dumping waste in a protected pond or driving 70 miles per hour in a 55 miles-per-hour zone cannot plead a lack of intent in his or her defense.

The "death by dealer" laws that we discussed in the opening to this chapter are an example of strict liability legislation. These laws hold that people who distribute drugs that lead to fatal overdoses are "strictly liable" for those deaths, regardless of whether there was any intent to kill. Opponents of this type of legislation argue that the *mens rea* requirement is too important to be discarded in homicide prosecutions. "Heroin distributers are not murderers, and they're not murderers when their customers die from an overdose," says Rutgers University professor Douglas Husak.[26]

Protecting Minors One of the most controversial strict liability crimes is **statutory rape,** in which an adult engages in a sexual encounter with a minor. In most states, even if the minor consents to the sexual act, the crime still exists because, being underage, he or she is considered incapable of making a rational decision on the matter.[27] Therefore, statutory rape has been committed even if the adult was unaware of the minor's age or was misled to believe that the minor was older.

Statutory Rape A strict liability crime in which an adult engages in a sexual act with a minor.

Actus Reus (pronounced *ak*-tus *ray*-uhs). A guilty (prohibited) act.

ACCOMPLICE LIABILITY Under certain circumstances, a person can be charged with and convicted of a crime that he or she did not actually commit. This occurs when the suspect has acted as an *accomplice*, helping another person commit the crime. Generally, to be found guilty as an accomplice, a person must have had "dual intent." This level of *mens rea* includes *both*:

1. The intent to aid the person who committed the crime, and
2. The intent that such aid would lead to the commission of the crime.[28]

Assume that Jerry drives Jason to a bank that Jason intends to rob. If Jerry has no knowledge of Jason's criminal plan, he does not fulfill the second prong of the "dual intent" test. As for the ***actus reus,*** the accomplice must help the primary actor in either a physical sense (for example, by providing the getaway car) or a psychological sense (for example, by encouraging her or him to commit the crime).[29]

In some states, a person can be convicted as an accomplice even without intent if the crime was a "natural and probable consequence" of his or her actions.[30]

This principle has led to a proliferation of **felony-murder** legislation. Felony-murder is a form of first degree murder that applies when a person participates in a serious felony that results in the death of a human being. Under felony-murder law, if two men rob a bank, and the first man intentionally kills a security guard, the second man can be convicted of first degree murder as an accomplice to the bank robbery, even if he had no intent to hurt anyone.

Along these same lines, if a security guard accidentally shoots and kills a customer during a bank robbery, the bank robbers can be charged with first degree murder because they committed the underlying felony. Felony-murder laws have come under criticism because they punish individuals for unintended acts or acts committed by others. Nevertheless, the criminal codes of more than thirty states include some form of the felony-murder rule.

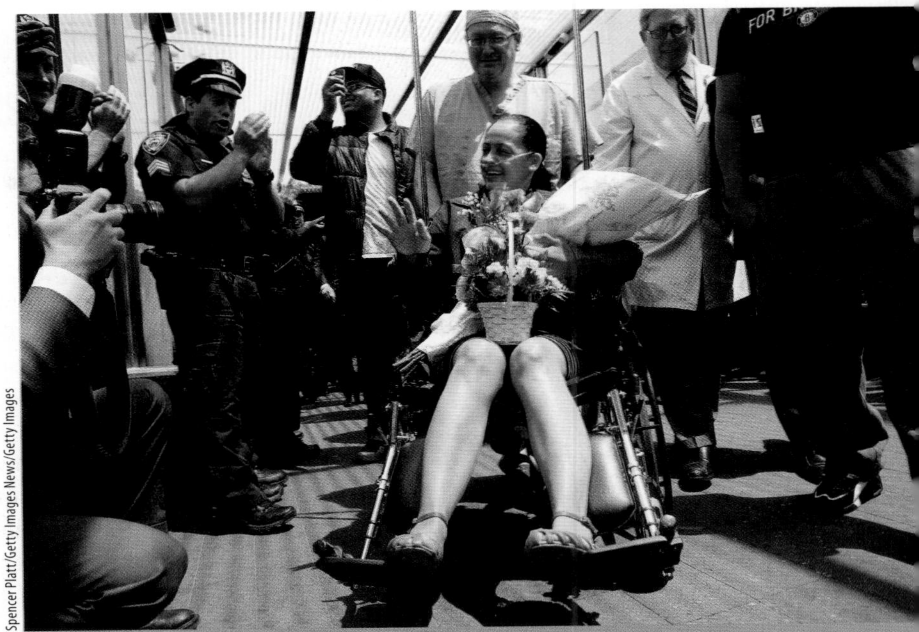

Spencer Platt/Getty Images News/Getty Images

New York City Police Department officer Rosa Rodriguez was injured responding to a fire started by teenager Marcell Dockery. Because her partner was killed in the blaze, Dockery was convicted of felony-murder and could spend the rest of his life behind bars. **Is this a fair result of the felony-murder rule, the felony in this instance being arson? Why or why not?**

3-5c Concurrence

According to criminal law, there must be *concurrence* between the guilty act and the guilty intent. In other words, the guilty act and the guilty intent must occur together.[31] Suppose, for example, that a woman intends to murder her husband with poison in order to collect his life insurance. Every evening, this woman drives her husband home from work.

On the night she plans to poison him, however, she swerves to avoid a cat crossing the road and runs into a tree. She survives the accident, but her husband is killed. Even though her intent was realized, the incident would be considered an accidental death because she had not planned to kill him by driving the car into a tree.

3-5d Causation

Criminal law also requires that the criminal act cause the harm suffered. In 1998, for example, thirteen-year-old Don Collins doused eight-year-old Robbie Middleton with gasoline and set him on fire, allegedly to cover up a sexual assault. Thirteen years later, after years of skin grafts and other surgeries, Middleton died from his burns. A Montgomery County, Texas, judge ruled that, despite the passage of time, Collins could be charged with Middleton's murder. In 2015, he was convicted and sentenced to forty years behind bars.

3-5e Attendant Circumstances

In certain crimes, **attendant circumstances**—also known as accompanying circumstances—are relevant to the *corpus delicti*. Most states, for example, differentiate between simple assault and the more serious offense of aggravated assault, depending on the attendant circumstance of whether the defendant used a weapon such as a gun or a knife while committing the crime.

Criminal law also classifies degrees of property crimes based on the attendant circumstance of the amount stolen. According to federal statutes, the theft of less than $1,000 from a bank is a misdemeanor, while the theft of any amount over $1,000 is a felony.[32] (To get a better understanding of the role of attendant circumstances in criminal statutes, see Figure 3.3.) Attendant circumstances must be proved beyond a reasonable doubt, just like any other element of a crime.[33]

In most cases, a person's motive for committing a crime is irrelevant—a court will not try to read the accused's mind. Over the past few decades,

Felony-Murder An unlawful homicide that occurs during the attempted commission of a felony.

Attendant Circumstances The facts surrounding a criminal event that must be proved to convict the defendant of the underlying crime.

FIGURE 3.3 ATTENDANT CIRCUMSTANCES IN CRIMINAL LAW

Intent	Act	Attendant Circumstances

Whoever intentionally confines, restrains, or detains another against that person's will is guilty of felony false imprisonment.

Most criminal statutes incorporate three of the elements we have discussed in this section: the act (*actus reus*), the intent (*mens rea*), and attendant circumstances. This diagram of the federal false imprisonment statute should give you an idea of how these elements combine to create the totality of a crime.

however, nearly every state and the federal government have passed *hate crime laws* that make the suspect's motive an important attendant circumstance to his or her criminal act. In general, **hate crime laws** provide for greater sanctions against those who commit crimes motivated by bias against a person based on race, ethnicity, religion, gender, sexual orientation, disability, or age.

The Federal Bureau of Investigation recorded almost 7,200 hate crimes in 2015. More than half of those incidents involved the victim's race, ethnicity, or ancestry, with another fifth focused on the victim's sexual orientation.[34]

3-5f Harm

For most crimes to occur, some harm must have been done to a person or to property. A certain number of crimes are actually categorized depending on the harm done to the victim, regardless of the intent behind the criminal act.

Consider two offenses, both of which involve one person hitting another on the back of the head with a tire iron. In the first instance, the victim dies, and the offender is charged with murder. In the second, the victim is only knocked unconscious, and the offender is charged with battery. Because the harm in the second instance is less severe, so is the crime with which the offender is charged, even though the acts are exactly the same. Furthermore, most states have different degrees of battery depending on the extent of the injuries suffered by the victim.

Hate Crime Laws Statutes that provide for greater sanctions against those who commit crimes motivated by bias against an individual or a group based on race, ethnicity, religion, gender, sexual orientation, disability, or age.

Inchoate Offenses Conduct deemed criminal without actual harm being done, provided that the harm that would have occurred is one the law tries to prevent.

Conspiracy A plot by two or more people to carry out an illegal or harmful act.

Many acts are deemed criminal even if no harm is done, so long as the harm that could have been done is against the law. Such acts are called **inchoate offenses.** An attempted crime is an inchoate offense. When Jenkins solicits Peterson to murder Jenkins's business partner, Jenkins has committed an inchoate offense, even if Peterson fails to carry out the act.

Threats and *conspiracies* also fall into the category of inchoate offenses. Simply stated, a criminal **conspiracy** exists when two or more people agree to engage in an illegal act. The United States Supreme Court has ruled that a person can be convicted of criminal conspiracy even though police intervention made the completion of the illegal plan impossible.[35]

ETHICS CHALLENGE

Some critics contend that hate crime laws are unethical because they seem to indicate that certain victims are more worthy of protection than others. Do you agree with this criticism? Why or why not?

3-6 WHICH DEFENSES ARE AVAILABLE UNDER CRIMINAL LAW?

After Robert Conley III was arrested and charged with assault for allegedly attacking Salvador Gomez with a golf club in Saginaw, Michigan, his lawyer argued that Conley could not possibly have committed the crime. The defense attorney produced four witnesses who swore that at 3:30 a.m. on the morning of June 3, 2016—the time of the incident— Conley was at home.

In other words, the lawyer claimed that Conley had an **alibi,** or evidence that he was elsewhere at the time of the crime, to prove his innocence. Alibis are just one of a number of established defenses for wrongdoing in our criminal courts. These defenses generally rely on one of two arguments: (1) the defendant is not responsible for the crime, or (2) the defendant was justified in committing the crime.

3-6a Excuse Defenses

LO3-3 List and briefly define the most important excuse defenses for crimes.

The idea of responsibility plays a significant role in criminal law. In certain circumstances, the law recognizes that even though an act is inherently criminal, society will not punish the actor because he or she does not have the requisite mental condition. In other words, the law "excuses" the person for his or her behavior. Insanity, intoxication, and mistake are the most important excuse defenses today, but we start our discussion of the subject with one of the first such defenses recognized by American law: infancy.

INFANCY The term **infancy,** as used in the law, refers to a person who has not reached the legal age of majority—that is, who is not legally considered to be an adult. Under the earliest state criminal codes of the United States, children younger than seven years of age could never be held legally accountable for crimes. Those between seven and fourteen years old were presumed to lack the capacity for criminal behavior, while anyone over the age of fourteen was tried as an adult. Thus, early American criminal law recognized infancy as a defense in which wrongdoing was excused when the wrongdoers were assumed to be too young to fully understand the consequences of their actions.

With the creation of the juvenile justice system in the early 1900s, the infancy defense became redundant, as youthful delinquents were automatically treated differently than adult offenders. Today, most states either designate an age (typically eighteen) under which wrongdoers are sent to juvenile court or allow judges and prosecutors to decide whether minors will be charged as adults on a case-by-case basis. We will explore the concept of infancy as it applies to the modern American juvenile justice system in much greater detail in Chapter 13.

INSANITY After Jody Kossow fatally stabbed her eight-year-old son, Thomas, more than fifty times with a kitchen knife, she called 911 and told the dispatcher that police should hurry to the crime scene because "Satan was after" her. In 2017, a Winnebago County, Illinois, judge ruled that Kossow suffered from a severe mental illness that prevented her from knowing that her actions were wrong. As a result, Kossow was sent to a psychiatric hospital rather than prison. Thus, **insanity** may be a defense to a criminal charge when the defendant's state of mind is such that she or he cannot claim legal responsibility for her or his actions.

Measuring Sanity The general principle of the insanity defense is that a person is excused for his or her criminal wrongdoing if, as a result of a mental disease or defect, he or she

- Does not perceive the physical nature or consequences of his or her conduct;
- Does not know that his or her conduct is wrong or criminal; or
- Is not sufficiently able to control his or her conduct so as to be held accountable for it.[36]

Although criminal law has traditionally accepted the idea that an insane person cannot be held responsible for criminal acts, society has long debated what standards should be used to measure sanity for the purposes of a criminal trial. This lack of consensus is reflected in the diverse tests employed by different American jurisdictions to determine insanity. The tests include the following:

1. *The* M'Naghten *rule*. Derived from an 1843 British murder case, the ***M'Naghten* rule** states that a person is legally insane and therefore not criminally responsible if, at the time of the offense, he or she was not able to distinguish between right and wrong.[37] As Figure 3.4 shows, half of the states still use a version of the *M'Naghten* rule. One state, New Hampshire, uses a slightly different version of this rule called the "product test." Under this standard, a defendant is not guilty if the unlawful act was the product of a mental disease or defect.
2. *The ALI/MPC test*. In the early 1960s, the American Law Institute

Alibi Proof that a suspect was somewhere other than the scene of the crime at the time of the crime, typically offered to demonstrate that the suspect was not guilty of the crime.

Infancy The status of a person who is below the legal age of majority. Under early American law, infancy excused young wrongdoers of criminal behavior because presumably they could not understand the consequences of their actions.

Insanity A defense for criminal liability that asserts a lack of criminal responsibility due to mental instability.

***M'Naghten* Rule** A test of criminal responsibility, derived from *M'Naghten's* Case in 1843, that relies on the defendant's inability to distinguish right from wrong.

FIGURE 3.4 INSANITY DEFENSES

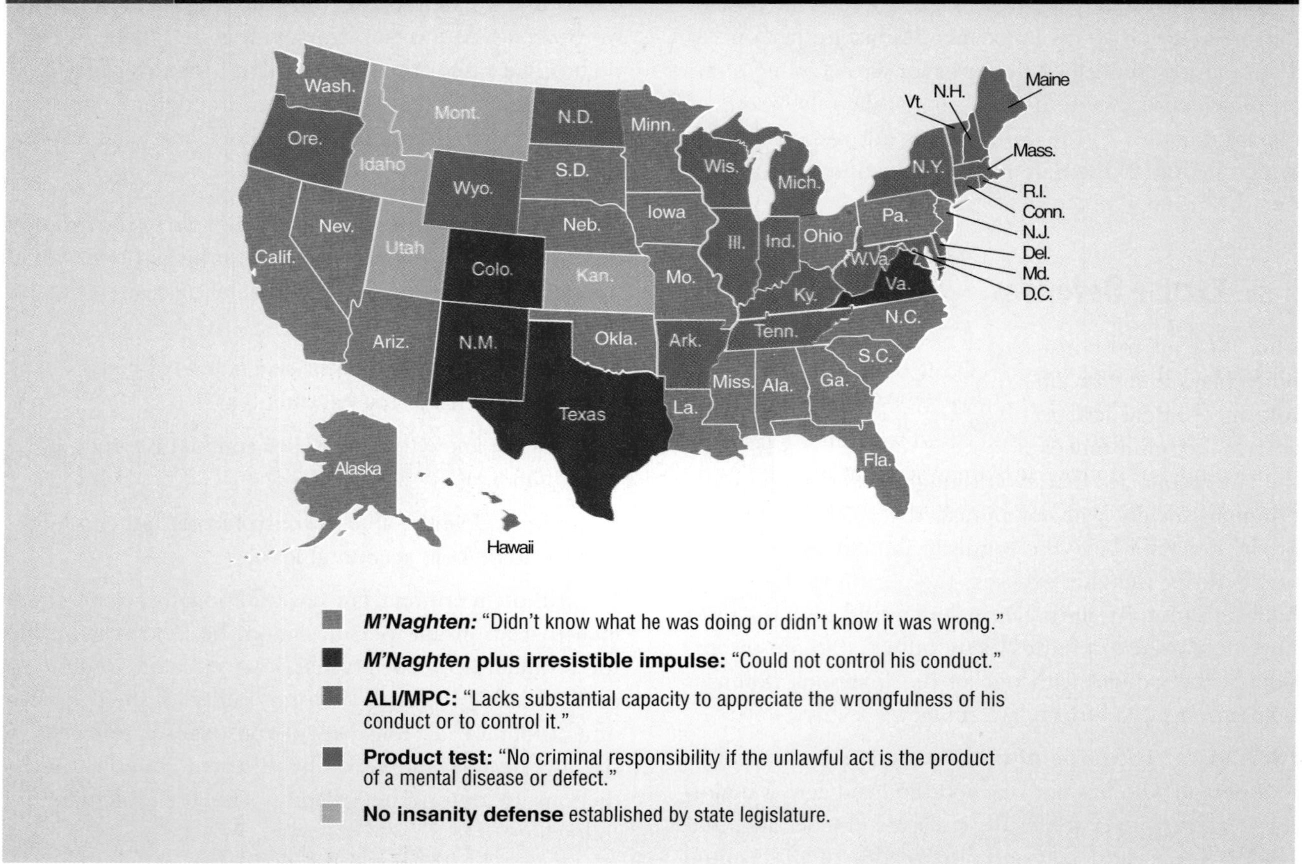

Source: Bureau of Justice Statistics, *The Defense of Insanity: Standards and Procedures, State Court Organization*, 1998 (Washington, D.C.: U.S. Department of Justice, June 2000).

(ALI) included an insanity standard in its Model Penal Code (MPC). Also known as the **substantial-capacity test**, the **ALI/MPC test** requires that the defendant lack "substantial capacity" either to "appreciate the wrongfulness" of his or her conduct or to conform that conduct "to the requirements of the law."[38]

3. *The irresistible-impulse test.* Under the **irresistible-impulse test,** a person may be found insane even if he or she was aware that a criminal act was "wrong," provided that some "irresistible impulse" resulting from a mental deficiency drove him or her to commit the crime.[39]

Substantial-Capacity Test (ALI/MPC Test) A test for the insanity defense that states that a person is not responsible for criminal behavior when he or she "lacks substantial capacity" to understand that the behavior is wrong or to know how to behave properly.

Irresistible-Impulse Test A test for the insanity defense under which a defendant who knew his or her action was wrong may still be found insane if he or she was unable, as a result of a mental deficiency, to control the urge to complete the act.

Competency Hearing A court proceeding to determine mental competence.

The ALI/MPC test is considered the easiest standard of the three for a defendant to meet because the defendant needs only to show a lack of "substantial capacity" to be released from criminal responsibility. Defense attorneys generally consider it more difficult to prove that the defendant could not distinguish "right" from "wrong" or that he or she was driven by an irresistible impulse.

Determining Competency Whatever the standard, the insanity defense is rarely entered and is even less likely to result in an acquittal, as it is difficult to prove.[40] Psychiatry is far more commonly used in the courtroom to determine the *competency* of a defendant to stand trial. If a judge believes that the defendant is unable to understand the nature of the proceedings or to assist in his or her own defense, the trial will not take place.

When a **competency hearing** (held to determine whether the defendant is competent to stand trial) reveals that the defendant is in fact incompetent, criminal proceedings come to a halt. For example, in August 2016, an El Paso County, Colorado, judge ruled that Robert Dear, Jr., suffered from a delusional disorder and therefore was not fit to stand trial. Dear had been charged with eight counts of first degree murder resulting from a shooting rampage at a Colorado Springs Planned Parenthood clinic eight months earlier. As a result of the judge's decision, Dear will be held indefinitely at a mental institution rather than face further criminal proceedings.

AP Images/*The Tennessean*, John Partipilo, Pool

Corey Batey, far right, was one of four University of Vanderbilt football players charged with raping an unconscious woman. His defense attorney unsuccessfully claimed that Batey was so drunk on the night in question that he was easily manipulated by the others into committing the crime. **Why do you think that the intoxication defense failed in this instance?**

INTOXICATION The law recognizes two types of **intoxication,** whether from drugs or from alcohol: *voluntary* and *involuntary*.

Involuntary Intoxication Involuntary intoxication occurs when a person is physically forced to ingest or is injected with an intoxicating substance, or is unaware that a substance contains drugs or alcohol. Involuntary intoxication is a viable defense to a crime if the substance leaves the person unable to form the mental state necessary to understand that the act committed while under the influence was wrong.[41]

Several years ago, for instance, the Ramsey County, Minnesota, district attorney's office dropped child assault charges against Jozetta R. Byrd after determining that the defendant's wrongdoing was the result of a negative reaction to her asthma medication. Because the drug rendered Byrd unable to "determine right from wrong," she was not criminally responsible for attacking her two young children.[42]

Voluntary Intoxication Voluntary drug or alcohol intoxication is also used to excuse a defendant's actions, though it is not a defense in itself. Rather, it is used when the defense attorney wants to show that the defendant was so intoxicated that *mens rea* was negated. In other words, the defendant could not possibly have had the state of mind that a crime requires.

Many courts are reluctant to allow voluntary intoxication arguments to be presented to juries. After all, the defendant, by definition, voluntarily chose to enter an intoxicated state. Indeed, thirteen states have eliminated voluntary intoxication as a possible defense, a step that has been criticized by many legal scholars but was upheld by the United States Supreme Court in *Montana v. Egelhoff* (1996).[43]

MISTAKE Ordinarily, ignorance of the law or a *mistaken idea* about what the law requires is not a valid defense. Such was the case when retired science teacher Eddie Leroy Anderson and his son dug for arrowheads near their favorite campground site in Idaho, unaware that the land was a federally protected archaeological site. Facing two years in prison for this mistake, they pleaded guilty and were given a year's probation and a $1,500 fine each. "Folks need to pay attention to where they are," said U.S. attorney Wendy Olson.[44]

Mistake of Law As the above example suggests, strict liability crimes specifically preclude the *mistake of law* defense, because the offender's intent is irrelevant. For practical reasons, the mistake of law defense is rarely allowed under any circumstances. If "I didn't know" was a valid defense, the courts would be clogged with defendants claiming ignorance of all aspects of criminal law. In some rare instances, however, people who claim that they honestly did not know that they were breaking a law may have a valid defense if (1) the law was not published or reasonably known to the public or (2) the person relied on an official statement of the law that was erroneous.[45]

Mistake of Fact A *mistake of fact*, as opposed to a *mistake of law*, operates as a defense when it negates the mental state necessary to commit a crime. If, for example, Oliver mistakenly walks off with Julie's briefcase because he thinks it is his, there is no theft. Theft requires knowledge that the property belongs to another.

Intoxication A defense for criminal liability in which the defendant claims that the taking of intoxicants rendered him or her unable to form the requisite intent to commit a criminal act.

In 2016, to use a real-life example, Hamilton County, Ohio, prosecutors declined to prosecute a father who mistook his fourteen-year-old son for an intruder and fatally shot the boy. The mistake-of-fact defense has proved very controversial in rape and sexual assault cases, in which the accused claims a mistaken belief that the sex was consensual, while the victim insists that he or she was coerced.

3-6b Justification Defenses

> **LO3-4** Describe the four most important justification criminal defenses.

In certain instances, a defendant will accept responsibility for committing an illegal act, but contend that—given the circumstances—the act was justified. In other words, even though the guilty act and the guilty intent may be present, the particulars of the case relieve the defendant of criminal liability. In 2015, for example, there were 770 "justified" killings of persons who were in the process of committing a felony: 442 were killed by law enforcement officers and 328 by private citizens.[46] Four of the most important justification defenses are duress, self-defense, necessity, and entrapment.

DURESS **Duress** exists when the *wrongful* threat of one person induces another person to perform an act that she or he would otherwise not perform. In such a situation, duress is said to negate the *mens rea* necessary to commit a crime. For duress to qualify as a defense, the following requirements must be met:

1. The threat must be of serious bodily harm or death.
2. The harm threatened must be greater than the harm caused by the crime.
3. The threat must be immediate and inescapable.
4. The defendant must have become involved in the situation through no fault of his or her own.[47]

Note that some scholars consider duress to be an excuse defense, because the threat of bodily harm negates any guilty intent on the part of the defendant.[48]

When ruling on the duress defense, courts often examine whether the defendant had the opportunity to avoid the threat in question. In one case, the defendant claimed that an associate threatened to kill him and his wife unless he participated in a marijuana deal. Although this contention was proved true during the course of the trial, the court rejected the duress defense because the defendant made no apparent effort to escape, nor did he report his dilemma to the police. In sum, the drug deal was avoidable—the defendant could have made an effort to extricate himself, but he did not, thereby surrendering the protection of the duress defense.[49]

> **Duress** Unlawful pressure brought to bear on a person, causing the person to perform an act that he or she would not otherwise perform.
>
> **Self-Defense** The legally recognized privilege to protect one's self or property from injury by another.

JUSTIFIABLE USE OF FORCE—SELF-DEFENSE A person who believes he or she is in danger of being harmed by another is justified in defending himself or herself with the use of force, and any criminal act committed in such circumstances can be justified as **self-defense.** Other situations that also justify the use of force include the defense of another person, the defense of one's dwelling or other property, and the prevention of a crime.

In all these situations, it is important to distinguish between *nondeadly* and *deadly* force. As the terms themselves suggest, nondeadly force is unlikely to cause death or great bodily harm, while deadly force is likely to cause death or great bodily harm.

The Amount of Force Generally speaking, people can use the amount of nondeadly force that seems necessary to protect themselves, their dwellings, or other property or to prevent the commission of a crime. Deadly force can be used in self-defense if there is a *reasonable belief* that imminent death or bodily harm will otherwise result, if the attacker is using unlawful force (an example of lawful force is that exerted by a police officer), if the defender has not initiated or provoked the attack, and if there is no other possible response or alternative way out of the life-threatening situation.[50]

Deadly force normally can be used to defend a dwelling only if an unlawful entry is violent and the person believes deadly force is necessary to prevent imminent death or great bodily harm. In some jurisdictions, it is also a viable defense if the person believes deadly force is necessary to prevent the commission of a felony (such as arson) in the dwelling.

Authorities will often take an expansive view of lawful deadly force when it is used to protect another person. So, earlier this decade, a New Orleans man was not charged with any crime after he fatally shot an offender who was sexually assaulting a woman—the first man's companion—at gunpoint.

The Duty to Retreat When a person is outside his or her home or in a public space, the rules for self-defense change somewhat. Until relatively recently, almost all jurisdictions required someone who is attacked under these circumstances to "retreat to the wall" before fighting

CAREER PREP

Criminal Court Judge

Job Description:

- **Preside over trials and hearings in federal, state, and local courts. Ensure that all proceedings are fair and protect the legal rights of everyone involved.**
- **Rule on admissibility of evidence, monitor the testimony of witnesses, and settle disputes between prosecutors and defense attorneys.**

What Kind of Training Is Required?

- **A law degree and several years of legal experience.**
- **Depending on the jurisdiction, judges are either appointed or elected.**

Annual Salary Range?

- **$118,000–$205,000**

Junial Enterprises, 2010/Used under license from Shutterstock.com

SOCIAL MEDIA CAREER TIP

Find groups on Facebook and LinkedIn in which people are discussing the criminal justice career or careers that interest you. Participate in the discussions to get information and build contacts.

back. In other words, under the **duty to retreat,** one who is being assaulted may not resort to deadly force if she or he has a reasonable opportunity to "run away" and thus avoid the conflict. Only when this person has run into a "wall," literally or otherwise, may deadly force be used in self-defense.

Many states have changed their laws to eliminate the duty to retreat. For example, a Florida law did away with the duty to retreat outside the home, stating that citizens have "the right to stand [their] ground and meet force with force, including deadly force," if they "reasonably" fear for their safety.[51] The Florida law also allows a person to use deadly force against someone who unlawfully intrudes into her or his house (or vehicle), even if that person does not fear for her or his safety.[52]

Proponents of "stand your ground" laws argue that they strengthen the concept of self-defense by making it less likely that persons who are defending themselves will be charged with crimes. Critics counter that by encouraging people to take violent action against their attackers rather than attempting to flee, the laws have created a "nation where disputes are settled by guns instead of gavels, and where suspects are shot by civilians instead of arrested by police."[53]

NECESSITY The **necessity** defense requires courts to weigh the harm caused by the crime actually committed against the harm that would have been caused by the criminal act avoided. If the avoided harm is greater than the committed harm, then the defense has a chance of succeeding. A Broward County, Florida, jury, for example, recently acquitted a defendant on charges of growing marijuana at his home because the defendant claimed he needed the marijuana to control his severe anorexia. In the eyes of the jurors, the defendant's medical necessity outweighed his alleged crimes.[54] Murder is the one crime for which the necessity defense is not applicable under any circumstances.

Duty to Retreat The requirement that a person claiming self-defense prove that she or he first took reasonable steps to avoid the conflict that resulted in the use of deadly force.

Necessity A defense against criminal liability in which the defendant asserts that circumstances required her or him to commit an illegal act.

ENTRAPMENT **Entrapment** is a justification defense that criminal law allows when a police officer or government agent deceives a defendant into wrongdoing. Although law enforcement agents can legitimately use various forms of subterfuge—such as informants or undercover agents—to gain information or apprehend a suspect in a criminal act, the law places limits on these strategies. Police cannot persuade an innocent person to commit a crime, nor can they coerce a suspect into doing so, even if they are certain she or he is a criminal.

The guidelines for determining entrapment were established in the 1932 case of *Sorrells v. United States*.[55] The case, which took place during Prohibition when the sale of alcoholic beverages was illegal, involved a federal law enforcement agent who repeatedly urged the defendant to sell him bootleg whiskey. The defendant initially rejected the agent's overtures, stating that he "did not fool with whiskey." Eventually, however, he sold the agent a half-gallon of the substance and was summarily convicted of violating the law. The United States Supreme Court held that the agent had improperly induced the defendant to break the law and reversed his conviction.

This case set the precedent for focusing on the defendant's outlook in entrapment cases. In other words, the Court decided that entrapment occurs if a defendant who is not predisposed to commit the crime is convinced to do so by an agent of the government.[56]

3-7 HOW DO CRIMINAL PROCEDURES PROTECT OUR CONSTITUTIONAL RIGHTS?

Entrapment A defense in which the defendant claims that he or she was induced by a public official—usually an undercover agent or police officer—to commit a crime that he or she would otherwise not have committed.

Substantive Criminal Law Law that defines crimes and punishments.

Procedural Criminal Law Law that governs procedures for investigating and prosecuting crimes.

Bill of Rights The first ten amendments to the U.S. Constitution.

To this point, we have focused on **substantive criminal law,** which defines the acts that the government will punish. We will now turn our attention to **procedural criminal law.** (The section that follows will provide only a short overview of criminal procedure. In later chapters, many other constitutional issues will be examined in more detail.)

Criminal law brings the force of the state, with all its resources, to bear against the individual. Criminal procedures, drawn from the ideals stated in the Bill of Rights, are designed to protect the constitutional rights of individuals and to prevent the arbitrary use of this power by the government.

3-7a The Bill of Rights

For various reasons, proposals related to the rights of individuals, including rights related to criminal procedure, were rejected during the framing of the U.S. Constitution in 1787. The need for a written declaration of the rights of individuals eventually caused the first Congress to draft twelve amendments to the Constitution and submit them for approval by the states. Ten of these amendments, commonly known as the **Bill of Rights,** were adopted in 1791. Since then, seventeen more amendments have been added.

The Bill of Rights, as interpreted by the United States Supreme Court, has served as the basis for procedural safeguards of the accused in this country. These safeguards include the following:

1. The Fourth Amendment protection from unreasonable searches and seizures.
2. The Fourth Amendment requirement that no warrants for a search or an arrest can be issued without probable cause.
3. The Fifth Amendment requirement that no one can be deprived of life, liberty, or property without "due process" of law.
4. The Fifth Amendment prohibition against *double jeopardy* (trying someone twice for the same criminal offense).
5. The Fifth Amendment guarantee that no person can be required to be a witness against (incriminate) himself or herself.
6. The Sixth Amendment guarantees of a speedy trial, a trial by jury, a public trial, the right to confront witnesses, and the right to a lawyer at various stages of criminal proceedings.
7. The Eighth Amendment prohibitions against excessive bails and fines and cruel and unusual punishments.

The Bill of Rights initially offered citizens protection only against the federal government. Over the years, however, the procedural safeguards of most of the provisions of the Bill of Rights have been applied to the actions of state governments through the Fourteenth Amendment.[57] Furthermore, the states, under certain circumstances, have the option to grant even more protections than are required by the federal Constitution. As these protections are crucial to criminal justice procedures in the United States, they will be afforded much more attention in Chapter 6, with regard to police action, and in Chapter 8, with regard to the criminal trial.

alexmillos/Shutterstock.com

In 2016, a group of sex offenders filed suit claiming that their due process rights were violated by a federal law that proposed to mark the passports of all sex offenders with a "unique identifier" identifying their status. **Would this law violate the substantive due process rights of sex offenders? Why or why not?**

3-7b Due Process

Both the Fifth and Fourteenth Amendments provide that no person should be deprived of "life, liberty, or property without due process of law." This **due process clause** basically requires that the government not act unfairly or arbitrarily. In other words, the government cannot rely on individual judgment and impulse when making decisions but must stay within the boundaries of reason and the law. Not surprisingly, disagreements as to the meaning of these provisions have plagued courts, politicians, and citizens since this nation was founded and will undoubtedly continue to do so.

To understand due process, it is important to consider its two types: procedural due process and substantive due process.

LO3-5 Explain the importance of the due process clause in the criminal justice system.

PROCEDURAL DUE PROCESS According to **procedural due process**, the law must be carried out according to a *method* that is fair and orderly. It requires that certain procedures be followed in administering and executing a law so that an individual's basic freedoms are not violated. Consider a recent case involving the University of Michigan. The university ruled that a sophomore named Drew Sterrett had engaged in sexual intercourse with another student without her consent. Sterret responded by suing the university in federal court, claiming that it had violated his due process rights in coming to a conclusion that would limit his future "education, employment, and career opportunities."

In his lawsuit, Sterrett contended that he had never been provided with the charges against him in writing. In addition, he had not been given a chance to question his accuser or to know the names of the witnesses who had testified against him. These procedural due process rights, as we will see in Chapter 8, are bedrocks of the American criminal justice system. Eventually, following judicial proceedings, the University of Michigan vacated all its findings against Sterrett.[58]

SUBSTANTIVE DUE PROCESS Fair procedures would obviously be of little use if they were used to administer unfair laws. For example, suppose a law requires everyone to wear a red shirt on Mondays. You wear a blue shirt on Monday, and you are arrested, convicted, and sentenced to one year in prison. The fact that all proper procedures were followed and your rights were given their proper protections would mean very little because the law that you broke was unfair and arbitrary.

Thus, **substantive due process** requires that the laws themselves be reasonable. The idea is that if a law is unfair or arbitrary, even if properly passed by a legislature, it must be declared unconstitutional. In the 1930s, for example, Oklahoma instituted the Habitual Criminal Sterilization Act. Under this

Due Process Clause The provisions of the Fifth and Fourteenth Amendments to the Constitution that guarantee that no person shall be deprived of life, liberty, or property without due process of law.

Procedural Due Process A provision in the Constitution that states that the law must be carried out in a fair and orderly manner.

Substantive Due Process The constitutional requirement that laws must be fair and reasonable in content and must further a legitimate governmental objective.

statute, a person who had been convicted of three felonies could be "rendered sexually sterile" by the state (that is, the person would no longer be able to produce children). The United States Supreme Court held that the law was unconstitutional, as there are "limits to the extent which a legislatively represented majority may conduct biological experiments at the expense of the dignity and personality and natural powers of a minority."[59]

STUDY TOOLS 3

LOCATED IN TEXTBOOK

- ☐ Rip out the Chapter Review Card.
- ☐ Review with the Chapter Quiz following this chapter.

LOCATED AT WWW.CENGAGEBRAIN.COM

- ☐ Review key terms flash cards.
- ☐ Read the chapter on all your favorite devices.
- ☐ Complete an Exam to test your knowledge.
- ☐ Check out Visual Summaries and You Decide activities to explore chapter concepts.

Quiz

1. The U.S. ________________________ is the supreme law of the United States.

2. The body of law created by judicial decisions is known as ________________________ law.

3. In contrast to criminal law, ________________________ law is concerned with disputes between private individuals or other private entities.

4. A ________________________ is a serious crime punishable by more than a year in prison or the death penalty.

5. A person found guilty of a ________________________ will usually spend less than a year in jail or pay a fine.

6. With strict liability crimes, a defendant is guilty even if he or she lacked the ________________________ to perform a criminal act.

7. Criminal law recognizes that a defendant may not be responsible for a criminal act if her or his mental state was impaired by________________________, or mental instability.

8. Defendants may claim that they were justified in committing a crime because they were acting in ________________________ - ________________________ to protect themselves or others from serious bodily harm.

9. ________________________ occurs when a government agent deceives a defendant into committing a crime.

10. The ____________ ____________ clause requires that the U.S. government follow certain procedures to ensure fairness and reasonableness before depriving its citizens of "life, liberty, or property."

Answers to the Chapter 3 Quiz can be found in the Answers section in the back of the book.

4 Law Enforcement Today

Eduardo Munoz Alvarez/Getty Images News/Getty Images

LEARNING OBJECTIVES

After studying this chapter, you will be able to . . .

4-1 List the four basic responsibilities of the police.

4-2 Identify the differences between the police academy and field training as learning tools for recruits.

4-3 Describe the challenges facing women who choose law enforcement as a career.

4-4 Indicate some of the most important law enforcement agencies under the control of the Department of Homeland Security.

4-5 Analyze the importance of private security today.

After finishing this chapter, go to **PAGE 88** for **STUDY TOOLS**

Local Hero

When he first got to Ohio State University (OSU), Alan Horujko planned to be an engineering major. His career path changed, however, when he started volunteering as an unarmed student safety officer with the OSU Police Department. Among other training, this position gave him a chance to patrol areas of the Columbus campus and prepare for active shooter situations. After a taste of law enforcement, "I just couldn't see myself sitting in a cubicle," Horujko said. Three years after his 2012 graduation, Horujko was hired as an OSU police officer. In his application for the position, he wrote that it would be an "honor to give something back to the . . . school that has already given so much to me."

On the morning of November 28, 2016, Horujko did just that. While assisting fire fighters responding to a gas leak on campus, the second-year officer watched as a small gray Honda plowed into a nearby crowd of pedestrians. The driver, a student named Abdul Razak Ali Artan, got out of the car and began stabbing bystanders with a butcher knife. (Earlier, Artan had posted online that he was "sick and tired" of seeing Muslims "killed and tortured" by the U.S. military.) Horujko drew his weapon and ordered Artan to drop the knife. The other man refused. After checking that the scene was free of civilians, Horujko fired three times, killing Artan and ending the threat.

In total, eleven people were hospitalized as a result of Artan's attack. Following protocol, Horujko was placed on administrative leave while the Columbus Department of Public Safety investigated the fatal shooting. Certainly, there was little doubt in the community that Horujko's actions were necessary and justified. "We appreciate your service and bravery," wrote one well-wisher on the OSU Emergency Management Department's Facebook page. "Thank you for protecting our children," wrote another.

AP Images/Ohio State University Police

On November 28, 2016, Ohio State University police officer Alan Horujko fatally shot a suspect who was attacking pedestrians on campus. *What factors went into Officer Horujko's decision to use deadly force? Was his decision correct? Why or why not?*

4-1 WHAT DO POLICE DO?

"There has never been a more dangerous or complicated and challenging time to be a police officer," said Columbus mayor Andrew Ginther of Officer Alan Horujko's timely measures. "We had a dynamic well-trained professional today save the lives of many of our residents and students."[1]

Even when they are not engaged in high-profile acts of courage, police officers are the most visible representatives of our criminal justice system. Indeed, they symbolize the system for many Americans who may never see the inside of a courtroom or a prison cell. Still, the general perception of a "cop's life" is often shaped by television dramas and films. In reality, police spend a great deal of time on such mundane tasks as responding to noise complaints, confiscating firecrackers, and poring over paperwork.

Sociologist Egon Bittner warned against the tendency to see the police primarily as agents of law enforcement and crime control. A more inclusive accounting of "what the police do," Bittner believed, would recognize that they provide "situationally justified force in society."[2] In other words, the function of the police is to solve any problem that may *possibly*, though not *necessarily*, require the use of force.

Within Bittner's rather broad definition of "what the police do," we can pinpoint four basic responsibilities of the police:

1. To enforce laws.
2. To provide services.
3. To prevent crime.
4. To preserve the peace.

LO4-1 List the four basic responsibilities of the police.

As will become evident over the next two chapters, there is a great deal of debate among legal and other scholars and law enforcement officers over which responsibilities deserve the most police attention and what methods police should employ in meeting those responsibilities.

4-1a Enforcing Laws

In the public mind, the primary role of the police is to enforce society's laws—hence, the term *law enforcement officer*. In their role as "crime fighters," police officers have a clear mandate to seek out and apprehend those who have violated the law. The crime-fighting responsibility is so dominant that all police activity—from the purchase of new automobiles to a plan to hire more minority officers—must often be justified in terms of its law enforcement value.[3]

Police officers also see themselves primarily as "crime fighters," a perception that often leads people into what they believe will be an exciting career in law enforcement. Although the job certainly offers challenges unlike any other, police officers normally do not spend the majority of their time in law enforcement duties. After surveying a year's worth of dispatch data from the Wilmington (Delaware) Police Department, researchers Jack Greene and Carl Klockars found that officers spent only about half of their shifts enforcing the law or dealing with crimes. The rest of their time was spent on order maintenance, service provision, traffic patrol, and medical assistance.[4]

Furthermore, information provided by the Uniform Crime Reports shows that most arrests are made for "crimes of disorder" or public annoyances rather than violent or property crimes. In 2015, for example, police made about 8.8 million arrests for drunkenness, liquor law violations, disorderly conduct, vagrancy, loitering, and other minor offenses, but only about 505,000 arrests for violent crimes.[5]

4-1b Providing Services

The popular emphasis on crime fighting tends to overshadow the fact that a great deal of a police officer's time is spent providing services for the community. The motto "To Serve and Protect" has been adopted by thousands of local police departments, and the *Law Enforcement Code of Ethics* recognizes the duty "to serve the community" in its first sentence.[6] The services that police provide are numerous—a partial list would include directing traffic, performing emergency medical procedures, counseling those involved in domestic disputes, providing directions to tourists, and finding lost children.

As we will see in the next section, many police departments have adopted a strategy called *community policing*. This strategy requires officers to provide assistance of a sort that is not, at first glance, directly related to law enforcement. For example, police officers often find themselves on the front lines when it comes to dealing with substance abuse and mental illness. Law enforcement agents in numerous jurisdictions carry naloxone, a drug that can instantly alleviate the effects of an opioid overdose. Over a recent one-year period, local police officers throughout Pennsylvania used naloxone to reverse more than six hundred such overdoses.[7]

In cities such as Houston, Los Angeles, and Minneapolis, local police officers are teaming up with mental health specialists to handle emergency calls involving mentally ill persons.[8] (The feature *Discretion in Action—Handle with Care* considers the best course of action for police confronted with a suspect suffering from mental illness.)

4-1c Preventing Crime

Perhaps the most controversial responsibility of the police is to *prevent* crime. According to Jerome Skolnick, co-director of the Center for Research in Crime and Justice at the New York University School of Law, there are two predictable public responses when crime rates begin to rise in a community. The first is to punish convicted criminals with stricter laws and more severe penalties. The second is to demand that the police "do something" to prevent crimes from occurring in the first place. Is it, in fact, possible for the police to "prevent" crimes? The strongest response that Professor Skolnick is willing to give to this question is "maybe."[9]

On a limited basis, police can certainly prevent some crimes. If a rapist is dissuaded from attacking a solitary woman because a patrol car is cruising the area, then the police officer behind the wheel has prevented a crime. Furthermore, exemplary police work can have a measurable effect. "Quite simply, cops count," says William Bratton, who has directed police departments in Boston, Los Angeles, and New York. "[T]he quickest way to impact crime is with a well-led, managed, and appropriately resourced police force."[10] In Chapter 5,

DISCRETION IN ACTION

Handle with Care

THE SITUATION Terri lives in a group home for people who suffer from mental illness. After she stops taking her medication, a social worker stops by to check on Terri's well-being. She responds by threatening the social worker, yelling, "Get out of here! I have a knife, and I'll kill you if I have to!" The social worker contacts the police, and Officers Helton and Ramirez take the call. Using a master key to open Terri's locked door, the officers find her holding a five-inch kitchen knife and screaming, "I am going to kill you. I don't need help. Get out." Officers Helton and Ramirez, who do not have their weapons drawn, leave the room and ponder their next move.

THE LAW Under the Fourth Amendment, as you will see in Chapter 6, law enforcement agents have the right to enter a home or dwelling without permission from a judge in emergency situations. The potential for injury to an occupant of that home or dwelling is one such situation.

WHAT WOULD YOU DO? On the one hand, Terri has threatened to kill three people, possesses a deadly weapon, and may harm herself. (Plus, if she escapes from her room, which is on the ground floor and has a window, she could harm others.) On the other hand, police officers should not assume that a person suffering from mental illness necessarily poses a threat to herself or to society. Furthermore, the goal here is not to arrest Teresa, but rather to move her to a mental health facility for involuntary treatment.

Officers Helton and Ramirez have several options. They can reenter Terri's room and try to subdue her themselves. Or they can call for police backup. Or they can request the assistance of mental health experts, thereby lessening the chance that they will need to use force against Terri. Which is the best option? Why?

To see how two police officers in San Francisco reacted in similar circumstances, go to Example 4.1 in Appendix A.

we will study a number of policing strategies that have been credited, by some, for decreasing crime rates in the United States.

In general, however, the deterrent effects of police presence are unclear. One study found no relationship between the size of the police presence in a neighborhood and the residents' perceived risk of being arrested for wrongdoing.[11] Furthermore, Carl Klockars has written that the "war on crime" is a war that the police cannot win because they cannot control the factors—such as unemployment, poverty, immorality, inequality, political change, and lack of educational opportunities—that contribute to criminal behavior in the first place.[12]

4-1d Preserving the Peace

To a certain extent, the fourth responsibility of the police, that of preserving the peace, is related to preventing crime. Police have the legal authority to use the power of arrest, or even force, in situations in which a crime has not yet occurred but might occur in the immediate future.

In the words of James Q. Wilson, the police's peacekeeping role (which Wilson believed to be the most important role of law enforcement officers) often takes on a pattern of simply "handling the situation."[13] For example, when police officers arrive on the scene of a loud, late-night house party, they may feel the need to disperse the party and even arrest some of the partygoers for disorderly conduct. By their actions, the officers have lessened the chances that serious and violent crimes will take place later in the evening.

The same principle is often used in dealing with domestic disputes, which, if they escalate, can lead to homicide. Such situations, to use Wilson's terminology again, need "fixing up," and police can use the power of arrest, or threat, or coercion, or sympathy to do just that.

ETHICS CHALLENGE

Do law enforcement agents have an ethical obligation to provide offenders with medical assistance? What if a police officer's partner has been killed by a suspect during a shootout, and the suspect—also shot—is bleeding profusely nearby? Ethically, must that officer do everything in his or her power to save the suspect's life? Why or why not?

CJ and TECHNOLOGY

High-Tech Cops

When patrol cars came into common use by police departments in the 1930s, they changed the face of American policing. Nine decades later, the technology associated with patrol cars continues to evolve. The vast majority of police cars in the United States are equipped with mobile data terminals that allow police officers to access information such as calls for service, suspects' outstanding warrants and criminal records, and neighborhood crime data.

About two-thirds of police departments also attach video cameras to their patrol automobiles, and many are able to "live-stream" video content from these devices. Another mounted camera commonly found on police autos automatically reads the license plates of nearby vehicles and performs an instant background check on both car and driver.

In addition to their sophisticated transportation, today's police officers enjoy a multitude of other technological advantages. As we saw in Chapter 1, mobile biometric technology provides officers with the ability to immediately identify a suspect using fingerprints or facial features. Advances in through-the-wall sensor devices are increasingly allowing law enforcement agents to track people's movements within buildings. A new generation of handheld translation devices is helping officers in cities where English is not the primary language of many residents. These devices contain hundreds of preset police commands in a variety of dialects, and some even feature voice-activated translation capabilities.

Thinking about Police Technology

Handheld thermography cameras measure changes in body temperature to determine whether a person is in pain or is injured and, if so, to pinpoint which part of the body is affected. How might police officers use such devices to investigate violent crimes and assist victims?

4-1e Policing Today

Even as the four basic responsibilities of the police just discussed have remained fairly stable, the manner in which these duties are carried out is constantly changing. American law enforcement today faces challenges that would have been unfamiliar even fifteen years ago, and it has had to develop new areas of expertise to meet these challenges effectively. In particular, the process of collecting, analyzing, and mapping crime data has become a hallmark of law enforcement in the twenty-first century.

INTELLIGENCE-LED POLICING Based on hard-earned experience and criminological studies, law enforcement officials know that two strategies are particularly effective in reducing crime: focusing on repeat offenders and focusing on high-crime neighborhoods. Police departments across the nation are increasingly relying on technology to put this knowledge to good use.

Intelligence-Led Policing (ILP) An approach that measures the risk of criminal behavior associated with certain individuals or locations so as to predict when and where such criminal behavior is most likely to occur in the future.

Thanks to data gathered by its Real-Time Analysis Critical Response Division, for example, the Los Angeles Police Department (LAPD) recently was able to determine that its Newton division was a "hot spot" for drug crime and gang activity. In response, the LAPD launched Operation LASER, which flooded the Newton area with more patrol officers. Over a ten-month period, Operation LASER resulted in a dramatic decrease in gun-related murders and other crimes, including robbery and aggravated assault.[14]

The LAPD's approach to crime in Newton is known as predictive policing, or **intelligence-led policing (ILP),** because it relies on data—or intelligence—concerning past crime patterns to predict future crime patterns. In theory, ILP is relatively simple. Just as commercial fishers are most successful when they concentrate on the areas of the ocean where the fish are, law enforcement does well to focus its scarce resources on the areas where the most crime occurs. With programs such as LASER and other "hot spot" technologies that we will discuss in the next chapter, police administrators are able to deploy small forces to specific locations, rather than blanketing an entire city with random patrols. Doing "more with less" in this manner is a particularly important consideration as police budgets shrink around the country.

THE WARRIOR-GUARDIAN SPLIT Some law enforcement veterans are wary of the influence that ILP has gained within the profession. "If it becomes all about the science," says Los Angeles Police Department deputy chief Michael Downing, "I worry we'll lose the important nuances."[15]

The continued importance of the human factor within law enforcement culture is, however, confirmed by what Samuel Walker calls the "war going on for the soul of policing in America."[16] One side of this war promotes protecting law enforcement officers and citizens through aggression and use of force. The other side concentrates on de-escalation and avoidance of conflict.

Spencer Platt/Getty Images News/Getty Images

Members of a police SWAT team search for a suspected terrorist in Watertown, Massachusetts. **What are the arguments for and against providing local police with military training and weaponry? Explain your answers.**

The Warrior Mentality In the summer of 2016, a police office named Jeronimo Yanez shot and killed an unarmed African American driver named Philando Castile following a traffic stop in St. Anthony, Minnesota. In the public uproar that followed, some pinpointed a training course entitled "The Bulletproof Warrior" that Yanez had completed two years earlier. The course advocated an aggressive approach to policing while emphasizing the constant dangers of police work. The course booklet, for example, warns that "the will to survive is often trained out of the psyches of" law enforcement agents and rejects the "myth" that "an officer must use the 'least intrusive' option when using force."[17]

This hyperaggressive style of policing is often referred to as **militarism,** as it meshes military training and weaponry with traditional law enforcement strategies. The militarizing of local police departments started with the Los Angeles Police Department's first Special Weapons and Tactics (SWAT) units in the late 1960s. These units, trained and armed like special military forces, were initially designed to deal with extreme circumstances such as riots, hostage situations, and active-shooter scenarios. Today, SWAT teams are used around 50,000 times a year, most often to serve drug-related warrants in private homes.[18]

The Guardian Mentality To counterbalance militarism and the warrior approach, many law enforcement agencies across the country are turning toward a guardian mentality of policing. As the name implies, the guardian approach stresses nonconfrontational tactics to strengthen the bonds between police officers and the communities that they "guard over." In the words of Seth Stoughton, a former police officer who now teaches law at the University of South Carolina, guardians are officers "who treat people humanely, who show them respect, who explain their actions, [and who] can improve the perceptions of officers, or their department, even when they are arresting someone."[19]

THE CHALLENGES OF COUNTERTERRORISM The trend toward SWAT unit militarization intensified after the terrorist attacks of September 11, 2001, when the federal government began to consider local police the "front lines" of a new kind of war. Since 2001, the Department of Defense (DOD) has donated billions of dollars worth of military equipment to local police departments in all fifty states. In addition, the DOD distributed more than $34 billion in "terrorism grants" to local departments to purchase military gear between 2001 and 2014.[20]

ILP principles are also having an impact on law enforcement antiterrorism tactics. More than one hundred local and state police organizations now operate intelligence units, with at least one in each state. The New York Police Department, in a class by itself, has a permanent counterterrorism force, known as the Critical Response Command, made up of nearly 500 members. This group of experienced officers engages in "hostile surveillance" of suspects, and its arsenal includes special cars mounted with semiautomatic assault rifles.

Most local police departments, however, do not have the resources to

Militarism The use of military training, tactics, and weaponry in policing.

make counterterrorism a priority. The Federal Bureau of Investigation (FBI), even with its significant resources, also struggles in this field. FBI agents conduct 10,000 assessments of terrorist suspects each year and are engaged in about 1,000 open investigations of potential "homegrown violent extremists" at any given time.[21] Nonetheless, the agency has been unable to prevent major domestic terrorist attacks in Boston, Orlando, Garland (Texas), and New York City in recent years, despite having previously investigated the suspect in each of these cases.

LAW ENFORCEMENT 2.0 For the most part, as you will see in subsequent chapters, the FBI has been successful in uncovering and preventing domestic terrorist plots. Nearly every one of these successful anti-terrorism investigations has relied on information gathered by federal agents on the Internet. It has also become commonplace for police agents to create fake profiles online as part of traditional criminal investigations. Federal drug agents, for example, have set up false Facebook pages using the identities of known drug dealers to "friend" their unwitting criminal associates.

Social media is a crucial public relations tool, as well. To build bridges with the public, the FBI operates a Facebook page and an official Twitter account. Indeed, the vast majority of all law enforcement agencies in the United States use social media to interact with the communities they serve.[22]

ETHICS CHALLENGE

The user agreements of both Facebook and Instagram ban law enforcement agents from going "undercover" online by impersonating others or setting up fake accounts. As you just read, this has not stopped police officers from engaging in the practice. Is this an ethical means of conducting a criminal investigation? Why or why not?

4-2 HOW DOES SOMEONE BECOME A POLICE OFFICER?

Recruitment The process by which law enforcement agencies develop a pool of qualified applicants from which to select new employees.

In 1961, police expert James H. Chenoweth commented that the methods used to hire police officers had changed little since 1829, when the first version of the modern police force was created in London, England.[23] The past half-century, however, has seen a number of improvements in the way that police administrators handle the task of **recruitment,** or the development of a pool of qualified applicants from which to select new officers.

Efforts have been made to diversify police rolls, and recruits in most police departments undergo a substantial array of tests and screens—discussed next—to determine their aptitude. Furthermore, annual starting salaries that can exceed $70,000, along with the opportunities offered by an interesting profession in the public service field, have attracted a wide variety of applicants to police work.

4-2a Basic Requirements

The selection process involves a number of steps, and each police department has a different method of choosing candidates. Most agencies, however, require at a minimum that a police officer:

- Be a U.S. citizen.
- Not have been convicted of a felony.
- Have or be eligible to have a driver's license in the state where the department is located.
- Be at least twenty-one years of age.
- Meet weight and eyesight requirements.

In addition, few departments will accept candidates older than forty-five years of age.

BACKGROUND CHECKS AND TESTS Beyond these minimum requirements, police departments usually engage in extensive background checks, including drug tests; a review of applicants' educational, military, and driving records; credit checks; interviews with spouses, acquaintances, and previous employers; and a background search to determine whether applicants have been convicted of any criminal acts. Police agencies generally impose physical requirements as well: normally, applicants must be able to pass a physical agility or fitness test.

In some departments, particularly those that serve large metropolitan areas, applicants must take a psychological screening test to determine if they are suited to law enforcement work. Generally, such tests measure applicants' ability to handle stress, follow rules, use good judgment, and avoid off-duty behavior that would reflect negatively on the department.[24]

Along these same lines, many American police agencies now review an applicant's social media activity on sources such as Facebook, Instagram, and Twitter. "A single posting on Facebook in poor taste won't automatically eliminate someone from our hiring process," explained then Arlington (Texas) deputy chief Lauretta Hill. "But if we see a pattern of behavior or something that raises a red flag, it lets us know that we need to dig a little deeper during our background investigation."[25]

EDUCATIONAL REQUIREMENTS One of the most dramatic differences between today's police recruits and those of several generations ago is their level of education. In the 1920s, few had attended college. In the 2010s, 84 percent of all local police departments require at least a high school diploma, and 10 percent require a degree from a two-year college.[26] Although a four-year degree is necessary for certain elite law enforcement positions, such as a Federal Bureau of Investigation special agent, only about 4 percent of large local police departments have such a requirement.[27] Those officers with four-year degrees do, however, generally enjoy an advantage in hiring and promotion, and often receive higher salaries than their less educated co-employees.

Not all police observers believe that education is a necessity for police officers. In the words of one police officer, "Effective street cops learn their skills on the job, not in a classroom."[28] By emphasizing a college degree, say some, police departments discourage those who would make solid officers but lack the necessary education. Indeed, more than half of local police departments that do have a degree requirement will consider military service as an alternative.[29]

FIGURE 4.1 THE MAIN ELEMENTS OF A LAW ENFORCEMENT ACADEMY CURRICULUM

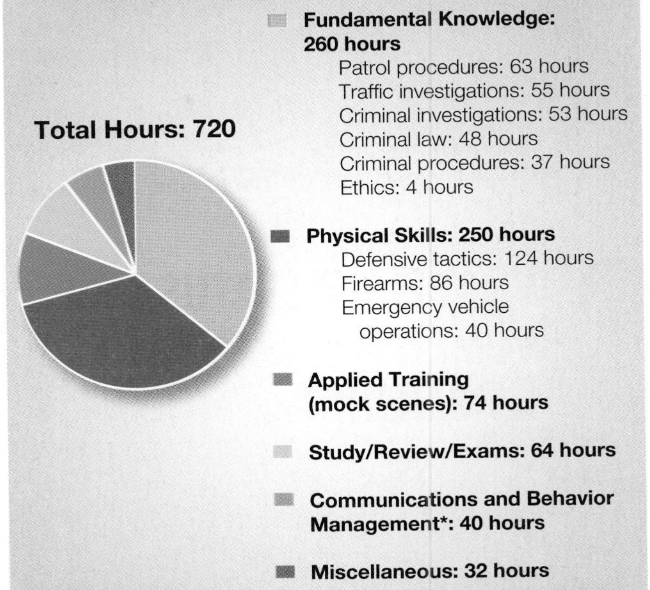

* This title refers to training in leadership and crisis management skills.

As this figure shows, a typical police academy cadet spends most of her or his time learning about the basic necessities of police work, such as defensive tactics, firearms, and patrol procedures.

Source: Adapted from Sue Rahr and Stephen K. Rice, *New Perspectives in Policing* (Washington, D.C.: National Institute of Justice, April 2015), Figure 1, page 8.

4-2b Training

LO4-2 Identify the differences between the police academy and field training as learning tools for recruits.

If an applicant successfully navigates the application process, he or she will be hired on a *probationary* basis. During this **probationary period,** which can last from six to eighteen months depending on the department, the recruit can be fired without cause if he or she proves inadequate to the challenges of police work.

Almost every state requires that police recruits pass through a training period while on probation. During this time, they are taught the basics of police work and are under constant supervision by superiors. The training period usually has two components: the police academy and field training.

ACADEMY TRAINING The *police academy*, run by either the state or a police agency, provides recruits with a controlled, militarized environment in which they receive their introduction to the world of the police officer. They are taught the laws of search, seizure, arrest, and interrogation; how and when to use weapons; the procedures for securing a crime scene and interviewing witnesses; first aid; self-defense; and other essentials of police work.

About half of all police academies favor a *stress-based* approach to training. This approach relies on a military model that emphasizes intensive physical demands and psychological pressures.[30] (See Figure 4.1 for a breakdown of a standard police academy curriculum.)

IN THE FIELD **Field training** takes place outside the confines of the police academy. A recruit is paired with an experienced police officer known as a field training officer (FTO). The goal of field training is to help rookies apply the

Probationary Period A period of time at the beginning of a police officer's career during which she or he may be fired without cause.

Field Training The segment of a police recruit's training in which he or she is removed from the classroom and placed on the beat, under the supervision of a senior officer.

concepts they have learned in the academy "to the streets," with the FTO playing a supervisory role to make sure that nothing goes awry.

That is, while the academy introduces recruits to the formal rules of police work, field training gives the rookies their first taste of the informal rules. In fact, the initial advice to recruits from some FTOs is often along the lines of "O.K., kid. Forget everything you learned in the classroom. You're in the real world now." Nonetheless, the academy is a critical component in the learning process, as it provides rookies with a road map to the job.

4-3 WHAT IS THE STATUS OF WOMEN AND MINORITIES IN POLICING?

For most of this nation's history, the typical American police officer was white and male. As recently as 1968, African Americans represented only 5 percent of all sworn officers in the United States, and the percentage of "women in blue" was even lower.[31] Only within the past thirty years has this situation been addressed, with many police departments actively trying to recruit women, as well as African Americans, Latinos, Asian Americans, and members of other minority groups.

The result, as you will see, has been a steady though not spectacular increase in the diversity of the nation's police forces. When it comes to issues of gender, race, and ethnicity, however, mere statistics rarely tell the entire story.

4-3a Gender and Law Enforcement

In 1987, about 7.6 percent of all local police officers were women. By 2013, that percentage had risen to 12.2 percent—17.6 percent in departments serving populations of more than one million people.[32] That increase seems less impressive, however, when one considers that women make up more than half of the population of the United States, meaning that they are still severely underrepresented in law enforcement.

ADDED SCRUTINY There are several reasons for the low levels of women serving as police officers in the United States. First and foremost, our culture generally sees policing as "man's work." For that reason, many qualified women never consider entering the field. When women do find employment in law enforcement, their levels of job satisfaction and promotion are often stifled by lack of role models. According to the National Association of Women Law Enforcement Executives, only about 220 women hold top leadership positions in America's approximately 14,000 local police agencies.[33] Consequently, female police officers have few superiors who might be able to mentor them in what can be a hostile work environment.

LO4-3 Describe the challenges facing women who choose law enforcement as a career.

In addition to the dangers and pressures facing all law enforcement agents, which we will discuss in the next chapter, women must deal with an added layer of scrutiny. Many male police officers feel that their female counterparts are mentally soft, physically weak, and generally unsuited for the rigors of the job. At the same time, male officers often try to protect female officers by keeping them out of hazardous situations, thereby denying the women the opportunity to prove themselves.[34]

TOKENISM Women in law enforcement also face the problem of *tokenism*, or the belief that they have been hired or promoted to fulfill diversity requirements and have not earned their positions. Tokenism creates pressure to prove the stereotypes wrong. When comparing

Mario Tama/Getty Images News/Getty Images

A female New York City police recruit tries on her bulletproof vest during a training session. **Do you believe that female police officers can be just as effective as men in protecting citizens from crime? Why or why not?**

the arrest patterns of male and female officers over a twelve-month period in Cincinnati, Ohio, for example, researchers noted several interesting patterns. Although overall arrest rates were similar, female officers were much more likely than their male counterparts to arrest suspects who were "non-deferential" or hostile. Also, the presence of a supervisor greatly increased the likelihood that a female officer would make an arrest.

Such patterns, the researchers concluded, show that female officers feel pressure to demonstrate that they are "good cops" who cannot be intimidated because of their gender.[35] One officer said that her female colleagues "go into that physical-arrest mode quicker [because] you want to prove that you can do it."[36] Similarly, women who rise through the law enforcement ranks often face questions concerning their worthiness. According to Tampa (Florida) police chief Jane Castor, "No matter how qualified you are or how much experience you have . . . people will say that you were promoted—in part, if not fully—because you're a woman."[37]

In fact, most of the negative attitudes toward women police officers are based on prejudice rather than actual experience. A number of studies have shown that there is very little difference between the performance of men and women in uniform.[38]

SEXUAL HARASSMENT According to a female officer interviewed by researcher Teresa Lynn, "The guys can view you as a sex object."[39] Anecdotal evidence suggests that this attitude is commonplace in police departments and often leads to **sexual harassment** of female police officers. Sexual harassment involves a pattern of unwelcome sexual advances or obscene remarks.

Such conduct can impact the recipient's career. One victim of sexual comments and physical contact by a superior said that when she rebuffed his advances, "he would retaliate by criticizing my reports or judgment."[40]

Despite having to deal with problems such as sexual harassment, outdated stereotypes, and tokenism, female police officers have generally shown that they are capable law enforcement officers, willing to take great risks if necessary to do their job. The names of nearly three hundred women are included on the National Law Enforcement Memorial in Washington, D.C.

4-3b Race and Ethnicity in Law Enforcement

As Figure 4.2 shows, like women, members of minority groups have been slowly increasing their presence in local police departments since the late 1980s. A closer look at the statistics shows that the percentage of African American police officers has remained relatively stable since 1993, while the numbers of Latino Americans and Asian Americans on police rolls nearly doubled during that same period.[41]

By most measures, members of minority groups are better represented than women in policing. Cities such as Atlanta and Washington, D.C., have local police departments that closely match their civilian populations in terms of diversity. Furthermore, in 2013, nearly one in three police recruits nationwide were members of an ethnic or racial minority.[42] On other measures, such as promotion, minorities in law enforcement continue to seek parity.[43]

DOUBLE MARGINALITY During a protest outside Fourth Precinct police headquarters in north Minneapolis, a young African American woman turned her attention to a black police officer guarding the station. "[You're] helping them kill us, your own race!" she shouted, calling the officer an Uncle Tom and encouraging him to commit suicide.[44]

The woman's insults highlight the problem of **double marginality.** This term refers to a situation in which minority officers are viewed with suspicion by both sides:

1. White police officers believe that minority officers will give members of their own race or ethnicity better treatment on the streets.
2. Those same minority officers face hostility from members of their own community who are under the impression that black and Latino officers are traitors to their race or ethnicity.

In response, minority officers may feel the need to act more harshly toward minority offenders to prove that they are not biased in favor of their own racial or ethnic group.[45]

THE BENEFITS OF A DIVERSE POLICE FORCE In 1986, Supreme Court justice John Paul Stevens spoke for many in the criminal justice system when he observed that "an integrated police force could develop a better relationship [with a racially diverse citizenry] and therefore do a more effective job of maintaining law and order than a force composed of white officers."[46] Despite the effects of double marginality, African American officers may have more

Sexual Harassment A repeated pattern of unwelcome sexual advances and/or obscene remarks. Under certain circumstances, sexual harassment is illegal and can be the basis for a civil lawsuit.

Double Marginality The situation in which minority law enforcement officers face suspicion both from their white colleagues and from members of the minority community to which they belong.

FIGURE 4.2 POLICE DIVERSITY IN AMERICAN CITIES

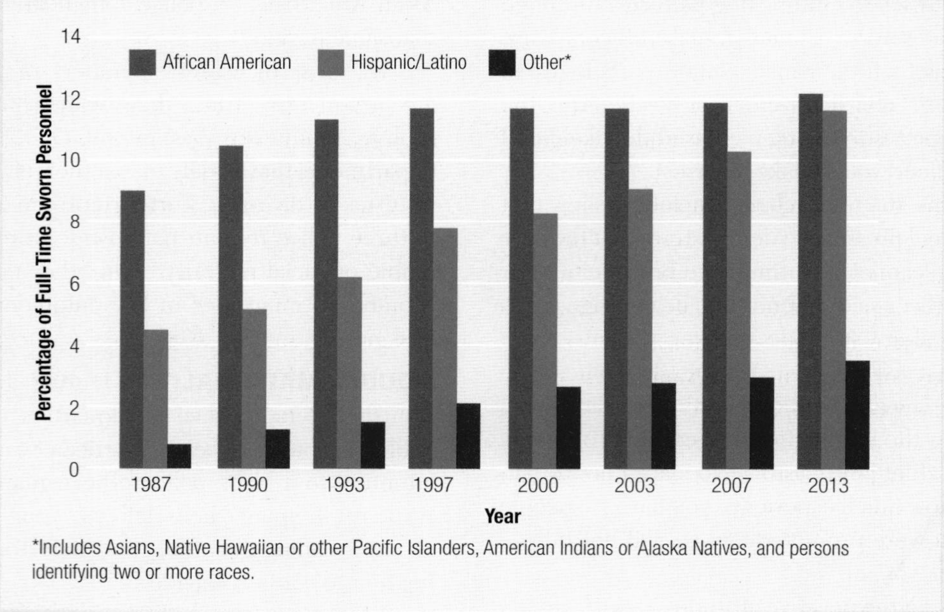

This graph shows that the percentage of members of some minority groups that make up local police department forces in the United States has been steadily growing since the late 1980s.

Source: Bureau of Justice Statistics, *Local Police Departments, 2013: Personnel, Policies, and Practices* (Washington, D.C.: U.S. Department of Justice, May 2015), Figure 5, page 5

credibility in a predominantly black neighborhood than white police officers, leading to better community-police relations and a greater ability to solve and prevent crimes.

Certainly, in the Mexican American communities typical of border states such as Arizona, Texas, and California, many Latino officers are able to gather information that would be very difficult for non-Spanish-speaking officers to collect. Finally, the best argument for a diverse police force is that members of minority groups represent a broad source of talent in this country, and such talent can only enhance the overall effectiveness of American law enforcement.

4-4 WHAT ARE THE DIFFERENT KINDS OF LAW ENFORCEMENT AGENCIES?

On January 9, 2017, Markeith Loyd killed Orlando police lieutenant Debra Clayton outside a shopping center as she tried to arrest him for murder. Over the next nine days, hundreds of law enforcement agents took part in a manhunt for Loyd, including officers from the Orange County Sheriff's Department, the Orlando Police Department, the Florida Department of Law Enforcement, the Federal Bureau of Investigation, and the U.S. Marshals Service. Loyd was finally captured when several dozen police officers, sheriffs' deputies, and state and federal agents surrounded him in an abandoned house on Orlando's west side.

As the effort to capture Loyd shows, Americans are served by a multitude of police organizations. Overall, there are about 18,000 law enforcement agencies in the United States, employing about 880,000 officers.[47] For the most part, these agencies operate on three different levels: local, state, and federal. Each level has its own set of responsibilities, which we shall discuss starting with local police departments.

4-4a Municipal Law Enforcement Agencies

About three-quarters of all *sworn officers*, or officers with arrest powers, work in police departments serving cities with populations of under 1 million residents.[48] While the

New York City Police Department employs about 35,000 police personnel, 90 percent of all local police departments have fifty or fewer law enforcement officers.[49]

Of the three levels of law enforcement, municipal agencies have the broadest authority to apprehend criminal suspects, maintain order, and provide services to the community. Whether the local officer is part of a large force or the only law enforcement officer in the community, he or she is usually responsible for a wide spectrum of duties, from responding to noise complaints to investigating homicides.

Larger police departments often assign officers to specialized task forces or units that deal with a particular crime or area of concern. For example, in Washington, D.C., the police department features a Lesbian, Gay, Bisexual, and Transgender (LGBT) Liaison Unit that handles anti-LGBT crimes in the city. The Knoxville (Tennessee) Police Department has a squad devoted to combating Internet crimes against children, while the three hundred officers assigned to the New York City Police Department's Emergency Service Unit are trained in suicide rescue, hostage negotiation, and SCUBA operations.

4-4b Sheriffs and County Law Enforcement

The **sheriff** is a very important figure in American law enforcement. Almost every one of the more than three thousand counties in the United States (except those in Alaska and Connecticut) has a sheriff. In every state except Rhode Island and Hawaii, sheriffs are elected by members of the community for two- or four-year terms and are paid a salary set by the state legislature or county board.

As elected officials who do not necessarily need a background in law enforcement, modern sheriffs resemble their counterparts from the political era of policing in many ways. Simply stated, the sheriff is also a politician. When a new sheriff is elected, she or he will sometimes repay political debts by appointing new deputies or promoting those who have given her or him support.

SIZE AND RESPONSIBILITY OF SHERIFFS' DEPARTMENTS Like municipal police forces, sheriffs' departments vary in size. The largest is the Los Angeles County Sheriff's Department, with more than 9,200 deputies. Of the esimated 3,012 sheriffs' departments in the country, sixteen employ more than 1,000 officers, while about 450 employ fewer than ten.[50]

Keep in mind that cities, which are served by municipal police departments, often exist within counties, which are served by sheriffs' departments. Therefore, police officers and sheriffs' deputies often find themselves policing the same geographical areas. Police departments, however, are generally governed by a local political entity, such as a mayor's office, while most sheriffs' departments are assigned their duties by state law. About 80 percent of all sheriffs' departments are responsible for investigating violent crimes in their jurisdictions. Other common responsibilities of a sheriff's department include:

- Investigating drug crimes.
- Maintaining the county jail.
- Carrying out civil and criminal processes within county lines, such as serving eviction notices and court summonses.
- Keeping order in the county courthouse.
- Enforcing orders of the court, such as overseeing the isolation of a jury during a trial.[51]

It is easy to confuse sheriffs' departments and local police departments. Both law enforcement agencies are responsible for many of the same tasks, including crime investigation and routine patrol. There are differences, however. Sheriffs' departments are more likely to be involved in county court and jail operations and to perform certain services such as search and rescue. Local police departments, for their part, are more likely to perform traffic-related functions than are sheriffs' departments.[52]

THE COUNTY CORONER Another elected official on the county level is the **coroner**, or medical examiner. Duties vary from county to county, but the coroner has a general mandate to investigate "all sudden, unexplained, unnatural, or suspicious deaths" reported to the office. The coroner is ultimately responsible for determining the cause of death in these cases. Coroners also perform autopsies and assist other law enforcement agencies in homicide investigations.

4-4c State Police and Highway Patrols

The most visible state law enforcement agency is the state police or highway patrol agency. Historically, state police agencies were created for three reasons:

1. To assist local police agencies, which often did not have adequate resources or training to handle their law enforcement tasks.

Sheriff The primary law enforcement officer in a county, usually elected to the post by a popular vote.

Coroner The medical examiner of a county, usually elected by popular vote.

AP Photo/Travis Morisse/The Hutchinson News

Local police officer Todd Geist of Medicine Lodge, Kansas, diverts traffic from a road closed by a grass fire. **In what ways are local police departments and sheriffs' departments similar? In what ways do these two law enforcement agencies differ?**

2. To investigate criminal activities that crossed jurisdictional boundaries (such as when bank robbers committed a crime in one county and then fled to another part of the state).
3. To provide law enforcement in rural and other areas that did not have local or county police agencies.

Today, there are twenty-three state police agencies and twenty-six highway patrols in the United States. State police agencies have statewide jurisdiction and are authorized to perform a wide variety of law enforcement tasks. Often, they provide the same services as city or county police departments and are restricted only by the boundaries of the state.

In contrast, highway patrols have limited authority. Their duties are generally defined either by their jurisdiction or by the specific types of offenses they have the authority to control. As their name suggests, most highway patrols concentrate primarily on regulating traffic. Specifically, they enforce traffic laws and investigate traffic accidents. Furthermore, they usually limit their activity to patrolling state and federal highways.

4-4d Federal Law Enforcement Agencies

U.S. Customs and Border Protection (CBP) The federal agency responsible for protecting U.S. borders and facilitating legal trade and travel across those borders.

Employees of federal agencies do not make up a large proportion of the nation's law enforcement personnel. In fact, the New York City Police Department has about one-fifth as many employees as all of the federal law enforcement agencies combined. Nevertheless, the influence of these federal agencies is substantial.

Unlike local police departments, which must deal with all forms of crime, federal agencies have been authorized, usually by Congress, to enforce specific laws or attend to specific situations. The U.S. Coast Guard, for example, patrols the nation's waterways, while the U.S. Postal Inspection Service investigates and prosecutes crimes perpetrated through the use of the U.S. mail.

In this section, we discuss the elements and duties of the most important federal law enforcement agencies, which are grouped according to the federal department or bureau to which they report. (See Figure 4.3 for the current federal law enforcement "lineup.")

THE DEPARTMENT OF HOMELAND SECURITY Comprising twenty-two federal agencies, the Department of Homeland Security (DHS) coordinates national efforts to protect the United States against international and domestic terrorism. While most of the agencies under DHS control are not specifically linked with the criminal justice system, the department does oversee three agencies that play an important role in counter-terrorism and crime fighting: U.S. Customs and Border Protection, U.S. Immigration and Customs Enforcement, and the U.S. Secret Service.

LO4-4 Indicate some of the most important law enforcement agencies under the control of the Department of Homeland Security.

U.S. Customs and Border Protection (CBP) The federal government spends about $20 billion annually to enforce immigration law.[53] A large chunk of these funds go to **U.S. Customs and Border Protection (CBP),** which polices the flow of goods and people across U.S. international borders. In general terms, this means that the agency has two primary goals:

1. To keep undocumented immigrants, illegal drugs, and drug traffickers from crossing our borders.
2. To facilitate the smooth flow of legal trade and travel.

Consequently, CBP officers are stationed at all 328 ports of entry to the United States. The officers have widespread authority to investigate and search all international passengers, whether they arrive on airplanes, ships, or other forms of transportation. The officers also have the responsibility of inspecting luggage

FIGURE 4.3 FEDERAL LAW ENFORCEMENT AGENCIES

A number of federal agencies employ law enforcement officers who are authorized to carry firearms and make arrests. The most prominent ones are under the control of the U.S. Department of Homeland Security, the U.S. Department of Justice, and the U.S. Department of the Treasury.

Department of Homeland Security

DEPARTMENT NAME	APPROXIMATE NUMBER OF OFFICERS	MAIN RESPONSIBILITIES
U.S. Customs and Border Protection (CBP)	44,000	(1) Prevent the illegal flow of people and goods across America's international borders; (2) facilitate legal trade and travel
U.S. Immigration and Customs Enforcement (ICE)	12,000	Uphold public safety and homeland security by enforcing the nation's immigration and customs laws
U.S. Secret Service	4,500	(1) Protect the president, the president's family, former presidents and their families, and other high-ranking politicians; (2) combat currency counterfeiters

Department of Justice

DEPARTMENT NAME	APPROXIMATE NUMBER OF OFFICERS	MAIN RESPONSIBILITIES
Federal Bureau of Investigation (FBI)	14,000	(1) Protect national security by fighting international and domestic terrorism; (2) enforce federal criminal laws such as those dealing with cyber crime, public corruption, and civil rights violations
Drug Enforcement Administration (DEA)	5,200	Enforce the nation's laws regulating the sale and use of drugs
Bureau of Alcohol, Tobacco, Firearms and Explosives (ATF)	2,500	(1) Combat the illegal use and trafficking of firearms and explosives; (2) investigate the illegal diversion of alcohol and tobacco products
U.S. Marshals Service	4,300	(1) Provide security at federal courts; (2) protect government witnesses; (3) apprehend fugitives from the federal court or corrections system

Department of the Treasury

DEPARTMENT NAME	APPROXIMATE NUMBER OF OFFICERS	MAIN RESPONSIBILITIES
Internal Revenue Service (IRS)	3,200	Investigate potential criminal violations of the nation's tax code

and cargo to ensure compliance with immigration and trade laws.

The U.S. Border Patrol, a branch of the CBP, has the job of policing the Mexican and Canadian borders between official ports of entry. Every year, hundreds of thousands of non-U.S. citizens attempt to enter the country illegally by crossing these large, underpopulated regions, particularly in the southern part of the country. In 2016, Border Patrol agents apprehended about 415,000 illegal border crossers, down from a high of nearly 1.7 million in 2000.[54]

To a large degree, this decrease reflects the recent economic downturn, which removed some of the monetary incentives for foreign nationals looking for work in the United States. In addition, CBP has "shrunk" the border, focusing the efforts of many of the nation's 21,000 Border Patrol agents on areas where illegal crossings are most likely to occur. Agents working those areas are supported by helicopters, drones, surveillance towers, reconnaissance planes with infrared radar, and highly sensitive cameras.

U.S. Immigration and Customs Enforcement (ICE) The CBP shares responsibility for locating and apprehending persons in the United States illegally with special agents from **U.S. Immigration and Customs Enforcement (ICE).** While the CBP focuses almost exclusively on the nation's borders, ICE has a broader mandate to investigate and to enforce immigration and customs laws. Simply stated, the CBP covers the borders, and ICE covers everything else.

ICE's duties include detaining undocumented aliens and deporting (removing) them from the United States, as well as ensuring that those without

U.S. Immigration and Customs Enforcement (ICE) The federal agency that enforces the nation's immigration and customs laws.

John Moore/Getty Images News/Getty Images

In Roma, Texas, a U.S. Border Patrol agent speaks with undocumented immigrants from Central America who have just crossed into the United States illegally. **What is the main difference in the duties of a U.S. Border Patrol agent and a U.S. Immigration and a Customs Enforcement (ICE) agent?**

permission do not work or gain other benefits in this country. ICE is also responsible for investigating and preventing **human trafficking.** This term broadly describes the crime of coercing a person to go from one country to another for the purpose of performing some form of labor—often prostitution—for the trafficker.

Recently, ICE has been aggressively removing undocumented immigrants from the United States. In 2016, for example, the agency conducted about 240,000 removals, 58 percent of which involved someone who had been convicted of a crime.[55] The federal government is also increasingly relying on local police departments to detain immigration law violators. Numerous municipalities are resisting this policy initiative, on the ground that it damages the relationship between local police and the immigrant communities they serve.

Human Trafficking The practice of illegally transporting a person from one country to another for the purpose of forced labor or sexual exploitation.

U.S. Secret Service A federal law enforcement organization with the primary responsibility of protecting the president, the president's family, the vice president, and other important political figures.

Infrastructure The services and facilities that support the day-to-day needs of modern life, such as electricity, food, transportation, and water.

The U.S. Secret Service When it was created in 1865, the **U.S. Secret Service** was primarily responsible for combating currency counterfeiters. In 1901, the agency was given the added responsibility of protecting the president of the United States, the president's family, the vice president, the president-elect, and former presidents. These duties have remained the cornerstone of the agency's role, with several expansions. After a number of threats against presidential candidates in the 1960s and early 1970s, including the shootings of Robert Kennedy of New York and Governor George Wallace of Alabama, in 1976 Secret Service agents became responsible for protecting those political figures as well.

In addition to its special plainclothes agents, the agency also directs two uniformed groups of law enforcement officers. The Secret Service Uniformed Division protects the grounds of the White House and its inhabitants, and the Treasury Police Force polices the Treasury Building in Washington, D.C. To aid its battle against counterfeiters and forgers of government bonds, the agency has the use of a laboratory at the Bureau of Engraving and Printing in the nation's capital.

Additional DHS Agencies In addition to the three already discussed—CBP, ICE, and the U.S. Secret Service—three other DHS agencies play a central role in preventing and responding to crime and terrorist-related activity:

- The *U.S. Coast Guard* defends the nation's coasts, ports, and inland waterways. It also combats illegal drug shipping and enforces immigration law at sea.
- The *Transportation Security Administration* is responsible for the safe operation of our airline, rail, bus, and ferry services. It also operates the Federal Air Marshals program, which places undercover federal agents on commercial flights.
- The *Federal Emergency Management Agency* is the lead federal agency in preparing for and responding to disasters such as hurricanes, floods, terrorist attacks, and *infrastructure* concerns. Our national **infrastructure** includes all of the facilities and systems that provide the daily necessities of modern life, such as electric power, food, water, transportation, and telecommunications.

THE DEPARTMENT OF JUSTICE The U.S. Department of Justice, created in 1870, is still the primary federal law enforcement agency in the country. With the

CAREER PREP

Federal Bureau of Investigation (FBI) Agent

Job Description:

- Primary role is to oversee intelligence and investigate federal crimes. Agents might track the movement of stolen goods across state lines, examine accounting and business records, listen to legal wiretaps, and conduct undercover investigations.
- Special agent careers are divided into five paths: intelligence, counterintelligence, counterterrorism, criminal, and cyber crime.

Courtesy Federal Bureau of Investigation/Department of Justice

What Kind of Training Is Required?

- A bachelor's and master's degree, plus three years of work experience, along with a written and oral examination, medical and physical examinations, a psychological assessment, and an exhaustive background investigation.
- Critical skills required in one or more of the following areas: accounting, finance, computer science/information technology, engineering, foreign language(s), law, law enforcement, intelligence, military, and/or physical sciences.

Annual Salary Range?

- $65,000–$75,000

SOCIAL MEDIA CAREER TIP
Don't forget about your phone! Every week, call at least three people from your social media networks and talk with them about your career interests. This kind of personal contact can be far more useful than an exchange of posts.

responsibility of enforcing criminal law and supervising the federal prisons, the Justice Department plays a leading role in the American criminal justice system. To carry out its responsibilities to prevent and control crime, the department has a number of law enforcement agencies, including the Federal Bureau of Investigation, the Drug Enforcement Administration, the Bureau of Alcohol, Tobacco, Firearms and Explosives, and the U.S. Marshals Service.

The Federal Bureau of Investigation (FBI) Initially created in 1908 as the Bureau of Investigation, this agency was renamed the **Federal Bureau of Investigation (FBI)** in 1935. One of the primary investigative agencies of the federal government, the FBI has jurisdiction over nearly two hundred federal crimes, including white-collar crimes, espionage (spying), kidnapping, extortion, interstate transportation of stolen property, bank robbery, interstate gambling, and civil rights violations.

With its network of agents across the country and the globe, the FBI is also uniquely positioned to combat worldwide criminal activity such as terrorism and drug trafficking. In fact, since 2001, the agency has shifted its focus from traditional crime to national security. Between that year and 2009, the FBI doubled its roster of counterterrorism agents, while reducing its

Federal Bureau of Investigation (FBI) The branch of the Department of Justice responsible for investigating violations of federal law.

number of criminal investigations. In 2014, the agency even officially changed its primary function from "law enforcement" to "national security."[56]

The Drug Enforcement Administration (DEA) The mission of the **Drug Enforcement Administration (DEA)** is to enforce domestic drug laws and regulations and to assist other federal and foreign agencies in combating illegal drug manufacture and trade on an international level. The agency also enforces the provisions of the Controlled Substances Act (CSA). The CSA specifies five categories of drugs based on the substances' medical use, potential for abuse, and addictive qualities.[57] It also sets penalties for the manufacture, sale, distribution, possession, and consumption of these drugs.

CAREER TIP Illegal drug manufacturers often try to outwit the DEA by creating new psychoactive substances that are not yet illegal under federal law. Consequently, the agency employs *forensic chemists* to identify these new illegal drugs and support their investigation by DEA special agents.

The DEA operates a network of six regional laboratories used to test and categorize seized drugs. Local law enforcement agencies have access to the DEA labs and often use them to ensure that information about particular drugs that will be presented in court is accurate and up to date. In recent years, Congress has given the FBI more authority to enforce drug laws, and the two agencies now share a number of administrative controls.

The Bureau of Alcohol, Tobacco, Firearms and Explosives (ATF) As its name suggests, the Bureau of Alcohol, Tobacco, Firearms and Explosives (ATF) is primarily concerned with the illegal sale, possession, and use of firearms and the control of untaxed tobacco and liquor products. The Firearms Division of the agency has the responsibility of enforcing the Gun Control Act of 1968, which sets the circumstances under which firearms may be sold and used in this country.

The bureau also regulates all gun trade between the United States and foreign nations, and collects taxes on all firearm importers, manufacturers, and dealers. In keeping with these duties, the ATF is also responsible for policing the illegal use and possession of explosives. Furthermore, the ATF is charged with enforcing federal gambling laws.

Drug Enforcement Administration (DEA) The federal agency responsible for enforcing the nation's laws and regulations regarding narcotics and other controlled substances.

The U.S. Marshals Service The oldest federal law enforcement agency is the U.S. Marshals Service. In 1789, President George Washington assigned thirteen U.S. Marshals to protect his attorney general. That same year, Congress created the office of the U.S. Marshals and Deputy Marshals. Originally, the U.S. Marshals acted as the main law enforcement officers in the western territories. Following the Civil War (1861–1865), when most of these territories had become states, these agents were assigned to work for the U.S. district courts, where federal crimes are tried.

The relationship between the U.S. Marshals Service and the federal courts continues today and forms the basis for the officers' main duties, which include:

1. Providing security at federal courts for judges, jurors, and other courtroom participants.
2. Controlling property that has been ordered seized by federal courts.
3. Protecting government witnesses who put themselves in danger by testifying against the targets of federal criminal investigations. This protection is sometimes accomplished by relocating the witnesses and providing them with different identities.
4. Transporting federal prisoners to detention institutions.
5. Investigating violations of federal fugitive laws.[58]

THE DEPARTMENT OF THE TREASURY The Department of the Treasury, formed in 1789, is mainly responsible for all financial matters of the federal government. It pays all the federal government's bills, borrows funds, collects taxes, mints coins, and prints paper currency.

The largest bureau of the Treasury Department, the Internal Revenue Service (IRS), is concerned with violations of tax laws and regulations. The bureau's criminal investigation division focuses on various forms of tax evasion and tax fraud, as well as prosecuting identity theft and public corruption. Each year, the IRS's criminal investigation division gains about 2,800 convictions in cases involving these types of wrongdoing.[59]

4-4e Private Security

LO4-5 Analyze the importance of private security today.

Even with increasing numbers of local, state, and federal law enforcement officers, the police do not have the ability to prevent every crime. Recognizing this, many businesses and citizens have decided to

CAREER PREP

U.S. Marshal

Job Description:

- Provide security at federal courts, control property that has been ordered seized by federal courts, and protect government witnesses who put themselves in danger by testifying against the targets of federal criminal investigations.
- Transport federal prisoners to detention institutions and hunt and capture fugitives from federal law.

What Kind of Training Is Required?

- A bachelor's degree or three years of qualifying experience, which includes work in law enforcement, correctional supervision, and volunteer teaching or counseling.
- A rigorous seventeen-and-a-half-week basic training program at the U.S. Marshals Service Training Academy in Glynco, Georgia.

iStockPhoto.com/Stephen Mulcahey

Annual Salary Range?

- $45,000–$55,000

GETTING LINKEDIN
Employment as an FBI or DEA agent or a U.S. Marshal is reserved for applicants with significant law enforcement experience. On LinkedIn, the most common federal law enforcement position advertised is that of a Transportation Security Officer—a recent search found more than 200 such postings, from Memphis, Tennessee, to Oakland, California.

hire private guards for their properties and homes. In fact, according to ASIS International, an industry-research firm, demand for **private security** generates revenues of approximately $377 billion a year.[60] More than 10,000 firms employing around 2 million people provide private security services in this country, compared with about 1.1 million public law enforcement employees.

PRIVATIZING LAW ENFORCEMENT As there are no federal regulations regarding private security, each state has its own rules. In several states, including California and Florida, prospective security guards must have at least forty hours of training. Ideally, a security guard—lacking the extensive training of a law enforcement agent—should only observe and report criminal activity unless use of force is needed to prevent a felony.

As a rule, private security is not designed to replace law enforcement. It is intended to deter crime rather than stop it. A uniformed security guard patrolling a shopping mall parking lot or a bank lobby has one primary function—to convince a potential criminal to search out a shopping mall or bank that does not have private security. For the same reason, many citizens hire security personnel to drive marked cars through their neighborhoods, making them a less attractive target for burglaries, robberies, vandalism, and other crimes.

SECONDARY POLICING As mentioned, although some states have minimum training requirements for private security officers, such training lags far behind the requirements to be a public officer. Consequently, there is a high demand for **secondary policing,** an umbrella term that covers the work that off-duty cops do when

Private Security The provision of policing services by private companies or individuals.

Secondary Policing The situation in which a police officer accepts off-duty employment from a private company or government agency.

"moonlighting" for private companies or government agencies.

Generally speaking, police officers operate under the same rules whether they are off duty or on duty. In addition, 83 percent of local police departments in the United States have written policies for secondary policing.[61] For example, among other restrictions, Seattle police officers cannot work (on duty or off duty) longer than eighteen consecutive hours in a twenty-four-hour period and must clear all private employment with a superior.[62]

Off-duty police officers commonly provide traffic control and pedestrian safety at road construction sites, as well as crowd control at large-scale functions such as music festivals and sporting events. They are also often hired to protect private properties and businesses, just like their nonpublic counterparts.

Mario Tama/Getty ImagesNews/Getty Images

A private security guard patrols the Manhattan Mall in New York City. **Why is being visible such an important aspect of many private security jobs?**

CONTINUED HEALTH OF THE INDUSTRY

Indicators point to continued growth for the private security industry. In general, three factors drive this growth:

1. The problem of crime in the workplace. According to the National Retail Security Survey, American retailers lose about $45 billion a year because of shoplifting and employee theft.[63]
2. Budget cuts in states and municipalities that have forced reductions in the number of public police, thereby raising the demand for private ones.
3. A rising awareness of private security products (such as home burglar alarms) and services as cost-effective protective measures.[64]

Another reason for the industry's continued health is terrorism. Private security is responsible for protecting more than three-fourths of the nation's likely terrorist targets, such as power plants, financial centers, dams, malls, oil refineries, and transportation hubs.

CAREER TIP *Loss prevention* is a catchall phrase used by retail companies to describe their efforts to reduce shoplifting and cash theft in their stores. Retailers need loss prevention *security officers* to keep an eye on suspicious shoppers and loss prevention *detectives* to investigate shoplifting and employee theft.

STUDY TOOLS 4

LOCATED IN TEXTBOOK

- ☐ Rip out the Chapter Review Card.
- ☐ Review with the Chapter Quiz following this chapter.

LOCATED AT WWW.CENGAGEBRAIN.COM

- ☐ Review key terms flash cards.
- ☐ Read the chapter on all your favorite devices.
- ☐ Complete an Exam to test your knowledge.
- ☐ Check out Visual Summaries and You Decide activities to explore chapter concepts.

Quiz

1. In the opinion of many civilians and law enforcement officers, the primary duty of the police is to ______________________ criminal law.

2. In reality, police officers spend a great deal of their time providing ______________________ such as directing traffic and providing emergency medical aid.

3. ______________________-led policing is an umbrella term referring to the law enforcement practice of relying on data concerning past crime patterns to predict future crimes.

4. During the ______________________ period, which can last as long as eighteen months, police recruits attend a police academy to learn the rules of police work.

5. Minority law enforcement officers often face the problem of ______________________ marginality, which means that they are viewed with suspicion by both white colleagues and members of their home communities.

6. Municipal police departments and ______________________ departments are both considered "local" organizations and have many of the same responsibilities.

7. On the state level, the authority of the ______________________ patrol is usually limited to enforcing traffic laws.

8. Nationally, agents from the ______________________ have the authority to investigate and make arrests regarding all federal crimes.

9. A federal law enforcement agency called the ______________________ regulates the sale and possession of guns in the United States.

10. Private security is designed to ______________________ crime rather than stop it.

Answers to the Chapter 4 Quiz can be found in the Answers section in the back of the book.

5 Problems and Solutions in Modern Policing

Allison Shelley/Getty Images News/Getty Images

LEARNING OBJECTIVES

After studying this chapter, you will be able to . . .

5-1 Explain why police officers are allowed discretionary powers.

5-2 List the three primary purposes of police patrol.

5-3 Describe how forensic experts use DNA fingerprinting to solve crimes.

5-4 Clarify the concepts of nondeadly force, deadly force, and reasonable force in the context of police use of force.

5-5 Explain what an ethical dilemma is, and name four categories of ethical dilemmas that a police officer typically may face.

After finishing this chapter, go to **PAGE 110** for **STUDY TOOLS**

In a Split Second . . .

The standoff started with a 911 call to the Albuquerque Police Department (APD) about an illegal campsite at the foot of the Sandia Mountains. When officers arrived on the scene, they found the culprit, James Boyd, to be angry, uncooperative, and armed with two pocketknives. Ordered to drop the knives, he replied, "Don't attempt to give me, the Department of Defense, another directive." As day turned to early evening, APD officers tried to negotiate a resolution. Boyd, who had spent much of his adult life moving between jails and psychiatric hospitals, responded with threats. "I'm bulletproof," he said. "Somebody's dying tonight and it ain't going to be me."

Four hours after the initial call, the APD decided to end the encounter. A K-9 unit moved toward Boyd and attempted to subdue him with a stun grenade. Boyd seemed unfazed by the small explosion and, as APD police officer Dominique Perez testified in court two years later, possibly moved a hand toward his waistband. Perez, perceiving "an immediate deadly threat" to a K-9 officer who was trying to retrieve his dog nearby, fired at Boyd. Another officer, Keith Sandy, thought Boyd "was going to attack us from a different angle" and also opened fire. Six of the shots from the two officers struck Boyd, killing him.

Ten months later, Perez and Sandy were charged with second degree murder. If convicted, they would face fifteen years in prison. At trial, prosecutors relied heavily on a video from Perez's helmet camera. Shown frame by frame, the video seemed to indicate that Boyd had turned his back to the officers before being shot. Perez countered that, in real time, the situation was not so straightforward. "The way it happened that day, it happened in the blink of an eye, at the speed of life," he testified. After hearing the evidence, jurors could not decide whether Boyd's shooting was justified, and, on October 12, 2016, Judge Alisa Hadfield declared a mistrial. "These are two good men," said one of the officers' defense attorneys following the trial. "Let [them] get on with their lives."

Former Albuquerque police officers Keith Sandy, left, and Dominique Perez, right, confer with legal counsel during their second degree murder trial for killing James Boyd. *Given the facts of the case, do you think the police officers' deadly use of force was justified?*

AP Images/Juan Labreche

5-1 HOW DO LAW ENFORCEMENT AGENTS USE DISCRETION?

Certainly, the Albuquerque police officers just discussed would have preferred not to have shot and killed James Boyd, regardless of the consequences. Their decisions were made in a split second, under stressful circumstances, and without the benefit of hindsight. That is, the officers relied on their discretion, a concept you were introduced to in Chapter 1. Not all police discretion involves situations as serious as the ones that led to the death in Albuquerque, but it is a crucial aspect of all areas of law enforcement.

5-1a Justification for Police Discretion

Despite the possibility of mistakes, courts generally have upheld the patrol officer's freedom to decide "what law to enforce, how much to enforce it, against whom, and on what occasions."[1] This judicial support of police discretion is based on the following factors:

- Police officers are considered trustworthy and are therefore assumed to make honest decisions, regardless of contradictory testimony by a suspect.
- Experience and training give officers the ability to determine whether a certain activity poses

LO5-1 Explain why police officers are allowed discretionary powers.

a threat to society and to take any reasonable action necessary to investigate or prevent such activity.

- Due to the nature of their jobs, police officers are very knowledgeable about human behavior and, by extension, criminal behavior.
- Police officers may find themselves in danger of personal, physical harm and must be allowed to take reasonable and necessary steps to protect themselves.[2]

Steve Allen Travel Photography / Alamy Stock Photo

Why might police officers dislike policies restricting their discretion to engage in high-speed chases? Why might officers welcome such policies?

Dr. Anthony J. Pinizzotto, a psychologist with the Federal Bureau of Investigation (FBI), and Charles E. Miller, an instructor in the bureau's Criminal Justice Information Services Division, take the justification for discretion one step further. These two experts argue that many police officers have a "sixth sense" that helps them handle on-the-job challenges. Pinizzotto and Miller believe that although "intuitive policing" is often difficult to explain to those outside law enforcement, it is a crucial part of policing and should not be discouraged by civilian administrators.[3]

5-1b Factors of Police Discretion

There is no doubt that subjective factors influence police discretion. The officer's beliefs, values, personality, and background all enter into his or her decisions. To a large extent, however, a law enforcement agent's actions are determined by the rules of policing set down in the U.S. Constitution and enforced by the courts. These rules are of paramount importance and will be discussed in great detail in Chapter 6.

ELEMENTS OF DISCRETION Assuming that most police officers stay on the right side of the Constitution in most instances, four other factors generally enter the discretion equation in any particular situation.[4] First, and most important, is the nature of the criminal act. The less serious a crime, the more likely a police officer is to ignore it. A person driving 60 miles per hour in a 55-miles-per-hour zone, for example, is much less likely to be ticketed than someone doing 80 miles per hour.

Policy A set of guiding principles designed to influence the behavior and decision making of police officers.

A second element often considered is the attitude of the wrongdoer toward the officer. A motorist who is belligerent toward a highway patrol officer is much more likely to be ticketed than one who is contrite and apologetic. Third, the relationship between the victim and the offender can influence the outcome. If the parties are in a familial or other close relationship, police officers may see the incident as a personal matter and be hesitant to make an arrest. The fourth factor of the discretion equation is departmental policy.

LIMITING POLICE DISCRETION Departmental policy can have the effect of limiting police discretion. A **policy** is a set of guiding principles that law enforcement agents must adhere to in stated situations. If a police administrator decides that all motorists who exceed the speed limit by 10 miles per hour will be ticketed, that policy will certainly influence the patrol officer's decisions.

Policies must be flexible enough to allow for officer discretion, but at the same time be specific enough to provide the officer with a clear sense of her or his duties and obligations. For example, nearly every local police department in the United States has a policy limiting officers' discretion to engage in high-speed automobile chases of suspects, which can place other drivers and pedestrians in grave danger.[5]

DISCRETION AND USE OF FORCE Following the public outcry that resulted from James Boyd's death, described in the opening of this chapter, the Albuquerque

Police Department dramatically changed its use-of-force policy. The revised standards include a section on "de-escalation," requiring that "officers shall use advisements, warnings, verbal persuasion, and other tactics as alternatives to higher levels of force, if feasible."[6]

Many local police departments have implemented use-of-force policies. For instance, a number of police departments forbid using chokeholds or strangleholds, or firing at a moving vehicle unless someone in the vehicle poses a deadly threat. Another common requirement is that officers give a verbal warning before using deadly force.

5-2 HOW DO POLICE OFFICERS FIGHT CRIME?

Albuquerque police administrators placed Officers Dominique Perez and Keith Sandy, whose fatal shooting of suspect James Boyd was discussed in the opening of this chapter, on *administrative leave* pending an investigation into the incident. As you might recall from the opening of the preceding chapter, Ohio State University police officials took the same course of action with Officer Alan Horujko after he was involved in a fatal shooting. While on administrative leave, Perez, Sandy, and Horujko were temporarily relieved of their duties.

This step does not necessarily imply that the officers were suspected of any wrongdoing. Most law enforcement agencies react similarly when a firearm is fired in the line of duty, both to allow for a full investigation of the event and to give the officer a chance to recover from what can be a traumatic experience.

Administrative leave is a *bureaucratic* response to an officer-involved shooting. In a **bureaucracy,** formal rules govern an individual's actions and relationships with coemployees. The ultimate goal of any bureaucracy is to reach its maximum efficiency—in the case of a police department, to provide the best service for the community within the confines of its limited resources, such as staff and budget. Although some police departments are experimenting with alternative structures based on a partnership between management and the officers in the field, most continue to rely on the hierarchical structure described below.

FIGURE 5.1 A TYPICAL POLICE DEPARTMENT CHAIN OF COMMAND

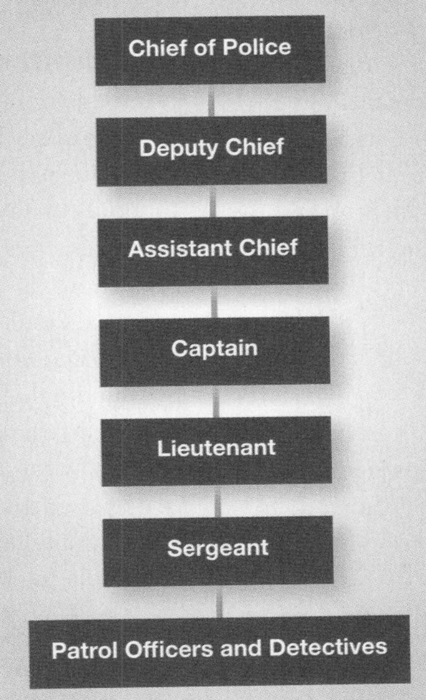

Most American police departments follow this model of the chain of command, though smaller departments with fewer employees often eliminate several of these categories.

5-2a The Structure of the Police Department

Each police department is organized according to its environment: the size of its jurisdiction, the type of crimes it must deal with, and the demographics of the population it must police. The Metropolitan Police Department of Washington, D.C., operates an Asian Liaison Unit that works within that city's Asian community, while the Evansville, Indiana, Police Department has set up a "No Meth" task force. Geographic location also influences police organization. The San Diego Police Department has a Harbor Patrol Unit, which would be unproductive in Grand Forks, North Dakota—as would be the Grand Forks Police Department's snowmobile patrol in Southern California.

CHAIN OF COMMAND Whatever the size or location of a police department, it needs a clear rank structure and strict accountability to function properly. One of the goals of the police reformers, especially beginning in the 1950s, was to lessen the corrupting influence of politicians. The result was a move toward a militaristic organization of police.[7] As you can see in Figure 5.1, a typical police department is based on a "top-down" chain of command that leads from the police chief down to detectives and patrol officers. In this formalized structure, all persons are aware of their place in the chain of command and of their duties and responsibilities within the organization.

Bureaucracy A hierarchically-structured administrative organization that carries out specific functions.

Delegation of authority is a critical component of the chain of command, especially in larger departments. The chief of police delegates authority to division chiefs, who delegate authority to commanders, and on down through the organization. This structure creates a situation in which nearly every member of a police department is directly accountable to a superior. As was the original goal of police reformers, these links encourage discipline and control, and lessen the possibility that any individual police employee will have the unsupervised freedom to abuse her or his position.[8]

Furthermore, experts suggest that no single supervisor should be responsible for too many employees. The ideal number of subordinates for a police sergeant, for example, is eight to ten patrol officers. This number is often referred to as the *span of control*. If the span of control rises above fifteen, then it is assumed that the superior officer will not be able to effectively manage his or her team.[9]

LAW ENFORCEMENT IN THE FIELD To a large extent, the main goal of any police department is the most efficient organization of its *field services*. Also known as "operations" or "line services," field services include patrol activities, investigations, and special operations. According to Henry M. Wrobleski and Karen M. Hess, most police officers are "generalists." That is, most officers are assigned to general areas and perform all field service functions within the boundaries of their beats.

Larger departments may be more specialized, with personnel assigned to specific types of crime, such as illegal drug activity or white-collar crime, rather than geographic locations. Smaller departments, which make up the bulk of local law enforcement agencies, rely almost exclusively on general patrol.[10]

5-2b Police on Patrol

Every police department has a patrol unit, and patrol is usually the largest division in the department. More than two-thirds of the sworn officers (officers authorized to make arrests and use force) in local police departments in the United States have patrol duties.[11]

"Life on the street" is not easy. Patrol officers must be able to handle any number of difficult situations, and experience is often the best and, despite training programs, the only teacher. As one patrol officer commented:

> You never stop learning. You never get your street degree. The person who says . . . they've learned it all is the person that's going to wind up dead or in a very compromising position. They've closed their minds.[12]

It may take a patrol officer years to learn when a gang is "false flagging" (trying to trick rival gang members into the open) or what to look for in a suspect's eyes to sense if he or she is concealing a weapon. This learning process is the backdrop to a number of different general functions that a patrol officer must perform on a daily basis.

THE PURPOSE OF PATROL As police accountability expert Samuel Walker has noted, the basic purposes of the police patrol have changed very little since 1829, when Sir Robert Peel founded the modern police department. These purposes include:

1. The deterrence of crime by maintaining a visible police presence.
2. The maintenance of public order and a sense of security in the community.
3. The twenty-four-hour provision of certain services that are not crime related.[13]

The first two goals—deterring crime and keeping order—are generally accepted as legitimate police functions. The third, however, has been more controversial.

COMMUNITY CONCERNS The extent to which noncrime incidents dominate patrol officers' time is evident in the Police Services Study, a survey of 26,000 calls to police in sixty different neighborhoods. The study found that only one out of every five calls involved the report of criminal activity.[14]

There is some debate over whether community services should be allowed to dominate patrol officers' duties. The question, however, remains: If the police do not handle these problems, who will? Few cities have the financial resources to hire public servants to deal specifically with, for example, finding shelter for homeless persons. Furthermore, the police are on call twenty-four hours a day, seven days a week, making them uniquely accessible to citizens.

LAW ENFORCEMENT AND MENTAL ILLNESS Of particular concern is the frequency with which police officers on patrol find themselves acting as psychiatric social workers. According to various studies, between 7 percent and 10 percent of all police-public contacts involve people with mental illness.[15] If law enforcement officers are not properly trained or otherwise prepared for these encounters, fatalities can result, as in the case described in the opening of this chapter. By one estimate,

LO5-2 List the three primary purposes of police patrol.

Delegation of Authority
A principle of command in which personnel take orders from and are responsible to those in positions of power directly above them.

at least half of the people justifiably killed by the police each year are mentally ill.[16]

To better prepare officers for dealing with such situations, a number of law enforcement agencies have instituted mandatory *crisis intervention team (CIT)* training programs. CIT teaches officers to recognize behavioral cues associated with mental illness and develop strategies of de-escalation, primarily with the goal of preventing the use of force against mentally ill civilians. More than three thousand state and local police departments have established crisis intervention teams, which often include the following elements:

1. Law enforcement officers who have completed the CIT program.
2. Access to mental health professionals who are "on call" to respond to police requests for assistance.
3. Drop-off locations, such as hospitals or mobile crisis vehicles, that provide mental health services beyond the expertise of law enforcement agencies.[17]

Rod Lamkey Jr/AFP/Getty Images

Given that most patrol shifts end without an officer making a single arrest, what activities take up most of a patrol officer's time?

On the positive side, it appears that the crisis intervention model is favorably viewed by police officers and can result in reduced arrest rates for mentally ill persons.[18] At the same time, such programs may be beyond the limited financial and personnel resources of small law enforcement agencies in rural areas.

PATROL ACTIVITIES To recap, the purposes of police patrols are to prevent and deter crime and also to provide social services. How can the police best accomplish these goals? Of course, each department has its own methods and strategies, but William Gay, Theodore Schell, and Stephen Schack divide routine patrol activity into four general categories:[19]

1. *Preventive patrol.* By maintaining a presence in a community, either in a car or on foot, patrol officers attempt to prevent crime from occurring. This strategy, which O. W. Wilson called "omnipresence," was a cornerstone of early policing philosophy and still takes up roughly 40 percent of patrol time.
2. *Calls for service.* Patrol officers spend nearly a quarter of their time responding to 911 calls for emergency service or other citizen problems and complaints.
3. *Administrative duties.* Paperwork takes up nearly 20 percent of patrol time. In Albuquerque, officers now spend 15 percent to 20 percent of their shifts saving and logging footage from their lapel cameras.[20]
4. *Officer-initiated activities.* Incidents in which the patrol officer initiates contact with citizens, such as stopping motorists and pedestrians and questioning them, account for 15 percent of patrol time.

5-2c Police Investigations

Investigation is the second main function of police, along with patrol. Whereas patrol is primarily preventive, investigation is reactive. After a crime has been committed and the patrol officer has gathered the preliminary information from the crime scene, the responsibility of finding "who dunnit" is delegated to the investigator, generally known as the **detective.**

The most common way for someone to become a detective is to be promoted from patrol officer. Detectives have not been the focus of nearly as much reform attention as their patrol counterparts, mainly because the scope of the detective's job is limited to law enforcement, with less emphasis given to social services and order maintenance.

AGGRESSIVE INVESTIGATION STRATEGIES Detective bureaus also have the option of implementing aggressive strategies. For example, if detectives suspect that a person was involved in the robbery of a Mercedes-Benz

Detective The primary police investigator of crimes.

CAREER PREP

Fish and Wildlife Service Officer

Job Description:

- Protect the integrity of America's natural habitats by policing the millions of acres of public land in this country, including wildlife refuges, fish hatcheries, waterfowl management areas, and wetland districts.
- Investigate wildlife crimes, particularly the illegal hunting, poaching, and sale of federally protected resources such as endangered species, migratory birds, marine mammals, and species of international concern.

What Kind of Training Is Required?

- Completion of an eighteen-week basic Land Management Police Training Academy course, a two-week Refuge Officer Basic School course, and a ten-week Field Training and Evaluation Program.
- The U.S. Fish and Wildlife Service offers students summer jobs that provide the experience necessary for a career in this field, with either a federal or a state agency.

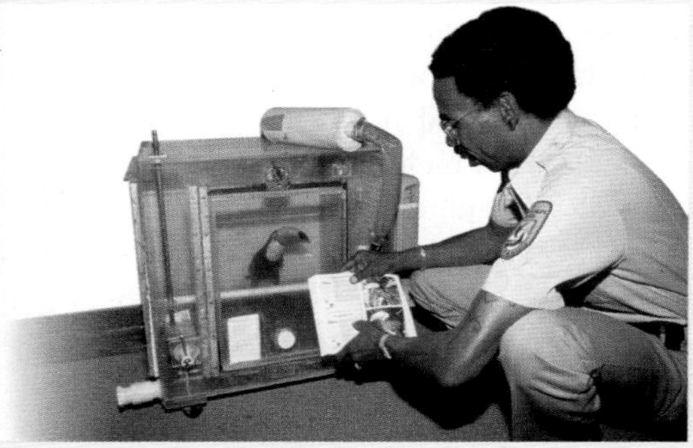

John Hollingsworth & Karen/National Conservation Training Center Publications & Training Materials/U.S. Fish and Wildlife Service

Annual Salary Range?

- $43,000–$65,000

Social Media Career Tip
When people search for your name, they generally won't click past the first page. Regularly check to see where your online material appears and whether you want this material to be on the Internet.

parts warehouse, one of them might pose as a "fence"—or purchaser of stolen goods. In what is known as a "sting" operation, the suspect is deceived into thinking that the detective (fence) wants to buy stolen car parts. After the transaction takes place, the suspect can be arrested.

Perhaps the most dangerous and controversial operation a law enforcement agent can undertake is to go *undercover*, or to assume a false identity in order to obtain information concerning illegal activities. Though each department has its own guidelines on when undercover operations are necessary, all that is generally required is the suspicion that illegal activity is taking place. Today, undercover officers are commonly used to infiltrate large-scale narcotics operations or those run by organized crime.

Confidential Informant (CI)
A human source for police who provides information concerning illegal activity in which he or she is involved.

In some situations, a detective bureau may not want to take the risk of exposing an officer to undercover work or may believe that an outsider cannot infiltrate an organized crime network. When the police need access and information, they have the option of turning to a **confidential informant (CI).** A CI is a person who is involved in criminal activity and gives information about that activity and those who engage in it to the police. As many as 80 percent of all illegal drug cases in the United States involve confidential informants. "They can get us into places we can't go," says one police administrator. "Without them, narcotics cases would practically cease to function."[21]

PREVENTIVE POLICING AND DOMESTIC TERRORISM Aggressive investigative strategies also play a crucial role in the federal government's efforts to combat domestic terrorism. Because would-be terrorists often need help to procure the weaponry necessary for their schemes, they are natural targets for well-placed informants and undercover agents. "We're not going to wait for the person to mobilize on his own time line," says Michael B. Steinbach, executive director of the FBI's National Security Branch.[22] According to an analysis by the *New York Times*, about two-thirds of all federal prosecutions involving those suspected of supporting the Islamic State terrorist organization have relied on evidence gathered by undercover operatives or informants.[23]

The recent conviction of Emanuel Lutchman provides an example of *preventive policing*, a popular counterterrorism strategy employed by the federal government. FBI agents arrested Lutchman for conspiring with members of the Islamic State to attack a Rochester, New York, restaurant on New Year's Eve, 2015. Prior to the arrest, a paid FBI informant had driven Lutchman to a Walmart to buy a machete, knives, ski masks, and other supplies needed for the planned attack. In January 2017, Lutchman pleaded guilty to providing material support to the Islamic State and was sentenced to twenty years in federal prison.

With preventive policing, then, the goal is not to solve the crime after it has happened. Rather, the goal is to prevent the crime from happening in the first place. Inevitably, such tactics raise the issue of entrapment. As you learned in Chapter 3, entrapment is a possible defense for criminal behavior when a government agent plants the idea of committing a crime in the defendant's mind. In the case just described, Lutchman's family pointed out that the suspect suffered from mental illness and that the FBI informant had to "loan" him $40 to purchase the supplies for the attack. "He didn't have money to buy Pampers for his son," Lutchman's grandmother said. "How would he find money to go buy these [weapons]?"[24]

Although the entrapment defense has been raised often in domestic terrorism cases involving informants and undercover agents, it has yet to succeed. The government has been uniformly successful in proving that these defendants were predisposed to commit the crime regardless of any outside influence.

5-2d Clearance Rates and Cold Cases

The ultimate goal of all law enforcement activity is to *clear* a crime, or secure the arrest and prosecution of the offender. Even a cursory glance at **clearance rates,** which show the percentage of reported crimes that have been cleared, reveals that investigations succeed only part of the time. In 2015, just 62 percent of homicides and 46 percent of total violent crimes were solved, while police cleared only 19 percent of property crimes.[25] For the most part, the different clearance rates for different crimes reflect the resources that a law enforcement agency expends on each type of crime. The police generally investigate a murder or a rape more vigorously than the theft of an automobile or a computer.

As a result of low clearance rates, police departments are saddled with an increasing number of **cold cases,** or criminal investigations that are not cleared after a certain amount of time. (The length of time before a case becomes "cold" varies from department to department. In general, a cold case must be "somewhat old" but not "so old that there can be no hope of ever solving it."[26])

Even using the various technologies we will explore in the next section, cold case investigations rarely succeed. A RAND study found that only about one in twenty cold cases results in an arrest, and only about one in a hundred results in a conviction.[27]

5-2e Forensic Investigations and DNA

Although the crime scene typically offers a wealth of evidence, some of it is incomprehensible to a patrol officer or detective without assistance. For that aid, law enforcement officers rely on experts in **forensics,** the practice of using science and technology to investigate crimes. Forensic experts apply their knowledge to items found at the crime scene to determine crucial facts such as:

- The cause of death or injury.
- The time of death or injury.
- The type of weapon or weapons used.
- The identity of the crime victim, if that information is otherwise unavailable.
- The identity of the offender (in the best-case scenario).

To assist forensic experts, many police departments operate or are affiliated with crime laboratories. Indeed, there are approximately four hundred publicly funded crime laboratories in the United States.

CRIME SCENE FORENSICS The first law enforcement agent to reach a crime scene has the important task of protecting any **trace evidence** from contamination. Trace evidence

Clearance Rates A comparison of the number of crimes cleared by arrest and prosecution with the number of crimes reported during any given time period.

Cold Case A criminal investigation that has not been solved after a certain amount of time.

Forensics The application of science to establish facts and evidence during the investigation of crimes.

Trace Evidence Evidence such as a fingerprint, blood, or hair found in small amounts at a crime scene.

is generally very small—often invisible to the naked human eye—and often requires technological aid for detection. Hairs, fibers, blood, fingerprints, broken glass, and footprints are all examples of trace evidence. A study released by the National Institute of Justice confirmed that when police are able to link such evidence to a suspect, the likelihood of a conviction rises dramatically.[28]

CAREER TIP A *bloodstain pattern analyst* can learn a great deal about a violent crime by examining where blood landed at the scene, the size and consistency of the drops, and the pattern of the blood spatter.

Police will also search a crime scene for bullets and spent cartridge casings. These items can provide clues as to how far the shooter was from the target. They can also be compared with information stored in national firearms databases to determine, under some circumstances, the gun used and its most recent owner. The study of firearms and its application to solving crimes goes under the general term **ballistics.** A new generation of ballistics technology allows technicians to create a 3D image of a bullet and match that image to the gun from which the original was fired.

FINGERPRINT RELIABILITY For more than a century, the most important piece of trace evidence has been the human fingerprint. Because no two fingerprints are alike, they are considered reliable sources of identification. Forensic scientists compare a fingerprint lifted from a crime scene with that of a suspect and declare a match if there are between eight and sixteen "points of similarity."

This method of identification, though highly reliable, is not infallible.[29] It is often difficult to lift a suitable print from a crime scene, and researchers have uncovered numerous cases in which innocent persons were convicted based on evidence obtained through faulty fingerprinting procedures.[30]

THE DNA REVOLUTION The technique of **DNA fingerprinting,** or using a suspect's DNA to match the suspect to a crime, emerged in the mid-1990s and has now all but replaced fingerprint evidence in many types of criminal investigations. The shift has been a boon to crime fighters: One law enforcement agent likened DNA fingerprinting to "the finger of God pointing down" at a guilty suspect.[31]

Ballistics The study of firearms, including the firing of the weapon and the flight of the bullet.

DNA Fingerprinting The identification of a person based on a sample of her or his DNA, the genetic material found in the cells of all living things.

LO5-3 Describe how forensic experts use DNA fingerprinting to solve crimes.

DNA, which is the same in each cell of a person's body, provides a "genetic blueprint" or "code" for every living organism. DNA fingerprinting is useful in criminal investigations because no two people, save for identical twins, have the same genetic code. Therefore, lab technicians can compare the DNA sample of a suspect with the evidence found at the crime scene. The technicians will look for thirteen points on the DNA fingerprint called "markers." If the match is negative, it is certain that the two samples did not come from the same source.

If the match is positive for each of the thirteen markers, the lab will determine the odds that the DNA sample could have come from someone other than the suspect. Those odds are so high—sometimes reaching 30 billion to one—that a match is practically conclusive.[32]

The DNA fingerprinting process begins when forensic technicians gather blood, semen, skin, saliva, or hair from the scene of a crime. Blood cells and sperm are rich in DNA, making them particularly useful in murder and rape cases. DNA has also been extracted from sweat on dirty laundry, skin cells on eyeglasses, and saliva on used envelope seals. Once a suspect is identified, her or his DNA can be used to determine whether she or he can be placed at the crime scene. In 2016, for example, investigators in Chicago connected Losardo Lucas to a home invasion that had taken place two years earlier by obtaining DNA from a cigarette butt he was careless enough to leave behind.

DNA IN ACTION The ability to find genetic information on such a wide variety of evidence, as well as the genetic information's longevity and accuracy, greatly increases the chances that a crime will be solved. Indeed, police no longer need a witness or even a suspect in custody to solve crimes. What they do need is a piece of evidence and a database.

In 1990, for example, eleven-year-old Robin Cornell and thirty-two-year-old Lisa Story were murdered in a Cape Coral, Florida, apartment that Story was sharing with Cornell's mother. For over twenty-five years, local police were unable to establish any meaningful leads on the killer. In August 2016, however, authorities collected a DNA sample from Joseph Zieler, who had been arrested in North Fort Myers, Florida, on a charge of felony aggravated battery for shooting his son with a pellet gun. Zieler's DNA matched a stored DNA sample taken from the Cape Coral crime scene, and he was charged with, among other crimes, double murder.

CAREER PREP

Forensic Scientist

Job Description:

- Examine, test, and analyze tissue samples, chemical substances, physical materials, and ballistics evidence collected at a crime scene.
- Testify as an expert witness on evidence or laboratory techniques in criminal trials.

What Kind of Training Is Required?

- A bachelor's degree in science, particularly chemistry, biology, biochemistry, or physics.
- Certification programs (usually two years' additional study) can help prospective applicants specialize as forensic consultants, fingerprint technicians, forensic investigators, and laboratory technicians.

Annual Salary Range?

- $52,000–$85,000

iStockPhoto.com/Nancy Catherine Walker

Getting LinkedIn

Although openings for forensic scientists at law enforcement agencies are scarce, LinkedIn consistently features postings for such positions at private laboratories. Such laboratories assist clients—such as doctors' offices, drug-testing facilities, and hospitals—that have a need for forensic laboratory services.

Databases and Cold Hits The identification of Joseph Zieler is an example of what police call a **cold hit,** which occurs when law enforcement officers find a suspect "out of nowhere" by comparing DNA evidence from a crime scene against the contents of a database. The largest and most important database is the National Combined DNA Index System (CODIS). Operated by the FBI since 1998, CODIS gives local and state law enforcement agencies access to the DNA profiles of almost 16 million people who have been connected to criminal activity. As of November 2016, the database had produced about 355,000 cold hits nationwide.[33]

DNA Collection Policies Authorities in all fifty states are required to collect DNA samples from offenders who have been convicted of felonies. In addition, more than half the states authorize the collection of DNA from those who have been arrested for a crime but not yet convicted.

In 2013, the U.S. Supreme Court upheld the practice of taking DNA samples from arrestees, as practiced in twenty-eight states and by the federal government, reasoning that such procedures are necessary to identify suspects.[34] The ruling is having the practical effect of greatly increasing DNA profiles stored in CODIS and other law enforcement databases.

Cold Hit The establishment of a connection between a suspect and a crime, often through the use of DNA evidence, in the absence of an ongoing criminal investigation.

ETHICS CHALLENGE

In speaking with a domestic terrorism suspect, an undercover FBI agent says, "Allah has more work for you to do," adding, "Revelation is going to come in your dreams that you have to do this thing." The "thing" is to shoot down American military airplanes with handheld missiles. Is this ethical behavior on the part of the FBI agent? Why or why not? What should happen to the suspect if he proceeds to purchase a handheld missile launcher on the black market?

CJ and TECHNOLOGY

911 Apps

To address some of the problems with existing cellphone 911 service, dozens of 911 enhancement apps have been created over the past few years. Most of these apps claim to connect the user to 911 more quickly and with greater location accuracy. They also provide "extras" not traditionally associated with 911 systems. For example, the 911 Help SMS app calls 911 while simultaneously notifying predetermined family members and friends with texts that include the caller's GPS coordinates.

Personal safety apps can be tailored for specific crimerelated circumstances. The bSafe app will privately alert friends that the user has safely reached his or her destination. When bSafe's alarm is triggered, the app immediately notes the user's GPS location and starts broadcasting video taken by the user's cellphone.

In addition, several apps are specifically designed to help domestic violence victims by giving them an easy and silent way to send text messages to law enforcement and trusted contacts. Such apps are often disguised as generic news apps to hide their purpose from any potential abuser who may have access to the phone.

Thinking about 911 Apps

Can you think of any class of crime victims besides domestic violence victims that would benefit from a specialized app? If you were to design a 911 app to help this group, what features would you include?

5-2f Patrol Strategies

While law enforcement officers do not like to think of themselves as being at the "beck and call" of citizens, that is the operational basis of much police work. All police departments practice **incident-driven policing,** in which calls for service are the primary instigators of action. Ideally, about one-third of a patrol officer's time should be taken with responding to calls for service.[35] In practice, the percentage is often much greater. During a typical eight-hour shift, for example, a Philadelphia patrol police officer will answer eighty 911 calls for service.[36]

911 TECHNOLOGY Nearly all the police departments in the country use **computer-aided dispatch (CAD)** systems to manage their incidence response strategies. With CAD, a 911 dispatcher enters the information from a caller into his or her computer, which prioritizes the emergency based on its nature. CAD also verifies the caller's address and phone number, and determines the closest patrol unit to the site of the emergency. In many jurisdictions, the details, including any previous 911 calls from the location, are then sent to a *mobile digital terminal* in the police officer's patrol car.

Incident-Driven Policing A reactive approach to policing that emphasizes a speedy response to calls for service.

Computer-Aided Dispatch (CAD) A method of dispatching police patrol units to the site of 911 emergencies with the assistance of a computer program.

CAREER TIP Although they are responsible for a crucial aspect of policing, *911 dispatchers* generally are not sworn police officers and do not need any law enforcement experience. Rather, they receive special training in dealing with emergency calls.

About 70 percent of 911 calls are made with wireless phones and often cannot be tracked using existing technology.[37] As utility companies increasingly abandon copper landlines for fiber-optic cables, however, more police departments will be able to adopt Next Generation 911. This system makes it possible for CAD to receive text messages, videos, photos, and location data about crime incidents.

Consider just one example of how text-to-911 can work. In Black Hawk County, Iowa, a woman locked herself in her bedroom when someone broke into her home. Afraid that a noise would alert the intruder to her location, she texted 911, and police officers were able to arrest him without further incident.[38]

RANDOM AND DIRECTED PATROL Of course, officers do not sit at the station waiting for incident calls. Earlier in this chapter, we noted that the majority of police officers are assigned to patrol duties. Most of these officers work **random patrol,** making the rounds of a specific area with the general goal of detecting and preventing crime. Every police department in the United States randomly patrols its jurisdiction using automobiles. In addition, 53 percent utilize foot patrols, 32 percent bicycle patrols, 16 percent motorcycle patrols, 4 percent boat patrols, and 1 percent horse patrols.[39]

In contrast to random patrols, **directed patrols** target specific areas of a city and often attempt to prevent a specific type of crime. Directed patrols have found favor among law enforcement experts as being a more efficient use of police resources than random patrols, as indicated by the Philadelphia Foot Patrol Experiment.

During this experiment, extra foot patrols were utilized in sixty Philadelphia locations plagued by high levels of violent crime. During three months of directed patrols, arrests increased by 13 percent in the targeted areas, and violent crime decreased by 23 percent. In addition, an estimated fifty-three violent crimes were prevented over the three-month period.[40]

"HOT SPOTS" AND CRIME MAPPING The target areas for directed patrols are often called **hot spots** because they contain greater numbers of criminals and have higher-than-average levels of victimization. On one level, focusing on hot spots seems relatively straightforward. As one police captain puts it, "We pick the areas that have the most shootings, the most robberies, and the most property crimes, and we put additional cops in those areas to bring down crime."[41]

On another level, to be effective, these strategies must be relatively sophisticated. They often rely on complicated algorithms and computer-based **crime mapping** to locate and identify hot spots and "cool" them down. Crime mapping uses geographic information systems (GIS) to track criminal acts as they occur in time and space. Once sufficient information has been gathered, it is analyzed to predict future crime patterns.

THE RISE OF COMPSTAT Computerized crime mapping was popularized when the New York Police Department launched CompStat in the mid-1990s. Still in use, CompStat starts with police officers reporting the exact location of crime and other crime-related information to department officials. These reports are then fed into a computer, which prepares grids of a particular city or neighborhood and highlights areas with a high incidence of serious offenses. (See Figure 5.2 for an example of a GIS crime map.)

In New York and many other cities, the police department holds "Crime Control Strategy Meetings" during which precinct commanders are held accountable for CompStat's data-based reports in their districts.

In theory, this system provides the police with accurate information about patterns of crime and gives them the ability to "flood" hot spots with officers at short notice. Police departments in forty-three of the nation's fifty largest cities are using CompStat,[42] and Wesley Skogan, a criminologist at Northwestern University, believes that CompStat and similar technologies were the most likely cause of declines in big-city crime during the first decade of the 2000s.[43]

5-2g Arrest Strategies

Like patrol strategies, arrest strategies can be divided into two categories that reflect the intent of police administrators. **Reactive arrests** are arrests made by police officers, usually on general patrol, who observe a criminal act or respond to a call for service. **Proactive arrests** occur when the police take the initiative to target a particular type of criminal or behavior. "The hypothesis," explains Lawrence Sherman, "is that a high certainty of arrest for a narrowly defined set of offenses or offenders will accomplish more than low arrest certainty for a broad range of targets."[44]

The popularity of proactive theories was solidified by a magazine article that James Q. Wilson and George L. Kelling wrote in 1982.[45] In their piece, entitled "Broken Windows," Wilson and Kelling argued that reform-era policing strategies focused on violent crime to the detriment of the vital police role of promoting the quality of life in neighborhoods. As a result, many communities, particularly in large cities, had fallen into a state of disorder and disrepute, with two very important consequences.

First, these neighborhoods—with their broken windows, dilapidated buildings, and lawless behavior by residents—were sending out "signals" that criminal activity was tolerated. Second, this

Random Patrol A patrol strategy that relies on police officers monitoring a certain area with the goal of detecting crimes in progress or preventing crime due to their presence.

Directed Patrol A patrol strategy designed to focus on a specific type of criminal activity in a specific geographic area.

Hot Spots Concentrated areas of high criminal activity that draw a directed police response.

Crime Mapping Technology that allows crime analysts to identify trends and patterns of criminal behavior within a given area.

Reactive Arrests Arrests that come about as part of the ordinary routine of police patrol and responses to calls for service.

Proactive Arrests Arrests that occur because of concerted efforts by law enforcement agencies to respond to a particular type of offender or criminal behavior.

disorder was spreading fear among law-abiding citizens, dissuading them from leaving their homes or attempting to improve their surroundings. Thus, the **broken windows theory** recommends maintaining order in these neighborhoods by cracking down on "quality-of-life" crimes such as panhandling, public drinking and urinating, loitering, and graffiti painting. Only by encouraging directed arrest strategies with regard to quality-of-life crime, Wilson and Kelling argued, could American cities be rescued from rising crime rates.

5-2h Community Policing

In "Broken Windows," Wilson and Kelling insisted that, to reduce fear and crime in high-risk neighborhoods, police had to rely on the cooperation of citizens. Today, a majority of police departments rely on a broad strategy known as **community policing** to improve relations with citizens and fight crime at the same time.

Community policing can be defined as an approach that promotes community-police partnerships, proactive problem solving, and community engagement to address issues such as fear of crime and the causes of such fear in a particular area. Neighborhood watch programs, in which police officers and citizens work together to prevent local crime and disorder, are a popular version of a community policing initiative.

Under community policing, patrol officers have the freedom to improvise. They are expected to develop personal relationships with residents and to encourage those residents to become involved in making the community a safer place. For example, beset by incidents of excessive force and high levels of citizen mistrust, the Albuquerque Police Department recently created six "neighborhood policing teams" to improve community relations. Each of these teams—made up of a sergeant and six patrol officers—works with residents to develop plans addressing specific problems in individual neighborhoods.[46]

To improve trust within their communities, a number of police departments also have turned to *collaborative reform*. In this offshoot of community policing, law enforcement officials form partnerships with local leaders to address difficult issues such as police use of force and arrest policies. In 2012, in response to unacceptable numbers of police shootings of unarmed civilians, the Las Vegas Metropolitan Police

Broken Windows Theory The theory that, by cracking down on quality-of-life crimes, law enforcement convinces both criminals and law-abiding citizens that lawlessness will no longer be tolerated in a particular area.

Community Policing A policing philosophy that emphasizes community support for and cooperation with the police in preventing crime.

FIGURE 5.2 A GIS CRIME MAP

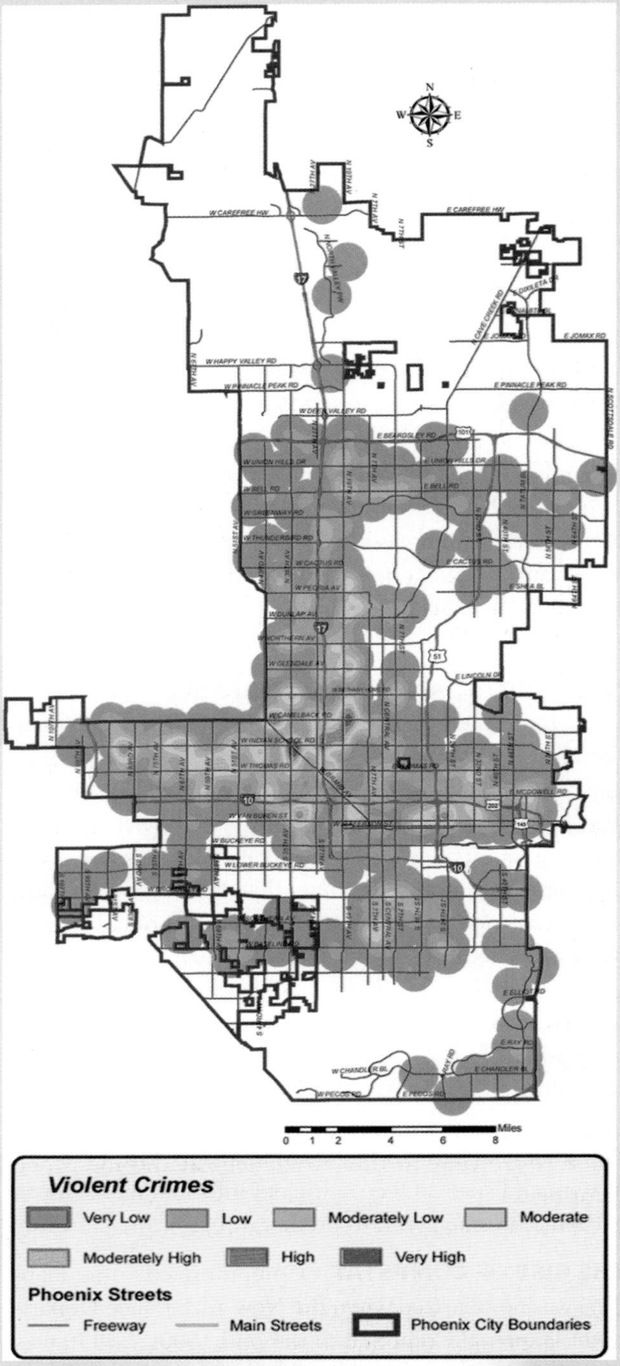

This crime map shows the incidence of gang-activity hot spots in Phoenix, Arizona.

Source: Phoenix Police Department

Department (LVMPD) entered into a collaborative reform agreement with the federal government. This accord led to seventy-two LVMPD reforms. Many of them related to improved use-of-force training, as well as increased public involvement in reviews of deadly force incidents. Within two years, the number of officer-involved shootings in Las Vegas had dropped 36 percent.[47]

5-2i Problem-Oriented Policing

Similar in spirit to community policing, **problem-oriented policing** is a strategy based on the premise that police departments devote too many of their resources to reacting to calls for service and too few to "acting on their own initiative to prevent or reduce community problems."[48] To rectify this situation, problem-oriented policing moves beyond simply responding to incidents and attempts instead to control or even solve the root causes of criminal behavior.

Boston Globe/Getty Images

A Grant County (Washington) sheriff's deputy allows local children to sit on his motorcycle during the annual Mattawa Community Days celebration. **How can establishing friendly relations with citizens help law enforcement agencies reduce crime?**

Problem-oriented policing encourages police officers to stop looking at their work as a day-to-day proposition. Rather, they should try to shift the patterns of criminal behavior in a positive direction. For example, instead of responding to a 911 call concerning illegal drug use by simply arresting the offender—a short-term response—the patrol officers should also look at the long-term implications of the situation.

They should analyze the pattern of similar arrests in the area and interview the arrestee to determine the reasons, if any, that the site was selected for drug activity.[49] Then additional police action should be taken to prevent further drug sales at the identified location.

5-3 WHAT ARE THE CHALLENGES OF BEING A POLICE OFFICER?

"Nowadays, we're in a culture where everything's against the police, or at least in the areas I patrol," said Ernie Williams, an officer with the Philadelphia Police Department. "Social media, news outlets, they're really coming down on the police. And we still gotta come to work. I pray nobody's going to get shot or hurt, but the reality is, someone probably is. We still have a job to do. And at times it can be a very difficult job."[50]

Officer Williams was reacting to anti-police publicity that spread throughout the country following a number of high-profile encounters in which unarmed suspects were injured or killed by law enforcement agents. The negative force of these incidents—often captured on smartphone video recordings—was made worse by the fact that, in many cases, the police officer was white and the suspect was a member of a minority group. "Any cop that uses his gun now has to worry about being indicted and losing his job and family," remarked a New York City police officer.[51] This frustration underscores many of the work-related issues that bind police officers together while at the same time potentially alienating them from the society that they are sworn to protect and serve.

5-3a Police Subculture

In a national poll of police officers, 86 percent of the nearly eight thousand respondents agreed that the American public does not understand the risks

Problem-Oriented Policing A policing philosophy that requires police to identify potential criminal activity and develop strategies to prevent or respond to that activity.

and challenges of police work.[52] This "disconnect" between law enforcement and civilians is one of the hallmarks of **police subculture.**

This broad term describes the basic assumptions and values that permeate law enforcement agencies and are taught to new members of a law enforcement agency as the proper way to think, perceive, and act. Every organization has a subculture, with values shaped by the particular aspects and pressures of that organization. In the police subculture, those values are formed in an environment characterized by danger, stress, boredom, and violence.

AP Photo/Cliff Owen

Family and colleagues mourn at the funeral of Prince William County (Virginia) police officer Ashley Guindon, who was fatally shot by a suspect. **How might violence against police officers contribute to the "blue curtain" between law enforcement and the public?**

From the first day on the job, rookies begin the process of **socialization,** in which they are taught the values and rules of police work. This process is aided by a number of rituals that are common to the law enforcement experience. Police theorist Harry J. Mullins believes that the following rituals are critical to the police officer's acceptance, and even embrace, of police subculture:

- Attending a police academy.
- Working with a senior officer, who passes on the "lessons" of police work and life to the younger officer.
- Making the initial felony arrest.
- Using force to make an arrest for the first time.
- Using or witnessing deadly force for the first time.
- Witnessing major traumatic incidents for the first time.[53]

Each of these rituals makes it clear to the police officer that this is not a "normal" job. The only other people who can understand the stresses of police work are fellow officers, and consequently law enforcement officers tend to insulate themselves from civilians. Eventually, the insulation breeds mistrust, and the police officer develops an "us versus them" outlook toward those outside the force.

In turn, this outlook creates what sociologist William Westly called the **blue curtain,** also known as the "blue wall of silence" or simply "the code."[54] This curtain separates the police from the civilians they are meant to protect.

Police Subculture The values and perceptions that are shared by members of a police department and, to a certain extent, by all law enforcement agents.

Socialization The process through which a police officer is taught the values and expected behavior of the police subculture.

Blue Curtain A metaphorical term used to refer to the value placed on secrecy and the general mistrust of the outside world shared by many police officers.

5-3b The Physical Dangers of Police Work

Police officers learn early in their careers that nothing about their job is "routine"—they face the threat of physical harm every day. According to the Officer Down Memorial Page, 140 law enforcement officers died in the line of duty in 2016.[55] In addition, about 50,000 assaults were committed against police officers in 2015, with 28 percent of these assaults resulting in an injury.[56] These numbers are troubling, but not necessarily surprising. As police experts John S. Dempsey and Linda S. Forst point out, police "deal constantly with what may be the most dangerous species on this planet—the human being."[57]

Despite perceptions to the contrary, a high percentage of deaths and injuries suffered by police officers are not the result of assaults by criminal suspects. Generally speaking, half of all law enforcement officer injuries are due to accidents, and about two-thirds of those injuries occur when officers are doing something other than making an arrest.[58] In particular, from 2006 to 2015, 603 police officers died from traffic-related accidents, compared with 521 who died from gunfire.[59]

Eight Long Minutes

The use of dogs to find evidence that would otherwise stay hidden is a common and crucial aspect of American law enforcement. As with their human handlers, however, the actions of sniffer dogs are bound by the rules of police procedure. If these rules are not closely followed, a court has the option to undo an otherwise valid arrest. For example, just after midnight on March 27, 2012, police officer Morgan Struble observed a car driven by Dennys Rodriguez veer onto the shoulder of Nebraska State Highway 275. Struble proceeded to perform a routine traffic stop, questioning Rodriguez and running a records check. After issuing Rodriguez a written warning, the police officer asked for permission to walk Floyd, a drug-sniffing dog, around the vehicle. Rodriguez refused.

Struble then had the driver turn off the engine, exit the vehicle, and wait by the patrol car while Struble radioed for backup. When the second police officer arrived, eight minutes later, Struble led Floyd twice around the car.

Midway through the second pass, the dog signaled the presence of drugs. A subsequent search of the vehicle uncovered a large bag of methamphetamine, and Rodriguez was arrested and charged with a drug crime. In court, Rodriguez's lawyers moved to suppress the bag of methamphetamine as evidence. They argued that Struble had no good reason to improperly prolong the traffic stop for the purpose of conducting a sniff search.

Several years ago, in *Rodriguez v. United States*, the United States Supreme Court agreed. According to the Court, Struble erred when he waited eight minutes to search Rodriguez's vehicle without any reasonable suspicion (a concept discussed later in the chapter) that the driver had committed a crime. "A police stop exceeding the time needed to handle the matter for which the stop was made violates the Constitution's shield against unreasonable seizures," explained Justice Ruth Bader Ginsberg. In other words, under the circumstances, the eight-minute interval between Struble's written warning and Floyd's sniff search was eight minutes too long.

The United States Supreme Court has ruled that sniff searches of automobiles by police dogs must be done in a reasonable amount of time and in a reasonable manner. *Do you agree with the Court that, in this case, Officer Struble acted unreasonably in searching Rodriguez's car? Why or why not?*

Aliaksei Smalenski/Shutterstock.com

6-1 HOW DOES THE FOURTH AMENDMENT RESTRICT POLICE DISCRETION?

In *Rodriguez v. United States*, the Supreme Court did not address whether Dennys Rodriguez was guilty or innocent of the charges against him. That was for the trial court to decide. Rather, the Court ruled that the Nebraska police officer had overstepped the boundaries of his authority by using a drug-sniffing dog to discover the bag of methamphetamine in Rodriguez's vehicle.[1] In the previous chapter, we discussed the importance of discretion for police officers. This discretion, as we noted, is not absolute. A law enforcement agent's actions are largely determined by the rules for policing set down in the U.S. Constitution and enforced by the courts.

To understand these rules, law enforcement officers must understand the Fourth Amendment, which reads as follows:

> The right of the people to be secure in their persons, houses, papers, and effects, against unreasonable searches and seizures, shall not be violated, and no Warrants shall issue, but upon probable cause, supported by Oath or affirmation, and particularly describing the place to be searched, and the persons or things to be seized.

This amendment contains two critical legal concepts: a prohibition against *unreasonable* **searches and seizures** and the requirement of **probable cause** to issue a warrant. (A warrant is written permission from a judge to engage in a search or arrest, as will be covered extensively later in the chapter.)

6-1a Reasonableness

Law enforcement personnel use searches and seizures to look for and collect the evidence prosecutors need to convict individuals suspected of crimes. As you have just read, when police are conducting a search or seizure, they must be *reasonable*. Though courts have spent innumerable hours scrutinizing the word, no specific meaning for *reasonable* exists. A thesaurus can provide useful synonyms—logical, practical, sensible, intelligent, plausible—but because each case is different, those terms are relative.

In the *Rodriguez* case, the Supreme Court accepted the argument that the search had been so unreasonable as to violate the Fourth Amendment's prohibition against unreasonable searches and seizures. That does not mean that the police officers' actions would have been unreasonable under any circumstances. Indeed, a decade before its *Rodriguez* ruling, the Court accepted a dog sniff search under similar circumstances.

In that case, while an Illinois state trooper was writing a driver a speeding ticket, a K-9 officer walked a police dog around the vehicle. After a signal from the dog, the officer found a large amount of marijuana in the car's trunk. Because the sniff search took place *at the same time* as the "course of a routine traffic stop," the Court upheld the driver's conviction for narcotics trafficking.[2]

CAREER TIP Law enforcement dogs provide invaluable services other than sniffing out illegal narcotics, such as detecting bombs, mines, and missing persons. These animals are prepared for their law enforcement duties by *K-9 (canine) trainers.*

Search and Seizure A legal term, as found in the Fourth Amendment to the U.S. Constitution, that generally refers to the search for and confiscation of evidence by law enforcement agents.

Probable Cause Reasonable grounds to believe the existence of facts warranting certain actions, such as the search or arrest of a person.

6-1b Probable Cause

The concept of reasonableness is linked to probable cause. The Supreme Court has ruled, for example, that any arrest or seizure is unreasonable unless it is supported by probable cause.[3] The burden of probable cause requires more than mere suspicion on a police officer's part. The officer must know of facts and circumstances that would reasonably lead to "the belief that an offense has been or is being committed."[4]

SOURCES OF PROBABLE CAUSE Probable cause cannot be retroactively applied. It must exist at the moment a police officer takes a certain action. Suppose, for example, a police officer stops a person for jaywalking, finds several ounces of marijuana in the person's pocket, and arrests him for marijuana possession. The arrest will probably be disallowed, even if the officer says the person "looked suspicious." Remember, suspicion does not equal probable cause. If, however, an informant tipped the officer off that the person was a drug dealer, probable cause might exist, and the arrest could be valid.

Several sources that may provide probable cause include:

LO6-1 Outline the four major sources that may provide probable cause.

1. *Personal observation.* Police officers may use their personal training, experience, and expertise to infer probable cause from situations that may not be obviously criminal. If, for example, a police officer observes several people in a car slowly circling a certain building in a high-crime area, that officer may assume that the people are "casing" the building in preparation for a burglary. Probable cause could be established for detaining the suspects.
2. *Information.* Law enforcement officers receive information from victims, eyewitnesses, informants, and official sources such as police bulletins or broadcasts. Such information, as long as it is believed to be reliable, is a basis for probable cause.
3. *Evidence.* In certain circumstances, which will be examined later in this chapter, police have probable cause for a search and seizure based on evidence—such as a shotgun—in plain view.
4. *Association.* In some circumstances, if the police see a person with a known criminal background in a place where criminal activity is openly taking place, they have probable cause to stop that person. Generally, however, association is not adequate to establish probable cause.[5]

THE PROBABLE CAUSE FRAMEWORK In a sense, the concept of probable cause allows police officers to do their job effectively. Most arrests are made without a warrant, which requires probable cause, because most arrests are the result of quick police reaction to the commission of a crime. Indeed, it would not be practical to expect a police officer to obtain a warrant before making

5-3c Stress and the Mental Dangers of Police Work

In addition to physical dangers, police work entails considerable mental pressure and stress. The conditions that cause stress—such as worries over finances or relationships—are known as **stressors.** Each profession has its own set of stressors, but police are particularly vulnerable to occupational pressures and stress factors such as the following:

- The constant fear of being a victim of violent crime.
- Exposure to violent crime and its victims.
- The need to comply with the law in nearly every job action.
- Lack of community support.
- Negative media coverage.

Police officers may face a number of internal pressures as well, including limited opportunities for career advancement, excessive paperwork, and low wages and benefits.[60]

Both male and female law enforcement agents experience these stressors, as well as others such as lack of sleep and chaotic private lives. Some stressors are, however, unique to female police officers, for reasons we touched on in the last chapter. These challenges include sexism, sexual harassment, the constant demand to prove oneself, and lack of acceptance in the male-dominated police subculture.[61]

Police stress can manifest itself in different ways. A University at Buffalo study found that the stresses of law enforcement often lead to high blood pressure and heart problems.[62] Interviewing a random sample of 184 officers from eleven different law enforcement agencies, public health expert Elizabeth Mumford found that over half of both female and male police officers "screened positive for alcohol misuse."[63]

If stress becomes overwhelming, an officer may suffer from **burnout,** becoming listless and ineffective as a result of mental and physical exhaustion. Another problem related to stress is *post-traumatic stress disorder (PTSD)*. Often recognized in war veterans and rape victims, PTSD is an anxiety disorder that develops in reaction to a traumatic event.

Finally, though some studies suggest that police officers have higher rates of suicide than the general population, it appears that most develop an extraordinary ability to handle the difficulties of the profession and persevere.[64]

5-3d Police Use of Force

It is generally accepted that not only is police use of force inevitable, but that law enforcement agents who are unwilling to use force cannot do their jobs effectively. "The police officer always causes the trouble," stated an appeals court in one well-known use-of-force case. "But it is trouble which the police officer is sworn to cause, which society pays him to cause and which, if kept within constitutional limits, society praises the officer for causing."[65]

INCIDENCE OF FORCE In general, the use of physical force by law enforcement personnel is very rare, occurring in only about 1.6 percent of the 44 million annual police-public encounters. Still, the Department of Justice estimates that law enforcement officers threaten to use force or use force in encounters with 715,000 civilians a year.[66] Federal researchers have also determined that almost 1,350 potential arrest-related deaths took place in the United States from June 2015 to March 2016.[67]

Of course, police officers are often justified in using force to protect themselves and other citizens. As we noted previously, they are the targets of tens of thousands of assaults each year. Law enforcement agents are also usually justified in using force to make an arrest, to prevent suspects from escaping, to restrain suspects or other individuals for their own safety, and to protect property.[68]

At the same time, few observers would be naïve enough to believe that the police are *always* justified in the use of force. A survey of emergency room physicians found that 98 percent believed that they had treated patients who were victims of excessive police force.[69]

How, then, is "misuse" of force to be defined? To provide guidance for officers in this tricky area, nearly every law enforcement agency designs a *use-of-force matrix*. As the example in Figure 5.3 shows, such a matrix presents officers with the proper force options for different levels of contact with a civilian.

TYPES OF FORCE To comply with the various, and not always consistent, laws concerning the use of force, a police officer must understand that there are two kinds of force: *nondeadly force* and *deadly force*. The vast majority of force used by law enforcement is nondeadly force—that is, force that is not likely to cause death or great bodily harm. In

Stressors The aspects of police work and life that lead to feelings of stress.

Burnout A mental state that occurs when a person suffers from exhaustion and has difficulty functioning normally as a result of overwork and stress.

FIGURE 5.3 THE ORLANDO (FLORIDA) POLICE DEPARTMENT'S USE-OF-FORCE MATRIX

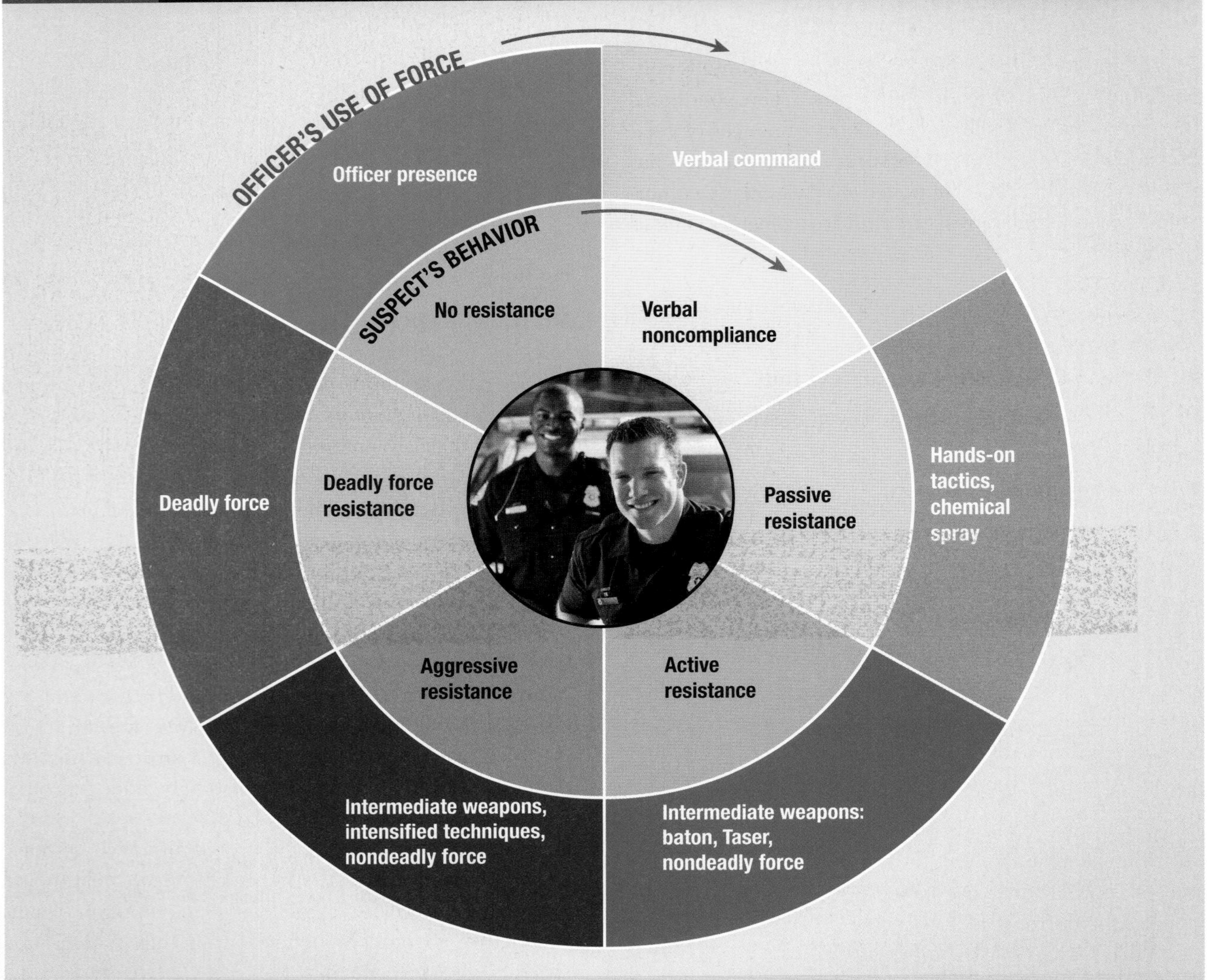

iStock.com/kali9

Like most local law enforcement agencies, the Orlando Police Department has a policy to guide its officers' use of force. Such policies instruct an officer on how to react to an escalating series of confrontations with a civilian and are often expressed visually, as shown here.

Source: Michael E. Miller, "Taser Use and the Use-of-Force Continuum," *Police Chief* (September 2010), 72.

most states, the use of nondeadly force is regulated by the concept of **reasonable force,** which allows the use of nondeadly force when a reasonable person would assume that such force was necessary for the officer to carry out her or his legal duties.

Reasonable Force The degree of force that is appropriate to protect the police officer or other citizens and is not excessive.

Deadly Force Force applied by a police officer that is likely or intended to cause death.

LO5-4 Clarify the concepts of nondeadly force, deadly force, and reasonable force in the context of police use of force.

So, for example, when New York City police officer James Frascatore threw ex-professional tennis player James Blake to the ground several years ago, the officer was not stripped of his badge because he used force on a suspect who was innocent. Frascatore was disciplined because his superiors felt that tackling an unarmed, compliant suspect as part of an investigation into a fraudulent credit card operation was excessive and unreasonable.

In contrast with nondeadly force, **deadly force** is force that an objective police officer realizes will place the subject in direct threat of serious injury or death.

A law enforcement agent is justified in using deadly force if she or he reasonably believes that such force is necessary to protect herself, himself, or another person from serious harm.[70] Generally speaking, the key question in use-of-force cases is: Did the officer behave reasonably, under the circumstances?

Photo by Mike McGregor/Contour by Getty Images

In many large cities, "hot spots" of crime—discussed earlier in the chapter—are located in low-income, minority neighborhoods. **Given this reality, how might such data-driven policing contribute to tension between the police and members of minority communities?**

THE UNITED STATES SUPREME COURT AND USE OF FORCE The United States Supreme Court set the standards for the use of deadly force by law enforcement officers in *Tennessee v. Garner* (1985).[71] The case involved an incident in which Memphis police officer Elton Hymon shot and killed a suspect who was trying to climb over a fence after stealing ten dollars from a residence. Hymon testified that he had been trained to shoot to keep a suspect from escaping, and indeed Tennessee law at the time allowed police officers to apprehend fleeing suspects in this manner.

In reviewing the case, the Supreme Court focused not on Hymon's action but on the Tennessee statute itself, ultimately finding it unconstitutional:

> When the suspect poses no immediate threat to the officer and no threat to others, the use of deadly force is unjustified. . . . It is not better that all felony suspects die than that they escape.[72]

The Court's decision forced twenty-three states to change their fleeing felon rules, but it did not completely eliminate police discretion in such situations. Police officers still may use deadly force if they have probable cause to believe that the fleeing suspect poses a threat of serious injury or death to the officers or others. (We will discuss the concept of probable cause in the next chapter.)

In essence, the Court recognized that police officers must be able to make split-second decisions without worrying about the legal ramifications. Four years after the *Garner* case, the Court tried to clarify this concept in *Graham v. Connor* (1989), stating that the use of any force should be judged by the "reasonableness of the officer on the scene, rather than with the 20/20 vision of hindsight."[73] In 2004, the Court modified this rule by suggesting that an officer's use of force could be "reasonable" even if, by objective measures, the force was not needed to protect the officer or others in the area.[74]

USE OF FORCE AND POLICE BIAS When polled, African Americans consistently express less confidence in police than do whites.[75] This mistrust can be at least partially attributed to a number of recent use-of-force incidents caught on videotape during which unarmed young black men were killed by law enforcement officers. Such videos "corroborate what African Americans have been saying for years" about rampant police bias, says Paul Butler, a Georgetown University Law School professor.[76]

Racial Profiling Two studies released in July 2016 seem to confirm these suspicions. The first, conducted by the Center for Policing Equity, showed that police were 3.6 times as likely to use force against black suspects as against whites.[77] The second, carried out by Harvard economics professor Roland G. Fryer, Jr., found that blacks were 50 percent more likely to be exposed to nonlethal force, such as being handcuffed or pushed to the ground. (Fryer's research did not find any racial differences in the victims of police shootings.)[78]

In addition, a recent Justice Department study indicated that, although police pull over white, black, and Latino drivers at similar rates, blacks and Latinos are more than three times more likely to be searched following the stop.[79] Such statistics support the controversial contention that **racial profiling** by police

Racial Profiling The practice of targeting people for police action based solely on their race, ethnicity, or national origin.

DISCRETION IN ACTION

Deadly Force

THE SITUATION On the day of his death, twelve-year-old Tamir was playing with a pellet gun in a park. Someone called 911 to report Tamir's behavior, saying that the gun was "probably fake" and that the person pointing it at other people was "probably a juvenile." This information was not passed along to Officer Loehmann, who arrived at the park with his partner on the lookout for an armed adult male.

Grainy video, taken by a surveillance camera, shows Loehmann stepping out of the police car and immediately firing twice at Tamir, killing the boy. The video also shows that, just before he is shot, Tamir reaches into his waistband and pulls out the pellet gun, possibly either to show the officers that it is not a real gun or to give it to them.

THE LAW Police officers are authorized to use deadly force when they reasonably believe such force is necessary to protect themselves or third parties from serious bodily harm.

WHAT WOULD YOU DO? Officer Loehmann claims that he believed the pellet gun to be real and believed that Tamir—large for his age—was going to shoot him or his partner. Lawyers for Tamir's family counter that Loehmann rushed into the situation and shot Tamir immediately, without first assessing whether the boy actually posed a threat.

If you were the district attorney in this jurisdiction, would you recommend to a grand jury (described in Chapter 8) that Loehmann be charged with criminal homicide? Remember, your decision rests on whether you think the officer's actions were reasonable under the circumstances.

To see how a district attorney in Cleveland, Ohio, decided this case, go to Example 5.1 in Appendix A.

in the United States is widespread. Racial profiling occurs when a police action is based on the race, ethnicity, or national origin of the suspect rather than any reasonable suspicion that he or she has broken the law.

Sanctioning Improper Police Force In situations where a police officer does act with evident bias, he or she may be subject to federal prosecution or civil actions. A **civil rights violation** involves the denial of the rights afforded to all Americans by the United States Constitution. Because the Constitution prohibits government officials from discriminating against citizens on the basis of race or ethnicity, many police lawsuits involve members of minority groups.[80]

Police officers can also be held criminally liable for misconduct, as we saw at the beginning of this chapter with regard to the two Albuquerque officers charged with second degree murder for allegedly killing a homeless man. The fact that those charges did not result in conviction is instructive. According to data gathered by Philip M. Stinson, an associate professor of criminal justice at Bowling Green State University, between 2005 and 2015 on-duty police officers fatally shot about eleven thousand people. During that time only seventy-five officers were charged with committing a homicide, and only twenty-six were convicted.[81]

Civil Rights Violation Any interference with a citizen's constitutional rights by a civil servant such as a police officer.

Police Corruption The abuse of authority by a law enforcement officer for personal gain.

The main reason behind this trend is the legal standard for police use of force that we discussed earlier in the chapter. As you may recall, such force is justified if the officer has a *reasonable* belief that is it necessary.

Consequently, as the U.S. Justice Department has noted, "Mistake, panic, misperception, or even poor judgment by a police officer does not provide a basis for prosecution."[82] (See the feature *Discretion in Action—Deadly Force* to better understand the mechanics of determining whether law enforcement agents are criminally liable for their actions.)

5-4 HOW IMPORTANT IS ETHICS IN POLICING?

If excessive force is a "strong" misuse of authority by law enforcement, then "soft" misuse of this authority manifests itself in **police corruption.** For general purposes, police corruption can be defined as the misuse of authority by a law enforcement officer "in a manner

California Governor Jerry Brown presents a Medal of Valor to El Cajon police officer Jarred Slocum, who was shot and wounded by a suspect while entering a burning home. **What role does the concept of duty play in a law enforcement agent's decision, regardless of her or his own safety, to protect the life of another person?**

designed to produce personal gain." Drug investigations, for example, often uncover temptingly large amounts of illegal drugs and cash. Former FBI agent Scott M. Bowman pleaded guilty in 2016 to improperly "confiscating" $136,000 in cash that had been seized by the agency during drug raids.

5-4a Ethical Dilemmas

> **LO5-5** Explain what an ethical dilemma is, and name four categories of ethical dilemmas that a police officer typically may face.

Police corruption is intricately connected with the ethics of law enforcement officers. As you saw in Chapter 1, ethics has to do with fundamental questions of the fairness, justice, rightness, or wrongness of any action. Given the significant power that police officers hold, society expects very high standards of ethical behavior from them.

Some police actions are obviously unethical, such as the behavior of the FBI agent who stole $136,000. Most ethical dilemmas that a police officer will face are not so clear cut. According to criminologists Joycelyn M. Pollock and Ronald F. Becker, any of the following situations can present an ethical dilemma:

- The officer does not know the right course of action.
- The course of action the officer considers right is difficult.
- The wrong choice is very tempting.[83]

Because of the many rules that govern policing—the subject of the next chapter—police officers often find themselves tempted by a phenomenon called **noble cause corruption.** This type of corruption occurs when, in the words of John

> **Noble Cause Corruption**
> Knowing misconduct by a police officer with the goal of attaining what the officer believes is a "just" result.

P. Crank and Michael A. Caldero, "officers do bad things because they believe the outcomes will be good."[84] Examples of noble cause corruption include planting evidence or lying in court to help convict someone the officer knows to be guilty.

5-4b Elements of Ethics

Pollock and Becker, both of whom have extensive experience as ethics instructors for police departments, further identify four categories of ethical dilemmas, involving discretion, duty, honesty, and loyalty.[85]

- *Discretion*. The law provides rigid guidelines for how police officers must act and how they cannot act, but it does not offer guidelines for how officers should act in many circumstances. As mentioned at the beginning of this chapter, police officers often use discretion to determine how they should act, and ethics plays an important role in guiding discretionary actions.
- *Duty*. The concept of discretion is linked with **duty,** or the obligation to act in a certain manner. Society, by passing laws, can make a police officer's duty clearer and, in the process, help eliminate discretion from the decision-making process. But an officer's duty will not always be obvious, and ethical considerations can often supplement "the rules" of being a law enforcement agent.
- *Honesty*. Of course, honesty is a critical attribute for an ethical police officer. A law enforcement agent must make hundreds of decisions in a day, and most of them require him or her to be honest in order to do the job properly.
- *Loyalty*. What should a police officer do if he or she witnesses a partner using excessive force on a suspect? The choice often sets loyalty against ethics, especially if the officer does not condone the violence.

Duty A police officer's moral sense that she or he should behave in a certain manner.

Although an individual's ethical makeup is determined by a multitude of personal factors, police departments can create an atmosphere that is conducive to professionalism and thus to ethical behavior. Brandon V. Zuidema and H. Wayne Duff, both captains with the Lynchburg (Virginia) Police Department, believe that law enforcement administrators can encourage ethical policing by:

1. Incorporating ethics into the department's mission statement.
2. Conducting internal training sessions in ethics.
3. Accepting "honest mistakes" and helping the officer learn from those mistakes.
4. Adopting a zero-tolerance policy toward unethical decisions when the mistakes are not so honest.[86]

ETHICS CHALLENGE

Beating a suspect to get information that would save the life of a crime victim is an example of noble cause corruption, discussed in this section. Can you think of any circumstances in which such actions are ethically defensible? Explain your answer.

STUDY TOOLS 5

LOCATED IN TEXTBOOK

- ☐ Rip out the Chapter Review Card.
- ☐ Review with the Chapter Quiz following this chapter.

LOCATED AT WWW.CENGAGEBRAIN.COM

- ☐ Review key terms flash cards.
- ☐ Read the chapter on all your favorite devices.
- ☐ Complete an Exam to test your knowledge.
- ☐ Check out Visual Summaries and You Decide activities to explore chapter concepts.

Quiz

1. When a police administration wants to limit officer discretion, it can institute a departmental _______________ to guide an officer's decision making in certain situations, such as high-speed chases.

2. One of the primary functions of patrol officers is to _______________ crime by maintaining a visible presence in the community.

3. The science of crime investigation is known as _______________.

4. The technique of _______________ fingerprinting involves crime labs using samples of a person's genetic material to match suspects to crimes.

5. All modern police departments practice _______________-driven policing, in which officers respond to calls for service after a crime has occurred.

6. Most patrol officers are assigned to _______________ patrols, in which they cover designated areas and react to incidents they encounter.

7. _______________ policing is a popular strategy in which officers are encouraged to develop partnerships with citizens to prevent and combat crime.

8. The police subculture is shaped by the physical dangers, such as assault, and the mental dangers, such as high levels of _______________, that officers face every day.

9. Police use of nondeadly force is regulated by the concept of _______________ force, or the amount of force that a rational person would consider necessary in a given situation.

10. _______________ _______________ corruption occurs when police officers engage in conduct they know to be wrong in the belief that it will produce a positive, desired outcome.

Answers to the Chapter 5 Quiz can be found in the Answers section in the back of the book.

6 Police and the Constitution:

The Rules of Law Enforcement

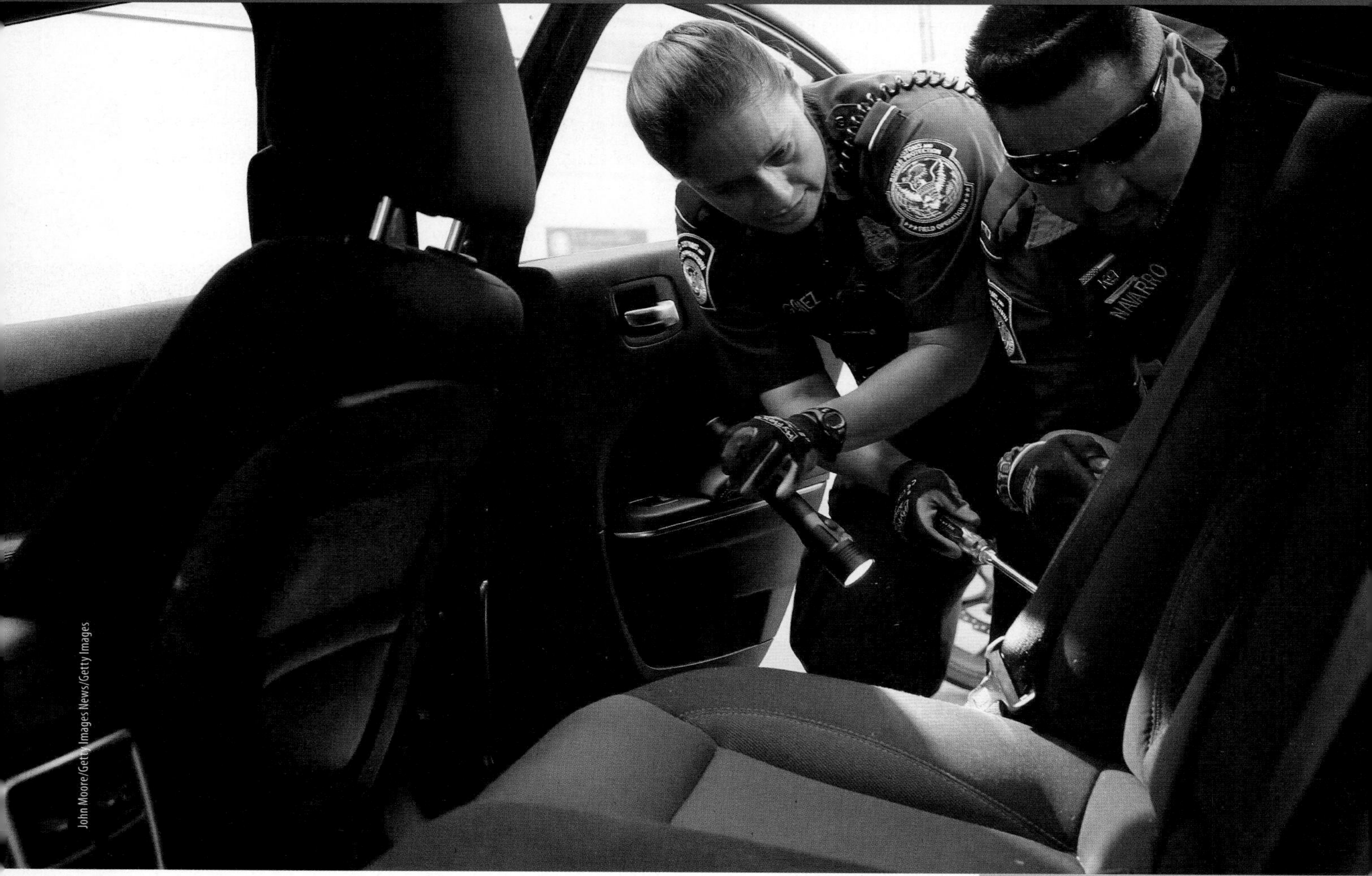

LEARNING OBJECTIVES

After studying this chapter, you will be able to . . .

- **6-1** Outline the four major sources that may provide probable cause.
- **6-2** Explain when searches can be made without a warrant.
- **6-3** Distinguish between a stop and a frisk, and indicate the importance of the case *Terry v. Ohio*.
- **6-4** List the four elements that must be present for an arrest to take place.
- **6-5** Indicate situations in which a *Miranda* warning is unnecessary.

After finishing this chapter, go to **PAGE 132** for **STUDY TOOLS**

CAREER PREP

Environmental Protection Agency Criminal Investigation Division Special Agent

Job Description:

- **Enforce the nation's environmental laws protecting air, water, and land resources.**
- **Investigate cases that involve negligent, knowing, or willful violations of federal environmental laws.**

What Kind of Training Is Required?

- **Eight weeks of basic federal law enforcement and criminal investigation training at the Federal Law Enforcement Training Center in Glynco, Georgia.**
- **An additional eight weeks of training in conducting investigations of the criminal provisions of federal environmental laws.**

Annual Salary Range?

- **$50,000–$100,000**

Image Source/Corbis

SOCIAL MEDIA CAREER TIP

For your profile photo, stick with a close-up, business-appropriate photo in which you are smiling and wearing something you would wear as a potential employee. Avoid symbols, party photos, long-distance shots, and baby pictures.

an arrest on the street. Thus, probable cause provides a framework that limits the situations in which police officers can make arrests, but also gives officers the freedom to act within that framework.

In 2003, the Supreme Court reaffirmed this freedom by ruling that Baltimore (Maryland) police officers acted properly when they arrested all three passengers of a car in which cocaine had been hidden in the back seat. "A reasonable officer," wrote Chief Justice William H. Rehnquist, "could conclude that there was probable cause to believe" that the defendant, who had been sitting in the front seat, was in "possession" of the illicit drug despite his protestations to the contrary.[6]

Once an arrest is made, the arresting officer must prove to a judge that probable cause existed. In *County of Riverside v. McLaughlin* (1991),[7] the Supreme Court held that this judicial determination of probable cause must be made within forty-eight hours after the arrest, even if this two-day period includes a weekend or holiday.

6-1c The Exclusionary Rule

Historically, the courts have looked to the Fourth Amendment for guidance in regulating the activity of law enforcement officers. The courts' most potent legal tool in this endeavor is the **exclusionary rule,** which prohibits the use of illegally seized evidence. According to this rule, any evidence obtained by an unreasonable search or seizure is inadmissible (may not be used) against a defendant in a criminal trial.[8] Even highly incriminating evidence, such as a knife stained with the victim's blood, usually cannot be introduced at a trial if illegally obtained.

Furthermore, any physical or verbal evidence police acquire by using illegally obtained evidence—known as the **fruit of the poisoned tree**—is also inadmissible.

Exclusionary Rule A rule under which any evidence that is obtained in violation of the accused's rights, as well as any evidence derived from illegally obtained evidence, will not be admissible in criminal court.

Fruit of the Poisoned Tree Evidence that is acquired through the use of illegally obtained evidence and is therefore inadmissible in court.

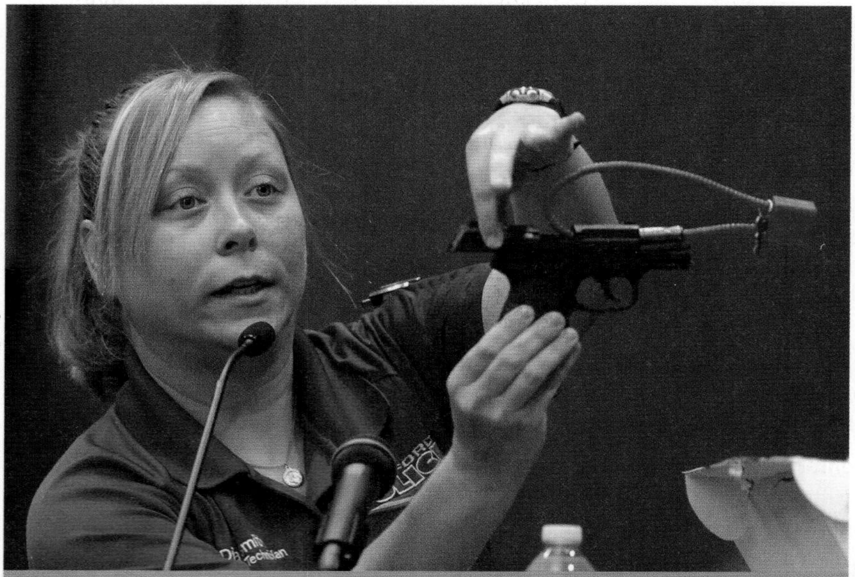

Orlando Sentinel/Tribune News Service/Getty Images

Suppose that this gun—used by a defendant to murder a victim—was found as the result of an improper police search. **Why might the exclusionary rule keep evidence of the gun's existence out of court?**

For example, if the police use the existence of the bloodstained knife to get a confession out of a suspect, that confession will be excluded as well.

One of the implications of the exclusionary rule is that it forces police to gather evidence properly. If they follow appropriate procedures, they are more likely to be rewarded with a conviction. If they are careless or abuse the rights of the suspect, they are unlikely to get a conviction. A strict application of the exclusionary rule, therefore, will permit guilty people to go free because of police carelessness or honest errors.

In practice, relatively few apparently guilty suspects benefit from the exclusionary rule. Research shows that about 1 percent of felony arrestees avoid incarceration because of improper police searches and seizures.[9]

THE "INEVITABLE DISCOVERY" EXCEPTION Critics of the exclusionary rule maintain that, regardless of statistics, the rule hampers the police's ability to gather evidence and causes prosecutors to release numerous suspects before their cases make it to court. Several Supreme Court decisions have mirrored this view and provided exceptions to the exclusionary rule.

"Inevitable Discovery" Exception The legal principle that illegally obtained evidence can be admissible in court if police using lawful means would inevitably have discovered it.

"Good Faith" Exception The legal principle that evidence obtained with the use of a technically invalid search warrant is admissible during trial if the police acted in good faith.

The **"inevitable discovery" exception** was established in the wake of the disappearance of ten-year-old Pamela Powers of Des Moines, Iowa, on Christmas Eve, 1968. The primary suspect in the case, a religious fanatic named Robert Williams, was tricked by a detective into leading police to the site where he had buried Powers. The detective convinced Williams that if he did not lead police to the body, he would soon forget where it was buried. This would deny his victim a "Christian burial."

Initially, in *Brewer v. Williams* (1977),[10] the Court ruled that the evidence (Powers's body) had been obtained illegally because Williams's attorney had not been present during the interrogation that led to his confession. Several years later, in *Nix v. Williams* (1984),[11] the Court reversed itself, ruling that the evidence was admissible because the body would eventually ("inevitably") have been found by lawful means.

THE "GOOD FAITH" EXCEPTION The scope of the exclusionary rule has been further diminished by two cases involving faulty warrants. In the first, *United States v. Leon* (1984),[12] the police seized evidence on authority of a search warrant that had been improperly issued by a judge. In the second, *Arizona v. Evans* (1995),[13] due to a computer error, a police officer detained Isaac Evans on the mistaken belief that he was subject to an arrest warrant. As a result, the officer found a marijuana cigarette on Evans's person and, after a search of his car, discovered a bag of marijuana.

In both cases, the Court allowed the evidence to stand under a **"good faith" exception** to the exclusionary rule. Under this exception, evidence acquired by a police officer using a technically invalid warrant is admissible if the officer was unaware of the error. In these two cases, the Court said that the officers acted in "good faith." By the same token, if police officers use a search warrant that they know to be technically incorrect, the good faith exception does not apply, and the evidence can be suppressed.

ETHICS CHALLENGE

Explain the exclusionary rule in terms of its impact on the ethical behavior of law enforcement agents.

6-2 WHAT ARE THE RULES FOR SEARCHES AND SEIZURES?

How far can law enforcement agents go in searching and seizing private property? Consider the steps taken by Jenny Stracner, an investigator with the Laguna Beach (California) Police Department. After receiving information that a suspect, Greenwood, was engaged in drug trafficking, Stracner enlisted the aid of the local trash collector in procuring evidence. Instead of taking Greenwood's trash bags to be incinerated, the collector agreed to give them to Stracner. The officer found enough drug paraphernalia in the garbage to obtain a warrant to search the suspect's home. Subsequently, Greenwood was arrested and convicted on narcotics charges.[14]

Remember, the Fourth Amendment is quite specific in forbidding unreasonable searches and seizures. Were Stracner's search of Greenwood's garbage and her seizure of its contents "reasonable"? The Supreme Court thought so, holding that Greenwood's garbage was not protected by the Fourth Amendment.[15]

6-2a The Role of Privacy in Searches

A crucial concept in understanding search and seizure law is *privacy*. By definition, a **search** is a governmental intrusion on a citizen's reasonable expectation of privacy. The recognized standard for a "reasonable expectation of privacy" was established in *Katz v. United States* (1967).[16]

The case dealt with the question of whether the defendant was justified in his expectation of privacy in the calls he made from a public phone booth. The Supreme Court held that "the Fourth Amendment protects people, not places," and Katz prevailed.

In his concurring opinion, Justice John Harlan, Jr., set a two-pronged test for a person's expectation of privacy:

1. The individual must prove that she or he expected privacy.
2. Society must recognize that expectation as reasonable.[17]

Accordingly, the Court agreed with Katz's claim that he had a reasonable right to privacy in a public phone booth. Even though the phone booth was a public place, accessible to anyone, Katz had taken clear steps to protect his privacy.

Despite the *Katz* ruling, simply taking steps to preserve one's privacy is not enough to protect against law enforcement intrusion. The steps must be reasonably certain to ensure privacy. If a person is unreasonable or mistaken in expecting privacy, he or she may forfeit that expectation. For instance, in *California v. Greenwood* (1988),[18] described at the beginning of this section, the Court did not believe that the suspect had a reasonable expectation of privacy when it came to his garbage bags.

The Court noted that when we place our trash on a curb, we expose it to any number of intrusions by "animals, children, scavengers, snoops, and other members of the public."[19] In other words, if Greenwood had truly intended for the contents of his garbage bags to remain private, he would not have left them on the side of the road.

Note also that, under the **private search doctrine,** law enforcement officers do not need a warrant to go through personal items that have already been searched by a third-party civilian. The reasoning behind this doctrine is that once a private search has taken place, the owner of the searched items no longer has a reasonable expectation of privacy.[20] So, for example, if an airline employee opens an unclaimed suitcase, finds illegal drugs, and then calls the police, no warrant is required for law enforcement officers to search the baggage and seize the contraband.[21]

Knumina Studios/Shutterstock.com

Should law enforcement be able to use police helicopters to determine if people are carrying out illegal behavior within fenced-in backyards? Why or why not?

Search The process by which police examine a person or property to find evidence that will be used to prove guilt in a criminal trial.

Private Search Doctrine The legal principle that a private search eliminates an owner's reasonable expectation of privacy regarding the object searched.

6-2b Search and Seizure Warrants

Remember, one of the purposes of the Fourth Amendment is to protect citizens from unreasonable police searches. To ensure that they will not be retroactively accused of unreasonably infringing on a suspect's privacy rights during a search, law enforcement officers can obtain a **search warrant.** A search warrant is a court order that authorizes police to search a certain area.

Before a judge or magistrate will issue a search warrant, law enforcement officers must provide:

- Information showing probable cause that a crime has been or will be committed.
- Specific information on the premises to be searched, the suspects to be found and the illegal activities taking place at those premises, and the items to be seized.

The purpose of a search warrant is to establish, before the search takes place, that a *probable cause to search* justifies infringing on the suspect's reasonable expectation of privacy.

PARTICULARITY OF SEARCH WARRANTS The drafters of the Bill of Rights specifically did not want law enforcement officers to have the freedom to make "general, exploratory" searches through a person's belongings.[22] Consequently, the Fourth Amendment requires that a warrant describe with "particularity" the place to be searched and the things—either people or objects—to be seized.

This "particularity" requirement places a heavy burden on law enforcement officers. Before going to a judge to ask for a search warrant, they must prepare an **affidavit** in which they provide specific, written information on the property that they wish to search and seize. They must know the specific address of any place they wish to search. General addresses of apartment buildings or office complexes are not sufficient.

Furthermore, courts generally frown on vague descriptions of goods to be seized. For example, several years ago, a federal court ruled that a warrant permitting police to search a home for "all handguns, shotguns and rifles" and "evidence showing street gang membership" was too broad. As a result, the seizure of a shotgun was disallowed for lack of a valid search warrant.[23]

A **seizure** is the act of taking possession of a person or property by the government because of a (suspected) violation of the law. In general, four categories of items can be seized by use of a search warrant:

1. Items resulting from the crime, such as stolen goods.
2. Items that are inherently illegal for anybody to possess (with certain exceptions), such as narcotics and counterfeit currency.
3. Items that can be called "evidence" of the crime, such as a bloodstained sneaker or a ski mask.
4. Items used in committing the crime, such as an ice pick or a printing press used to make counterfeit bills.[24]

See Figure 6.1 for an example of a search warrant.

REASONABLENESS DURING A SEARCH AND SEIZURE No matter how " particular" a warrant is, it cannot provide for all the conditions that are bound to come up during its service. Consequently, the law gives law enforcement officers the ability to act "reasonably"

FIGURE 6.1 EXAMPLE OF A SEARCH WARRANT

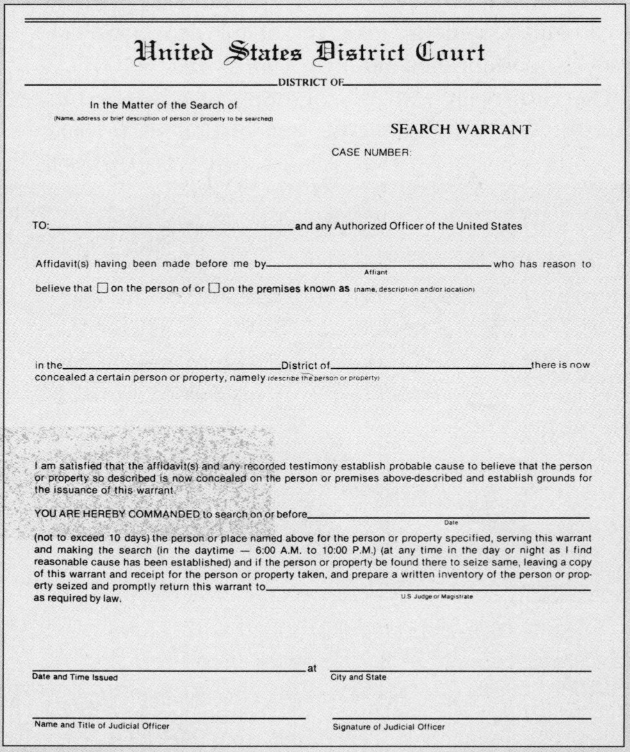

United States District Court

_____ DISTRICT OF _____

In the Matter of the Search of
(Name, address or brief description of person or property to be searched)

SEARCH WARRANT

CASE NUMBER:

TO: _____ and any Authorized Officer of the United States

Affidavit(s) having been made before me by _____ (Affiant) who has reason to believe that ☐ on the person of or ☐ on the premises known as (name, description and/or location)

in the _____ District of _____ there is now concealed a certain person or property, namely (describe the person or property)

I am satisfied that the affidavit(s) and any recorded testimony establish probable cause to believe that the person or property so described is now concealed on the person or premises above-described and establish grounds for the issuance of this warrant.

YOU ARE HEREBY COMMANDED to search on or before _____ (Date)

(not to exceed 10 days) the person or place named above for the person or property specified, serving this warrant and making the search (in the daytime — 6:00 A.M. to 10:00 P.M.) (at any time in the day or night as I find reasonable cause has been established) and if the person or property be found there to seize same, leaving a copy of this warrant and receipt for the person or property taken, and prepare a written inventory of the person or property seized and promptly return this warrant to _____ (U.S. Judge or Magistrate) as required by law.

_____ at _____
Date and Time Issued — City and State

_____ _____
Name and Title of Judicial Officer — Signature of Judicial Officer

Search Warrant A written order, based on probable cause and issued by a court, commanding that police officers or criminal investigators search a specific person, place, or property to obtain evidence.

Affidavit A written statement of facts, confirmed by the oath or affirmation of the party making it and made before a person having the authority to administer the oath or affirmation.

Seizure The forcible taking of a person or property in response to a violation of the law.

during a search and seizure in the event of unforeseeable circumstances. For example, if a police officer is searching an apartment for a stolen MacBook Pro laptop computer and notices a vial of crack cocaine sitting on the suspect's bed, that contraband is considered to be in "plain view" and can be seized.

Note, though, that if law enforcement officers have a search warrant that authorizes them to search for a stolen laptop computer, they are not justified in opening small drawers. Because a computer cannot fit in a small drawer, an officer has no reasonable basis for searching one. Hence, officers are restricted in where they can look by the items they are searching for.

CAREER TIP There is some debate as to whether taking blood from a possible drunk driver constitutes a search under the Fourth Amendment. In many jurisdictions, only a licensed *phlebotomist*—not a police officer—is authorized to draw blood from a person suspected of driving under the influence.

6-2c Searches and Seizures without a Warrant

LO6-2 Explain when searches can be made without a warrant.

Although the Supreme Court has established the principle that searches conducted without warrants are unreasonable *per se* (by definition), it has set "specifically established" exceptions to the rule.[25] In fact, most searches take place in the absence of a judicial order. Warrantless searches and seizures can be lawful when police are in "hot pursuit" of a subject or when they search bags of trash left at the curb for regular collection. Because of the magnitude of smuggling activities in "border areas" such as airports, seaports, and international boundaries, a warrant normally is not needed to search property in those places.

Furthermore, in *Brigham City v. Stuart* (2006),[26] the Court held unanimously that police officers do not need a warrant to enter a private home in an emergency, such as when they reasonably fear for the safety of the inhabitants. The two most important circumstances in which a warrant is not needed, though, are (1) searches incidental to arrests and (2) consent searches.

SEARCHES INCIDENTAL TO AN ARREST The most frequent exception to the warrant requirement involves **searches incidental to arrests,** so called because nearly every time police officers make an arrest (a procedure discussed in detail later in the chapter), they also search the suspect. As long as the original arrest was based on probable cause, these searches are valid for two reasons, established by the Supreme Court in *United States v. Robinson* (1973):

1. The need for a police officer to find and confiscate any weapons a suspect may be carrying.
2. The need to protect any evidence on the suspect's person from being destroyed.[27]

Law enforcement officers are, however, limited in the searches they may make during an arrest. These limits were established by the Supreme Court in *Chimel v. California* (1969).[28] In that case, police arrived at Chimel's home with an arrest warrant but not a search warrant. Even though Chimel refused their request to "look around," the officers searched the entire three-bedroom house for nearly an hour, finding stolen coins in the process. Chimel was convicted of burglary and appealed, arguing that the evidence of the coins should have been suppressed.

The Supreme Court held that the search was unreasonable. In doing so, the Court established guidelines as to the acceptable extent of searches incidental to arrests. Primarily, the Court ruled that police may search any area within the suspect's "immediate control" to confiscate any weapons or evidence that the suspect could destroy. The Court found, however, that there was no justification

> for routinely searching rooms other than that in which the arrest occurs—or, for that matter, for searching through all desk drawers or other closed or concealed areas in that room itself. Such searches, in the absence of well-recognized exceptions, may be made only under the authority of a search warrant.[29]

The exact interpretation of the "area within immediate control" has been left to individual courts, but in general it has been taken to mean the area within the reach of the arrested person. Thus, the Court is said to have established the "arm's reach doctrine" in its *Chimel* decision.

SEARCHES WITH CONSENT **Consent searches,** the second most common type of warrantless searches, take place when individuals voluntarily give law enforcement officers permission

Searches Incidental to Arrests Searches for weapons and evidence that are conducted on persons who have just been arrested.

Consent Searches Searches by police that are made after the subject of the search has agreed to the action.

to search their persons, homes, or belongings. The most relevant factors in determining whether consent is voluntary are

1. The age, intelligence, and physical condition of the consenting suspect.
2. Any coercive behavior by the police, such as the language used to request consent.
3. The length of the questioning and its location.[30]

If a court finds that a person has been physically threatened or otherwise coerced into giving consent, the search is invalid.[31] Furthermore, the search must be reasonable. In 2007, the North Carolina Supreme Court invalidated a consent search that turned up a packet of cocaine. As part of this search, the police had pulled down the suspect's underwear and shone a flashlight on his groin.

The court ruled that a reasonable person in the defendant's position would not consent to such an intrusive examination.[32] (Figure 6.2 provides an overview of the circumstances under which warrantless searches have traditionally been allowed.)

6-2d Searches of Automobiles

In *Carroll v. United States* (1925),[33] the Supreme Court ruled that the law could distinguish among automobiles, homes, and persons in questions involving police searches. In the years since its *Carroll* decision, the Court has established that the Fourth Amendment does not require police to obtain a warrant to search automobiles or other movable vehicles when they have probable cause to believe that a vehicle contains contraband or evidence of criminal activity.[34]

The reasoning behind such leniency is straightforward: Requiring a warrant to search an automobile places too heavy a burden on police officers. By the time the officers could communicate with a judge and obtain the warrant, the suspects could have driven away and destroyed any evidence. Consequently, the Court has consistently held that someone in a vehicle does not have the same reasonable expectation of privacy as someone at home or even in a phone booth.

WARRANTLESS SEARCHES OF AUTOMOBILES For nearly three decades, police officers believed that if they lawfully arrested the driver of a car, they could legally make a warrantless search of the car's entire front and back compartments. This understanding was based on the Supreme Court's ruling in *New York v. Benton* (1981),[35] which seemed to allow this expansive interpretation of the "area within immediate control" with regard to automobiles.

In *Arizona v. Gant* (2009), however, the Court announced that its *Benton* decision had been misinterpreted. Such warrantless searches are allowed only in two situations:

1. The person being arrested is close enough to the car to grab or destroy evidence or a weapon inside the car.

FIGURE 6.2 EXCEPTIONS TO THE SEARCH WARRANT REQUIREMENT

Incident to Lawful Arrest Police officers may search the area within the immediate control of a person after they have arrested him or her.	**Automobile Exception** If police officers have probable cause to believe that an automobile contains evidence of a crime, they may, in most instances, search the vehicle without a warrant.
Consent Police officers may search a person without a warrant if that person voluntarily agrees to be searched and has the legal authority to authorize the search.	**Plain View** If police officers are legally engaged in police work and happen to see evidence of a crime in "plain view," they may seize it without a warrant.
Stop and Frisk Police officers may frisk, or "pat down," a person if they suspect that the person may be involved in criminal activity or poses a danger to those in the immediate area.	**Abandoned Property** Any abandoned property, such as a hotel room that has been vacated or contraband that has been discarded, may be searched and seized by police officers without a warrant.
Hot Pursuit If police officers are in "hot pursuit," or chasing a person they have probable cause to believe committed a crime, and that person enters a building, the officers may search the building without a warrant.	**Border Searches** Law enforcement officers on border patrol do not need a warrant to search vehicles crossing the border.

In many instances, it would be impractical for police officers to leave a crime scene, go to a judge, and obtain a search warrant before conducting a search. Therefore, under the above circumstances, a search warrant is not required.

DISCRETION IN ACTION

A Valid Pretext?

THE SITUATION You are a police officer patrolling an area of Washington, D.C., that is marked by extremely high rates of drug-related crime. You become suspicious of a truck with temporary license plates being driven slowly by a young African American male.

Although you do not consider yourself racially biased, you are well aware, from experience, that in this neighborhood many young black men in these types of vehicles with temporary plates are drug dealers. These suspicions do not, however, reach the level of probable cause needed to pull over the truck. Then, the driver fails to signal while making a right turn.

THE LAW As far as Fourth Amendment law is concerned, any subjective reasons that a police officer might have for stopping a suspect, including any motive based on racial stereotyping or bias, are irrelevant. As long as the officer has objective probable cause to believe a traffic violation or other wrongdoing has occurred, the stop is valid.

WHAT WOULD YOU DO? You are convinced that the driver of the truck is selling illegal drugs, and you want to stop and search him. The failure to signal gives you a valid pretext to pull over the truck, even though your real reasons for the stop would be its slow pace, its temporary plates, the race of its driver, and the level of drug crime in the neighborhood. What do you do?

To see how the United States Supreme Court reacted to an officer's decision in a similar situation, go to Example 6.1 in Appendix A.

2. The arresting officer reasonably believes that the car contains evidence pertinent to the same crime for which the arrest took place.[36]

So, for example, a police officer will no longer be able to search an automobile for contraband if the driver has been arrested for failing to pay previous speeding tickets—unless the officer reasonably believes the suspect has the ability to reach and destroy any such contraband.

As you can imagine, the law enforcement community reacted negatively to the restrictions outlined in the *Gant* decision.[37] Police officers, however, still can conduct a warrantless search of an automobile based on circumstances other than the incidental-to-an-arrest doctrine. These circumstances include probable cause of criminal activity, consent of the driver, and "protective searches" to look for weapons if police officers have a reasonable suspicion that such weapons exist.[38]

PRETEXTUAL STOPS Several years ago, a police officer in Starke, Florida, pulled over professional football player Letroy Guion for "failure to maintain a single lane." While writing a ticket, the officer smelled marijuana, providing him with legal justification to conduct a search. The search uncovered 357 grams of pot, about $190,000 in cash, and an illegally owned firearm in Guion's truck.

It is important to understand that such automobile stops and searches are a valid part of police work. As long as an officer has probable cause to believe that a traffic law has been broken, her or his "true" motivation for making a stop is irrelevant.[39] So, even if the police officer does not have a legally sufficient reason to search for evidence of a crime such as drug trafficking, the officer can use a minor traffic violation to pull over the car and investigate his or her "hunch." (To learn more about such "pretextual stops," see the feature *Discretion in Action—A Valid Pretext?*)

6-2e The Plain View Doctrine

As we have already seen several times in this chapter, the Constitution, as interpreted by our courts, provides very little protection to evidence *in plain view*. For example, suppose a traffic officer pulls over a person for speeding, looks in the driver's side window, and clearly sees what appears to be a bag of heroin resting on the passenger seat. In this instance, under the **plain view doctrine,** the officer would be justified in seizing the drugs without a warrant.

Plain View Doctrine The legal principle that objects in plain view of a law enforcement agent who has the right to be in a position to have that view may be seized without a warrant and introduced as evidence.

CJ and TECHNOLOGY

Tactical Camera Spheres

The size and shape of a baseball, with a hard rubber shell and a six-lens camera, the Explorer could be a game changer for police tactical operations. When activated—stationary or in motion—the Explorer's camera snaps images at fifteen frames per second. Software uploads these images to a mobile device, such as a smartphone or tablet, and combines them so that they can be viewed instantaneously as a single, panoramic picture. Various models also have video-streaming capabilities and sensors that can detect hazards such as high carbon monoxide levels.

Law enforcement agents who have used Explorer appreciate the device's simplicity. "You are able to throw it into a room or hallway, somewhere you need to gather immediate tactical intelligence but there's a risk to sending an officer in," says Mark Clevette, Commander of Special Operations for the Maine Department of Corrections. "The safety advantage is obvious."

Thinking about Tactical Camera Spheres

What are some of the circumstances in which Explorer "balls" would be useful to law enforcement? Under what circumstances might law enforcement need to obtain a search warrant before deploying these devices to gather intelligence?

The plain view doctrine was first put forward by the Supreme Court in *Coolidge v. New Hampshire* (1971).[40] The Court ruled that law enforcement officers may make a warrantless seizure of an item if four criteria are met:

1. The item is positioned so as to be detected easily by an officer's sight or some other sense.
2. The officer is legally in a position to notice the item in question.
3. The discovery of the item is inadvertent. That is, the officer had not intended to find the item.
4. The officer immediately recognizes the illegal nature of the item.

No interrogation or further investigation is allowed under the plain view doctrine.

Advances in technology that allow law enforcement agents to "see" beyond normal human capabilities have raised new issues in regard to plain view principles. *Thermal imagers*, for example, measure otherwise invisible levels of infrared radiation. These devices are particularly effective in detecting marijuana plants grown indoors because of the heat thrown off by the "grow lights" that the plants need to survive.

Electronic Surveillance The use of electronic equipment by law enforcement agents to record private conversations or observe conduct that is meant to be private.

The question for the courts has been whether a warrantless search of a dwelling through its walls by means of a thermal imager violates Fourth Amendment protections of privacy. According to the Supreme Court, an item is not in plain view if law enforcement agents need the aid of this technology to "see" it.[41] Thus, information from a thermal imager is not by itself justification for a warrantless search.

6-2f Electronic Surveillance

During the course of a criminal investigation, law enforcement officers may decide to use **electronic surveillance,** or electronic devices such as wiretaps or hidden microphones ("bugs"), to monitor and record conversations, observe movements, and trace or record telephone calls.

BASIC RULES: CONSENT AND PROBABLE CAUSE Given the invasiveness of electronic surveillance, the Supreme Court has generally held that the practice is prohibited by the Fourth Amendment. In *Burger v. New York* (1967),[42] however, the Court ruled that it is permissible under certain circumstances. That same year, *Katz v. United States* (discussed at the beginning of this section) established that recorded conversations are inadmissible as evidence unless certain procedures are followed.

In general, law enforcement officers can use electronic surveillance only if consent is given by one of the parties to be monitored, or, in the absence of such consent, with a warrant.[43] For the warrant to be valid, it must:

1. Detail with "particularity" the conversations that are to be overheard.
2. Name the suspects and the places that will be under surveillance.
3. Show probable cause to believe that a specific crime has been or will be committed.[44]

Once the specific information has been gathered, the law enforcement officers must end the electronic surveillance immediately.[45] In any case, the surveillance cannot last more than thirty days without a judicial extension.

AP Images/Jose Luis Magana

What is your opinion of the Supreme Court's ruling that police officers need a warrant to search the contents of arrestees' cell phones in most circumstances?

FORCE MULTIPLIERS Certain pervasive forms of electronic surveillance are allowed under the theory that people who are in public places have no reasonable expectation of privacy. This theory, generally upheld by American courts,[46] allows for the use of a number of technological *force multipliers*, or devices that allow law enforcement agencies to expand their capabilities without a significant increase in personnel.

Perhaps the most pervasive force multiplier is closed-circuit television surveillance (CCTV). This form of surveillance relies on strategically placed video cameras to record and transmit all activities in a targeted area. New York City's CCTV system uses about three thousand cameras to cover much of that city's midtown and downtown areas. Several other large cities, such as Boston and Los Angeles, employ hundreds of public surveillance cameras.

Another popular force multiplier involves computerized infrared cameras that take digital photos of license plates. Usually mounted on police cars, these *automatic license plate recognition (ALPR)* devices convert the images to text. Then the numbers are instantly checked against databases that contain records of the license plates of stolen cars and automobiles driven by a wide variety of targets, from wanted felons to citizens with unpaid parking tickets. In heavy-traffic areas, ALPR units can check thousands of license plates each hour.

6-2g Cell Phones and the Fourth Amendment

Given the pervasiveness of cell phones in everyday life and the amount of information stored on these "mobile computers," it should come as no surprise that the devices raise a number of questions about privacy and police searches. In *California v. Riley* (2014),[47] the Supreme Court ruled, unanimously, that police officers need a warrant to search the contents of cell phones belonging to suspects they have just arrested. As we saw earlier in this section, law enforcement agents may, in many instances, carry out a warrantless search of an arrestee following an arrest.

Because of the vast amounts of personal information on cell phones, however, the Court decided that these items deserve greater protections than items such as wallets and cigarette packs. Furthermore, once a cell phone has been secured by police, the arrestee will not be able to "delete incriminating data," and the "data on the phone can endanger no one"—the two primary justifications for warrantless searches incidental to an arrest.[48]

In his opinion, Chief Justice John G. Roberts acknowledged that the Court's decision would "have an impact on the ability of law enforcement to combat crime." But, he added, "Privacy comes at a cost."[49] Practically, the ruling does not mean the end of cell phone searches. Rather, it means that police will need to get a warrant before engaging in such searches. Alternatively, they will need the consent of the cell phone owner.

6-3 WHEN CAN POLICE STOP AND FRISK A SUSPECT?

Two experienced Chicago police officers were standing by their patrol car when a woman approached. She told the officers that she had just purchased illegal drugs from a man and provided them with the suspect's physical description and the location of his drug-selling activity. The police officers went to the location—in an area known to both as a hot spot for drug dealing—and saw a man matching the woman's description clasp hands with another man. Believing that they had just witnessed a drug deal, the officers stopped the suspect, patted him down, and, after finding heroin, made an arrest.

LO6-3 Distinguish between a stop and a frisk, and indicate the importance of the case *Terry v. Ohio*.

Under the circumstances, these two law enforcement agents believed that they had *reasonable suspicion* that the man had committed a crime. When reasonable suspicion exists, police officers may *stop and frisk* a suspect. In a stop and frisk, law enforcement officers (1) briefly detain a person they reasonably believe to be suspicious, and (2) if they believe the person to be armed, proceed to pat down, or "frisk," that person's outer clothing.

6-3a The Elusive Definition of Reasonable Suspicion

Like so many elements of police work, the decision of whether to stop a suspect is based on the balancing of conflicting priorities. On the one hand, a police officer feels a sense of urgency to act when he or she believes that criminal activity is occurring or is about to occur. On the other hand, law enforcement agents do not want to harass innocent individuals, especially if doing so runs afoul of the U.S. Constitution. In stop-and-frisk law, this balancing act rests on the fulcrum of reasonable suspicion.

TERRY V. OHIO The precedent for the ever-elusive definition of a "reasonable" suspicion in stop-and-frisk situations was established in *Terry v. Ohio* (1968).[50] In that case, a detective named McFadden observed two men (one of whom was Terry) acting strangely in downtown Cleveland. The men walked repeatedly past a certain store, peered into the window, and then stopped at a street corner to confer. At one point, while they were talking, another man joined the conversation and then left quickly.

Several minutes later, the three men met again at another corner a few blocks away. Detective McFadden believed the trio was planning to break into the store. He approached them, told them who he was, and asked for identification. After receiving a mumbled response, the detective frisked the three men and found handguns on two of them, who were tried and convicted of carrying concealed weapons.

Stop A brief detention of a person by law enforcement agents for questioning.

The Supreme Court upheld the conviction, ruling that Detective McFadden had reasonable cause to believe that the men were armed and dangerous and that swift action was necessary to protect himself and other citizens in the area.[51] The Court accepted McFadden's interpretation of the unfolding scene as based on objective facts and practical conclusions. It therefore concluded that his suspicion was reasonable.

THE "TOTALITY OF THE CIRCUMSTANCES" TEST For the most part, the judicial system has refrained from placing restrictions on police officers' ability to make stops. In the *Terry* case, the Supreme Court did say that an officer must have "specific and articulable facts" to support the decision to make a stop, but added that the facts may be "taken together with rational inferences."[52] The Court has consistently ruled that because of their practical experience, law enforcement agents are in a unique position to make such inferences and should be given a good deal of freedom in doing so.

In the years since the *Terry* case was decided, the Court has settled on a "totality of the circumstances" test to determine whether a stop is based on reasonable suspicion.[53] In 2002, for example, the Court ruled that a U.S. Border Patrol agent's stop of a minivan in Arizona was reasonable.[54] On being approached by the Border Patrol car, the driver had stiffened, slowed down his van, and avoided making eye contact with the agent. Furthermore, the children in the van waved at the officer in a mechanical manner, as if ordered to do so. The agent pulled over the van and found 128 pounds of marijuana.

In his opinion, Chief Justice William Rehnquist pointed out that such conduct might have been unremarkable on a busy city highway, but on an unpaved road thirty miles from the Mexican border it was enough to reasonably arouse the agent's suspicion.[55] The justices also made clear that the need to prevent terrorist attacks is part of the "totality of the circumstances." Therefore, law enforcement agents have considerable leeway to make stops near U.S. borders.

6-3b A Stop

The terms *stop* and *frisk* are often used in concert, but they describe two separate acts. A **stop** takes place when a law enforcement officer has reasonable suspicion that criminal activity has taken place or is about to take place.

Because an investigatory stop is not an arrest, there are limits to how long police can detain someone who has been stopped. For example, in one situation an airline

John Moore/Getty Images News/Getty Images

A police officer frisks a suspect in New London, Connecticut. **What is the main purpose behind a frisk? When are police justified in frisking someone?**

traveler and his luggage were detained for ninety minutes while the police waited for a drug-sniffing dog to arrive. The Supreme Court ruled that the initial stop of the passenger was constitutional, but that the ninety-minute wait was excessive.[56]

In 2004, the Court held that police officers could require suspects to identify themselves during a stop that is otherwise valid under the *Terry* ruling.[57] The case involved a Nevada rancher who was fined $250 for refusing to give his name to a police officer investigating a possible assault. The defendant argued that such requests force citizens to incriminate themselves against their will, which is prohibited, as we shall see later in the chapter, by the Fifth Amendment. Justice Anthony Kennedy wrote, however, that "asking questions is an essential part of police investigations" that would be made much more difficult if officers could not determine the identity of a suspect.[58] The ruling validated "stop-and-identify" laws in twenty states and numerous cities and towns.

6-3c A Frisk

The Supreme Court has stated that a **frisk** should be a protective measure. Police officers cannot conduct a frisk as a "fishing expedition" simply to try to find items besides weapons, such as illegal narcotics, on a suspect.[59]

A frisk does not necessarily follow a stop and in fact may occur only when the officer is justified in thinking that the safety of police officers or other citizens may be endangered. So, in the case of the two Chicago police officers that opened this section, an Illinois appeals court ruled that while the initial stop was acceptable, the officers had violated the suspect's right by frisking him. The state court was unwilling to accept the contention that the suspect was involved in a drug transaction and "drugs and guns go together" as sufficient grounds for a pat-down.[60]

As with stops, frisks must be supported by reasonable suspicion. The Illinois court rejected the argument that the Chicago police officers had objective reasons to fear for their safety. In the *Terry* case, by contrast, the Supreme Court accepted that Detective McFadden reasonably believed that the three suspects posed a threat. Crucially, the suspects had refused to answer McFadden's questions. Although this refusal was within their rights because they had not been arrested, it provided the officer with sufficient motive for the frisk.

In 2009, the Court extended the "stop-and-frisk" authority by ruling that a police officer could order a passenger in a car that had been pulled over for a traffic violation to submit to a pat-down.[61] To do so, the officer must have a reasonable suspicion that the suspect may be armed and dangerous.

6-4 WHAT ARE THE RULES FOR MAKING AN ARREST?

As happened in the *Terry* case, discussed earlier, a stop and frisk may lead to an **arrest.** An arrest is the act of apprehending a suspect for the purpose of detaining him or her on a criminal charge.

It is important to understand the difference between a stop and an arrest. In the eyes of the law, a stop is a relatively brief intrusion on a citizen's rights, whereas an arrest involves a deprivation of liberty and calls for a full range of constitutional protections. (See Figure 6.3 to better understand how a stop differs from an arrest.) Consequently, while a stop can be made based on reasonable suspicion, a law enforcement officer needs probable cause, as defined earlier, to make an arrest.[62]

Frisk A pat-down or minimal search by police to discover weapons.

Arrest The act of depriving a person suspected of criminal activity of his or her liberty.

FIGURE 6.3 THE DIFFERENCE BETWEEN A STOP AND AN ARREST

Both stops and arrests are considered seizures because both police actions restrict an individual's freedom to "walk away." Both must be justified by a showing of reasonableness. You should be aware, however, of the differences between a stop and an arrest. During a stop, police can interrogate the person and make a limited search of his or her outer clothing. If certain events occur during the stop, such as the discovery of an illegal weapon, then officers may arrest the person. If an arrest is made, the suspect comes under police control and is protected by the U.S. Constitution in a number of ways that will be discussed later in the chapter.

PhotoDisc / Getty Images

	Stop	Arrest
Justification	Reasonable suspicion	Probable cause
Warrant	None	Required in some, but not all, situations
Intent of Officer	To investigate suspicious activity	To make a formal charge against the suspect
Search	May frisk, or "pat down," for weapons	May conduct a full search for weapons or evidence
Scope of Search	Outer clothing only	Area within the suspect's immediate control or "reach"

6-4a Elements of an Arrest

When is somebody under arrest? The easy—and incorrect—answer would be whenever the police officer says so. In fact, the state of being under arrest depends not only on the actions of the law enforcement officer but also on the perception of the suspect.

Suppose Mr. Smith is stopped by plainclothes detectives, driven to the police station, and detained for three hours for questioning. During this time, the police never tell Mr. Smith he is under arrest, and in fact, he is free to leave at any time. But if Mr. Smith or any other reasonable person *believes* he is not free to leave, then, according to the Supreme Court, that person is in fact under arrest and should receive the necessary constitutional protections.[63]

Criminal justice professor Rolando V. del Carmen of Sam Houston State University has identified four elements that must be present for an arrest to take place:

1. The *intent* to arrest. In a stop, though it may entail slight inconvenience and a short detention period, there is no intent on the part of the law enforcement officer to deprive the suspect of her or his freedom. Therefore, there is no arrest. As *intent* is a subjective term, it is sometimes difficult to determine whether the police officer intended to arrest. In situations when the intent is unclear, courts often rely—as in our hypothetical case of Mr. Smith—on the perception of the arrestee.[64]
2. The *authority* to arrest. State laws give police officers the authority to place citizens under custodial arrest, or take them into *custody*, a concept defined later in the chapter.
3. *Seizure or detention.* A necessary part of an arrest is the detention of the subject. Detention is considered to have occurred as soon as the arrested individual submits to the control of the officer, whether peacefully or under the threat or use of force.
4. The *understanding* of the person that she or he has been arrested. Through either words—such as "you are now under arrest"—or actions, the person taken into custody must understand that an arrest has taken place. When a suspect has been forcibly subdued by the police, handcuffed, and placed in a patrol car, he or she is believed to understand that an arrest has been made. This understanding may be lacking if the person is intoxicated, insane, or unconscious.[65]

Arrest Warrant A written order, based on probable cause and issued by a judge or magistrate, commanding that the person named on the warrant be arrested by the police.

LO6-4 List the four elements that must be present for an arrest to take place.

6-4b Arrests with a Warrant

When law enforcement officers have established probable cause to arrest an individual who is not in police custody, they obtain an **arrest warrant** for that person. An arrest warrant, similar to a search warrant, contains information such as the name of the person suspected and the crime he or she is suspected of having committed. (See Figure 6.4 for an example of an arrest warrant.) Judges or magistrates issue arrest warrants after first determining that the law enforcement officers have indeed established probable cause.

ENTERING A DWELLING There is a perception that an arrest warrant gives law enforcement officers the authority

FIGURE 6.4 EXAMPLE OF AN ARREST WARRANT

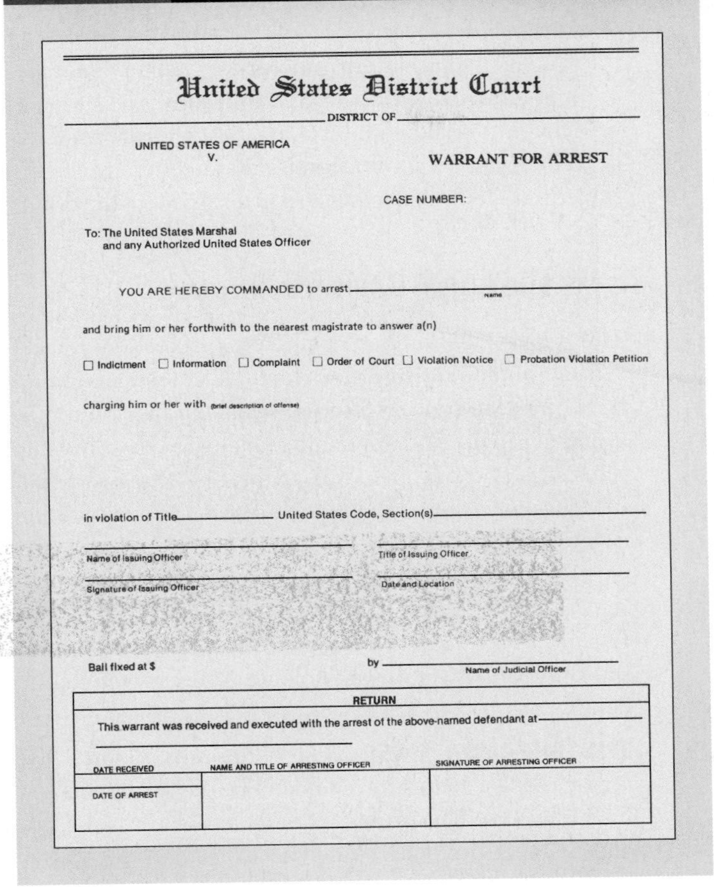
United States District Court

DISTRICT OF

UNITED STATES OF AMERICA
V.

WARRANT FOR ARREST

CASE NUMBER:

To: The United States Marshal
and any Authorized United States Officer

YOU ARE HEREBY COMMANDED to arrest ____ Name

and bring him or her forthwith to the nearest magistrate to answer a(n)

☐ Indictment ☐ Information ☐ Complaint ☐ Order of Court ☐ Violation Notice ☐ Probation Violation Petition

charging him or her with (brief description of offense)

in violation of Title ____ United States Code, Section(s) ____

Name of Issuing Officer — Title of Issuing Officer

Signature of Issuing Officer — Date and Location

Bail fixed at $ ____ by ____ Name of Judicial Officer

RETURN		
This warrant was received and executed with the arrest of the above-named defendant at		
DATE RECEIVED	NAME AND TITLE OF ARRESTING OFFICER	SIGNATURE OF ARRESTING OFFICER
DATE OF ARREST		

to enter a dwelling without first announcing themselves. This is not accurate. In *Wilson v. Arkansas* (1995),[66] the Supreme Court reiterated the common law requirement that police officers must knock and announce their identity and purpose before entering a dwelling.

Under certain conditions, known as **exigent circumstances,** law enforcement officers need not announce themselves. As determined by the courts, these circumstances arise when officers have a reasonable belief of any of the following:

- The suspect is armed and poses a strong threat of violence to the officers or others inside the dwelling.
- Persons inside the dwelling are in the process of destroying evidence or escaping because of the presence of the police.
- A felony is being committed at the time the officers enter.[67]

THE WAITING PERIOD The Supreme Court severely weakened the practical impact of the "knock-and-announce" rule with its decision in *Hudson v. Michigan* (2006).[68] In that case, Detroit police did not knock before entering the defendant's home with a warrant. Instead, they announced themselves and then waited only three to five seconds before making their entrance, not the fifteen to twenty seconds suggested by a prior Court ruling.[69] Hudson argued that the drugs found during the subsequent search were inadmissible because the law enforcement agents did not follow proper procedure.

By a 5–4 margin, the Court disagreed. In his majority opinion, Justice Antonin Scalia stated that an improper "knock and announce" is not unreasonable enough to provide defendants with a "get-out-of-jail-free card" by disqualifying evidence uncovered on the basis of a valid search warrant.[70] In other words, the exclusionary rule does not apply. Legal experts still advise, however, that police observe a reasonable waiting period after knocking and announcing to be certain that any evidence found during the subsequent search will stand up in court.[71]

IMPROPER STOPS AND ARRESTS What if a police officer makes a stop without reasonable suspicion, and that stop leads to a valid arrest? The Supreme Court addressed this issue in *Utah v. Strieff* (2016).[72] The case arose when a South Salt Lake, Utah, police officer stopped Edward Strieff as Strieff was leaving a house under surveillance for "narcotics activity." As often happens after a stop, the officer ran a warrant check and found that Strieff was wanted for a minor traffic violation. The officer arrested Strieff and, searching him, found a baggie containing illegal drugs.

Because no reasonable suspicion supported the initial stop, Strieff's lawyers argued that this evidence should be suppressed under the exclusionary rule. The Supreme Court reasoned, however, that the goal of the exclusionary rule is to deter *deliberate* police misconduct. In this situation, as Justice Clarence Thomas noted, the officer was "at most negligent."[73] Therefore, the Court ruled that the illegal drugs found on Strieff were admissible, creating what could be called a "negligence" exception to the exclusionary rule. Disagreeing with the majority opinion, Justice Sonia Sotomayor argued that "the Fourth Amendment does not tolerate an officer's unreasonable searches and seizures just because he did not know any better."[74]

6-4c Arrests without a Warrant

Arrest warrants are not always required, and in fact, most arrests are made on the scene without a warrant. A law enforcement

Exigent Circumstances
Situations that require extralegal or exceptional actions by the police.

officer may make a **warrantless arrest** in any of these circumstances:

1. The offense is committed in the presence of the officer.
2. The officer has probable cause to believe that the suspect has committed a particular crime.
3. The time lost in obtaining a warrant would allow the suspect to escape or destroy evidence, and the officer has probable cause to make an arrest.[75]

The type of crime also comes to bear. As a general rule, officers can make a warrantless arrest for a crime they did not see if they have probable cause to believe that a felony has been committed. For misdemeanors, the crime must have been committed in the presence of the officer.

According to a 2001 Supreme Court ruling, even an arrest for a misdemeanor that involves "gratuitous humiliations" imposed by a police officer "exercising extremely poor judgment" is valid as long as the officer can satisfy probable cause requirements.[76] That case involved a Texas mother who was handcuffed, taken away from her two young children, and placed in jail for failing to wear her seat belt.

6-5 WHAT ARE THE *MIRANDA* RIGHTS?

Warrantless Arrest An arrest made without a warrant for the action.

Interrogation The direct questioning of a suspect to gather evidence of criminal activity and to try to gain a confession.

Admission A statement acknowledging that certain facts concerning a crime are true but falling short of a confession.

Confession A statement acknowledging that the suspect participated in some aspect of a crime.

Coercion The use of physical force or mental intimidation to compel a person to do something—such as confess to committing a crime—against her or his will.

***Miranda* Rights** The constitutional rights of accused persons taken into custody by law enforcement officials, including the right to remain silent and the right to counsel.

After the Pledge of Allegiance, there is perhaps no recitation that comes more readily to the American mind than the *Miranda* warning:

> You have the right to remain silent. If you give up that right, anything you say can and will be used against you in a court of law. You have the right to speak with an attorney and to have the attorney present during questioning. If you so desire and cannot afford one, an attorney will be appointed for you without charge before questioning.

The *Miranda* warning is not a mere prop. It strongly affects one of the most important aspects of any criminal investigation—the **interrogation,** or questioning of a suspect from whom the police want to get information concerning a crime.

The goal of an interrogation is to gain an *admission* or, preferably, a *confession*. An **admission** is a statement verifying information about some aspect of the underlying crime, while a **confession** is a statement in which the subject admits to being involved in an aspect of the crime.

6-5a The Legal Basis for *Miranda*

The Fifth Amendment guarantees protection against self-incrimination. In other words, a defendant cannot be required to provide information about his or her own criminal activity. A defendant's choice *not* to incriminate himself or herself cannot be interpreted as a sign of guilt by a jury in a criminal trial. A confession is by definition a statement of self-incrimination.

How, then, to reconcile the Fifth Amendment with the critical need of law enforcement officers to gain confessions? The answer lies in the concept of **coercion,** or the use of physical or psychological duress to obtain a confession.

THE *MIRANDA* CASE The Supreme Court first asserted that a confession could not be physically coerced in a 1936 case concerning a defendant who was beaten and whipped until he confessed to a murder.[77] It was not until 1966, however, that the Court handed down its landmark decision in *Miranda v. Arizona*.[78]

The case involved Ernesto Miranda, a produce worker who had been arrested three years earlier in Phoenix and charged with kidnapping and rape. Detectives questioned Miranda for two hours before gaining a confession of guilt. At no time was Miranda informed that he had a right to have a lawyer present. The Court overturned Miranda's conviction, stating that police interrogations are, by their very nature, coercive and therefore deny suspects their constitutional right against self-incrimination by "forcing" them to confess.

***MIRANDA* RIGHTS** The ***Miranda* rights,** established in this case, are based on what University of Columbia law professor H. Richard Uviller called *inherent coercion*. This term refers to the assumption that even if a police officer does not lay a hand on a suspect, the general atmosphere of an interrogation is in and of itself coercive.[79]

Though the *Miranda* case is best remembered for the procedural requirement it established, at the time the Supreme Court was more concerned about the treatment of suspects during interrogation. The Court found that routine police interrogation strategies, such as leaving suspects alone in a room for several hours before questioning them, were inherently coercive.

Therefore, the Court reasoned, every suspect needed protection from coercion, not just those who had been physically abused. The *Miranda* warning is a result of this need. In theory, if the warning is not given to a suspect before an interrogation, the fruits of that interrogation, including a confession, are invalid.

Joe Raedle/Getty Images News/Getty Images

Study the details of this photo of a Miami Beach, Florida, police officer and a suspect. **Why must the officer "Mirandize" the suspect before asking her any questions, even if the officer never formally places the suspect under arrest?**

6-5b When a *Miranda* Warning Is Required

As we shall see, a *Miranda* warning is not always necessary. Generally, *Miranda* requirements apply only when a suspect is in **custody.** In a series of rulings since *Miranda*, the Supreme Court has defined custody as an arrest or a situation in which a reasonable person would not feel free to leave.[80] Consequently, a **custodial interrogation** occurs when a suspect is under arrest or is deprived of her or his freedom in a significant manner.

A *Miranda* warning is required before a custodial interrogation takes place. Thus, if four police officers enter a suspect's bedroom at 4:00 A.M., wake him, and form a circle around him, then they must give him a *Miranda* warning before questioning. Even though the suspect has not been arrested, he will "not feel free to go where he please[s]."[81]

6-5c When a *Miranda* Warning Is Not Required

A *Miranda* warning is not necessary in a number of situations:

LO6-5 Indicate situations in which a *Miranda* warning is unnecessary.

1. When the police do not ask the suspect any questions that are *testimonial* in nature. Such questions are designed to elicit information that may be used against the suspect in court. Note that "routine booking questions," such as the suspect's name, address, height, and eye color, do not require a *Miranda* warning. Even though answering these questions may provide incriminating evidence, the Supreme Court has held that they are absolutely necessary if the police are to do their jobs.[82] (Imagine the officer not being able to ask a suspect her or his name.)
2. When the police have not focused on a suspect and are questioning witnesses at the scene of a crime.
3. When a person volunteers information before the police have asked a question.
4. When the suspect has given a private statement to a friend or some other acquaintance. *Miranda* does not apply to these statements so long as the government did not orchestrate the situation.
5. During a stop and frisk, when no arrest has been made.
6. During a traffic stop.[83]

In 1984, the Supreme Court also created a "public-safety exception" to the *Miranda* rule. The case involved a police officer who, after feeling an empty shoulder holster on a man he had just arrested, asked the suspect the location of the gun without informing him of his *Miranda* rights. The Court ruled that the gun was admissible as evidence because the police's duty to protect the public is more important than a suspect's *Miranda* rights.[84]

In 2013, federal law enforcement agents relied on this exception to question Boston Marathon bomber Dzhokhar Tsarnaev from his hospital bedside without first "Mirandizing" him.

Custody The forceful detention of a person or the person's perception that he or she is not free to leave the immediate vicinity.

Custodial Interrogation The questioning of a suspect after that person has been taken into custody.

Once the agents were satisfied that Tsarnaev knew of no other active plots or threats to public safety, they read the suspect his *Miranda* rights in the presence of a lawyer.[85]

WAIVING *MIRANDA* Suspects can *waive* their Fifth Amendment rights and speak to a police officer, but only if the waiver is made voluntarily. Silence on the part of a suspect does not mean that his or her *Miranda* protections have been relinquished. To waive their rights, suspects must state—either in writing or orally—that they understand those rights and that they will voluntarily answer questions without the presence of counsel.

To ensure that the suspect's rights are upheld, prosecutors are required to prove by a preponderance of the evidence that the suspect "knowingly and intelligently" waived his or her *Miranda* rights.[86] To make the waiver perfectly clear, police will ask suspects two questions in addition to giving the *Miranda* warning:

1. Do you understand your rights as I have read them to you?
2. Knowing your rights, are you willing to talk to another law enforcement officer or me?

If the suspect indicates that she or he does not want to speak to the officer, thereby invoking her or his right to silence, the officer must *immediately* stop any questioning.[87] Similarly, if the suspect requests a lawyer, the police can ask no further questions until an attorney is present.[88]

CLEAR INTENT The suspect must be absolutely clear about her or his intention to stop the questioning or have a lawyer present. In *Davis v. United States* (1994),[89] the Supreme Court upheld the interrogation of a suspect after he said, "Maybe I should talk to a lawyer." The Court found that this statement was too ambiguous, explaining that police officers should not be required to "read the minds" of suspects who make vague declarations.

Along these same lines, in *Berghuis v. Thompkins* (2010),[90] the Court upheld the conviction of a suspect

CAREER PREP

Detective

Job Description:

- **Collect evidence and obtain facts pertaining to criminal cases.**
- **Conduct interviews, observe suspects, examine records, and help with raids and busts. Some detectives are assigned to multiagency task forces that deal with specific types of crime, like drug trafficking or gang activity.**

What Kind of Training Is Required?

- **Two to five years of experience as a police officer are required before taking the test to become a detective.**
- **Larger departments require sixty units of college credit or an associate's degree.**

Annual Salary Range?

- **$48,000–$98,000**

iStockPhoto.com/Karen Mower

GETTING LINKEDIN
The most common detective position offered on LinkedIn is in the field of "loss prevention," which, as you learned in Chapter 4, involves preventing shoplifting at private businesses. Like public law enforcement officers, loss prevention detectives "utilize CCTV equipment," "use the latest in advanced interviewing and interrogation techniques," and "work independently," to quote a posting from a retail store in Hampshire County, Massachusetts.

who implicated himself in a murder after remaining mostly silent during nearly three hours of police questioning. The defendant claimed that he had invoked his *Miranda* rights by being uncommunicative with the interrogating officers. The Court disagreed, saying that silence is not enough—a suspect must actually state that he or she wishes to cut off questioning for the *Miranda* protections to apply.

Rudy Matchinga/Shutterstock.com

For the most part, interviews of criminal suspects in American police interrogation rooms such as this one are based on the premise that the person being interrogated is guilty of a crime. **Why do you agree or disagree with this strategy? What are some of its benefits and drawbacks?**

6-5d False Confessions

While observing more than two hundred interrogations over a nine-month period in northern California, University of San Francisco law professor Richard Leo noted that more than 80 percent of the suspects waived their *Miranda* rights.[91] Apparently, the suspects wanted to appear cooperative, a "willingness to please" that contributes to the troubling phenomenon of *false confessions* in the American criminal justice system.

COERCION AND FALSE CONFESSIONS

A **false confession** occurs when a suspect admits to a crime that she or he did not actually commit. Given that juries tend to place a great deal of weight on confessions, sometimes to the exclusion of other evidence, false confessions can have disastrous consequences for the defendant in court.[92] About one in four wrongful convictions overturned by DNA evidence resulted at least partially from a false confession.[93]

The Reid Technique According to Saul Kassin, a professor of psychology at Williams College in Williamstown, Massachusetts, there are three general types of false confessions:

1. *Voluntary.* The suspect is seeking attention, or is delusional and thinks he or she did commit the crime.
2. *Internalized.* The suspect is a vulnerable person, suffering from the stress of the interrogation, who comes to believe that he or she committed the crime.
3. *Compliant.* The suspect knows he or she is innocent, but decides—under police influence—that it is in his or her best interests to confess to the crime.

Kassin believes that the last two categories of false confessions are often "coerced."[94]

Indeed, the Reid Technique, used widely by American law enforcement, is premised on the assumption that all interrogation subjects are guilty. Police officers trained in this method reject any denials during the interrogation. They are also taught to minimize the moral seriousness of the crime, and to present the suspect's actions as the lesser of two evils. ("Was this your idea, or did your buddies talk you into it?") When the suspect finally does admit to the crime, he or she is to be congratulated and immediately asked for corroborating details.[95]

Pressure Points Critics believe that the Reid Technique creates feelings of helplessness in the suspect and turns a confession into an "escape hatch" from the unpleasantness of the interrogation.[96] In 1985, for example, after forty hours of questioning with no attorney present, eighteen-year-old Christopher Abernathy, who was learning disabled, signed a written confession to having killed fifteen-year-old Kristina Hickey.

Almost immediately, Abernathy disavowed the confession, saying that he only made it because the interrogating officers said doing so was the only way he could go home and see his mother. Nonetheless, he was eventually sentenced

False Confession A confession of guilt when the confessor did not, in fact, commit the crime.

ETHICS CHALLENGE

Several years ago, police in Troy, New York, told a suspect that his son's life could be saved only if the suspect explained how the boy had injured his head. In fact, the child was already brain dead, which the suspect did not know when he admitted to slamming his son's head against a mattress. Law enforcement agents can use deception when interviewing suspects to gain a confession. Even so, did the Troy police behave ethically in this instance? Explain your answer.

to life in prison for the crime. Abernathy stayed behind bars until 2015, when a Cook County (Illinois) judge dismissed the charges against him based on the initial coercive questioning and more recent DNA evidence showing that someone else most likely killed Hickey.[97]

Another potential problem with the Reid Technique, noted earlier, is that it is predicated on the assumption that the suspect is guilty.[98] Because both guilty and innocent suspects show stress when being interrogated by police, the interrogator may be "fooled" by an innocent person's evasive and nervous behavior.

RECORDING CONFESSIONS The mandatory videotaping of interrogations has been offered as a means to promote police accountability. Nineteen states, as well as federal agencies such as the Bureau of Alcohol, Tobacco, Firearms and Explosives, the Federal Bureau of Investigation, and the U.S. Marshals Service, mandate the recording of interrogations for certain felonies.[99]

In theory, such recordings will make clear any improper tactics used by law enforcement to gain a confession. In reality, this strategy might not live up to reformers' expectations. As Professor Jennifer Mnookin of the University of California, Los Angeles, points out, there is no guarantee that "judges or jurors can actually tell the difference between true and false confessions, even with the more complete record of interactions that recorded interrogations provide."[100]

STUDY TOOLS 6

LOCATED IN TEXTBOOK

- ☐ Rip out the Chapter Review Card.
- ☐ Review with the Chapter Quiz following this chapter.

LOCATED AT WWW.CENGAGEBRAIN.COM

- ☐ Review key terms flash cards.
- ☐ Read the chapter on all your favorite devices.
- ☐ Complete an Exam to test your knowledge.
- ☐ Check out Visual Summaries and You Decide activities to explore chapter concepts.

Quiz

1. The Fourth Amendment has been interpreted to require ____________ ____________ that a crime has been or will be committed before a search warrant can be issued.

2. Judges rely on the ____________ rule to keep evidence that has been improperly obtained by the police out of criminal courts.

3. A search is a government intrusion on the ____________ of an individual.

4. Law enforcement agents do not need a judge's prior approval to conduct a search if the subject of the search gives her or his ____________.

5. A police officer can "stop" a suspect if the officer has a ____________ suspicion that a criminal act is taking place or is about to take place.

6. Following a stop, a police officer may ____________ the suspect for weapons as a protective measure.

7. An arrest occurs when a law enforcement officer takes a suspect into ____________ on a criminal charge.

8. If a police officer has prior knowledge of a suspect's criminal activity, he or she must obtain a ____________ from a judge or magistrate before arresting the suspect.

9. In most instances, a *Miranda* warning must be read to a suspect ____________ a custodial interrogation takes place.

10. A suspect can ____________ her or his *Miranda* rights, but this must be done "knowingly and intentionally."

Answers to the Chapter 6 Quiz can be found in the Answers section in the back of the book.

7 Courts and the Quest for Justice

trekandshoot/Shutterstock.com

LEARNING OBJECTIVES

After studying this chapter, you will be able to . . .

- **7-1** Define *jurisdiction* and contrast geographic and subject-matter jurisdiction.
- **7-2** Explain the difference between trial and appellate courts.
- **7-3** Explain briefly how a case is brought to the United States Supreme Court.
- **7-4** List the different names given to public prosecutors, and indicate the general powers they have.
- **7-5** Explain why defense attorneys must often defend clients they know to be guilty.

After finishing this chapter, go to **PAGE 153** for **STUDY TOOLS**

Text Message

"When are you doing it?" seventeen-year-old Michelle Carter asked her eighteen-year-old boyfriend, Carter Roy, in one of the thousands of texts the two shared. "You always say you're gonna do it, but you never do." On July 13, 2014, Roy finally did "it," committing suicide by carbon monoxide poisoning in his truck behind a Fairhaven, Massachusetts, KMart. Earlier that day, Carter had texted to Roy, "Tonight is the night," and "It's painless and quick." Furthermore, the two were speaking on the phone when Roy got out of his truck, afraid that the carbon monoxide was working. "I [expletive] told him to get back in," Carter apparently later admitted to a friend.

No criminal statute in Massachusetts applies specifically to Carter's behavior. Nonetheless, Bristol County prosecutors charged her with involuntary manslaughter for "strongly influencing" and "encouraging" Roy to commit suicide. New England School of Law professor David Siegel called the charge "a square peg in a round hole," noting that the state would need to prove that, with her goading, Carter consciously disregarded a "substantial and unjustifiable" risk of causing Roy's death. "What we have here is a young man who made a voluntary decision to end his own life," argued Joseph Cataldo, Carter's defense attorney. "His death was not caused by Michelle Carter."

According to Professor Siegel, prosecutors wanted to use the courts to "send a message" that, despite the lack of a specific law prohibiting it, Carter's behavior was unacceptable. In April 2016, a Massachusetts appeals court seemed to agree. Rejecting the defense's claim that no crime had taken place, the court ruled that there was sufficient evidence of a "direct, causal link" between Carter's actions and Roy's death for the case to go to trial. Thirteen months later, Juvenile Court Judge Lawrence Moniz determined that Carter created and then failed to set right the "toxic environment" that led to Roy's death, and found her guilty of involuntary manslaughter.

Michelle Carter, shown here in a Taunton, Massachusetts, courtroom, was convicted of involuntary manslaughter for encouraging her boyfriend to kill himself. "It's a sad story, a tragedy, but it's not manslaughter," said Carter's defense attorney of the charges. *Do you agree? Why or why not?*

AP Images/Patrick Whittemore/The Boston Herald

7-1 WHAT ROLE DO COURTS PLAY IN SOCIETY?

After the Massachusetts appeals court ruled that Michelle Carter's manslaughter trial could move forward, Carter Roy's family expressed a sense of relieved anticipation. "I hope that justice will be served," said Roy's grandfather, Conrad Roy, Sr.[1]

Famed jurist Roscoe Pound once characterized "justice" as society's demand "that serious offenders be convicted and punished," while at the same time "the innocent and unfortunate are not oppressed."[2] This somewhat idealistic definition obscures the fact that there are two sides to each court proceeding. While Roy, Sr., understandably has strong feelings about Carter's fate, American legal traditions allow a person accused of any crime, no matter how heinous, the chance to prove his or her innocence before a neutral decision maker. On a practical level, then, a court is a place where arguments are settled. At best, the court provides a just environment in which the basis of the argument can be decided through the application of the law.

Courts have extensive powers in our criminal justice system: They can bring to bear the authority of the state to seize property and to restrict individual liberty. Given that the rights to own property and to enjoy personal freedom are enshrined in the U.S. Constitution, a court's *legitimacy* in taking such measures must be unquestioned by society.

This legitimacy is based on two factors: impartiality and independence.[3] In theory, each party involved in a courtroom dispute must have an equal chance to present its case and must be secure in the belief that no outside factors are going to influence the decision rendered by the court. In reality, as we shall see over the next three chapters, it does not always work that way.

7-1a Due Process and Crime Control in the Courts

As mentioned earlier, the criminal justice system has two sets of underlying values: due process and crime control. Due process values focus on protecting the rights of the individual, whereas crime control values stress the punishment and repression of criminal conduct. The competing nature of these two value systems is often evident in the nation's courts.

THE DUE PROCESS FUNCTION The primary concern of early American courts was to protect the rights of the individual against the power of the state. Memories of injustices suffered at the hands of the British monarchy were still strong, and most of the procedural rules that we have discussed in this textbook were created with the express purpose of giving the individual a "fair chance" against the government in any courtroom proceedings.

Therefore, the due process function of the courts is to protect individuals from the unfair advantages that the government—with its immense resources—automatically enjoys in legal battles. Seen in this light, constitutional guarantees such as the right to counsel, the right to a jury trial, and protection from self-incrimination are equalizers in the "contest" between the state and the individual.

THE CRIME CONTROL FUNCTION Advocates of crime control distinguish between the court's obligation to be fair to the accused and its obligation to be fair to society. The crime control function of the courts emphasizes punishment and retribution—criminals must suffer for the harm done to society, and it is the courts' responsibility to see that they do so. Given this responsibility to protect the public, deter criminal behavior, and "get criminals off the streets," the courts should not be concerned solely with giving the accused a fair chance.

Rather than using due process rules as "equalizers," then, the courts should use them as protection against blatantly unconstitutional acts. For example, a detective who beats a suspect with a tire iron to get a confession has obviously infringed on the suspect's constitutional rights. If, however, the detective uses trickery to gain a confession, the court should allow the confession to stand because it is not in society's interest that law enforcement agents be deterred from outwitting criminals.

7-1b The Rehabilitation Function

A third view of the court's responsibility is based on the "medical model" of the criminal justice system. In this model, criminals are analogous to patients, and the courts perform the role of physicians who dispense "treatment."[4] The criminal is seen as sick, not evil, and therefore treatment is morally justified.

AP Images/The Press of Atlantic City, Dale Gerhard

Why is it important that American criminal courtrooms, such as this one in Cape May, New Jersey, are places of impartiality and independence?

Of course, treatment varies from case to case, and some criminals require harsh penalties such as incarceration. In other cases, however, it may not be in society's best interest for the criminal to be punished according to the formal rules of the justice system. Perhaps the criminal can be rehabilitated to become a productive member of society and thus save taxpayers the costs of incarceration or other punishment.

7-1c The Bureaucratic Function

To a certain extent, the crime control, due process, and rehabilitation functions of a court are secondary to its bureaucratic function. In general, a court may have the goal of protecting society or protecting the rights of the individual, but on a day-to-day basis that court has the more pressing task of dealing with the cases brought before it.

Like any bureaucracy, a court is concerned with speed and efficiency, and loftier concepts such as justice can be secondary to a judge's need to wrap up a particular case before six o'clock so that administrative deadlines can be met. Indeed, many observers feel that the primary adversarial relationship in the courts is not between the two parties involved but between the ideal of justice and the reality of bureaucratic limitations.[5]

7-2 HOW DO AMERICAN COURTS OPERATE?

One of the most often cited limitations of the American judicial system is its complex nature. In truth, the United States does not have a single judicial system, but fifty-two different systems—one for each state, the District of Columbia, and the federal government.

As each state has its own unique judiciary with its own set of rules, some of which may conflict with the federal judiciary, it is helpful at this point to discuss some basics—the concept of jurisdiction, trial and appellate courts, and the dual court system.

7-2a Jurisdiction

In Latin, *juris* means "law," and *diction* means "to speak." Thus, **jurisdiction** literally refers to the power "to speak the law." Before any court can hear a case, it must have jurisdiction over the persons involved in the case or its subject matter. The jurisdiction of every court, even the United States Supreme Court, is limited in some way.

LO7-1 Define *jurisdiction* and contrast geographic and subject-matter jurisdiction.

GEOGRAPHIC JURISDICTION One limitation is geographic. Generally, a court can exercise its authority over residents of a certain area. A state trial court, for example, normally has jurisdictional authority over crimes committed in a particular area of the state, such as a county or a district. A state's highest court (often called the state supreme court) has jurisdictional authority over the entire state, and the United States Supreme Court has jurisdiction over the entire country.

For the most part, criminal jurisdiction is determined by legislation. The U.S. Congress or a state legislature can determine what acts are illegal within the geographic boundaries it controls, thus giving federal or state courts jurisdiction over those crimes.

Federal versus State Jurisdiction Most criminal laws are state laws, so the majority of all criminal trials are heard in state courts. Many acts that are illegal under state law, however, are also illegal under federal law. What happens when more than one court system has jurisdiction over the same criminal act?

As a general rule, when Congress "criminalizes" behavior that is already prohibited under a state criminal code, the federal and state courts both have jurisdiction over that crime unless Congress indicates otherwise in the initial legislation. Thus, **concurrent jurisdiction,** which occurs when two different court systems have simultaneous jurisdiction over the same case, is quite common.

For instance, both the federal courts and the South Carolina state court system have jurisdiction over Dylann Roof, who killed nine African American parishioners during bible study at a Charleston church in June 2015. South Carolina does not have a hate crimes law, and federal officials felt that the racial component of Roof's actions needed to be addressed. Thus, the federal government decided to pursue the case. In January 2017, a federal judge sentenced Roof to be executed after he was found guilty of, among other counts, federal hate crimes resulting in death. Three months later, South Carolina authorities allowed Roof to plead guilty to all related state charges, clearing the way for the defendant to begin his imprisonment on federal death row.[6]

Jurisdiction The authority of a court to hear and decide cases within an area of the law or a geographic territory.

Concurrent Jurisdiction The situation that occurs when two or more courts have the authority to preside over the same criminal case.

Susana Gonzalez/Bloomberg/Getty Images

In 2017, Mexico extradited notorious drug trafficker Joaquin "El Chapo" Guzman, shown here with Mexican security forces, to the United States. **Should the possibility that Guzman was responsible for distributing large amounts of cocaine into this country give the American court system jurisdiction over him? Why or why not?**

State versus State Jurisdiction Multiple states can also claim jurisdiction over the same defendant or criminal act, depending on state legislation and the circumstances of the crime. For example, if Billy is standing in State A and shoots Frances, who is standing in State B, the two states could have concurrent jurisdiction to try Billy for murder.

Similarly, if a property theft takes place in State A but police recover the stolen goods in State B, concurrent jurisdiction could exist. Some states have also passed laws stating that they have jurisdiction over their own citizens who commit crimes in other states, even if there is no other connection between the home state and the criminal act.[7]

The concept of jurisdiction encourages states to cooperate with each other regarding fugitives from the law. In 2016, for example, Cody Masiello was suspected by authorities of carjacking a driver at gunpoint in Seaside Heights, New Jersey. About three weeks after the alleged crime, Pennsylvania state troopers arrested Masiello across the state line in Saylorsburg. Pennsylvania officials subsequently *extradited* Masiello back to New Jersey to face the carjacking charges. **Extradition** is the formal process by which one legal authority, such as a state or a nation, transfers a fugitive or a suspect to another legal authority that has a valid claim on that person.

Extradition The process by which one jurisdiction surrenders a person accused or convicted of violating another jurisdiction's criminal law to the second jurisdiction.

INTERNATIONAL JURISDICTION Under international law, each country has the right to create and enact criminal law for its territory. Therefore, the notion that a nation has jurisdiction over any crimes committed within its borders is well established. The situation becomes more delicate when one nation feels the need to go outside its own territory to enforce its criminal law. International precedent does, however, provide several bases for expanding jurisdiction across international borders.

For example, antiterrorism efforts have been guided by the principle that the United States has jurisdiction over persons who commit crimes against Americans even when the former are citizens of foreign countries and live outside the United States. In 2016, Spanish authorities agreed to extradite Ali Charaf Damache to the United States because of charges that he had recruited U.S. citizens to engage in international terrorist activities. Furthermore, some behavior, such as piracy and genocide, is considered a crime against all nations collectively and, according to *universal jurisdiction*, can be prosecuted by any nation having custody of the wrongdoer.

SUBJECT-MATTER JURISDICTION Jurisdiction over subject matter also acts as a limitation on the types of cases a court can hear. State court systems include courts of *general* (unlimited) *jurisdiction* and courts of *limited jurisdiction*. Courts of general jurisdiction have no restrictions on the subject matter they may address. These courts deal with the most serious felonies and civil cases. Courts of limited jurisdiction, also known as lower courts, handle misdemeanors and civil matters under a certain amount, usually $1,000.

Many states have created special subject-matter courts that only dispose of cases involving a specific crime. For example, a number of jurisdictions have established drug courts to handle an overload of illicit narcotics arrests. Furthermore, under the Uniform Code of Military Justice, the U.S. military has jurisdiction over active personnel who commit crimes, even if those crimes occur outside the course of duty.[8] In such cases, military officials can either attempt to *court-martial* the suspect in military court or allow civilian prosecutors to handle the case in state or federal court.

CAREER TIP For those interested in both a military and a law enforcement career, the *U.S. Army's Criminal Investigation Command* is responsible for investigating crimes involving military personnel.

7-2b Trial and Appellate Courts

LO7-2 Explain the difference between trial and appellate courts.

Another distinction is between courts of original jurisdiction and courts of appellate, or review, jurisdiction. Courts having *original jurisdiction* are courts of the first instance, or **trial courts.** Almost every case begins in a trial court. It is in this court that a trial (or a guilty plea) takes place, and the judge imposes a sentence if the defendant is found guilty. Trial courts are primarily concerned with *questions of fact*. They are designed to determine exactly what events occurred that are relevant to questions of the defendant's guilt or innocence.

Courts having *appellate jurisdiction* act as reviewing courts, or **appellate courts.** In general, cases can be brought before appellate courts only on appeal by one of the parties in the trial court. (Note that because of constitutional protections against being tried twice for the same crime, prosecutors who lose in criminal trial court cannot appeal the verdict.) An appellate court does not use juries or witnesses to reach its decision. Instead, its judges make a decision on whether the lower court's ruling should be *affirmed* or *reversed*. If the ruling is reversed, it may also be *remanded* (sent back to the original court for a new trial). Appellate judges present written explanations for their decisions, and these **opinions** of the court are the basis for a great deal of the precedent in the criminal justice system.

It is important to understand that appellate courts do not determine the defendant's guilt or innocence—they make judgments only on questions of procedure. In other words, they are concerned with *questions of law* and normally accept the facts as established by the trial court. Only rarely will an appeals court question a jury's decision. Instead, the appellate judges will review how the facts and evidence were provided to the jury and rule on whether errors were made in the process.

7-2c The Dual Court System

America's system of federalism allows the federal government and the governments of the fifty states to hold separate authority in many areas. As a result, the federal government and each of the fifty states, as well as the District of Columbia, have their own separate court systems. Because of the split between the federal courts and the state courts, the United States is said to have a **dual court system.** (See Figure 7.1 to get a better idea of how federal and state courts operate as distinct yet parallel entities.)

Federal and state courts both have limited jurisdiction. Generally, federal courts preside over cases involving violations of federal law, and state courts preside over cases involving violations of state law. The distinction is not always clear, however. Federal courts have jurisdiction over nearly five thousand crimes, many of which also can be found in state criminal codes.

As we saw earlier in this section, when such *concurrent jurisdiction* exists, both sides can try the defendant under their own laws, or one side can step aside and let the other decide the fate of the defendant. Because the federal court system has greater resources than most state court systems, federal criminal charges often take precedence over state criminal charges for practical reasons.

7-3 HOW DO STATES ORGANIZE THEIR COURTS?

Typically, a state court system includes several levels, or tiers, of courts. State courts may include:

1. Lower courts, or courts of limited jurisdiction.
2. Trial courts of general jurisdiction.
3. Appellate courts.
4. The state's highest court.

As previously mentioned, each state has a different judicial structure,

Trial Courts Courts in which most cases begin and in which questions of fact are examined.

Appellate Courts Courts that review decisions made by lower courts, such as trial courts; also known as *courts of appeals*.

Opinions Written statements by appellate judges expressing the reasons for the court's decision in a case.

Dual Court System The separate but interrelated court system of the United States, made up of the courts on the national level and the courts on the state level.

FIGURE 7.1 THE DUAL COURT SYSTEM

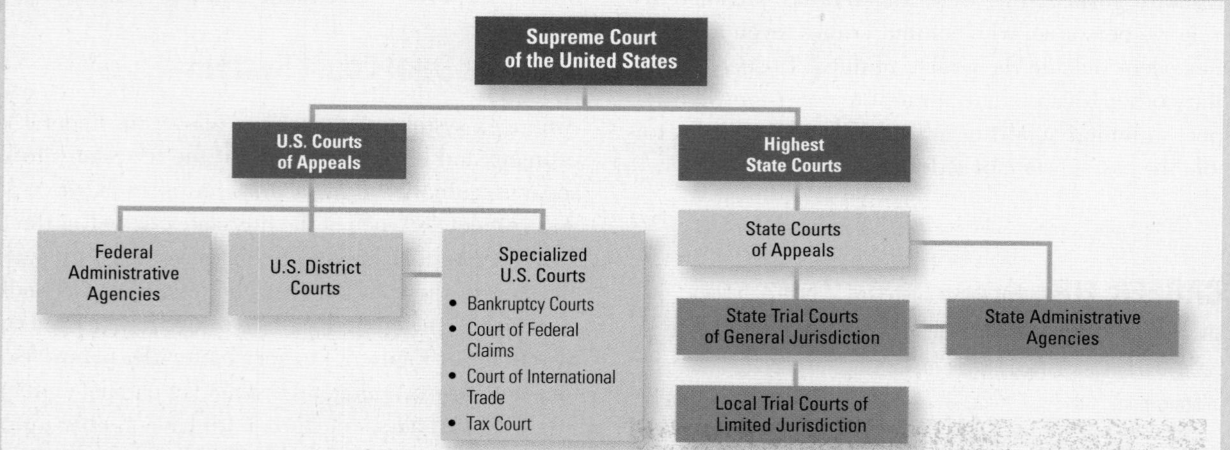

in which different courts have different jurisdictions, but there are enough similarities to allow for a general discussion. Figure 7.2 shows a typical state court system.

7-3a Courts of Limited Jurisdiction

Most states have local trial courts that are limited to trying cases involving minor criminal matters, such as traffic violations, prostitution, and drunk and disorderly conduct. Although these minor courts sometimes keep no written record of the trial proceedings and cases are decided by a judge rather than a jury, defendants have the same rights as in other trial courts.

Most minor criminal cases are decided in these lower courts. Courts of limited jurisdiction can also be responsible for the preliminary stages of felony cases. Arraignments, bail hearings, and preliminary hearings often take place in these lower courts.

MAGISTRATE COURTS **Magistrates,** or, in some states, municipal court judges, preside over courts whose jurisdiction is limited to disputes between private individuals and to crimes punishable by small fines or short jail terms. In certain regions, such as rural areas, *justices of the peace* perform a similar function. In most jurisdictions, magistrates are responsible for providing law enforcement agents with search and seizure warrants.

Magistrates A public civil officer or official with limited judicial authority within a particular geographic area, such as the authority to issue an arrest warrant.

Problem-Solving Courts Lower courts that have jurisdiction over one specific area of criminal activity, such as illegal drugs or domestic violence.

SPECIALTY COURTS As mentioned earlier, many states have created courts that have jurisdiction over very narrowly defined areas of criminal justice. These so-called **problem-solving courts** not only remove many cases from the rest of the court system but also allow court personnel to become experts in a particular subject. Problem-solving courts include:

1. Drug courts, which deal only with illegal substance crimes.
2. Veterans courts, designed to handle factors that are often linked to criminal behavior by those who have served in the U.S. military, such as post-traumatic stress disorder and substance abuse.
3. Juvenile courts, which specialize in crimes committed by minors. (We will discuss juvenile courts in more detail in Chapter 13.)
4. Domestic violence courts, which deal with crimes such as child and spousal abuse.
5. Mental health courts, which focus primarily on the treatment and rehabilitation of offenders with mental health problems.

Many state and local governments are searching for cheaper alternatives to locking up nonviolent offenders in prison or jail. Because problem-solving courts offer a range of treatment options for wrongdoers, these courts are becoming increasingly popular in today's more budget-conscious criminal justice system. For example,

FIGURE 7.2 A TYPICAL STATE COURT SYSTEM

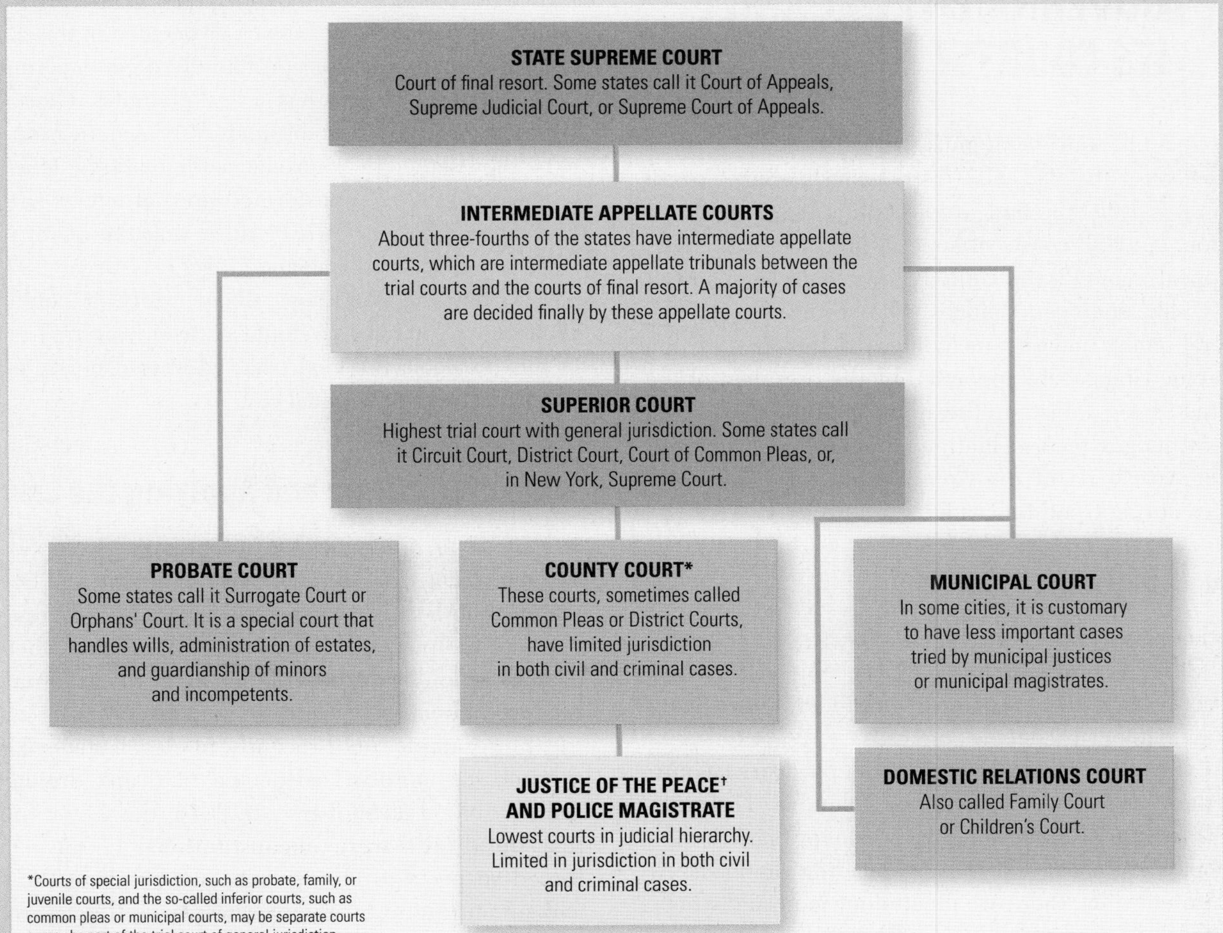

*Courts of special jurisdiction, such as probate, family, or juvenile courts, and the so-called inferior courts, such as common pleas or municipal courts, may be separate courts or may be part of the trial court of general jurisdiction.

†Justices of the peace do not exist in all states. Their jurisdiction varies greatly from state to state when they do exist.

about three thousand drug courts are now operating in the United States, a number that is expected to increase as the financial benefits of diverting drug law violators from correctional facilities become more attractive to politicians.

7-3b Trial Courts of General Jurisdiction

State trial courts that have general jurisdiction may be called county courts, district courts, superior courts, or circuit courts. In Ohio, the name is the court of common pleas, and in Massachusetts, the trial court. (The name sometimes does not correspond with the court's functions. For example, in New York the trial court is called the supreme court, whereas in most states the supreme court is the state's highest court.) Courts of general jurisdiction have the authority to hear and decide cases involving many types of subject matter, and they are the setting for criminal trials.

7-3c State Courts of Appeals

Every state has at least one court of appeals (known as an appellate, or reviewing, court), which may be an intermediate appellate court or the state's highest court. About three-fourths of the states have intermediate appellate courts. The highest appellate court in a state is usually called the supreme court, but in both New York and Maryland, the highest state court is called the court of appeals. The decisions of each state's highest court on all questions of state law are final. Only when issues of federal law or constitutional procedure are involved can the United States Supreme Court overrule a decision made by a state's highest court.

7-4 HOW DOES THE FEDERAL GOVERNMENT ORGANIZE ITS COURTS?

The federal court system is basically a three-tiered model consisting of (1) U.S. district courts (trial courts of general jurisdiction) and various courts of limited jurisdiction, (2) U.S. courts of appeals (intermediate courts of appeals), and (3) the United States Supreme Court.

Unlike state court judges, who are usually elected, federal court judges—including the justices of the Supreme Court—are appointed by the president of the United States, subject to the approval of the Senate. All federal judges receive lifetime appointments (because under Article III of the Constitution they "hold their offices during Good Behavior").

7-4a U.S. District Courts

On the lowest tier of the federal court system are the U.S. district courts, or federal trial courts. These are the courts in which cases involving federal laws begin and a judge or jury decides the case.

Every state has at least one federal district court, and there is one in the District of Columbia. The number of judicial districts varies over time, primarily owing to population changes and corresponding caseloads. At the present time, there are ninety-four judicial districts. The federal system also includes other trial courts of limited jurisdiction, such as the Tax Court and the Court of International Trade.

7-4b U.S. Courts of Appeals

In the federal court system, there are thirteen U.S. courts of appeals—also referred to as U.S. circuit courts of appeals. The federal courts of appeals for twelve of the circuits hear appeals from the district courts located within their respective judicial circuits (see Figure 7.3). The Court of Appeals for the Thirteenth Circuit, called the Federal Circuit, has national appellate jurisdiction over certain types of cases, such as cases in which the U.S. government is a defendant.

The decisions of the circuit courts of appeals are final unless a further appeal is pursued and granted. In that case, the matter is brought before the Supreme Court.

Judicial Review The power of a court to review the actions of the executive and legislative branches and, if necessary, declare those actions unconstitutional.

7-4c The United States Supreme Court

Although the United States Supreme Court reviews a minuscule percentage of the cases decided in this country each year, its decisions profoundly affect the criminal justice system. To give just a few examples, *Gideon v. Wainwright* (1963)[9] established every American's right to be represented by counsel in a criminal trial; *Miranda v. Arizona* (1966)[10] transformed pretrial interrogations; *Furman v. Georgia* (1972)[11] ruled that the death penalty was unconstitutional; and *Gregg v. Georgia* (1976)[12] spelled out the conditions under which it could be allowed. As you have no doubt noticed from references in this textbook, the Court has addressed nearly every important facet of criminal law.

7-4d Interpreting and Applying the Law

The Supreme Court "makes" criminal justice policy in two important ways: through *judicial review* and by virtue of its authority to interpret the law. **Judicial review** refers to the power of the Court to determine whether a law or action by the other branches of the government is constitutional.

For example, until recently, in eleven states it was a crime for motorists suspected of drunk driving to refuse a blood alcohol test. In 2016, the Court found that these laws were unconstitutional because they forced suspects to choose between breaking the law and submitting to overly invasive warrantless searches of their bodies.[13]

STATUTORY INTERPRETATION As the final interpreter of the Constitution, the Supreme Court must also determine the meaning of certain statutory provisions when applied to specific situations. In 1994, for example, Congress passed a law that gives a victim of child pornography the ability to seek restitution from offenders to the extent that he or she has been harmed by the illegal behavior.[14] Twenty years later, the Court overturned a $3.4 million award to a woman whose childhood rape had been videotaped and widely disseminated on the Internet.

The offender in the case had pleaded guilty to having images of child pornography on his computer, including two images of the victim. The Court ruled that, under the 1994 law, the offender could not be held responsible for all of the damages the victim had suffered.[15]

JURISDICTION OF THE SUPREME COURT The United States Supreme Court consists of nine justices—a chief justice and eight associate justices. The Supreme Court has original, or trial, jurisdiction only in rare

FIGURE 7.3 GEOGRAPHIC BOUNDARIES OF THE FEDERAL CIRCUIT COURTS OF APPEALS

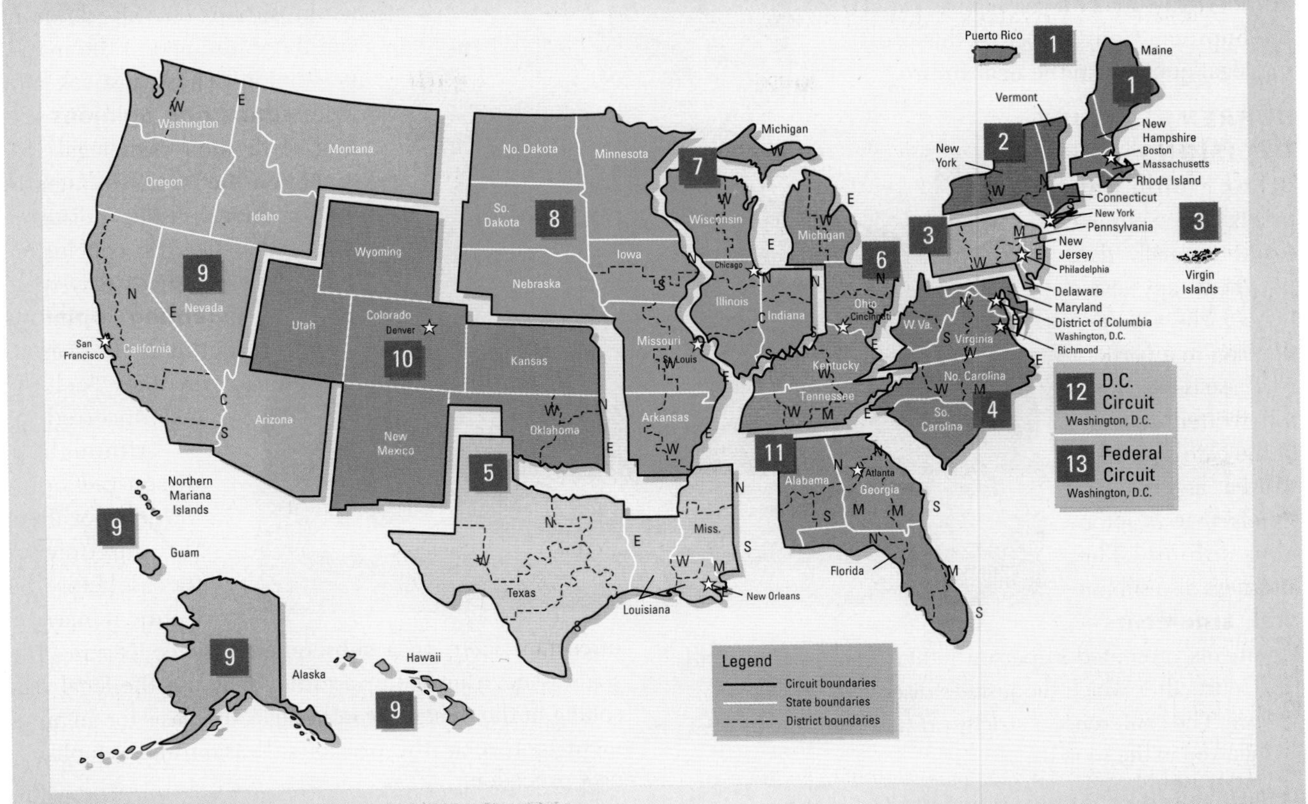

Source: Administrative Office of the United States Courts.

instances (set forth in Article III, Section 2, of the Constitution). In other words, only rarely does a case originate at the Supreme Court level.

Most of the Court's work is as an appellate court. It has appellate authority over cases decided by the U.S. courts of appeals, as well as over some cases decided in the state courts when federal questions are at issue.

WHICH CASES REACH THE SUPREME COURT?

There is no absolute right to appeal to the United States Supreme Court. Although thousands of cases are filed with the Supreme Court each year, in 2015–2016 the Court heard only eighty-two. With a **writ of *certiorari*** (pronounced sur-shee-uh-*rah*-ree), the Supreme Court orders a lower court to send it the record of a case for review. A party can petition the Supreme Court to issue a writ of *certiorari*, but whether the Court will do so is entirely within its discretion. More than 90 percent of the petitions for writs of *certiorari* (or "certs," as they are popularly called) are denied. A denial is not a decision on the merits of a case, nor does it indicate agreement with the lower court's opinion. Therefore, the denial of the writ has no value as a precedent.

LO7-3 Explain briefly how a case is brought to the United States Supreme Court.

The Court will not issue a writ unless at least four justices approve of it. This is called the **rule of four.** Although the justices are not required to give their reasons for refusing to hear a case, frequently the discretionary decision is based on whether the legal issue involves a "substantial federal question." Often, such questions arise when lower courts split on a particular issue.

For example, different federal and state courts have produced varying opinions on the question of whether the private search doctrine applies to digital storage devices, such as computers. Recall from the preceding chapter that under this doctrine, law enforcement officers do not need a warrant to go through personal items that have already been searched by a third-party civilian. Given how often private

Writ of *Certiorari* A request from a higher court asking a lower court for the record of a case.

Rule of Four A rule of the United States Supreme Court that the Court will not issue a writ of *certiorari* unless at least four justices approve of the decision to hear the case.

third-party searches of computer files turn up incriminating evidence, such as child pornography, many legal experts expect the Supreme Court to clarify this pressing legal question in the near future.[16]

SUPREME COURT DECISIONS Like other appellate courts, the Supreme Court normally does not hear any evidence. The Court's decision in a particular case is based on the written record of the case and the written arguments (briefs) that the attorneys submit. The attorneys also submit **oral arguments**—arguments presented in person rather than on paper—to the Court, after which the justices discuss the case in *conference*. The conference is strictly private—only the justices are allowed in the room.

AP Images/Lawrence Jackson

John G. Roberts, Jr., pictured here, is the seventeenth chief justice of the United States Supreme Court. **What does it mean to say that Roberts and the eight associate members of the Court "make criminal justice policy"?**

Majorities and Pluralities When the Court has reached a decision, the chief justice, if in the majority, assigns the task of writing the Court's opinion to one of the justices. When the chief justice is not in the majority, the most senior justice voting with the majority assigns the writing of the Court's opinion. The opinion outlines the reasons for the Court's decision, the rules of law that apply, and the decision.

From time to time, the justices agree on the outcome of a case, but no single reason for that outcome gains five votes. When this occurs, the rationale that gains the most votes is called the *plurality* opinion. Plurality opinions are problematic, because they do not provide a strong precedent for lower courts to follow. Although still relatively rare, the incidence of plurality opinions has increased over the past fifty years as the Court has become more ideologically fractured.[17]

Oral Arguments The verbal arguments presented in person by attorneys to an appellate court.

Concurring Opinions Separate opinions prepared by judges who support the decision of the majority but who want to make a particular point or to voice disapproval of the grounds on which the decision was made.

Dissenting Opinions Separate opinions in which judges disagree with the conclusion reached by the majority of the court and expand on their own views about the case.

Concurrence and Dissent Often, one or more justices who agree with the Court's decision may do so for reasons different from those outlined in the majority opinion. These justices may write **concurring opinions** setting forth their own legal reasoning on the issue. Frequently, one or more justices disagree with the Court's conclusion. These justices may write **dissenting opinions** outlining the reasons why they feel the majority erred.

Although a dissenting opinion does not affect the outcome of the case before the Court, it may be important later. In a subsequent case concerning the same issue, a justice or attorney may use the legal reasoning in the dissenting opinion as the basis for an argument to reverse the previous decision and establish a new precedent.

7-5 HOW DO JUDGES FUNCTION IN THE COURT SYSTEM?

Supreme Court justices are the most visible and best-known American jurists, but in many ways they are unrepresentative of the profession as a whole. Few judges enjoy a three-room office suite fitted with a fireplace and a private bath, as does each Supreme Court justice. Few judges have four clerks to assist them. Few judges get a yearly vacation that stretches from July through September. Most judges, in fact, work at the lowest level of the system, in criminal trial courts, where they are burdened with overflowing caseloads and must deal daily with the pettiest of criminals.

One attribute a Supreme Court justice and a criminal trial judge in any small American city do have in common is the expectation that they will be just. Of all the participants in the criminal justice system, no single person is held to the same high standards as the judge. From her or his lofty perch in the courtroom, the judge is counted on to be "above the fray" of the bickering defense attorneys and prosecutors.

When the other courtroom contestants rise at the entrance of the judge, they are placing the burden of justice squarely on the judge's shoulders.

7-5a The Roles and Responsibilities of Trial Judges

One of the reasons that judicial integrity is considered so important is the amount of discretionary power a judge has over the court proceedings. Nearly every stage of the trial process includes a decision or action to be taken by the presiding judge.

BEFORE THE TRIAL A great deal of the work done by a judge takes place before the trial even starts, free from public scrutiny. These duties, some of which you have seen from a different point of view in the section on law enforcement agents, include determining the following:

1. Whether there is sufficient probable cause to issue a search or arrest warrant.
2. Whether there is sufficient probable cause to authorize electronic surveillance of a suspect.
3. Whether enough evidence exists to justify the temporary incarceration of a suspect.
4. Whether a defendant should be released on bail, and if so, the amount of the bail.
5. Whether to accept pretrial motions by prosecutors and defense attorneys.
6. Whether to accept a plea bargain.

During these pretrial activities, the judge takes on the role of the *negotiator*.[18] As most cases are decided through plea bargains rather than through trial proceedings, the judge often offers his or her services as a negotiator to help the prosecution and the defense "make a deal." The amount at which bail is set is often negotiated as well. Throughout the trial process, the judge usually spends a great deal of time in his or her *chambers*, or office, negotiating with the prosecutors and defense attorneys.

DURING THE TRIAL When the trial starts, the judge takes on the role of *referee*. In this role, she or he is responsible for seeing that the trial unfolds according to the dictates of the law and that the participants in the trial do not overstep any legal or ethical bounds.

Furthermore, the judge is expected to be neutral, determining the admissibility of testimony and evidence on a completely objective basis. The judge also acts as a *teacher* during the trial, explaining points of law to the

CJ and TECHNOLOGY

Lie Detection in Court

In 1935, Professor Leonarde Keeler relied on a polygraph test to show a jury that two defendants were lying when they denied attempting to kill a sheriff in Portage, Wisconsin. After the trial ended in convictions, Professor Keeler claimed that the "findings of the lie detector are as acceptable . . . as fingerprint testimony."

Eight decades later, that prediction has yet to come true. Although polygraphs—devices that monitor changes in respiration, pulse, and blood pressure—are commonly used to determine truthfulness as part of police investigations and job screenings, the technology has not been permitted as evidence in criminal courtrooms. The problem is that polygraphs are often inaccurate and thus too unreliable for use in court.

Besides polygraph tests, other forms of lie-detector technology have also been developed. For example, some researchers presume that the brain "works harder" in telling a lie than in telling the truth. Therefore, functional magnetic resonance imaging, which (as we discussed in Chapter 2) measures blood flow in the brain, should be able to detect falsehoods. Most recently, software designed by researchers at the University of Michigan purports to use a speaker's words and gestures to determine whether he or she is telling the truth. Neither technology, however, has proven sufficiently dependable to convince "gatekeeper" judges to allow it as evidence in criminal trials.

Thinking about Lie Detection in Court

The University of Michigan software described above boasts a 75 percent accuracy rate in determining whether the subject is telling the truth. Are judges justified in keeping the potential results of this software out of court? Why or why not?

jury. If the trial is not a jury trial, then the judge must also make decisions concerning the guilt or innocence of the defendant.

At the close of the trial, if the defendant is found guilty, the judge must decide on the length of the sentence and the type of sentence. (Different types of sentences, such as incarceration, probation, and other forms of community-based corrections, will be discussed in Chapters 9 and 10.) The sentencing phase also gives the judge a chance to make personal comments about the proceedings, if he or she wishes.

Bikeriderlondon/ShutterStock.com

In your own words, explain how a judge acts as a "referee" when he or she is presiding over a criminal trial.

THE ADMINISTRATIVE ROLE Judges are also *administrators* and are responsible for the day-to-day functioning of their courts. A primary administrative task of a judge is scheduling. Each courtroom has a **docket,** or calendar of cases, and it is the judge's responsibility to keep the docket current. This entails not only scheduling the trial, but also setting pretrial motion dates and deciding whether to grant attorneys' requests for *continuances*, or additional time to prepare for the trial.

Judges must also keep track of the immense paperwork generated by each case and manage the various employees of the court. Some judges are even responsible for the budgets of their courtrooms.[19] In 1939, Congress, recognizing the burden of such tasks, created the Administrative Office of the United States Courts to provide administrative assistance for federal court judges.[20] Most state court judges, however, do not have the luxury of similar aid, though they are supported by a court staff.

CAREER TIP High-level judges, including Supreme Court justices, enjoy the services of *law clerks*, who prepare reports for the judges on the legal issues of cases and help the judges research and write opinions. Law clerks are often recent law school graduates beginning their legal careers.

Docket The list of cases entered on a court's calendar and thus scheduled to be heard by the court.

Partisan Elections Elections in which candidates are affiliated with and receive support from political parties.

Nonpartisan Elections Elections in which candidates are presented on the ballot without any party affiliation.

Missouri Plan A method of selecting judges that combines appointment and election.

7-5b Selection of Judges

In the federal court system, all judges are appointed by the president and confirmed by the Senate. It is difficult to make a general statement about how judges are selected in state court systems, because the procedure varies widely from state to state. In some states, such as New Jersey, all judges are appointed by the governor and confirmed by the upper chamber of the state legislature.

In other states, such as Alabama, **partisan elections** are used to choose judges. In these elections, a judicial candidate declares allegiance to a political party, usually the Democrats or the Republicans, before the election. States such as Kentucky that conduct **nonpartisan elections** do not require a candidate to affiliate herself or himself with a political party in this manner.

In 1940, Missouri became the first state to combine appointment and election in a so-called merit selection process. When all jurisdiction levels are counted, nineteen states and the District of Columbia now utilize the **Missouri Plan,** as merit selection has been labeled. The Missouri Plan consists of three basic steps:

- When a vacancy on the bench arises, candidates are nominated by a nonpartisan committee of citizens.
- The names of the three most qualified candidates are sent to the governor or executive of the state judicial system, and that person chooses who will be the judge.

- A year after the new judge has been installed, a "retention election" is held so that voters can decide whether the judge deserves to keep the post.[21]

The goal of the Missouri Plan is to eliminate partisan politics from the selection procedure, while at the same time giving the citizens a voice in the process.

7-5c Diversity on the Bench

One of the supposed benefits of judicial elections is that they make judges more representative of the communities in which they serve. According to the Brennan Center for Justice in New York City, however, "Americans who enter the courtroom often face a predictable presence on the bench: a white male."[22]

Overall, about 58 percent of all state appellate judges are white males.[23] In many states, members of minority groups are underrepresented in comparison to the demographics of the general population. California, for example, is nearly 38 percent Latino and 15 percent Asian American. The state judiciary, however, is only 9.9 percent Latino and 6.5 percent Asian American.[24] In Texas, minority women make up 28 percent of the population but fill only 12 percent of judgeships, and, for minority men, the numbers are 29 percent and 14 percent, respectively.[25]

Members of minority groups are also underrepresented in the federal judiciary, though not to the same extent as in the states. Of the approximately 1,700 federal judges in this country, about 13 percent are African American, 7 percent are Latino, and less than 3 percent are Asian American. Furthermore, about one-quarter are women.[26] Of the 111 justices who have served on the United States Supreme Court, two have been African American: Thurgood Marshall (1967–1991) and Clarence Thomas (1991–present). In 2009, Sonia Sotomayor became the first Latina appointed to the Court and the third woman, following Sandra Day O'Connor (1981–2006) and Ruth Bader Ginsburg (1993–present). A year later, Elena Kagan became the fourth woman appointed to the Court.

ETHICS CHALLENGE

In every state that has judicial elections, judges are allowed to receive campaign contributions from lawyers who appear before them in court. What ethical issues arise from this situation? Some states ban judges from making personal requests for funds, though such requests can still be made by the judges' campaign committees. Does this strategy remove—or at least lessen—the risk of corruption? Why or why not?

7-6 WHAT IS THE COURTROOM WORK GROUP?

Television dramas often depict the courtroom as a battlefield, with prosecutors and defense attorneys spitting fire at each other over the loud and insistent protestations of a frustrated judge. Consequently, many people are somewhat disappointed when they witness a real courtroom at work. Rarely does anyone raise his or her voice, and the courtroom professionals appear—to a great extent—to be cooperating with each other. In Chapter 5, we discussed the existence of a police subculture, based on the shared values of law enforcement agents. A courtroom subculture exists as well, centered on the **courtroom work group.**

The most important feature of any work group is that it is a *cooperative* unit, whose members establish shared values and methods that help the group efficiently reach its goals. Though cooperation is not a concept usually associated with criminal courts, it is in fact crucial to the adjudication process.

7-6a Members of the Courtroom Work Group

The courtroom work group is made up of those individuals who are involved with the defendant from the time she or he is arrested until sentencing. The most prominent members are the judge, the prosecutor, and the defense attorney. Three other court participants complete the work group:

1. The *bailiff of the court* is responsible for maintaining security and order in the judge's chambers and the courtroom. Bailiffs lead the defendant in and out of the courtroom and attend to the needs of the jurors during the trial. The bailiff, often a member of the local sheriff's department but sometimes an employee of the court, also delivers summonses in some jurisdictions.
2. The *clerk of the court* has an exhausting list of responsibilities. Any plea, motion, or other matter to be acted on by the judge must go through the clerk. The large amount of paperwork generated during a trial, including transcripts, photographs, evidence, and any other records, is maintained by the clerk. The clerk also issues subpoenas for jury duty and coordinates the jury selection process. In the federal court

Courtroom Work Group The social organization consisting of the judge, prosecutor, defense attorney, and other court workers.

CAREER PREP

Bailiff

Job Description:

- Maintain order and provide security in the courtroom during trials, and escort and guard jurors and prevent them from having improper contact with the public.
- Open and close court, call cases, call witnesses, and generally "direct the traffic" of the trial.

What Kind of Training Is Required?

- At minimum, a high school diploma or GED.
- Supplemental training at a vocational school or a police academy, or a two- or four-year college degree with an emphasis on criminal justice.

Annual Salary Range?

- $32,000–$54,000

iStockPhoto.com/Alina Solovyova-Vincent

SOCIAL MEDIA CAREER TIP

Networking is crucial. Develop as many useful social media contacts as possible, and cultivate those contacts. Also, reciprocate. If you help others establish online contacts, they are likely to remember you and return the favor.

system, judges select clerks, while state clerks are either appointed or, in nearly a third of the states, elected.

3. *Court reporters* record every word that is said during the course of the trial. They also record any depositions, or pretrial question-and-answer sessions in which a party or a witness answers an attorney's questions under oath.

7-6b The Judge in the Courtroom Work Group

The judge is the dominant figure in the courtroom and therefore exerts the most influence over the values and norms of the work group. A judge who runs a "tight ship" follows procedure and restricts the freedom of attorneys to deviate from regulations, while a *"laissez-faire"* judge allows more leeway to members of the work group. A judge's personal philosophy also affects the court proceedings. If a judge has a reputation for being "tough on crime," both prosecutors and defense attorneys will alter their strategies accordingly.

Public Prosecutor An individual, acting as a trial lawyer, who initiates and conducts cases in the government's name and on behalf of the people.

Although preeminent in the work group, a judge must still rely on other group members. To a certain extent, the judge is the least informed member of the trio. Like a juror, the judge learns the facts of the case as they are presented by the attorneys. If the attorneys do not properly present the facts, then the judge is hampered in making rulings.

7-6c The Prosecution

If, as we suggested earlier, the judge is the referee of the courtroom, then the prosecutor and the defense attorney are its two main combatants. On the side of the government, acting in the name of "the people," the **public prosecutor** tries cases against criminal defendants.

The public prosecutor in federal criminal cases is called a U.S. attorney. In cases tried in state or local courts, the public prosecutor may be referred to as a *prosecuting attorney, state attorney, district attorney, county attorney,* or *city attorney*. Given their great autonomy, prosecutors are generally considered the most dominant figures in the American criminal justice system.

LO7-4 List the different names given to public prosecutors, and indicate the general powers they have.

Give several reasons why experience as a prosecutor would make someone, such as United States Supreme Court justice Sonia Sotomayor, a more effective judge.

A DUTY OF FAIRNESS In some jurisdictions, the district attorney is the chief law enforcement officer, with broad powers over police operations. Prosecutors have the power to bring the resources of the state to bear against the individual and hold the legal keys to meting out or withholding punishment.

Ideally, this power is balanced by a duty of fairness and a recognition that the prosecutor's ultimate goal is not to win cases, but to see that justice is done. In *Berger v. United States* (1935), Justice George Sutherland said of the prosecutor, "It is as much his duty to refrain from improper methods calculated to produce a wrongful conviction as it is to use every legitimate means to bring about a just one."[27]

THE *BRADY* RULE To lessen the opportunity for "improper" behavior by prosecutors, the United States Supreme Court established the *Brady* rule more than half a century ago. This rule holds that prosecutors are not permitted to keep evidence from the defendant and her or his attorneys that may be useful in showing innocence.[28]

For example, in 1998 Michael Wearry was sentenced to death for killing a pizza-delivery driver named Eric Walber near Baton Rouge, Louisiana. Prosecutors had no physical evidence linking Wearry to the crime and relied heavily on the testimony of two jailhouse informants.

As it turned out, one of the informants held a grudge against Wearry, while the other sought to trade his testimony for a lesser punishment in another crime. Furthermore, medical reports of Walber's death contradicted the prosecution's version of events. Because prosecutors failed to disclose any of this information to defense attorneys, in 2016 the United States Supreme Court reversed Wearry's conviction and granted him a new trial.[29]

THE OFFICE OF THE PROSECUTOR When he or she is acting as an *officer of the law* during a criminal trial, there are limits on the prosecutor's conduct, as you will see in the next chapter. During the pretrial process, however, prosecutors hold a great deal of discretion in deciding the following:

1. Whether an individual who has been arrested by the police will be charged with a crime.
2. The level of the charges to be brought against the suspect.
3. If and when to stop the prosecution.

There are more than eight thousand prosecutors' offices around the country, serving state, county, and municipal jurisdictions. Even though the **attorney general** is the chief law enforcement officer in any state, she or he has limited control (and, in some states, no control) over prosecutors within the state's boundaries.

Each jurisdiction has a chief prosecutor, who is sometimes appointed but more often elected. As an elected official, he or she typically serves a four-year term, though in some states, such as Alabama, the term is six years. In smaller jurisdictions, the chief prosecutor has several assistants, and they work closely together. In larger ones, the chief prosecutor may have numerous *assistant prosecutors*, many of whom he or she rarely meets.

Assistant prosecutors—for the most part, young attorneys recently graduated from law school—may be assigned to particular sections of the organization. These sections include general criminal prosecutions or areas of *special prosecution*, such as narcotics or gang crimes.

THE PROSECUTOR AS ELECTED OFFICIAL The chief prosecutor's autonomy is not absolute. As an elected official, she or he

Attorney General The chief law officer of a state; also, the chief law officer of the nation.

must answer to the voters. (There are exceptions: U.S. attorneys are nominated by the president and approved by the Senate, and chief prosecutors in Alaska, Connecticut, New Jersey, Rhode Island, and the District of Columbia are either appointed or hired as members of the attorney general's office.) In many jurisdictions, the prosecutor must declare a party affiliation and is expected to reward fellow party members with positions in the district attorney's office if elected.

The post of prosecutor is also considered a "stepping-stone" to higher political office, and many prosecutors have gone on to serve in legislatures or as judges. Sonia Sotomayor, the first Latina member of the United States Supreme Court, started her legal career in 1979 as an assistant district attorney in New York City. While at that job, she first came to public attention by helping to prosecute the "Tarzan Murderer," an athletic criminal responsible for at least twenty burglaries and four killings.

7-6d The Defense Attorney

The media provide most people's perception of defense counsel: the idealistic public defender who nobly serves the poor, the "ambulance chaser," or the celebrity attorney in the $3,000 suit. These stereotypes, though not entirely fictional, tend to obscure the crucial role that the **defense attorney** plays in the criminal justice system.

Most persons charged with crimes have little or no knowledge of criminal procedure. Without assistance, they would be helpless in court. By acting as a staunch advocate for her or his client, the defense attorney (ideally) ensures that the government proves every point against that client beyond a reasonable doubt, even for cases that do not go to trial. In sum, the defense attorney provides a counterweight against the state in our adversary system.

THE RESPONSIBILITIES OF THE DEFENSE ATTORNEY The Sixth Amendment right to counsel is not limited to the actual criminal trial. In a number of instances, the United States Supreme Court has held that defendants are entitled to representation as soon as their rights may be denied, which, as we have seen, includes the custodial interrogation and lineup identification procedures.[30] Therefore, an important responsibility of the defense attorney is to represent the defendant at the various stages of the custodial process, such as arrest, interrogation, lineup, and arraignment. Other responsibilities include:

Defense Attorney The lawyer representing the defendant.

Public Defenders Court-appointed attorneys who are paid by the state to represent defendants who cannot afford private counsel.

- Investigating the incident for which the defendant has been charged.
- Communicating with the prosecutor, which includes negotiating plea bargains.
- Preparing the case for trial.
- Submitting defense motions, including motions to suppress evidence.
- Representing the defendant at trial.
- Negotiating a sentence, if the client has been convicted.
- Determining whether to appeal a guilty verdict.[31]

DEFENDING THE GUILTY At one time or another in their careers, all defense attorneys will face a difficult question: Must I defend a client whom I know to be guilty? According to the American Bar Association's code of legal ethics, the answer is almost always, "yes."[32] The most important responsibility of the criminal defense attorney is to be an advocate for her or his client. As such, the attorney is obligated to use all ethical and legal means to achieve the client's desired goal, which is usually to avoid or lessen punishment for the charged crime.

LO7-5 Explain why defense attorneys must often defend clients they know to be guilty.

As Supreme Court justice Byron White once noted, defense counsel has no "obligation to ascertain or present the truth." Rather, our adversary system insists that the defense attorney "defend the client whether he is innocent or guilty."[33] Indeed, if defense attorneys refused to represent clients whom they believed to be guilty, the Sixth Amendment guarantee of a criminal trial for all accused persons would be rendered meaningless. (To learn more about the difficult situations that can arise with a guilty defendant, see the feature *Discretion in Action—The Repugnant Client*.)

THE PUBLIC DEFENDER Generally speaking, there are two different types of defense attorneys: (1) private attorneys, who are hired by individuals, and (2) **public defenders,** who work for the government. The distinction is not absolute, as many private attorneys accept employment as public defenders, too.

The modern role of the public defender was established by the Supreme Court's interpretation of the Sixth Amendment in *Gideon v. Wainwright* (1963).[34] In that case, the Court ruled that no defendant can be "assured a fair trial unless counsel is provided for him," and therefore the state must provide a public defender to those who cannot afford to hire one for themselves.

Subsequently, the Court extended this protection to juveniles in *In re Gault* (1967)[35] and those faced with

DISCRETION IN ACTION

The Repugnant Client

THE SITUATION Gerard Marrone is the defense attorney for Levi Aron, charged with kidnapping, murdering, and dismembering eight-year-old Leiby Kletzky in Brooklyn, New York. There is little question of Aron's guilt, as he provided the police with a signed confession and has no alibi for his whereabouts at the time of the crime. Marrone is uncertain about whether he wants to continue representing this "horrific" client. "You can't look at your kids and then look at yourself in the mirror, knowing that a little boy, who's close in age to my eldest son, was murdered so brutally," Marrone said about his conflicted feelings.

THE LAW The Sixth Amendment requires that all criminal defendants are entitled to the right to assistance of counsel. Nonetheless, no state or federal law requires defense attorneys to represent clients they know to be guilty of committing a crime. The American Bar Association (ABA) Model Rule of Professional Conduct, which provides informal guidance to the nation's lawyers, does not mandate representation of a client that an attorney finds "repugnant."

WHAT WOULD YOU DO? Despite the ABA's advice about "repugnant" clients, the criminal justice system would not be able to function if lawyers refused to represent guilty defendants. Many believe that attorneys are ethically obligated to take on unpopular cases and clients to ensure the integrity of the American judicial system.

At the same time, a lawyer must be guided by his or her own conscience. If a client is so repugnant to the lawyer as to impair the quality of representation, then perhaps the lawyer should drop the case. Given these opposing viewpoints, would you continue to represent Levi Aaron if you were in Gerard Marrone's position?

To see Gerard Marrone's eventual decision, go to Example 7.1 in Appendix A.

imprisonment for committing misdemeanors in *Argersinger v. Hamlin* (1972).[36] The impact of these decisions has been substantial: About 90 percent of all criminal defendants in the United States are represented by public defenders or other appointed counsel.[37]

Eligibility Issues Although the Supreme Court's *Gideon* decision obligated the government to provide attorneys for indigent (poor) defendants, it offered no guidance on just how poor the defendant needs to be to qualify for a public defender. In theory, counsel should be provided for those who are unable to hire an attorney themselves without "substantial hardship."[38] In reality, each jurisdiction has its own guidelines, and a defendant refused counsel in one area might be entitled to it in another.

New York State recently changed its standards so that any defendant with an annual income below about $30,000 is eligible for public counsel. Previously, these services were denied if the defendant owned a car or a house, often regardless of her or his income.[39]

Defense Counsel Programs In most areas, the county government is responsible for providing indigent defendants with attorneys. Three basic types of programs are used to allocate defense counsel:

1. *Assigned counsel programs*, in which local private attorneys are assigned clients on a case-by-case basis by the county.
2. *Contracting attorney programs*, in which a particular law firm or group of attorneys is hired to regularly assume the representative and administrative tasks of indigent defense.
3. *Public defender programs*, in which the county assembles a salaried staff of full-time or part-time attorneys and creates a public (taxpayer-funded) agency to provide services.[40]

Much to the surprise of many indigent defendants, these programs are not entirely without cost. Government agencies can charge fees for "free" legal counsel when the fees will not impose a "significant legal financial hardship" on the defendant. In at least forty-three states and the District of Columbia, therefore, local public defender offices have the option of charging some form of so-called cost recoupment.[41]

In South Dakota, indigent defendants are billed $92 an hour for the services of a public defender, regardless of the outcome of the case. A defendant can be jailed for failing to cover these costs even if she or he is found innocent of the original charge.[42]

CAREER PREP

Public Defender

Job Description:

- **Interview low-income applicants for legal services and, if they are eligible, engage in negotiation, trial, and /or appeal of legal issues on their behalf.**
- **Exercise initiative, sound judgment, and creativity in attempting to solve the legal problems of the poor.**

What Kind of Training Is Required?

- **A law degree and membership in the relevant state bar association.**
- **Commitment and dedication to the needs of low-income and elderly clients.**

Annual Salary Range?

- **$44,000–$97,000**

StockPhoto.com/BirdofPrey

GETTING LINKEDIN

Although most public defenders work on a city or county level, there are seventy-nine federal public defender organizations with 3,300 employees. Given its national reach, LinkedIn is an excellent source of information about job openings for federal public defenders.

ATTORNEY-CLIENT PRIVILEGE To defend a client effectively, a defense attorney must have access to all the facts concerning the case, even those that may be harmful to the defendant. To promote the unrestrained flow of information between the two parties, legislatures and lawyers themselves have constructed rules of **attorney-client privilege.** These rules require that communications between a client and his or her attorney be kept confidential, unless the client consents to the disclosure.

The Privilege and Confessions Attorney-client privilege does not stop short of confessions. Indeed, if, on hearing any statement that points toward guilt, the defense attorney could alert the prosecution or try to resign from the case, attorney-client privilege would be rendered meaningless. Even if the client says, "I have just killed seventeen women. I selected only pregnant women so I could torture them and kill two people at once. I did it. I liked it. I enjoyed it," the defense attorney must continue to do his or her utmost to serve that client.[43]

Attorney-Client Privilege
A rule of evidence requiring that communications between a client and his or her attorney be kept confidential, unless the client consents to disclosure.

Without attorney-client privilege, observes legal expert John Kaplan, lawyers would be forced to give their clients the equivalent of the *Miranda* warning before representing them.[44] In other words, lawyers would have to make clear what clients could or could not say in the course of preparing for trial, because any incriminating statement might be used against the client in court. Such a development would have serious ramifications for the criminal justice system.

The Exception to the Privilege The scope of attorney-client privilege is not all-encompassing. In *United States v. Zolin* (1989),[45] the Supreme Court ruled that lawyers may disclose the contents of a conversation with a client if the client has provided information concerning a crime that has yet to be committed. This exception applies only to communications involving a crime that is ongoing or will occur in the future.

If the client reveals a past crime, the privilege is still in effect, and the attorney may not reveal any details of that particular criminal act.

This aspect of the privilege can, admittedly, have tragic consequences. In 1956, for example, Darrel Parker was convicted of raping and killing his wife in Lincoln, Nebraska. These crimes had actually been committed by Wesley Peery, who admitted as much to his attorney. Parker spent fourteen years in prison, however, and was not exonerated until Peery died of a heart attack, allowing his attorney to make the confession public.

ETHICS CHALLENGE

Leon, the defendant, is on trial for having sex with an underage girl. Leon is represented by Daniel, the defense attorney, A jury finds Leon not guilty. A year later, as part of a dispute over legal fees, Daniel tells a judge that, in private conversations, Leon admitted to having sex with numerous underage girls, including members of his family. Should these conversations be covered by attorney-client privilege? Did Daniel behave unethically in sharing them with a court? Explain your answers.

Pat Greenhouse/The Boston Globe/Getty Images

Defense attorney Jill Corey appears in Quincy, Massachusetts, District Court with her client. **Why are the rules of attorney-client privilege necessary for a defense attorney to properly do his or her job?**

STUDY TOOLS 7

LOCATED IN TEXTBOOK

- ☐ Rip out the Chapter Review Card.
- ☐ Review with the Chapter Quiz following this chapter.

LOCATED AT WWW.CENGAGEBRAIN.COM

- ☐ Review key terms flash cards.
- ☐ Read the chapter on all your favorite devices.
- ☐ Complete an Exam to test your knowledge.
- ☐ Check out Visual Summaries and You Decide activities to explore chapter concepts.

Quiz

1. The due process function of American courts is to protect ______________________ in light of the various advantages that the prosecution enjoys during legal proceedings.

2. The ______________________ ______________________ function of the courts emphasizes punishment and the concept that criminals must suffer for the harm they do to society.

3. Before any court can hear a case, it must have ______________________ over the persons involved or the subject matter of the dispute.

4. The American court system is a dual court system composed of ______________________ courts and state courts.

5. When it agrees to hear an appeal of a lower court decision, the United States Supreme Court issues a writ of ______________________.

6. When a Supreme Court justice agrees with the Court's decision but for different reasons than those outlined in the majority opinion, he or she will write a ______________________ opinion setting forth his or her legal reasoning.

7. In some states, judges are nominated by the state's ______________________ and approved by the state legislature.

8. Public ______________________ initiate and conduct cases on behalf of society against the defendant.

9. The Sixth Amendment states that every person accused of a crime in the United States has a right to the assistance of ______________________.

10. Those defendants who cannot afford to hire a defense attorney are provided with ______________________ defenders by the government.

Answers to the Chapter 7 Quiz can be found in the Answers section in the back of the book.

8 Pretrial Procedures and the Criminal Trial

AP Images/Amanda Rossmann/The Cincinnati Enquirer

LEARNING OBJECTIVES

After studying this chapter, you will be able to …

8-1 Identify the steps involved in the pretrial criminal process.

8-2 Indicate why prosecutors, defense attorneys, and defendants often agree to plea bargains.

8-3 Identify the basic protections enjoyed by criminal defendants in the United States.

8-4 Contrast challenges for cause and peremptory challenges during *voir dire*.

8-5 List the standard steps in a criminal jury trial.

After finishing this chapter, go to **PAGE 179** for **STUDY TOOLS**

The Holdout

Three times, the judge asked the jurors to come up with a verdict. Three times, the jurors failed to do so. Consequently, on May 8, 2015, after a four-month trial and eighteen days of jury deliberation, Justice Maxwell Riley had no choice but to declare a mistrial in the murder case of Pedro Hernandez. Thirty-three years earlier, in his own words, Hernandez had lured six-year-old Etan Patz into the basement of the New York City bodega where he worked and strangled the boy. Eleven of the jurors accepted this confession as proof of Hernandez's guilt. One did not. "Ultimately I couldn't find enough evidence that was not circumstantial to convict," Adam Sirois, the holdout, said afterwards. "I couldn't get there."

In fact, Etan's body was never found. Neither were the boy's clothes or the small tote bag that he was carrying when he disappeared. Prosecutors had no forensic evidence from a crime scene. The only proof they could offer was a videotaped confession in which the defendant said, "Something took over me and I squeezed [Patz] more and more." Hernandez's attorneys claimed that this confession was a fantasy made up by their client, who was suffering from mental problems. For Sirois, the holdout juror, the main issue was that police interviewed Hernandez for more than six hours before turning on the videotape and getting the confession. "We needed to see the full interrogation to determine if the story [the defendant] eventually told police originated with him or if it was coached to him by the detectives," said Sirois.

Following the mistrial, the other jurors expressed hope that prosecutors would retry Hernandez and find a resolution "for the Patz family, for the Hernandez family, [and] for the City of New York." They got their wish. On February 14, 2017, after a second, three-month trial and nine days of jury deliberation, a different set of jurors found Hernandez guilty of murdering Etan. Eventually, he was sentenced to life in prison without parole.

AP Images/Mark Lennihan

A photograph of six-year-old Etan Patz hangs on an angel figurine as part of a memorial held for the boy several years ago in the SoHo neighborhood of New York City. *Do you agree with the policy that jurors must vote unanimously to find a defendant such as Pedro Hernandez guilty? Or should an 11–1 vote, as occurred in Hernandez's first trial, be sufficient? Why?*

8-1 WHAT HAPPENS AFTER ARREST?

Not surprisingly, given the extraordinary nature of the case and history of Etan Patz's disappearance, Pedro Hernandez's murder trials attracted national attention. Those who followed the proceedings might have come away with a skewed version of how the criminal justice system works, however. According to the "*wedding cake*" model of our court system, only the top, and smallest, "layer" of trials comes close to meeting constitutional standards of procedural justice.[1]

In these celebrity trials, such as Hernandez's, committed (and expensive) attorneys argue minute technicalities for days, with numerous (and expensive) expert witnesses taking the stand for both sides. On the bottom, largest layer of the wedding cake, the vast majority of defendants are dealt with informally, and the end goal seems to be speed rather than justice. Indeed, as you will see in this chapter, trial by jury is quite rare. Instead, the fate of most criminal suspects in this country is decided during pretrial procedures, which start almost as soon as the police have identified a suspect.

LO8-1 Identify the steps involved in the pretrial criminal process.

8-1a The Initial Appearance

After an arrest has been made, the first step toward determining the suspect's guilt or innocence is the **initial appearance.** During this brief proceeding, the magistrate informs the defendant of the charges that have been brought against him or her and explains his or her constitutional rights—particularly, the right to remain silent (under the Fifth Amendment) and the right to be represented by counsel (under the Sixth Amendment). At this point, if the defendant cannot afford to hire a private attorney, a public defender may be appointed, or private counsel may be hired by the state to represent the defendant.

As the U.S. Constitution does not specify how soon a defendant must be brought before a magistrate after arrest, it has been left to the judicial branch to determine the timing of the initial appearance. The Supreme Court has held that the initial appearance must occur "promptly," which in most cases means within forty-eight hours of booking.[2]

8-1b Pretrial Detention

In misdemeanor cases, a defendant may decide to plead guilty and be sentenced during the initial appearance. Otherwise, the magistrate will usually release those charged with misdemeanors on their promise to return at a later date for further proceedings. For felony cases, however, the defendant is not permitted to make a plea at the initial appearance because a magistrate's court does not have jurisdiction to decide felonies.

Furthermore, in most instances the defendant will be released only if she or he posts **bail**—an amount paid by the defendant to the court and retained by the court until the defendant returns for further proceedings. Defendants who cannot afford bail are generally kept in a local jail or lockup until the date of their trial, though many jurisdictions are searching for alternatives to this practice because of overcrowded incarceration facilities.

THE PURPOSE OF BAIL Bail is provided for under the Eighth Amendment. The amendment does not, however, guarantee the right to bail. Instead, it states that "excessive bail shall not be required." This has come to mean that the bail amount must be reasonable compared with the seriousness of the wrongdoing. It does *not* mean that the amount of bail must be within the defendant's ability to pay.

At the same time, in theory, bail is not intended to be a punitive measure. That is, bail is not meant to be a sort of fine that a defendant must pay to avoid waiting for her or his trial in jail. Rather, bail is designed to provide an incentive for the accused to return to court and participate in her or his legal proceedings.

SETTING BAIL There is no uniform system for setting bail. Each jurisdiction has its own *bail tariffs*, or general guidelines concerning the proper amount of bail. For misdemeanors, the police usually follow a preapproved bail schedule created by local judicial authorities.

In felony cases, the primary responsibility to set bail lies with the judge. As Figure 8.1 shows, bail amounts generally rise according to the seriousness of the underlying offense, with murder suspects facing the highest cost of pretrial freedom.

PREVENTIVE DETENTION In addition to encouraging defendants to return to court, bail may sometimes serve another purpose: the protection of the community. That is, if a judge feels that the defendant would

FIGURE 8.1 AVERAGE BAIL AMOUNTS FOR VIOLENT FELONIES

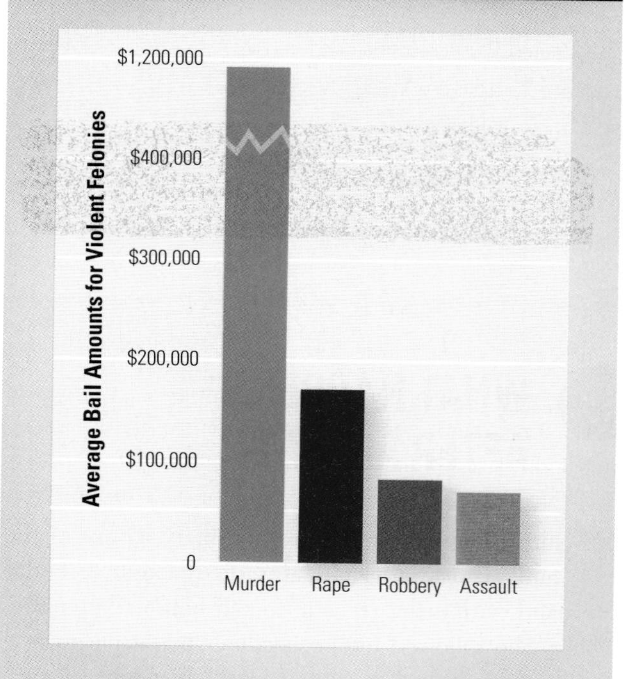

These figures represent the mean bail amounts for the seventy-five largest counties in the nation.

Source: Adapted from Bureau of Justice Statistics, *Felony Defendants in Large Urban Counties, 2009—Statistical Tables* (Washington, D.C.: U.S. Department of Justice, December 2013), Table 16, page 19.

Initial Appearance An accused's first appearance before a judge or magistrate following arrest.

Bail The dollar amount or conditions set by the court to ensure that an individual accused of a crime will appear for further criminal proceedings.

pose a threat if he or she were released before trial, the judge will set bail at a level the suspect cannot possibly afford. "The bail is really being set to keep the person in custody," admits Judge W. Kent Hamlin of Superior Court in Fresno County, California.[3] For example, in 2016, a judge set bail at $5.1 million for Damin Pashilk, a construction worker charged with seventeen counts of arson for allegedly setting a series of devastating fires in Northern California.

Alternatively, more than thirty states and the federal government have passed **preventive detention** legislation to achieve the same effect. These laws allow judges to act "in the best interests of the community" by denying bail to arrestees with prior records of violence, thus keeping them in custody prior to trial.[4]

Chris Johnson/Hemera/Getty Images

If a defendant "skips" bail by failing to appear at trial, the bail bond agent sometimes hires a fugitive-recovery agent to find the defendant and return him or her to court. **Are there any circumstances under which a fugitive-recovery agent should be allowed to use deadly force in apprehending a runaway defendant? Explain your answer.**

8-1c Posting Bail

To gain pretrial release, a defendant must pay the full amount of the bail in cash to the court. The money, called a *cash bond*, will be returned when the suspect appears for trial.

Given the large amount of funds required, and the relative lack of wealth of many criminal defendants, a defendant can rarely post bail in cash. Another option is to use real property, such as a house, instead of cash as collateral. These **property bonds** are also rare because most courts require property valued at double the bail amount. Thus, if bail is set at $5,000, the defendant (or the defendant's family and friends) will have to produce property valued at $10,000.

8-1d Bail Bond Agents

If unable to post bail with cash or property, a defendant may arrange for a **bail bond agent** to post a bail bond on the defendant's behalf. The bond agent, in effect, promises the court that he or she will turn over to the court the full amount of bail if the defendant fails to return for further proceedings. The defendant usually must give the bond agent a certain percentage of the bail (frequently 10 percent) in cash.

This amount, which is often not returned to the defendant later, is considered payment for the bond agent's assistance and assumption of risk. Depending on the amount of the bail bond, the defendant may also be required to sign over to the bond agent rights to certain property (such as a car, a valuable watch, or other asset) as security for the bond.

8-1e Bail Reform

One of the most consistent criticisms of bail is that the system is biased against low-income defendants who may not have the financial means to "buy" their temporary freedom. Numerous studies show that defendants detained in jail have worse trial outcomes than those who are able to gain pretrial release.[5] Furthermore, higher bail bond amounts make it more likely that members of minority groups will be kept in jail prior to their trials.[6]

To remedy this situation, bail reformers want to increase the use of **release on recognizance (ROR).** With ROR, the judge, relying on various **risk assessment** factors, decides that the defendant

Preventive Detention The retention of an accused person in custody due to fears that she or he will commit a crime if released before trial.

Property Bonds An alternative to posting bail in cash, in which the defendant gains pretrial release by providing the court with property as assurance that he or she will return for trial.

Bail Bond Agent A businessperson who agrees, for a fee, to pay the bail amount if the accused fails to appear in court as ordered.

Release on Recognizance (ROR) A judge's order that releases an accused person from jail with the understanding that he or she will return of his or her own will for further proceedings.

Risk Assessment A method for determining the likelihood that an offender will be involved in future wrongdoing.

is not at risk to "jump" bail and does not pose a threat to the community. The defendant is then released at no cost with the understanding that he or she will return at the time of the trial. A study of nearly two thousand defendants in Colorado found that ROR is just as effective as traditional bail bonds in protecting the public and ensuring appearance at trial, with significantly lower costs.[7]

8-2 HOW DOES A PROSECUTOR LINK A DEFENDANT TO A CRIME?

Once the initial appearance has been completed and bail has been set, the prosecutor must establish *probable cause*. In other words, the prosecutor must show that a crime was committed and link the defendant to that crime. There are two formal procedures for establishing probable cause at this stage of the pretrial process: preliminary hearings and grand juries.

8-2a The Preliminary Hearing

During the **preliminary hearing,** the defendant appears before a judge or magistrate who decides whether the evidence presented is sufficient for the case to proceed to trial. Normally, every person arrested has a right to this hearing within a reasonable amount of time after his or her initial arrest—usually, no later than ten days if the defendant is in custody or within thirty days if he or she has gained pretrial release.

Preliminary Hearing An initial hearing in which a magistrate decides if there is probable cause to believe that the defendant committed the crime with which he or she is charged.

Discovery Formal investigation by each side prior to trial.

Grand Jury A group of citizens called to decide if there is probable cause to believe that the defendant committed a crime.

Information The formal charge against the accused issued by the prosecutor after a preliminary hearing has found probable cause.

Indictment A charge or written accusation, issued by a grand jury, that probable cause exists to believe that a named person has committed a crime.

THE PRELIMINARY HEARING PROCESS The preliminary hearing is conducted in the manner of a mini-trial. Typically, a police report of the arrest is presented by a law enforcement officer, supplemented with evidence provided by the prosecutor. Because the burden of proving probable cause is relatively light (compared with proving guilt beyond a reasonable doubt), prosecutors rarely call witnesses during the preliminary hearing, saving them for the trial.

During this hearing, the defendant has a right to be represented by counsel, who may cross-examine witnesses and challenge any evidence offered by the prosecutor. In most states, defense attorneys can take advantage of the preliminary hearing to begin the process of **discovery,** in which they are entitled to have access to any evidence in the possession of the prosecution relating to the case. Discovery is considered a keystone in the adversary process, as it allows the defense to see the evidence against the defendant prior to making a plea.

WAIVING THE HEARING The preliminary hearing often seems rather perfunctory. It usually lasts no longer than five minutes, and the judge or magistrate rarely finds that probable cause does not exist. For this reason, defense attorneys commonly advise their clients to waive their right to a preliminary hearing.

Once a judge has ruled affirmatively, in many jurisdictions the defendant is bound over to the **grand jury,** a group of citizens called to decide whether probable cause exists. In other jurisdictions, the prosecutor issues an **information,** which replaces the police complaint as the formal charge against the defendant for the purposes of a trial.

8-2b The Grand Jury

The grand jury does not determine the guilt or innocence of the defendant. Rather, it determines whether the evidence presented by the prosecution is sufficient to provide probable cause that a crime occurred. If a majority of the jurors find sufficient evidence, the grand jury will issue an **indictment** (pronounced in-*dyte*-ment). Like an information in a preliminary hearing, the indictment becomes the formal charge against the defendant.

The federal government and about one-third of the states require grand jury indictments to bring felony charges. In most of the other states, a grand jury is optional. When a grand jury is not used, the discretion of whether to charge is left to the prosecutor, who must then present his or her argument at the preliminary hearing.

SPECIAL FEATURES OF GRAND JURIES Grand juries are *impaneled*, or created, for a period of time usually not exceeding three months. For the most part, grand jury proceedings are dominated by the prosecution, which can present a wide variety of evidence against the defendant, including photographs, documents, tangible objects, and the testimony of witnesses. Generally speaking, grand juries differ from trials in that:

1. Jurors can ask the district attorney and the judge questions about relevant law and can request that witnesses be recalled to the stand to testify a second time.
2. The defense cannot cross-examine prosecution witnesses, though it can present its own witnesses.
3. The proceedings are closed (secret). Witnesses can speak publicly, but only about their own testimony. Members of the grand jury are not allowed to speak to the media.

A "RUBBER STAMP" Clearly, the procedural rules of the grand jury favor prosecutors. The exclusionary rule (see Chapter 6) does not apply in grand jury investigations, so prosecutors can present evidence that would be disallowed at any subsequent trial. Furthermore, the grand jury is given the prosecution's version of the facts, with the defense having only a limited ability to offer counterarguments.

In the words of one observer, a grand jury would indict a "ham sandwich" if the government asked it to do so.[8] Overall, defendants are indicted at a rate of more than 99 percent,[9] leading to the common characterization of the grand jury as little more than a "rubber stamp" for the prosecution.

CAREER TIP If a grand jury needs more evidence, it can issue a document called a subpoena, ordering a person to appear in court and answer its questions. The task of delivering the subpoena is often left to a *process server*, whose career is based on the challenge of finding people who may not want to be found.

8-2c Case Attrition

Prosecutorial discretion includes the power *not* to prosecute cases. Generally speaking, of every one hundred felony arrests in the United States, only thirty-five of the arrestees are prosecuted, and only eighteen of these prosecutions lead to incarceration.

Consequently, fewer than one in three adults arrested for a felony sees the inside of a prison or jail cell. This phenomenon is known as **case attrition,** and it is explained in part by prosecutorial discretion.

SCARCE RESOURCES About half of the adult felony cases brought to prosecutors by police are dismissed through a *nolle prosequi* (Latin for "unwilling to pursue"). Another option is **deferred prosecution,** in which a prosecutor agrees to delay further legal action as long as the defendant meets certain conditions.

For example, if the charges involve possession of an illegal drug, the conditions may include getting substance abuse counseling and having no further contact with the criminal justice system for six months. If the defendant holds up his or her end of the agreement, then the case is usually dismissed, with the original charges expunged from the defendant's criminal record.

Why would the district attorney choose not to prosecute cases? In the section on law enforcement, you learned that the police do not have the resources to arrest every lawbreaker in the nation. Similarly, district attorneys do not have the resources to prosecute every arrest. They must choose how to distribute their scarce resources.

SCREENING FACTORS Most prosecutors have a *screening* process for deciding when to prosecute and when not to prosecute. This process varies a bit from jurisdiction to jurisdiction, but most prosecutors consider several factors in making the decision:[10]

- The most important factor in deciding to prosecute is not whether the prosecutor believes the suspect is guilty but whether there is *sufficient evidence for conviction*. If prosecutors have strong physical evidence and a number of reliable and believable witnesses, they are quite likely to prosecute.
- Prosecutors also rely heavily on *offense seriousness* to guide their priorities, preferring to take on felony offenses rather than misdemeanors. In other words, everything else being equal, a district attorney will prosecute a rapist instead of a jaywalker because the former presents a greater threat to society than does the latter. A prosecutor will also be more likely to prosecute someone with an extensive record of wrongdoing than a first-time offender.
- Sometimes a case is dropped even when it involves a serious crime and a wealth of evidence exists against the suspect. These situations usually involve *uncooperative victims*. Domestic violence cases are particularly difficult to prosecute because the victims may want to keep the matter private, fear reprisals, or have a strong desire to protect their abuser. In one study of Chicago domestic violence cases, prosecutors won

Case Attrition The process through which prosecutors, by deciding whether to prosecute each person arrested, effect an overall reduction in the number of persons prosecuted.

Deferred Prosecution When a prosecutor agrees to delay criminal proceedings against a defendant as long as the defendant meets certain requirements.

CAREER PREP

Trial Court Administrator

Job Description:

- Oversee court operations, budget and accounting, technology, emergency management, and human resources.
- Establish and maintain working relationships with judges, state attorneys, public defenders, clerks, other state and federal courts (including the United States Supreme Court), law enforcement agencies, and the public.

What Kind of Training Is Required?

- A bachelor of arts in court administration, management, or a related area, and five years of professional experience in court administration or government administration, plus five years in a supervisory capacity.
- A law degree, master's degree, or certification by the Institute of Court Management may substitute for nonsupervisory experience.

Annual Salary Range?

- $40,000–$70,000

eurobanks/Shutterstock.com

GETTING LINKEDIN

Sheriffs' departments are often involved in operating county-level courts (see Chapter 4), and these departments also hire trial court administrators. One LinkedIn posting by the Hillsborough County (Florida) Sheriff's Office for a court operations assistant focused on information technology skills and "considerable knowledge of court procedures."

convictions 73 percent of time when the victim participated in court proceedings and only 23 percent of the time when the victim refused to cooperate.[11]

CAREER TIP Many cities have shelters that provide therapeutic and practical services for both victims and perpetrators of domestic violence. These organizations rely on *domestic violence counselors* to provide such services.

- *Unreliability of victims* can also affect a charging decision. If the victim of an alleged battery charge has an extensive criminal record and is unlikely to show up in court to testify, prosecutors may be reluctant to pursue the matter.
- A prosecutor may be willing to drop a case or reduce the charges against *a defendant who is willing to testify against other offenders*. Federal law encourages this kind of behavior by offering sentencing reductions to defendants who provide "substantial assistance in the investigation or prosecution of another person who has committed an offense."[12]

ETHICS CHALLENGE

What are the potential ethical pitfalls of the practice, common among prosecutors, of reducing the charges against a defendant who is willing to testify against other offenders?

8-3 WHY DO SO MANY DEFENDANTS PLEAD GUILTY?

Based on the information (delivered during the preliminary hearing) or indictment (handed down by the grand jury), the prosecutor submits a motion to the court to order the defendant to appear before the trial court for an **arraignment.** Due process of law, as guaranteed by the Fifth Amendment, requires that a criminal defendant be informed of the charges brought against her or him and be offered an opportunity to respond to those charges. The arraignment is one of the ways in which due process requirements are satisfied by criminal procedure law.

At the arraignment, the defendant is informed of the charges and must respond by pleading not guilty or guilty. In some but not all states, the defendant may also enter a plea of ***nolo contendere,*** which is Latin for "I will not contest it." The plea of *nolo contendere* is neither an admission nor a denial of guilt. (The consequences for someone who pleads guilty and for someone who pleads *nolo contendere* are the same in a criminal trial, but the latter plea cannot be used in a subsequent civil trial as an admission of guilt.)

Most frequently, the defendant pleads guilty to the initial charge or to a lesser charge that has been agreed on through plea bargaining between the prosecutor and the defendant. If the defendant pleads guilty, no trial is necessary, and the defendant is sentenced based on the crime he or she has admitted committing.

8-3a Plea Bargaining in the Criminal Justice System

Plea bargaining most often takes place after the arraignment and before the beginning of the trial. In its simplest terms, it is a process by which the accused, represented by defense counsel, and the prosecutor work out a mutually satisfactory disposition of the case, subject to court approval.

Usually, plea bargaining involves the defendant's pleading guilty to the charges against her or him in return for a lighter sentence, but other variations are possible as well. The defendant can agree to plead guilty in exchange for having the charge against her or him reduced from, say, felony burglary to the lesser offense of breaking and entering. Or a person charged with multiple counts may agree to plead guilty if the prosecutor agrees to drop one or more of the counts. Whatever the particulars, the results of a plea bargain are generally the same: The prosecutor gets a conviction, and the defendant a lesser punishment.

In *Santobello v. New York* (1971),[13] the Supreme Court held that plea bargaining "is not only an essential part of the process but a highly desirable part for many reasons." Some observers would agree, but with ambivalence. They understand that plea bargaining offers the practical benefit of saving court resources, but question whether it is the best way to achieve justice.[14]

8-3b Motivations for Plea Bargaining

Given the high rate of plea bargaining—accounting for 97 percent of criminal convictions in state courts[15]—it follows that the prosecutor, defense attorney, and defendant each have strong reasons to engage in the practice.

LO8-2 Indicate why prosecutors, defense attorneys, and defendants often agree to plea bargains.

PROSECUTORS AND PLEA BARGAINING In most cases, a prosecutor has a single goal after charging a defendant with a crime: conviction. If a case goes to trial, no matter how certain a prosecutor may be that the defendant is guilty, there is always a chance that a jury or judge will disagree. Plea bargaining removes this risk. Furthermore, the prosecutorial screening process described earlier in the chapter is not infallible.

Sometimes, a prosecutor will find that the evidence against the accused is weaker than first thought or will uncover new information that changes the complexion of the case. In these situations, the prosecutor may decide to drop the charges or, if he or she still feels that the defendant is guilty, turn to plea bargaining to "save" a questionable case.

The prosecutor's role as an administrator also comes into play. She or he may be interested in the quickest, most efficient manner to dispose of caseloads, and plea bargains reduce the time and money spent on each case. Personal philosophy can affect the proceedings as well. A prosecutor who feels that a mandatory minimum sentence for a particular crime, such as

Arraignment A court proceeding in which the suspect is formally charged with the criminal offense stated in the indictment.

Nolo Contendere Latin for "I will not contest it." A plea in which a criminal defendant chooses not to challenge, or contest, the charges brought by the government.

Plea Bargaining The process by which the accused and the prosecutor work out a mutually satisfactory conclusion to the case.

marijuana possession, is too strict may plea bargain in order to lessen the penalty. Similarly, some prosecutors will consider plea bargaining only in certain instances—for burglary and theft, for example, but not for more serious felonies such as rape and murder.

DEFENSE ATTORNEYS AND PLEA BARGAINING Political scientist Milton Heumann has said that a defense attorney's most important lesson is that "most of his [or her] clients are guilty."[16] Given this stark reality, favorable plea bargains are often the best a defense attorney can do for clients, aside from helping them to gain acquittals.

Some have suggested that defense attorneys have other, less savory motives for convincing a client to plead guilty. These motives include a desire to increase profit margins by quickly disposing of cases[17] or a wish to ingratiate themselves with the other members of the courtroom work group by showing their "reasonableness."[18]

DEFENDANTS AND PLEA BARGAINING The plea bargain allows the defendant a measure of control over his or her fate. In September 2016, for example, Danny Heinrich pleaded guilty to federal child pornography charges that will keep him in prison for at least twenty years. As part of the plea bargain, prosecutors agreed not to charge Heinrich for murdering eleven-year-old Jacob Wetterling nearly twenty-seven years earlier—a crime for which, if convicted, he could have spent the rest of his life behind bars. As Figure 8.2 shows, defendants who plea bargain receive significantly lighter sentences on average than those who are found guilty at trial.

VICTIMS AND PLEA BARGAINING One of the major goals of the victims' rights movement has been to increase the role of victims in the plea bargaining process. In recent years, the movement has had some success in this area. About half of the states now allow for victim participation in plea bargaining. Many have laws similar to a North Carolina statute that requires the district attorney's office to offer victims "the opportunity to consult with the prosecuting attorney" and give their views on "plea possibilities."[19]

On the federal level, the Crime Victims' Rights Act grants victims the right to be "reasonably heard" during the process.[20] In the case just discussed, Jacob Wetterling's parents approved Danny Heinrich's relatively lenient plea bargain on the condition that he give a detailed confession of how he murdered Jacob and reveal the whereabouts of the boy's remains.[21]

In general, crime victims have mixed emotions regarding plea bargains. On the one hand, any form of "negotiated justice" that lessens the offender's penalty may add insult to the victim's emotional and physical injuries. On the other hand, trials can bring up events and emotions that some victims would rather not have to reexperience.

FIGURE 8.2 SENTENCING OUTCOMES FOR GUILTY PLEAS

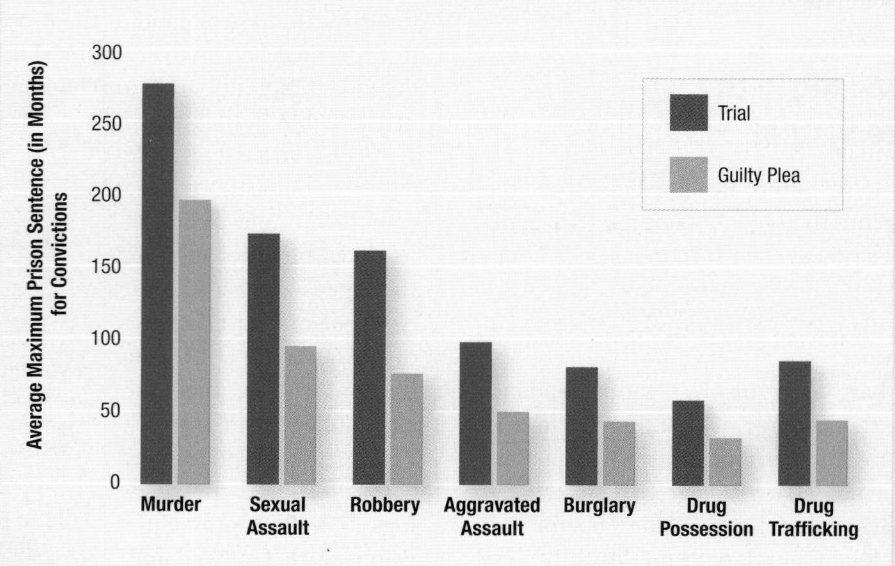

Source: Bureau of Justice Statistics, *Felony Sentences in State Courts, 2006—Statistical Tables* (Washington, D.C.: U.S. Department of Justice, December 2009), Table 4.3.

GOING TO TRIAL Despite the large number of defendants who eventually plead guilty, the plea of not guilty is fairly common at the arraignment. This is true even when the facts of the case seem stacked against the defendant. Generally, a not guilty plea in the face of strong evidence is part of a strategy to do one of the following:

1. Gain a more favorable plea bargain,
2. Challenge a crucial part of the evidence on constitutional grounds, or
3. Submit one of the affirmative defenses discussed in Chapter 3.

Of course, if either side is confident in the strength of its arguments and evidence, it will be more willing to go to trial. Both prosecutors and defense attorneys may favor a trial to gain publicity, and sometimes public pressure after an extremely violent or high-profile crime will force a chief prosecutor (who is, remember, normally an elected official) to take a weak case to trial.

Also, some defendants may insist on their right to a trial, regardless of their attorneys' advice. In the remainder of this chapter, we will examine what happens to the roughly 3 percent of indictments that do lead to the courtroom.

8-4 WHAT ARE THE SPECIAL FEATURES OF CRIMINAL TRIALS?

Criminal trial procedures are designed to protect criminal defendants against the power of the state by providing them with a number of rights. Many of the significant rights of the accused are spelled out in the Sixth Amendment, which reads, in part, as follows:

LO8-3 Identify the basic protections enjoyed by criminal defendants in the United States.

> In all criminal prosecutions, the accused shall enjoy the right to a speedy and public trial, by an impartial jury of the State and the district wherein the crime shall have been committed, ... and to be informed of the nature and cause of the accusation; to be confronted with the witnesses against him; to have compulsory process for obtaining witnesses in his favor; and to have the Assistance of Counsel for his defense.

In the last chapter, we discussed the Sixth Amendment's guarantee of the right to counsel. In this section, we will examine the other important aspects of the criminal trial, beginning with two protections explicitly stated in the Sixth Amendment: the right to a speedy trial by an impartial jury.

8-4a A "Speedy" Trial

As you have just read, the Sixth Amendment requires a speedy trial for those accused of a criminal act. The reason for this requirement is obvious: Depending on various factors, the defendant may lose his or her right to move freely and may be incarcerated prior to trial. Also, the accusation that a person has committed a crime jeopardizes that person's reputation in the community. If the defendant is innocent, the sooner the trial is held, the sooner his or her innocence can be established in the eyes of the court and the public.

The Sixth Amendment does not specify what is meant by the term *speedy*. The United States Supreme Court has refused to quantify "speedy" as well, ruling instead in *Barker v. Wingo* (1972)[22] that only in situations in which the delay is unwarranted and proved to be prejudicial can the accused claim a violation of Sixth Amendment rights.

Note that the Sixth Amendment's guarantee of a speedy trial does not apply until a person has been accused of a crime. Citizens are protected against unreasonable delays before accusation by **statutes of limitations.** These legislative time limits require prosecutors to charge a defendant with a crime within a certain amount of time after the illegal act took place.

If the statute of limitations on a particular crime is ten years, and the police do not identify a suspect until ten years and one day after the criminal act occurred, then that suspect cannot be charged with that particular offense. In general, murder and other offenses that carry the death penalty are not governed by statutes of limitations.

8-4b The Role of the Jury

The Sixth Amendment also states that anyone accused of a crime shall be judged by "an impartial jury." In *Duncan v. Louisiana* (1968),[23] the Supreme Court solidified this right by ruling that in all felony cases, the defendant is entitled to a **jury trial.** The Court has, however, left it to the individual states to decide whether juries are required for misdemeanor cases.[24] If the defendant waives her or his right to trial by jury, a **bench trial** takes place in which a judge decides questions of legality and fact, and no jury is involved.

The typical American jury consists of twelve persons. About half the states allow fewer than twelve persons on criminal juries,

Statutes of Limitations Laws limiting the amount of time prosecutors have to bring criminal charges against a suspect after the crime has occurred.

Jury Trial A trial before a judge and a jury.

Bench Trial A trial conducted without a jury, in which a judge makes the determination of the defendant's guilt or innocence.

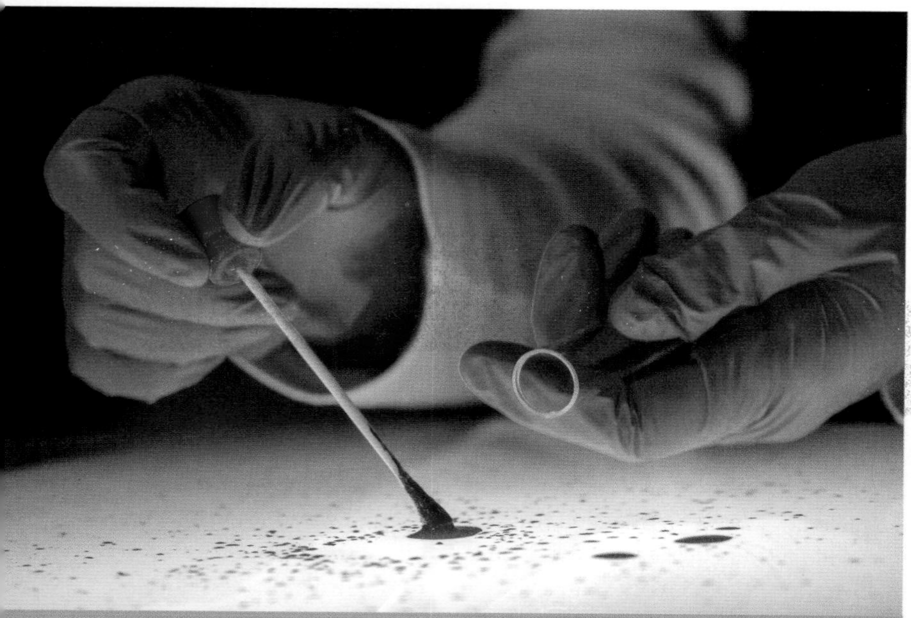

The collection of DNA in hair, saliva, and, as shown here, blood, allows crime labs to more accurately and easily match a suspect to evidence at a crime scene. **What are the arguments for and against abolishing statutes of limitations for any crime in which DNA evidence is available?**

though rarely for serious felony cases. In federal courts, defendants are entitled to have the case heard by a twelve-member jury unless both parties agree in writing to a smaller jury.

In most jurisdictions, jury verdicts in criminal cases must be *unanimous* for **acquittal** or conviction. If the jury cannot reach unanimous agreement on whether to acquit or convict the defendant, the result is a *hung jury*. When this occurs, the prosecution has the option to retry the case, which is what happened with defendant Pedro Hernandez in the case discussed in the opening of this chapter.

The Supreme Court has held that unanimity is not a rigid requirement. It declared that jury verdicts must be unanimous in federal criminal trials, but has given states leeway to set their own rules.[25] As a result, Louisiana and Oregon continue to require only ten votes for conviction in criminal cases.

8-4c The Privilege against Self-Incrimination

In addition to the Sixth Amendment, which specifies the protections we have just discussed, the Fifth Amendment to the Constitution also provides important safeguards for the defendant. The Fifth Amendment states that no person "shall be compelled in any criminal case to be a witness against himself." Therefore, a defendant has the right not to testify at his or her own trial—in popular parlance, to "take the Fifth." Because defense attorneys often are wary of exposing their clients to prosecutor's questions in court, defendants rarely take the witness stand.

Acquittal A declaration following a trial that the individual accused of the crime is innocent in the eyes of the law and thus is absolved from the charges.

It is important to note not only that the defendant has the right to "take the Fifth," but also that the decision to do so should not prejudice the jury in the prosecution's favor. The Supreme Court came to this controversial conclusion while reviewing *Adamson v. California* (1947),[26] a case involving the convictions of two defendants who had declined to testify in their own defense against charges of robbery, kidnapping, and murder. The prosecutor in the *Adamson* proceedings frequently and insistently brought this silence to the notice of the jury in his closing argument, insinuating that if the pair had been innocent, they would not have been afraid to testify.

The Court ruled that such tactics effectively invalidated the Fifth Amendment by using the defendants' refusal to testify as a ploy to insinuate guilt. As a result, judges are required to inform the jury that an accused's decision to remain silent cannot be held against him or her. This protection only covers post-arrest and trial silence, however. In 2013, the Supreme Court ruled that prosecutors can inform a jury that a defendant refused to answer police questions *before* being arrested, a process detailed in Chapter 6.[27]

8-4d The Presumption of Innocence

The presumption in criminal law is that a defendant is innocent until proved guilty. The burden of proving guilt falls on the state (the public prosecutor). Even if a defendant did in fact commit the crime, she or he will be "innocent" in the eyes of the law unless the prosecutor can substantiate the charge with sufficient evidence to convince a jury (or judge, in a bench trial) of the defendant's guilt.

Sometimes, especially when a case involves a high-profile crime, pretrial publicity may have convinced many members of the community—including potential jurors—that a defendant is guilty. In these instances, a judge has the authority to change the venue of the trial to increase the likelihood of an unbiased jury. For example, the case of Justin Ross Harris, charged with intentionally killing his infant son by leaving the boy in the back seat of an overheated SUV, received intense local media scrutiny. As a result, a Cobb County, Georgia, judge moved Harris's 2016 trial to coastal Glynn County, about 275 miles south of Atlanta, where the alleged crime occurred.

8-4e A Strict Standard of Proof

In a criminal trial, the defendant is not required to prove his or her innocence. As mentioned earlier, the burden of proving the defendant's guilt lies entirely with the state. Furthermore, the state must prove the defendant's guilt *beyond a reasonable doubt*. In other words, the prosecution must show that, based on all the evidence, the defendant's guilt is clear and unquestionable. Explaining his reservations about Pedro Hernandez's guilt in the case that opened this chapter, holdout juror Adam Sirois said that, despite the defendant's confessions, "I could not get beyond reasonable doubt."[28]

In *In re Winship* (1970),[29] a case involving the due process rights of juveniles, the Supreme Court ruled that the Constitution requires the reasonable doubt standard because it reduces the risk of convicting innocent people and therefore reassures Americans of the law's moral force and legitimacy. This high standard of proof in criminal cases reflects a fundamental social value—the belief that it is worse to convict an innocent individual than to let a guilty one go free. The consequences to the life, liberty, and reputation of an accused person from an erroneous conviction for a crime are substantial, and this has been factored into the process. Placing a high standard of proof on the prosecutor reduces the margin of error in criminal cases (at least in one direction).

8-5 HOW IS THE JURY SELECTED?

The initial step in a criminal trial involves choosing the jury. The main goal of jury selection is to produce a cross section of the population in the jurisdiction where the crime was committed. Besides having to live in the jurisdiction where the case is being tried, there are very few restrictions on eligibility to serve on a jury.

State legislatures generally set the requirements, and they are similar in most states. For the most part, jurors must be

1. Citizens of the United States.
2. Eighteen years of age or over.
3. Free of felony convictions.
4. Healthy enough to function in a jury setting.
5. Sufficiently intelligent to understand the issues of a trial.
6. Able to read, write, and comprehend the English language (with one exception—New Mexico does not allow non-English-speaking citizens to be eliminated from jury lists simply because of their lack of English-language skills).

The **master jury list**, sometimes called the *jury pool*, is made up of all the eligible jurors in a community. This list is usually drawn from voter-registration lists or driver's license rolls, which have the benefit of being easily available and up-to-date.

The next step in gathering a jury is to draw together the ***venire*** (Latin for "to come"). The *venire* is composed of all those people who are notified by the clerk of the court that they have been selected for jury duty. Those selected to be part of the *venire* are ordered to report to the courthouse on the date specified by the notice.

8-5a *Voir Dire*

At the courthouse, prospective jurors are gathered, and the process of selecting those who will actually hear the case begins. This selection process is not haphazard. The court ultimately seeks jurors who are free of any biases that may affect their willingness to listen to the facts of the case impartially.

To this end, both the prosecutor and the defense attorney have some input into the ultimate makeup of the jury. Each attorney questions prospective jurors in a proceeding known as ***voir dire*** (French for "to speak the truth"). During *voir dire*, jurors are required to provide the court with a significant amount of personal information, including home address, marital status, employment status, arrest record, and life experiences.

QUESTIONING POTENTIAL JURORS The *voir dire* process involves both written and oral questioning of potential jurors. Attorneys fashion their inquiries in such a manner as to uncover any biases on the parts of prospective jurors and to find persons who might identify with the plights of their respective sides.

As one attorney noted, though a lawyer will have many chances to talk to a jury as a whole, *voir dire* is his or her only chance to talk with the individual jurors. (To better understand the specific kinds of questions asked during this process, see Figure 8.3.)

Master Jury List The list of citizens in a court's district from which a jury can be selected.

Venire The group of citizens from which the jury is selected.

Voir Dire The preliminary questions that the trial attorneys ask prospective jurors to determine whether they fit to serve on the jury.

FIGURE 8.3 SAMPLE JUROR QUESTIONNAIRE

87. Have you, a family member, or a close friend ever seen a mental health professional, therapist, or counselor for emotional, psychological, or psychiatric difficulties?

89. Have you, a family member, or a close friend ever taken medication for psychiatric, psychological, or emotional difficulties?

93. Do you recall reading any books, magazines, or newspaper articles or seeing any television programs or movies about psychiatrists, psychologists, or other mental health professionals?

94. Is there anything about your answers to [these] questions that makes you believe you cannot be a fair and impartial juror in this matter?

Louis Lanzano/AP Images

In the murder trial of Pedro Hernandez, featured at the beginning of the chapter, defense attorneys planned to show that their client's mental problems made Hernandez (pictured here) particularly susceptible to giving police a false confession. Therefore, as the above excerpts from the juror questionnaire shows, the lawyers were interested in learning potential jurors' views on the subject of mental illness.

Source: Supreme Court of the State of New York, County of New York.

CHALLENGING POTENTIAL JURORS During *voir dire*, the attorney for each side may exercise a certain number of challenges to prevent particular persons from serving on the jury. Both sides can exercise two types of challenges: challenges "for cause" and peremptory challenges.

LO8-4 Contrast challenges for cause and peremptory challenges during *voir dire*.

Challenges for Cause If a defense attorney or prosecutor concludes that a prospective juror is unfit to serve, the attorney may exercise a **challenge for cause** and request that that person not be included on the jury.

Attorneys must provide the court with a sound, legally justifiable reason for why potential jurors are "unfit" to serve. For example, jurors can be challenged for cause if they are mentally incompetent or are proved to have a prior link—be it personal or financial—with the defendant or victim.

Peremptory Challenges Each attorney may also exercise a limited number of **peremptory challenges.** These challenges are based solely on an attorney's subjective reasoning, and the attorney usually is not required to give any legally justifiable reason for wanting to exclude a particular person from the jury.

Challenge for Cause A *voir dire* challenge for which an attorney states the reason why a prospective juror should not be included on the jury.

Peremptory Challenges *Voir dire* challenges to exclude potential jurors from serving on the jury without any supporting reason or cause.

Because of the rather random nature of peremptory challenges, each state limits the number that an attorney may utilize: between five and ten for felony trials (depending on the state) and between ten and twenty for trials that could possibly result in the death penalty (also depending on the state). Once an attorney's peremptory challenges are used up, he or she must accept forthcoming jurors, unless a challenge for cause can be used.

8-5b Race and Gender Issues in Jury Selection

For many years, prosecutors used their peremptory challenges as an instrument of segregation in jury selection. Prosecutors were able to keep African Americans off juries in cases in which an African American was the defendant. The argument that African Americans—or members of any other minority group—would be partial toward one of their own was tacitly supported by the Supreme Court. Despite its own assertion, made in *Swain v. Alabama* (1965),[30] that blacks have the same right to appear on a jury as whites, the Court mirrored the apparent racism of society as a whole by protecting the questionable actions of many prosecutors.

THE *BATSON* REVERSAL The Supreme Court reversed this policy in 1986 with *Batson v. Kentucky*.[31] In that case, the Court declared that the Constitution prohibits prosecutors from using peremptory challenges to strike possible jurors on the basis of race. Under the

AP Images/CJ Gunther

Why is it important for a defendant to be tried by a jury of her or his "peers"?

Batson ruling, the defendant must prove that the prosecution's use of a peremptory challenge was racially motivated. Doing so requires a number of legal steps:[32]

1. First, the defendant must make a *prima facie* case that there has been discrimination during *venire*. (*Prima facie* is Latin for "at first sight." Legally, it refers to a fact that is presumed to be true unless contradicted by evidence.)
2. To do so, the defendant must show that he or she is a member of a recognizable racial group and that the prosecutor has used peremptory challenges to remove members of this group from the jury pool.
3. Then, the defendant must show that these facts and other relevant circumstances raise the possibility that the prosecutor removed the prospective jurors solely because of their race.
4. If the court accepts the defendant's charges, the burden shifts to the prosecution to prove that its peremptory challenges were race neutral. If the court finds against the prosecution, it rules that a *Batson* violation has occurred.

The Court has revisited the issue of race a number of times in the years since its *Batson* decision. In *Powers v. Ohio* (1991),[33] it ruled that a defendant may contest race-based peremptory challenges even if the defendant is not of the same race as the excluded jurors. In *Georgia v. McCollum* (1992),[34] the Court placed defense attorneys under the same restrictions as prosecutors when making race-based peremptory challenges.

WOMEN ON THE JURY In *J.E.B. v. Alabama ex rel. T.B.* (1994),[35] the Supreme Court extended the principles of the *Batson* ruling to cover gender bias in jury selection. The case was a civil suit for paternity and child support brought by the state of Alabama. Prosecutors used nine of their ten challenges to remove men from the jury, while the defense made similar efforts to remove women. When challenged, the state defended its actions by referring to what it called the rational belief that men and women might have different views on the issues of paternity and child support. The Court disagreed and held this approach to be unconstitutional.

8-6 WHAT HAPPENS DURING A CRIMINAL TRIAL?

Once the jury members have been selected, the judge swears them in and the trial itself can begin. (See Figure 8.4 for a preview of the stages of a jury trial that will be detailed in this section.) A rather pessimistic truism among attorneys is that every case "has been won or lost when the jury is sworn." This reflects the belief that jurors' values are the major, if not dominant, factor in the decision of guilt or innocence.[36]

LO8-5 List the standard steps in a criminal jury trial.

In actuality, it is difficult to predict how a jury will go about reaching a decision. Despite a number of studies on the question, researchers have not been able to identify any definitive consistent patterns of jury behavior. Sometimes, jurors in a criminal trial will follow instructions to find a defendant guilty unless there is a reasonable doubt, and sometimes they seem to follow instinct or prejudice and apply the law any way they choose.

FIGURE 8.4 THE STEPS OF A JURY TRIAL

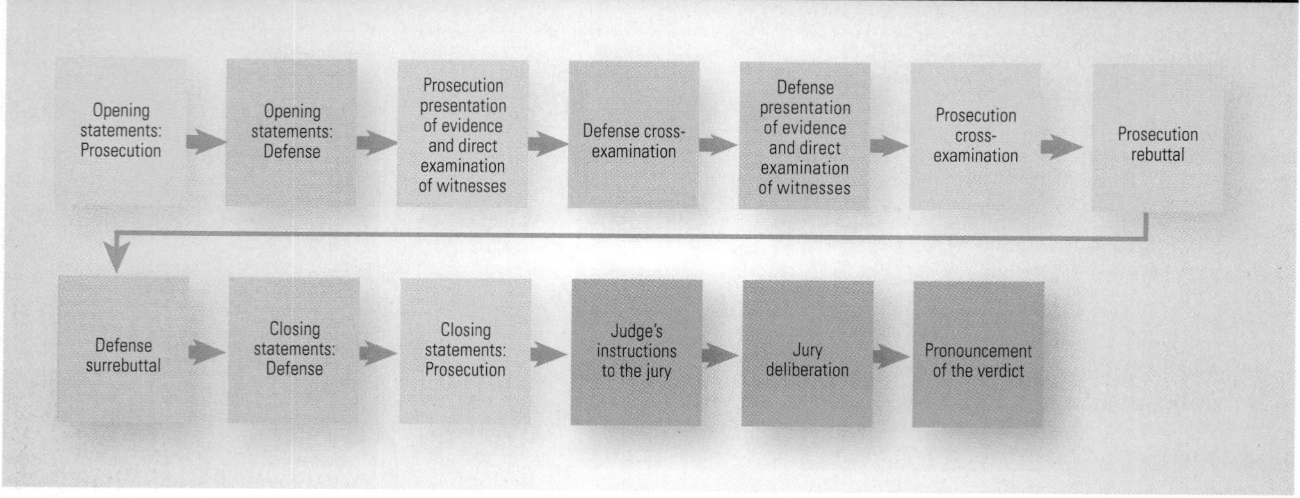

8-6a Opening Statements

Attorneys may choose to open the trial with a statement to the jury, though they are not required to do so. In these **opening statements,** the attorneys give a brief version of the facts and the supporting evidence that they will present during the trial. Because some trials can last for weeks or even months, it is extremely helpful for jurors to hear a summary of what will unfold. In short, the opening statement is a kind of "road map" that describes the destination that each attorney hopes to reach and outlines how she or he plans to reach it.

8-6b The Role of Evidence

Once the opening statements have been made, the prosecutor begins the trial proceedings by presenting the state's *evidence* against the defendant. **Evidence** is anything that is used to prove the existence or nonexistence of a fact. Courts have complex rules about what types of evidence may be presented and how the evidence may be brought out during the trial. For the most part, evidence can be broken down into two categories: testimony and real evidence. **Testimony** consists of statements by competent witnesses. **Real evidence,** presented to the court in the form of exhibits, includes any physical items—such as the murder weapon or a bloodstained piece of clothing—that affect the case.

Rules of evidence are designed to ensure that testimony and exhibits presented to the jury are relevant, reliable, and not unfairly prejudicial against the defendant. One of the tasks of the defense attorney is to challenge evidence presented by the prosecution by establishing that the evidence is not reliable.

Of course, the prosecutor also tries to demonstrate the irrelevance or unreliability of evidence presented by the defense. The final decision on whether evidence is allowed before the jury rests with the judge, in keeping with his or her role as the "referee" of the adversary system.

TESTIMONIAL EVIDENCE A person who is called to testify on factual matters that would be understood by the average citizen is referred to as a **lay witness.** If asked about the condition of a victim of an assault, for example, a lay witness could relate certain facts, such as "she was bleeding from her forehead" or "she was unconscious on the ground for several minutes."

A lay witness could not, however, give information about the medical extent of the victim's injuries, such as whether she suffered from a fractured skull or internal bleeding. Coming from a lay witness, such testimony would be inadmissible.

When the matter in question requires scientific, medical, or technical skill beyond the scope of the average person, prosecutors and defense attorneys may call an **expert witness** to the stand. The expert witness is

Opening Statements The attorneys' statements to the jury at the beginning of the trial.

Evidence Anything that is used to prove the existence or nonexistence of a fact.

Testimony Verbal evidence given by witnesses under oath.

Real Evidence Evidence that is brought into court and seen by the jury, as opposed to evidence that is described for a jury.

Lay Witness A witness who can truthfully and accurately testify on a fact in question without having specialized training or knowledge.

Expert Witness A witness with professional training or substantial experience qualifying her or him to testify on a certain subject.

CAREER PREP

Jury Consultant

Job Description:

- **Pretrial: Research jurors' backgrounds, assist with juror selection, create favorable potential juror profiles, develop *voir dire* questions, and organize mock trials to aid trial attorneys.**
- **During trial: Carefully watch jurors' body language and behavior to determine if the client trial lawyer is communicating her or his arguments successfully, coach witnesses, and help trial lawyers develop strategies.**

What Kind of Training Is Required?

- **Minimum of a bachelor's degree (although a master's degree or a Ph.D. is ideal) in sociology, political science, criminology, psychology, or behavioral science. Research and data analysis skills are also crucial for this profession.**
- **A strongly developed intuition. Jury consultants are not hired for their expertise in criminal law but for their insight into human behavior, decision making, and motivational patterns.**

iStockphoto.com/Alina Solovyova-Vincent

Annual Salary Range?

- **$44,000–$100,000**

SOCIAL MEDIA CAREER TIP
You need to differentiate yourself from everyone else online by providing unique, relevant, high-quality content on a regular basis. You should network with a purpose, not just to share fun things.

an individual who has professional training, advanced knowledge, or substantial experience in a specialized area, such as medicine, computer technology, or ballistics.

DIRECT VERSUS CIRCUMSTANTIAL EVIDENCE Two types of testimonial evidence may be brought into court: direct evidence and circumstantial evidence. **Direct evidence** is evidence that has been witnessed by the person giving testimony. "I saw Bill shoot Chris" is an example of direct evidence.

Circumstantial evidence is indirect evidence that, even if believed, does not establish the fact in question but only the degree of likelihood of the fact. In other words, circumstantial evidence can create an inference that a fact exists.

Suppose, for example, that the defendant owns a gun that shoots bullets of the type found in the victim's body. This circumstantial evidence, by itself, does not establish that the defendant committed the crime. Combined with other circumstantial evidence, however, it may do just that. For instance, if other circumstantial evidence indicates that the defendant had a motive for harming the victim and was at the scene of the crime when the shooting occurred, the jury might conclude that the defendant committed the crime.

RELEVANCE Evidence will not be admitted in

Direct Evidence Evidence that establishes the existence of a fact that is in question without relying on inference.

Circumstantial Evidence Indirect evidence that is offered to establish, by inference, the likelihood of a fact that is in question.

court unless it is relevant to the case being considered. **Relevant evidence** is evidence that tends to prove or disprove a fact in question. Forensic proof that the bullets found in a victim's body were fired from a gun discovered in the suspect's pocket at the time of arrest, for example, is certainly relevant. The suspect's prior record, showing a conviction for armed robbery ten years earlier, is, as we shall soon see, irrelevant to the case at hand and in most instances will be ruled inadmissible by the judge.

Evidence also may be excluded if it would tend to distract the jury from the main issues of the case, mislead the jury, or cause jurors to decide the issue on an emotional basis. For example, several years ago, during the murder trial of former professional football player Aaron Hernandez, Judge Susan Garsh ruled that texts sent by Odin Lloyd, the victim, to his sister on the night of Odin's death were inadmissible.

The texts read, "U saw who I'm with," and "NFL [National Football League]," referring to Hernandez. Judge Garsh kept this evidence from the jury because the texts suggested, without proof, that Lloyd was warning his sister that Hernandez was responsible for any harm that might befall him that night.[37]

EVIL CHARACTER Defense attorneys are likely to have some success precluding prosecutors from using prior purported criminal activities or actual convictions to show that the defendant has criminal propensities or an "evil character."[38] During the trial of Aaron Hernandez, mentioned earlier, the prosecution was denied the opportunity to tell the jury that the defendant faced a civil lawsuit for shooting another friend following an argument in a South Florida nightclub two years earlier. "This case is about Odin Lloyd and no one else," said Hernandez's defense attorney while arguing against the introduction of this evidence.[39]

Concerns of this kind are codified in the Federal Rules of Evidence, which state that evidence of "other crimes, wrongs, or acts is not admissible to prove the character of a person in order to show action in conformity therewith." Such evidence is allowed only when it does not apply to character construction and focuses instead on "motive, opportunity, intent, preparation, plan, knowledge, identity, or absence of mistake or accident."[40]

Although this legal concept has come under a great deal of criticism, it is consistent with the presumption-of-innocence standards discussed earlier.

Relevant Evidence Evidence tending to make a fact in question more or less probable than it would be without the evidence.

John Tlumacki/The Boston Globe/Getty Images

Several years ago, Aaron Hernandez—shown here in a Bristol County, Massachusetts, courtroom—was found guilty of fatally shooting Odin Lloyd and sentenced to life in prison without parole. During his trial, Judge Susan Garsh ruled that a photograph from the celebrity gossip website TMZ that depicted Hernandez holding a gun was inadmissible as evidence. **Why do you think the judge made this decision?**

Arguably, if a prosecutor is allowed to establish that the defendant has shown antisocial or even violent traits in the past, this will prejudice the jury against the defendant in the present trial.

Even if the judge instructs jurors that this prior evidence is irrelevant, human nature dictates that it will probably have a "warping influence" on the jurors' perception of the defendant.[41] Therefore, whenever possible, defense attorneys will keep such evidence from the jury.

8-6c The Prosecution's Case

Because the burden of proof is on the state, the prosecution is generally considered to have a more difficult task than the defense. The prosecutor attempts to establish guilt beyond a reasonable doubt by presenting the *corpus delicti* (Latin for "body of the offense") of the crime to the jury. *Corpus delicti* is a legal term that refers to the substantial facts that show a crime has been committed. By establishing such facts through the presentation of relevant and nonprejudicial evidence, the prosecutor hopes to convince the jury of the defendant's guilt.

DIRECT EXAMINATION OF WITNESSES Witnesses are crucial to establishing the prosecutor's case against the defendant. The prosecutor will call witnesses to the stand and ask them questions pertaining to the sequence of events that the trial is addressing. This form of questioning is known as **direct examination.** During direct examination, the prosecutor will usually not be allowed to ask *leading questions*—questions that might suggest to the witness a particular desired response.

A leading question might be something like "So, Mrs. Williams, you noticed the defendant threatening the victim with a broken beer bottle?" If Mrs. Williams answers "yes" to this question, she has, in effect, been "led" to the conclusion that the defendant was, in fact, threatening with a broken beer bottle. The fundamental purpose behind testimony is to establish what actually happened, not what the trial attorneys would like the jury to believe happened. (A properly worded query would be, "Mrs. Williams, please describe the defendant's manner toward the victim during the incident.")

COMPETENCE AND RELIABILITY OF WITNESSES The rules of evidence include certain restrictions and qualifications pertaining to witnesses. Witnesses must have sufficient mental competence to understand the significance of testifying under oath.

They must also be reliable in the sense that they are able to give a clear and sound description of the events in question. If not, the prosecutor or defense attorney will make sure that the jury is aware of these shortcomings through *cross-examination*.

8-6d Cross-Examination

After the prosecutor has directly examined her or his witnesses, the defense attorney is given the chance to question these witnesses. The Sixth Amendment states, "In all criminal prosecutions, the accused shall enjoy the right ... to be confronted with witnesses against him." This **confrontation clause** gives the accused, through his or her attorneys, the right to cross-examine witnesses. **Cross-examination** refers to the questioning of an opposing witness during trial, and both sides of a case are allowed to conduct cross-examination.

QUESTIONING WITNESSES Cross-examination allows the attorneys to test the truthfulness of opposing witnesses and usually entails efforts to create doubt in the jurors' minds that a witness is reliable (see Figure 8.5). After the defense has cross-examined a prosecution witness, the prosecutor may want to reestablish any reliability that might have been lost. The prosecutor can do so by again questioning the witness, a process known as *redirect examination*.

Following the redirect examination, the defense attorney will be given the opportunity to ask further questions of prosecution witnesses, or *recross examination*. Thus, each side has two opportunities to question a witness. The attorneys need not do so, but only after each side has been offered the opportunity will the trial move on to the next witness or the next stage.

HEARSAY Cross-examination is also linked to problems presented by *hearsay* evidence. **Hearsay** can be defined as any testimony given about a statement made by someone else. An example of hearsay would be: "Jenny told me that Bill told her that he was the killer." Literally, it is what someone heard someone else say. For the most part, hearsay is not admissible as evidence.

When a witness offers hearsay, the person making the original remarks is not in court and therefore cannot be cross-examined. If such testimony were allowed, the defendant's Sixth Amendment right to confront witnesses against him or her would be violated.

There are a number of exceptions to the hearsay rule, and as a result a good deal of hearsay evidence finds its way into criminal trials. For example, a hearsay statement is usually admissible if there seems to be little risk of a lie. Therefore, a statement made by someone who believes that his or her death is imminent—a "dying declaration" or a suicide note—is often allowed in court even though it is hearsay.[42] Similarly, the rules of most states allow hearsay when the statement contains an admission of wrongdoing *and* the speaker is not available to testify in court. The logic behind this exception is that a person generally does not make a statement against her or his own best interests unless it is true.[43]

8-6e The Defendant's Case

After the prosecution has finished presenting its evidence, the defense attorney may offer the defendant's case. Because the burden is on the state to prove

Direct Examination The examination of a witness by the attorney who calls the witness to the stand to testify.

Confrontation Clause The part of the Sixth Amendment that guarantees all defendants the right to confront witnesses testifying against them during the criminal trial.

Cross-Examination The questioning of an opposing witness during trial.

Hearsay A statement made by an out-of-court speaker that is later offered in court by a witness (not the speaker) concerning a matter before the court.

FIGURE 8.5 THE CROSS-EXAMINATION

During Michael Dunn's trial for the murder of Jordan Davis outside a convenience store in Jacksonville, Florida, the defendant claimed he had fatally shot Davis in self-defense. Crucially, Dunn insisted that Davis had pointed a shotgun at him, though no such weapon was found at the crime scene. When Dunn took the stand, the prosecution cross-examined him about what he said to his fiancée, Rhonda Rouer, following the shooting.

Prosecutor: How did you describe the weapon [to her]? Did you say [Davis and his friends] had a sword? Did you say they had a machete?

Dunn: Gun.

Prosecutor: A gun. You used the word "gun"?

Dunn: Multiple times.

Later in the trial, the prosecution called Rouer (pictured here) as a witness. In her testimony, she stated that Dunn never mentioned that he had been threatened with a shotgun, or any other kind of weapon, during the confrontation. Dunn was convicted of first degree murder and sentenced to life in prison without parole.

AP Images/*Florida Times-Union*, Bob Mack

the accused's guilt, the defense is not required to offer any case at all. It can simply "rest" without calling any witnesses or producing any real evidence, and ask the jury to decide the merits of the case on what it has seen and heard from the prosecution.

CREATING A REASONABLE DOUBT Defense lawyers most commonly defend their clients by attempting to expose weaknesses in the prosecutor's case. Remember that if the defense attorney can create reasonable doubt concerning the client's guilt in the mind of just a single juror, the defendant has a good chance of gaining an acquittal or at least a *hung jury*, a circumstance explained later in the chapter.

Even if the prosecution can present seemingly strong evidence, a defense attorney may succeed by creating reasonable doubt. In an illustrative case, Jason Korey bragged to his friends that he had shot and killed Joseph Brucker in Pittsburgh, Pennsylvania, and a great deal of circumstantial evidence linked Korey to the killing. The police, however, could find no direct evidence. They could not link Korey to the murder weapon, nor could they match his footprints to those found at the crime scene.

Michael Foglia, Korey's defense attorney, explained his client's bragging as an attempt to gain attention, not a true statement. Though this explanation may strike some as unlikely, in the absence of physical evidence it did create doubt in the jurors' minds, and Korey was acquitted. (For a better idea of how this strategy works in court, see the feature *Discretion in Action—Shadow of a Doubt?*)

OTHER DEFENSE STRATEGIES The defense can choose among a number of strategies to generate reasonable doubt in the jurors' minds. It can present an *alibi defense*, by submitting evidence that the accused was not at or near the scene of the crime at the time the crime was committed. Another option is to attempt an *affirmative defense*, by presenting facts that add to the ones offered by the prosecution. Possible affirmative defenses, which we discussed in detail in Chapter 3, include self-defense, insanity, duress, and entrapment.

With an affirmative defense strategy, the defense attempts to prove that the defendant should be found not guilty because of certain circumstances surrounding the crime. An affirmative strategy can be difficult to carry out because it forces the defense to prove the reliability of its own evidence, not simply disprove the evidence offered by the prosecution.

The defense is often willing to admit that a certain criminal act took place, especially if the defendant has already confessed. In this case, the primary question of the trial becomes not whether the defendant is guilty, but what the defendant is guilty of. In these situations, the defense strategy focuses on obtaining the lightest possible penalty for the defendant. This strategy is partially

DISCRETION IN ACTION

Shadow of a Doubt?

THE SITUATION Twelve-year-old Garrett was killed in his mother's apartment moments after he returned from a nearby afternoon basketball game. The boy screamed for help, according to neighbors, before being strangled to death. Oral, the local soccer coach, is eventually charged with Garrett's murder. Oral insists he is innocent. No direct evidence—such as fingerprints, trace DNA samples, or witnesses—places Oral at the crime scene.

In court, prosecutors rely heavily on security camera footage that shows Garrett walking by Oral's car in a parking lot. Oral's car then briefly follows Garrett and turns left, toward the boy's apartment, instead of right, toward Oral's home. As for motive, prosecutors contend that Oral was punishing Garrett's mother, who had recently broken up with him. At trial, Garrett's mother testifies that she ended the relationship in part because Garrett did not like Oral.

THE LAW To find a defendant guilty, a judge or jury must find beyond a reasonable doubt that she or he committed a crime.

WHAT WOULD YOU DO? You are Oral's defense attorney. Your job is to create reasonable doubt in the jurors' minds that your client killed Garrett. Oral tells you that he was in the parking lot scouting a local soccer team on a field that the boy passed on the way home. You also discover that a police dog brought to the crime scene followed a scent to a nearby river nowhere near your client's house and that video footage shows a white man in a hoodie near Garrett's home at the time of the murder. (Oral is African American.) Finally, your client was not arrested until two-and-a-half years after Garrett's death.

Taking all these factors into consideration, what argument will you make before the jury to create reasonable doubt?

To see how a defense attorney argued in a case with similar facts that took place in Potsdam, New York, go to Example 8.1 in Appendix A.

responsible for the high percentage of proceedings that end in plea bargains.

8-6f Rebuttal and Surrebuttal

After the defense closes its case, the prosecution is permitted to bring new evidence forward that was not used during its initial presentation to the jury. This is called the **rebuttal** stage of the trial. When the rebuttal stage is finished, the defense is given the opportunity to cross-examine the prosecution's new witnesses and introduce new witnesses of its own. This final act is part of the *surrebuttal*.

After these stages have been completed, the defense may offer a *motion for a directed verdict*, asking the judge to find in the defendant's favor. If this motion is rejected, and it almost always is, the case is closed, and the opposing sides offer their closing arguments.

8-6g Closing Arguments

In their **closing arguments,** the attorneys summarize their presentations and argue one final time for their respective cases. In most states, the defense attorney goes first, and then the prosecutor. (In Colorado, Kentucky, and Missouri, the order is reversed.) An effective closing argument includes all of the major points that support the government's or the defense's case. It also emphasizes the shortcomings of the opposing party's case.

Rebuttal Evidence given to counteract or disprove evidence presented by the opposing party.

Closing Arguments Arguments made by each side's attorney after the cases for the plaintiff and defendant have been presented.

ETHICS CHALLENGE

As you learned in this section, expert witnesses are paid for their testimony by either the prosecution or the defense. In your opinion, what ethical problems, if any, does this common practice raise? What role does cross-examination play in limiting any potential problems with partisan expert witnesses?

8-7 WHAT HAPPENS AT THE END OF A CRIMINAL TRIAL?

After closing arguments, the outcome of the trial is in the hands of the jury. Before the jurors begin their deliberations, the judge gives the jury a **charge,** summing up the case and instructing the jurors on the rules of law that apply to the issues in the case.

These charges, also called jury instructions, are usually prepared during a special *charging conference* involving the judge and the trial attorneys. In this conference, the attorneys suggest the instructions they would like the jurors to receive, but the judge makes the final decision as to the charges submitted. If the defense attorney disagrees with the charges sent to the jury, he or she can enter an objection, thereby setting the stage for a possible appeal.

8-7a Jury Deliberation

After receiving the charge, the jury begins its deliberations. Jury deliberation is a somewhat mysterious process, as it takes place in complete seclusion. Most of what is known about how a jury deliberates comes from mock trials or interviews with jurors after the verdict has been reached.

A general picture of the deliberation process constructed from this research shows that jurors are not necessarily predisposed to argue with one another over the fate of the defendant. In approximately three out of every ten cases, the initial vote by the jury led to a unanimous decision. In 90 percent of the remaining cases, the majority eventually dictated the decision.[44]

One of the most important instructions that a judge normally gives the jurors is that they should seek no outside information during deliberation. The idea is that jurors should base their verdict *only* on the evidence that the judge has deemed admissible. In extreme cases, the judge will order that the jury be *sequestered*, or isolated from the public, during the trial and deliberation stages of the proceedings. **Sequestration** is used when deliberations are expected to be lengthy, or when the trial is attracting a high amount of interest and the judge wants to keep the jury from being unduly influenced. Juries are usually sequestered in hotels and kept under the watch and guard of officers of the court.

Charge The judge's instructions to the jury following the attorneys' closing arguments.

Sequestration The isolation of jury members during a trial to ensure that their judgment is not tainted by outside information.

Verdict A formal decision made by the jury.

Hung Jury A jury whose members are so irreconcilably divided in their opinions that they cannot reach a verdict.

***Allen* Charge** An instruction by a judge to a deadlocked jury that asks the jurors in the minority to reconsider the majority opinion.

Appeal The process of seeking a higher court's review of a lower court's decision for the purpose of correcting or changing this decision.

8-7b The Verdict

Once it has reached a decision, the jury issues a **verdict.** The most common verdicts are guilty and not guilty, though, as we have seen, juries may signify different degrees of guilt if instructed to do so. Following the announcement of a guilty or not guilty verdict, the jurors are discharged, and the jury trial proceedings are finished.

When a jury in a criminal trial is unable to agree on a unanimous verdict—or a majority verdict, in certain states—it returns with no decision. This is known as a **hung jury.** Following a hung jury, the judge will declare a mistrial, and the case will be tried again in front of a different jury if the prosecution decides to pursue the matter a second time. As you may recall, this is what happened with defendant Pedro Hernandez, whose multiple trials for the murder of six-year-old Etan Patz we discussed at the opening of the chapter.

A judge can do little to reverse a hung jury, considering that "no decision" is just as legitimate a verdict as guilty or not guilty. In some states, however, if there are only a few dissenters to the majority view, a judge can send the jury back to the jury room under a set of rules set forth more than a century ago by the Supreme Court in *Allen v. United States* (1896).[45]

The ***Allen* charge,** as this instruction is called, asks the jurors in the minority to reconsider the majority opinion. Many jurisdictions do not allow *Allen* charges on the ground that they improperly coerce jurors with the minority opinion to change their minds.[46]

8-7c Appeals

Even if a defendant is found guilty, the trial process is not necessarily over. In our criminal justice system, a person convicted of a crime has a right to appeal. An **appeal** is the process of seeking a higher court's review of a lower court's decision for the purpose of correcting or changing the lower court's judgment. A defendant who loses a case

CJ and TECHNOLOGY

Wireless Devices in the Courtroom

One former juror, fresh from trial, complained that the members of the courtroom work group had not provided the jury with enough information to render a fair verdict. "We felt deeply frustrated at our inability to fill those gaps in our knowledge," he added.

Until recently, frustrated jury members have lacked the means to carry out their own investigations in court. Today, however, jurors with smartphones and tablet computers can easily access news stories and online research tools. With these wireless devices, they can look up legal terms, blog and tweet about their experiences, and sometimes even try to contact other participants in the trial through "friend" requests on social media websites.

This access can cause serious problems for judges, whose responsibility it is to ensure that no outside information taints the jury's decision. Over the past several years, jurors have used smartphones to pull up images of a crime scene on Google Earth, measure the distance between a defendant's home and the crime scene on MapQuest, and look up the definitions of technical terms such as *reasonable doubt* and *retinal detachment*. In many such cases, the presiding judge feels obligated to declare a mistrial, as these instances of juror misconduct could have improperly influenced the final verdict.

Thinking about Wireless Devices in the Courtroom
The Sixth Amendment guarantees the accused the right to trial by an "impartial jury." How does the use of wireless devices in the courtroom threaten this right?

in a trial court cannot automatically appeal the conviction. The defendant normally must first be able to show that the trial court acted improperly on a question of law.

At the state level, an appellate court upholds the decision of the trial court in 52 percent of all appeals.[47] Common reasons for appeals include the introduction of tainted evidence by the prosecution or faulty jury instructions delivered by the trial judge. In 2017, for example, Justin Ross Harris appealed his conviction for killing his young son by leaving the boy in a hot car, mentioned earlier in the chapter. Among other issues, Harris's lawyers claimed that the trial judge created an "unduly prejudicial atmosphere" by showing the jury "ghoulish images of a dead child with his eyes open" and "macabre autopsy photos."[48]

DOUBLE JEOPARDY The appeals process is available only to the defense. If a jury finds the accused not guilty, the prosecution cannot appeal to have the decision reversed. To do so would infringe on the defendant's Fifth Amendment rights against multiple trials for the same offense.

This guarantee against being tried a second time for the same crime is known as protection from **double jeopardy.** The prohibition against double jeopardy means that once a criminal defendant is found not guilty of a particular crime, the government may not reindict the person and retry him or her for the same crime.

The prohibition against double jeopardy is not, however, absolute. There are several circumstances in which, for practical purposes, a defendant can find herself or himself back in court after a jury has failed to find her or him guilty of committing a particular crime:

1. One state's prosecution will not prevent a different state or the federal government from prosecuting the same crime.
2. Acquitted defendants can be sued in *civil court* for circumstances arising from the alleged wrongdoing on the theory that they are not being tried for the same *crime* twice.
3. A hung jury is not an acquittal for purposes of double jeopardy. So, if a jury is deadlocked, the government is free to set a new trial.

THE APPEALS PROCESS There are two basic reasons for the appeals process. The first is to correct an error made during the initial trial. The second is to review policy. Because of this second

Double Jeopardy To twice place at risk (jeopardize) a person's life or liberty.

function, the appellate courts are an important part of the flexible nature of the criminal justice system. When existing law has ceased to be effective or no longer reflects the values of society, an appellate court can effectively change the law through its decisions and the precedents that it sets.[49] A classic example was the *Miranda v. Arizona* decision (see Chapter 6), which, although it failed to change the fate of the defendant (he was found guilty on retrial), had a far-reaching impact on custodial interrogation of suspects.

It is also important to understand that once the appeals process begins, the defendant is no longer presumed innocent. The burden of proof has shifted, and the defendant is obligated to prove that her or his conviction should be overturned. The method of filing an appeal differs slightly among the fifty states and the federal government, but the five basic steps are similar enough for summarization in Figure 8.6. For the most part, defendants are not required to exercise their right to appeal. The one exception involves the death sentence. Given the seriousness of capital punishment, the defendant is required to appeal the case, regardless of his or her wishes.

FIGURE 8.6 THE STEPS OF AN APPEAL

1. The defendant, or *appellant*, files a **notice of appeal**—a short written statement outlining the basis of the appeal.
2. The appellant transfers the trial court record to the appellate court. This record contains items such as evidence and a transcript of the testimony.
3. Both parties file **briefs**. A brief is a written document that presents the party's legal arguments.
4. Attorneys from both sides present **oral arguments** before the appellate court.
5. Having heard from both sides, the judges of the appellate court retire to deliberate the case and make their decision. As described in Chapter 7, this decision is issued as a **written opinion**. Appellate courts generally do one of the following:
   - **Uphold** the decision of the lower court.
   - **Modify** the lower court's decision by changing only a part of it.
   - **Reverse** the decision of the lower court.
   - **Reverse and remand** the case, meaning that the matter is sent back to the lower court for further proceedings.

8-7d Wrongful Convictions

The appeals process is primarily concerned with "legal innocence." That is, appeals courts focus on how the law was applied in a case, rather than on the facts of the case. But what if a defendant who is factually innocent has been found guilty at trial? For the most part, such **wrongful convictions** can be righted only with the aid of new evidence suggesting that the defendant was not, in fact, guilty. When such new evidence is uncovered, a prosecutor's office can choose to reopen the case and redress the initial injustice.

DNA EXONERATIONS In Chapter 5, we saw how DNA fingerprinting has been a boon for law enforcement. According to the Innocence Project, a New York–based legal group, as of February 2017, the procedure has also led to the exoneration of 394 convicts in the United States.[50] The five most common reasons[51] for wrongful convictions later overturned by DNA evidence:

1. *Eyewitness misidentification*, which research shows to be a factor in nearly three-fourths of all cases in which a falsely convicted person has been exonerated by DNA evidence.[52]
2. *False confessions*, which are often the result of overly coercive police interrogation techniques or a suspect's mental illness.
3. *Faulty forensic evidence* produced by crime labs, which analyze evidence of everything from bite marks to handwriting samples to ballistics. Since the arrest of Keith Harward in 1982, at least twenty-four other defendants whose convictions were based wholly or partly on bite-mark evidence have been exonerated.[53]
4. *False informant testimony*, provided by "jailhouse snitches" and other offenders who are motivated to lessen their own punishment by incriminating other suspects.
5. *Law enforcement misconduct* by overzealous or corrupt police officers and prosecutors.

Wrongful Conviction The conviction, either by verdict or by guilty plea, of a person who is factually innocent of the charges.

HABEAS CORPUS In 2009, the United States Supreme Court ruled that convicts have no constitutional right to DNA testing that may prove their innocence.[54] Nonetheless, most states allow prisoners access to such testing if there is a reasonable possibility of a wrongful conviction.

In addition, even after the appeals process is exhausted, a convict may have access to a procedure

AP Images/Daniel Sangjib Min/Richmond Times-Dispatch

In 2016, after spending more than thirty-three years behind bars, Keith Harward was released from a Virginia prison when DNA evidence proved him innocent of the violent crimes for which he was initially convicted. **Should prosecutors be punished for bringing charges against defendants such as Harward who turn out to be innocent? If so, what would be an appropriate punishment? Explain your answers.**

known as ***habeas corpus*** (Latin for "you have the body"). *Habeas corpus* is a judicial order that commands a corrections official to bring a prisoner before a federal court so that the court can hear the convict's claim that he or she is being held illegally. A writ of *habeas corpus* differs from an appeal in that it can be filed only by someone who is imprisoned. In recent years, defense attorneys have successfully used the *habeas corpus* procedure for a number of their death row clients who have new DNA evidence proving their innocence.[55]

Habeas Corpus An order that requires corrections officials to bring an inmate before a court and explain why he or she is being held in prison.

STUDY TOOLS 8

LOCATED IN TEXTBOOK

- ☐ Rip out the Chapter Review Card.
- ☐ Review with the Chapter Quiz following this chapter.

LOCATED AT WWW.CENGAGEBRAIN.COM

- ☐ Review key terms flash cards.
- ☐ Read the chapter on all your favorite devices.
- ☐ Complete an Exam to test your knowledge.
- ☐ Check out Visual Summaries and You Decide activities to explore chapter concepts.

Quiz

1. Following the initial appearance, in most cases the defendant will be detained until trial unless he or she can post ________________________.

2. In some states, a group of citizens called a ________________________ ________________________ determines whether the prosecution has established probable cause that the defendant committed the crime in question.

3. A ________________________ ________________________ occurs when the prosecution and the defense work out an agreement that resolves the case with the defendant admitting guilt.

4. If a defendant waives his or her right to a jury trial, a ________________________ trial takes place in which the judge decides questions of law and fact.

5. To gain a "guilty" verdict, the prosecution must prove that the defendant is guilty beyond a ________________________ ________________________.

6. The process by which the prosecution and defense choose a jury is called ________________________ ________________________.

7. Evidence will not be admitted into a criminal trial unless it is relevant and does not unfairly ________________________ the jury against the defendant.

8. ________________________ examination takes places when, for example, the prosecution questions those witnesses that it has called to strengthen its case.

9. ________________________-examination takes place when, for example, defense attorneys question those witnesses that have been called to the stand by the prosecution.

10. If a defendant is convicted, she or he has the option of filing an ________________________ claiming that the trial court acted improperly on a question of law during the proceedings.

Answers to the Chapter 8 Quiz can be found in the Answers section in the back of the book.

9 Punishment and Sentencing

Pat Greenhouse/The Boston Globe/Getty Images

LEARNING OBJECTIVES

After studying this chapter, you will be able to . . .

- **9-1** List and contrast the four basic philosophical reasons for sentencing criminals.
- **9-2** Contrast indeterminate with determinate sentencing.
- **9-3** Explain some of the reasons why sentencing reform has occurred.
- **9-4** Describe the goal of mandatory minimum sentencing guidelines and explain why these laws have become unpopular in recent years.
- **9-5** Identify the two stages that make up the bifurcated process of death penalty sentencing.

After finishing this chapter, go to **PAGE 202** for **STUDY TOOLS**

Questionable Judgment

"In 2006, I sentenced a man to eighteen years in prison," federal district Judge Stefan Underhill wrote a decade later. "I have been wrestling with that decision ever since." Judge Underhill worried that neither society nor the defendant—a gang enforcer who killed a potential witness before turning his life around—benefited from such a long stint behind bars. This admission gained little attention, as judges rarely face public disapproval for being too harsh when sentencing, particularly for a confessed murderer.

Excessive judicial leniency, however, is another story. In 2016, for example, Santa Clara County (California) Judge Aaron Persky came under withering criticism for sentencing Stanford University freshman and first-time offender Brock Turner to six months in jail. Turner had been found guilty of raping a twenty-three-year-old woman behind a dumpster on the Stanford campus. Judge Persky defended his decision by saying that Turner had "less moral culpability" because he was drunk at the time of the assault. Court documents seemed to show that the judge took into consideration Turner's considerable skill as a collegiate swimmer in handing down the light sentence. The victim responded, "How fast Brock swims does not lessen the severity of what happened to me, and should not lessen the severity of his punishment."

Five months later, Judge John McKeon of Valley County (Montana) District Court faced comparable public outrage after he sentenced a father to sixty days in jail for repeatedly raping his twelve-year-old daughter. The judge relied on a state law that recommends probation for sex offenders if such a disposition "affords a better opportunity for rehabilitation of the offender and for the ultimate protection of the victim and society." Reacting to an online petition to remove him from office that had collected about 265,000 supporters, Judge McKeon said that though his ruling was not "popular," it was "just and proper." More than 1.3 million people signed a similar online petition to remove Judge Persky as part of the Brock Turner sentencing controversy.

In 2016, Judge Aaron Persky sentenced Brock Turner (shown here leaving a Santa Clara, California, jail) to six months behind bars for sexual assault. The judge justified his sentencing decision by saying that a long prison term would not make Turner any less likely to commit another violent crime in the future. *What is your opinion of this reasoning?*

REUTERS/Stephen Lam

9-1 WHY DO WE PUNISH CRIMINALS?

LO9-1 List and contrast the four basic philosophical reasons for sentencing criminals.

Professor Herbert Packer has said that punishing criminals serves two ultimate purposes: the "deserved infliction of suffering on evil doers" and "the prevention of crime."[1] Even this straightforward assessment raises several questions. How does one determine the sort of punishment that is "deserved"? How can we be sure that certain penalties "prevent" crime? Should criminals be punished solely for the benefit of society, or should their well-being also be taken into consideration? Why did Brock Turner and the Montana father receive such light sentences for acts that have resulted in many other defendants spending decades behind bars?

Sentencing laws indicate how any given society has answered these questions, but do not tell us why they were answered in that manner. To understand why, we must first consider the four basic philosophical reasons for sentencing—retribution, deterrence, incapacitation, and rehabilitation.

9-1a Retribution

The oldest and most common justification for punishing someone is that he or she "deserved it"—as the Old Testament states, "an eye for an eye and a tooth for a tooth." Under a system of justice that favors

retribution, a wrongdoer who has freely chosen to violate society's rules must be punished for the infraction.

Retribution relies on the principle of **just deserts,** which holds that the severity of the punishment must be in proportion to the severity of the crime. Retributive justice is not the same as *revenge*. Whereas revenge implies that the wrongdoer is punished only with the aim of satisfying a victim or victims, retribution is more concerned with the needs of society as a whole.

One problem with retributive ideas of justice lies in proportionality. Whether or not one agrees with the death penalty, the principle behind it is easy to fathom: The punishment (death) often fits the crime (murder). But what about the theft of an automobile? How does one fairly determine the amount of time the thief must spend in prison for that crime? Should the type of car or the wealth of the car owner matter? Theories of retribution often have a difficult time providing answers to such questions.

Irfan Khan/*Los Angeles Times*/Getty Images

A Los Angeles judge recently sentenced Dr. Hsui-Ying Tseng (pictured here) to thirty years to life in prison for improperly prescribing drugs to three of her patients who fatally overdosed. **How does the theory of deterrence justify Tseng's punishment?**

9-1b Deterrence

Whereas the goal of retribution is only to punish the wrongdoer, the goal of **deterrence** is to prevent future crimes. By "setting an example," society is sending a message to potential criminals that certain actions will not be tolerated.

Deterrence can take two forms: general and specific. The basic idea of *general deterrence* is that by punishing one person, society discourages others from committing a similar crime. *Specific deterrence* assumes that an individual, after being punished once for a certain act, will be less likely to repeat that act because she or he does not want to be punished again. Proponents of harsh sentences for nonviolent drug crimes often rely on general deterrence principles to argue that such punishments discourage illegal drug possession and distribution by others.[2]

Both forms of deterrence have proved problematic in practice. General deterrence assumes that a person commits a crime only after a rational decision-making process in which he or she implicitly weighs the benefits of the crime against the possible costs of the punishment. This is not necessarily the case, especially for young offenders who tend to value the immediate rewards of crime over the possible future consequences. The argument for specific deterrence is somewhat weakened by the fact that a relatively small number of habitual offenders are responsible for the majority of certain criminal acts.

Retribution The philosophy that those who commit criminal acts should be punished for breaking society's rules to the extent required by just deserts.

Just Deserts A sanctioning philosophy based on the assertion that criminal punishment should be proportionate to the severity of the crime.

Deterrence The strategy of preventing crime through the threat of punishment.

Incapacitation A strategy for preventing crime by detaining wrongdoers in prison, thereby separating them from the community and reducing criminal opportunities.

9-1c Incapacitation

"Wicked people exist," said James Q. Wilson. "Nothing avails except to set them apart from innocent people."[3] Wilson's blunt statement summarizes the justification for **incapacitation** as a form of punishment.

As a purely practical matter, incarcerating criminals guarantees that they will not be a danger to society, at least for the length of their prison terms. Such reasoning is partially responsible for the dramatic increase of life sentences without the possibility of parole in the criminal justice system. Since 1984, the inmate population serving life without parole has quadrupled, to nearly 160,000, encompassing one of every nine individuals behind bars in the United States.[4]

CJ and TECHNOLOGY

Electronic Eavesdropping

"Our society is going through a technological transformation," notes Adam Schwartz, a civil liberties lawyer. "We are at a time where tens of millions of Americans carry around a telephone or other device in their pocket that has an audio-video capacity. Ten years ago, [we] weren't walking around with all these devices." This widespread ability to record interactions with others has increased the possibility that Americans are breaking the law, often without their knowledge. The criminal codes of twelve states require the consent of all parties involved before any conversation can be recorded.

In some cases, the penalties for breaking these laws can be quite harsh. Under the Illinois Eavesdropping Act, audio-recording a civilian without consent is a Class 4 felony, punishable by up to three years in prison. Audio-recording an Illinois law enforcement official who is performing her or his duties without consent is a Class 1 felony, punishable by up to fifteen years in prison.

Thinking about Electronic Eavesdropping
What is the purpose behind making electronic eavesdropping a criminal act deserving of punishment?

Several studies do support incapacitation's efficacy as a crime-fighting tool. Criminologist Isaac Ehrlich of the University at Buffalo estimated that a 1 percent increase in sentence length will produce a 1 percent decrease in the crime rate.[5] More recently, Avinash Singh Bhati of the Urban Institute in Washington, D.C., found that higher levels of incarceration lead to fewer violent crimes but have little impact on property crime rates.[6]

Incapacitation as a theory of punishment does suffer from several weaknesses. Unlike retribution, it offers no proportionality with regard to a particular crime. Giving a burglar a life sentence would certainly ensure that she or he would not commit another burglary. Does that justify such a severe penalty?

Furthermore, incarceration protects society only until the criminal is freed. Many studies have shown that, on release, offenders may actually be more likely to commit crimes than before they were imprisoned.[7] In that case, incapacitation may increase likelihood of crime, rather than diminish it.

9-1d Rehabilitation

For many, **rehabilitation** is the most "humane" goal of punishment. This line of thinking reflects the view that crime is a "social phenomenon" caused not by the inherent criminality of a person, but by factors in that person's surroundings. By removing wrongdoers from their environment and intervening to change their values and personalities, the rehabilitative model suggests that criminals can be "treated" and possibly even "cured" of their proclivities toward crime.

Studies of the effectiveness of rehabilitation are too varied to be easily summarized. It does, however, appear that, in most instances, criminals who receive treatment are less likely to reoffend than those who do not.[8]

9-1e Restorative Justice

Restorative justice strategies attempt to repair the damage that a crime does to the victim, the victim's family, and society as a whole. This outlook relies on the efforts of the offender to "undo" the harm caused by the criminal act through an apology and **restitution,** or monetary compensation for losses suffered by the victim. Five features differentiate restorative justice from the mainstream criminal justice system:

1. *Offender involvement.* Offenders are given the opportunity to take responsibility for and address the reasons behind their behavior in ways that do not involve the corrections system.
2. *Victim involvement.* Victims have a voice in determining how the offender should atone for her or his crime.

Rehabilitation The philosophy that society is best served when wrongdoers are provided the resources needed to eliminate their criminal behavior.

Restorative Justice An approach to punishment designed to repair the harm done to the victim and the community by the offender's criminal act.

Restitution Monetary compensation for damages done to the victim by the offender's criminal act.

CAREER PREP

Mediation Specialist

Job Description:

- **Complement the standard adjudication of a crime by acting as a third party facilitator between the victim and the offender. Help resolve their conflicts through a face-to-face discussion of the criminal act.**
- **Encourage the increased presence of restorative justice in the criminal justice system.**

Golden Pixels LLC/Shutterstock.com

What Kind of Training Is Required?

- **No formal licensing or certification process exists for mediators. Rather, training is available through independent mediation programs and mediation organizations. Some colleges and universities offer advanced degrees in conflict management and dispute resolution.**
- **Skills required include the ability to communicate, negotiate, solve problems, and analyze difficult situations. Successful mediators are also highly intuitive and able to meet clients' emotional needs during difficult times.**

Annual Salary Range?

- **$50,000–$70,000**

SOCIAL MEDIA CAREER TIP

Be aware of your e-mail address/screen name/login name and what it represents. Stay away from nicknames. Use a professional and unique name to represent yourself consistently across social media platforms.

3. *Victim-offender interaction*. On a voluntary basis, victims and offenders meet to discuss and better understand the circumstances of the crime. This meeting allows the victim to express her or his feelings related to the offense.
4. *Community involvement*. Community members also affected by the crime can participate in the process and request an apology and restitution from the offender.
5. *Problem-solving practices*. Participants in the process—including victims, offenders, and community members—can develop strategies for solving the problems that led to the crime in question.[9]

Although restorative justice is theoretically available for all types of criminal behavior, it almost always involves property crime, public order crime, and, particularly, offenses committed by juveniles. Rarely, if ever, will restorative justice principles be applied to violent crime.

ETHICS CHALLENGE

In Iran, convicted criminals can buy their freedom from their victims. Several years ago, for example, a man found guilty of murdering a rival during a knife fight had the charges against him dropped after he paid the victim's family $50,000. Does this practice have any ethical benefits for society? How does it differ from the American practice of restitution, described in this section? Explain your answers.

9-2 WHAT IS THE STRUCTURE OF THE SENTENCING PROCESS?

Philosophy not only is integral to explaining *why* we punish criminals, but also influences *how* we do so. The history of criminal sentencing in the United States has been characterized by shifts in institutional power among the three branches of the government. When public opinion moves toward more severe strategies of retribution, deterrence, and incapacitation, legislatures have responded by asserting their power over determining sentencing guidelines. In contrast, periods of rehabilitation are marked by a transfer of this power to judges.

9-2a Legislative Sentencing Authority

Because legislatures are responsible for making laws, these bodies are also initially responsible for passing the criminal codes that determine the length of sentences.

INDETERMINATE SENTENCING Penal codes with **indeterminate sentencing** policies set a minimum and maximum amount of time that a person must spend in prison. For example, the indeterminate sentence for aggravated assault could be three to nine years, or six to twelve years, or twenty years to life.

Within these parameters, a judge can prescribe a particular term, after which an administrative body known as the *parole board* decides at what point the offender is to be released. A prisoner is aware that he or she is eligible for *parole* as soon as the minimum time has been served and that good behavior can further shorten the sentence.

> **LO9-2** Contrast indeterminate with determinate sentencing.

DETERMINATE SENTENCING Disillusionment with the somewhat vague nature of indeterminate sentencing often leads politicians to support **determinate sentencing,** or fixed sentencing. As the name implies, in determinate sentencing an offender serves exactly the amount of time to which she or he is sentenced (minus "good time," described below). For example, if the legislature deems that the punishment for a first-time armed robber is ten years, then the judge has no choice but to impose a sentence of ten years, and the criminal will serve ten years minus good time before being freed.

"GOOD TIME" AND TRUTH IN SENTENCING Often, the amount of time prescribed by a judge bears little relation to the amount of time the offender actually spends behind bars. In states with indeterminate sentencing, parole boards have broad powers to release prisoners once they have served the minimum portion of their sentence. Furthermore, most states offer prisoners the opportunity to reduce their sentences by doing **"good time"**—or behaving well—as determined by prison administrators. (See Figure 9.1 for an idea of the effects of good-time regulations and other early-release programs on state prison sentences.)

Sentence-reduction programs promote discipline within a correctional institution and reduce overcrowding, so many prison officials welcome them. The public, however, may react negatively to news that a violent criminal has served a shorter term than ordered by a judge and pressure elected officials to "do something."

In Illinois, for example, some inmates were serving less than half their sentences by receiving a one-day reduction in their term for each day of "good time." Under pressure from victims' groups, the state legislature passed a **truth-in-sentencing law** that requires murderers and others convicted of serious crimes to complete at least 85 percent of their sentences with no time off for good behavior.[10]

As their name suggests, the primary goal of these laws is to provide the public with more accurate information about the actual amount of time an offender will spend behind bars. The laws also keep convicts incapacitated for longer periods of time. Fifteen years after Illinois passed its truth-in-sentencing law, those murderers subject to the legislation were spending an average of seventeen months more in prison than those not subject to the legislation. For sex offenders, the difference was 3.5 years.[11] Today, forty states have instituted some form of truth-in-sentencing laws, though the continued popularity of such statutes is being undermined by the pressures of overflowing prisons.

9-2b Judicial Sentencing Authority

During the pretrial procedures and the trial itself, the judge's role is somewhat passive and reactive. She or he is primarily a "procedural watchdog," ensuring

Indeterminate Sentencing Imposition of a sentence that prescribes a range of years rather than a specified number of years to be served.

Determinate Sentencing Imposition of a sentence that is fixed by a sentencing authority and cannot be reduced by judges or other corrections officials.

"Good Time" A reduction in time served by prisoners based on good behavior, conformity to rules, and other positive behavior.

Truth-in-Sentencing Law Legislative attempts to ensure that convicts will serve approximately the terms to which they were initially sentenced.

FIGURE 9.1 AVERAGE SENTENCE LENGTH AND ESTIMATED TIME TO BE SERVED IN STATE PRISON

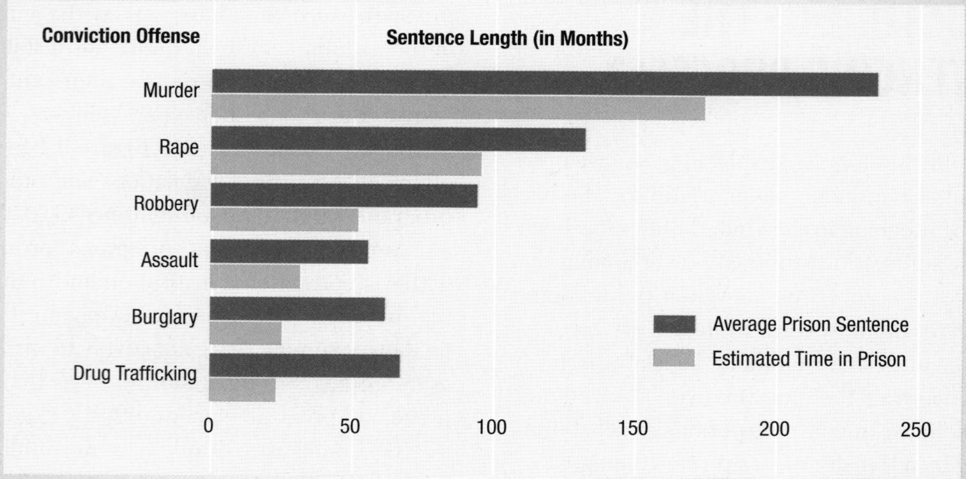

Source: *National Corrections Reporting Program: Sentence Length of State Prisoners, by Offense, Admission Type, Sex, and Race*, "Table 9: First Releases from State Prison, 2009." *www.bjs.gov*. Bureau of Justice Statistics: May 5, 2011, Web.

that the rights of the defendant are not infringed while the prosecutor and defense attorney dictate the course of action. At a traditional sentencing hearing, however, the judge is no longer an arbiter between the parties. She or he is now called on to exercise the ultimate authority of the state in determining the defendant's fate.

INDIVIDUALIZED JUSTICE When theories of rehabilitation hold sway over the criminal justice system, indeterminate sentencing practices are guided by the theory of "individualized justice." Just as a physician gives specific treatment to individual patients depending on their particular health needs, the hypothesis goes, a judge needs to consider the specific circumstances of each individual offender in choosing the best form of punishment.

Taking the analogy one step further, just as the diagnosis of a qualified physician should not be questioned, a qualified judge should have absolute discretion in making the sentencing decision. *Judicial discretion* rests on the assumption that a judge should be given ample leeway in determining punishments that fit both the crime and the criminal.[12] As we shall see later in the chapter, the growth of determinate sentencing has severely restricted judicial discretion in many jurisdictions.

JUDICIAL DISPOSITIONS Within whatever legislative restrictions apply, the sentencing judge has a number of options when it comes to choosing the proper form of punishment. These sentences, or *dispositions*, include:

1. *Imprisonment*. Whether for the purpose of retribution, deterrence, incapacitation, or rehabilitation, a common form of punishment in American history has been imprisonment. In fact, it is used so commonly today that judges—and legislators—are having to take factors such as prison overcrowding into consideration when making sentencing decisions. The issues surrounding imprisonment will be discussed in Chapters 11 and 12.
2. *Probation*. One of the effects of prison overcrowding has been a sharp rise in the use of probation, in which an offender is permitted to live in the community under supervision and is not incarcerated. (Probation is covered in Chapter 10.) *Alternative sanctions* (also discussed in Chapter 10) combine probation with other dispositions, such as electronic monitoring, house arrest, boot camps, and shock incarceration.
3. *Fines*. Fines can be levied by judges in addition to incarceration and probation or independently of other forms of punishment. Fines are generally considered a form of judicial leniency for nonviolent offenders. This disposition has, however, come under criticism recently for its often stark alternatives: pay or go to jail.[13] Although technically unconstitutional,[14] the widespread practice of incarcerating those who cannot pay their fines unavoidably discriminates against indigent defendants.

Whereas fines are payable to the government, restitution and community service are seen as reparations to the injured party or to the community. As noted earlier, restitution is a direct payment to the victim or victims of a crime. Community service consists of "good works"—such as cleaning up highway litter or tutoring disadvantaged youths—that benefit the entire community.

DISCRETION IN ACTION

Pledge Night

THE SITUATION Michael was a nineteen-year-old pledge of the Pi Delta Psi fraternity. At an early December weekend retreat in Pennsylvania's Pocono Mountains, Michael and the other pledges were blindfolded, outfitted with backpacks weighted with sand, and forced to cross a frozen yard while taking blows from fraternity members. During the ritual, Michael kicked one of the men tackling him. In retaliation, fraternity members struck him more forcefully and pushed him to the ground, each knock amplified by the weight of the backpack.

Michael lost consciousness. While some of the fraternity members searched the Internet for terms like "Concussion can't wake up," others tried to hide evidence linking them to his injuries. After an hour, three members took Michael to a nearby hospital, where he eventually died from brain damage. A doctor at the hospital determined that his head injuries were so severe that they would have required "hundreds of pounds" of force. At trial, one of the fraternity members known to have struck Michael was found guilty of third degree murder, or "acting with extreme indifference to human life."

THE LAW Under state sentencing guidelines, the penalties for third degree murder without a deadly weapon can range from six to forty years in prison. These guidelines are, however, not mandatory.

WHAT WOULD YOU DO? You are the sentencing judge in this trial. You have several factors to consider. The defendant had no previous criminal record. As his lawyer argued, "This was a scared kid who clearly had no intention to commit any crimes that weekend. When the accident occurred, he used bad judgment."

At the same time, the defendant did help try to cover up the crime and lied to police about his involvement in Michael's death. Furthermore, a harsh punishment would send the message that the criminal justice system does not condone violent fraternity hazing. Choosing from the dispositions in the text, how would you sentence the defendant?

To see how a judge in Monroe County, Pennsylvania, decided the outcome of a similar case, go to Example 9.1 in Appendix A.

Along with restitution, *apologies* play an important role in restorative justice, discussed previously. An apology is seen as an effort by the offender to recognize the wrongness of her or his conduct and acknowledge the impact that it has had on the victim and the community. (See the feature *Discretion in Action—Pledge Night* to learn more about one judge's sentencing decision.)

9-2c The Sentencing Process

The decision of how to punish a wrongdoer is the end result of what Yale Law School professor Kate Stith and federal appeals court judge José A. Cabranes call the "sentencing ritual."[15] The two main participants in this ritual are the judge and the defendant, but prosecutors, defense attorneys, and probation officers also play roles in the proceedings.

Individualized justice requires that the judge consider all the relevant circumstances in making sentencing decisions. Therefore, judicial discretion is often tantamount to *informed* discretion—without the aid of the other members of the courtroom work group, the judge would not have sufficient information to make the proper sentencing choice.

THE PRESENTENCE INVESTIGATIVE REPORT For judges operating under indeterminate sentencing guidelines, information in the **presentence investigative report** is a valuable component of the sentencing ritual. Compiled by a probation officer, the report describes the crime in question, notes the suffering of any victims, and lists the defendant's prior offenses (as well as any alleged but uncharged criminal activity).

The report also contains a range of personal data such as family background, work history, education, and community activities—information that is not admissible as

Presentence Investigative Report An investigative report on an offender's background that assists a judge in determining the proper sentence.

evidence during trial. In putting together the presentence investigative report, the probation officer is supposed to gain a "feel" for the defendant and communicate these impressions of the offender to the judge.

The report also includes a sentencing recommendation. For example, as part of the case discussed in the opening of this chapter, a county probation officer recommended a "moderate jail sentence" for Brock Turner. Her presentence report cited Turner's "lack of a criminal history, his youthful age, and his expressed remorse and empathy toward the victim."[16]

This practice has been criticized as giving probation officers too much power in the sentencing process, because less diligent judges might simply rely on the recommendation in determining punishment.[17] For the most part, however, judges do not act as if they were bound by the presentence investigative report.

SENTENCING AND THE JURY Juries also play an important role in the sentencing process. As we will see later in the chapter, it is the jury, and not the judge, that generally decides whether a convict eligible for the death penalty will in fact be executed.

Additionally, six states—Arkansas, Kentucky, Missouri, Oklahoma, Texas, and Virginia—allow juries, rather than judges, to make the sentencing decision even when the death penalty is not an option. In these states, the judge gives the jury instructions on the range of penalties available, and then the jury makes the final decision.[18]

9-2d Factors of Sentencing

The sentencing ritual strongly lends itself to the concept of individualized justice. With inputs—sometimes conflicting—from the prosecutor, attorney, and probation officer, the judge can be reasonably sure of getting the "full picture" of the crime and the criminal. In making the final decision, however, most judges consider two factors above all others: the seriousness of the crime and any mitigating or aggravating circumstances.

"Real Offense" The actual offense committed, as opposed to the charge levied by a prosecutor as the result of a plea bargain.

Mitigating Circumstances Any circumstances accompanying the commission of a crime that may justify a lighter sentence.

Aggravating Circumstances Any circumstances accompanying the commission of a crime that may justify a harsher sentence.

THE SERIOUSNESS OF THE CRIME As would be expected, the seriousness of the crime is the primary factor in a judge's sentencing decision. The more serious the crime, the harsher the punishment, for society demands no less. Each judge has his or her own methods of determining the seriousness of the offense. Many judges simply consider the "conviction offense," basing their sentence on the crime for which the defendant was convicted.

Other judges—some mandated by statute—focus instead on the **"real offense"** in determining the punishment. The "real offense" is based on the actual behavior of the defendant, regardless of the official conviction. For example, through a plea bargain, a defendant may plead guilty to simple assault when in fact he hit his victim in the face with a baseball bat. A judge, after reading the presentence investigative report, could decide to sentence the defendant as if he had committed aggravated assault, which is the "real offense." Though many prosecutors and defense attorneys are opposed to "real offense" procedures, which can render a plea bargain meaningless, there is considerable belief in criminal justice circles that they bring a measure of fairness to the sentencing decision.[19]

MITIGATING AND AGGRAVATING CIRCUMSTANCES When deciding the severity of punishment, judges and juries are often required to evaluate the *mitigating and aggravating circumstances* surrounding the case. **Mitigating circumstances** are those circumstances, such as the fact that the defendant was coerced into committing the crime, that allow a lighter sentence to be handed down. In contrast, **aggravating circumstances,** such as a prior record, blatant disregard for the safety of others, or the use of a weapon, can lead a judge or jury to inflict a harsher penalty than might otherwise be warranted.

iStockPhoto.com/Alina Solovyova-Vincent/Alina555

Generally speaking, jurors hand down harsher sentences than judges, particularly for drug-related crimes and sexual assaults. **Why do you think this is the case?**

CAREER PREP

Gang Investigator

Job Description:

- Conduct assessments and refer at-risk youth to appropriate activities, programs, or agencies as an alternative to their becoming involved in criminal activity. Also, counsel troubled youths and their families.
- Serve as a liaison between the police department and schools and community organizations regarding gangs and other youth-related matters.

What Kind of Training Is Required?

- At a minimum, a high school diploma and any combination of training, education, and experience equivalent to three to five years' social service employment involving youth. A law enforcement background is also very helpful.
- Preferred candidates will have a bachelor's degree in counseling, criminal justice, or another social science field. Bilingual (English/Spanish) skills are desired.

Pressmaster/ShutterStock.com

Annual Salary Range?

- $70,000–$80,000

GETTING LINKEDIN

"Gang intelligence" is a growing field in both the public and the private sectors. A LinkedIn posting for a gang SME (subject-matter expert) by a private company in Sacramento, California, required "Experience in identifying emerging threats or trends related to gangs operating inside and outside of prisons and their effect on communities."

CAREER TIP To emphasize the mitigating circumstances that might have contributed to a client's criminality, defense attorneys often rely on *behavioral specialists* as expert witnesses. These health-care experts focus on diagnosing and treating problem behavior.

Aggravating circumstances play an important role in a prosecutor's decision to charge a suspect with capital murder. The criminal code of every state that employs the death penalty contains a list of aggravating circumstances that make an offender eligible for execution.

Most of these codes require that the murder take place during the commission of a felony, or create a grave risk of death for multiple victims, or interfere with the duties of law enforcement.[20] As you will see later in the chapter, mitigating factors such as mental illness and youth can spare an otherwise death-eligible offender from capital punishment.

JUDICIAL PHILOSOPHY Most states and the federal government spell out mitigating and aggravating circumstances in statutes, but there is room for judicial discretion in applying the law to particular cases. Judges are not uniform, or even consistent, in their opinions of which circumstances are mitigating or aggravating.

One judge may believe that a fourteen-year-old is not fully responsible for his or her actions, while another may believe that teenagers should be treated as adults by criminal courts. A recent study of sentencing practices in Florida suggests that defendants who look less "trustworthy" are subjected to harsher sentences from state judges.[21]

9-3 WHAT ARE SOME PROBLEMS WITH SENTENCING?

For some, the natural differences in judicial philosophies, when combined with a lack of institutional control, raise important questions. Why should a bank robber in South Carolina and a bank robber in Michigan receive different sentences? Even federal indeterminate sentencing guidelines seem overly vague: a bank robber can receive a prison term from one day to twenty years, depending almost entirely on the judge.[22] Furthermore, if judges have freedom to use their discretion, do they not also have the freedom to misuse it?

Purported improper judicial discretion is often the first reason given for two phenomena that plague the criminal justice system: *sentencing disparity* and *sentencing discrimination*. Though the two terms are often used interchangeably, they describe different statistical occurrences—the causes of which are open to debate.

LO9-3 Explain some of the reasons why sentencing reform has occurred.

9-3a Sentencing Disparity

Justice would seem to demand that those who commit similar crimes should receive similar punishments. **Sentencing disparity** occurs when this expectation is not met in one of three ways:

1. Criminals receive similar sentences for different crimes of unequal seriousness.
2. Criminals receive different sentences for similar crimes.
3. Mitigating or aggravating circumstances have a disproportionate effect on sentences.

Sentencing Disparity A situation in which those convicted of similar crimes do not receive similar sentences.

Sentencing Discrimination A situation in which the length of a sentence appears to be influenced by a defendant's race, gender, economic status, or other nonrelevant factor.

Most of the blame for sentencing disparities is placed at the feet of the judicial profession. Even with the restrictive presence of the sentencing reforms we will discuss shortly, judges have a great deal of influence over the sentencing decision, whether they are making that decision themselves or instructing the jury on how to do so.

Like other members of the criminal justice system, judges are individuals, and their discretionary sentencing decisions reflect that individuality. Besides judicial discretion, several other causes have been offered as explanations for sentencing disparity, including differences between geographic jurisdictions and between federal and state courts.

GEOGRAPHIC DISPARITIES For offenders, the amount of time spent in prison often depends as much on where the crime was committed as on the crime itself. A comparison of the sentences for drug trafficking reveals that someone convicted of the crime in Washington State faces an average of 64 months in prison, whereas a similar offender in Mississippi can expect an average of 121 months.[23]

The average sentences imposed in the Fourth Circuit, which includes North Carolina, South Carolina, Virginia, and West Virginia, are consistently harsher than those in the Ninth Circuit, comprising most of the western states: 31 months longer for convictions related to firearms and 34 months longer for all offenses.[24] Such disparities can be attributed to a number of different factors, including local attitudes toward crime and financial resources available to cover the expenses of incarceration.

FEDERAL VERSUS STATE COURT DISPARITIES Because of different sentencing guidelines, the punishment for the same crime in federal and state courts can also be dramatically different. In North Carolina, for example, a defendant convicted of distributing child pornography in state court will rarely face a prison sentence of more than two years. If it is a first offense, he or she will most likely be placed on probation. Federal courts, however, have a mandatory five-year minimum prison term for any child pornography distribution conviction, with punishments often reaching twenty years because of aggravating circumstances.[25] Figure 9.2 shows the sentencing disparities for certain crimes in the two systems.

9-3b Sentencing Discrimination

Sentencing discrimination occurs when disparities can be attributed to extralegal variables such as the defendant's gender, race, or economic standing.

RACE AND SENTENCING At first glance, racial discrimination would seem to be rampant in sentencing practices. Research by Cassia Spohn of Arizona State University

FIGURE 9.2 AVERAGE MAXIMUM SENTENCES FOR SELECTED CRIMES IN STATE AND FEDERAL COURTS

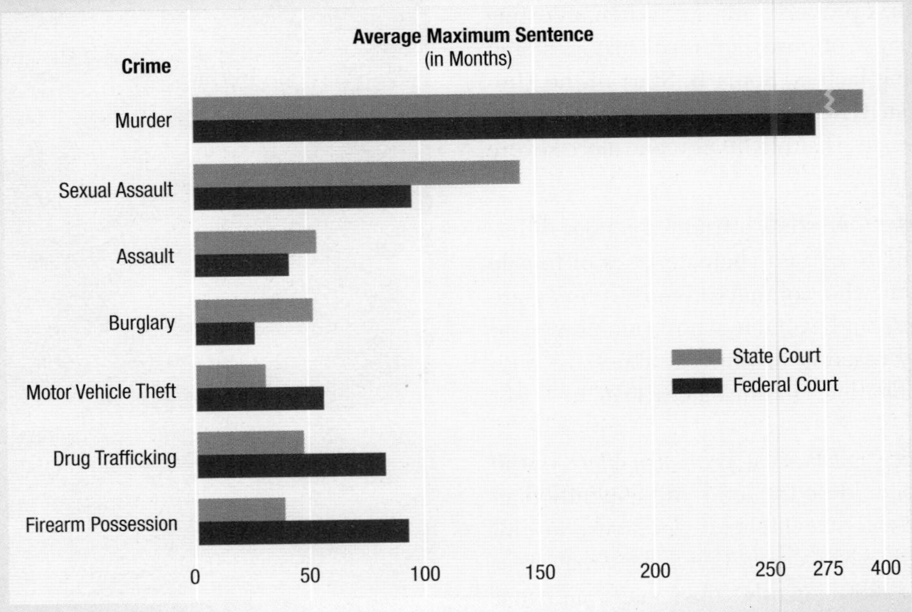

Source: Bureau of Justice Statistics, *Felony Defendants in Large Urban Counties, 2009—Statistical Tables* (Washington, D.C.: U.S. Department of Justice, December 2013), Table 25, page 30; and "Statistical Information Packet, Fiscal Year 2009, First Circuit," Table 7. *www.ussc.gov*. United States Sentencing Commission: 2010, Web.

and David Holleran of the College of New Jersey suggests that minorities pay a "punishment penalty" when it comes to sentencing.[26] In Chicago, Spohn and Holleran found that convicted African Americans were 12.1 percent more likely and convicted Latinos were 15.3 percent more likely to go to prison than convicted whites. Another report released by the Illinois Disproportionate Justice Impact Study Commission found that African Americans were nearly five times more likely to be sentenced to prison than whites for low-level drug crimes in that state.[27]

Nationwide, sentences imposed on African American males are about 20 percent more severe than those imposed on white males for similar crimes.[28] Black and Latino defendants are also significantly more likely to be incarcerated than white defendants for comparable wrongdoing.[29] Furthermore, race seems to play a meaningful role in determining which capital crimes are punished by death sentences.[30]

Such numbers, while significant, may not be the result of blatant sentencing bias. For example, the large numbers of Latinos in federal prison are a direct result of immigration laws, which disproportionately target that demographic. Furthermore, Spohn and Holleran found that the rate of imprisonment rose significantly for minorities who were young and unemployed. This led them to conclude that the disparities between races were not the result of "conscious" discrimination on the part of the sentencing judges. Rather, faced with limited time to make decisions and limited information about the offenders, the judges would resort to stereotypes, considering not just race, but age and unemployment as well.[31]

WOMEN AND SENTENCING Few would argue that race or ethnicity should be a factor in sentencing decisions—the system should be "color-blind." Does the same principle apply to women? In other words, should the system be "gender-blind" as well—at least on a policy level? Congress answered that question in the Sentencing Reform Act of 1984, which emphasized the ideal of gender-neutral sentencing.[32] In practice, however, this ideal has not been realized.

CAREER TIP When a mother becomes involved with the criminal justice system, the state can decide to place her children in a foster home. The professionals who oversee this process and look out for the best interests of the children, and their families, are called *foster care case workers.*

Gender Differences Women who are convicted of crimes are less likely to go to prison than men, and those who are incarcerated tend to serve shorter sentences. According to government data, on average, a woman receives a sentence that is twenty-nine months shorter than that of a man for a violent crime and nine months shorter for a property crime.[33] When adjusting for comparable arrest offenses, criminal histories, and other presentencing factors, Sonja B. Starr of the University of Michigan Law School found that male convicts receive sentences that are 60 percent more severe than those for women.[34]

The Chivalry Effect One study attributes gender differences in sentencing to certain characteristics of female criminality. Women who commit property crimes are usually accessories, and women who commit violent crimes are usually reacting to physical abuse. In both situations, the mitigating circumstances lead to lesser punishment.[35]

Other evidence suggests that a *chivalry effect*, or the idea that women should be treated more leniently than men, plays a large role in sentencing decisions. Several self-reported studies have shown that judges may treat female defendants more "gently" than males and that with women, judges are influenced by mitigating factors, such as marital status and family background, that they would ignore with men.[36]

In certain situations, however, a woman's gender may seem to work against her. In 2016, for example, married couple Christopher and Lonna Barton pleaded guilty to selling "Molly," a synthetic hallucinogen and amphetamine. A Baker County (Florida) judge sentenced Christopher to three years in prison and Lonna to seven years in prison.

Explaining the discrepancy, Lonna's defense attorney said he believed that his client had received extra punishment because, in separate proceedings, she had been found guilty of neglect that contributed to the death of her infant son.[37] According to Keith Crew, a professor of sociology and criminology at the University of Northern Iowa, defendants who are seen as bad mothers often "get the hammer" from judges and juries.[38]

AP Images/The Oakland Press, Vaughn Gurganian

A judge in Pontiac, Michigan, gave seventy-five-year-old Sandra Layne a harsher sentence than required by state guidelines for the second-degree murder of her seventeen-year-old grandson. **How might a woman's gender work against her in sentencing situations involving family-related violent crimes?**

9-4 HOW HAVE POLITICIANS TRIED TO "FIX" SENTENCING?

Sentencing Guidelines
Legislatively determined guidelines that judges are required to follow when sentencing those convicted of specific crimes.

Judicial discretion, then, has both positive and negative aspects. Although it allows judges to impose a wide variety of sentences to fit specific criminal situations, it appears to fail to rein in some judges' subjective biases, which can lead to disparity and perhaps discrimination. Critics of judicial discretion believe that its costs (the lack of equality) outweigh its benefits (providing individualized justice). As Columbia law professor John C. Coffee noted:

> If we wish the sentencing judge to treat "like cases alike," a more inappropriate technique for the presentation could hardly be found than one that stresses a novelistic portrayal of each offender and thereby overloads the decisionmaker in a welter of detail.[39]

In other words, Professor Coffee feels that judges are given too much information in the sentencing process, making it impossible for them to be consistent in their decisions. It follows that limiting judicial discretion would not only simplify the process but lessen the opportunity for disparity or discrimination. This attitude has spread through state and federal legislatures, causing extensive changes in sentencing procedures within the American criminal justice system.

9-4a Sentencing Guidelines

In an effort to eliminate the inequities of disparity by removing judicial bias from the sentencing process, many states and the federal government have turned to **sentencing guidelines,** which require judges to dispense legislatively determined sentences based on factors such as the seriousness of the crime and the offender's prior record.

FIGURE 9.3 A PORTION OF MASSACHUSETTS'S SENTENCING GUIDELINES

Sentencing Guidelines Grid

Level	Illustrative Offenses	Sentence Range				
6	Manslaughter (Involuntary) Armed Robbery (No Gun) A&B DW* (Significant Injury)	40–60 Months	45–67 Months	50–75 Months	60–90 Months	80–120 Months
5	Unarmed Robbery Unarmed Burglary Stalking in Violation of Order Larceny ($50,000 and over)	12–36 Months IS-IV IS-III IS-II	24–36 Months IS-IV IS-III IS-II	36–54 Months	48–72 Months	60–90 Months
	Criminal History Scale	A No/Minor Record	B Moderate Record	C Serious Record	D Violent/Repetitive	E Serious Violent

Intermediate Sanction Levels	
IS-IV	24-Hour Restriction
IS-III	Daily Accountability
IS-II	Standard Supervision

*A&B DW = Assault and Battery, Dangerous Weapon

The numbers in each cell represent the range from which the judge selects the maximum sentence (Not More Than).

The minimum sentence (Not Less Than) is two-thirds of the maximum sentence and constitutes the initial parole eligibility date.

Source: "Massachusetts Sentencing Grid." *www.mass.gov*. Massachusetts Court System: visited February 18, 2017, Web.

STATE SENTENCING GUIDELINES About twenty states employ some form of sentencing guidelines. In general, these guidelines remove discretionary power from state judges by turning sentencing into a mathematical exercise. Members of the courtroom work group use a *grid* to determine the proper sentence.

Figure 9.3 shows the grid established by the Massachusetts sentencing commission. One axis ranks the type of crime, while the other identifies the offender's criminal history. The red boxes indicate the "incarceration zone." A prison sentence is required for crimes in this zone.

The yellow boxes identify the "discretionary zone," in which the judge can decide between incarceration, probation, and various intermediate sanctions. As you will learn in the next chapter, intermediate sanctions include home confinement, fines, and electronic monitoring.

FEDERAL SENTENCING GUIDELINES In 1984, Congress passed the Sentencing Reform Act (SRA),[40] paving the way for federal sentencing guidelines that went into effect three years later. Similar in many respects to the state guidelines, the SRA also eliminated parole for federal prisoners and severely limited early release from prison due to good behavior.[41] The impact of the SRA and the state guidelines was dramatic. Sentences became harsher—by 2004, the average federal prison sentence was fifty months, more than twice as long as in 1984.[42]

Much to the disappointment of supporters of sentencing reform, a series of United States Supreme Court decisions handed down midway though the first decade of the 2000s held that federal sentencing guidelines were advisory only.[43] Five years after these Court decisions, according to the U.S. Sentencing Commission, African American defendants were receiving sentences about 20 percent longer than white males who were convicted of similar crimes.[44] Similarly, a study released in 2015 shows that judicial leniency for white males and all women has increased significantly in federal courts, with sentence lengths moving in the opposite direction for black males.[45]

JUDICIAL DEPARTURES In essence, the Supreme Court decisions just mentioned gave federal judges the ability to "depart" from federal sentencing guidelines. Federal judges are taking advantage of this discretion, deviating from sentencing guidelines in almost half of all cases before them.[46] This "escape hatch" of judicial discretion, called a **departure,** is available to state judges as well as their federal counterparts. Judges in Massachusetts, for example, can depart from the grid in Figure 9.3 if a case involves mitigating or aggravating circumstances.[47]

Departure A stipulation in sentencing guidelines that allows a judge to adjust his or her sentencing decision based on the special circumstances of a particular case.

9-4b Mandatory Sentencing Guidelines

LO9-4 Describe the goal of mandatory minimum sentencing guidelines and explain why these laws have become unpopular in recent years.

In an attempt to close even the limited loophole of judicial discretion offered by departures, politicians (often urged on by their constituents) have passed sentencing laws even more contrary to the idea of individualized justice. These **mandatory (minimum) sentencing guidelines** further limit a judge's power to deviate from determinate sentencing laws by setting firm standards for certain crimes.

STATE AND FEDERAL MANDATORY MINIMUMS The mandatory minimum "movement" started in the early 1970s in New York state, which was experiencing a wave of heroin-related crime. Governor Nelson Rockefeller pushed through a series of mandatory drug sentences, the most draconian being a fifteen-years-to-life punishment for anyone convicted of possessing four ounces of any illegal narcotic other than marijuana.[48] Today, nearly every state has mandatory sentencing laws, most related to crimes involving the sale or possession of illegal drugs.

The federal government passed its Anti-Drug Abuse Act[49] in the mid-1980s, in response to the cocaine overdose death of a well-known basketball player named Len Bias. Federal mandatory minimums are guided by a set of "triggers" based on the amount of drugs involved, the offender's criminal history, and many other attendant circumstances.

These triggers include selling drugs to someone under twenty-one years of age, using a minor as part of "drug operations," and carrying a firearm during the drug-related crime.[50] This legislation has given a great deal of power to federal prosecutors, who, by using their discretion to add penalty enhancements, are able to coerce defendants into plea bargaining rather than risking a lengthy prison sentence.[51]

"THREE-STRIKES" LEGISLATION **Habitual offender laws** are a form of mandatory sentencing found in twenty-six states and used by the federal government. Also known as "three-strikes-and-you're-out" laws, these statutes require that any person convicted of a third felony must serve a lengthy prison sentence. In many cases, the underlying crime does not have to be of a violent or dangerous nature.

Mandatory (Minimum) Sentencing Guidelines Statutorily determined punishments that must be applied to those who are convicted of specific crimes.

Habitual Offender Laws Statutes that require lengthy prison sentences for those who are convicted of repeated felonies.

Jim West/Alamy Stock Photo

Through a ballot initiative, California voters decided to revise the state's "three strikes" law so that only a violent or serious third felony will trigger the automatic life sentence. **Do you think that the new version of California's habitual offender law is fairer than the old one? Why or why not?**

Under Washington's habitual offender law, for example, a "persistent offender" is automatically sentenced to life even if the third felony offense happens to be "vehicular assault" (an automobile accident that causes injury), unarmed robbery, or attempted arson, among other lesser felonies.[52] Consequently, about 44 percent of the nearly 670 inmates serving life without parole in that state were sentenced for a third strike.[53] In California, convicts have been sent to prison for life for third offenses that include shoplifting a pair of tube socks, stealing a slice of pizza, and possessing .14 grams of methamphetamine.[54]

The Supreme Court validated the most punitive aspects of habitual offender laws with its decision in *Lockyer v. Andrade* (2003).[55] That case involved the sentencing under California's "three-strikes" law of Leandro

Andrade to fifty years in prison for stealing $153 worth of videotapes. Writing for the majority in a bitterly divided 5–4 decision, Justice Sandra Day O'Connor concluded that Andrade's punishment was not so "objectively" unreasonable that it violated the Constitution.[56] Basically, the justices who upheld the law said that if the California legislature—and by extension the California voters—felt that the law was reasonable, then the judicial branch was in no position to disagree.

REFORMING MANDATORY MINIMUMS Somewhat ironically, in 2012 California voters decided that the state's three-strikes law was indeed unreasonable. That year, by a two-thirds vote, Californians passed a ballot initiative revising the law. Now, a life sentence will be imposed only when the third felony conviction is for a serious or violent crime.

Furthermore, the measure authorizes judges to resentence those approximately 3,000 inmates who are serving life prison terms in California prisons because of a nonviolent "third strike." As of February 2016, about 2,100 of these inmates had been released from prison.[57]

The California ballot initiative reflects nationwide discontent with mandatory minimum sentencing statutes. These laws are often unpopular with judges because of the limitations they place on judicial discretion. They are also seen as contributing heavily to the explosive, and costly, growth of the U.S. prison population since the 1980s, which we will discuss in in a future chapter. In addition, the country's minority population seems to have borne the brunt of harsh sentencing legislation—nearly 70 percent of all convicts subject to mandatory minimum sentences are African American or Latino.[58]

In response to these issues, nearly thirty states have reformed their mandatory sentencing laws since 2000. In general, these reforms take one of three approaches:[59]

1. *Expanding judicial discretion*. In Iowa, judges can depart from mandatory minimum sentences for certain drug crimes when no violence or threat of violence was present.[60]
2. *Limiting habitual offender "triggers."* In Nevada, misdemeanor convictions no longer count toward a five-year mandatory minimum sentence for a third conviction.[61]
3. *Repealing or revising mandatory minimum sentences*. In 2009, New York repealed the "Rockefeller drug laws," eliminating mandatory minimum sentences for low-level drug offenders.[62]

On the federal level, the U.S. Congress is considering several bills that would allow federal judges to depart from mandatory minimum sentences for nonviolent drug offenses.[63]

9-4c Victim Impact Evidence

The final piece of the sentencing puzzle involves victims and victims' families. As mentioned in Chapter 2, crime victims traditionally were banished to the peripheries of the criminal justice system. This situation has changed dramatically with the emergence of the victims' rights movement over the past several decades.

Victims are now given the opportunity to testify—in person or through written testimony—during sentencing hearings about the suffering they experienced as the result of the crime. These **victim impact statements (VISs)** have proved extremely controversial, however, and legal experts have had a difficult time determining whether they cause more harm than good.

BALANCING THE PROCESS The Crime Victims' Rights Act gives victims the right to be reasonably heard during the sentencing process,[64] and many state victims' rights laws contain similar provisions.[65] In general, these laws allow a victim to tell his or her side of the story to the sentencing body, be it a judge, jury, or parole officer.

In nonmurder cases, the victim can personally describe the physical, financial, and emotional impact of the crime. When the charge is murder or manslaughter, relatives or friends can give personal details about the victim and describe the effects of her or his death. In almost all instances, the goal of the VIS is to increase the harshness of the sentence.

Most of the debate surrounding VISs centers on their use in the sentencing phases of death penalty cases. Supporters point out that the defendant has always been allowed to present character evidence in the hope of dissuading a judge or jury from capital punishment. According to some, a VIS balances the equation by giving survivors a voice in the process.

Presenting a VIS is also said to have psychological benefits for victims, who are no longer forced to sit in silence as decisions that affect their lives are made by others.[66] Finally, on a purely practical level, a VIS may help judges and juries make informed sentencing decisions by providing them with an understanding of all of the consequences of the crime.

THE RISKS OF VICTIM EVIDENCE Opponents of the use of VISs claim that they interject dangerously prejudicial evidence into the sentencing process, which should be governed by reason, not emotion. The inflammatory nature of a VIS, they say, may distract judges and juries from the

Victim Impact Statement (VIS) A statement to the sentencing body in which the victim is given the opportunity to describe how the crime has affected her or him.

facts of the case, which should be the only basis for a sentence.[67]

In fact, research has shown that hearing victim impact evidence makes jurors more likely to impose the death penalty.[68] The Supreme Court, however, has given its approval to the use of VISs, allowing judges to decide whether the statements are admissible on a case-by-case basis, just as they do with any other type of evidence.[69]

ETHICS CHALLENGE

Critics contend that victim impact statements unethically introduce the idea of a victim's "social value" into the courtroom. That is, judges and juries may feel compelled to base the punishment on the worthiness of the victim (his or her standing in the community, role as a family member, and the like) rather than the circumstances of the crime. What is your opinion of this argument?

9-5 WHAT IS THE STATUS OF CAPITAL PUNISHMENT IN THE UNITED STATES?

Few topics in the criminal justice system inspire such heated debate as **capital punishment,** or the use of the death penalty. Opponents such as legal expert Stephen Bright wonder whether "there comes a time when a society gets beyond some of the more primitive forms of punishment."[70] They point out that the United States is the sole Western democracy that continues the practice, putting it among China, Iran, Iraq, and Saudi Arabia on the list of nations that carry out the most executions.[71]

Critics also claim that a process whose subjects are chosen by "luck and money and race" cannot serve the interests of justice.[72] Proponents believe that the death penalty serves as the ultimate deterrent for violent criminal behavior and that the criminals who are put to death are the "worst of the worst" and deserve their fate.

Today, about 2,900 convicts are living on "death row" in American prisons, meaning they have been sentenced to death and are awaiting execution. In the 1940s, as many as two hundred people were put to death in the United States in one year. As Figure 9.4 shows, the most recent high-water mark was ninety-eight in 1999. Despite declines since then, certain states and the federal government still regularly seek the death penalty for offenders convicted of capital crimes. Consequently, the questions that surround the death penalty—Is it fair? Is it humane? Does it deter crime?—will continue to mobilize both its supporters and its detractors.

Capital Punishment The use of the death penalty to punish wrongdoers for certain crimes.

9-5a Methods of Execution

In its early years, when the United States adopted the practice of capital punishment from England, it also adopted English methods, which included drawing and quartering and boiling the convict alive. By the nineteenth century, these techniques had been deemed "barbaric" and were replaced by hanging. Indeed, the history of capital punishment in America is marked by attempts to make the act more humane. The 1890s saw the introduction of electrocution as a less painful method of execution than hanging, and in 1890 in Auburn Prison, New York, William Kemmler was the first American to die in an electric chair.

The "chair" remained the primary form of execution until 1977, when Oklahoma became the first state to adopt lethal injection. Today, this method dominates executions in all thirty-one states that employ the death penalty. Fourteen states authorize at least two different methods of execution, meaning that electrocution (eight states), lethal gas (five states), hanging (three states), and the firing squad (two states) are still used on very rare occasions.[73]

For about three decades, states used a similar three-drug process to carry out lethal injections. The process—which involves a sedative, a paralyzing agent, and a drug that induces heart failure—was designed to be as painless as possible for the condemned convict.

More recently, however, the companies that manufacture these three drugs have refused to sell them for execution purposes. This has forced state officials to experiment with untested replacement drugs, a development that—as we shall soon see—has added an element of uncertainty to capital punishment in the United States.

9-5b The Death Penalty and the Supreme Court

The United States Supreme Court's attitude toward the death penalty has been shaped by two decisions made more than a century ago. First, in 1890, the Court established that as long as they are not carried out in an "inhuman" or "barbarous" fashion, executions are not forbidden by the Eighth Amendment.[74] Since that case, the Court has never ruled that any method of execution is unconstitutionally "cruel and unusual."

FIGURE 9.4 EXECUTIONS IN THE UNITED STATES, 1976 TO 2016

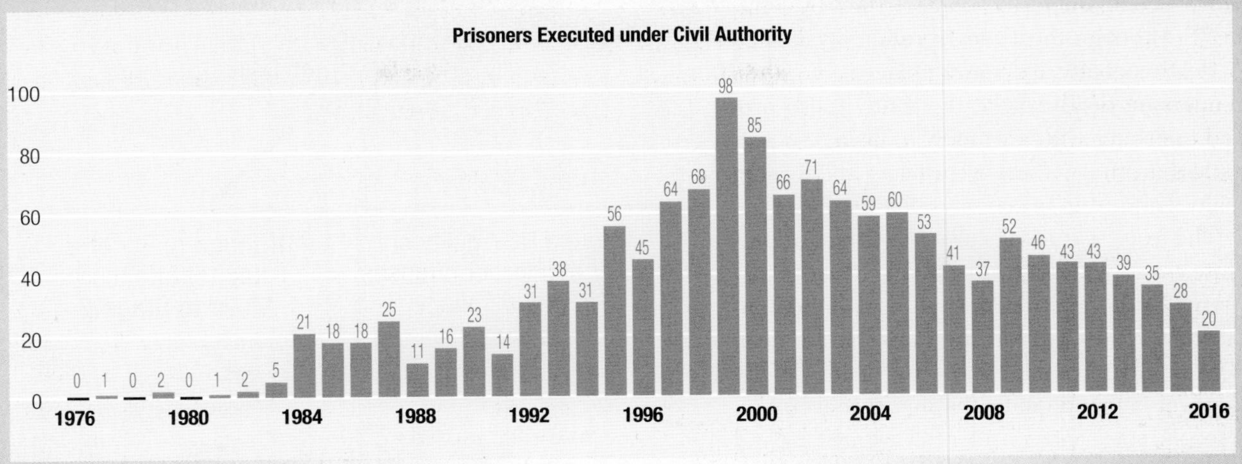

Source: Death Penalty Information Center.

Then, in *Weems v. United States* (1910),[75] the Court made a ruling that further clarified the meaning of "cruel and unusual" as prohibited by the Eighth Amendment, though the facts of the case did not involve capital punishment. The defendant had been sentenced to fifteen years of hard labor, a heavy fine, and a number of other penalties for the relatively minor crime of falsifying official records. The Court overturned the sentence, ruling that the penalty was too harsh considering the nature of the offense. Ultimately, in the *Weems* decision, the Court set three important precedents concerning sentencing:

1. Cruel and unusual punishment is defined by the changing norms and standards of society and therefore is not based on historical interpretations.
2. Courts may decide whether a punishment is unnecessarily cruel with regard to physical pain.
3. Courts may decide whether a punishment is unnecessarily cruel with regard to psychological pain.[76]

In *Baze v. Rees* (2008),[77] the Supreme Court ruled that the mere possibility of pain "does not establish the sort of 'objectively intolerable risk of harm' that qualifies as cruel and unusual" punishment. That ruling, however, applied to the three-drug process described earlier. For a variety of reasons, manufacturers in America and Europe now refuse to sell those drugs to the states.

Consequently, state corrections systems have been forced to try new lethal injection protocols, with controversial results. In December 2016, using a replacement anesthetic called midazolam, Alabama authorities took thirty minutes to execute convicted murderer Robert Smith, Jr. For thirteen minutes, Smith, who was supposed to be heavily sedated, coughed and moved, raising questions of whether he was conscious during the procedure.

Similarly lengthy ordeals by condemned convicts in Arizona, Oklahoma, and Ohio bolstered claims by medical experts that midazolam cannot be relied upon to mask the pain suffered during lethal injection.[78] Nevertheless, in 2015 the Supreme Court approved use of the drug, once again holding that a method of capital punishment was not cruel and unusual.[79] Writing for the Court's 5–4 majority, Justice Samuel Alito pointed out that rejecting all available means for executions would be the same as ending the practice, which remains constitutional. In her dissent, Justice Sonia Sotomayor accused her colleagues of sanctioning "the chemical equivalent of being burned alive."[80]

9-5c Death Penalty Sentencing

In the 1960s, the Supreme Court became increasingly concerned about what it saw as serious flaws in the way the states administered capital punishment. Finally, in 1967, the Court put a moratorium on executions until it could "clean up" the process. The chance to do so came with the *Furman v. Georgia* case, decided in 1972.[81]

THE BIFURCATED PROCESS In its *Furman* decision, by a 5–4 margin, the Supreme Court essentially held that the death penalty, as administered by the states, violated the Eighth Amendment. Justice Potter Stewart was particularly eloquent in his concurring opinion, stating that the sentence of death was so arbitrary as to be comparable to "being struck by lightning."[82] Although the *Furman* ruling invalidated the death penalty for more than six hundred offenders on death row at the time, it also provided the states with a window to make the process less arbitrary, thereby bringing their death penalty statutes up to constitutional standards.

The result was a two-stage, or *bifurcated*, procedure for capital cases. In the first stage, a jury determines the guilt or innocence of the defendant for a crime that has, by state statute, been determined to be punishable by death. If the defendant is found guilty, the jury reconvenes in the second stage and considers all aggravating and mitigating factors to decide whether the death sentence is in fact warranted. (See Figure 9.5 to get a better idea of how these two stages work.)

Therefore, even if a jury finds the defendant guilty of a crime, such as first degree murder, that *may be* punishable by death, in the second stage it can decide that the circumstances surrounding the crime justify only a punishment of life in prison.

LO9-5 Identify the two stages that make up the bifurcated process of death penalty sentencing.

FIGURE 9.5 THE BIFURCATED DEATH PENALTY PROCESS

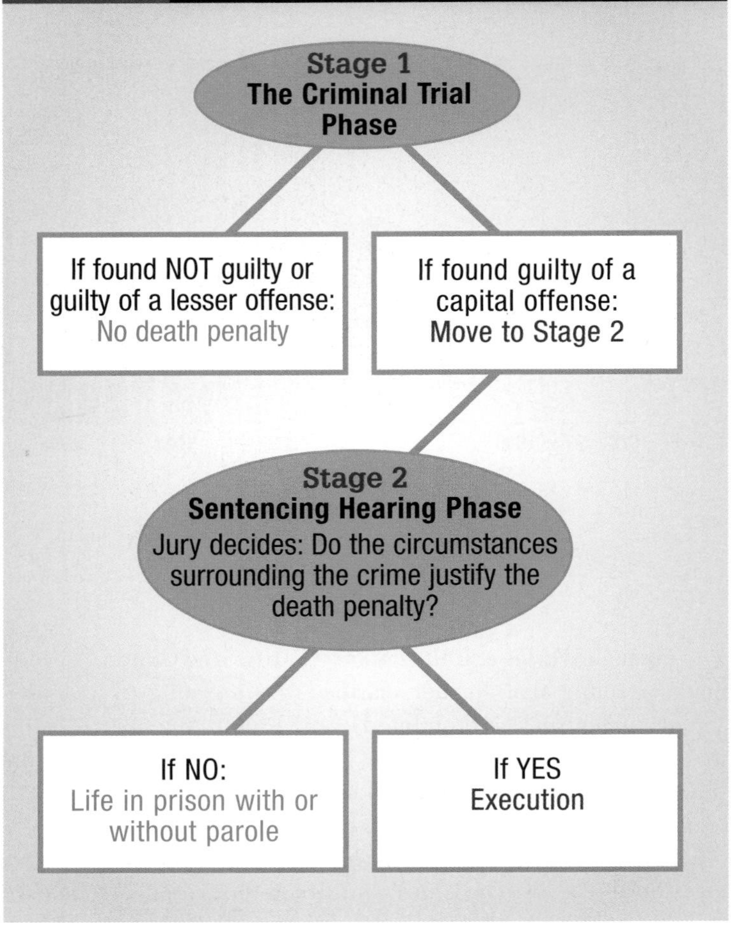

9-5d The Extent of Capital Punishment

Today, thirty-one states and the federal government have capital punishment laws based on the bifurcated process. State governments are responsible for almost all executions in this country. The federal government has carried out only three death sentences since 1963, and usually seeks capital punishment only for high-profile defendants such as Dylann Roof, sentenced to die in 2017 for killing nine African American parishioners at a church in Charleston, South Carolina, two years earlier.

Even a cursory glance at the data shows that the death penalty states do not impose capital punishment at a consistent rate. As Figure 9.6 shows, a convict's likelihood of being executed is strongly influenced by geography. Five states—Florida, Missouri, Oklahoma, Texas, and Virginia—account for more than two-thirds of all executions.

THE JURY'S ROLE The Supreme Court reaffirmed the important role of the jury in death penalties in *Ring v. Arizona* (2002).[83] The case involved Arizona's bifurcated process: After the jury determined a defendant's guilt or innocence, it would be dismissed, and the judge alone would decide whether execution was warranted.

The Court found that this procedure violated the defendant's Sixth Amendment right to a jury trial, ruling that juries must be involved in *both* stages of the bifurcated process. The decision invalidated death penalty laws in Arizona, Colorado, Idaho, Montana, and Nebraska, forcing legislatures in those states to hastily revamp their procedures.

The only state that routinely allows a measure of judicial discretion when it comes to capital punishment is Alabama, where jurors only recommend the final sentencing outcome in capital cases, pending a judge's approval. This practice may, however, be resting on uncertain legal ground. The Supreme Court recently struck down the part of Florida's execution procedure that gave judges rather than juries the final say in death penalty decisions.[84]

MITIGATING CIRCUMSTANCES Several mitigating circumstances will prevent a defendant found guilty of

FIGURE 9.6 EXECUTIONS BY STATE, 1976–2016

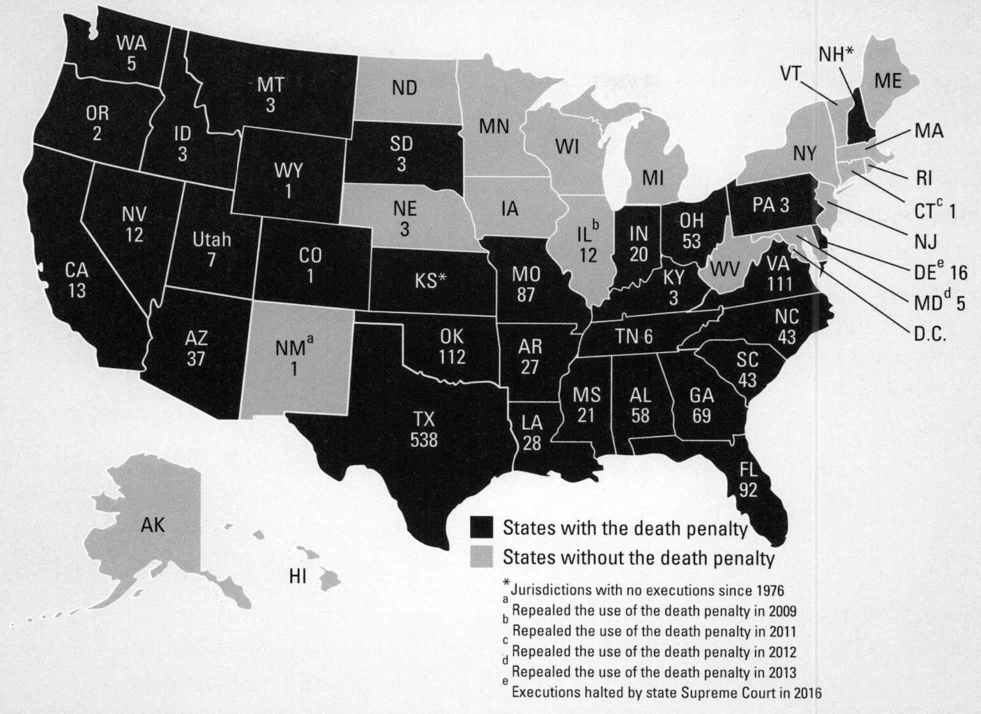

Source: Death Penalty Information Center.

first degree murder from receiving the death penalty. In 1986, the United States Supreme Court held that the Constitution prohibits the execution of a person who is insane.[85] Sixteen years later, in *Atkins v. Virginia* (2002),[86] the Court similarly ended the death penalty for mentally handicapped defendants.

This later decision underscored the continuing importance of the *Weems* test, discussed earlier in this section. In 1989, the Court had rejected the argument that execution of a mentally handicapped person was "cruel and unusual" under the Eighth Amendment.[87] At the time, only two states barred execution of the mentally handicapped. Thirteen years later, eighteen states had such laws, and the Court decided that this increased number reflected "changing norms and standards of society."

Following the *Atkins* case, many observers, including four Supreme Court justices, hoped that the same reasoning would be applied to the question of whether convicts who committed the relevant crime when they were juveniles may be executed. These hopes were realized in 2005 when the Court issued its *Roper v. Simmons* decision, which effectively ended the execution of those who committed crimes as juveniles.[88]

As in the *Atkins* case, the Court relied on the "evolving standards of decency" test, noting that a majority of the states, as well as every other civilized nation, prohibited the execution of offenders who committed their crimes before the age of eighteen. The *Roper* ruling required that seventy-two convicted murderers in twelve states be resentenced and took the death penalty "off the table" for dozens of pending cases in which prosecutors were seeking capital punishment for juvenile criminal acts.

9-5e The Future of the Death Penalty

As noted earlier in the chapter, the number of executions carried out each year in the United States has decreased dramatically since 1999. Other statistics also indicate a decline in death penalty activity. In 2016, only thirty people were sentenced to death, a drop of nearly 40 percent from the previous year's already historically low tally.[89] Furthermore, 2016 marked the first year in nearly forty years that no state carried out ten or more executions, and only five states carried out at least one execution, the lowest number since 1992.[90]

THE DECLINE IN EXECUTIONS We have already addressed some of the reasons for the diminishing presence of executions in the criminal justice system. With its decisions in the *Atkins* (2002) and *Roper* (2005) cases, the United States Supreme Court removed the possibility that hundreds of mentally handicapped and juvenile offenders could be sentenced to death. Over the past several years, at least seven states—Arizona, Arkansas, Louisiana, Mississippi, Montana, Ohio, and Oklahoma—temporarily shut down their death chambers to deal with issues surrounding their lethal injection drugs.

Other factors in the declining use of capital punishment in the United States include:

1. *The life-without-parole alternative*. In the early 1970s, only seven states allowed juries to sentence offenders to life in prison without parole instead of death. Now, every state provides this option, and juries seem to prefer this form of incapacitation to execution.[91]
2. *Plummeting murder rates*. The number of murders committed in this country is currently half what it was in the early 1990s.[92] As murder is the most common capital crime, this reduction has led to a decline in the number of offenders eligible for the death penalty.
3. *High costs*. Because of the costs of intensive law enforcement investigations, extensive *voir dire* (see Chapter 8), and lengthy appellate reviews, pursuing capital punishment can be very expensive for states. Nevada recently determined that its death penalty cases cost twice as much as similar cases without the death penalty, resulting in a $76 million price tag for state taxpayers between 1976 and 2014.[93]

CHANGING NORMS AND STANDARDS In August 2016, Delaware's Supreme Court ruled that the state's death penalty procedures were unconstitutional because they gave judges too great a role in the capital punishment sentencing process.[94] As a result of this ruling, Delaware became the seventh state to end capital punishment since 2004, along with Connecticut, Illinois, Maryland, New Jersey, New Mexico, and New York.

In addition, the majority of states that do carry out executions have not done so in recent years. According to the Pew Research Center, in 2016 public support for the death penalty dipped below 50 percent for the first time in forty years.[95] Under the circumstances, is it possible that the "norms and standards" of our society are turning against capital punishment, raising the possibility of a new evaluation under the *Weems* test?

Probably not. Only two Supreme Court justices—Stephen Breyer and Ruth Bader Ginsberg—have openly questioned the constitutionality of capital punishment.[96] In 2016, the Court refused to hear a case on whether the practice violates the Eighth Amendment's prohibition on cruel and unusual punishment.[97] Also in 2016, the residents of Nebraska voted to reinstate the death penalty after a year-long hiatus.

Finally, public support for executions tends to rise when the penalty is linked with certain crimes, such as the killing of children or law enforcement officers.[98] Therefore, future strategies for capital punishment in the United States may focus not on rejection but rather on reform.

Robert J Daveant/Shutterstock.com

How would you describe your attitude toward the death penalty? Do you think it is a fair way to punish those who commit murder? Why or why not?

STUDY TOOLS 9

LOCATED IN TEXTBOOK

- ☐ Rip out the Chapter Review Card.
- ☐ Review with the Chapter Quiz following this chapter.

LOCATED AT WWW.CENGAGEBRAIN.COM

- ☐ Review key terms flash cards.
- ☐ Read the chapter on all your favorite devices.
- ☐ Complete an Exam to test your knowledge.
- ☐ Check out Visual Summaries and You Decide activities to explore chapter concepts.

Quiz

1. The goal of the sentencing doctrine called ________________ is to prevent future crimes by "setting an example" with punishments for convicted criminals.

2. A sentencing doctrine known as ________________ suggests that offenders can be "treated" for their criminal tendencies and possibly "cured" of them.

3. ________________ sentences set a minimum and maximum amount of time a convict must spend behind bars, giving corrections officials the discretion to release the inmate within that time period.

4. A determinate sentence indicates the exact length of incapacitation, minus possible reductions for ________________ ________________.

5. ________________ circumstances can allow for a lighter sentence, while aggravating circumstances can lead to the imposition of a harsher penalty.

6. Sentencing ________________ occurs when similar crimes are punished with dissimilar sentences.

7. Sentencing ________________ is the result of judicial consideration of extralegal variables such as the defendant's race or gender.

8. With the aim of limiting judicial discretion, many states and the federal government have enacted sentencing ________________.

9. By a large margin,________________ ________________ is the most widespread method of execution in the United States today.

10. Following the "norms and standards" guidelines it established with the *Weems* decision, in 2005 the United States Supreme Court prohibited the execution of persons who were ________________ at the time of their crime.

Answers to the Chapter 9 Quiz can be found in the Answers section in the back of the book.

10 Probation, Parole, and Intermediate Sanctions

LEARNING OBJECTIVES

After studying this chapter, you will be able to . . .

10-1 Explain the justifications for community-based corrections programs.

10-2 Describe the three general categories of conditions placed on a probationer.

10-3 Identify the main differences between probation and parole.

10-4 Explain which factors influence the decision to grant parole.

10-5 List the three levels of home monitoring.

After finishing this chapter, go to **PAGE 222** for **STUDY TOOLS**

A Significant Departure

According to nineteen-year-old Chevelle Nesbeth, the only reason she visited Jamaica was to please her boyfriend. Also according to Nesbeth, friends in Jamaica purchased her round-trip ticket and asked her to bring two suitcases back to the United States as a favor. As Nesbeth tells the story, she was as surprised as anyone when a search of this luggage at New York City's Kennedy International Airport uncovered about 1.3 pounds of cocaine. A federal jury, unimpressed with her apparent naïveté, found Nesbeth guilty of importation and possession of a controlled substance with intent to distribute.

Under federal sentencing guidelines, Nesbeth should have spent from thirty-three to forty-one months in prison for her crimes. Senior district judge Frederick Block decided to depart from those guidelines, however, and spared Nesbeth any incarceration. Instead, on May 25, 2016, he sentenced her to a year of probation, six months of home confinement, and one hundred hours of community service. Judge Block did call Nesbeth's criminal conduct "inexcusable." At the same time, he emphasized that her wrongdoing was "a marked deviation from an exemplary law-abiding life." Prior to her arrest, Nesbeth was attending school and planned to become a teacher. "She has a record of prior good works counseling and tending to young children," the judge noted. "She apparently was under the influence of her boyfriend, and there is no evidence that she was even to be paid for her crime or was motivated by financial gain."

Even without going to prison, Judge Block explained, Nesbeth was going to be severely punished for her wrongdoing. Because of her conviction, Nesbeth would temporarily lose her driver's license and become ineligible for student loans and work assistance. She and her family would be denied federally assisted housing and other benefits such as food stamps, potentially for the remainder of her life. Justifying his seemingly lenient ruling, the judge criticized these "collateral consequences" as serving "no useful function other than to further punish criminal defendants after they have completed their court-imposed sentences."

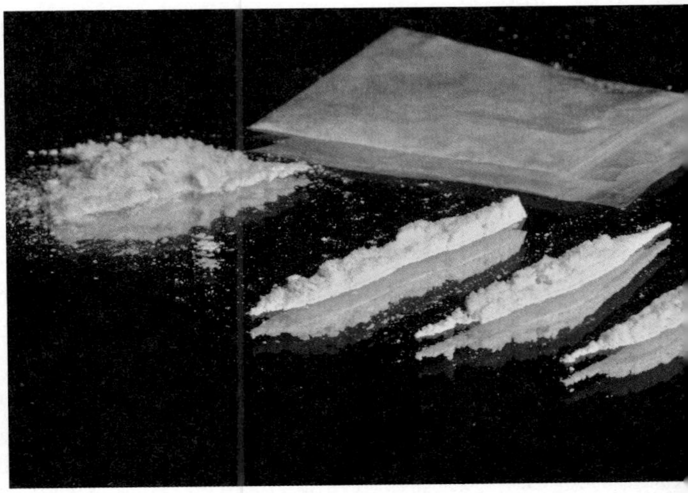

wawritto/Shutterstock.com

In May 2016, Judge Frederick Block decided that a defendant found guilty of importing and possessing 1.3 pounds of cocaine deserved a punishment of probation rather than incarceration. *Is this sentence in society's best interests? Why or why not?*

10-1 WHY DO WE NEED COMMUNITY CORRECTIONS?

After Judge Frederick Block refused to send Chevelle Nesbeth to prison for smuggling cocaine, the *New York Post* ran an editorial with the headline, "Brooklyn Judge Attempts to Rewrite Laws with an Outrageous Wrist-Slap for Felon."[1] In fact, as this chapter will make clear, the law allows a range of sentencing possibilities for American judges, including numerous options that keep offenders out of prison and jail.

For instance, about 3.8 million offenders are presently serving their sentences in the community on *probation* rather than behind bars. In addition, approximately 870,000 convicts in the United States have been *paroled*, meaning that they are finishing their prison sentences "on the outside" under the supervision of correctional officers.[2]

America, says University of Minnesota law professor Michael Tonry, is preoccupied with the "absolute severity of punishment" and the "widespread view that only imprisonment counts."[3] Consequently, **community corrections** such as probation and parole are often considered a less severe, and therefore a less worthy,

Community Corrections
The correctional supervision of offenders in the community as an alternative to sending them to prison or jail.

LO10-1 Explain the justifications for community-based corrections programs.

alternative to imprisonment. In reality, community corrections are crucial to our criminal justice system. One in fifty-three adults in this country is living under community supervision,[4] and few criminal justice matters are more pressing than the need to successfully reintegrate these offenders into society.

AP Images/LM Otero

In Dallas, street prostitutes such as the one shown here are often treated as crime victims and offered access to treatment and rehabilitation programs. **How might society benefit if such offenders are kept out of jail or prison through these kinds of diversion programs?**

10-1a Reintegration

A very small percentage of all convicted offenders have committed crimes that warrant life imprisonment or capital punishment. Most, at some point, will return to the community. Consequently, according to one group of experts, the task of the corrections system

> includes building or rebuilding solid ties between the offender and the community, integrating or reintegrating the offender into community life—restoring family ties, obtaining employment and an education, securing in the larger sense a place for the offender in the routine functioning of society.[5]

Considering that some studies have shown higher recidivism rates for offenders who are subjected to prison culture, a frequent justification of community-based corrections is that they help to reintegrate the offender into society.

Reintegration has a strong theoretical basis in rehabilitative theories of punishment. An offender is generally considered to be "rehabilitated" when he or she no longer represents a threat to other members of the community and therefore is believed to be fit to live in that community. In the context of this chapter and the two that follow, it will also be helpful to see reintegration as a process through which criminal justice officials such as probation and parole officers provide the offender with incentives to follow the rules of society.

These incentives can be positive, such as enrolling the offender in a drug treatment program. They can also be negative—in particular, the threat of a return to prison or jail for failure to comply. In all instances, criminal justice professionals must carefully balance the needs of the individual offender against the rights of law-abiding members of the community.

Reintegration A goal of corrections that focuses on preparing the offender for a return to the community unmarred by further criminal behavior.

Diversion An effort to keep offenders out of prison or jail by diverting them into programs that promote treatment and rehabilitation rather than punishment.

10-1b Diversion

Another justification for community-based corrections, based on practical considerations, is **diversion.** As you are already aware, many criminal offenses fall into the category of "petty," and it is well-nigh impossible, as well as unnecessary, to imprison every offender for every offense. Diversion programs not only relieve the pressure on overloaded courts and overcrowded jails and prisons, but also spare low-risk, nonviolent offenders the "collateral consequences" of a conviction, as described in the opening of this chapter.

In addition, the programs provide offenders with job training, counseling, and substance abuse treatment, thereby addressing the root causes of criminal behavior. Prosecutors in Cook County, Illinois, divert approximately five thousand participants from the criminal justice system on an annual basis, with 86 percent of felony defendants staying crime free for at least a year after completing the program.[6]

In his "strainer" analogy, corrections expert Paul H. Hahn likens this process to the workings of a kitchen strainer. With each "shake" of the corrections "strainer," the less serious offenders are diverted from incarceration. At the end, only the most serious convicts remain in prison.[7] The diversionary role of community-based punishments has become more pronounced as prisons and jails have filled up over the past several decades. In fact, probationers and parolees now account for about 70 percent of all adults in the American corrections systems.[8]

10-1c The "Low-Cost Alternative"

Not all of the recent expansion of community corrections can be attributed to acceptance of its theoretical underpinnings. Many politicians and criminal justice officials who do not look favorably on ideas such as reintegration and diversion have embraced programs to keep nonviolent offenders out of prison. The reason is simple: economics. The cost of constructing and maintaining prisons and jails, as well as housing and caring for inmates, has placed a great deal of pressure on corrections budgets across the country. States spend between $48 billion and $53 billion a year on their corrections systems, most of which goes to prison operating costs.[9]

Community corrections offer an enticing financial alternative to imprisonment. The Bureau of Prisons estimates that the federal government saves about $25,600 annually by shifting a nonviolent offender from incarceration to supervised release.[10] The average yearly cost of housing an inmate in North Carolina is $29,003, compared with $1,170 for community corrections.[11] The substance abuse programs affiliated with Cook County's diversion efforts, discussed above, save the county an estimated $1.5 million annually by keeping drug offenders out of jail.[12]

ETHICS CHALLENGE

Some jurisdictions charge mandatory fees to participate in a diversion program. For example, a woman in Topeka, Kansas, who struck a girl while driving—causing the victim brain damage and the loss of a leg—paid about $1,100 in fees to take part in one such program, leading to a dismissal of reckless battery charges. What are some ethical problems that arise when such fees are required of offenders, regardless of their ability to pay?

10-2 HOW DOES PROBATION WORK?

As Figure 10.1 shows, **probation** is the most common form of punishment in the United States. Although it is administered differently in various jurisdictions, probation can be generally defined as

FIGURE 10.1 PROBATION IN AMERICAN CORRECTIONS

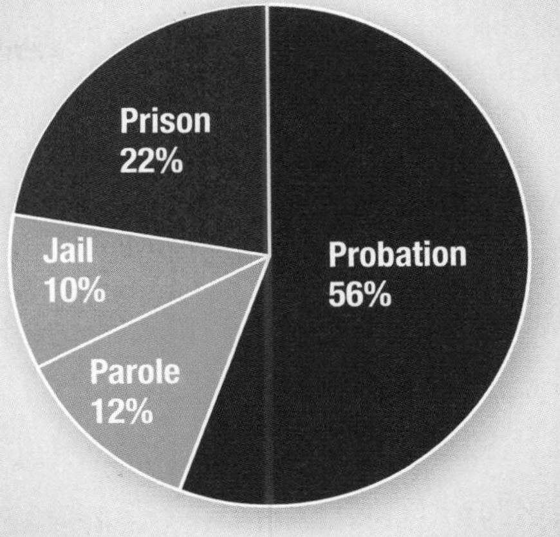

As this pie graph shows, the majority of convicts under the control of the American corrections system are on probation.

Source: Bureau of Justice Statistics, *Correctional Populations in the United States, 2015* (Washington, D.C.: U.S. Department of Justice, December 2016), Table 1, page 2.

> the legal status of an offender who, after being convicted of a crime, has been directed by the sentencing court to remain in the community under the supervision of a probation service for a designated period of time and subject to certain conditions imposed by the court or by law.[13]

The theory behind probation is that the legal system can treat certain offenders more economically and humanely by putting them under controls while still allowing them to live in the community. One of the advantages of probation has been that it provides for the rehabilitation of the offender while saving society the costs of incarceration.

Despite probation's widespread use, certain participants in the criminal justice system question its ability to reach its rehabilitative goals. Critics point to the immense number of probationers, some of whom are violent felons, as evidence that the system has outgrown its idealistic principles.[14]

10-2a Sentencing and Probation

Probation is basically an arrangement between sentencing authorities and the offender. In traditional probation, the offender agrees to comply with

Probation A criminal sanction in which a convict is allowed to remain in the community rather than be imprisoned.

certain terms for a specified amount of time in return for serving the sentence in the community. One of the primary benefits for the offender, besides not being sent to a correctional facility, is that the length of the probationary period is usually considerably shorter than the length of a prison term (see Figure 10.2).

The traditional form of probation is not the only arrangement that can be made. A judge can hand down a **suspended sentence,** under which a defendant who has been convicted and sentenced to be incarcerated is not required to serve the sentence immediately. Instead, the judge puts the offender on notice, keeping open the option of reinstating the original sentence and sending the offender to prison or jail if he or she reoffends. In practice, suspended sentences are quite similar to probation.

ALTERNATIVE SENTENCING ARRANGEMENTS Judges can also combine probation with incarceration. Such sentencing arrangements include:

- *Split sentences*. In **split sentence probation,** also known as *shock probation*, the offender is sentenced to a specific amount of time in prison or jail, to be followed by a period of probation.
- *Shock incarceration*. In this arrangement, an offender is sentenced to prison or jail with the understanding that after a period of time, she or he may petition the court to be released on probation. Shock incarceration is discussed more fully later in the chapter.
- *Intermittent incarceration*. With intermittent incarceration, the offender spends a certain amount of time each week, usually during the weekend, in a jail, workhouse, or other government institution.

Split sentences are sometimes useful for judges, as they combine the "treatment" aspects of probation with the "punishment" aspects of incarceration. According to the United States Sentencing Commission, about 3 percent of all sentences handed down by federal judges are split sentences.[15]

Suspended Sentence A judicially imposed condition in which an offender is not required to begin serving her or his prison term immediately after being sentenced.

Split Sentence Probation A sentence that consists of incarceration in a prison or jail, followed by a probationary period in the community.

Revocation The formal process that follows the failure of a probationer or parolee to comply with the terms of his or her probation or parole.

CHOOSING PROBATION Generally, research has shown that offenders are most likely to be denied probation if they:

- Are convicted on multiple charges.
- Were on probation or parole at the time of the arrest.
- Have two or more prior convictions.
- Are addicted to narcotics.
- Seriously injured the victim of the crime.
- Used a weapon during the commission of the crime.[16]

As might be expected, the chances of a felon being sentenced to probation are highly dependent on the seriousness of his or her crime. Only 19 percent of probationers in the United States have committed a violent crime, including domestic violence and sex offenses. The majority of probationers have been convicted of property crimes, drug offenses, or public order crimes such as drunk driving.[17]

Probation permits the judicial system to recognize that some offenders are less blameworthy than others. In 2016, for example, Lyvette Crespo pleaded guilty to voluntary manslaughter for killing her husband, Daniel, who had apparently been abusing her for many years.

A Los Angeles judge sentenced Crespo to only ninety days in jail, along with five years' probation, five hundred hours of community service, and completion of an anger management course. "Not every case is deserving of the max sentence," said an approving local prosecutor of Crespo's punishment, which could have been up to eleven years behind bars.[18]

10-2b Conditions of Probation

A judge may decide to impose certain conditions as part of a probation sentence. These conditions represent a "contract" between the judge and the offender, in which the latter agrees that if she or he does not follow certain rules, probation may be *revoked*. **Revocation** is the formal process by which probation is ended and a probationer is punished for his or her wrongdoing, often by being sent to jail or prison for the original term decided by the court.

Judges have a great deal of discretion to impose any terms of probation that they feel are necessary. In 2017, for example, an Idaho judge required a nineteen-year-old convicted of statutory rape to abstain from extramarital sex during the term of his probation. That same year, a federal judge ordered a white-collar criminal with a history of alcoholism not only to refrain from any drug or alcohol use as a condition of probation, but also to stay out of bars and disassociate himself from anybody he knew to be a consumer of alcohol.[19]

PRINCIPLES OF PROBATION A judge's personal philosophy is often reflected in the probation conditions that she or he creates for probationers. In *In re Quirk* (1997),[20] for example, the Louisiana Supreme Court

FIGURE 10.2 AVERAGE LENGTH OF SENTENCE: PRISON VERSUS PROBATION

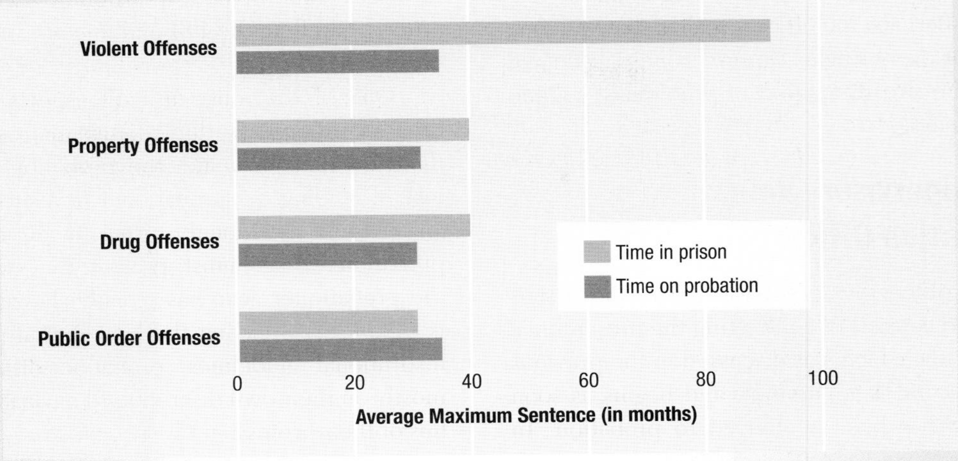

As you can see, the average probation sentence is much shorter than the average prison sentence for most crimes.

Source: Bureau of Justice Statistics, *Felony Defendants in State Courts, 2009—Statistical Tables* (Washington, D.C.: U.S. Department of Justice, December 2013), Table 25, page 30; and Table 27, page 31.

upheld the ability of a trial judge to impose church attendance as a condition of probation.

Though judges have a great deal of discretion in setting the conditions of probation, they do operate under several guiding principles. First, the conditions must be related to the dual purposes of probation, which most federal and state courts define as (1) the rehabilitation of the probationer and (2) the protection of the community. Second, the conditions must not violate the U.S. Constitution, as probationers are generally entitled to the same constitutional rights as other prisoners.[21]

Of course, probationers do give up certain constitutional rights when they consent to the terms of probation. Most probationers, for example, agree to spot checks of their homes for contraband such as drugs or weapons, and they therefore have a diminished expectation of privacy.[22]

TYPES OF CONDITIONS Obviously, probationers who break the law are very likely to have their probation revoked. Other, less serious infractions may also result in revocation. The conditions placed on a probationer fall into three general categories:

- *Standard conditions*, which are imposed on all probationers. These include reporting regularly to the probation officer, notifying the agency of any change of address, not leaving the jurisdiction without permission, and remaining employed.
- *Punitive conditions*, which usually reflect the seriousness of the offense and are intended to increase the punishment of the offender. Such conditions include fines, community service, restitution, drug testing, and home confinement (discussed later).
- *Treatment conditions*, which are imposed to reverse patterns of self-destructive behavior. Such treatment generally includes counseling for drug and alcohol abuse, anger management, and therapy for mental health issues, and is a component of approximately 27 percent of probation sentences in this country.[23]

LO10-2 Describe the three general categories of conditions placed on a probationer.

Some observers feel that judges have too much discretion in imposing overly restrictive conditions that no person, much less one who has exhibited antisocial tendencies, could meet. Citing prohibitions on drinking liquor, gambling, and associating with "undesirables," as well as requirements such as meeting early curfews, the late University of Delaware professor Carl B. Klockars claimed that if probation rules were taken seriously, "very few probationers would complete their terms without violation."[24]

As the majority of probationers do complete their terms successfully,[25] Klockars's statement suggests that either probation officers are unable to determine that violations are taking place, or many of them are exercising a great deal of discretion in reporting minor probation violations. Perhaps the officers realize that violating probationers for every single "slip-up" is unrealistic and would add to the already significant problem of jail and prison overcrowding.

10-2c The Supervisory Role of the Probation Officer

The probation officer has two bas[...] investigative and consists of conduc[...] investigation (PSI), which was discu[...] chapter. The second is supervisory [...] as the offender has been sentenc[...]

Roles of Probation officer
① investigative and consists of the presentence investigation (PSI)
② supervisory and begins as soon as the offender has been sentenced to probation
• Authority = ability to influence a person's actions w/o resorting to force
• caseload = # of clients a probation officer is responsible for at one time

smaller probation agencies, individual officers perform both tasks. In larger jurisdictions, the trend has been toward separating the responsibilities, with *investigating officers* handling the PSI and *line officers* concentrating on supervision.

One of the most difficult aspects of a probation officer's supervisory duties is an unavoidable *role conflict*. On the one hand, the probation officer has the task of guiding the probationer to a successful comple[...]erm. On the other hand, the [...]rotect the community from [...] already shown that he or she [...] law. Operating under vague [...]robation officers must rely [...]tion to navigate the complexi-

CAREE[...]

Probation ([...]

Job Description:

- **Work with offenders or clients wh[...] been sentenced to probation and will not go to prison or jail for their offenses. In some departments, investigate offender backgrounds, write presentence reports, and recommend sentences.**
- **Includes extensive fieldwork to meet with and monitor offenders. May be required to carry a firearm or other weapon for protection.**

What Kind of Training Is Required?

- **A bachelor's degree in criminal justice, social work, psychology, or a related field.**
- **Must be at least twenty-one years old, have no felony convictions, and have strong writing and interview skills. Experience in multicultural outreach is a plus.**

Annual Salary Range?

- **$30,000–$80,000**

Stephen Coburn/Shutterstock.com

GETTING LINKEDIN

A LinkedIn posting for a deputy chief probation officer in Alameda County, California, focuses on the importance of community-relations skills in this profession. The "ideal candidate" for the post has passion and sensitivity for the needs of Alameda County's "ethnically/culturally diverse urban population" and a "track record of building trust and consensus" among coworkers and clients.

THE USE OF AUTHORITY Not surprisingly, research shows that the ideal officer-offender relationship is based on mutual respect, honesty, and trust. In reality, these conditions are often hard to maintain between probation officers and their clients. Any incentive an offender might have to be completely truthful with a line officer is marred by one simple fact: self-reported wrongdoing can be used to revoke probation. Even probation officers whose primary mission is to rehabilitate are under institutional pressure to punish their clients for violating conditions of probation. One officer deals with this situation by telling his clients

> that I'm here to help them, to get them a job, and whatever else I can do. But I tell them too that I have a family to support and that if they get too far off track, I can't afford to put my job on the line for them. I'm going to have to violate them.[27]

Boston Globe/Getty Images

A Wareham, Massachusetts, probation officer checks her appointment schedule. **Why is mutual trust between probation officers and their clients often difficult to achieve?**

In the absence of trust, most probation officers rely on their **authority** to guide an offender successfully through the sentence. An officer's authority, or ability to influence a person's actions without resorting to force, is based partially on her or his power to revoke probation. It also reflects her or his ability to impose a number of lesser sanctions.

For example, if a probationer fails to attend a required alcohol treatment program, the officer can send him or her to a "lockup," or detention center, overnight. To be successful, a probation officer must establish this authority early in the relationship, as it is the primary tool for persuading the probationer to behave in an acceptable manner.

THE CASELOAD DILEMMA Even the most balanced, "firm but fair" approach to probation can be defeated by the problem of excessive *caseloads*. A **caseload** is the number of clients a probation officer is responsible for at any one time. Heavy probation caseloads seem inevitable. Unlike a prison cell, a probation officer can always take "just one more" client. Furthermore, the ideal caseload size is very difficult to determine because different offenders require different levels of supervision.

The consequences of disproportionate probation officer–probationer ratios are, in many instances, predictable. When burdened with large caseloads, probation officers find it practically impossible to rigorously enforce the conditions imposed on their clients. Lack of surveillance leads to lack of control, which can undermine the very basis of a probationary system.

Federal probation officers in western Oklahoma, for example, oversee about nine hundred probationers each, an increase of 17 percent since 2010. With fewer officers per probationer, fewer probation violations are being uncovered. "There is a tie between revocation rates going down and a shortage of officers in the community checking on people," said Steve Skinner, chief of the federal probation office in Oklahoma City.[28]

10-2d Revocation of Probation

The probation period can end in one of two ways. Either the probationer successfully fulfills the conditions of the sentence, or the probationer misbehaves and probation is revoked, resulting in a prison or jail term. As mentioned, probationers who break the law will generally have their probation revoked. The decision of whether to revoke after a **technical violation**—such as failing to report a change of address or testing positive for drug use—is often made at the discretion of the probation officer.

As we have seen, probationers do not always enjoy the same protections

Authority The power conferred on an agent of the law to enforce obedience.

Caseload The number of individual probationers or parolees under the supervision of a probation or parole officer.

Technical Violation An action taken by a probationer or parolee that, although not criminal, breaks the terms of probation or parole as designated by the court.

under the U.S. Constitution as other members of society. The United States Supreme Court has not stripped these offenders of all rights, however. In *Mempa v. Rhay* (1967),[29] the Court ruled that probationers were entitled to an attorney during the revocation process. Then, in *Morrissey v. Brewer* (1972) and *Gagnon v. Scarpelli* (1973),[30] the Court established a three-stage procedure by which the "limited" due process rights of probationers must be protected in potential revocation situations:

- *Preliminary hearing*. In this appearance before a "disinterested person" (often a judge), the facts of the violation or arrest are presented, and it is determined whether probable cause for revoking probation exists. This hearing can be waived by the probationer.
- *Revocation hearing*. During this hearing, the probation agency presents evidence to support its claim of violation, and the probationer can attempt to refute this evidence. The probationer has the right to know the charges being brought against him or her. Furthermore, probationers can testify on their own behalf and present witnesses in their favor, as well as confront and cross-examine adverse witnesses. A "neutral and detached" body must hear the evidence and rule on the validity of the proposed revocation.
- *Revocation sentencing*. If the presiding body rules against the probationer, then the judge must decide whether to impose incarceration and for what length of time. In a revocation hearing dealing with technical violations, the judge will often reimpose probation with stricter terms or intermediate sanctions.

In effect, this is a "bare-bones" approach to due process. Most of the rules of evidence that govern regular trials do not apply to revocation hearings.

Probation officers are not, for example, required to read offenders their *Miranda* rights before questioning them about crimes they may have committed during probation. In *Minnesota v. Murphy* (1984),[31] the Supreme Court ruled that a meeting between probation officer and client does not equal custody and, therefore, the Fifth Amendment protection against self-incrimination does not apply either.

10-2e Does Probation Work?

On August 27, 2016, Rodney Earl Sanders admitted to killing two nuns in Holmes County, Mississippi. A year earlier, Sanders had been arrested for felony driving-under-the-influence and was free on probation. Indeed, probationers are responsible for a significant amount of crime. According to the most recent data, 11 percent of all suspects arrested for violent crimes (and 13 percent of those arrested for murder) were on probation at the time of their apprehension.[32] Such statistics raise a critical question—is probation worthwhile?

To evaluate the effectiveness of probation, we must look again at its purpose. Generally, as we saw earlier, the goal of probation is to reintegrate and divert as many offenders as possible while at the same time protecting the public. Specifically, probation and other community corrections programs are evaluated by their success in preventing *recidivism*—the eventual rearrest of the probationer.[33] Given that most probationers are first-time, nonviolent offenders, the system is not designed to prevent relatively rare outbursts of violence, such as the murder committed by Rodney Earl Sanders.

RISK FACTORS FOR RECIDIVISM About 8 percent of all probationers exit probation by being sent to prison or jail.[34] There are several risk factors that make a probationer more likely to recidivate, including:

1. *Antisocial personality patterns*, meaning that the probationer is impulsive, pleasure seeking, restlessly aggressive, or irritable.
2. *Procriminal attitudes* such as negative opinions of authority and the law, as well as a tendency to rationalize prior criminal behavior.
3. *Social supports for crime*, including friends who are offenders and a living environment lacking in positive role models.[35]

Other important risk factors for recidivism include substance abuse and unemployment. By concentrating resources on those probationers who exhibit these risk factors, probation departments can succeed in lowering caseloads and overall recidivism rates.

"SWIFT AND CERTAIN" One of the problems with traditional methods of sanctioning probation violations is the length of the proceedings. If, for example, a probationer fails a drug test, it may take months before a penalty is enforced, weakening the link between wrongdoing and punishment. As criminologist James Q. Wilson pointed out, a parent does not discipline a child by saying, "Because [you've misbehaved], you have a 50-50 chance nine months from now of being grounded."[36]

A number of probation departments have implemented strategies that operate on the principle of providing "swift and certain" sanctions for probation violations. Perhaps the most successful of these strategies is Hawaii's Opportunity Probation with Enforcement (HOPE) program. The rules of HOPE are simple. Each substance abuse probationer must call the courthouse every day to learn if she or he is required to come in for a urine test for drugs, or *urinalysis*. If drugs are found in the probationer's system during one of these frequent tests, a short jail term—one to two weeks—is automatically imposed.[37] HOPE has resulted in large reductions in positive drug tests by probationers, and its 2,200 participants are significantly less likely to be rearrested than those not in the program.[38]

10-3 HOW DOES PAROLE WORK?

At any given time, about 870,000 Americans are living in the community on **parole**—the *conditional* release of a prisoner after a portion of his or her sentence has been served behind bars. Parole allows the corrections system to continue to supervise an offender who is no longer incarcerated. As long as parolees follow the conditions of their parole, they are allowed to finish their terms outside the prison. If parolees break the terms of their early release, however, they face the risk of being returned to a penal institution.

Parole is based on three concepts:[39]

1. *Grace.* The prisoner has no right to be given an early release, but the government has granted her or him that privilege.
2. *Contract of consent.* The government and the parolee enter into an arrangement whereby the latter agrees to abide by certain conditions in return for continued freedom.
3. *Custody.* Technically, though no longer incarcerated, the parolee is still the responsibility of the state. Parole is an extension of corrections.

Because of good-time credits and parole, most prisoners do not serve their entire sentence in prison. In fact, the average felon serves only about half of the term handed down by the court.

10-3a Comparing Probation and Parole

Both probation and parole operate under the basic assumption that the offender serves her or his time in the community rather than in a prison or jail. The main differences between the two concepts—which sound confusingly similar—involve their circumstances.

Probation is a sentence handed down by a judge following conviction and usually does not include incarceration. Parole is a conditional release from prison and occurs after an offender has already served some time in a correctional facility. (See Figure 10.3 for clarification.)

LO10-3 Identify the main differences between probation and parole.

CONDITIONS OF PAROLE In many ways, parole supervision is similar to probation supervision. Like probationers, offenders who are granted parole are placed under the supervision of community corrections officers and required to follow certain conditions. Parole conditions often mirror probation conditions. All parolees, for example, must comply with the law, and they are generally responsible for reporting to their parole officer at certain intervals.

The frequency of these visits, along with the other terms of parole, is spelled out in the **parole contract,** which sets out the agreement between the state and the paroled offender. Under the terms of the contract, the state agrees to conditionally release the inmate, and the future parolee agrees that her or his conditional release will last only as long as she or he abides by the contract.

PAROLE REVOCATION About a quarter of parolees return to prison before the end of their parole period, most because they were convicted of a new offense or had their parole revoked.[40] Property crimes are the most common reason that both male and female parolees return to incarceration, and men on parole are twice as likely as their female counterparts to have their parole revoked for a violent crime.[41]

Parole revocation is similar in many aspects to probation revocation. If the parolee commits a new crime, then a return to prison is very likely. If, however, the individual commits a technical violation by breaking a condition of parole, then parole authorities have discretion as to whether revocation proceedings should be initiated. A number of states, including Arkansas, Connecticut, Georgia, and Texas, have recently have taken steps to avoid reincarcerating parolees for technical violations as part of their continuing efforts to reduce prison populations.[42]

When authorities do attempt to revoke parole for a technical violation, they must provide the parolee with a revocation hearing.[43] Although this hearing does not provide the same due process protections as a criminal trial, the parolee does have the right to be notified of the charges, to present witnesses, to speak in his or her defense, and to question any hostile witnesses (so long as such questioning would not place these witnesses in danger).

In the first stage of the hearing, the parole authorities determine whether there is probable cause that a violation occurred. Then, they decide whether to return the parolee to prison.

Parole The conditional release of an inmate before his or her sentence has expired.

Parole Contract An agreement between the state and the offender that establishes the conditions of parole.

FIGURE 10.3 PROBATION VERSUS PAROLE

	Probation	Parole
Basic Definition	An **alternative to imprisonment** in which a person who has been convicted of a crime is allowed to serve his or her sentence in the community subject to certain conditions and supervision by a probation officer.	An **early release** from a correctional facility,[45] in which the convicted offender is given the chance to spend the remainder of her or his sentence under supervision in the community.
Timing	The offender is sentenced to a probationary term in place of a prison or jail term. If the offender breaks the conditions of probation, he or she is sent to prison or jail. Therefore, **probation generally occurs *before* imprisonment**.	Parole is a form of early release. Therefore, **parole occurs *after* an offender has spent time behind bars.**
Authority	**Probation is under the domain of the judiciary.** A judge decides whether to sentence a convict to probation, and a judge determines whether a probation violation warrants revocation and incarceration.	**Parole often falls under the domain of the parole board.** This administrative body determines whether the prisoner qualifies for early release and the conditions under which the parole must be served.
Characteristics of Offenders	As a number of studies have shown, probationers are normally less involved in the criminal lifestyle. Most of them are **first-time offenders who have committed nonviolent crimes.**	Many parolees have **spent months or even years in prison** and, besides abiding by conditions of parole, must make the difficult transition to "life on the outside."

Probation and parole have many aspects in common. In fact, probation and parole are so similar that many jurisdictions combine them into a single agency. There are, however, some important distinctions between the two systems, as noted above.

PROBATION AND PAROLE OFFICERS Unlike police officers or sheriffs' deputies, probation and parole officers generally do not wear uniforms. Instead, they have badges that identify their position and agency. The duties of probation officers and parole officers are so similar that many small jurisdictions combine the two posts into a single position.

Given the supervisory nature of their professions, probation and parole officers are ultimately responsible for protecting the community by keeping their clients from committing crimes. There is also an element of social work in their duties, and these officers must constantly balance the needs of the community with the needs of the offender.[44] Parole officers in particular are expected to help the parolee readjust to life outside the correctional institution by helping her or him find a place to live and a job, and seeing that she or he receives any treatment that may be necessary.

10-3b Discretionary Release

As you may recall from Chapter 9, corrections systems are classified by sentencing procedure—indeterminate or determinate. Indeterminate sentencing occurs when the legislature sets a range of punishments for particular crimes, and the judge and the parole board exercise discretion in determining the actual length of the prison term. For that reason, states with indeterminate sentencing are said to have systems of **discretionary release.**

Discretionary Release The release of an inmate into a community supervision program at the discretion of the parole board within limits set by law.

ELIGIBILITY FOR PAROLE Under indeterminate sentencing, parole is not a right but a privilege. This is a crucial point, as it establishes the terms of the relationship between the inmate and the corrections authorities during the parole process.

In *Greenholtz v. Inmates of the Nebraska Penal and Correctional Complex* (1979),[45] the Supreme Court ruled that inmates do not have a constitutionally protected right to expect parole, thereby giving states the freedom to set their own standards for determining parole eligibility. In most states that have retained indeterminate sentencing, a prisoner is eligible to be considered for parole release after serving a legislatively determined percentage of the minimum sentence—usually one-half or two-thirds—less any good time or other credits.

Not all convicts are eligible for parole. As we saw in Chapter 9, offenders who have committed the most serious crimes often receive life sentences without the possibility of early release. In general, life without parole is reserved for those who have been found guilty of first degree murder or are defined by statute as habitual offenders.

In addition, about 3,300 inmates convicted of nonviolent drug and property crimes have also received this sentence.[46] Today, about one-third of convicts serving life sentences have no possibility of parole.[47]

AP Images/Jim Cole

A parole board discusses the fate of a parolee in Concord, New Hampshire. **What role should crime victims have in the parole process, if any? Explain your answer.**

PAROLE PROCEDURES A convict does not apply for parole. Rather, different jurisdictions have different procedures for determining discretionary release dates. In many states, the offender is eligible for discretionary release at the end of his or her minimum sentence minus good-time credits.

In 2016, for example, Patrick Durocher was sentenced to three to five years in prison for sexually assaulting a woman on the campus of the University of Massachusetts Amherst. This means that Durocher will become eligible for parole after serving three years, less good time. In other states, parole eligibility is measured at either one-third or one-half of the maximum sentence, or it is a matter of discretion for the parole authorities.

In most, but not all, states, the responsibility for making the parole decision falls to the **parole board,** whose members are generally appointed by the governor. According to the American Correctional Association, the parole board has four basic roles:

1. To decide which offenders should be placed on parole.
2. To determine the conditions of parole and aid in the continuing supervision of the parolee.
3. To discharge the offender when the conditions of parole have been met.
4. If a violation occurs, to determine whether parole privileges should be revoked.[48]

Most parole boards are small, made up of three to seven members. In many jurisdictions, board members' terms are limited to between four and six years. The requirements for board members vary. Nearly half the states have no prerequisites, while others require a bachelor's degree or some expertise in the field of criminal justice.

THE PAROLE DECISION Parole boards use a number of criteria to determine whether a convict should be given discretionary release. These criteria include:

1. The nature and circumstances of the underlying offense and the offender's current attitude toward it.
2. The offender's prior criminal record.
3. The offender's attitude toward the victim and the victim's family members.
4. The offender's physical, mental, and emotional health.
5. The offender's behavior behind bars, including his or her participation in programs for self-improvement.[49]

In a system that uses discretionary parole, the actual release decision is made at a **parole grant hearing.**

During this hearing, the entire board or a subcommittee reviews relevant information on the convict. Sometimes, but not always, the offender is interviewed. "I really am sorry for all the crimes I committed," Darryl Dent told a New York parole board in March 2016. Dent was serving five to eleven years behind bars for stealing a wallet, his eighth petty theft conviction. "I'm tired of coming to jail. I'm 56 years old, and I don't want to spend the rest of my life in jail."[50]

Because the board members have only limited knowledge of each offender, key players in the case are often notified in advance of the parole hearing and asked to provide comments and recommendations. These participants include the sentencing judge, the attorneys at the trial, the victims, and any law enforcement officers who may be involved.

After these preparations, the typical parole hearing itself is very short—usually lasting just a few minutes. In most jurisdictions, there is little time for more lengthy proceedings.

Parole Board A body of appointed civilians that decides whether a convict should be granted conditional release before the end of his or her sentence.

Parole Grant Hearing A hearing in which the entire parole board or a subcommittee determines whether to grant parole.

DISCRECTION IN ACTION

Cause for Compassion?

The Situation Thirty-seven years ago, Susan was convicted of first degree murder and sentenced to life in prison for taking part in a grisly killing spree in Los Angeles. Over the course of two days, Susan and her accomplices killed seven people. Susan stabbed one of the victims—a pregnant woman—sixteen times and wrote the word "PIG" on a door using another victim's blood. During her trial, Susan testified that she "was stoned, man, stoned on acid" at the time of her crimes.

Now sixty-one years old, Susan is before your parole board, requesting release from prison. For most of her time behind bars, she has been a model prisoner, and she has apologized numerous times for her wrongdoing. Furthermore, her left leg has been amputated, the left side of her body is paralyzed, and she has been diagnosed with terminal brain cancer.

The Law You have a great deal of discretion in determining whether a prisoner should be paroled. Some of the factors you should consider are the threat the prisoner would pose to the community if released, the nature of the offense, and the level of remorse. In addition, California allows for "compassionate release" when an inmate is "terminally ill."

LO10-4 Explain which factors influence the decision to grant parole.

What Would You Do? Susan obviously poses no threat to the community and is a viable candidate for compassionate release. Should she be set free on parole? Or are some crimes so horrific that the convict should never be given parole, no matter what the circumstances? Explain your vote.

To see how a California parole board voted in a similar situation, go to Example 10.1 in Appendix A.

The New York parole board that ultimately rejected Darryl Dent's parole, for example, holds about twelve thousand hearings a year, conducting as many as forty in a single day.[51]

PAROLE DENIAL When parole is denied, the reasons usually involve poor prison behavior by the offender and/or the severity of the underlying crime.[52] After a parole denial, the entire process will generally be replayed at the next "action date," which depends on the nature of the offender's crimes and all relevant laws.

In 2016, for example, seventy-two-year-old Sirhan Sirhan was denied parole for the fifteenth time. Nearly five decades earlier, Sirhan had been convicted of murdering Senator Robert F. Kennedy at the Ambassador Hotel in Los Angeles and sentenced to life in prison. At his most recent parole hearing, Sirhan claimed that he did not remember shooting Kennedy, leading the California parole board to conclude that he did not show adequate remorse or understand the enormity of his crime.[53]

Mandatory Release Release from prison that occurs when an offender has served the full length of the sentence, minus adjustments for good time.

On rare occasions, a state governor will veto the decision of a parole board to grant supervised release. In 2016, for example, a California parole board recommended the release of sixty-six-year-old Leslie Van Houten, whose parole had been denied nineteen times for a double murder that took place in 1969.

Over the course of nearly five decades behind bars, Van Houten had been a model inmate, earning her bachelor's and master's degrees in prison and running a self-help group for incarcerated women. California governor Jerry Brown blocked Van Houten's parole, however, saying that "her role in these extraordinarily brutal crimes ... cannot be overlooked and lead me to believe she remains an unacceptable risk to society if released."[54] (See the feature *Discretion in Action—Cause for Compassion?* to learn more about the process of discretionary release.)

10-3c Parole Guidelines

Nearly twenty states have moved away from discretionary release systems to procedures that provide for **mandatory release.** Under mandatory release, offenders leave prison only when their prison terms have expired, minus adjustments for good time. No parole board is involved in this type of release, which is designed to eliminate discretion from the process.

Instead, in mandatory release, corrections officials rely on **parole guidelines** to determine the early release date. Similar to sentencing guidelines, parole guidelines determine a potential parolee's risk of recidivism using a mathematical equation. Under this system, inmates and corrections authorities know the *presumptive parole date* soon after the inmate enters prison. So long as the offender does not experience any disciplinary or other problems while incarcerated, he or she can be fairly sure of the time of release.

Note that a number of states and the federal government claim to have officially "abolished" parole through truth-in-sentencing laws. (As described in Chapter 9, this form of legislation requires certain statutorily determined offenders to serve at least 85 percent of their prison terms.) For the most part, however, these laws simply emphasize prison terms that are "truthful," not necessarily "longer."

Mechanisms for parole, by whatever name, are crucial to the criminal justice system for several reasons. First, they provide inmates with an incentive to behave properly in the hope of an early release. Second, they reduce the costs related to incarceration by keeping down the inmate population, a critical concern for prison administrators.[55]

10-4 WHAT ARE SOME TYPES OF INTERMEDIATE SANCTIONS?

Many observers feel that the most widely used sentencing options—imprisonment and probation—fail to reflect the immense diversity of crimes and criminals. **Intermediate sanctions** provide a number of additional sentencing options for wrongdoers who require stricter supervision than that supplied by probation, but for whom imprisonment would be unduly harsh and counterproductive. The intermediate sanctions discussed in this section are designed to match the specific punishment and treatment of an individual offender with a corrections program that reflects that offender's situation.

Dozens of different variations of intermediate sanctions are handed down each year. To cover the spectrum succinctly, two general categories of such sanctions will be discussed in this section: those administered primarily by the courts and those administered primarily by corrections departments, including day reporting centers, intensive supervision probation, shock incarceration, and home confinement. Remember that none of these sanctions is exclusive. They are often combined with imprisonment and probation and parole, and with each other.

10-4a Judicially Administered Sanctions

The lack of sentencing options is most frustrating for the person who, in the majority of cases, does the sentencing—the judge. Consequently, when judges are given the discretion to "color" a punishment with intermediate sanctions, they will often do so. In addition to imprisonment and probation, a judge has five sentencing options:

1. Fines.
2. Community service.
3. Restitution.
4. Pretrial diversion programs.
5. Forfeiture.

Fines, community service, and restitution were discussed in Chapter 9. In the context of intermediate sanctions, it is important to remember that these punishments are generally combined with incarceration or probation. For that reason, some critics feel the retributive or deterrent impact of such punishments is severely limited. Many European countries, in contrast, rely heavily on fines as the sole sanction for a variety of crimes.

PRETRIAL DIVERSION PROGRAMS Not every criminal violation requires the courtroom process. Consequently, some judges have the discretion to order an offender into a **pretrial diversion program** during the preliminary hearing. (As illustrated in the earlier example from Cook County, Illinois, prosecutors can also offer an offender the opportunity to join such a program in return for reducing or dropping the initial charges.)

These programs represent an "interruption" of the criminal proceedings and are generally reserved for young or first-time offenders who have been arrested on charges of illegal drug use, child or spousal abuse, or sexual misconduct. Pretrial diversion programs usually include extensive counseling, often in a treatment center. If the offender successfully follows the

Parole Guidelines Standards that are used in the parole process to measure the risk that a potential parolee will recidivate.

Intermediate Sanctions Sanctions that are more restrictive than probation and less restrictive than imprisonment.

Pretrial Diversion Program An alternative to trial in which the offender agrees to participate in a specified counseling or treatment program in return for withdrawal of the charges.

CAREER TIP In Nevada, judges can sentence problem gamblers to treatment rather than prison for gambling-related wrongdoing. This option has created a statewide demand for *pathological gambling therapists*, who help problem gamblers overcome their addictions.

conditions of the program, the criminal charges are dropped.

PROBLEM-SOLVING COURTS Many judges have found opportunities to divert low-level offenders by presiding over problem-solving courts. In these comparatively informal courtrooms, judges attempt to address problems such as drug addiction, mental illness, and homelessness that often lead to the eventual rearrest of the offender. About three thousand problem-solving courts are operating in the United States.

Although problem-solving courts cover a wide variety of subjects, from domestic violence to juvenile crime to mental illness, the most common problem-solving courts are drug courts. The specific procedures of drug courts vary widely, but most follow a general pattern. Either after arrest or on conviction, the offender is given the option of entering a drug court program or continuing through the standard courtroom process.

Those who choose the former come under the supervision of a judge who will oversee a mixture of treatment and sanctions designed to cure their addiction. When offenders successfully complete the program, the drug court rewards them by dropping all charges. Drug courts operate on the assumption that when a criminal addict's drug use is reduced, his or her drug-fueled criminal activity will also decline.

FORFEITURE In 1970, Congress passed the Racketeer Influenced and Corrupt Organizations Act (RICO) in an attempt to prevent the use of legitimate business enterprises as shields for organized crime.[56] As amended, RICO and other statutes allow judges to implement *forfeiture* proceedings in certain criminal cases.

Forfeiture The process by which the government seizes private property attached to criminal activity.

Day Reporting Center (DRC) A community-based corrections center to which offenders report on a daily basis for treatment, education, and rehabilitation.

Forfeiture is a process by which the government seizes property gained from or used in criminal activity. For example, if a person is convicted for smuggling cocaine into the United States from South America, a judge can order the seizure of not only the narcotics, but also the speedboat used to deliver the drugs to a pickup point off the coast of South Florida. In *Bennis v. Michigan* (1996),[57] the Supreme Court ruled that a person's home or car could be forfeited even though the owner was unaware that the property was connected to illegal activity.

Once property is forfeited, the government has several options. It can sell the property, with the proceeds going to the state and/or federal law enforcement agencies involved in the seizure. Alternatively, the government agency can use the property directly in further crime-fighting efforts or award it to a third party, such as an informant.

Forfeiture is financially rewarding for both federal and local law enforcement agencies. The U.S. Marshals Service manages about $3.1 billion worth of contraband and property impounded from criminals and criminal suspects. In 2015, the agency shared about $365 million of these funds with state and local law enforcement agencies, with an additional $605 million going to crime victims.[58]

10-4b Day Reporting Centers

Day reporting centers (DRCs) are mainly tools to reduce jail and prison overcrowding. Although the offenders are allowed to live in the community rather than jail or prison, they must spend all or part of each day at a reporting center. In general, being sentenced to a DRC is an extreme form of supervision. With offenders under a single roof, they are much more easily monitored and controlled. DRCs are instruments of rehabilitation as well. They often feature treatment programs for drug and alcohol abusers and provide counseling for a number of psychological problems, such as depression and anger management.

Scott Keeler/ Newscom/ZUMA Press/Largo/FL/USA

In Pinellas County, Florida, Judge Dee Anna Farnell congratulates graduates of her drug court program. **Why might those who see drug abuse as a public health issue be critical of drug courts?**

CAREER PREP

Substance Abuse Counselor

Job Description:

- Assess the background and needs of patients suffering from substance abuse and addiction, and craft and execute a plan for recovery.
- Lead group and one-on-one counseling sessions geared toward providing the patient with a sense of accountability and a desire to change the direction of her or his life.

Monkey Business/Fotolia

What Kind of Training Is Required?

- A bachelor's degree from a counselor program, often found in the department of education or psychology in undergraduate institutions, as well as two years of counseling in a related field or equivalent life experience.
- For licensing and employment with a government agency, a master's degree in substance abuse counseling or rehabilitation counseling is often required.

Annual Salary Range?

- $30,000–$60,000

SOCIAL MEDIA CAREER TIP
Manage your online reputation—or someone else will do it for you. Monitor your profile using tools such as iSearch, Pipl, and ZabaSearch. Check BoardTracker, BoardReader, and Omgili for information on what people are saying about you on message boards.

10-4c Intensive Supervision Probation

Over the past several decades, a number of jurisdictions have turned to **intensive supervision probation (ISP)** to solve the problems associated with burdensome caseloads discussed earlier in the chapter. ISP offers a more restrictive alternative to regular probation, with higher levels of face-to-face contact between offenders and officers and frequent modes of control such as urine tests for drugs.

In New Jersey, for example, ISP officers have caseloads of only 20 offenders (compared with 115 for other probation officers in the state) and are provided with additional resources to help them keep tabs on their charges.[59] Different jurisdictions have different methods of determining who is eligible for ISP, but a majority of states limit ISP to offenders who do not have prior probation violations.

10-4d Shock Incarceration

As the name suggests, **shock incarceration** is designed to "shock" criminals into compliance with the law. Following conviction, the offender is first sentenced to a prison or jail term.

Then, usually within ninety days, he or she is released and resentenced to probation. The theory behind shock incarceration is that by getting a taste of the brutalities of the daily prison grind, the offender will be shocked into a crime-free existence.

Intensive Supervision Probation (ISP) A form of probation in which the offender is placed under stricter and more frequent surveillance and control than in conventional probation.

Shock Incarceration A short period of incarceration that is designed to deter further criminal activity by "shocking" the offender with the hardships of imprisonment.

THE VALUE OF SHOCK In the past, shock incarceration was targeted primarily toward youthful, first-time offenders, who were thought to be more likely to be "scared straight" by a short stint behind bars. More recent data show, however, that 20 percent of all adults sentenced to probation spend some time in jail or prison before being released into the community.[60]

Critics of shock incarceration are dismayed by this trend. They argue that the practice needlessly disrupts the lives of low-level offenders who would not otherwise be eligible for incarceration and exposes them to the mental and physical hardships of prison life.[61] Furthermore, there is little evidence that shock probationers fare any better than regular probationers when it comes to recidivism rates.[62]

BOOT CAMPS Impact incarceration programs, or *boot camps*, are a variation on traditional shock incarceration. Instead of spending the "shock" period of incarceration in prison or jail, offenders are sent to a boot camp. Modeled on military basic training, these camps are generally located within prisons and jails, though some can be found in the community.

The programs emphasize strict discipline, manual labor, and physical training. They are designed to instill self-responsibility and self-respect in participants, thereby lessening the chances that they will return to a life of crime. More recently, boot camps have also emphasized rehabilitation, incorporating such components as drug and alcohol treatment programs, anger management courses, and vocational training.

CAREER TIP Although boot camps have fallen out of public favor somewhat, wilderness therapy programs for teenagers with behavioral problems such as drug or alcohol abuse or antisocial tendencies are flourishing. These programs rely on *field guides, outdoor instructors,* and *youth counselors.*

Home Confinement A community-based sanction in which offenders serve their terms of incarceration in their homes.

Electronic Monitoring A supervision technique in which the offender's whereabouts are kept under surveillance by an electronic device.

10-4e Home Confinement and Electronic Monitoring

Various forms of **home confinement**—in which offenders serve their sentences not in a government institution but at home—have existed for centuries. It has often served as a method of political control, used by totalitarian regimes to isolate and silence dissidents, and it continues to be used in this way. For purposes of general law enforcement, home confinement was impractical until relatively recently. After all, one could not expect offenders to keep their promises to stay at home, and the personnel costs of guarding them were prohibitive.

In the 1980s, however, the advent of **electronic monitoring,** which uses technology to guard the prisoner, made home confinement more viable. Today, all fifty states and the federal government have home monitoring programs, with about 125,000 offenders, including probationers and parolees, participating at any one time.[63]

THE LEVELS OF HOME MONITORING Home monitoring has three general levels of restriction:

LO10-5 List the three levels of home monitoring.

1. *Curfew*, which requires offenders to be in their homes at specific hours, usually at night.
2. *Home detention*, which requires that offenders remain home at all times, with exceptions being made for education, employment, counseling, and other specified activities such as the purchase of food or, in some instances, attendance at religious services.
3. *Home incarceration*, which requires the offender to remain home at all times, save for medical emergencies.

Under ideal circumstances, home confinement serves many of the goals of intermediate sanctions. It protects the community. It saves public funds and space in correctional facilities by keeping convicts out of institutional incarceration. It meets public expectations of punishment for criminals. Uniquely, home confinement also recognizes that convicts, despite their crimes, play important roles in the community, and allows them to continue in those roles. An offender, for example, may be given permission to leave confinement to care for elderly parents.

Home confinement is also lauded for giving sentencing officials the freedom to match the punishment with the needs of the offender. In 2016, for example, Rajat Gupta was allowed to serve the final six months of a two-year prison sentence for stock market fraud at his New York City apartment. Wearing an electronic ankle bracelet, Gupta could leave home to work, visit the doctor, or attend religious services. Indeed, home confinement is a popular punishment for white-collar criminals, who often need to earn funds to pay off significant court-ordered fines—nearly $20 million in Gupta's case.[64]

TYPES OF ELECTRONIC MONITORING According to some reports, the inspiration for electronic monitoring was a *Spider-Man* comic book in which the hero was trailed by the use of an electronic device on his arm. In 1979, a New Mexico judge named Jack Love, having read the comic, convinced an executive at Honeywell, Inc., to begin developing similar technology to supervise convicts.[65]

Two major types of electronic monitoring grew out of Love's initial concept. The first is a "programmed contact" system, in which the offender is contacted periodically by voice or text to verify his or her whereabouts. Verification may be obtained via a computer that uses voice or visual identification techniques, or the offender may be required to enter a code in an electronic box when called.

The second is a "continuously signaling" device, worn around the convict's wrist, ankle, or neck. A transmitter in the device sends out a continuous signal to a "receiver-dialer" device located in the offender's dwelling. If the receiver device does not detect a signal from the transmitter, it informs a central computer, and the police are notified.

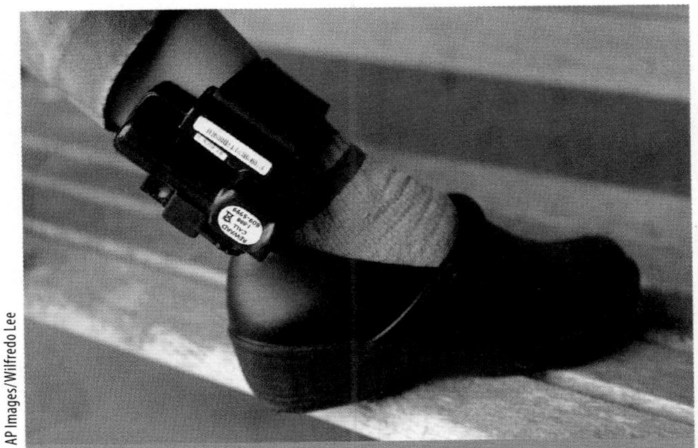

AP Images/Wilfredo Lee

How does an electronic monitoring device, such as the one shown here, meet the goals of intermediate sanctions?

TECHNOLOGICAL ADVANCES IN ELECTRONIC MONITORING As electronic monitoring technology has evolved, the ability of community corrections officials to target specific forms of risky behavior has greatly increased. Michigan courts, for example, routinely place black boxes in the automobiles of repeat traffic violators. Not only do these boxes record information about the offenders' driving habits for review by probation

CJ and TECHNOLOGY

Global Positioning System (GPS)

Global positioning system (GPS) technology is a form of tracking technology that relies on twenty-four military satellites orbiting thousands of miles above the earth. The satellites transmit signals to each other and to a receiver on the ground, allowing a monitoring station to determine the location of a receiving device to within a few feet. GPS provides a much more precise level of supervision than regular electronic monitoring. The offender wears a transmitter, similar to a traditional electronic monitor, around his or her ankle or wrist. This transmitter communicates with a portable tracking device, a small box that uses the military satellites to determine the probationer's movements.

GPS technology can be used either "actively" to constantly monitor the subject's whereabouts or "passively" to ensure that the offender remains within the confines of a limited area determined by a judge or probation officer. Inclusion and exclusion zones are also important to GPS supervision. Inclusion zones are areas such as a home or workplace where the offender is expected to be at certain times. Exclusion zones are areas such as parks, playgrounds, and schools where the offender is not permitted to go. GPS-linked computers can alert officials immediately when an exclusion zone has been breached and create a computerized record of the probationer's movements for review at a later time.

Despite the benefits of this technology, it is rarely used in the context of community corrections. According to the Bureau of Justice Statistics, only about eight thousand probationers are currently being tracked by GPS.

Thinking about GPS

How might GPS monitoring be used to improve and overhaul the American bail system, covered in Chapter 8?

Los Angeles County Probation Department

Explain the possible connection between higher levels of surveillance by probation and parole officers and greater numbers of probationers and parolees being incarcerated.

officers, but they also emit a loud beep when the car goes too fast or stops too quickly. Another device—an ankle bracelet—is able to test a person's sweat for alcohol levels and transmit the results over the Internet.

10-4f Widening the Net

As we have seen, most of the convicts chosen for intermediate sanctions are low-risk offenders. From the point of view of the corrections official doing the choosing, this makes sense. Such offenders are less likely to commit crimes and attract negative publicity. This selection strategy, however, appears to invalidate one of the primary reasons intermediate sanctions exist: to reduce prison and jail populations. If most of the offenders in intermediate sanctions programs would otherwise have received probation, then the effect on these populations is nullified. Indeed, studies have shown this to be the case.[66]

Widen the Net To increase the number of citizens who are under the control and surveillance of the American corrections system.

At the same time, intermediate sanctions broaden the reach of the corrections system. In other words, they increase rather than decrease the amount of control the state exerts over the individual. Suppose a person is arrested for a misdemeanor such as shoplifting and, under normal circumstances, would receive probation. With access to intermediate sanctions, the judge may add a period of home confinement to the sentence.

Critics contend that such practices **widen the net** of the corrections system by increasing the number of citizens who are under the control and surveillance of the state and also *strengthen the net* by increasing the government's power to intervene in the lives of its citizens.[67] Technological advances—such as the black boxes in automobiles, sweat-testing ankle bracelets, and GPS devices mentioned in this chapter—will only accelerate the trend.

ETHICS CHALLENGE

With criminal forfeiture, as described in this section, a defendant must be convicted of committing a crime before her or his property is confiscated. Under *civil forfeiture*, used by the federal government and many state governments, law enforcement agencies can confiscate property without the criminal conviction of its owner and can keep that property, even if the owner is ultimately found to be innocent of the crime. The government need only prove a "substantial connection" between the property and underlying crime for civil forfeiture to apply. What might be some of the ethical pitfalls of civil forfeiture?

STUDY TOOLS 10

LOCATED IN TEXTBOOK

- ☐ Rip out the Chapter Review Card.
- ☐ Review with the Chapter Quiz following this chapter.

LOCATED AT WWW.CENGAGEBRAIN.COM

- ☐ Review key terms flash cards.
- ☐ Read the chapter on all your favorite devices.
- ☐ Complete an Exam to test your knowledge.
- ☐ Check out Visual Summaries and You Decide activities to explore chapter concepts.

Quiz

1. Supporters of community corrections point to the role these programs play in ______________ nonviolent offenders from prison and jail.

2. Offenders sentenced to ______________ serve their sentence in the community under the supervision of the corrections system.

3. To a large extent, the effectiveness of community corrections programs is measured by ______________, or the rate at which participants are rearrested and/or reincarcerated.

4. ______________ refers to the conditional release of an inmate before the end of his or her sentence.

5. A ______________ violation of the terms of probation or parole makes the offender eligible to be sent, or returned, to prison.

6. In jurisdictions that have systems of discretionary release, a ______________ ______________ makes the parole decision.

7. In jurisdictions with ______________ release, offenders leave prison only when their prison terms have expired, minus adjustments for good time.

8. Judicially administered sanctions include fines, restitution, and ______________, a process in which the government seizes property connected to illegal activity.

9. Boot camps, or militaristic programs designed to instill self-responsibility, are a form of ______________ incarceration.

10. Home confinement has become more effective in recent years, thanks to technology known as ______________ ______________.

Answers to the Chapter 10 Quiz can be found in the Answers section in the back of the book.

11 Prisons and Jails

Pixinoo/Shutterstock.com

LEARNING OBJECTIVES

After studying this chapter, you will be able to …

11-1 Contrast the Pennsylvania and the New York penitentiary theories of the 1800s.

11-2 List and briefly explain the four types of prisons.

11-3 Identify some factors that have caused the prison population to grow dramatically in the last several decades.

11-4 Describe the arguments for and against private prisons.

11-5 Summarize the distinction between jails and prisons, and indicate the importance of jails in the American corrections system.

After finishing this chapter, go to **PAGE 242** for **STUDY TOOLS**

Downsizing?

To reform its criminal justice system, Maryland's legislature took two massive steps in 2016. First, nonviolent offenders who had been given severe prison sentences in the past would be eligible for early release. Second, mandatory minimum sentences for newly convicted nonviolent offenders were rescinded, meaning that those found guilty of intent to distribute illegal drugs would no longer automatically face ten years in prison. As a result, Maryland expects to reduce its prison population by nearly two thousand and save at least $80.5 million dollars in incarceration costs over the next decade.

Maryland is hardly the only state to have taken dramatic measures with regard to corrections and criminal justice. In 2010, South Carolina eliminated some mandatory minimums, changed low-level property crimes from felonies to misdemeanors, and made it less likely for probation and parole violators to be incarcerated. By 2016, these measures had led to an 18 percent drop in South Carolina's prison population and $18 million in corrections savings. Overall, between 2006 and 2016, twenty-eight states saw their prison populations decline, contributing to a small but significant trend in American corrections: fewer inmates. In 2015, the U.S. prison population fell by just over 2 percent, hitting its lowest level since 2005 and continuing a six-year downward course.

To be sure, these decreases do little to threaten our nation's title as "the globe's leading incarcerator." About 2.2 million Americans are in prison and jail. The United States locks up six times as many of its citizens as Canada does, and eight times as many as a number of European democracies. Still, the fact that politicians are willing to accept policies that reduce the number of inmates represents a sea change in the country's corrections strategies. "We're talking about using a scarce resource—beds in jails and prisons—in the most effective way. I would say to people, 'Who would you rather have [incarcerated]—a bank robber or an addict who is aggressively panhandling downtown?'" says Benjamin David, a district attorney from North Carolina. "This is not a political issue, it is a moral issue."

Justin Sullivan/Getty Images News/Getty Images

About 2.2 million inmates are incarcerated in prisons and jails in the United States. *Economic considerations aside, what is your opinion of America's dramatically high incarceration rates?*

11-1 HOW HAVE AMERICAN PRISONS EVOLVED?

Today's high rates of imprisonment—often referred to as evidence of "mass incarceration" in the United States—are the result of many criminal justice strategies that we have discussed in this textbook. These include truth-in-sentencing guidelines, relatively long sentences for gun and drug crimes, "three-strikes" habitual offender laws, and judicial freedom to incarcerate convicts for relatively minor criminal behavior.

At the base of all these policies is a philosophy that sees prisons primarily as instruments of punishment. The loss of freedom imposed on inmates is the penalty for the crimes they have committed. Punishment has not, however, always been the main reason for incarceration in this country.

11-1a English Roots

The prisons of eighteenth-century England, known as "bridewells" after London's Bridewell Palace, had little to do with punishment. These facilities were mainly used to hold debtors or those awaiting trial, execution, or banishment from the community. (In many ways, as will be made clear, these facilities resembled the modern jail.)

English courts generally imposed one of two sanctions on convicted felons: they turned them loose, or they executed them.[1] To be sure, most felons were released, pardoned either by the court or the clergy after receiving a whipping or a branding.

The correctional system in the American colonies differed very little from that of their motherland. If anything, colonial administrators were more likely to use corporal punishment than their English counterparts, and the death penalty was not uncommon in early America. The one dissenter was William Penn, who adopted the "Great Law" in Pennsylvania in 1682. Based on Quaker ideals of humanity and rehabilitation, this criminal code forbade the use of torture and mutilation as forms of punishment.

Instead, felons were ordered to pay restitution of property or goods to their victims. If the offenders did not have sufficient property to make restitution, they were placed in a prison, which was primarily a "workhouse."[2] The death penalty was still allowed under the "Great Law," but only in cases of premeditated murder. Penn proved to be an exception, however, and the path to reform was much slower in the colonies than in England.

11-1b Walnut Street Prison: The First Penitentiary

On William Penn's death in 1718, the "Great Law" was rescinded in favor of a harsher criminal code, similar to those of the other colonies. At the time of the American Revolution, however, the Quakers were instrumental in the first broad swing of the incarceration pendulum from punishment to rehabilitation. In 1776, Pennsylvania passed legislation ordering that offenders be reformed through treatment and discipline rather than simply beaten or executed.[3] Several states, including Massachusetts and New York, quickly followed Pennsylvania's example.

Pennsylvania continued its reformist ways by opening the country's first **penitentiary** in a wing of Philadelphia's Walnut Street Jail in 1790. The penitentiary operated on the assumption that silence and labor provided the best hope of rehabilitating the criminal spirit. Remaining silent would force the prisoners to think about their crimes, and eventually the weight of conscience would lead to repentance. At the same time, enforced labor would attack the problem of idleness—regarded as the main cause of crime by penologists of the time.[4] Consequently, inmates at Walnut Street were isolated from one another in solitary rooms and kept busy with constant menial chores.

Penitentiary An early form of correctional facility that emphasized separating inmates from society and from each other.

Separate Confinement A nineteenth-century penitentiary system developed in Pennsylvania in which inmates were kept separate from each other at all times, with daily activities taking place in individual cells.

CAREER TIP Just as criminologists study crime, *penologists* study the corrections system, often with a focus on prison management and inmate rehabilitation.

Eventually, the penitentiary at Walnut Street succumbed to the same problems that continue to plague institutions of confinement: overcrowding and excessive costs. As an influx of inmates forced more than one person to be housed in a room, maintaining silence became nearly impossible. By the early 1800s, officials could not find work for all of the convicts, so many were left idle.

11-1c The Great Penitentiary Rivalry: Pennsylvania versus New York

LO11-1 Contrast the Pennsylvania and the New York penitentiary theories of the 1800s.

The apparent lack of success at Walnut Street did little to dampen enthusiasm for the penitentiary concept. Throughout the first half of the nineteenth century, a number of states reacted to prison overcrowding by constructing new penitentiaries. Each state tended to have its own peculiar twist on the roles of silence and labor, and two such systems—those of Pennsylvania and New York—emerged to shape the debate over the most effective way to run a prison.

THE PENNSYLVANIA SYSTEM After the failure of Walnut Street, Pennsylvania constructed two new prisons: the Western Penitentiary near Pittsburgh (opened in 1826) and the Eastern Penitentiary in Cherry Hill, near Philadelphia (1829). The Pennsylvania system took the concept of silence as a virtue to new extremes. Based on the idea of **separate confinement,** these penitentiaries were constructed with back-to-back cells facing outward from the center. (See Figure 11.1 for the layout of the original Eastern Penitentiary.)

To protect each inmate from the corrupting influence of the others, prisoners worked, slept, and ate alone in their cells. Their only contact with other human beings came in the form of religious instruction from a visiting clergyman or prison official.[5]

FIGURE 11.1 THE EASTERN PENITENTIARY

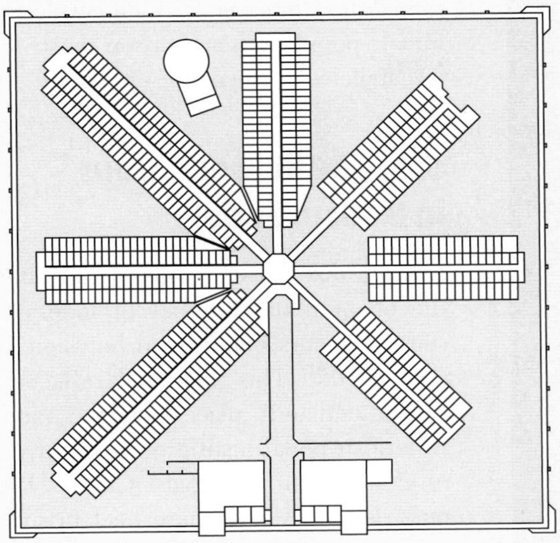

As you can see, the Eastern Penitentiary was designed in the form of a "wagon wheel," known today as the radial style. The back-to-back cells in each "spoke" of the wheel faced outward from the center to limit contact between inmates.

THE NEW YORK SYSTEM If Pennsylvania's prisons were designed to transform wrongdoers into honest citizens, those in New York focused on obedience. When New York's Newgate Prison (built in 1791) became overcrowded, the state authorized the construction of Auburn Prison, which opened in 1816. Auburn initially operated under many of the same assumptions that guided the penitentiary at Walnut Street.

Solitary confinement, however, seemed to lead to an inordinate amount of sickness, insanity, and even suicide among inmates, and it was abandoned in 1822. Nine years later, Elam Lynds became warden at Auburn and instilled the **congregate system,** also known as the Auburn system. Like Pennsylvania's separate confinement system, the congregate system was based on silence and labor. At Auburn, however, inmates worked and ate together, with silence enforced by prison guards.[6]

If either state can be said to have "won" the debate, it was New York. The Auburn system proved more popular, and a majority of the new prisons built during the first half of the nineteenth century followed New York's lead, though mainly for economic reasons rather than philosophical ones. New York's penitentiaries were cheaper to build because they did not require so much space.

Furthermore, inmates in New York were employed in workshops, whereas those in Pennsylvania toiled alone in their cells. Consequently, the Auburn system was better positioned to exploit prison labor in the early years of widespread factory production.

11-1d The Reformers and the Progressives

The Auburn system did not go unchallenged. In the 1870s, a group of reformers argued that fixed sentences, imposed silence, and isolation did nothing to improve prisoners. These critics proposed that penal institutions should offer the promise of early release as a prime tool for rehabilitation. Echoing the views of the Quakers a century earlier, the reformers presented an ideology that would heavily influence American corrections for the next century.

This "new penology" was put into practice at New York's Elmira Reformatory in 1876. At Elmira, good behavior was rewarded by early release, and misbehavior was punished with extended time under a three-grade system of classification. On entering the institution, the offender was assigned a grade of 2.

If the inmate followed the rules and completed work and school assignments, after six months he was moved up to grade 1, the necessary grade for release. If, however, the inmate broke institutional rules, he was lowered to grade 3. A grade 3 inmate needed to behave properly for three months before he could return to grade 2 and begin to work back toward grade 1 and eventual release.[7]

How Elmira worked

Although other penal institutions did not adopt the Elmira model, its theories came into prominence in the first two decades of the twentieth century thanks to the Progressive movement in criminal justice. The Progressives believed that criminal behavior was caused by social, economic, and biological factors and, therefore, a corrections system should have a goal of treatment, not punishment. Consequently, they trumpeted a **medical model** for prisons, which held that institutions should offer a variety of programs and therapies to cure inmates of their "ills," whatever the root causes. The Progressives were largely responsible for the spread of indeterminate sentences (Chapter 9), probation (Chapter 10), intermediate sanctions (Chapter 10), and parole (Chapter 10) in the first half of the twentieth century.

Congregate System A nineteenth-century penitentiary system developed in New York in which inmates were kept in separate cells during the night but worked together in the daytime in silence.

Medical Model A model of corrections in which the psychological and biological roots of an inmate's criminal behavior are identified and treated.

Library of Congress/Corbis Historical/VCG/Getty Images

Inmates of the Elmira Reformatory in New York attend a presentation at the prison auditorium. **To what extent do you believe that treatment should be a part of the incarceration of criminals?**

11-1e The Reassertion of Punishment

Even though the Progressives had a great influence on the corrections system as a whole, their theories had little impact on the prisons themselves. Many of these facilities had been constructed in the nineteenth century and were impervious to change. More important, prison administrators usually did not agree with the Progressives and their followers, so the day-to-day lives of most inmates varied little from the congregate system of Auburn Prison.

Academic attitudes began to shift away from the Progressives in the mid-1960s. Then, in 1974, the publication of Robert Martinson's famous "What Works?" essay provided opponents of the medical model with statistical evidence that rehabilitation efforts did nothing to lower recidivism rates.[8] This is not to say that Martinson's findings went unchallenged. A number of critics argued that rehabilitative programs could be successful.[9] In fact, Martinson himself retracted most of his claims in a little-noticed article published five years after his initial report.[10]

Attempts by Martinson and others to "set the record straight" went largely unnoticed, however, as crime rose sharply in the early 1970s. This trend led many criminologists and politicians to champion "get tough" measures to deal with criminals they now considered "incurable." By the end of the 1980s, the legislative, judicial, and administrative strategies that we have discussed throughout this text had positioned the United States for an explosion in inmate populations and prison construction unparalleled in the nation's history.

11-1f The Role of Prisons in Modern Society

For reasons that we will explain later in the chapter, the number of federal and state prisoners quadrupled between 1980 and 2010.[11] This increase reflects the varied demands placed on the modern American penal institution. As University of Connecticut sociologist Charles Logan once noted, Americans expect prisons to "correct the incorrigible, rehabilitate the wretched, . . . restrain the dangerous, and punish the wicked."[12]

Basically, prisons exist to make society a safer place. Whether this is to be achieved through retribution, deterrence, incapacitation, or rehabilitation—the four justifications of corrections introduced in Chapter 9—depends on the operating philosophy of the individual penal institution.

MODELS OF ORGANIZATION Three general models of prisons have emerged to describe the different schools of thought behind prison organization:

- The *custodial model* is based on the assumption that prisoners are incarcerated for reasons of incapacitation, deterrence, and retribution. All decisions within the prison—such as what form of recreation to provide the inmates—are made with an eye toward security and discipline, and the daily routine of the inmates is highly controlled. The custodial model has dominated the most restrictive prisons in the United States since the 1930s.
- The *rehabilitation model* stresses the ideals of individualized treatment that we discussed in Chapter 9 Security concerns are often secondary to the well-being of the individual inmate, and a number of treatment programs are offered to aid prisoners in changing their criminal and antisocial behavior. The rehabilitation model came into prominence during the 1950s and enjoyed widespread popularity until it began to lose general acceptance in the 1970s and 1980s.

- In the *reintegration model*, the correctional institution serves as a training ground for the inmate to prepare for existence in the community. Prisons that have adopted this model give the prisoners more responsibility during incarceration and offer halfway houses and work programs to help them reintegrate into society. This model is becoming more influential, as corrections officials react to problems such as prison overcrowding.[13]

DIFFERING PERSPECTIVES Critical views of the prison's role in society are at odds with these three "ideal" perspectives. Professor Alfred Blumstein argues that prisons create new criminals, especially with regard to nonviolent drug offenders. Not only do these nonviolent felons become socialized to the criminal lifestyle while in prison, but the stigma of incarceration makes it more difficult for them to obtain employment on release.

Their only means of sustenance "on the outside" is to apply the criminal methods they learned in prison.[14] A study by criminal justice professors Cassia Spohn of Arizona State University and David Holleran of the College of New Jersey found that convicted drug offenders who were sentenced to prison were 2.2 times more likely to be incarcerated for a new offense than those sentenced to probation.[15]

11-2 HOW ARE PRISONS ORGANIZED AND MANAGED?

The United States has a dual prison system that parallels its dual court system, which we discussed earlier in the textbook. The Federal Bureau of Prisons (BOP) currently operates about one hundred confinement facilities, ranging from prisons to immigration detention centers to community corrections institutions.[16] In the federal corrections system, a national director, appointed by the president, oversees six regional directors and a staff of nearly 40,000 employees.

All fifty states also operate state prisons, which number about 1,700 and make up more than 90 percent of the country's correctional facilities.[17] Governors are responsible for the organization and operation of state corrections systems, which vary widely based on each state's geography, demographics, and political culture.

Generally, offenders sentenced in federal court for breaking federal law serve their time in federal prisons, and offenders sentenced in state court for breaking state law serve their time in state prisons. As you can see in Figure 11.2, federal prisons hold relatively few violent felons, because relatively few federal laws involve violent crime. At the same time, federal prisons are much more likely to hold public order offenders, a group that includes violators of federal immigration law.

FIGURE 11.2 TYPES OF OFFENSES OF FEDERAL AND STATE PRISON INMATES

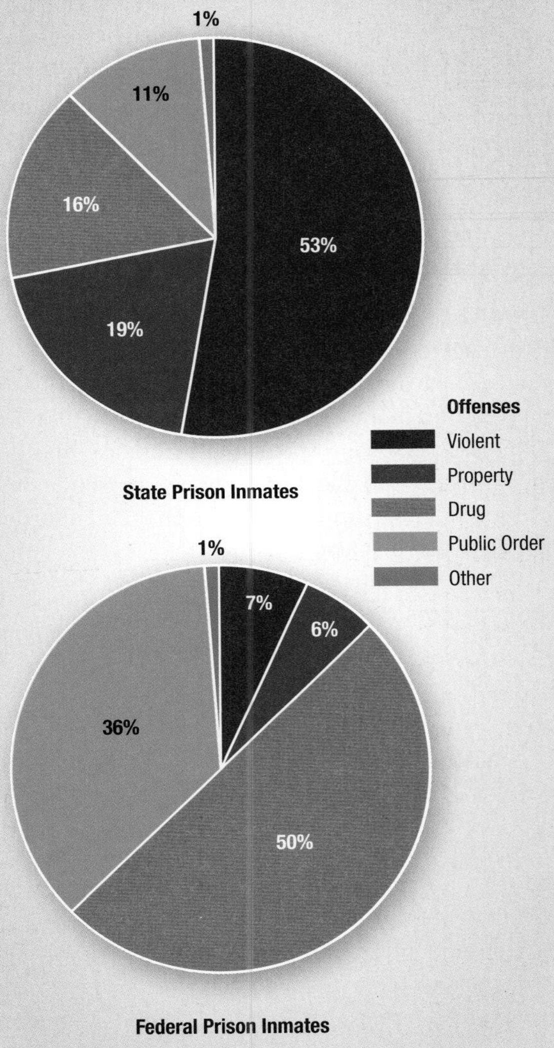

As the comparison above shows, state prisoners are most likely to have been convicted of violent crimes, while federal prisoners are most likely to have been convicted of drug and public order offenses.

Source: Bureau of Justice Statistics, *Prisoners in 2015* (Washington, D.C.: U.S. Department of Justice, December 2016), Table 9, page 14; and Table 10, page 15.

11-2a Prison Administration

Whether the federal government or a state government operates a prison, its administrators have the same general goals, summarized by Charles Logan as follows:

> The mission of a prison is to keep prisoners—to keep them in, keep them safe, keep them in line, keep them healthy, and keep them busy—and to do it with fairness, without undue suffering and as efficiently as possible.[18]

Considering the environment of a prison—an enclosed world inhabited by people who are generally violent and angry and would rather be anywhere else—Logan's mission statement is somewhat unrealistic. A prison staff must supervise the daily routines of hundreds or thousands of inmates, a duty that includes providing them with meals, education, vocational programs, and different forms of leisure. The smooth operation of this supervision is made more difficult—if not, at times, impossible—by budgetary restrictions, overcrowding, and continual inmate turnover.

FORMAL PRISON MANAGEMENT In some respects, the management structure of a prison is similar to that of a police department, as discussed in Chapter 5. Both systems rely on a hierarchical (top-down) *chain of command* to increase personal responsibility. Both assign different employees to specific tasks, though prison managers have much more direct control over their subordinates than do police managers.

The main difference is that police departments have a *continuity of purpose* that is sometimes lacking in prison organizations. All members of a police force are, at least theoretically, working to reduce crime and apprehend criminals. In a prison, this continuity is less evident. An employee in the prison laundry service and one who works in the visiting center have little in common. In some instances, employees may even have cross-purposes: A prison guard may want to punish an inmate, while a counselor in the treatment center may want to rehabilitate her or him.

Consequently, a strong hierarchy is crucial for any prison management team that hopes to meet Charles Logan's expectations. As Figure 11.3 shows, the **warden** (also known as a superintendent) is ultimately responsible for the operation of a prison. He or she oversees deputy wardens, who in turn manage the various organizational lines of the institution. The custodial employees, who deal directly with the inmates and make up more than half of a prison's staff, operate under a militaristic hierarchy, with a line of command passing from the deputy warden to the captain to the correctional officer.

Warden The prison official who is ultimately responsible for the organization and performance of a correctional facility.

GOVERNING PRISONS The implications of prison mismanagement can be severe. While studying a series of prison riots, sociologists Bert Useem and Peter Kimball found that breakdown in managerial control commonly preceded such acts of mass violence.[19] During the 1970s, for example, conditions at the State Penitentiary in New Mexico deteriorated significantly. Inmates were increasingly the targets of random and harsh treatment at the hands of the prison staff, while at the same time a reduction in structured activities left prison life "painfully boring."[20] The result, in 1980, was one of the most violent prison riots in the nation's history.

What sort of prison management is most suited to avoid such situations? Most prisons in the United States operate under an authoritarian management structure, characterized by a strong leader, extensive control of the prison environment, and harsh discipline for misbehaving inmates.[21] Political scientist John DiIulio believes that, in general, the sound governance of correctional facilities is a matter of order, amenities, and services:

- *Order* can be defined as the absence of misconduct such as murder, assault, and rape. Many observers, including DiIulio, believe that, having incarcerated a person, the state has a responsibility to protect that person from disorder in the correctional institution.
- *Amenities* are those comforts that make life "livable," such as clean living conditions, acceptable food, and entertainment. One theory of incarceration holds that inmates should not enjoy a quality of life comparable to life outside prison. Without the basic amenities, however, prison life becomes unbearable, and inmates are more likely to lapse into disorder.
- *Services* include programs designed to improve an inmate's prospects on release, such as vocational training, remedial education, and drug treatment. Again, many feel that a person convicted of a crime does not deserve to participate in these kinds of programs, but they have two clear benefits. First, they keep the inmate occupied and focused during her or his sentence. Second, they reduce the chances that the inmate will go back to a life of crime after she or he returns to the community.[22]

According to DiIulio, in the absence of order, amenities, and services, inmates will come to see their imprisonment as not only unpleasant but unfair, and they will

FIGURE 11.3 ORGANIZATIONAL CHART FOR A TYPICAL CORRECTIONAL FACILITY

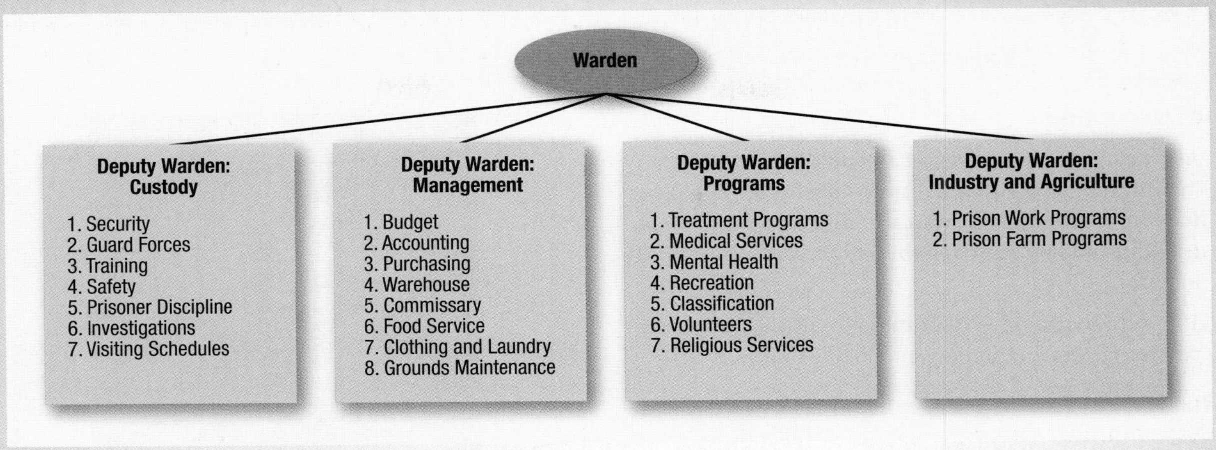

become much more difficult to control.[23] Furthermore, weak governance encourages inmates to come up with their own methods of regulating their lives. As we shall see in the next chapter, the result is usually high levels of violence and the expansion of prison gangs and other unsanctioned forms of authority.

CLASSIFICATION One of the most important aspects of prison administration occurs soon after a defendant has been convicted of a crime and sentenced to be incarcerated. In this **classification** process, an inmate's mental, physical, and security needs are evaluated to help determine the best correctional facility "fit."

The classification process usually takes four to eight weeks and is overseen by a corrections counselor, also known as a case manager. During this period, the inmate undergoes numerous tests and interviews to identify education levels, medical issues, drug/alcohol addictions, and any behavioral "red flags."

Taking the results of the process into consideration, prison administrators generally rely on three broad criteria for classification purposes:

1. The seriousness of the crime committed.
2. The risk of future criminal or violent conduct.
3. The need for treatment and rehabilitation programs.[24]

Classification is not a one-time operation. Inmates can, and often do, change their behavior patterns during the course of their incarceration. If an inmate acts more violently, or, conversely, shows an increasingly positive attitude, that inmate will need to be *reclassified*. Furthermore, the successful completion of prison rehabilitation programs may require an adjustment in the inmate's release plan, discussed in the next chapter.[25]

11-2b Types of Prisons

LO11-2 List and briefly explain the four types of prisons.

Following the classification process, an inmate is assigned a **custody level.** Corrections officials rely on this custody level to place the inmate in the appropriate correctional facility. In the federal prison system, an offender's custody level determines whether she or he is sent to one of six different types of prisons. Inmates in level 1 facilities are usually nonviolent and require the least amount of security, while inmates in level 6 facilities are the most dangerous and require the harshest security measures.

To simplify matters, most correctional facilities are designated as being one of three security levels—minimum, medium, or maximum. A fourth level—the supermaximum-security prison, known as the "supermax"—is relatively rare and extremely controversial due to its hyper-harsh methods of punishing and controlling the most dangerous prisoners.

MAXIMUM-SECURITY PRISONS In a certain sense, the classification of prisoners today owes a debt to the three-grade system developed at the Elmira Reformatory, discussed earlier in the chapter. Once wrongdoers enter a corrections facility, they are constantly graded on behavior. Those who serve "good time," as we have seen, are often rewarded with early release. Those

Classification The process through which prison officials screen each incoming inmate to best determine that inmate's security and treatment needs.

Custody Level The security designation given to new inmates.

CAREER PREP

Warden

Job Description:

- As chief managing officer of an adult correctional institution, the warden is responsible for the custody, feeding, clothing, housing, care, treatment, discipline, training, employment, rehabilitation, and wellbeing of inmates.
- The warden provides institutional staff with effective communications, training, and leadership.

What Kind of Training Is Required?

- A bachelor's degree in criminal justice, social work, psychology, or a related field.
- One or more years of work experience in the management of a major division of a correctional institution.

Annual Salary Range?

- $45,000–$100,000 (depending on size of institution and geographic region)

Micah May, 2000/Used under license from Shutterstock.com

SOCIAL MEDIA CAREER TIP

Regularly reevaluate your social media tools and the methods you use to keep up to date in your fields of interest. If you are still using the same tools as a year ago, you probably aren't keeping up with the latest developments in Internet technology.

who compile extensive misconduct records are usually housed, along with violent and repeat offenders, in **maximum-security prisons.**

The names of these institutions—Folsom, San Quentin, Sing Sing, Attica—conjure up foreboding images of concrete and steel jungles, with good reason. Maximum-security prisons are designed with full attention to security and surveillance. In these institutions, inmates' lives are programmed in a militaristic fashion to keep them from escaping or from harming themselves or the prison staff. About a quarter of the prisons in the United States are classified as maximum security, and these institutions house about a third of the country's prisoners.

Maximum-Security Prison A correctional institution designed and organized to control and discipline dangerous felons, as well as prevent escape.

The Design Maximum-security prisons tend to be large—holding more than a thousand inmates—and they have similar features. The entire operation is usually surrounded by concrete walls that stand twenty to thirty feet high and have also been sunk deep into the ground to deter tunnel escapes. Fences reinforced with razor-ribbon barbed wire that can be electrically charged may supplement these barriers. The prison walls are studded with watchtowers, from which guards armed with shotguns and rifles survey the movement of prisoners below.

Inmates live in cells, most of them with dimensions similar to those found in the Topeka Correctional Facility, a maximum-security prison in Topeka, Kansas: eight feet by fourteen feet with cinder block walls. The space contains bunks, a toilet, a sink, and possibly a cabinet or closet. Cells are located in rows of *cell blocks*, each of which forms its own security unit, set off by a series of gates and bars. A maximum-security institution is essentially a collection of numerous cell blocks, each constituting its own prison within a prison.

Most prisons, regardless of their design, have cell blocks that open into sprawling prison yards, where the inmates commingle daily. The "prison of the future," however, rejects this layout. Instead, it relies on a podular design, as evident at the Two Rivers Correctional Institution in Umatilla, Oregon. (Podular design is discussed in more detail later in the chapter.) At Two Rivers, which opened about a decade ago, fourteen housing units, called pods, contain ninety-six inmates each. Each unit has its own yard, so inmates rarely, if ever, interact with members of other pods. This design gives administrators the flexibility to, for example, place violent criminals in pod A and white-collar criminals in pod B without worrying about mixing the two different security levels.[26]

AP Images/Matt York

What security measures can you identify from this photo of a cell block at Arizona State Prison in Florence, Arizona?

Security Measures Within maximum-security prisons, inmates' lives are dominated by security measures. Whenever they move from one area of the prison to another, they do so in groups and under the watchful eye of armed correctional officers.

Television surveillance cameras may be used to monitor their every move, even when sleeping, showering, or using the toilet. They are subject to frequent pat-downs or strip searches at the guards' discretion. Constant "head counts" ensure that every inmate is where he or she should be. Tower guards—many of whom have orders to shoot to kill in the case of a disturbance or escape attempt—constantly look down on the inmates as they move around outdoor areas of the facility.

SUPERMAX PRISONS About thirty states and the Federal Bureau of Prisons (BOP) operate **supermax** (short for supermaximum-security) **prisons,** which are supposedly reserved for the "worst of the worst" of America's corrections population. Many of the inmates in these facilities are deemed high risks to commit murder behind bars—about a quarter of the occupants of the BOP's U.S. Penitentiary Administrative Maximum (ADX) in Florence, Colorado, have killed other prisoners or assaulted correctional officers elsewhere.

Supermax prisons are also used as punishment for offenders who commit serious disciplinary infractions in maximum-security prisons or who become involved with prison gangs. Although different jurisdictions have different definitions of what constitutes a supermax, the most reliable surveys estimate that about sixty such facilities exist in the United States, holding approximately 25,000 inmates.[27]

The main purpose of a supermax prison is to strictly control the inmates' movement, thereby limiting (or eliminating) situations that could lead to breakdowns in discipline. For the most part, supermax prisons operate in a state of perpetual **lockdown,** in which all inmates are confined to their cells and activities such as meals, recreational sports, and treatment programs are nonexistent. For the sixty minutes of each day that supermax inmates are allowed out of their cells (compared with twelve to sixteen hours in regular maximum-security prisons), they may either shower or exercise in an enclosed, concrete "yard" covered by plastic mesh. Prisoners are strip-searched before and after leaving their cells, and are placed in waist restraints and handcuffs on their way to and from the "yard" and showers.[28]

MEDIUM- AND MINIMUM-SECURITY PRISONS Medium-security prisons hold about 45 percent of the prison population and minimum-security prisons 20 percent. Inmates at **medium-security prisons** have for the most part committed less serious crimes than those housed in maximum-security prisons and are not considered high risks for escaping or causing harm.

Consequently, medium-security institutions are not designed for control to the same extent as

Supermax Prison A highly secure correctional facility that manages offenders who would pose a threat to the security and safety of other inmates and staff members if housed in the general inmate population.

Lockdown A disciplinary action taken by prison officials in which all inmates are ordered to their quarters and nonessential prison activities are suspended.

Medium-Security Prison A correctional institution that houses less dangerous inmates and therefore uses less restrictive measures to prevent violence and escapes.

maximum-security prisons and have a more relaxed atmosphere. These facilities also offer more educational and treatment programs and allow for more contact between inmates. Medium-security prisons are rarely walled, relying instead on high fences. Prisoners have more freedom of movement within the structures, and the levels of surveillance are much lower. Living quarters are less restrictive as well—many of the newer medium-security prisons provide dormitory housing.

A **minimum-security prison** seems at first glance to be more like a college campus than an incarceration facility. Most of the inmates at these institutions are first-time offenders who are nonviolent and well behaved. A high percentage are white-collar criminals. In addition, inmates are often transferred to minimum-security prisons as a reward for good behavior in other facilities.

Therefore, security measures are lax compared with even medium-security prisons. Unlike medium-security institutions, minimum-security prisons sometimes do not have armed guards. Prisoners are provided with amenities such as televisions and computers in their rooms. They also enjoy freedom of movement, and are allowed off prison grounds for educational or employment purposes to a much greater extent than those held in more restrictive facilities.

CAREER TIP Many colleges now offer degrees in *recreation management.* Although geared toward corporate fitness/wellness programs, this discipline also has a place in the corrections system. For example, Danbury Women's Prison has a track and a gymnasium that is used for Pilates and yoga classes.

11-3 WHAT TRENDS ARE DRIVING THE AMERICAN PRISON POPULATION?

LO11-3 Identify some factors that have caused the prison population to grow dramatically in the last several decades.

As Figure 11.4 shows, the number of Americans in prison or jail has increased dramatically in the past several decades. A number of different factors, described in this section, have been offered as reasons for this long-term trend, which has only recently begun to level off.

11-3a Factors in Prison Population Growth

John Pfaff, an expert on sentencing from Fordham University's School of Law, attributes much of the growth in the U.S. prison population to a greater willingness on the part of prosecutors to bring felony—rather than misdemeanor—charges against arrestees.[29] Other experts point to the enhancement and stricter enforcement of the nation's drug laws. In 1980, about 19,000 drug offenders were incarcerated in state prisons and 4,800 drug offenders were in federal prisons.

Minimum-Security Prison A correctional institution designed to allow inmates, most of whom pose low security risks, a great deal of freedom of movement and contact with the outside world.

Thirty-five years later, state prisons held about 209,000 inmates who had been arrested for drug offenses, and the number of drug offenders in federal prisons had risen to approximately 97,000 (representing about half of all inmates in federal facilities).[30]

INCREASED PROBABILITY OF INCARCERATION For most of the 1980s, crime rates in the United States were much higher than they are today. In addition, during that decade, the likelihood of incarceration in a state prison after arrest increased fivefold for drug offenses, threefold for weapons offenses, and twofold for crimes such as sexual assault, burglary, auto theft, and larceny.[31]

With more convicted offenders facing greater probability of imprisonment, the state inmate population was bound to grow.[32] In the federal criminal justice system, this trend has persisted. The proportion of convicted defendants being sent to federal prison rose from 54 percent in 1988 to 87 percent in 2015.[33]

INMATES SERVING MORE TIME In Chapter 9, we discussed a number of "get tough" sentencing laws passed in reaction to the crime wave of the 1970s and 1980s. These measures, including sentencing guidelines, mandatory minimum sentences, and truth-in-sentencing laws, have significantly increased the length of prison terms in the United States.[34]

Overall, inmates released from state prison in 2009 spent an average of nine months—about 36 percent—longer behind bars than inmates released in 1990.[35] On the federal level, in the fifteen years after the passage of the Sentencing Reform Act of 1984, the average time served in federal prison increased more than 50 percent.[36]

FEDERAL PRISON GROWTH The number of inmates in the federal prison population declined by about 7 percent (or 14,112 prisoners) in 2015.[37] This decrease is too small, however, to offset the longer-term expansion of the federal corrections system. Between 2000 and 2015,

FIGURE 11.4 THE INMATE POPULATION OF THE UNITED STATES

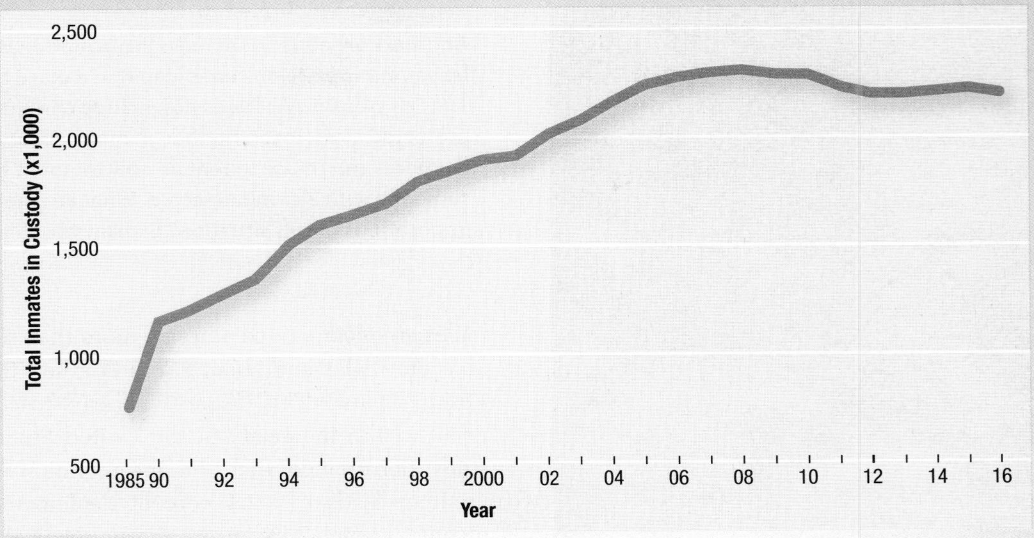

The total number of inmates in the United States has risen from 744,208 in 1985 to about 2.2 million in 2016.

Source: U.S. Department of Justice.

the federal prison population grew 56 percent, from about 125,000 to over 196,000.[38]

As already mentioned, an increase in federal drug offenders is largely responsible for the growth of the federal prison population. Because of mandatory minimum sentencing laws, federal drug traffickers spend an average of seventy-four months behind bars, considerably longer than those sentenced to state prisons.[39] Other factors driving federal prison population growth include the following:

1. Starting in 1987, Congress *abolished parole* in the federal corrections system, meaning that federal inmates must serve their entire sentences, minus good time credits.[40]
2. The number of federal inmates sentenced for *immigration violations* (covered by federal law rather than state law) increased by more than 850 percent from 1990 to 2015.[41]
3. In 2017, nearly 12,700 *female offenders* were behind bars in federal prison, about 75 percent more than in 1995.[42] Indeed, there were about the same number of women in federal prison for drug offenses in 2012 as there were for all offenses in 1995.[43]

11-3b Decarceration

To significantly reverse the trend of prison population growth, says Michael Tonry, a criminal justice professor at the University of Minnesota, there must be a national consensus that "too many people have been sent to prison for too long."[44] As we saw at the beginning of this chapter, policymakers in numerous jurisdictions have embraced strategies of *decarceration*, or the lowering of incarceration rates. In general, decarceration policies rely on three methods to reduce the number of offenders in prison:

1. Decreasing the probability that nonviolent offenders will be sentenced to prison.
2. Increasing the rate of release of nonviolent offenders from prison.
3. Decreasing the rate of imprisonment for probation and parole violators.[45]

For the most part, decarceration strategies have focused on reducing the number of nonviolent offenders behind bars. More than half the states have enacted "front-end" reforms to divert these offenders from prison or to shorten their length of incarceration.[46] Along those same lines, as many as 46,000 nonviolent federal offenders are expected to gain early release under federal sentencing guidelines established in 2015.[47]

Since the beginning of the decade, California has been implementing a "realignment" strategy to move nearly 60,000 low-level offenders from prison to some form of community corrections. As a result, the state's prison inmate population declined by 51 percent from 2006 to 2015.[48] Besides California, three other states (New Jersey, New York, and Rhode Island) have

Anurak Pongpatimet/shutterstock.com

What are some of the possible consequences of having a parent behind bars for the affected child and for society as a whole?

decreased their prison populations by over 20 percent in the twenty-first century.[49] In general, states are relying on *evidence-based practices*, or those strategies supported by statistical research, to decarcerate.

11-3c The Consequences of America's High Rates of Incarceration

Proponents of decarceration point out that mass incarceration can have severe social repercussions for communities and the families that make up those communities. About 2.7 million minors in this country—one in twenty-eight—have a parent in prison.[50] These children are at an increased risk of suffering from poverty, depression, and academic problems, as well as higher levels of juvenile delinquency and eventual incarceration themselves.[51]

Studies also link high imprisonment rates to increased incidence of sexually transmitted diseases and teenage pregnancy, as the separation caused by incarceration wreaks havoc on interpersonal relationships.[52] In addition, of course, incarceration has a harmful impact on offenders themselves. After being released from prison or jail, these men and women suffer from higher rates of physical and mental health problems than the rest of the population, and are more likely to struggle with addiction, unemployment, and homelessness.[53]

Because of the demographics of the U.S. prison population, these problems have a disproportionate impact on members of minority groups. African American males are incarcerated at a rate more than six times that of white males and about two and a half times that of Latino males.[54] This disparity appears to contribute to racial wealth inequality in the United States. A recent study determined that the incarceration of a family member leads to a 64 percent decline in household income, leaving African Americans relatively more susceptible to this form of economic hardship.[55]

Private Prisons Correctional facilities operated by private corporations instead of the government and, therefore, reliant on profits for survival.

ETHICS CHALLENGE

Another consequence of mass incarceration is that it leaves many ex-felons unable to find a place to live. The Fair Housing Act does not include criminals as a protected class, meaning that, in many circumstances, landlords can refuse to rent an apartment or house to someone with a criminal record. What are the ethical implications of this situation? Explain your answer.

11-4 WHAT ARE PRIVATE PRISONS?

As the prison population soared at the end of the twentieth century, state corrections officials faced a serious problem: too many inmates, not enough prisons. "States couldn't build space fast enough," explains corrections expert Martin Horn. "And so they had to turn to the private sector."[56] With corrections exhibiting every appearance of "a recession-proof industry," American businesses eagerly entered the market.

Today, **private prisons,** or prisons run by private firms to make a profit, are an important part of the criminal justice system. About two dozen private companies operate more than two hundred facilities across the United States. The two largest corrections firms, Corrections Corporation of America (CCA) and the GEO Group, Inc., manage approximately 190 correctional facilities and generate about $3.3 billion in annual revenue combined. By 2015, private penal institutions housed about 126,000 inmates, representing 8.3 percent of all prisoners in the state and federal corrections systems.[57]

11-4a Why Privatize?

It would be a mistake to automatically assume that private prisons are less expensive to run than public ones. Nevertheless, the incentive to privatize is primarily financial.

COST EFFICIENCY Private prisons can often be run more cheaply and efficiently than public ones for the following reasons:

> **LO11-4** Describe the arguments for and against private prisons.

- *Labor costs*. The wages of public employees account for nearly two-thirds of a prison's operating expenses. Although private corrections firms pay base salaries comparable to those of public prison employees, their nonunionized staffs receive lower levels of overtime pay, workers' compensation claims, sick leave, and healthcare insurance.
- *Competitive bidding*. Because of the profit motive, private corrections firms have an incentive to buy goods and services at the lowest possible price.
- *Less red tape*. Private corrections firms are not part of the government bureaucracy and therefore do not have to contend with the massive amount of paperwork that can clog government organizations.[58]

In 2015, the Bureau of Prisons estimated that, on average, it costs the federal government about $80 a day to house an inmate, compared with about $63 a day in a privately operated prison.[59] Similarly, research conducted at Temple University found that, by replacing public correctional facilities with private ones, states could save up to 45 percent in operating costs per prison.[60]

OVERCROWDING AND OUTSOURCING Private prisons are becoming increasingly attractive to state governments faced with the competing pressures of tight budgets and overcrowded corrections facilities. Lacking the funds to alleviate overcrowding by building more prisons, state officials are turning to the private institutions for help.

Several years ago, for example, the Oklahoma Corrections Department spent $2 million to purchase beds at private institutions to handle a prison population that was at 112 percent of capacity.[61] Often, the private prison is out of state, which leads to the "outsourcing" of inmates. Washington State recently alleviated its prison overcrowding problems by sending about a thousand inmates to private institutions in Michigan.[62]

11-4b The Argument against Private Prisons

The assertion that private prisons offer economic benefits is not universally accepted. A number of studies have found that private prisons are no more cost-effective than public ones.[63] Furthermore, opponents of private prisons worry that, despite the assurances of corporate executives, private corrections companies will "cut corners" to save costs, denying inmates important security guarantees in the process.

SAFETY CONCERNS Various studies have also uncovered disturbing patterns of misbehavior at private prisons. For example, in the year after CCA took over operations of Ohio's Lake Erie Correctional Institution from the state corrections department, the number of assaults against correctional officers and inmates increased by over 40 percent.[64] In addition, research conducted by Curtis R. Blakely of the University of South Alabama and Vic W. Bumphus of the University of Tennessee at Chattanooga found that a prisoner in a private correctional facility was twice as likely to be assaulted by a fellow inmate as a prisoner in a public one.[65]

PHILOSOPHICAL CONCERNS Other critics see private prisons as inherently unjust, even if they do save tax dollars or provide enhanced services. These observers believe that corrections is not simply another industry, like garbage collection or road maintenance, and that only the government has the authority to punish wrongdoers. In the words of John DiIulio:

> It is precisely because corrections involves the deprivation of liberty, precisely because it involves the legally sanctioned exercise of coercion by some citizens over others, that it must remain wholly within public hands.[66]

AP Images/Mark Humphrey

Do you agree with the argument that private prisons such as the Trousdale Turner Correctional Center in Hartsville, Tennessee, shown here, are inherently unjust, no matter what costs they may save taxpayers? Why or why not?

CJ and TECHNOLOGY

Video Visits

Thousands of prisons and jails in the United States offer "video visitation" to inmates. These communications take place via closed-circuit video systems located within the corrections facility. Administrators favor video visits because they promote safety and require less work for correctional staffers, who do not need to transport an inmate to a visiting area. There is also a profit motive. For example, Securus Technologies, which provides video communications to thousands of jails, typically charges a dollar a minute for such teleconferences. Twenty percent of this fee goes back to the correctional facility.

Opponents of visual visitation condemn the burden that these costs place on inmates' families, many of which are low income. They also point out that the practice tends to displace face-to-face visits, which have a number of benefits. Research shows that seeing friends and family members in person creates social bonds, lessens stress, and even reduces recidivism among inmates.

Thinking about Video Visits

In some instances, Securus has required that, before using its services, a jail must ban all in-person visitation, forcing inmates to rely on the video feeds to contact loved ones. What is your opinion of this situation, in which a private company is essentially dictating correctional policy?

Furthermore, some observers note, if a private corrections firm receives a fee from the state for each inmate housed in its facility, does that not give management an incentive to increase the amount of time each prisoner serves? Though government parole boards make the final decision on an inmate's release from private prisons, the company could manipulate misconduct and good behavior reports to maximize time served and, by extension, maximize profits.[67]

"You can put a dollar figure on each inmate that is held at a private prison," says Alex Friedmann of *Prison Legal News*. "They are treated as commodities. And that's very dangerous and troubling when a company sees the people it incarcerates as nothing more than a money stream."[68]

11-4c The Future of Private Prisons

The private prison industry will continue to play an important role in American corrections for two reasons. First, states experiencing shrinking corrections budgets and congested prisons rely on private correctional institutions to handle their inmate population overflow.

Jail A facility, usually operated by the county government, used to hold persons awaiting trial or those who have been found guilty of minor crimes (mostly misdemeanors).

Second, the federal government contracts with private facilities to house about two-thirds of the undocumented immigrants taken into custody by U.S. Immigration and Customs Enforcement. In 2016, private prisons held an average of about 20,000 such detainees on a typical day.[69]

This figure seems poised to increase because of an immigration law "crackdown" announced by the Department of Homeland Security in early 2017. As part of this strategy, the federal government will rely on private prisons to detain increasing numbers of noncitizens.[70]

11-5 WHAT ROLE DO JAILS PLAY IN THE CORRECTIONS SYSTEM?

LO11-5 Summarize the distinction between jails and prisons, and indicate the importance of jails in the American corrections system.

Although prisons and prison issues dominate the public discourse on corrections, there is an argument to be made that jails are the dominant penal institutions in the United States. In general, a prison is a facility designed to house people convicted of felonies for lengthy periods of time, while a **jail** is authorized to hold pretrial detainees and offenders who have committed misdemeanors. On any given day, about 730,000 inmates are in jail in this country, and jails admit approximately 11.7 million persons over the course of a year.[71] Nevertheless, jail funding is often the lowest priority for the

FIGURE 11.5 THE MAIN DIFFERENCES BETWEEN PRISONS AND JAILS

Prisons	Jails
1. . . . are operated by the federal and state governments.	. . . are operated by county and city governments.
2. . . . hold inmates who may have lived quite far away before being arrested.	. . . hold mostly inmates from the local community.
3. . . . house only those who have been convicted of a crime.	. . . house those who are awaiting trial or have recently been arrested, in addition to convicts.
4. . . . generally hold inmates who have been found guilty of serious crimes and received sentences of longer than one year.	. . . generally hold inmates who have been found guilty of minor crimes and are serving sentences of less than a year.
5. . . . often offer a wide variety of rehabilitation and educational programs for long-term prisoners.	. . . due to smaller budgets, tend to focus only on the necessities of safety, food, and clothing.

tight budgets of local governments, leading to severe overcrowding and other dismal conditions.

Many observers see this negligence as having far-reaching consequences for criminal justice. Jail is often the first contact that citizens have with the corrections system. It is at this point that treatment and counseling have the best chance to deter future criminal behavior.[72]

By failing to take advantage of this opportunity, says Professor Franklin Zimring of the University of California, Berkeley School of Law, corrections officials have created a situation in which "today's jail folk are tomorrow's prisoners."[73] (To better understand the role that these two correctional institutions play in the criminal justice system, see Figure 11.5.)

11-5a The Jail Population

Like their counterparts in state prisons, jail inmates are overwhelmingly young male adults. About 48 percent of jail inmates are white, 35 percent are African American, and 14 percent are Latino.[74] The main difference between state prison and jail inmates involves their criminal activity. As Figure 11.6 shows, jail inmates are more likely to have been convicted of nonviolent crimes than their counterparts in state prison.

PRETRIAL DETAINEES A significant number of those detained in jails—about 435,000 inmates on any given day[75]—technically are not prisoners. They are **pretrial detainees** who have been arrested by the police and, for a variety of reasons that we discussed in Chapter 8, are unable to post bail. Pretrial detainees are, in many ways, walking legal contradictions. According to the U.S. Constitution, they are innocent until proved guilty. At the same time, by being incarcerated while awaiting trial, they are denied a number of personal freedoms and are subjected to the poor conditions of many jails.

In *Bell v. Wolfish* (1979), the Supreme Court rejected the notion that this situation is inherently unfair by refusing to give pretrial detainees greater legal protections than sentenced jail inmates have.[76] In essence, the Court recognized that treating pretrial detainees differently from convicted jail inmates would place too much of a burden on corrections officials and was therefore impractical.[77]

SENTENCED JAIL INMATES According to the U.S. Department of Justice, about 38 percent of those in jail have been convicted of their current charges.[78] In other words, they have been found guilty of a crime, usually a misdemeanor, and sentenced to time in jail.

The typical jail term lasts between thirty and ninety days, and rarely does a prisoner spend more than one year in jail for any single crime. Often, a judge will credit the length of time the convict has spent in detention waiting for trial—known as **time served**—toward his or her sentence. This practice acknowledges two realities of jails:

1. Terms are generally too short to allow the prisoner to gain any benefit (that is, rehabilitation) from the jail's often limited or nonexistent treatment facilities. Therefore, the jail term can serve no purpose except to punish the wrongdoer. (Judges who believe jail time can serve purposes of deterrence and incapacitation may not agree with this line of reasoning.)
2. Jails are chronically overcrowded, and judges need to clear space for new offenders.

OTHER JAIL INMATES Pretrial detainees and those convicted of misdemeanors make up the majority of the jail population. Jail inmates

Pretrial Detainees Individuals who cannot post bail after arrest and are therefore forced to spend the time prior to their trial incarcerated in jail.

Time Served The period of time a person denied bail (or unable to pay it) has spent in jail prior to his or her trial.

FIGURE 11.6 TYPES OF OFFENSES OF PRISON AND JAIL INMATES

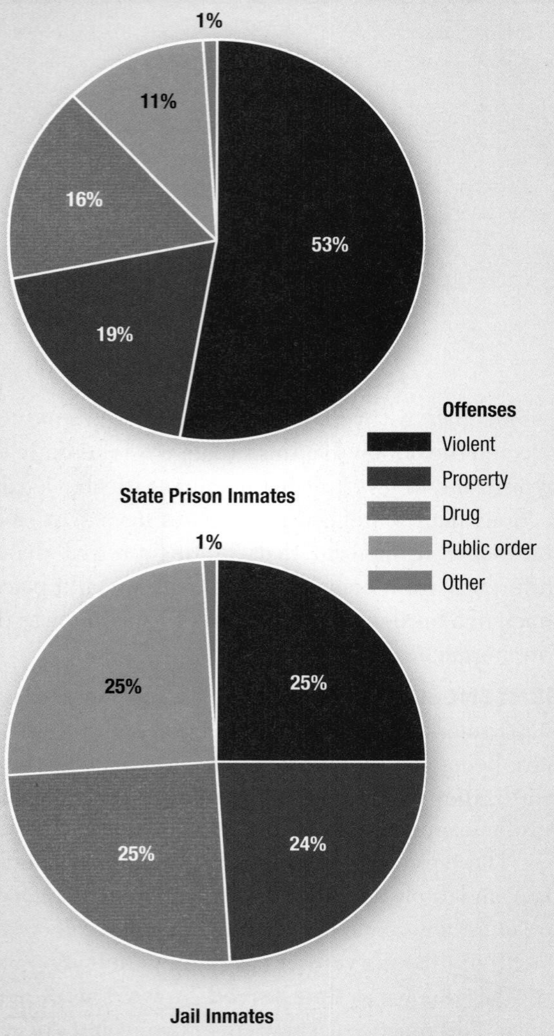

As the comparison above shows, jail inmates are more likely than state prisoners to have been convicted of nonviolent crimes. This underscores the main function of jails: to house less serious offenders for a relatively short period of time.

Source: Bureau of Justice Statistics, *Prisoners in 2015* (Washington, D.C.: U.S. Department of Justice, September 2014), Table 9, page 14; and Bureau of Justice Statistics, *Profile of Jail Inmates, 2002* (Washington, D.C.: U.S. Department of Justice, July 2004), 1.

also include probation and parole violators, mentally ill inmates, juveniles awaiting transfer to juvenile authorities, and immigration law violators being held for the federal government. Increasingly, jails are also called on to handle the overflow from state prisons that have reached or surpassed their population capacities.

11-5b Jail Administration

About 3,300 jails are in operation in the United States. The vast majority of these are managed on a county level by an elected sheriff. Most of the remainder are under the control of the federal government or local municipalities, and six state governments (Alaska, Connecticut, Delaware, Hawaii, Rhode Island, and Vermont) also manage jails.

The capacity of jails varies widely. With seven facilities encompassing four thousand square miles, the Los Angeles County Jail houses a daily average of about 19,000 inmates. Jails that large are, however, the exception rather than the rule. About half of all jails in this country house fewer than five hundred inmates.[79]

THE FEE SYSTEM Many jails operate on the principle of a **fee system,** in which a government agency reimburses the sheriff's department for the daily cost of housing and feeding each inmate. This practice is often problematic, because once the daily fee per inmate has been established (at, say, $8), the sheriff is free to divert some of those funds to other areas of need in her or his department. Also, it is not uncommon for sheriffs' departments to charge inmates "pay-to-stay" fees for aspects of their incarceration such as food, clothing, and medical and dental care.

THE "BURDEN" OF JAIL ADMINISTRATION Given that the public's opinion of jails ranges from negative to indifferent, some sheriffs neglect their jail management duties. Instead, they focus on high-visibility issues such as putting more law enforcement officers on the streets and improving security in schools. In fact, a jail usually receives publicity only after an escape or an incident in which inmates are abused by jailers.

Nonetheless, with their complex and diverse populations, jails are often more difficult to manage than prisons. Jails hold people who have never been incarcerated before and who exhibit a range of behavior—from nonviolent to extremely violent—that only adds to the unpredictable atmosphere. Jail inmates have a number of other problems, including:

1. *Mental illness*. About 60 percent of jail inmates have a history of mental illness, including symptoms of schizophrenia, depression, hallucinations, and suicidal tendencies.[80]
2. *Physical health problems and disabilities*. More than one-third of jail inmates report having a current medical problem such as an injury or ailments such as arthritis, asthma, or sexually transmitted diseases.[81]

Fee System A system in which the sheriff's department is reimbursed by a government agency for the costs of housing jail inmates.

CAREER PREP

Deputy Sheriff/Jail Division

Job Description:

- Be responsible for supervising jail inmates by ensuring that order, discipline, safety, and security are maintained.
- Transport or escort inmates and defendants from jail to courtrooms, attorneys' offices, or medical facilities.

What Kind of Training Is Required?

- Depending on the jurisdiction, possession of a high school diploma or bachelor's degree, as well as successful completion of written and physical examinations, training, and a probationary period.
- Some states require completion of a "jail academy" training course of up to sixteen weeks, including field training.

Annual Salary Range?

- $31,000–$73,000

iStock.com/kaupok

GETTING LINKEDIN

In one LinkedIn posting, the Dane County (Wisconsin) Sheriff's Office highlighted "supervision of jail inmates" as part of its job description for a potential deputy sheriff hire. Indeed, in many counties, a sheriff deputy's main duties involve keeping order at the county jail rather than traffic control or law enforcement.

Furthermore, about 40 percent have disabilities in areas such as hearing, vision, and cognition.[82]

3. *Substance abuse and dependency*. About two-thirds of jail inmates are dependent on alcohol or other drugs, and half of all convicted jail inmates were under the influence of drugs or alcohol at the time of their arrest.[83]

Given that most jails lack the resources and facilities to properly deal with these problems, the task of managing jail inmate populations falls disproportionately on untrained prison staff. Speaking of mentally ill inmates at Rikers Island, New York City's main jail complex, one corrections official said, "They need medication, treatment, [and] psychological help. They don't need a corrections officer."[84]

One problem that consistently plagues jails is the inability to live up to the American Correctional Association's requirement that they "operate effectively as self-contained communities in which all necessary goods are provided in a safe, secure, and controlled manner."[85]

As a result of these challenges, many jails need expensive upgrades to (1) add bed space for increased inmate populations and (2) provide better health and psychiatric care. So, for example, the new Muskegon (Michigan) County Jail, which opened in 2015, has 600 inmate beds (up from 370 in the old jail) and a "medical triage" center to better determine the health needs of inmates during the intake process.[86]

11-5c New-Generation Jails

For most of the nation's history, the architecture of a jail was secondary to its purpose of keeping inmates safely locked away. Consequently, most jails in the United States continue to resemble those from the days of the Walnut Street Jail in Philadelphia.

In this *traditional*, or *linear*, *design*, jail cells are located along a corridor. To supervise the inmates while they are in their cells, custodial officers must walk up and down the corridor, so the number of offenders they can see

Fred Thornhill/Reuters/Corbis

How does the layout of this direct supervision jail differ from that of the maximum-security prison pictured earlier in the chapter? What do these differences tell you about the security precautions needed for jail inmates as opposed to prison inmates?

at any one time is severely limited. With this limited supervision, inmates can more easily break institutional rules.

PODULAR DESIGN In the 1970s, planners at the Bureau of Federal Prisons decided to upgrade the traditional jail design with the goal of improving conditions for both the staff and the inmates. The result was the **new-generation jail,** which differs significantly from its predecessors.[87] The layout of the new facilities makes it easier for the staff to monitor cell-confined inmates. The basic structure of the new-generation jail is based on a podular design. Each "pod" contains "living units" for individual prisoners. These units, instead of lining up along a straight corridor, are often situated in a triangle so that a staff member in the center of the triangle has visual access to nearly all the cells.

Daily activities such as eating and showering take place in the pod, which also has an outdoor exercise area. Treatment facilities are also located in the pod, allowing greater access for the inmates.

During the day, inmates stay out in the open and are allowed back in their cells only when given permission. The officer locks the door to the cells from his or her control terminal.

New-Generation Jail A type of jail designed to encourage interaction between inmates and jailers and offering greater opportunities for treatment.

Direct Supervision Approach A process of prison and jail administration in which correctional officers are in continuous visual contact with inmates during the day.

DIRECT SUPERVISION APPROACH The podular design also enables a new-generation jail to be managed using a **direct supervision approach.**[88] One or more jail officers are stationed in the living area of the pod and are therefore in constant interaction with all prisoners in that particular pod. Some new-generation jails even provide a desk in the center of the living area, which sends a very different message to the prisoners than the traditional control booth.

Theoretically, jail officials who have constant contact with inmates will be able to stem misconduct quickly and efficiently, and will also be able to recognize "danger signs" from individual inmates and stop outbursts before they occur. (As noted earlier in the chapter, corrections officials are using aspects of podular design when building new prisons, for many of the same reasons that the trend has been popular in jails.)

ETHICS CHALLENGE

Jail officials routinely strip-search new inmates to (1) detect lice and other contagious diseases, (2) look for evidence of gang membership such as tattoos, and (3) prevent smuggling of drugs and weapons. These strip searches are highly invasive, often including close examination of the subject's genitals and rectum. Are there any ethical issues with conducting such searches on jail entrants who have not been convicted of a crime? Explain your answer.

STUDY TOOLS 11

LOCATED IN TEXTBOOK

☐ Rip out the Chapter Review Card.

☐ Review with the Chapter Quiz following this chapter.

LOCATED AT WWW.CENGAGEBRAIN.COM

☐ Review key terms flash cards.

☐ Read the chapter on all your favorite devices.

☐ Complete an Exam to test your knowledge.

☐ Check out Visual Summaries and You Decide activities to explore chapter concepts.

Quiz

1. In the second half of the 1800s, the Progressive movement introduced the ________________ model of prison management, which focused on rehabilitation rather than punishment.

2. The ________________ (also known as a superintendent) is at the top of a prison's command structure.

3. Using a process called ________________, prison administrators determine which correctional facility provides the best "fit" for the offender, based mostly on security concerns.

4. Offenders who have been convicted of violent crimes and repeat offenders are likely to be sent to ________________-security prisons.

5. If a prisoner assaults another inmate or a correctional officer, prison officials may decide to transfer that prisoner to a ________________ prison designed to hold the "worst of the worst."

6. Double the number of ________________ offenders are in federal prisons today than was the case two decades ago, due in large part to increased federal prosecution and incarceration of drug offenders.

7. Many states are adopting strategies of ________________ designed to reduce their inmate populations and the costs associated with their corrections systems.

8. Prison officials often feel pressure to send inmates to private prisons to alleviate ________________ of public correctional facilities.

9. Rather than having been convicted of any crime, a significant number of jail inmates are ________________ ________________ who are unable to post bail.

10. Most jails are operated on a local level by the county ________________.

Answers to the Chapter 11 Quiz can be found in the Answers section in the back of the book.

12 The Prison Experience and Prisoner Reentry

AP Images/Rich Pedroncelli

LEARNING OBJECTIVES

After studying this chapter, you will be able to …

- **12-1** Explain the concept of prison as a total institution.
- **12-2** Indicate some of the reasons for violent behavior in prisons.
- **12-3** Describe the hands-off doctrine of prisoner law and indicate two standards used to determine if prisoners' rights have been violated.
- **12-4** Contrast parole, expiration release, pardon, and furlough.
- **12-5** Explain the goal of prisoner reentry programs.

After finishing this chapter, go to **PAGE 264** for **STUDY TOOLS**

Two Strikes

In 2016, a coalition of community leaders and prison inmates calling themselves the Free Alabama Movement released a document entitled "Our Freedom Bill." Among other stipulations, this manifesto demanded the elimination of "all laws that permit slavery" in Alabama. This request was not quite as extreme as it might have seemed. While the Thirteenth Amendment to the U.S. Constitution, ratified in 1865, did abolish slavery, it provided an exception for jobs performed "as a punishment for a crime." As a result of this loophole, almost every prison inmate in the United States, if physically and mentally able, works for little or no compensation.

The variety of prison employment is enormous, from on-site maintenance and kitchen duty, to firefighting, to building products for companies such as McDonald's, Walmart, and Victoria's Secret. At the most, inmates in federal prisons receive salaries of up to $1.14 an hour. At the least, a number of states, including Alabama, do not pay inmates at all. To draw attention to this version of "slavery," on September 9, 2016, members of the Free Alabama Movement at the William C. Holman Correctional Facility in Atmore organized a strike. That day, about 75 inmates at Holman refused to work. Over the next several weeks, as news of this action spread through social media, approximately 24,000 prisoners in twelve other states joined the cause.

The inmate work strike was not the only sign of labor unrest at Holman prison that month. On September 24, nine correctional officers stayed home to protest the institution's chronic understaffing. Holman had already experienced a number of violent riots that year, and on September 1, an inmate had fatally stabbed a correctional officer following a dispute over food portions. "Officers are refusing to go in the cells because of the violence and won't respond to emergency situations because they think it's too dangerous," said one inmate, who claimed that four stabbings a day were taking place at Holman. "Basically, prisoners are just policing themselves."

AP Images/Gerald Herbert

A prisoner pushes a bin of greens inside a food-processing plant at the Louisiana State Penitentiary in Angola, where inmate workers are paid as little as two cents an hour. *Do you think it is fair that inmates receive low wages, or no wages, for doing work while incarcerated? Why or why not?*

12-1 HOW DO INMATES ADJUST TO LIFE IN PRISON?

In this chapter, we will look at the life of the imprisoned convict, starting with the realities of an existence behind bars and finishing with the challenges of returning to free society. Along the way, we will discuss violence in prison, correctional officers, women's prisons, different types of release, and several other issues that are at the forefront of American corrections today. To start, we must understand the forces that shape prison culture and how those forces affect the overall operation of the correctional facility.

Any institution, whether a school, a bank, or a police department, has an organizational culture—a set of values that help the people in the organization understand what actions are acceptable and what actions are unacceptable. According to a theory put forth by the influential sociologist Erving Goffman, prison cultures are unique because prisons are **total institutions** that encompass every aspect of an inmate's life. Unlike a student or a bank teller, a prisoner cannot leave the institution or have

LO12-1 Explain the concept of prison as a total institution.

Total Institution An institution, such as a prison, that provides all of the necessities for existence to those who live within its boundaries.

any meaningful interaction with outside communities. Others arrange every aspect of daily life, and all prisoners are required to follow this schedule in the same manner.[1]

Inmates develop their own argot, or way of speaking. They also have their own way of expressing themselves through body art (see Figure 12.1). They create their own economy, which, in the absence of currency, is based on the barter of valued commodities such as food, contraband, and sexual favors. They establish methods of determining power, many of which, as we shall see, involve violence. Isolated and heavily regulated, prisoners create a social existence that is, out of both necessity and design, separate from the outside world.

12-1a Adapting to Prison Society

On arriving at prison, each convict attends an orientation session and receives a "Resident's Handbook." The handbook provides information such as meal and official count times, disciplinary regulations, and visitation guidelines.

The norms and values of the prison society, however, cannot be communicated by the staff or learned from a handbook. As first described by Donald Clemmer in his classic 1940 work, *The Prison Community*, the process of **prisonization**—or adaptation to the prison culture—advances as the inmate gradually understands what constitutes acceptable behavior in the institution, as defined not by the prison officials but by other inmates.[2]

In studying prisonization, criminologists have focused on two areas: how prisoners change their behavior to adapt to life behind bars, and how life behind bars has changed because of inmate behavior. Sociologist John Irwin has identified several patterns of inmate behavior, each one driven by the inmate's personality and values:

1. Professional criminals adapt to prison by "doing time." In other words, they follow the rules and generally do whatever is necessary to speed up their release and return to freedom.
2. Some convicts, mostly state-raised youths or those frequently incarcerated in juvenile detention centers, are more comfortable inside prison than outside. These inmates serve time by "jailing," or establishing themselves in the power structure of prison culture.
3. Other inmates take advantage of prison resources such as libraries or drug treatment programs by "gleaning," or working to improve themselves to prepare for a return to society.
4. Finally, "disorganized" criminals exist on the fringes of prison society. These inmates may have mental impairments or low levels of intelligence, and find it impossible to adapt to prison culture on any level.[3]

Prisonization The socialization process through which a new inmate learns the accepted norms and values of the prison culture.

The process of categorizing prisoners has a theoretical basis, but it serves a practical purpose as well, allowing administrators to reasonably predict how different inmates will act in certain situations. An inmate who is "doing time" generally does not present the same security risk as one who is "jailing."

12-1b Who Is in Prison?

The culture of any prison is heavily influenced by its inmates. Their values, beliefs, and experiences will be reflected in the social order that exists behind bars. As we noted in the last chapter, the past several decades have seen incarceration rates of women and minority groups rise sharply.

Furthermore, the arrest patterns of inmates have changed over that time period. A prisoner today is much more likely to have been incarcerated on a drug charge or immigration violation than was the case in the 1980s. Today's inmate is also more likely to behave violently behind bars—a situation that will be addressed shortly.

AN AGING INMATE POPULATION In recent years, the most significant demographic change in the prison population involves age. Though the majority of inmates are still under thirty-four years old, the number of state and federal prisoners over the age of forty has increased dramatically since the mid-1990s. Several factors have contributed to this upsurge, including longer prison terms, mandatory prison terms, recidivism, and higher levels of crimes—particularly violent crimes—committed by older offenders.[4]

AN AILING INMATE POPULATION Overall, about half of those incarcerated in the United States (including federal and state prisoners and jail inmates) report having a chronic medical condition such as cancer, high blood pressure, diabetes, or asthma.[5] Furthermore, given the frailties of older inmates, prisons and jails are now holding more people with medical issues than in the past. Poor health is the cause of nine of ten inmate deaths in state prisons, with heart disease and cancer accounting for over half of these fatalities.[6] Not surprisingly, the mortality rates of inmates fifty-five and older from heart disease and cancer are significantly higher than those of any other age group.[7]

Corrections budgets are straining under the financial pressures caused by the health-care needs of aging inmates. In the federal prison system, the annual cost of housing an inmate who has health problems—many of

FIGURE 12.1 PRISON TATTOOS

1488 These numbers are worn by inmates who consider themselves white supremacists or Nazi sympathizers. The number 14 refers to the number of words in a speech made by white supremacist David Lane; 88 refers to the doubling of the eighth letter of the alphabet, as in "Heil Hitler."

14·88

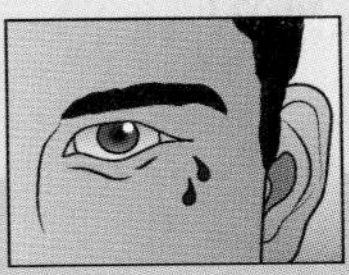

A teardrop Depending on the location of the prison, a teardrop can indicate that the wearer is serving a lengthy prison sentence or that the wearer has committed murder.

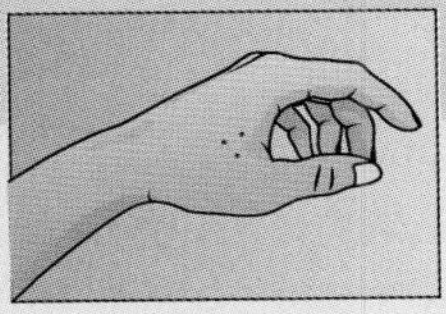

Three dots Typically found on the hands or around the eyes, this logo refers to "*mi vida loca*," or "my crazy life." It acknowledges an allegiance to the gang lifestyle.

A clock with no hands This image indicates that the wearer is spending a lengthy amount of time behind bars.

Playing cards Playing cards, as well as card suits (spades, clubs, hearts, and diamonds), have two meanings: (1) literally, that the inmate likes to participate in games of chance, such as poker, and (2) figuratively, that the inmate takes risks in real life.

Using makeshift needles and ink from contraband pens or melted plastic, many inmates have become proficient at the art of tattooing. These tattoos help establish the inmate's place in prison culture by symbolizing concepts such as toughness, racism, and the length of time spent behind bars.

Source: Correctionsone.com.

whom are over fifty-five years of age—is more than twice the cost of housing a prisoner in the general population.[8]

About half of the nearly $60 million that Virginia spends annually on off-site prison medical treatment goes for the care of older inmates.[9] Given the burden of inmate medical costs, state corrections officials may be tempted to cut such services whenever possible. As we will see later in the chapter, however, prisoners have a constitutional right to adequate health care.

ETHICS CHALLENGE

Do you feel that corrections officials are ethically obligated to provide all necessary health care to inmates? Consider the case of Prisoner X, who is serving life in prison for murder. He has fallen ill, and only a $1 million heart transplant will save his life. Should taxpayers pay for the heart transplant? Should Prisoner X receive the transplant instead of a law-abiding citizen who also needs a new heart? Explain your answers.

MENTAL ILLNESS BEHIND BARS Another factor in rising correctional healthcare costs is the high incidence of mental illness in American prisons and jails. During the 1950s and 1960s, nearly 600,000 mental patients lived in public hospitals, often against their will. A series of scandals spotlighting the poor medical services and horrendous living conditions in these institutions led to their closure and the elimination of much of the nation's state-run mental health infrastructure.[10] Many mentally ill people now receive no supervision whatsoever, and some inevitably commit deviant or criminal acts.

As a result, in the words of criminal justice experts Katherine Stuart van Wormer and Clemens Bartollas, jails and prison have become "the dumping grounds for people whose bizarre behavior lands them behind bars."[11] According to the federal government, half of state prison inmates and 60 percent of jail inmates have experienced mental health problems such as depression or psychosis at a recent point in their lives.[12]

As with aging and ailing prisoners, correctional facilities are required by law to provide treatment to mentally ill inmates, thus driving the costs associated with their confinement well above the average. For reasons that should become clear over the course of this chapter, correctional facilities are not designed to foster mental well-being, and indeed inmates with mental illnesses often find that their problems are exacerbated by the prison environment.[13]

12-1c Rehabilitation and Prison Programs

In Chapter 9, we saw that rehabilitation is one of the basic theoretical justifications for punishment. **Prison programs,** which include any organized activities designed to foster rehabilitation, benefit inmates in several ways. On a basic level, these programs get prisoners out of their cells and alleviate the boredom that marks prison and jail life. The programs also help inmates improve their health and skills, giving them a better chance of reintegration into society after release. Consequently, nearly every federal and state prison in the United States offers some form of rehabilitation.[14]

SUBSTANCE ABUSE TREATMENT As we have seen throughout this textbook, there is a strong link between crime and abuse of drugs and alcohol. According to the National Center on Addiction and Substance Abuse (CASA) at New York's Columbia University, 1.5 million prison and jail inmates in the United States meet the medical criteria for substance abuse or addiction. Also according to CASA, only 11 percent of these inmates have received any type of professional treatment behind bars.[15]

The most effective substance abuse programs for prisoners require trained staff, lengthy periods of therapy, expensive medication, and community aftercare, and carry a price tag of nearly $10,000 per inmate. If every eligible prisoner in the United States received such treatment, the cost would be $12.6 billion. Researchers at CASA contend, however, that "the nation would break even in a year" if just one in ten of these inmates remained substance and crime free and employed for one year after release from prison.[16]

VOCATIONAL AND EDUCATIONAL PROGRAMS Even if an ex-convict does stay substance free, he or she will have a difficult time finding a steady paycheck. Employers are only about half as likely to hire job applicants with criminal records as they are those with "clean sheets."[17]

Prison Programs Organized activities for inmates that are designed to improve their physical and mental health and/or provide them with vocational skills.

To overcome this handicap, more than half of all American prisons offer *vocational* training, or prison programs that provide inmates with skills necessary to find a job. Such programs commonly provide instruction in blue-collar fields such as landscaping, automobile repair, and electrical work. Nine out of ten prisons also attempt to educate their inmates, offering literacy training, GED (general equivalency degree) programs, and other types of instruction.[18]

Some evidence suggests that such efforts can have a positive effect on rates of reoffending. A recent study by the nonprofit Rand Corporation, summarizing thirty years of research, found that ex-inmates who participated in education programs from behind bars had a 43 percent lower chance of reoffending within three years after release than those who did not.[19] The same study found that participation in vocational training improved an inmate's chances of finding post-release employment by 28 percent.[20]

CAREER TIP Most *prison teachers* are either corrections employees who have obtained the necessary certification or civilians with teaching credentials and previous career experience.

12-2 HOW VIOLENT IS LIFE BEHIND BARS?

Prisons and jails are dangerous places to live. Prison culture is predicated on violence—one observer calls the modern penal institution an "unstable and violent jungle."[21] Correctional officers use the threat of violence (and, at times, actual violence) to control the inmate population. Sometimes, the inmates strike back. According to the Bureau of Labor Statistics, because of inmate assaults, correctional officers have one of the most dangerous jobs in the United States.[22]

Among the prisoners, violence is used to establish power and dominance. On occasion, this violence leads to death. Although misconduct varies from institution to institution, overall rates of inmate-on-inmate assault are two to three times higher than arrest rates for assault in the general U.S. adult population.[23]

With nothing but time on their hands, prisoners have been known to fashion deadly weapons out of everyday items such as toothbrushes and mop handles. Many inmates also bring the "code of the street," with its fixation on "respect, toughness, and retribution," into prison, making them likely both to engage in violent acts behind bars and to be victims of such violence.[24]

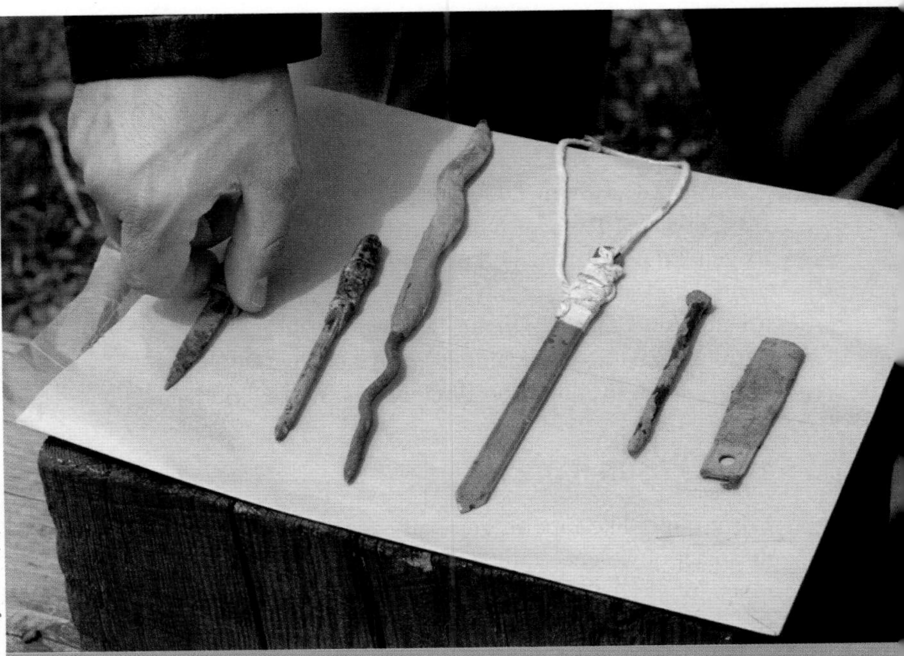

AP Images/David Duprey

A correctional official displays a set of homemade knives, also known as *shivs*, made by inmates at Attica Correctional Facility in Attica, New York. **How does the deprivation model explain high levels of prison violence?**

12-2a Violence in Prison Culture

Until the 1970s, prison culture emphasized "noninterference" and did not support inmate-on-inmate violence. Prison "elders" would themselves punish any of their peers who showed a proclivity toward assaulting fellow inmates. Today, in contrast, violence is used to establish the prisoner hierarchy by separating the powerful from the weak. Humboldt State University's Lee H. Bowker has identified several other reasons for violent behavior:

- It provides a deterrent against being victimized, as a reputation for violence may eliminate an inmate as a target of assault.
- It enhances self-image in an environment that does not respect other attributes, such as intelligence.
- In the case of rape, it gives sexual relief.
- It serves as a means of acquiring material goods through extortion or outright robbery.[25]

LO12-2 Indicate some of the reasons for violent behavior in prisons.

The **deprivation model** can be used to explain the high level of prison violence. According to this model, the stressful and oppressive conditions of prison life lead to aggressive behavior on the part of inmates. Prison researcher Stephen C. Light found that when conditions such as overcrowding worsen, inmate misconduct often increases.[26] In these circumstances, the violent behavior may not have any express purpose—it may just be a means of relieving tension.

12-2b Riots

The deprivation model is helpful in explaining collective violence but leaves some questions unanswered. As far back as the 1930s, sociologist Frank Tannenbaum noted that harsh prison conditions can cause tension to build among inmates until it eventually explodes in the form of mass violence.[27] Living conditions among prisons are fairly constant, however, so how can the seemingly spontaneous outbreak of prison riots be explained?

Researchers have addressed the seeming randomness of prison violence by turning to the concept of **relative deprivation.** These theories focus on the gap between what is expected in a certain situation and what is achieved. Criminologist Peter C. Kratcoski has argued that because prisoners enjoy such meager privileges to begin with, any further deprivation can spark disorder.[28] A number of prison experts have noted that collective violence occurs in response to heightened measures of security at corrections facilities.[29] Thus, the violence is primarily a reaction to additional reductions in freedom for inmates, who enjoy very little freedom to begin with.

Riots, which have been defined as situations in which a number of prisoners are beyond institutional control for a significant amount of time, are relatively rare. These incidents are marked by extreme levels of inmate-on-inmate violence and

Deprivation Model A theory that inmate aggression is the result of the frustration inmates feel at being deprived of freedom, consumer goods, and other staples of life outside the institution.

Relative Deprivation The theory that inmate aggression is caused when freedoms and services that the inmate has come to accept as normal are decreased or eliminated.

can often be attributed, at least in part, to poor living conditions and inadequate prison administration.

Alabama's Holman Correctional Facility, featured in the opening of this chapter, experienced no fewer than three riots in 2016, including one in which an inmate stabbed the warden. Designed to hold about six hundred inmates, Holman houses around one thousand in its general population, and prisoners have easy access to contraband weapons. "All I have is chemical spray and a baton, and the inmates have knives," said a Holman correctional officer, explaining why he and his colleagues are reluctant to administer discipline in the facility.[30]

12-2c Prison Rape

Prison rape, like rape in general, is considered primarily an act of violence rather than sex. Inmates subject to rape ("punks") are near the bottom of the prison power structure and, in some instances, may accept rape by one particularly powerful inmate in return for protection from others.[31] Abused inmates often suffer from rape trauma syndrome and a host of other psychological ailments, including suicidal tendencies. Many prisons do not offer sufficient medical treatment for rape victims, nor does the prison staff take the necessary measures to protect obvious targets of rape—young, slightly built, nonviolent offenders.

According to the most recent inmate survey, 3.1 percent of heterosexual inmates, 14 percent of homosexual inmates, and 40 percent of transgender inmates reported having been sexually assaulted by other inmates or prison staff.[32] The total number of rapes measured in this survey—about 80,000—is almost certainly an underrepresentation, as many such assaults go unreported due to shame or fear of retaliation.

12-2d Issues of Race and Ethnicity

"As a white person, I can't use or touch anything that a black person has used or touched," says ex-convict Steven Czifra of his life in a California prison. "If I drop my soap on the floor next to my bunk," Czifra explains, "I have to throw it away" because a black inmate probably has walked on the floor.[33]

Czifra is describing the "etiquette" observed in the prison between whites and blacks. Race plays a major role in prison life, and prison violence is often an outlet for racial tension. As prison populations have changed over the past decades, with African Americans and Latinos becoming the majority in many penal institutions, issues of race and ethnicity have become increasingly important to prison administrators and researchers.

Prison Gang A group of inmates who band together within the corrections system to engage in social and criminal activities.

SEPARATE WORLDS As early as the 1950s, researchers were noticing different group structures in inmate life. At that time, for example, prisoners at California's Soledad Prison informally segregated themselves according to geography as well as race: Tejanos (Mexicans raised in Texas), Chicanos, blacks from California, blacks from the South and Southwest, and the majority whites all formed separate social worlds.[34]

Leo Carroll, professor of sociology at the University of Rhode Island, has written extensively about how today's prisoners are divided into hostile groups, with race determining nearly every aspect of an inmate's life, including friends, job assignments, and cell location.[35]

PRISON GANGS In many instances, racial and ethnic identification is the primary focus of the **prison gang**—a clique of inmates who join together in an organizational structure to engage in illegal activity. Gang affiliation is often the cause of inmate-on-inmate violence. For decades, the California prison system has been plagued by feuds involving various gangs, such as the Mexican Mafia, composed of U.S.-born inmates of Mexican descent, and their enemies, a spin-off organization called La Nuestra Familia.

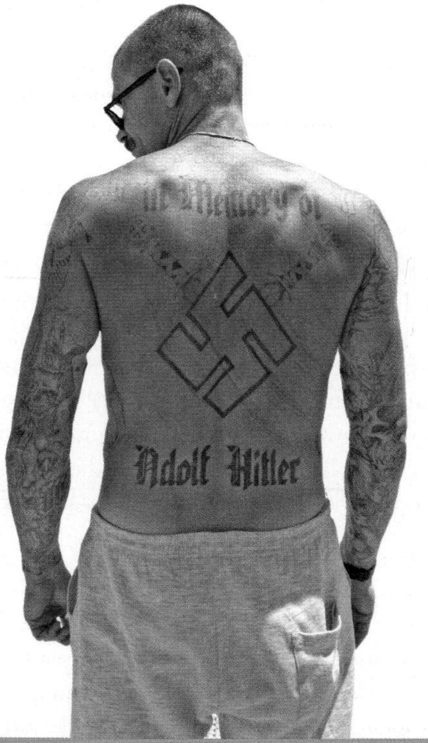

Mark Allen Johnson/ZUMA Press/Calipatria/CA/USA/Newscom

What are some of the reasons that an inmate such as this member of the Aryan Brotherhood would join a prison gang?

CJ and TECHNOLOGY

Contraband Cell Phones

One piece of technology has made the task of controlling prison gangs extremely difficult: the cell phone. Although inmates are prohibited from possessing these devices, cell phones are routinely used to arrange attacks, plan escapes, and operate illegal money-making schemes from behind bars.

The phones are usually smuggled in by visitors, who hide them in locations as varied as babies' diapers, food packages, soda cans, and body cavities. In Georgia, corrections officials found cell-phone parts stuffed into the body of a dead cat that had been thrown over a prison fence, and there have been numerous reports nationwide of drones being used to deliver the phones into prison yards.

Earlier this decade, forty-four inmates and correctional officers at the Baltimore City Detention Center were arrested for helping to operate the Black Guerrilla Family gang from within the prison using cell phones. In response, the state of Maryland started a managed access program to deal with the problem. This "cellular umbrella" antenna technology is designed to analyze all calls made from the prison and instantly block any that originate from a contraband phone. Authorities at the Mississippi State Penitentiary in Parchman estimate that between 2010 and 2015, its managed-access system, while not 100 percent effective, captured more than six million illicit transmissions.

Thinking about Contraband Cell Phones

It would be much easier—and cheaper—for corrections officials to combat contraband cell phones by disrupting *all* cell-phone activity in a prison or jail. However, this practice—called "jamming"—is illegal under federal law. What do you think is the reasoning behind this blanket prohibition of jamming?

In part, the prison gang is a natural result of life in the modern prison. As one expert says of these gangs:

> Their members have done in prison what many people do elsewhere when they feel personally powerless, threatened, and vulnerable. They align themselves with others, organize to fight back, and enhance their own status and control through their connection to a more powerful group.[36]

In addition to their important role in the social structure of correctional facilities, prison gangs participate in a wide range of illegal economic activities within these institutions, including prostitution, drug selling, gambling, and loan sharking. A study released in 2011 by Alan J. Drury and Matt DeLisi of Iowa State University found that gang members were more likely to be involved in prison misconduct than inmates who had been convicted of murder.[37]

The Prevalence of Prison Gangs There is little question that the nation's correctional institutions are hotbeds of gang activity. The most recent research conducted by the National Gang Crime Research Center places the proportion of gang members in state prisons and local jails at 30 percent of male inmates and 9 percent of female inmates. In the same survey, 87 percent of corrections officials answered "yes" to the question "Do you believe that some inmates may have voluntarily joined or may have been recruited into a gang while incarcerated?"[38]

Combating Prison Gangs In their efforts to combat the influence of prison gangs, over the past decade correctional officials have increasingly turned to the **security threat group (STG)** model. Generally speaking, an STG is an identifiable group with three or more individuals and a leadership structure that poses a threat to the safety of other inmates or members of the corrections community. About two-thirds of all prisons have a correctional officer who acts as an STG coordinator.[39] This official is responsible for the classification of individuals who are likely to be involved in STG (though not necessarily prison gang) activity and for taking measures to protect the prison community from these individuals.

In many instances, these measures are punitive. Prison officials, for example, have reduced overall levels of violence significantly by putting gang members in *solitary confinement*, away from the general prison population. Other punitive measures include restrictions on privileges such as family visits and prison program participation, as well as delays of parole eligibility.[40]

Security Threat Group (STG) A group of three or more inmates who engage in activity that poses a threat to the safety of other inmates or the prison staff.

12-3 HOW DO CORRECTIONAL OFFICERS MAINTAIN DISCIPLINE?

Ideally, the presence of correctional officers—the standard term used to describe prison guards—has the effect of lessening violence in American correctional institutions. Practically speaking, this is indeed the case. Without correctional officers, the prison would be a place of anarchy. But in the highly regulated, oppressive environment of the prison, correctional officers must use the threat of violence, if not actual violence, to instill discipline and keep order. Thus, the relationship between prison staff and inmates is marked by mutual distrust.

Consider the two following statements, the first made by a correctional officer and the second by a prisoner:

> [My job is to] protect, feed, and try to educate scum who raped and brutalized women and children . . . who, if I turn my back, will go into their cell, wrap a blanket around their cellmate's legs, and threaten to beat or rape him if he doesn't give sex, carry contraband, or fork over radios, money, or other goods willingly. And they'll stick a shank in me tomorrow if they think they can get away with it.[41]

> The pigs in the state and federal prisons . . . treat me so violently, I cannot possibly imagine a time I could ever have anything but the deepest, aching, searing hatred for them. I can't begin to tell you what they do to me. If I were weaker by a hair, they would destroy me.[42]

It may be difficult for an outsider to understand the emotions that fuel such sentiments. French philosopher Michel Foucault points out that discipline, both in prison and in the general community, is a means of social organization as well as punishment.[43]

Discipline is imposed when a person behaves in a manner that is contrary to the values of the dominant social group. Correctional officers and inmates have different concepts of the ideal structure of prison society, and, as the two quotations just cited demonstrate, this conflict generates intense feelings of fear and hatred, which often lead to violence.

12-3a Rank and Duties of Correctional Officers

The custodial staff at most prisons is organized according to four general ranks—captain, lieutenant, sergeant, and officer. In keeping with the militaristic model, captains are primarily administrators who deal directly with the warden on custodial issues. Lieutenants are the disciplinarians of the prison, responsible for policing and transporting the inmates. Sergeants oversee platoons of officers in specific parts of the prison, such as various cell blocks or work spaces.

Lucien X. Lombardo, professor of sociology and criminal justice at Old Dominion University, has identified six general job categories among correctional officers:[44]

1. *Block officers.* These employees supervise cell blocks containing as many as four hundred inmates, as well as the correctional officers on block guard duty. In general, the block officer is responsible for the well-being of the inmates. He or she tries to ensure that the inmates do not harm themselves or other prisoners and also acts as something of a camp counselor, dispensing advice and seeing that inmates understand and follow the rules of the facility.
2. *Work detail supervisors.* In most penal institutions, the inmates work in the cafeteria, the prison store, the laundry, and other areas. Work detail supervisors oversee small groups of inmates as they perform their tasks.
3. *Industrial shop and school officers.* These officers perform maintenance and security functions in workshop and educational programs. Their primary responsibility is to make sure that inmates are on time for these programs and do not cause any disturbances during the sessions.
4. *Yard officers.* Officers who work the prison yard usually have the least seniority, befitting the assignment's reputation as dangerous and stressful. These officers must be constantly on alert for breaches in prison discipline or regulations in the relatively unstructured environment of the prison yard.
5. *Tower guards.* These officers spend their entire shifts, which usually last eight hours, in isolated, silent posts high above the grounds of the facility. Although their only means of communication are walkie-talkies or cellular devices, the safety benefits of the position can outweigh the loneliness that comes with the job.
6. *Administrative building assignments.* Officers who hold these positions provide security at prison gates, oversee visitation procedures, act as liaisons for civilians, and handle administrative tasks such as processing the paperwork when an inmate is transferred from another institution.

CAREER PREP

Correctional Officer

Job Description:

- Ensure the safety of inmates and other employees of the correctional facility. This includes escorting inmates from their prison cells to other areas of the prison, standing guard over inmates after they have been removed from their cells, searching inmates for forbidden items, and patrolling the prison grounds.

What Kind of Training Is Required?

- At the state level, a high school diploma. At the federal level, a bachelor's degree or three years of full-time experience in counseling and supervision.
- Written, physical, and psychological examinations and a training period that can last up to six months, depending on the size of the correctional facility.

Annual Salary Range?

- $35,000–$70,000

Leah-Anne Thompson/Shutterstock.com

SOCIAL MEDIA CAREER TIP
Don't misrepresent facts or tell lies of omission online. Doing so in front of millions of online viewers ensures that you will almost certainly be caught, and such untruths can fatally damage career possibilities.

12-3b Discipline

Inmate discipline policies have three general goals:

1. To ensure a safe and orderly living environment.
2. To instill respect for authority of correctional officers and administrators.
3. To teach values and respectful behavior that influence the inmate's attitude when she or he is released from prison.[45]

As Erving Goffman noted in his essay on the "total institution," in the general society adults are rarely placed in a position where they are "punished" as a child would be.[46] Therefore, the strict disciplinary measures imposed on prisoners come as something of a shock and can provoke strong defensive reactions. Correctional officers who must deal with these responses often find that disciplining inmates is the most difficult and stressful aspect of their job. (To learn more about the potential hazards for correctional officers in dealing with inmates, see the feature *Discretion in Action—"Downing a Duck."*)

SANCTIONING PRISONERS As mentioned earlier, one of the first items that an inmate receives on entering a correctional facility is a manual that details the rules of the prison or jail, along with the punishment that will result from rule violations. These handbooks can be quite lengthy—running one hundred pages in some instances—and specific. Not only will a prison manual prohibit obvious misconduct such as violent or sexual activity, gambling, and possession of drugs or currency, but it also addresses matters of daily life such as personal hygiene, dress codes, and conduct during meals.

Correctional officers enforce the prison rules in much the same way that a highway patrol officer enforces traffic regulations. For a minor violation, the inmate may be "let off easy" with a verbal warning. More serious infractions will result in a "ticket," or a report forwarded to the institution's disciplinary committee.[47] The disciplinary committee generally includes several correctional officers and, in some instances, outside citizens or even inmates.

Although, as we shall see, the United States Supreme Court has ruled that inmates must be given a

DISCRETION IN ACTION

"Downing a Duck"

THE SITUATION You have just been hired as a correctional officer at a maximum-security prison. Most of the inmates at the facility are violent criminals serving lengthy sentences. During your first week, the inmates in your cell block do a poor job of keeping their living quarters clean, causing you to get a negative performance review and a tongue-lashing from your supervisor. An inmate named Rick consoles you and promises that he will use his influence to ensure that the other inmates "make you look good." He does so. Later, you are threatened by two prisoners who threaten to "get" you. Rick steps in and defuses the situation. You are grateful and begin to look at Rick as something of a friend.

When another inmates dies of a heart attack, Rick comes to you and asks for a favor. He and some other inmates have taken up a collection for the inmate's widow, and he wants you to deliver the money, with a sympathy card, to her on the outside.

THE LAW Prison regulations strictly prohibit inmates from possessing any form of money or currency. State law prohibits correctional officers from transporting any contraband outside the prison.

WHAT WOULD YOU DO? Clearly, you are legally required not only to refuse Rick's request, but also to report him and the other inmates for possession of cash. You also remember advice from a colleague, who warned that inmates are skilled at manipulating inexperienced correctional officers, a strategy called "downing a duck." At the same time, Rick has made your job much easier, and it is possible that he saved your life. While Rick's request may technically be against the rules, he is hardly asking you to do something immoral or unethical. How do you respond?

To see how prison employees in upstate New York reacted to friendly overtures from a pair of inmates, go to Example 12.1 in Appendix A.

"fair hearing" before being disciplined, the Court denied inmates the right to confront adverse witnesses or consult a lawyer during these hearings.[48] In practice, then, an inmate has very little ability to challenge the committee's decision.

SOLITARY CONFINEMENT Depending on the seriousness of the violation, sanctions can range from a loss of privileges such as visits from family members to the extreme unpleasantness of **solitary confinement,** also known as restrictive housing. In general, these terms refer to the confinement of an inmate alone in a small cell with minimal environmental stimulation or social interaction. In the past, solitary confinement was primarily a disciplinary tool. Today, however, prison officials use it as a form of preventive detention for inmates, such as gang members, who are deemed a security risk to themselves or others.

Although critics contend that solitary confinement causes severe damage to the mental health of prisoners, no federal laws control its use. Furthermore, most states have no legislation that controls the use of restrictive housing. On any given day, between 80,000 and 100,000 federal and state inmates are "in solitary" in the United States.[49]

Solitary Confinement A disciplinary practice that involves placing the punished inmate in a separate cell to isolate him or her from human contact.

USE OF FORCE Generally, courts have been unwilling to put too many restrictions on the use of force by correctional officers. As we saw earlier with police officers, correctional officers are given great leeway to use their experience to determine when force is warranted. In *Whitley v. Albers* (1986),[50] the Supreme Court held that the use of force by prison officials violates an inmate's Eighth Amendment protections only if the force amounts to "the unnecessary and wanton infliction of pain."

Excessive force can be considered "necessary" if the legitimate security interests of the penal institution are at stake. Consequently, an appeals court ruled that when officers at a Maryland prison formed an "extraction team" to remove the leader of a riot from his cell, beating him in the process, the use of force was justified given the situation.[51]

Legitimate Security Interests Courts have found that the "legitimate security interests" of a prison or jail justify the use of force when the correctional officer is

1. Acting in self-defense.
2. Acting to defend the safety of a third person, such as a member of the prison staff or another inmate.

3. Upholding the rules of the institution.
4. Preventing a crime such as assault, destruction of property, or theft.
5. Preventing an escape effort.[52]

In addition, most prisons and jails have written policies that spell out the situations in which their employees may use force against inmates. Following the lead of their counterparts in law enforcement, administrators in numerous correctional facilities are equipping their correctional officers with body cameras to provide more transparency in actual and alleged use-of-force incidents.

The "Malicious and Sadistic" Standard The judicial system has not given correctional officers total freedom of discretion to apply force. In *Hudson v. McMillan* (1992),[53] the Supreme Court ruled that minor injuries suffered by a convict at the hands of a correctional officer following an argument did violate the inmate's rights, because there was no security concern at the time of the incident. In other words, the issue is not *how much* force was used, but whether the officer used the force as part of a good faith effort to restore discipline or acted "maliciously and sadistically" to cause harm.

Kim Hairston/*Baltimore Sun*/MCT/Tribune News Service/Getty Images

What are some of the challenges that face female correctional officers who work in men's correctional facilities?

12-3c Female Correctional Officers

Security concerns were the main reason that, for many years, prison administrators refused to hire women as correctional officers in men's prisons. The consensus was that women were not physically strong enough to subdue violent male inmates and that their mere presence in the predominantly masculine prison world would cause disciplinary breakdowns.[54]

As a result, in the 1970s a number of women brought lawsuits against state corrections systems, claiming that they were being discriminated against on the basis of their gender. For the most part, these legal actions were successful in opening the doors to men's prisons for female correctional officers (and vice versa).[55] Today, more than 100,000 women work as correctional officers in prison and jails, many of them in constant close contact with male inmates.[56]

According to the data, female correctional officers are just as effective as their male counterparts in maintaining discipline in men's prisons. As reported in one study of Texas maximum-security prisons, inmates felt that female correctional officers were as competent as their male counterparts and exhibited "calm and cool" in pressurized situations.[57] Further evidence suggests that this calming influence on male inmates can lower levels of prison violence.[58]

12-3d Protecting Prisoners' Rights

The general attitude of the law toward inmates is summed up by the Thirteenth Amendment to the U.S. Constitution, which we mentioned in this chapter's opening feature:

> Neither slavery nor involuntary servitude, except as a punishment for crime whereof the party shall have been duly convicted, shall exist within the United States.

In other words, inmates do not have the same guaranteed rights as other Americans. For most of the nation's history, courts have followed the spirit of this amendment by applying the **"hands-off" doctrine** of prisoner law. This (unwritten) doctrine assumes that the care of inmates should be left to prison officials and that it is not the place of judges to intervene in penal administrative matters.

"Hands-Off" Doctrine The unwritten judicial policy that favors noninterference by the courts in the administration of prisons and jails.

At the same time, the United States Supreme Court has stated that "[t]here is no iron curtain between the Constitution and the prisons of this country."[59] Consequently, as with so many other areas of the criminal justice system, the treatment of prisoners is based on a balancing act—here, between the rights of prisoners and the security needs of the correctional institutions.

LO12-3 Describe the hands-off doctrine of prisoner law and indicate two standards used to determine if prisoners' rights have been violated.

Because inmates do not enjoy the same civil rights as other members of society, American courts tend to place more weight on security concerns. In 1984, for example, the Supreme Court ruled that arbitrary searches of prison cells are allowed under the Fourth Amendment because inmates have no reasonable expectation of privacy.[60] (See Chapter 6 for a review of this expectation.)

THE "DELIBERATE INDIFFERENCE" STANDARD As for those constitutional rights that inmates do retain, in 1976 the Supreme Court established the **"deliberate indifference"** standard. In the case in question, *Estelle v. Gamble*,[61] an inmate had claimed to be the victim of medical malpractice. In his majority opinion, Justice Thurgood Marshall wrote that prison officials violated a convict's Eighth Amendment rights if they "deliberately" failed to provide him or her with necessary medical care. At the time, the decision was hailed as a victory for prisoners' rights, and it continues to ensure that a certain level of health care is provided.

In 2016, for example, a U.S. District Court ruled that that prison officials at the Wallace Pack Unit in Navasota, Texas, were "deliberately indifferent" when they failed to provide inmates with drinking water that met "contemporary standards of decency." The facility's water supply contained between 2 and 4.5 times the amount of arsenic permitted by the federal Environmental Protection Agency.[62]

In general, however, courts have found it difficult to define "deliberate" in this context. Does it mean that prison officials "should have known" that an inmate was placed in harm's way, or does it mean that officials purposefully placed the inmate in that position?

"Deliberate Indifference" The standard for establishing a violation of an inmate's Eighth Amendment rights, requiring that prison officials were aware of harmful conditions in a correctional institution and failed to take steps to remedy those conditions.

"Identifiable Human Needs" The basic human necessities that correctional facilities are required by the Constitution to provide to inmates.

The Supreme Court seems to have taken the latter position. In *Wilson v. Seiter* (1991),[63] for example, inmate Pearly L. Wilson filed a lawsuit alleging that certain conditions of his confinement—including overcrowding; excessive noise; inadequate heating, cooling, and ventilation; and unsanitary bathroom and dining facilities—were cruel and unusual. The Court ruled against Wilson, stating that he had failed to prove that these conditions, even if they existed, were the result of "deliberate indifference" on the part of prison officials.

"IDENTIFIABLE HUMAN NEEDS" In its *Wilson* decision, the Supreme Court created the **"identifiable human needs"** standard for determining Eighth Amendment violations. The Court asserted that a prisoner must show that the institution has denied her or him a basic need such as food, warmth, or exercise.[64] The Court mentioned only these three needs, however, forcing the lower courts to determine for themselves what other needs, if any, fall into this category.

Because of the Supreme Court's *Estelle* decision, described earlier, prisoners do have a well-established right to "adequate" medical care. "Adequate" has been interpreted to mean a level of care comparable to what the inmate would receive if he or she were not behind bars.[65]

So, for example, several years ago, California agreed to provide sex reassignment surgery for transgender inmate Shiloh Quine, who is serving a life sentence without parole for murder. The state's medical expert had ruled that the medial procedure was necessary to "alleviate severe pain caused by her gender dysphoria."[66] Furthermore, in 2011, the Supreme Court asserted that the overcrowding of California's state prisons was so severe that it denied inmates satisfactory levels of health care.[67]

12-4 ARE WOMEN'S PRISONS DIFFERENT?

When the first women's prison in the United States opened in 1839 on the grounds of New York's Sing Sing institution, the focus was on rehabilitation. Prisoners were prepared for a return to society with classes on reading, knitting, and sewing. Early women's reformatories had few locks or bars, and several included nurseries for the inmates' young children.

Today, the situation is dramatically different. "Women's institutions are literally men's institutions, only we pull out the urinals," remarks Meda Chesney-Lind, a criminologist at the University of Hawaii.[68] Given the different circumstances surrounding male and female incarceration, this uniformity can have serious consequences for the women imprisoned in this country.

FIGURE 12.2 FEMALE PRISONERS IN THE UNITED STATES BY RACE, ETHNICITY, AND AGE

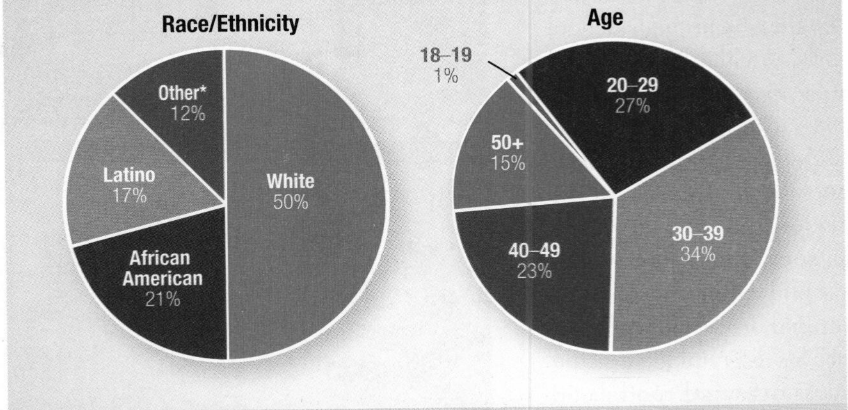

*Includes American Indians, Alaska Natives, Native Hawaiians, other Pacific Islanders, and persons identifying two or more races.

Source: Bureau of Justice Statistics, *Prisoners in 2015* (Washington, D.C.: U.S. Department of Justice, December 2016), Table 8, page 13.

12-4a Characteristics of Female Inmates

Male inmates outnumber female inmates by approximately twelve to one, and there are only about a hundred women's correctional facilities in the United States. Consequently, most research concerning the American corrections system focuses on male inmates and men's prisons. Enough data exist, however, to provide a useful portrait of women behind bars.

Female inmates are typically low income and undereducated, and have a history of unemployment. Female offenders are much less likely than male offenders to have committed a violent offense. Most are incarcerated for a nonviolent drug or property crime.[69] As Figure 12.2 shows, the demographics of female prisoners are similar to those of their male counterparts. That is, the majority of female inmates are under the age of forty, and the population is disproportionately African American.

The single factor that most distinguishes female prisoners from their male counterparts is a history of physical or sexual abuse. A self-reported study conducted by the federal government indicates that 55 percent of female jail inmates have been abused at some point in their lives, compared with only 13 percent of male jail inmates.[70] Fifty-seven percent of women in state prisons and 40 percent of women in federal prisons report some form of past abuse—both figures are significantly higher than those for male prisoners.[71] Health experts believe that these levels of abuse are related to the significant amount of drug and alcohol addiction that plagues the female prison population, as well as to the mental illness problems that such addictions can cause or exacerbate.[72]

12-4b The Motherhood Problem

Drug and alcohol use within a women's prison can be a function of the anger and depression many inmates experience due to being separated from their children. An estimated 147,000 American children have a mother in state prison, and the problem is much more pronounced for African American and Latino children than for white children.[73] Given the scarcity of women's correctional facilities, inmates are often housed at great distances from their children. One study found that almost two-thirds of women in federal prison are more than five hundred miles from their homes.[74]

Further research indicates that an inmate who serves her sentence more than fifty miles from her residence is much less likely to receive phone calls or personal visits from family members. For most inmates and their families, the costs of "staying in touch" are too high.[75] This kind of separation can have serious consequences for the children of inmates. When a father goes to prison, his children are likely to live with their mother. When a mother is incarcerated, however, her children are likely to live with other relatives or, in about 11 percent of the cases, be sent to foster care.[76]

Only nine states provide facilities where inmates and their infant children can live together, and in these facilities nursery privileges generally end once the child is eighteen months old. Even this limited contact seems to be of great benefit to the mother. A ten-year study released in 2009 showed that the recidivism rate for mothers separated from newborns was 50 percent, compared with only 17 percent for mothers who had nursery privileges.[77] "Nothing has made me want to change before," said one incarcerated mother. "Kids make you want to change."[78]

12-4c The Culture of Women's Prisons

After spending five years visiting female inmates in the Massachusetts Correctional Institution (MCI) at Framingham, journalist Cristina Rathbone observed that the medium-security facility seemed "more like a high school than a prison."[79] The prisoners were older and tougher than high school girls, but they still divided into cliques, with the "lifers" at the top of the hierarchy and "untouchables" such as child abusers at the bottom. Unlike in men's prisons, where the underground economy revolves around drugs and weapons, at MCI-Framingham the most treasured contraband items are clothing, food, and makeup.[80]

RJ Sangosti/Getty Images

Explain how a women's prison is typically different from a men's prison when it comes to levels of violence and social interactions between inmates.

THE PSEUDO-FAMILY Although both men's and women's prisons are organized with the same goals of control and discipline, the cultures within the two institutions are generally very different. As we have seen, male prison society operates primarily on the basis of power. Deprived of the benefits of freedom, male prisoners tend to create a violent environment that bears little relation to life on the outside.[81]

In contrast, researchers have found that women prisoners prefer to re-create their outside identities by forming social networks that resemble, as noted earlier, high school cliques or, more commonly, the traditional family structure.[82] In these pseudo-families, inmates often play specific roles, with the more experienced convicts acting as "mothers" to younger, inexperienced "daughters." As one observer noted, the younger women rely on their "moms" for emotional support, companionship, loans, and even discipline.[83]

SEXUAL VIOLENCE AND PRISON STAFF Compared with men's prisons, women's prisons have extremely low levels of race-based, gang-related physical aggression.[84] Furthermore, though rates of sexual victimization can be high, most such episodes involve abusive sexual contacts such as unwanted touching rather than sexual assault or rape.[85]

One form of serious prison violence that does plague women prisoners, however, is sexual misconduct by prison staff. Although no large-scale study on sexual abuse of female inmates by male correctional officers exists, a number of state-level studies suggest that it is widespread.[86] Dr. Kerry Kupers, who has studied the effects of prison sexual assault, believes that it contributes to the depression, anxiety, and other mental illnesses suffered by so many women prisoners.[87]

ETHICS CHALLENGE

A number of states place pregnant inmates in handcuffs or other forms of restraint as part of the procedure for childbirths that take place while the inmates are incarcerated. What might be some of the reasons for this practice? Do you feel it is an ethical way to treat these women during and after labor? Why or why not?

12-5 WHAT HAPPENS TO EX-INMATES?

On August 28, 2016, according to Chicago police, Derren Sorrells took aim at a man driving a car, fired, and missed. The bullet struck and killed a young mother who was pushing a stroller down a nearby sidewalk. Sorrells, who had earlier been sentenced to six years behind bars for possession of a stolen vehicle, had been paroled from prison only two weeks earlier.

In contrast, two years after serving a decade in federal prison for drug distribution, Dquan Rosario earned a job as an emergency medical technician in Essex County, New Jersey. "Instead of peddling drugs that are destroying lives, he's saving lives," said one of Rosario's supporters. "He's making the community better."[88]

Each year, about 640,000 inmates are released from American prisons. The challenge for ex-inmates is to ensure that their post-release experience mirrors that of Dquan Rosario rather than that of Derren Sorrells. More than in the past, however, ex-convicts are not facing this challenge alone. Given the benefits to society of reducing recidivism, corrections officials and community leaders are making unprecedented efforts to help newly released prisoners establish crime-free lives.

12-5a Types of Prison Release

The majority of all inmates leaving prison—about two-thirds—do so through one of the parole mechanisms discussed in Chapter 10. Of the remaining third, most are given an **expiration release.**[89] Also known as "maxing out," expiration release occurs when an inmate has served the maximum amount of time on the initial sentence, minus reductions for good-time credits, and is not subjected to community supervision.

LO12-4 Contrast parole, expiration release, pardon, and furlough.

Another, quite rare unconditional release is a **pardon,** a form of executive clemency. The president (on the federal level) and the governor (on the state level) can grant a pardon, or forgive a convict's criminal punishment. Most states have a board of pardons—affiliated with the parole board—that makes recommendations to the governor in cases in which it believes a pardon is warranted. The majority of pardons involve obvious miscarriages of justice, though sometimes a governor will pardon an individual to remove the stain of conviction from her or his criminal record.

Certain temporary releases also exist. Some inmates, who qualify by exhibiting good behavior and generally proving that they do not represent a risk to society, are allowed to leave the prison on **furlough** for a certain amount of time, usually between a day and a week. At times, a furlough is granted because of a family emergency, such as a funeral. Furloughs can be particularly helpful for an inmate who is nearing release and can use them to ease the readjustment period. Finally, certain alternative sentencing arrangements involve combinations of imprisonment and probation release. Generally, however, as you have seen, probationers experience community supervision in place of a prison term.

12-5b The Challenges of Reentry

What steps can corrections officials take to lessen the possibility that ex-convicts will reoffend following their release? Efforts to answer that question have focused on programs that help inmates make the transition from prison to the outside. In past years, these programs would have come under the general heading of "rehabilitation," but today corrections officials and criminologists refer to them as part of the strategy of **prisoner reentry.**

The concept of reentry has come to mean many things to many people. For our purposes, keep in mind the words of Joan Petersilia of the University of California at Irvine, who defines *reentry* as encompassing "all activities and programming conducted to prepare ex-convicts to return safely to the community and to live as law abiding citizens."[90] In other words, whereas rehab is focused on the individual offender, *reentry* encompasses the released convict's relationship with society.

BARRIERS TO REENTRY Perhaps the largest obstacle to successful prisoner reentry is the simple truth that life behind bars is very different from life on the outside. As one inmate explains, the "rules" of prison survival are hardly compatible with good citizenship:

> An unexpected smile could mean trouble. A man in uniform was not a friend. Being kind was a weakness. Viciousness and recklessness were to be respected and admired.[91]

The prison environment also insulates inmates. They are not required to make the day-to-day decisions that characterize a normal existence beyond prison walls. Bruce Western, a Harvard sociologist, describes one freed female offender who "frequently forgot to eat breakfast or lunch for several months because she was used to being called to meals in prison."[92]

Depending on the length of incarceration, a released inmate must

Expiration Release The release of an inmate from prison at the end of his or her sentence without any further correctional supervision.

Pardon An act of executive clemency that overturns a conviction and erases mention of the crime from the person's criminal record.

Furlough Temporary release from a prison for purposes of vocational or educational training, to ease the shock of release, or for personal reasons.

Prisoner Reentry A corrections strategy designed to prepare inmates for a successful return to the community and to reduce recidivism.

AP Images/John Harrell

Should all inmates be eligible for reentry programs, such as this job training program offered by the Indiana Department of Corrections, regardless of the seriousness of the crimes they committed? Why or why not?

adjust to an array of economic, technological, and social changes that took place while she or he was behind bars.

Common acts such as using an ATM or a smartphone may be completely alien to someone who has just completed a long prison term. According to Ann Jacobs, director of the Prisoner Reentry Institute at New York's John Jay College of Criminal Justice, ex-convicts often perceive themselves as "imposters" who are "incapable of living a normal life."[93]

HOUSING AND EMPLOYMENT Other obstacles hamper reentry efforts. Housing can be difficult to secure, as many private property owners refuse to rent to someone with a criminal record, and federal and state laws restrict public housing options for ex-convicts. Finding affordable housing is, in turn, closely linked with another crucial and difficult step in the reentry process—finding a job.[94]

Desistance The process through which criminal activity decreases and reintegration into society increases over a period of time.

criminal adjusts to society

The Council of State Governments has tabulated more than 46,000 federal and state restrictions imposed on convicted felons, about three-quarters of which are employment-related.[95] Furthermore, background checks of potential employees are commonplace in corporate America. As a result, according to research conducted by the Ella Baker Institute, about a quarter of former inmates remain unemployed five years after their release, with the vast majority of the rest able to find only part-time or temporary work.[96]

These economic barriers can be complicated by the physical and mental condition of the freed convict. We have already discussed the high incidence of substance abuse among prisoners and the health-care needs of aging inmates. We have also described the high incidence of mental illness among prisoners. One study concluded that as many as one in five Americans leaving jail or prison is seriously mentally ill.[97] (See Figure 12.3 for a list of the hardships commonly faced by former inmates in their first year out of prison.)

12-5c Promoting Desistance

One ex-inmate compared the experience of being released to entering a "dark room, knowing that there are steps in front of you and waiting to fall."[98] The goal of reentry is to act as a flashlight for convicts by promoting **desistance,** a general term used to describe continued abstinence from offending and reintroduction of offenders into society.

Certainly, the most important factor in the process is the individual convict. She or he has to *want* to desist and take steps to do so. In most cases, however, ex-inmates are going to need help—help getting an education, help finding and keeping a job, and help freeing themselves from harmful addictions to drugs and alcohol. Corrections officials are in a good position to offer this assistance, and their efforts in doing so form the backbone of the reentry movement.

REENTRY PLANNING BEHIND BARS In addition to the rehabilitation-oriented prison programs discussed earlier in the chapter, most correctional facilities offer "life skills" classes to inmates. This counseling covers topics

LO12-5 Explain the goal of prisoner reentry programs.

FIGURE 12.3 PRISONER REENTRY ISSUES

1. **Housing.** Nearly two-thirds of the men were living with family members, and about half considered their housing situation "temporary." Many were concerned about their living environment: Half said that drug dealing was a major problem in their neighborhoods, and almost 25 percent were living with drug and alcohol abusers.
2. **Employment.** After one year, only about one-third of the former inmates had a full-time job, and another 11 percent were working part time.
3. **Family and friends.** One in four of the men identified family support as the most important thing keeping them from returning to criminality. Another 16 percent said that avoiding certain people and situations was the most crucial factor in their continued good behavior.
4. **Programs and services.** About two-thirds of the former inmates had taken part in programs and services such as drug treatment and continuing education.
5. **Health.** More than half of the men reported suffering from a chronic health condition, and 29 percent showed symptoms of depression.
6. **Substance use.** About half of the men admitted to weekly drug use or alcohol intoxication. Men who had strong family ties and those who were required to maintain telephone contact with their parole officers were less likely to engage in frequent substance use.
7. **Parole violation and recidivism.** More than half of the former inmates reported that they had violated the conditions of their parole, usually by drug use or having contact with other parolees. Fifteen percent of the men returned to prison in the year after release. Four out of five of the returns were the result of a new crime.

Researchers from the Urban Institute in Washington, D.C., asked nearly three hundred former prisoners (all male) in the Cleveland, Ohio, area about the most pressing issues they faced in their first year after release. The answers provide a useful snapshot of the many challenges of reentry.

Source: Christy A. Visher and Shannon M. E. Courtney, *One Year Out: Experience of Prisoners Returning to Cleveland* (Washington, D.C.: Urban Institute, April 2007), 2.

such as finding and keeping a job, locating a residence, understanding family responsibilities, and budgeting.

After release, however, former inmates often find it difficult to continue with educational programs and counseling as they struggle to readjust to life outside prison. Consequently, parole supervising agencies operate a number of programs to facilitate offenders' desistance efforts while, at the same time, protecting the community to the greatest extent possible.

COMMUNITY-BASED REENTRY PROGRAMS As is made clear in Figure 12.3, work and lodging are crucial components of desistance. Corrections officials have several options in helping certain parolees—usually low-risk offenders—find employment and a place to live during the supervision period. Nearly a third of correctional facilities offer **work release programs,** in which prisoners nearing the end of their sentences are given permission to work at paid employment in the community.[99]

Inmates on work release either return to the correctional facility in the evening or, under certain circumstances, live in community residential facilities known as **halfway houses.** These facilities, also available to other parolees and those who have finished their sentences, are often remodeled hotels or private homes. They provide a less institutionalized living environment than a prison or jail for a small number of offenders (usually between ten and twenty-five). Halfway houses can be tailored to the needs of the former inmates. Many communities, for example, offer substance-free transitional housing for those whose past criminal behavior was linked to drug or alcohol abuse.

CAREER TIP Organizations such as the Fortune Society, which operates out of New York City, provide aid for ex-inmates who may be struggling after release. These entities rely on *reentry counselors* to help ex-convicts deal with issues such as substance abuse, anger management, and joblessness.

12-5d The Special Case of Sex Offenders

Despite the beneficial impact of reentry efforts, one group of wrongdoers has consistently been denied access to such programs: those convicted of sex crimes. The eventual return of these offenders to society causes such high levels of community anxiety that the criminal justice system has not yet figured out what to do with them.

FEAR OF SEX OFFENDERS Outraged that a halfway

Work Release Programs Temporary release of convicts from prison for purposes of employment.

Halfway Houses A community-based form of early release that places inmates in residential centers and allows them to reintegrate with society.

CAREER PREP

Halfway House Program Manager

Job Description:

- **Coordinate recreational, educational, and vocational counseling and other programs for residents. Also, maintain the security of the house and the residents.**
- **Serve as a mediator between the residents and the community and as an advocate for the halfway house with community groups.**

Scanrail1/Shutterstock.com

What Kind of Training Is Required?

- **A bachelor's degree or master's degree in social work, career counseling, criminal justice, or psychology.**
- **Also helpful are internships, volunteer work with a halfway house, or community service work through an agency.**

Annual Salary Range?

- **$41,000–$61,000**

GETTING LINKEDIN

Halfway house employees are expected to be quite versatile. Among the requirements listed in a LinkedIn posting for a resident counselor in Des Moines, Iowa, was the ability to provide "education and treatment support" in the areas of "chemical dependency, daily living skills, parenting, self-sufficiency, behavioral/mental health, and relationships."

house for sex offenders was operating in their midst, residents of a Mesa, Arizona, neighborhood posted signs reading, "Sex Offenders, Felons, and Pedophiles," with arrows pointing toward the home.

"It's a safety issue," explained one neighbor. "There is still that lingering effect that they could possibly strike again."[100] Such attitudes reflect the widespread belief that convicted sex offenders cannot be "cured" of their criminality and therefore are destined to continue committing sex offenses after their release from prison.

It is true that the medical health profession has had little success in treating the "urges" that lead to sexually deviant or criminal behavior.[101] This has not, however, translated into rampant recidivism among sex offenders compared with other types of criminals. According to the U.S. Department of Justice, the rearrest rates of rapists (46 percent) and those convicted of other forms of sexual assault (41 percent) are among the lowest for all offenders.[102]

Furthermore, after analyzing eighty-two recidivism studies, Canadian researchers R. Karl Hanson and Kelly Morton-Bourgon found that only 14 percent of sex offenders were apprehended for another sex crime after release from prison or jail. On average, such offenders were significantly more likely to be rearrested for nonsexual criminal activity, if they were rearrested at all.[103]

CONDITIONS OF RELEASE Whatever their recidivism rates, sex offenders are subject to extensive community supervision after being released from prison. Generally, they are supervised by parole officers and live under the same threat of revocation as other parolees. Specifically, many sex offenders—particularly child molesters—have the following special conditions of release:

- No contact with children under the age of eighteen.
- Psychiatric treatment.

- Must stay a certain distance from schools or parks where children are present.
- Cannot own toys that may be used to lure children.
- Cannot have a job or participate in any activity that involves children.

Furthermore, more than half of the states and hundreds of municipalities have passed *residency restrictions* for convicted sex offenders. These laws ban sex offenders from living within a certain distance of places where children naturally congregate.

SEX OFFENDER NOTIFICATION LAWS

Perhaps the most dramatic step taken by criminal justice authorities to protect the public from sex crimes involves *sex offender registries*, or databases that contain sex offenders' names, addresses, photographs, and other information. The movement to register sex offenders started in the mid-1990s, after seven-year-old Megan Kanka of Hamilton Township, New Jersey, was raped and murdered by a twice-convicted pedophile (an adult sexually attracted to children) who had moved into her neighborhood after being released from prison on parole.

The next year, in response to public outrage, the state passed a series of laws known collectively as the New Jersey Sexual Offender Registration Act, or "Megan's Law."[104] Today, all fifty states and the federal government have a **sex offender notification law,** which requires local law authorities to alert the public when a sex offender has been released into the community.

AP Images/Francis Specker

Residents of Phelan, California, protest the opening of a proposed group home for sex offenders in their neighborhood. **What are some of the reasons that community members fear the nearby presence of freed sex offenders? Are these fears justified? Why or why not?**

Active and Passive Notification No two sex offender notification laws have exactly the same provisions, but all are designed with the goal of allowing the public to learn the identities of convicted sex offenders living in their midst. In general, the laws demand that a paroled sex offender notify local law enforcement authorities on taking up residence in a state.

In Georgia, for example, paroled sex offenders are required to present themselves to both the local sheriff and the superintendent of the public school district where they plan to live.[105] This registration process must be renewed every time the parolee changes address.

The authorities, in turn, notify the community of the sex offender's presence through the use of one of two models. Under the "active" model, the authorities directly notify the community or community representatives. Traditionally, this notification has taken the form of bulletins or posters, distributed and posted within a certain distance from the offender's home. Now, however, a number of states use e-mail alerts to fulfill notification

Sex Offender Notification Law Legislation that requires law enforcement authorities to provide notice when convicted sex offenders are released into the community.

obligations. In the "passive" model, information on sex offenders is made open and available for public scrutiny.

Prevalence of Sex Offender Registries In 2006, Congress passed the Adam Walsh Child Protection and Safety Act, which established a national registry of sex offenders.[106] In addition, all fifty states operate sex offender registries with data on registered sex offenders in their jurisdictions. (For an idea of how this process works, you can visit the Federal Bureau of Investigation's Sex Offender Registry website.) The total number of registered sex offenders in the United States is about 800,000.

CIVIL CONFINEMENT To many, any type of freedom, even if encumbered by notification requirements, is too much freedom for a sex offender. "The issue is, what can you do short of putting them all in prison for the rest of their lives?" complained one policymaker.[107]

In fact, a number of states have devised a legal method to keep sex offenders off the streets for, if not their entire lives, then close to it. These **civil confinement** laws allow corrections officials to lock up sex offenders in noncorrectional facilities such as psychiatric hospitals after the conclusion of their prison terms. Under these laws, corrections officials can keep sexual criminals confined for an unspecified amount of time as long as they are deemed a danger to society. In practice, civil confinement laws essentially give the state the power to detain this class of criminal indefinitely—a power upheld by the United States Supreme Court in 2010.[108]

Civil Confinement The practice of confining individuals against their will if they present a danger to the community.

keeping sex offenders in non correctional facilities, such as psychiatric hospitals, if they present a danger to the community.

STUDY TOOLS 12

LOCATED IN TEXTBOOK

- ☐ Rip out the Chapter Review Card.
- ☐ Review with the Chapter Quiz following this chapter.

LOCATED AT WWW.CENGAGEBRAIN.COM

- ☐ Review key terms flash cards.
- ☐ Read the chapter on all your favorite devices.
- ☐ Complete an Exam to test your knowledge.
- ☐ Check out Visual Summaries and You Decide activities to explore chapter concepts.

Quiz

1. Prison culture is different from the cultures of schools or workplaces because prison is a ________________________ ________________________ that dominates every aspect of the inmate's life.

2. In recent decades, the prison culture has been affected by the increased average age of inmates, which has led to skyrocketing ________________________-________________________costs for federal and state corrections systems.

3. The concept of ________________________, based on the gap between an inmate's expectations and reality, is used to explain the conditions that lead to prison riots.

4. Correctional officers may use force against inmates when a ________________________ security interest is being served.

5. Courts will not accept any force on the part of correctional officers that is "________________________ and sadistic."

6. To prove that prison officials violated constitutional prohibitions against cruel and unusual punishment, the inmate must first show that the officials demonstrated " ________________________ indifference" in taking or not taking an action.

7. While levels of physical violence are relatively low in women's prisons, female inmates do face a greater threat of sexual assault from ________________________ ________________________ than male inmates do.

8. One way in which the corrections system tries to help inmates prepare for release is by offering ________________________ programs that include job training and work release opportunities.

9. Corrections officials promote desistance by allowing certain low-risk offenders to live in ________________________ houses, where they can receive specialized attention and treatment.

10. Sex offender ________________________ laws mandate that law enforcement officials alert the public when a sex offender has moved into the community.

Answers to the Chapter 12 Quiz can be found in the Answers section in the back of the book.

13 The Juvenile Justice System

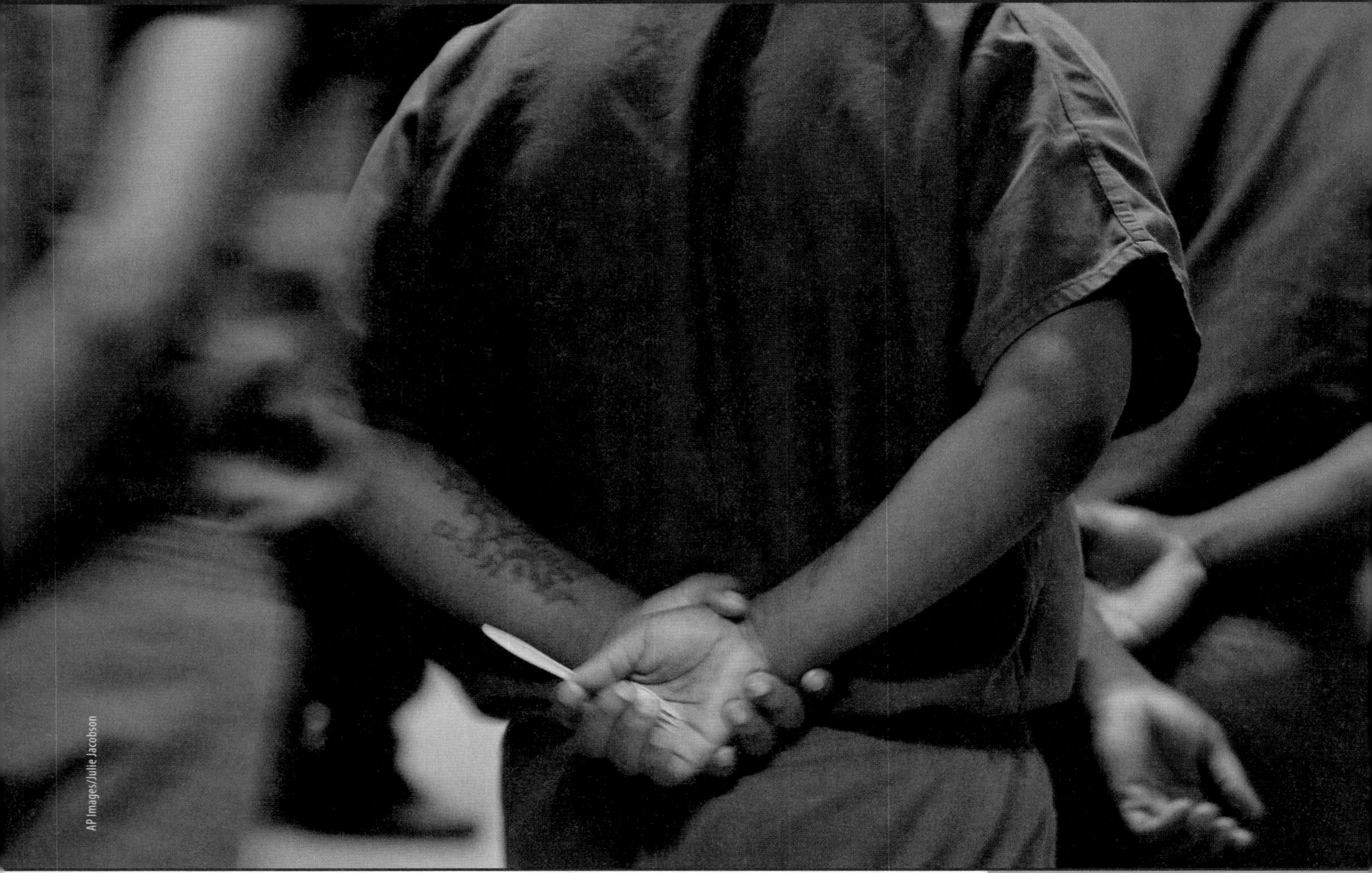

LEARNING OBJECTIVES

After studying this chapter, you will be able to …

- **13-1** List the four major differences between juvenile courts and adult courts.
- **13-2** Identify and briefly describe the single most important U.S. Supreme Court case with respect to juvenile justice.
- **13-3** Describe the reasoning behind recent U.S. Supreme Court decisions that have lessened the harshness of sentencing outcomes for violent juvenile offenders.
- **13-4** Describe the one variable that always correlates highly with juvenile crime rates.
- **13-5** Describe the four primary components of pretrial juvenile justice procedure.

After finishing this chapter, go to **PAGE 286** for **STUDY TOOLS**

Bad Thing. Good Kid?

"I know I committed a truly horrible crime and I am sorry for that," said Paul Gingerich, his voice breaking while he addressed a courtroom in Kosciusko County, Indiana. "I will never stop being sorry and I know sorry will never be enough." Six years earlier, in the same courtroom, a twelve-year-old Gingerich had pleaded guilty to shooting and killing Phil Danner, the stepfather of his fifteen-year-old friend Colt Lundy. (Gingerich and Lundy, who also took part in the murder, wanted to run away together and saw Danner as an impediment to these plans.) For his crimes, a judge sentenced Gingerich to twenty-five years behind bars.

The decision to punish such a young boy so harshly spurred calls for the reform of Indiana's juvenile justice system. As a result, the state legislature passed "Paul's Law," named in honor of Gingerich. This statute gives Indiana judges the discretion to remove violent juvenile offenders from adult prison at the age of eighteen if there is evidence that the offender is susceptible to changing her or his ways. "Adolescent development research proves that children are fundamentally different than adults," said a supporter of Paul's Law. "They are more prone to risk-taking behavior, more susceptible to peer pressure, and they are uniquely capable of rehabilitation."

In 2016, an eighteen-year-old Gingerich petitioned to have his sentence readjusted under Paul's Law. He had spent the five years since Danner's murder in the Pendleton Juvenile Correctional Facility, amassing an impressive record of good behavior and successful therapy. After hearing evidence of Gingerich's rehabilitation, Judge James Heuer decided that the young man would spend only three hundred days in adult prison before serving the remainder of his sentence—nearly two decades—under home detention. "I am willing to bet the mortgage on Paul Gingerich," said Monica Foster, his lawyer, noting that any misstep would land her client back behind bars. "He is a good kid who did a very bad thing."

In Indiana, juvenile court judges have the ability to remove an eighteen-year-old violent juvenile offender from adult prison if there is evidence that the young inmate can be rehabilitated. *What is your opinion of this form of judicial discretion?*

AP Images/Daniel Mears/Detroit News

13-1 WHY DO WE HAVE A SEPARATE JUSTICE SYSTEM FOR JUVENILES?

A difficult question—asked every time a youthful offender such as Paul Gingerich commits a heinous act of violence—lies at the heart of the juvenile justice debate: Should such acts by youths be given the same weight as those committed by adults, or should they be seen as "mistakes" that can be corrected by care and counseling?

From its earliest days, the American juvenile justice system has operated as an uneasy compromise between "rehabilitation and punishment, treatment and custody."[1] At the beginning of the 1800s, juvenile offenders were treated the same as adult offenders—they were judged by the same courts and sentenced to the same severe penalties. This situation began to change soon after, as urbanization and industrialization created an immigrant underclass that was, at least in the eyes of many reformers, predisposed to deviant activity. Certain members of the Progressive movement, known as the child savers, began to take steps to "save" children from these circumstances, introducing the idea of rehabilitating delinquents in the process.

13-1a The Child-Saving Movement

In general, the child savers favored the doctrine of ***parens patriae,*** which holds that the state has not only a right but also a duty to care for children who are neglected, delinquent, or in some other way disadvantaged. Juvenile offenders, the child savers believed, required treatment, not punishment, and they were horrified at the thought of placing children in prisons with hardened adult criminals. In 1967, then Supreme Court justice Abe Fortas said of the child savers:

> They believed that society's role was not to ascertain whether the child was "guilty" or "innocent," but "What is he, how has he become what he is, and what had best be done in his interest and in the interest of the state to save him from a downward career." The child—essentially good, as they saw it—was made "to feel that he is the object of [the government's] care and solicitude," not that he was under arrest or on trial.[2]

Child-saving organizations convinced local legislatures to pass laws that allowed them to take control of children who exhibited criminal tendencies or had been neglected by their parents. To separate these children from the environment in which they were raised, the organizations created a number of institutions, the best known of which was New York's House of Refuge.

Opening in 1825, the House of Refuge implemented many of the same reformist measures popular in the penitentiaries of the time, meaning that its charges were subjected to the healthful influences of hard study and labor. Although the House of Refuge was criticized for its harsh discipline (which caused many boys to run away), similar institutions sprang up throughout the Northeast during the middle of the 1800s.

13-1b The Illinois Juvenile Court

The efforts of the child savers culminated with the passage of the Illinois Juvenile Court Act in 1899. The Illinois legislature created the first court specifically for juveniles, guided by the principles of *parens patriae* and based on the belief that children are not fully responsible for criminal conduct and are capable of being rehabilitated.[3]

The Illinois Juvenile Court and those in other states that followed in its path were (and, in many cases, remain) drastically different from adult courts:

LO13-1 List the four major differences between juvenile courts and adult courts.

- *No juries.* The matter was decided by judges who wore regular clothes instead of black robes and sat at a table with the other participants rather than behind a bench. Because the primary focus of the court was on the child and not the crime, the judge had wide discretion in disposing of each case.
- *Different terminology.* To reduce the stigma of criminal proceedings, "petitions" were issued instead of "warrants." The children were not "defendants" but "respondents," and they were not "found guilty" but "adjudicated delinquent."
- *No adversarial relationship.* Instead of trying to determine guilt or innocence, the parties involved in the juvenile court worked together in the best interests of the child, with the emphasis on rehabilitation rather than punishment.
- *Confidentiality.* To avoid "saddling" the child with a criminal past, juvenile court hearings and records were kept sealed, and the proceedings were closed to the public.

By 1945, every state had a juvenile court system modeled after the first Illinois court. For the most part, these courts were able to operate without interference until the 1960s and the onset of the juvenile rights movement.

Parens Patriae A doctrine that holds that the state has a responsibility to look after the well-being of children and to assume the role of parent if necessary.

Status Offender A juvenile who has engaged in behavior deemed unacceptable for those under a certain statutorily determined age.

13-1c Status Offending

After the first juvenile court was established in Illinois, the Chicago Bar Association described its purpose as, in part, to "exercise the same tender solicitude and care over its neglected wards that a wise and loving parent would exercise with reference to his [or her] own children under similar circumstances."[4] In other words, the state was given the responsibility of caring for those minors whose behavior seemed to show that they could not be controlled by their parents.

As a result, many **status offenders** found themselves in the early houses of refuge, and these offenders continue to be placed in state-run facilities today. A status offense is an act that, when committed by a juvenile, is considered illegal and grounds for possible state custody. The same act, when committed by an adult, does not warrant law enforcement action. (See Figure 13.1 for an idea of which status offenses are most commonly brought to the attention of authorities.)

CAREER TIP Most states have attendance laws that require students to be in school during school hours. These states employ *truancy officers* to enforce such laws by working with parents and investigating suspicious patterns of absence.

FIGURE 13.1 STATUS OFFENSES

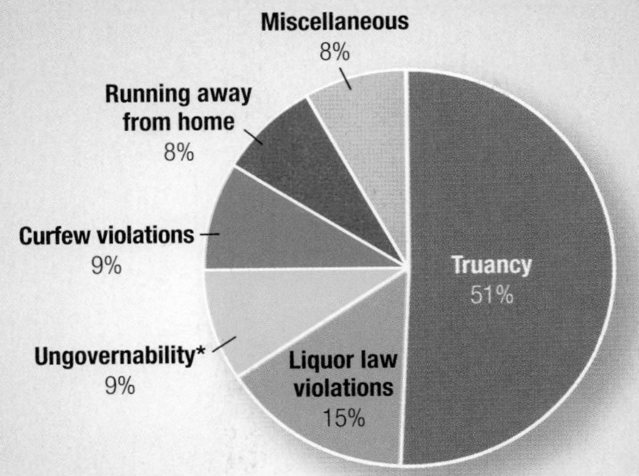

* Being beyond the control of parents, teachers, or other adult authority figures.

About 109,000 status offenses are processed by juvenile courts in the United States each year. The most common, as this graph shows, are truancy (skipping school) and liquor-related offenses.

Source: Sarah Hockenberry and Charles Puzzanchera, *Juvenile Court Statistics, 2013* (Pittsburgh, Pa.: National Center for Juvenile Justice, July 2015), 66.

13-1d Juvenile Delinquency

In contrast to status offending, **juvenile delinquency** refers to conduct that would also be criminal if committed by an adult. According to federal law and the laws of most states, a juvenile delinquent is someone who has not yet reached his or her eighteenth birthday—the age of adult criminal responsibility—at the time of the offense in question. In two states (New York and North Carolina), persons aged sixteen are considered adults, and five other states confer adulthood on seventeen-year-olds for purposes of criminal law.

Under certain circumstances, discussed later in this chapter, children under these ages can be tried in adult courts and incarcerated in adult prisons and jails. Remember, from the opening of this chapter, that Paul Gingerich was twelve years old when he was charged as an adult and sentenced to a long term in prison for his role in the murder of Phil Danner. By contrast, in most cases, an offender who is adjudicated as a juvenile and held in a juvenile corrections facility cannot be held past her or his eighteenth or twenty-first birthday, depending on the jurisdiction, regardless of the seriousness of the underlying wrongdoing.

13-1e Constitutional Protections and the Juvenile Court

Though the ideal of the juvenile court seemed to offer the "best of both worlds" for juvenile offenders, in reality the lack of procedural protections led to many children being arbitrarily punished not only for crimes, but for status offenses as well. Juvenile judges were treating all violators similarly, which led to many status offenders being incarcerated in the same institutions as violent delinquents. In response to a wave of lawsuits demanding due process rights for juveniles, the United States Supreme Court issued several rulings in the 1960s and 1970s that significantly changed the juvenile justice system.

KENT V. UNITED STATES The first decision to extend due process rights to children in juvenile courts was *Kent v. United States* (1966).[5] The case concerned sixteen-year-old Morris Kent, who had been arrested for breaking into a woman's house, stealing her purse, and raping her. Because Kent was on juvenile probation, the state sought to transfer his trial for the crime to an adult court.

Without giving any reasons for his decision, the juvenile judge consented to this strategy, and Kent was sentenced in the adult court to a thirty- to ninety-year prison term. The Supreme Court overturned the sentence, ruling that juveniles have a right to counsel and a hearing in any instance in which the juvenile judge is considering sending the case to an adult court. The Court stated that, in such cases, a child receives "the worst of both worlds," getting neither the "protections accorded to adults" nor the "solicitous care and regenerative treatment" offered in the juvenile system.[6]

IN RE GAULT The *Kent* decision provided the groundwork for *In re Gault* one year later. Considered by many to be the single most important case concerning juvenile justice, *In re Gault* involved a fifteen-year-old boy who was arrested for allegedly making a lewd phone call while on probation.[7]

In its decision, the Supreme Court held that juveniles facing a loss of liberty were entitled to many of the same basic procedural safeguards granted to adult offenders in this country. These safeguards include notice of charges, the right to counsel, the privilege

LO13-2 Identify and briefly describe the single most important U.S. Supreme Court case with respect to juvenile justice.

Juvenile Delinquency Illegal behavior committed by a person who is under an age limit specified by statute.

CAREER PREP

Youth Worker

Job Description:

- Provide safety, security, custodial care, discipline, and guidance for youths held in juvenile correctional facilities.
- Play a critical role in the rehabilitation of youthful offenders and, as a result, have a potentially great impact on their success during and after incarceration.

What Kind of Training Is Required?

- A bachelor's degree in human services, behavioral science, or a related field.
- Professional communication skills and commitment and dedication to the needs of adolescent offenders and their families.

Annual Salary Range?

- $33,000—$55,000

iStock.com/lisafx

SOCIAL MEDIA CAREER TIP

Potential employers want information about you, but they do not want your life story. To capitalize on two primary benefits of social media, personalize your message and be concise.

against self-incrimination, and the right to confront and cross-examine witnesses.

OTHER IMPORTANT COURT DECISIONS Over the next ten years, the Supreme Court handed down three more important rulings on juvenile court procedure. The ruling in *In re Winship* (1970)[8] required the government to prove "beyond a reasonable doubt" that a juvenile had committed an act of delinquency, raising the burden of proof from a "preponderance of the evidence."

In *Breed v. Jones* (1975),[9] the Court held that the Fifth Amendment's double jeopardy clause prevented a juvenile from being tried in an adult court for a crime that had already been adjudicated in juvenile court. In contrast, the decision in *McKeiver v. Pennsylvania* (1971)[10] represented an instance in which the Court did not move the juvenile court further toward the adult model. In that case, the Court ruled that the Constitution did not give juveniles the right to a jury trial.

13-2 HOW IS DELINQUENCY DETERMINED?

In the eyes of many observers, the net effect of the Supreme Court decisions during the 1966–1975 period was to move juvenile justice away from the ideals of the child savers. As a result of these decisions, many young offenders would find themselves in a formalized system that is often indistinguishable from its adult counterpart.

At the same time, though the Court has recognized that minors charged with crimes possess certain constitutional rights, it has failed to dictate at what age these rights should be granted. Consequently, the legal status of children in the United States varies depending on where they live, with each state making its own policy decisions on the crucial questions of age and competency.

13-2a The Age Question

In Chapter 3, we saw that early American criminal law recognized infancy as a defense against criminal charges. At that time, on attaining fourteen years of age, a youth was considered an adult and treated accordingly by the criminal justice system. During the "get tough on crime" movement of the 1990s, many states took steps that promoted sending young offenders to adult courts.

Recently, however, states are moving in the opposite direction. From 2009 to 2016, six states raised the age at which offenders are treated as adults from seventeen to eighteen. Today, forty-three states treat offenders under the age of eighteen as juveniles (see Figure 13.2).

The consequences of this shift are significant. Suppose, for example, that a seventeen-year-old gets into a fight at school. In Alabama, where the juvenile age limit is eighteen, her parents will be notified, and if necessary, her case will be handled by a juvenile court. In neighboring Georgia, where the age limit is seventeen, she might be arrested, charged with battery, and housed in a local jail until she can post bail. There is a good chance she will be expelled from school for missing multiple days of class, and she will almost certainly be burdened with an arrest record for the rest of her life.

Regardless of a state's age limits, young offenders of *any* age who commit violent crimes can be *transferred* to adult court by means of a process we will discuss later in the chapter. Those defendants can, and often do, receive lengthy sentences to be served in adult prisons.

When young offenders who remain in juvenile court are found guilty, they receive "limited" sentences that usually expire when they turn eighteen or twenty-one. In addition, young offenders who are processed in the juvenile justice system have significantly lower recidivism rates than those sent to the adult system.[11]

13-2b The Culpability Question

Many researchers believe that by the age of fourteen, an adolescent has the same ability as an adult to make a competent decision. Nevertheless, according to some observers, a juvenile's capacity to understand the difference between "right" and "wrong" does not mean that she or he should be held to the same standards of competency as an adult.

FIGURE 13.2 AGE LIMIT FOR JUVENILE COURT JURISDICTION

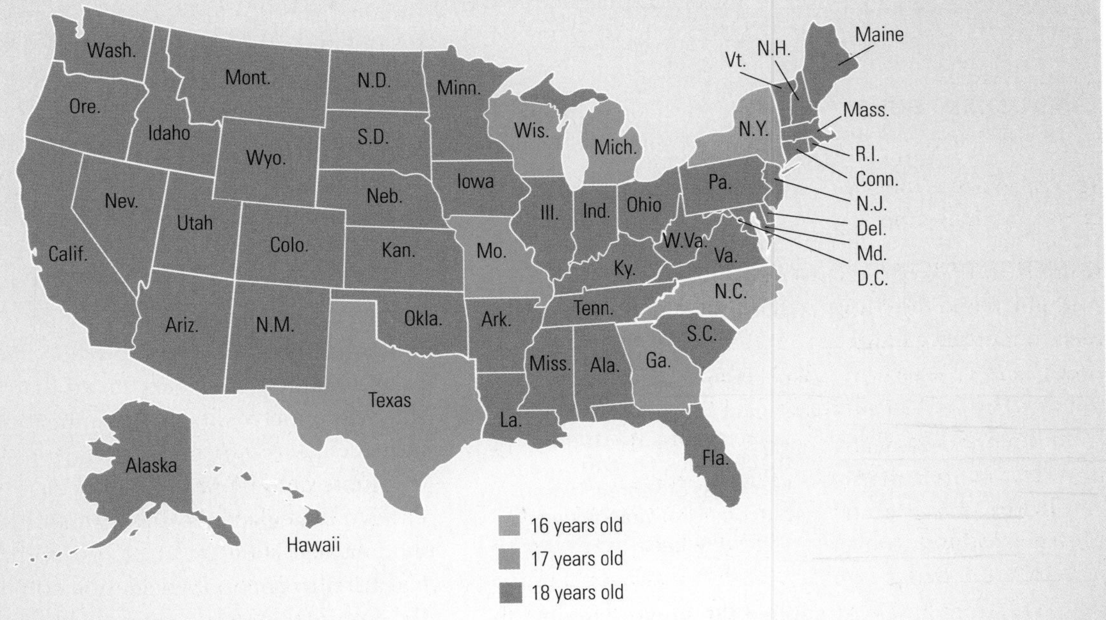

For the majority of states, eighteen years is the age under which youthful offenders will be considered juveniles and have their cases adjudicated in juvenile court.

Source: "Juvenile Age of Jurisdiction and Transfer to Adult Court Laws." *www.ncsl.org*. National Conference of State Legislatures: February 1, 2017, Web.

JUVENILE BEHAVIOR A study released in 2003 by the Research Network on Adolescent Development and Juvenile Justice found that 33 percent of juvenile defendants in criminal courts had the same low level of understanding of legal matters as mentally ill adults who had been found incompetent to stand trial.[12] Legal psychologist Richard E. Redding believes that

> adolescents' lack of life experience may limit their real-world decision-making ability. Whether we call it wisdom, judgment, or common sense, adolescents may not have nearly enough.[13]

Juveniles are generally more impulsive, more likely to engage in risky behavior, and less likely to calculate the long-term consequences of any particular action. Furthermore, adolescents are far more likely to respond to peer pressure than are adults, meaning that they often engage in the same criminal or delinquent behavior as their friends.[14] Accordingly, they are arrested as part of a group at much higher rates than adults.[15]

AP images/Dubuque Telegraph Herald, Dave Kettering

Isaiah Sweet, center, was sentenced to life in prison without parole for murdering his grandparents with an assault rifle when he was seventeen years old. **According to the Supreme Court's *Miller* ruling, is Sweet's sentence constitutional? Why or why not? What else would you need to know to answer this question?**

Furthermore, juveniles are less likely than adults to display remorse immediately following a violent act. As a result, they are often penalized by the courts for showing "less grief than the system demands."[16]

DIMINISHED GUILT The "diminished culpability" of juveniles was one of the reasons given by the United States Supreme Court in its landmark decision in *Roper v. Simmons* (2005).[17] That case forbade the execution of offenders who were under the age of eighteen when they committed their crimes. In his majority opinion, Justice Anthony Kennedy wrote that because minors cannot fully comprehend the consequences of their actions, the two main justifications for the death penalty—retribution and deterrence—do not "work" with juvenile wrongdoers.[18]

LO13-3 Describe the reasoning behind recent U.S. Supreme Court decisions that have lessened the harshness of sentencing outcomes for violent juvenile offenders.

The Supreme Court applied the same reasoning in two later cases that have dramatically affected the sentencing of violent juvenile offenders. First, in *Graham v. Florida* (2010),[19] the Court held that juveniles who commit crimes that do not involve murder may not be sentenced to life in prison without the possibility of parole. According to Justice Kennedy, who wrote the majority opinion, state officials must give these inmates "some meaningful opportunity to obtain release based on demonstrated maturity and rehabilitation."[20]

Then, with *Miller v. Alabama* (2012),[21] the Court banned laws in twenty-eight states that made life-without-parole sentences *mandatory* for juveniles convicted of murder. The case focused on the fate of Evan Miller, who was fourteen years old when he killed a neighbor with a baseball bat. The ruling did not signify that juvenile offenders such as Miller could not, under any circumstances, be sentenced to life without parole. Rather, the Court stated that judges must have the discretion to weigh the mitigating factors in each individual case.

For example, Miller had been abused by his stepfather and neglected by his alcoholic and drug-addicted mother, had spent most of his life in foster care, and had tried to commit suicide four times.[22] According to the Court, this type of personal history must be taken into account when determining the proper sentence for a juvenile murderer. Such mitigating factors may indicate that the offender has the potential to be rehabilitated and therefore should be afforded the possibility of parole.

13-3 HOW MUCH JUVENILE DELINQUENCY IS THERE IN THE UNITED STATES?

When asked, juveniles will admit to a wide range of illegal or dangerous behavior, including carrying weapons, getting involved in physical fights, driving after drinking alcohol, and stealing or deliberately damaging school property.[23] Has the juvenile justice system been effective in controlling and preventing this kind of misbehavior, as well as more serious acts? Answering this question requires us to examine recent trends in the extent of juvenile delinquency.

13-3a Delinquency by the Numbers

According to the Uniform Crime Reporting program, in 2015 juveniles accounted for 10.2 percent of violent crime arrests and 8.5 percent of criminal activity arrests in general.[24] As Figure 13.3 shows, juvenile arrest rates for violent crimes have fluctuated dramatically over the past three decades. In the 2000s, with a few exceptions, juvenile crime in the United States has decreased at a rate similar to that of adult crime, as discussed earlier in this textbook. From 2004 to 2013, juvenile court delinquency caseloads declined by 37 percent.[25]

Not surprisingly, the drop in juvenile arrests and court appearances has led to fewer juveniles behind bars. The national population of juvenile inmates decreased 52 percent between 1997 and 2014, allowing officials in some states, including California, Ohio, and Texas, to close juvenile detention facilities.[26]

THE DECLINE OF JUVENILE CRIME A number of theories have been put forth to explain the downturn in juvenile offending. Some observers point to the increase in police action against "quality-of-life" crimes such as loitering, which they believe stops juveniles before they have a chance to commit more serious crimes.

Similarly, about 80 percent of American municipalities enforce juvenile curfews, which restrict the movement of minors during certain hours, usually after dark.[27] In 2015, law enforcement made about 45,000 arrests for curfew and loitering law violations.[28]

FIGURE 13.3 ARREST RATES OF JUVENILES

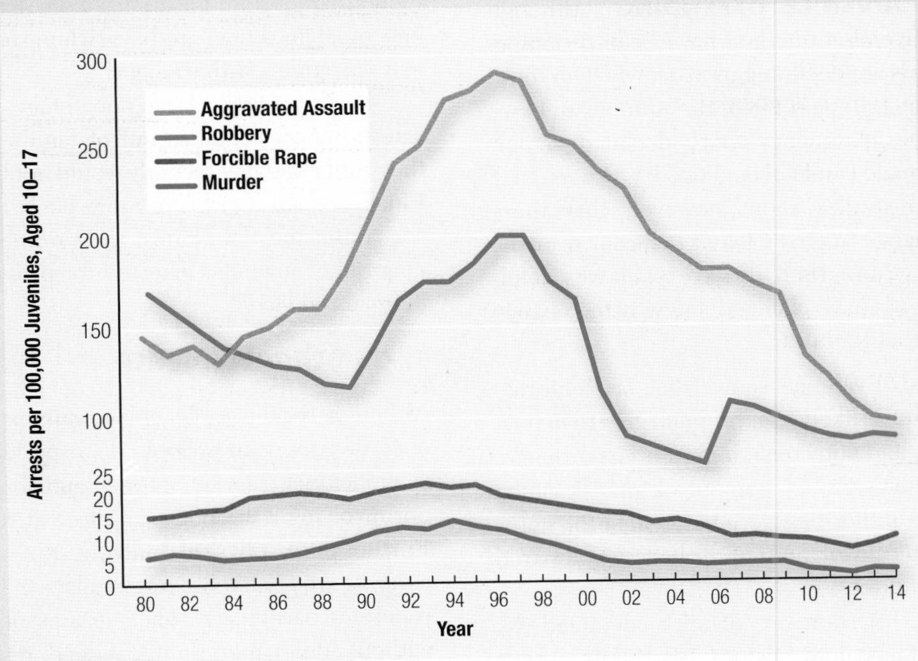

After rising dramatically in the mid-1990s, juvenile arrest rates for violent crimes have—with a few exceptions—continued to drop steadily in the 2000s.

Source: "Statistical Briefing Book: Juvenile Arrest Rates." *www.ojjdp.gov*. Office of Juvenile Justice and Delinquency Prevention: visited March 22, 2017, Web.

Furthermore, hundreds of local programs designed to educate children about the dangers of drugs and crime operate across the country. The results of such community-based efforts are difficult, if not impossible, to measure—it cannot be assumed that children would have become delinquent if they had not participated. Nevertheless, these programs are generally considered a crucial element of keeping youth crime under control.[29]

Scott Olson/Getty Images News/Getty Images

A police officer interviews two teenage girls who were involved in a fight in Tucson, Arizona. **Do you think that law enforcement is likely to treat girls more harshly than boys for this type of misbehavior? Why or why not?**

RACE AND JUVENILE OFFENDING As is the case in the criminal justice system, African Americans are overrepresented in the juvenile justice system. The total delinquency case rate for black juveniles is more than double that for white juveniles.[30] African American youths are more likely to be arrested for every major category of crime than are white youths, and more than six in every ten juvenile offenders in state custody is a member of a minority group.[31]

GENDER AND JUVENILE OFFENDING Although overall rates of juvenile offending have been dropping, arrest rates for girls are declining more slowly than those for boys. Between 1997 and 2013, the number of cases involving males in delinquency courts declined 47 percent, while the female caseload declined by 34 percent.[32]

Self-reported studies show, however, that there has been little change in girls' violent behavior over the past few decades.[33] How, then, do we explain why delinquency rates for girls have changed and why the change is different from that for boys?

Detention Trends Evidence shows that law enforcement officers are more likely to apprehend girls than boys for status offenses and nonviolent behavior. According to the most recent statistics, 37 percent of girls detained by juvenile justice authorities were being held for status offenses and technical violations of probation, compared with 25 percent of boys.[34]

Furthermore, 21 percent of girls detained by authorities were taken into custody for simple assault and public order offenses, compared to just 12 percent of boys.[35] Criminologists who focus on issues of gender hypothesize that such behavior is considered normal for boys, but is seen as deviant for girls and therefore more deserving of punishment.[36]

Family- and Gender-Based Delinquency A significant amount of data also suggest that police are much more likely to make arrests in situations involving domestic violence than was the case several decades ago. Experts have found that girls are four times more apt to fight with parents or siblings than are boys, who usually engage in violent encounters with strangers.

Consequently, a large percentage of female juvenile arrests for assault arise out of family disputes—arrests that until relatively recently would not have been made.[37] Finally, because girls are more likely to be exploited in sex trafficking operations, they represent a significant majority of juveniles arrested for prostitution and commercialized vice.[38]

13-3b School Violence

Although serious violence on campus is rare, 65 percent of American schools do experience at least one such incident each school year, and about 450,000 fights not involving a weapon take place at schools annually.[39] Furthermore, physical bullying, threats, and weapon-carrying are relatively commonplace in the learning environment, particularly when groups of students gather without adult supervision.[40] Indeed, research shows that juveniles are most likely to be victims of violent crime on school days between 3 P.M. and 4 P.M.—in other words, just after the end of classes.[41]

SECURITY MEASURES Victimization rates of students for nonfatal crimes have declined significantly

CJ and TECHNOLOGY

Gunshot Detectors in Schools

The sad—and frightening—reality concerning school shootings is that they are almost impossible to predict, making them very difficult to stop. An estimated two-thirds of such incidents in American schools are over before police are able to engage the shooter. The challenge, then, is to link schools with local law enforcement agencies to speed up the response time to active shooters.

With this goal in mind, several years ago California's Newark Memorial High School became the first school in the United States to install gunshot-detection sensors on campus grounds. This technology uses microphones, computer software, a clock, and satellite positioning technology to pinpoint the precise location and time of gunfire. When the system is "triggered" by a gunshot, the school's security camera immediately provides a live feed of the event to a local law enforcement agency.

Ideally, this will give police a good idea of the suspect's description and location, as well as the danger posed to students and staff. "[The technology] won't stop a school shooting but it'll get us to the shooter quicker," says Newark Police Commander Mike Carroll.

Thinking about Gunshot Detectors in Schools
Suppose a school attack involves a knife, a hidden bomb, or some other "silent" weapon. What kind of technological "trigger" could be used to alert local law enforcement in these situations?

over the past twenty-five years.[42] In part, this downturn reflects general crime trends.

Additionally, since the fatal shootings of fourteen students and a teacher at Columbine High School near Littleton, Colorado, in 1999, many schools have improved security measures. From 1999 to 2013, the percentage of American schools using security cameras to monitor their campuses increased from 19 to 64 percent. In addition, three-quarters of public schools control access to school buildings by locking or monitoring their doors.[43]

DISCIPLINARY MEASURES The Columbine shootings also led many schools to adopt "zero tolerance" policies when it comes to student behavior. These policies require strict punitive measures, such as suspension, expulsion, or referral to the police, for *any* breach of the school's disciplinary code. As a result, according to research conducted by the Vera Institute of Justice, one in nine secondary school students are suspended or expelled each year.[44]

The many critics of zero-tolerance policies point out that only 5 percent of serious school disciplinary actions involve possession of a weapon.[45] Examples of less-serious student behavior resulting in expulsion include incidents in which a seven-year-old ate a Pop-Tart into the shape of a gun, a young boy fired an imaginary bow and arrow, and a six-year-old boy kissed a six-year-old girl on the hand.[46]

This trend of reacting harshly to minor infractions may have serious repercussions for society. Students who have been expelled for any amount of time are at a much greater risk for future involvement in the juvenile justice system than those who have not faced such disciplinary measures.[47]

13-3c Bullying

A disproportionate number of young people who do bring guns or other weapons to school report that they have been *bullied* by other students.[48] **Bullying** can be broadly defined as repeated, aggressive behavior that contains at least one of the following elements:

1. *Physical abuse,* such as hitting, punching, or damaging the subject's property.
2. *Verbal abuse,* such as teasing, name calling, intimidation, or homophobic or racist remarks.
3. *Social and emotional abuse,* such as spreading false rumors, social exclusion, or playing jokes designed to humiliate.
4. *Cyber abuse,* which includes any form of bullying that takes place online or through the use of devices such as smartphones. (We will explore the issue of *cyberbullying* more fully in the next chapter's discussion of cyber crime.)

Bullying has traditionally been seen more as an inevitable rite of passage among adolescents than as potentially criminal

Bullying Overt acts taken by students with the goal of intimidating, harassing, or humiliating other students.

behavior. In recent years, however, society has become more aware of the negative consequences of bullying, underscored by a number of high-profile "bullycides."

In October 2016, for example, eleven-year-old Bethany Thompson fatally shot herself in Cable, Ohio, apparently after enduring sustained teasing for having a "crooked smile" because of a brain tumor operation. According to research conducted at Yale University, juveniles who have been bullied are between two and nine times more likely to commit suicide than those who have not been bullied.[49]

ETHICS CHALLENGE

A municipal ordinance in Shawano, Wisconsin, allows city officials to fine parents who are told that their children are behaving like bullies and do nothing to stop the behavior. The penalty for a first offense is $366. What is your opinion of this law? Is it ethical? Is it enforceable? Explain your answers.

13-4 WHY DO JUVENILES COMMIT CRIMES?

An influential study conducted by Professor Marvin Wolfgang and several colleagues in the early 1970s introduced the "chronic 6 percent" to criminology. The researchers found that out of one hundred boys, six will become chronic offenders, meaning that they will be arrested five or more times before their eighteenth birthdays. Furthermore, the researchers determined that these chronic offenders are responsible for half of all crimes and two-thirds of all violent crimes within any given cohort (a group of persons who have similar characteristics).[50]

Does this "6 percent rule" mean that no matter what steps society takes, six out of every hundred juveniles are "bad seeds" and will act delinquently? Or does it point to a situation in which a small percentage of children may be more likely to commit crimes under certain circumstances?

Most criminologists favor the second interpretation. In this section, we will examine the four factors that have traditionally been used to explain juvenile criminal behavior and violent crime rates: age, substance abuse, family problems, and gangs. Keep in mind, however, that the factors influencing delinquency are not limited to these areas (see Figure 13.4). Researchers are constantly interpreting and reinterpreting statistical evidence to provide fresh perspectives on this very important issue.

FIGURE 13.4 RISK FACTORS FOR JUVENILE DELINQUENCY

Family	• Single parent/lack of parental role model • Parental or sibling drug/alcohol abuse • Extreme economic deprivation • Family members in a gang or in prison
School	• Academic frustration/failure • Learning disability • Negative labeling by teachers • Disciplinary problems
Community	• Social disorganization (refer to Chapter 2) • Presence of gangs and obvious drug use in the community • Availability of firearms • High crime/constant feeling of danger • Lack of social and economic opportunities
Peers	• Delinquent friends • Friends who use drugs or who are members of gangs • Lack of "positive" peer pressure
Individual	• Mental illness • Tendency toward aggressive behavior • Inability to concentrate or focus/easily bored/hyperactive • Alcohol or drug use • Fatalistic/pessimistic viewpoint

The characteristics listed here are generally accepted as "risk factors" for juvenile delinquency. In other words, if one or more of these factors are present in a juvenile's life, he or she has a greater chance of exhibiting delinquent behavior—though such behavior is by no means a certainty.

13-4a The Age-Crime Relationship

Crime statistics are fairly conclusive on one point: The older a person is, the less likely he or she will exhibit criminal behavior. Self-reported studies confirm that most people are involved in some form of criminal behavior—however "harmless"—during their early years. In fact, Terrie Moffitt of Duke University has said that "it is statistically aberrant to refrain from crime during adolescence."[51] So why do the vast majority of us not become chronic offenders?

AGING OUT According to many criminologists, particularly Travis Hirschi and Michael Gottfredson, any group of at-risk persons—regardless of gender, race, intelligence, or class—will commit fewer crimes as they grow older.[52] This process is known as **aging out** (or, sometimes, *desistance*, a term we introduced in the preceding chapter). Professor Robert J. Sampson and his colleague John H. Laub believe that this phenomenon is explained by certain events, such as marriage, employment, and military service, that force delinquents to "grow up" and forgo criminal acts.[53]

LO13-4 Describe the one variable that always correlates highly with juvenile crime rates.

AGE OF ONSET Another view sees the **age of onset,** or the age at which a youth begins delinquent behavior, as a consistent predictor of future criminal behavior. One study compared recidivism rates between juveniles first judged to be delinquent before the age of fifteen and those first adjudicated delinquent after the age of fifteen. Of the seventy-one subjects who made up the first group, 32 percent became chronic offenders. Of the sixty-five who made up the second group, none became chronic offenders.[54]

Furthermore, according to the Office of Juvenile Justice and Delinquency Prevention, the earlier a youth enters the juvenile justice system, the more likely he or she will become a violent offender.[55] This research suggests that juvenile justice resources should be concentrated on the youngest offenders, with the goal of preventing crime and reducing the long-term risks for society.

13-4b Substance Abuse

As we have seen throughout this textbook, substance abuse plays a strong role in criminal behavior for adults. The same can certainly be said for juveniles.

A STRONG CORRELATION Drug use is associated with a wide range of antisocial and illegal behaviors by juveniles, from school suspensions to large-scale theft.[56] Nearly all young offenders (94 percent) entering juvenile detention self-report drug use at some point in their lives, and 85 percent have used drugs in the previous six months.[57] According to the Arrestee Drug Abuse Monitoring Program, nearly 60 percent of male juvenile detainees and 46 percent of female juvenile detainees test positive for drug use at the time of their offense.[58]

Drug use is a particularly strong risk factor for girls. Some 75 percent of young women incarcerated in juvenile facilities report regular drug and alcohol use—starting at the age of fourteen—and one study found that 87 percent of female teenage offenders need substance abuse treatment.[59]

STRONG CAUSATION? The correlation between substance abuse and offending for juveniles seems obvious. Does this mean that substance abuse *causes* juvenile offending? Researchers make the point that most youths who become involved in antisocial behavior do so before their first experience with alcohol or drugs. Therefore, it would appear that substance abuse is a form of delinquent behavior rather than its cause.[60] Still, one study of adolescent offenders did find that substance abuse treatment reduces criminal behavior in the short term, suggesting that, at the least, the use of illegal drugs is an integral component of the juvenile delinquent lifestyle.[61]

13-4c Child Abuse and Neglect

Abuse by parents also plays a substantial role in juvenile delinquency. **Child abuse** can be broadly defined as the infliction of physical, emotional, and/or sexual damage on a child. **Child neglect** is a form of abuse that occurs when caregivers deprive a child of necessities such as love, shelter, food, and proper care. According to the National Survey of Children's Exposure to Violence, one in ten children in the United States experiences mistreatment at the hands of a close family member before reaching eighteen years of age.[62]

Children in homes characterized by violence or neglect suffer from a variety of physical, emotional, and mental health problems at a much greater rate than their peers.[63] This, in turn, increases their chances of engaging in delinquent behavior. One survey of violent juveniles showed that 75 percent had been subjected to severe abuse by a family member and 80 percent had witnessed violence in their homes.[64] Nearly half of all juveniles—and 80 percent of girls—sentenced to life in prison suffered high rates of abuse.[65]

Cathy Spatz Widom, a professor of psychology at John Jay College of Criminal Justice, compared the arrest records of two groups of subjects—one made up of 908 cases of substantiated parental abuse and neglect, and the other made up of 667 children who had not been abused or neglected. Widom found that those who had been abused or neglected were 53 percent more likely to be arrested as juveniles than those who had not.[66] Simply put, according to researchers Janet Currie of Columbia University and Erdal Tekin

Aging Out A term used to explain the fact that criminal activity declines with age.

Age of Onset The age at which a juvenile first exhibits delinquent behavior.

Child Abuse Mistreatment of children involving physical, emotional, and/or sexual damage.

Child Neglect A form of child abuse in which the child is denied certain necessities such as shelter, food, care, and love.

of Georgia State University, "child maltreatment roughly doubles the probability that an individual engages in many types of crime."[67]

13-4d Gangs

When youths cannot find the stability and support they require in the family structure, they often turn to their peers. This is just one explanation for why juveniles join **youth gangs.** Although jurisdictions may have varying definitions, for general purposes a youth gang is viewed as a group of three or more persons who (1) self-identify as an entity separate from the community by adopting special clothing, vocabulary, hand signals, and names and (2) engage in criminal activity. According to research conducted by criminologists David C. Pyrooz and Gary Sweeten, there are just over a million gang members between the ages of five and seventeen in the United States.[68]

3 or more people

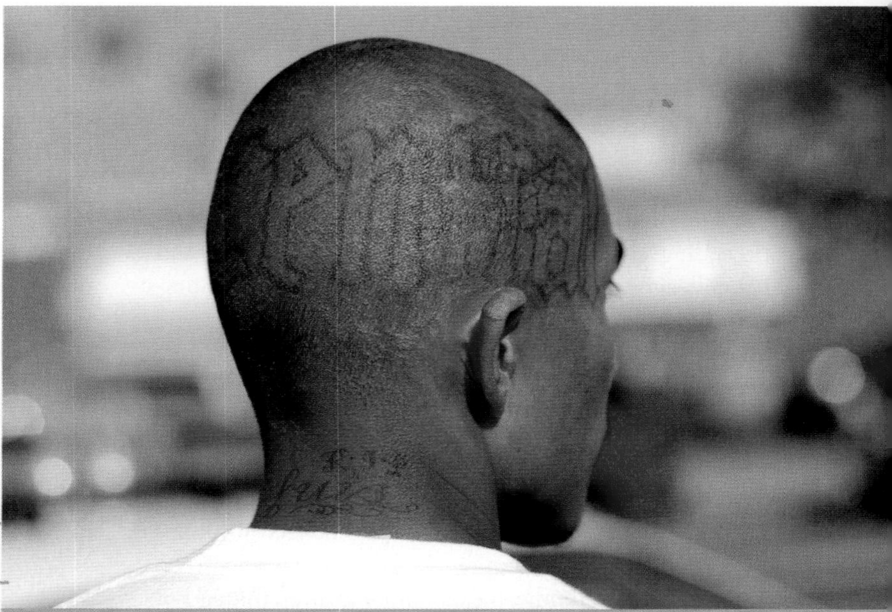

Kevork Djansezian/Getty Images News/Getty Images

In Los Angeles, a gang member signifies his allegiance to the "Street Villains" through a series of elaborate tattoos. **What role does identity play in a juvenile's decision to join a gang?**

A study of criminal behavior among juveniles in Seattle found that gang members were considerably more likely to commit crimes than at-risk youths who shared many characteristics with gang members but were not affiliated with any gang. The survey also found that gang members were much more likely to own firearms or have friends who did than non–gang members.[69] In addition, on reaching adulthood, youth gang members have worse outcomes than their peers in a number of areas, including drug abuse, likelihood of arrest and incarceration, and general health.[70]

WHO JOINS GANGS? The average gang member is eighteen years old, though members are often older in cities with long traditions of gang activity, such as Chicago and Los Angeles. Although it is difficult to determine with any certainty the makeup of gangs as a whole, one recent survey found that 53 percent of all gang members in the United States are Latino, 32 percent are African American, and 10 percent are white, with the remaining 5 percent belonging to other racial or ethnic backgrounds.[71]

3 or more people

Youth Gang A self-formed group of youths with several identifiable characteristics, including a gang name and other recognizable symbols, a geographic territory, and participation in illegal activities.

Though gangs tend to have racial or ethnic characteristics—that is, one group predominates in each gang—many researchers do not believe that race or ethnicity is the dominant factor in gang membership. Instead, gang members seem to come from lower-class or working-class communities, mostly in urban areas but with an increasing number from the suburbs and rural counties.

WHY JOIN GANGS? The decision to join a gang, like the decision to engage in any sort of antisocial or criminal behavior, is a complex one, and the factors that go into it vary depending on the individual. Generally, however, the reasons for gang membership involve one or more of the following:

1. *Identity.* Being part of a gang often confers a status that the individual feels he or she could not attain outside the gang.
2. *Protection.* Many gang members live in neighborhoods marked by high levels of crime and violence, and a gang guarantees support and retaliation in case of an attack.
3. *Fellowship.* The gang often functions as an extension of the family and provides companionship that may not be available at home.
4. *Criminal activity.* Many gang members enjoy financial rewards because of the gang's profits and protection.
5. *Intimidation.* Some gang members are pressured or forced to join the gang, often to act as "foot soldiers" in the gang's criminal enterprises.[72]

To help gang members leave their gang, "desistance experts" often focus on counteracting the same pressures that initially led to gang membership. For example, gang members with intimate partners and children are encouraged to commit to their "real family" rather than their "gang family." Help in gaining legal employment can also reduce some of the financial incentives for gang members to continue their illegal activities.[73]

13-5 WHAT HAPPENS AFTER A JUVENILE IS ARRESTED?

In an attempt to stem the tide of violent crime in their city, Chicago police officers spend hours monitoring the social media accounts of local gang members, who often use that format to boast about past and future criminal activity. Most commonly, however, contact between juvenile offenders and law enforcement takes place on the streets, initiated by a police officer on patrol who either apprehends the juvenile while he or she is committing a crime or answers a call for service. The youth is then passed on to an officer of the juvenile court, who must decide how to handle the case. (See Figure 13.5 for an overview of the juvenile justice process.)

13-5a Police Discretion and Juvenile Crime

Police arrest about 580,000 youths under the age of eighteen each year.[74] In most states, police officers must have probable cause to believe that the minor has committed an offense, just as they would if the suspect was an adult. Police power with regard to juveniles is greater than with adults, however, because police can take youths into custody for status offenses, such as possession of alcohol or truancy. In these cases, the officer is acting *in loco parentis*, or in the place of the parent. The officer's role is not necessarily to punish the youths, but to protect them from harmful behavior.

Police officers also have a great deal of discretion in deciding what to do with juveniles who have committed crimes or status offenses. Juvenile justice expert Joseph Goldstein labels this discretionary power **low-visibility decision making** because it relies on factors that the public is not generally in a position to understand or criticize. When a grave offense has

Low-Visibility Decision Making A term used to describe the discretionary power police have in determining what to do with misbehaving juveniles.

FIGURE 13.5 THE JUVENILE JUSTICE PROCESS

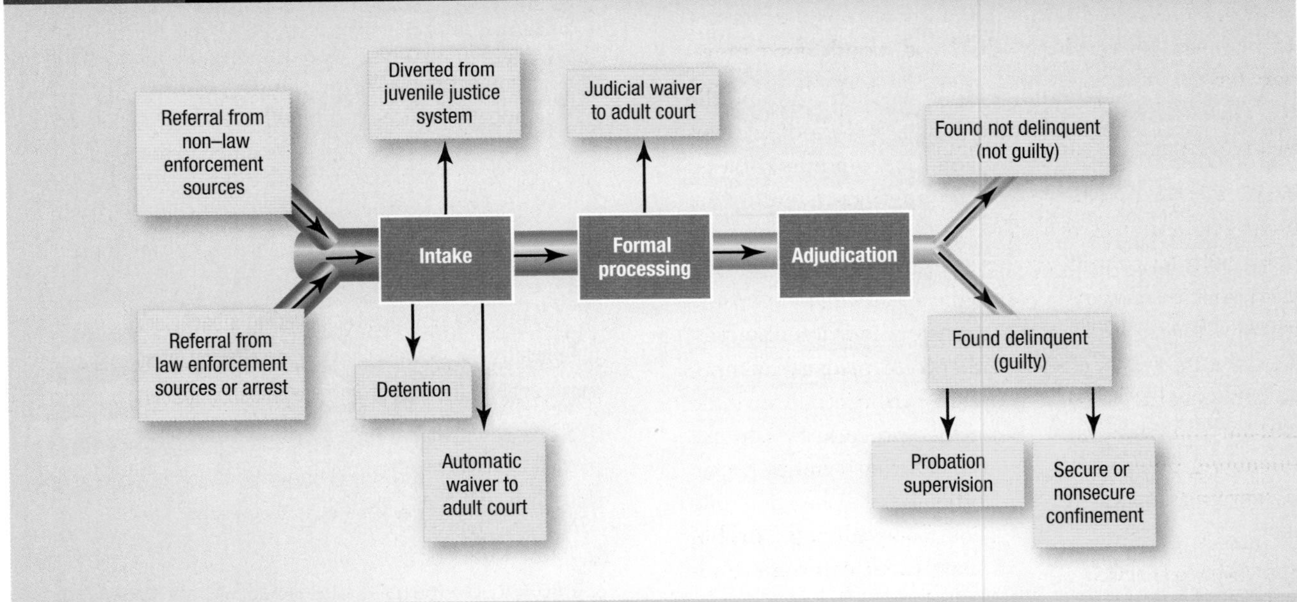

This diagram shows the possible tracks that a young person may take after her or his first contact with the juvenile justice system (usually a police officer).

Source: Office of Juvenile Justice and Delinquency Prevention.

taken place, a police officer may decide to formally arrest the juvenile, send him or her to juvenile court, or place the youth under the care of a social-service organization. In less serious situations, the officer may simply issue a warning or take the offender to the police station and release the child into the custody of her or his parents.

In making these discretionary decisions, police generally consider the following factors:

- The nature of the child's offense.
- The offender's past history of involvement with the juvenile justice system.
- The setting in which the offense took place.
- The ability and willingness of the child's parents to take disciplinary action.
- The attitude of the offender.
- The offender's gender.

Law enforcement officers notify the juvenile court system that a particular young person requires its attention through a process known as a **referral.** Anyone with a valid reason, including parents, relatives, welfare agencies, and school officials, can refer a juvenile to the juvenile court. The vast majority of cases in juvenile courts, however, are referred by the police.[75]

13-5b Intake

As noted earlier, if, following arrest, a police officer feels the offender warrants the attention of the juvenile justice process, the officer will refer the youth to juvenile court. Once this step has been taken, a complaint is filed with a special division of the juvenile court, and the **intake** process begins. Intake may be followed by diversion to a community-based program, transfer to an adult court, or detention to await trial in juvenile court. Thus, intake, diversion, transfer, and detention are the four primary components of pretrial juvenile justice procedure.

Referral The notification process through which a law enforcement officer or other concerned citizen makes the juvenile court aware of a juvenile's unlawful or unruly conduct.

Intake The process by which an official of the court must decide whether to file a petition, release the juvenile, or place the juvenile under some other form of supervision.

Petition The document filed with a juvenile court alleging that the juvenile is a delinquent or a status offender and requesting that the court either hear the case or transfer it to an adult court.

During intake, an official of the juvenile court—usually a probation officer, but sometimes a judge—must decide, in effect, what to do with the offender. The intake officer has several options during intake:

LO13-5 Describe the four primary components of pretrial juvenile justice procedure.

1. Simply dismiss the case, releasing the offender without taking any further action. This occurs in about one in three cases, usually because the judge cannot determine a sufficient reason to continue.[76]
2. Divert the offender to a social-services program, such as drug rehabilitation or anger management.
3. File a **petition** for a formal court hearing. The petition is the formal document outlining the charges against the juvenile.
4. Transfer the case to an adult court, where the offender will be tried as an adult.

With regard to status offenses, judges have sole discretion to decide whether to process the case or *divert* the youth to another juvenile service agency.

13-5c Pretrial Diversion

In the early 1970s, Congress passed the first Juvenile Justice and Delinquency Prevention (JJDP) Act, which ordered the development of methods "to divert juveniles from the traditional juvenile justice system."[77] Within a few years, hundreds of diversion programs had been put into effect. Today, diversion refers to the process of removing low-risk offenders from the formal juvenile justice system by placing them in community-based rehabilitation programs.

Diversion programs vary widely but fall into three general categories:

1. *Probation.* In this program, the juvenile is returned to the community but placed under the supervision of a juvenile probation officer. If the youth breaks the conditions of probation, he or she can be returned to the formal juvenile system.

CAREER TIP Besides needing a bachelor's degree in a field such as criminal justice, psychology, or social work, applicants for the post of *juvenile probation officer* often need experience working with young people. Such experience can be gained by volunteering with organizations such as the Boys & Girls Club, YMCA, and Big Brothers Big Sisters.

2. *Treatment and aid.* Many juveniles have behavioral or medical conditions that contribute to their delinquent behavior, and many diversion programs offer remedial education, drug and alcohol treatment, and other forms of counseling to alleviate these problems.

3. *Restitution.* In these programs, the offender "repays" her or his victim, either directly or symbolically through community service.[78]

Proponents of diversion programs include many labeling theorists, who believe that contact with the formal juvenile justice system "labels" the youth a delinquent, which leads to further delinquent behavior.

13-5d Transfer to Adult Court

One side effect of diversionary programs is that the youths who remain in the juvenile courts are more likely to be seen as "hardened" and thus less amenable to rehabilitation. This, in turn, increases the likelihood that such an offender will be transferred to an adult court, a process in which the juvenile court waives jurisdiction over the youth. In the 1980s and 1990s, when the American juvenile justice system shifted away from ideals of treatment and toward punishment, transfer to adult court was one of the most popular means of "getting tough" on delinquents.

INCIDENCE OF TRANSFER The proportion of juveniles waived to adult court for property crimes has decreased steadily in the past two decades. About 4,000 delinquent cases are now waived to adult criminal court each year—less than 1 percent of all cases that reach juvenile court. This figure is down significantly from 1994, when the number of such cases peaked at 13,600.[79]

As might be expected, the majority of transfer cases involve juveniles, such as Paul Gingerich, who have committed a violent offense.[80] In the opening of this chapter, we discussed how Gingerich was charged as an adult for, at the age of twelve, participating in the murder of a friend's stepfather.

METHODS OF TRANSFER There are three types of transfer laws, and most states use more than one of them, depending on the jurisdiction and the seriousness of the offense. Juveniles are most commonly transferred to adult courts through **judicial waiver,** in which the juvenile judge is given the power to determine whether a young offender's case will be waived to adult court. The judge makes this decision based on the offender's age, the nature of the offense, and any criminal history. All but five states employ judicial waiver.

Twenty-nine states have taken the waiver responsibility out of judicial hands through **automatic transfer,** also known as *legislative waiver*. In these states, the legislatures have designated certain conditions—usually involving serious crimes such as murder and rape—under which a juvenile case is automatically "kicked up" to adult court. In Rhode Island, for example, a juvenile aged sixteen or older with two prior felony adjudications will automatically be transferred on being accused of a third felony.[81]

Fifteen states also allow for **prosecutorial waiver,** in which prosecutors are allowed to choose whether to initiate proceedings in juvenile or criminal court when certain age and offense conditions are met. (See *Discretion in Action—Juvenile Drunk Driving* for further insight into prosecutorial waiver procedures.)

13-5e Detention

If a decision is made that the offender will face adjudication in a juvenile court, the intake official must decide what to do with him or her until the start of the trial. Generally, the juvenile is released into the custody of parents or a guardian—most jurisdictions favor this practice in lieu of setting money bail for youths. The intake officer may also place the offender in **detention,** or temporary custody in a secure facility, until the disposition process begins.

Once a juvenile has been detained, most jurisdictions require that a **detention hearing** be held within twenty-four hours. During this hearing, the offender has several due process safeguards, including the right to counsel, the right against self-incrimination, and the right to cross-examine and confront witnesses.

In justifying its decision to detain, the court will usually address one of three issues:

1. Whether the child poses a danger to the community.
2. Whether the child will return for the adjudication process.
3. Whether detention will provide protection for the child.

The Supreme Court upheld the practice of preventive detention (see Chapter 8) for juveniles in *Schall v. Martin* (1984)[82] by ruling that youths can be detained if they are deemed a "risk" to the

Judicial Waiver The process in which the juvenile judge, based on the facts of the case at hand, decides that the alleged offender should be transferred to adult court.

Automatic Transfer The process by which a juvenile is transferred to adult court as a matter of state law.

Prosecutorial Waiver A procedure by which the prosecutor has discretion to decide whether a case will be heard by a juvenile court or an adult court.

Detention The temporary custody of a juvenile in a secure facility after a petition has been filed and before the adjudicatory process begins.

Detention Hearing A hearing to determine whether a juvenile should be detained, or remain detained, while waiting for the adjudicatory process to begin.

DISCRETION IN ACTION

Juvenile Drunk Driving

THE SITUATION James, a seventeen-year-old high school senior, gets behind the wheel of his father's car with a blood alcohol concentration of .12, well over the state limit for driving under the influence (DUI). He slams headfirst into another car, killing the driver. Initially, he is charged with vehicular homicide as a juvenile.

THE LAW In this state, prosecutors have the discretion to waive juvenile offenders to adult court if the alleged offender is sixteen years old or older at the time of the alleged offense and is charged with a felony, such as vehicular manslaughter.

WHAT WOULD YOU DO? You are a prosecutor with the discretionary power to transfer James from juvenile court to adult court. On the one hand, James has no previous criminal record, did not intend to kill his victim, and has shown extreme remorse for his actions. Furthermore, he is a juvenile and, as such, is seen by the law as less culpable than an adult. On the other hand, his careless actions resulted in a homicide, and trying him as an adult might deter other juveniles from committing DUI crimes. Do you keep James in juvenile court or waive him to adult court? Why?

To learn what a prosecutor in Denver, Colorado, did in a similar situation, see Example 13.1 in Appendix A.

safety of the community or to their own welfare. About one-third of juveniles involved in violent offenses are detained before trial.[83]

13-6 HOW ARE JUVENILES TRIED AND PUNISHED?

In just over half of all referred cases, the juvenile is eventually subject to formal proceedings in juvenile court.[84] As noted earlier, changes in the juvenile justice system since *In re Gault* (1967) have led many to contend that juvenile courts have become indistinguishable, both theoretically and practically, from adult courts.[85] About half the states, for example, permit juveniles to request a jury trial under certain circumstances. Juvenile justice proceedings can still be distinguished from the adult system of criminal justice, however, and these differences are evident in the adjudication and disposition of the juvenile trial.

Adjudicatory Hearing The process through which a juvenile court determines whether there is sufficient evidence to support the initial petition.

Disposition Hearing A hearing in which the juvenile judge or officer decides the appropriate punishment for a youth found to be delinquent or a status offender.

13-6a Adjudication

During the adjudication stage of the juvenile justice process, a hearing is held to determine whether the offender is delinquent or in need of some form of court supervision. Most state juvenile codes dictate a specific set of procedures that must be followed during the **adjudicatory hearing,** with the goal of providing the respondent with "the essentials of due process and fair treatment." Consequently, the respondent in an adjudicatory hearing has the right to notice of charges, counsel, and confrontation and cross-examination, along with the privilege against self-incrimination.

Furthermore, "proof beyond a reasonable doubt" must be established to find the child delinquent. When the child admits guilt—that is, admits to the charges of the initial petition—the judge must ensure that the admission was voluntary.

At the close of the adjudicatory hearing, the judge is generally required to rule on the legal issues and evidence that have been presented. Based on this ruling, the judge determines whether the respondent is delinquent or in need of court supervision.

Alternatively, the judge can dismiss the case based on a lack of evidence. It is important to remember that finding a child delinquent is *not* the same as convicting an adult of a crime. A delinquent does not face the same restrictions imposed on adult convicts in some states, such as limits on the right to vote and to run for political office.

13-6b Disposition

Once a juvenile has been adjudicated delinquent, the judge must decide what steps will be taken toward treatment and/or punishment. Most states provide for a *bifurcated* process in which a separate **disposition hearing** follows the adjudicatory hearing. Depending on state law, the juvenile may be entitled to counsel at the disposition hearing.

SENTENCING JUVENILES In an adult trial, the sentencing phase is primarily concerned with protecting the community from the convict. In contrast, a juvenile judge uses the disposition hearing to determine a sentence that will serve the needs of the child. For assistance in this crucial process, the judge will order the probation department to gather information on the juvenile and present it in the form of a **predisposition report.** The report usually contains information concerning the respondent's family background, the facts surrounding the delinquent act, and interviews with social workers, teachers, and other important figures in the child's life.

JUDICIAL DISCRETION In keeping with the rehabilitative tradition of the juvenile justice system, juvenile judges generally have a great deal of discretion in choosing one of several disposition possibilities. A judge can tend toward leniency, delivering only a stern reprimand or warning before releasing the juvenile into the custody of parents or other legal guardians.

Otherwise, the choice is among incarceration in a juvenile correctional facility, probation, or community treatment. In most cases, the seriousness of the offense is the primary factor used in determining whether to incarcerate a juvenile, though history of delinquency, family situation, and the offender's attitude are all relevant.

13-6c Juvenile Corrections

In general, juvenile corrections are based on the concept of **graduated sanctions**—that is, the severity of the punishment should fit the crime. Consequently, status and first-time offenders are diverted or placed on probation, repeat offenders find themselves in intensive community supervision or treatment programs, and serious and violent offenders are placed in correctional facilities. (See Figure 13.6 to get a better idea of how graduated sanctions apply to the juvenile justice system.)

JUVENILE PROBATION The majority of all adjudicated delinquents (64 percent) will never receive a disposition more severe than being placed on probation.[86] These statistics reflect a general understanding among juvenile court judges and other officials that a child should normally be removed from her or his home only as a last resort.

The organization of juvenile probation is very similar to adult probation, and juvenile probationers are increasingly subjected to electronic monitoring and other supervisory tactics. The main difference between the two programs

Predisposition Report A report prepared during the disposition process that provides the judge with relevant background material to aid in the disposition decision.

Graduated Sanctions A continuum of disposition options used in juvenile corrections with the goal of ensuring that the juvenile's punishment matches the wrongdoing in severity.

FIGURE 13.6 THE GRADUATED SANCTIONS MODEL

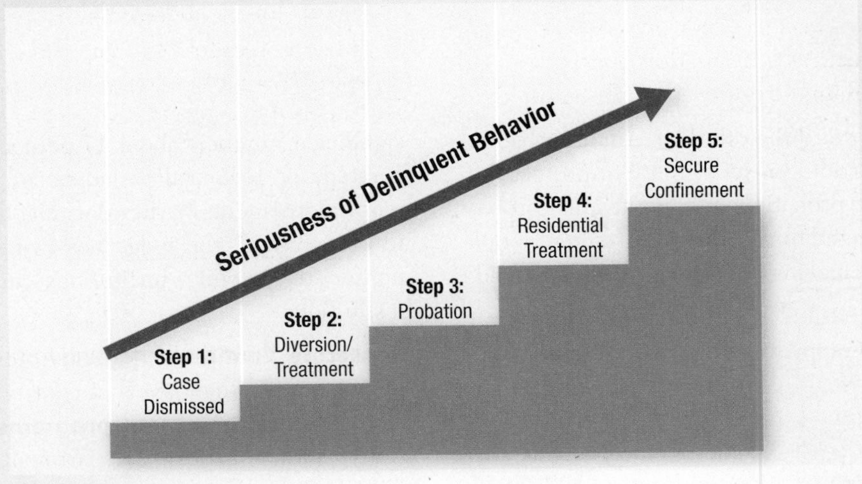

In juvenile corrections, the severity of punishment is directly related to the seriousness of the delinquent behavior.

CAREER PREP

Juvenile Detention Officer

Job Description:

- **Oversee the detention of juvenile offenders being held in temporary custody before the adjudicatory process begins. Observe the behavior of and, when necessary, counsel the juvenile offenders to ensure their safety during the detention period.**
- **Maintain personal relationships with the juvenile offenders so as to supervise their progress in educational, recreational, and therapeutic activities while housed at the detention center.**

What Kind of Training Is Required?

- **A high school diploma plus at least three years of work experience involving children of school age (seven to seventeen years) or one year of college education for each year of experience lacking.**
- **Physical agility and strength, as well as a firm manner in dealing with juveniles who may present severe disciplinary problems.**

Annual Salary Range?

- **$29,000–$62,000**

PhotoDisc

GETTING LINKEDIN

Increasingly, juvenile detention centers are used to house undocumented non-citizen children who are in the United States illegally without their parents. As a result, a number of juvenile detention centers are advertising on LinkedIn for "bilingual detention specialists" to coordinate cases involving these young people.

lies in the attitude toward the offender. Adult probation officers have an overriding responsibility to protect the community from the probationer, while juvenile probation officers are expected to take the role of a mentor or a concerned relative in looking after the needs of the child.

CONFINING JUVENILES About 54,000 American youths (down from approximately 107,000 in 1995) are incarcerated in public and private juvenile correctional facilities in the United States.[87] Most of these juveniles have committed offenses against people or property, but a significant number (about 17 percent) have been incarcerated for technical violations of their probation or parole agreements.[88] After deciding that a juvenile needs to be confined, the judge has two sentencing options: nonsecure juvenile institutions and secure juvenile institutions.

Residential Treatment Program A government-run facility for juveniles whose offenses are not deemed serious enough to warrant incarceration in a training school.

Nonsecure Confinement Some juvenile delinquents do not require high levels of control and can be placed in **residential treatment programs.** These programs, run by either probation departments or social-services departments, allow their subjects freedom of movement in the community. Generally, the juveniles must follow certain rules, such as avoiding alcoholic beverages and returning to the facility for curfew.

Melanie Stetson Freeman/The Christian Science Monitor/Getty Images

Juvenile inmates wait to go into the gym at the Juvenile Detention Center in Toledo, Ohio. **Why might young offenders who are transferred to adult correctional facilities have higher recidivism rates than those who remain in juvenile facilities?**

Residential treatment programs can be divided into four categories:

1. *Foster care programs,* in which the juveniles live with couples who act as surrogate parents.
2. *Group homes,* which generally house between twelve and fifteen youths and provide treatment, counseling, and education services by a professional staff.
3. *Family group homes,* which combine aspects of foster care and group homes, meaning that a single family, rather than a group of professionals, looks after the needs of the young offenders.
4. *Rural programs,* which include wilderness camps, farms, and ranches where between thirty and fifty children are placed in an environment that provides recreational activities and treatment programs.

Secure Confinement Secure facilities are comparable to the adult prisons and jails we discussed earlier in the textbook. These institutions go by a confusing array of names depending on the state in which they are located, but the two best known are boot camps and training schools.

A **boot camp** is the juvenile version of shock probation. As we noted in Chapter 10, boot camps are modeled after military training for new recruits. Boot camp programs are based on the theory that giving wayward youths a taste of the "hard life" of military-like training for short periods of time, usually no longer than 180 days, will "shock" them out of a life of crime. At a typical youth boot camp, inmates are grouped in platoons and live in dormitories. They spend eight hours a day training, drilling, and doing hard labor, and also participate in programs such as basic adult education and job skills training.

No juvenile correctional facility is called a "prison." This does not mean that all such facilities lack any resemblance to prisons. The facilities that most closely mimic the atmosphere of an adult correctional facility are **training schools,** alternatively known as youth

Boot Camp A variation on traditional shock incarceration in which juveniles (and some adults) are sent to secure confinement facilities modeled on military basic training camps.

Training School A correctional institution for juveniles found to be delinquent or status offenders.

camps, youth development centers, industrial schools, and several other similar titles.

Whatever the name, these institutions claim to differ from their adult countparts by offering a variety of programs to treat and rehabilitate the young offenders. In reality, training schools are plagued by many of the same problems as adult prisons and jails, including high levels of inmate-on-inmate violence, substance abuse, gang conflict, and overcrowding.

ETHICS CHALLENGE

Los Angeles County recently passed an ordinance allowing the use of solitary confinement as a brief "cooling-off" measure for juvenile offenders. This step can be taken only after consultation with a mental heath professional. Is this an ethical approach to solitary confinement (discussed in Chapter 12) for juveniles? Why or why not?

AFTERCARE Juveniles leave correctional facilities either through an early release program or because they have served their sentences. Juvenile corrections officials recognize that many of these children, like adults, need assistance in readjusting to the outside world. In addition, about two-thirds of youths who come in contact with the juvenile justice system have behavioral health problems, such as alcohol abuse, serious depression, trauma related to exposure to violence, risk for suicide, and disorders related to low self-control.[89]

Aftercare The variety of therapeutic, educational, and counseling programs made available to juvenile delinquents after they have been released from a correctional facility.

For all these reasons, released juveniles are often placed in **aftercare** programs. Based on the same philosophy that drives the prisoner reentry movement (discussed in the preceding chapter), aftercare programs are designed to offer services for the released juveniles, while at the same time supervising them to reduce the chances of recidivism.

The ideal aftercare program includes community support groups, education and employment aid, and continued monitoring to ensure that the juvenile is able to deal with the demands of freedom. Statistics suggest, however, that the aftercare needs of young offenders often go unmet. Nearly 60 percent of those who have been referred to juvenile court are "re-referred" before turning eighteen.[90]

STUDY TOOLS 13

LOCATED IN TEXTBOOK

- ☐ Rip out the Chapter Review Card.
- ☐ Review with the Chapter Quiz following this chapter.

LOCATED AT WWW.CENGAGEBRAIN.COM

- ☐ Review key terms flash cards.
- ☐ Read the chapter on all your favorite devices.
- ☐ Complete an Exam to test your knowledge.
- ☐ Check out Visual Summaries and You Decide activities to explore chapter concepts.

Quiz

1. At its inception, the American juvenile justice system was guided by the principles of *parens patriae*, which holds that the ________________ has a responsibility to look after children when their parents cannot do so.

2. When a juvenile engages in wrongdoing that would not be a crime if done by an adult, she or he has committed a ________________.

3. The U.S. Supreme Court relied on the concept of "diminished culpability" when, in 2005, it prohibited the ________________ ________________ for offenders who were juveniles when they committed their crimes.

4. Experts focus on the process of ________________ ________________ to explain why young people commit fewer offenses as they grow older.

5. Youth who become involved in ________________ are more likely to engage in criminal activity than those who do not.

6. If the circumstances are serious enough, a police officer can formally ________________ an offending juvenile.

7. In less serious circumstances, a police officer can ________________ the juvenile to the juvenile court system.

8. If a juvenile court judge believes that the seriousness of the offense so warrants, he or she can transfer the juvenile into the adult court system through a process called judicial ________________.

9. A juvenile offender's delinquency is determined during the ________________ hearing, which is similar in many ways to an adult trial.

10. If the juvenile is found to be delinquent, her or his sentence is determined during ________________ the hearing.

Answers to the Chapter 13 Quiz can be found in the Answers section in the back of the book.

14 Today's Challenges in Criminal Justice

Sean Gallup/Getty Images News/Getty Images

LEARNING OBJECTIVES

14-1 Outline the three major reasons why the Internet is conducive to the dissemination of child pornography.

14-2 Define *malware*, and identify the main way in which worms differ from viruses and Trojans.

14-3 Summarize the three federal laws that have been particularly influential on our nation's counterterrorism strategies.

14-4 Explain how background checks, in theory, protect the public from firearm-related violence.

14-5 Indicate some of the ways that white-collar crime is different from violent or property crime.

After finishing this chapter, go to **PAGE 307** for **STUDY TOOLS**

"REVENGE PORN"

A few months after Norma broke up with her boyfriend, she found out that he had posted sexually explicit selfies of her on an X-rated website called PornHub. Along with the photos, he included her first and last names, her phone number, her hometown, and a solicitation for oral sex. "I cannot get back my privacy that had been invaded when those pictures were online," Norma told a court in Newark, New Jersey. "I do not know how many people saw them, I do not know how many people saved them, and every single day I think about the fact that other people have seen me in my most private state."

Norma's ex-boyfriend was charged under New Jersey's so-called "revenge porn" law and sentenced to five years' probation. The legislation makes it a crime for one person to disclose online the image of another person in which her or his "intimate parts are exposed" without that person's approval. Thirty-three other states and Washington, D.C., also have laws that criminalize *nonconsensual pornography*, which can broadly be defined as the distribution of sexually graphic images of individuals without their consent. These laws cover many forms of wrongdoing, including stealing and selling nude images of celebrities and *sextortion*, in which the offender threatens to post explicit photographs online if the victim does not provide more such images, sexual favors, or money.

Victims of nonconsensual pornography suffer in numerous ways beyond the shame of exposure. They may find it difficult to find work, given that most employers now consult search engines to collect information on job applicants. Their personal relationships with family and friends who have viewed the images may be strained. And, crucially, they may be placed in physical danger. Several years ago, fifty men showed up at the home of a Maryland woman whose ex-husband posted fake ads using her image online, including one that said, "Rape Me and My Children."

MyImages - Micha/Shutterstock.com

California's nonconsensual pornography law includes a provision that the images are shown "with the intent to cause emotional distress." *What might be some of the unintended consequences of a "revenge porn" law that does not feature an intent requirement?*

14-1 WHAT IS CYBER CRIME?

The Internet is teeming with *cyberdeviance*—behavior that, while not technically illegal, falls outside society's norms. By one measure, pornography websites receive more visitors than Amazon, Netflix, and Twitter combined.[1] Activities such as "sexting," or sharing sexually explicit photos online, are commonplace and generally are not illegal. Even filming sex acts and placing the videos on the Internet, if consensual, is beyond the reach of criminal law.

Without consent, the legal equation changes. In 2016, for example, Benjamin Barber, an Oregon resident, posted pornographic footage of himself engaging in sex with a former partner on multiple websites. Because the partner did not give her consent, Barber was charged with five counts of "unlawful dissemination of an intimate image" and sentenced to six months in jail.

If Barber had posted the videos several years earlier, he probably would not have been arrested. In 2015, however, Oregon passed a nonconsensual pornography law, and Barber's behavior went from deviant to illegal.[2] In other words, he had committed a **cyber crime,** the broad term that we will use in this section to describe any criminal activity carried out by the use of a computer in the virtual community of the Internet.

Cyber Crime A crime that occurs online, in the virtual community of the Internet, as opposed to in the physical world.

placing videos of child pornography on the internet.

14-1a Crime and the Internet

Peter C. Vey/The New Yorker Collection/The Cartoon Bank

"You know, you can do this just as easily online."

As this textbook has made clear, committing a crime in the "real world" is difficult and full of uncertainty. A robber, for example, must plan out the logistics of the crime, determine a suitable victim with items worth taking, and accept the risk of law enforcement intervention. Technology makes cyber crime considerably easier. With relatively basic knowledge of how computers operate, a person can conduct a wide range of wrongdoing without leaving the relative safety of home.[3]

Technology also acts as a "force multiplier," allowing for the targeting of numerous victims. "Robbing one person at a time using a knife or a gun doesn't scale well," notes Marc Goodman of the Future Crimes Institute. "But now one person can rob millions at the click of a button."[4]

The example of *child pornography* shows how cyber crime has raised the stakes for the criminal justice system. (Child pornography is the illegal production and sale of material depicting sexually explicit conduct involving a child.) In the late 1970s, about 250 child pornography magazines were circulating in the United States, and it was relatively easy for law enforcement to confiscate hard copies of these publications.[5] With the advent of the Internet, however, child pornography became much easier to disseminate. The reasons for this include:

1. ***Speed.*** The Internet is a quick means of sending visual material over long distances. Child pornographers can deliver their material faster and more securely online than through regular mail.
2. ***Security.*** Any illegal material that passes through the hands of a mail carrier is inherently in danger of being discovered. This risk is significantly reduced with e-mail. Furthermore, Internet sites that offer child pornography can protect their customers with passwords, which keep random Web surfers (or law enforcement agents) from stumbling on the sites or chat rooms.
3. ***Anonymity.*** Obviously, anonymity is the most important protection offered by the Internet for sellers and buyers of child pornography, as it is for any person engaged in illegal behavior in cyberspace.[6]

LO14-1 Outline the three major reasons why the Internet is conducive to the dissemination of child pornography.

Because of these factors, courts and lawmakers have had a difficult time controlling not only child pornography but also a wide variety of other online wrongdoing. In this section, we will focus on three general areas of online offending, as identified by cyber crime expert David Wall: (1) cyber trespass, (2) cyber deception and theft, and (3) cyber violence.[7]

14-1b Cyber Trespass

In ea… Berk… stude… cybe… store… that… alert… whic… pute… for fi… are c… card… spen… men…

• Cyber trespass = unauthorized person illegaly gains entry to computer systems
• Hack = using a computer system to gain illegal access to another computer system
• Vulnerabilities = allows hackers to enter the targeted system without permission →
• Malware = malicious software, software desingned to distrupt or damage a computer system
Ex: virus →

CJ and TECHNOLOGY

Hacking the "Internet of Things"

The "Internet of things" (IoT) is set to dominate our daily lives in the near future. The term refers to objects that contain tiny computer chips that wirelessly connect them to the Internet. The roster of Web-connected items—including automobiles, refrigerators, televisions, pacemakers, light bulbs, and smoke detectors—is already extensive. It is estimated that the IoT will include fifty billion devices worldwide by 2020, up from twenty billion in 2017.

The tiny computers that form the basis of the IoT do not have as much processing power or memory as desktop computers or even smartphones. Consequently, the security software on these systems tends to be unsophisticated and easily bypassed by malware such as Mirai, which scours the Web for vulnerabilities. In October 2016, Mirai was able to gain access to hundreds of thousands of IoT devices with simple passwords such as "admin" or "12345." It used these captured devices to launch an attack on Dyn, a New Hampshire–based company that helps route Internet traffic.

The result: temporary outages at popular websites such as Netflix, PayPal, Spotify, and Twitter. "When the Internet apocalypse comes, your smart thermostat may be to blame," remarked one observer after the attack.

Thinking about Hacking the "Internet of Things"

The dangers of a remotely controlled automobile or heart monitor are obvious. Experts warn that smart light bulbs are also susceptible to easy hacking. Using your imagination, describe the national security risks posed by a large number of malware-infected light bulbs.

HACKING The individuals who breached security at UC Berkeley are known as *hackers*. A **hack** is the act of using one computer system to gain illegal access to another computer system. In general, hackers take advantage of flaws in computer software or hardware, known as *vulnerabilities*, that allow them to enter the targeted system without permission.

Hacking is unnervingly frequent in the United States. Each hour, government agencies, businesses, and individuals are subjected to hundreds of hacking attempts. Over the past several years, cybercriminals have successfully hacked the White House, the U.S. State Department, and the Pentagon, not to mention dozens of large companies such as Yahoo, Apple, and Verizon.

MALWARE Hackers rely on malicious software, or *malware*, to carry out their illegal activities. Over the past few decades, a dizzying array of malware has been developed, and more complex forms of this software are introduced each year. For our purposes, the four general categories of malware that follow provide a helpful introduction to the subject.

> **LO14-2** Define *malware*, and identify the main way in which worms differ from viruses and Trojans.

1. A **worm** is a software program that is capable of reproducing itself as it spreads from one computer to the next.
2. A **virus** is also able to reproduce itself but must be attached to an "infested" host file to travel from one computer network to another.
3. **Trojans** are, at first glance, useful pieces of software that do damage when installed and activated on a computer.
4. **Botnets** allow a hacker to "take over" another computer without the knowledge of the targeted computer's owner. That computer is then used to spread malware, thus hiding the hacker's identity.

For the most part, viruses, Trojans, and botnets require a careless act, such as clicking on a file or attachment, to spread to targeted computers. Worms, in contrast, can

Hack The illegal use of one computer system to gain access to another computer system and steal or manipulate the data in the targeted system.

Worm A computer program that can automatically replicate itself and interfere with the normal use of a computer. A worm does not need to be attached to an existing file to move from one network to another.

Virus A computer program that can replicate itself and interfere with the normal use of a computer. A virus cannot exist as a separate entity and must attach itself to another program to move through a network.

Trojan Malware that appears to be beneficial to a computer user, but causes damage to the computer when it is installed and activated.

Botnet A network of computers that have been appropriated without the knowledge of their owners and used to spread harmful programs via the Internet.

move from computer to computer without further human action.

14-1c Cyber Deception and Theft

Not all hacking is geared toward monetary gain, but it certainly can be used to that end. In 2016, for example, hackers managed to gain access to a computer network that arranges for transfers of funds between banks. With this access, they drained $81 million from accounts at the Bangladesh Bank before being discovered. Thus, *cyber deception and theft*, which involves the illegal acquisition of information or resources using computer networks, plays a significant role in cyber crime.

CYBER CONSUMER FRAUD The expanding world of e-commerce has created many benefits for consumers. It has also led to some challenging problems, including fraud conducted via the Internet. In general, fraud is any misrepresentation knowingly made with the intention of deceiving another person.

FIGURE 14.1 FRAUDULENT ACTIVITY ON THE INTERNET

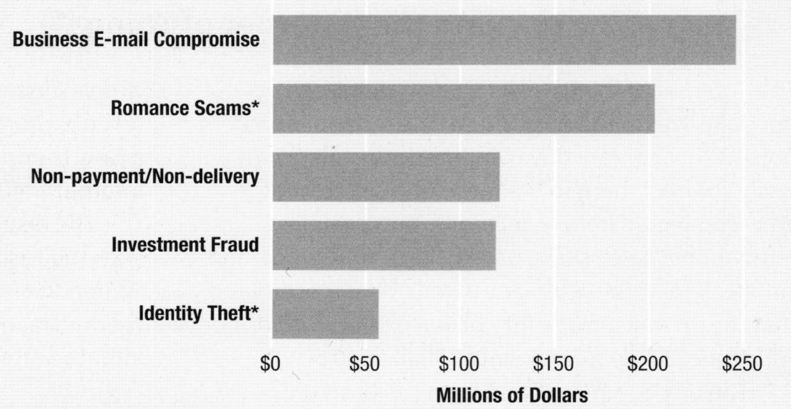

Business E-mail Compromise: Victims, mostly businesses, are instructed via e-mail to redirect invoice payments to nonexistent suppliers.

Non-payment/Non-delivery: Victims are scammed at e-commerce websites; either (1) goods and services are shipped, and payment is never rendered, or (2) payment is sent, and goods and services are never received.

Investment Fraud: Deceptive practices that convince victims to make investments or purchases (such as for real estate) on the basis of false information, usually promising a large return with minimal financial risk.

*Described in the text.

In its most recent annual report on cyber crime, the Internet Crime Complaint Center highlighted five "frequently reported Internet crimes." These crimes, along with the annual total losses reported by their victims, are detailed above.

Source: Internet Crime Complaint Center, *IC3 2015 Internet Crime Report* (Glen Allen, Va.: National White Collar Crime Center, 2016), 16, 226–230.

Furthermore, the victim must reasonably rely on the fraudulent information to her or his detriment. **Cyber fraud,** then, is fraud committed over the Internet. Scams that were once conducted solely by mail or phone can now be found online, and new technology has led to increasingly more creative ways to commit fraud.

Cyber Fraud Any misrepresentation knowingly made over the Internet with the intention of deceiving another and on which a reasonable person would and does rely to his or her detriment.

Data Breach The illegal appropriation of protected or confidential information.

Identity Theft The theft of personal information, such as a person's name, driver's license number, or Social Security number.

Online dating scams, for example, have increased dramatically in recent years, with fraudsters creating fake profiles to deceive unwitting romantic partners. According to the Internet Crime Complaint Center (IC3), operated as a partnership between the FBI and the National White Collar Crime Center, in 2015 online romance scam artists defrauded victims out of more than $200 million.[10]

In one case, the FBI arrested a Houston resident for defrauding numerous older women he met on Internet dating websites out of millions of dollars. First, he would profess to fall in love with his victims. Then, he would offer to take over management of their personal finances, which he would steal as soon as the funds were naively placed in his control. (See Figure 14.1 to learn about the costs associated with other common forms of cyber fraud.)

CYBER THEFT A **data breach** is an incident in which unauthorized persons access and steal confidential or protected information. In cyberspace, those who carry out data breaches are not subject to the physical limitations of the "real" world. A thief with network access can steal data stored in a networked computer from anywhere on the globe. Only the speed of the connection and the thief's computer equipment limit the quantity of data that can be stolen.

Identity Theft This freedom from physical limitations has led to a marked increase in **identity theft,** which occurs when the wrongdoer steals a form of identification—such as a name, date of birth, or Social Security number—and uses the information to access the victim's financial resources. According to the federal government, about 7 percent of Americans aged sixteen and older are victims of identity theft each year.[11]

The vast majority of identity theft victims (86 percent) experience data breaches involving existing bank and credit card accounts.[12] Online, an identity thief can steal financial information by fooling websites into thinking that he or she is the true account holder. For example, important personal information such as one's birthday, hometown, or employer that is available on social media sites such as Facebook can be used to convince a third party to reveal the victim's Social Security or bank account number.

Password Protection The more personal information a cyber criminal obtains, the easier it is for him or her to find a victim's online user name. Once the online user name has been compromised, it is easier to steal a victim's password, which is often the last line of defense to financial information. Internet users should be wary of any links contained within e-mails sent from an unknown source, as these links can sometimes be used to illegally obtain personal information. (See Figure 14.2 for some hints on how to protect your online passwords.)

FIGURE 14.2 PROTECTING ONLINE PASSWORDS

1. **Don't** use existing words such as your pet's name or your hometown. Such words are easy for computer identity theft programs to decode.
2. **Do** use at least eight characters in your passwords, with a nonsensical combination of upper-and lower-case letters, numbers, and symbols. A weak password is "scout1312." A strong password is "4X$dQ%3Z9j."
3. **Don't** use the same username and password for different Web accounts. If you do, then each account is in danger if one account is compromised.
4. **Do** use a different password for each Web account. If necessary, write down the various passwords and keep the list in a safe place.
5. **Don't** use information that can be easily found online or guessed at in choosing the questions that Web sites use to verify your password. That is, don't select questions such as "What is your birthday?" or "What is your city of birth?" Instead, choose questions with obscure answers that you are certain to remember or can easily look up.
6. **Don't** log on to any website if you are connected to the Internet via a wireless network (Wi-Fi) that is not itself password protected.

Once an online password has been compromised, the information on the protected website is fair game for identity thieves. By following these simple rules, you can strengthen the protection provided by your online passwords.

Phishing A distinct form of identity theft known as **phishing** adds a different wrinkle to this particular form of cyber crime. In a phishing attack, the perpetrators "fish" for financial data and passwords from consumers by posing as a legitimate business such as a bank or credit-card company. The "phisher" sends an e-mail asking the recipient to "update" or "confirm" vital information, often with the threat that an account or some other service will be discontinued if the information is not provided. Once the unsuspecting target enters the information, the phisher can use it to masquerade as the person or to extract funds from his or her bank or credit account.

The preferred method of phishing is through the use of **spam,** the unsolicited "junk e-mails" that flood virtual mailboxes with advertisements, solicitations, and other messages. Although 86 percent of the world's e-mail traffic still involves spam, filter systems are now able to block most unwanted e-mails.[13]

To get around these filters, phishers are increasingly using tactics that target small groups of recipients rather than blasting fake e-mails to millions of people at a time. Phishing scams affect not only e-mail but also other areas, such as text messaging and social networking sites. According to the security firm Proofpoint, phishing on social media sites increased 150 percent from 2015 to 2016.[14]

Another form of phishing, called *spear phishing*, can be difficult to detect because the messages seem to have come from co-workers, friends, or family members. Several years ago, a cybergang infiltrated the security systems of a number of banks worldwide by sending bank employees e-mails containing links to news clips, apparently sent by colleagues. When the employees clicked on the links, they inadvertently downloaded software onto their computers that allowed the cyber thieves to drain hundreds of millions of dollars from accounts in the affected banks.[15]

PIRATING INTELLECTUAL PROPERTY ONLINE

Most people think of wealth in terms of houses, land, cars, stocks, and bonds. Wealth, however, also includes **intellectual property,** which consists of the products that result from intellectual, creative processes. The government provides various forms of protection for intellectual

Phishing Sending an unsolicited e-mail that falsely claims to be from a legitimate organization in an attempt to acquire sensitive information from the recipient.

Spam Bulk e-mails, particularly of commercial advertising, sent in large quantities without the consent of the recipient.

Intellectual Property Property resulting from intellectual, creative processes.

property, such as copyrights and patents. These protections ensure that a person who writes a book or a song or creates a software program is financially rewarded if that product is sold in the marketplace.

Intellectual property such as books, films, music, and software is vulnerable to "piracy"—the unauthorized copying and use of the property. In the past, copying intellectual products was time consuming, and the quality of the pirated copies was clearly inferior.

In today's online world, however, things have changed. Simply clicking a mouse can now reproduce millions of unauthorized copies, and pirated duplicates of copyrighted works obtained via the Internet are often exactly the same as the original, or close to it. The Business Software Alliance estimates that 39 percent of all business software is pirated, costing software makers more than $52 billion in 2015.[16]

SpeedKingz/Shutterstock.com

Should states pass laws making cyberbullying a criminal offense? What might be some of the problems with such policies?

14-1d Cyber Violence

Cyber violence, our final category of cyber crime, focuses on the use of the Internet to cause harm. Although this form of cyber hostility may have financial consequences, those who engage in it are primarily interested in bringing about emotional harm, embarrassment, or shame.[17]

CYBERBULLYING As texting and social networking sites such as Snapchat and Instagram have become an integral part of youth culture, so, it seems, has *cyberbullying*. A twenty-first century update on traditional bullying, which we discussed in the preceding chapter, **cyberbullying** uses electronic means to cause social embarrassment or emotional harm. The practice has become even more prevalent in recent years with the advent of social networking apps such as Yik Yak that allow users to make cruel, rude, and sexually suggestive comments about their peers anonymously.

To many, cyberbullying can be even more harmful than "old school" bullying. Not only does the anonymity of cyberspace seem to embolden offenders, causing them to be more vicious than they would be in person, but also the hurtful information spreads quickly to a large audience.

"It's really horrifying the next day after the message has been sent around, and you're the laughingstock of the school," said one young victim. "You have no idea why or what's funny."[18] According to the Cyberbullying Research Center, about a quarter of American students aged twelve to seventeen had been the subject of "mean or hurtful comments online" in the thirty days before being surveyed.[19]

CYBERSTALKING In the opening of this chapter, we discussed "revenge porn," a form of cyberbullying that involves the nonconsensual publication online of explicit sexual images. Revenge porn is often a component of **cyberstalking**, which occurs when one person uses e-mail, text messages, or some other form of electronic communication to cause a victim to reasonably fear for her or his safety or the safety of her or his immediate family. According to the most recent federal data on the subject, about 850,000 Americans are targets of cyberstalking each year.[20]

Nearly all the states, as well as the federal government, have passed laws to combat this form of criminal behavior. Most of these statutes require that the offender pose a **true threat** to his or her victim—that is, that the victim can be said to reasonably fear for his or her safety.[21] In the absence of a true threat, the communication is protected by the First Amendment.

A U.S. appeals court applied this test in a 1997 case involving a University of Michigan student. That student,

Cyberbullying To bully electronically by sending repeated, hurtful messages via texting or the Internet

Cyberstalking The crime of stalking committed in cyberspace through the use of e-mail, text messages, or other forms of electronic communication.

True Threat An act of speech or expression that is not protected by the First Amendment because it is done with the intention of placing a specific victim or group of victims in fear of unlawful violence.

DISCRETION IN ACTION

Facebook Fantasy?

THE SITUATION After Anthony's wife, Tara, leaves him, taking their children with her, Anthony's online behavior becomes increasingly erratic. He begins posting violent rap lyrics on Facebook aimed at Tara, including: "If I only knew then what I know now . . . I would have smothered your ass with a pillow. Dumped your body in the back seat. Dropped you off in Toad Creek and made it look like a rape and murder." He also writes that he would like to see a Halloween costume of his wife's "head on a stick." In due course, Anthony is arrested for breaking a federal law that makes it a crime to transmit "any communication containing . . . any threat to injure the person of another."

THE LAW According to the United States Supreme Court's interpretation of the First Amendment, Anthony's Facebook posts can be considered a "true threat," and therefore a criminal act, only if they represent "a serious expression of an intent to commit an act of unlawful violence to a particular individual or group of individuals."

WHAT WOULD YOU DO? You are a juror at Anthony's trial. You hear him testify that his remarks were nothing more than a form of therapy to help "deal with the pain" of separation from his family. "I would never hurt my wife," he says. "I felt like I was being stalked," counters Tara during her testimony. "I felt extremely afraid for [my life] and my children's lives."

This case poses a difficult question: If a person makes a statement that one might reasonably take as a threat, but that was not intended by the speaker as a threat, is it a true threat? Your answer will help determine whether you vote to convict Anthony of breaking federal law.

To see how the United States Supreme Court ruled in this case, see Example 14.1 in Appendix A.

Abraham Alkhabaz, posted a graphic story online in which a woman with the same name as one of his classmates was raped and murdered. Alkhabaz was eventually arrested by federal agents and charged with communicating threats across state lines to injure another person.

The federal court overturned this arrest due to lack of evidence showing that the defendant would actually have carried out his violent fictional imaginings.[22] (See the feature *Discretion in Action—Facebook Fantasy?* to apply the true threat doctrine to a more recent case of possible online stalking and harassment.)

CYBERTERRORISM In the spring of 2016, approximately eight hundred members of the Arkansas Library Association (ALA) were surprised to learn that they had become international news. Supporters of the extremist terrorist organization ISIS had hacked the ALA's computer system and published the members' names, home addresses, and e-mail addresses on a "hit list" app. If the subjects of this action were concerned about being targeted by terrorists, it did not show. One library director called the hacking "vaguely amusing," adding, "Our credit card information didn't get stolen apparently, so we're glad for that."[23]

Homeland security experts worry that such relatively harmless incidents are a precursor to a much more serious **cyberattack** by a terrorist organization. Cyberattacks are designed to damage a nation's infrastructure, which includes its power companies, water treatment plants, airports, chemical plants, and oil refineries. In a worst-case scenario, a cyberattack could allow a terrorist organization to seize control of the federal air traffic control system, or shut down national power grids. "This is a much bigger threat over time than losing some credit cards to cyber criminals," said one security expert.[24]

One of the potential methods of carrying out such a large-scale cyberattack is a *distributed denial of service (DDoS)*. As part of a DDoS, hackers flood a targeted system with malware, much of it meaningless electronic "traffic," causing the system to crash and become inaccessible. Hackers in Iran, for example, are suspected to have launched DDoS attacks at a number of targets in the United States, including several major banks, a small dam in New York State, and a Las Vegas casino whose owner had been critical of the country's rulers.[25]

Cyberattack An attempt to damage or disrupt computer systems or electronic networks operated by computers.

14-1e Fighting Cyber Crime

During the 2013 holiday season, hackers used a malware program called Kaptoxa to steal credit- and debit-card data from at least 70 million customers of the retail giant Target. In response, the company hired private contractors to plug its security holes and erase the malware from its compromised systems.

Ideally, of course, corporations should have software already in place to prevent hacking operations, and most do. Businesses spend billions of dollars a year to *encrypt* their vital information, or encode it in such a way that only authorized parties have access to it. **Encryption** is seen as the best strategy for protecting the "Internet of things," whose vulnerabilities were discussed in this chapter's *CJ & Technology* feature.

Companies also hire outside experts to act as hackers and attempt to gain access to their systems, a practice known as "penetration testing." In 2016, the passenger-referral company Uber launched a "bug bounty" program that pays as much as $10,000 to anybody who can find security weaknesses in its mobile app.[26]

Even the most thorough private protection services often lag behind the ingenuity of the hacker community, however. In the Target attack, for example, the malware was programmed to constantly erase itself, making it practically impossible to detect. "The dynamics of the Internet and cyberspace are so fast that we have a hard time staying ahead of the adversary," admits former U.S. Secret Service agent Robert D. Rodriguez.[27]

THE "ZERO-DAYS" PROBLEM The Internet was designed to promote connectivity, not security. As more and more online threats to companies such as Target have developed, those businesses have had to respond with increasingly novel defenses. Facebook, for example, has constructed ThreatData, a defense system that monitors new worms, viruses, and malicious websites to create a constantly updated "blacklist" of blocked malware.

Still, it is virtually impossible to protect against "zero days," the industry term for new vulnerabilities that security software cannot detect and for which there are no existing defenses. The Internet security consulting firm Symantec uncovered an average of one new zero-day vulnerability per week in 2015.[28]

Clearly, private industry needs government help to fight off cyber criminals. With hundreds of millions of users in every corner of the globe transferring unimaginable amounts of information almost instantaneously, however, the Internet has proved resistant to government regulation. In addition, although a number of countries have tried to "control" the Internet, the U.S. government has generally adopted a hands-off attitude to better promote the free flow of ideas and encourage the growth of electronic commerce. Thus, in this country, cyberspace is largely unregulated, making efforts to fight cyber crime all the more difficult.

Encryption The translation of computer data into a secret code with the goal of protecting those data from unauthorized parties.

FEDERAL LAW ENFORCEMENT AND CYBER CRIME Aside from investigating reports of online harassment and child pornography in their jurisdictions, local police do not play a large role in combatting cyber crime. Simply put, most police departments and sheriffs' departments do not have the training or the resources to effectively manage cyber crime investigations.[29] Consequently, the federal government has traditionally taken the lead in law enforcement efforts against cyber crime.

The FBI has the primary responsibility for enforcing federal criminal statutes involving computer crime and leads the federal government's law enforcement efforts to combat cyber criminals. Since 2002, the Bureau has operated a Cyber Division dedicated to investigating computer-based crimes. The Cyber Division and its administrators coordinate the FBI's efforts in cyberspace, specifically its investigations into cyber terrorism and intellectual property theft. The division also has jurisdiction over the Innocent Images National Initiative (IINI), the agency's online child-pornography subdivision.

Additionally, through its Financial Crimes division, the Secret Service is heavily involved in combatting cyber crime. The Secret Service has three primary investigatory responsibilities in this area: (1) cyber fraud against financial institutions such as banks and credit unions, (2) access-device fraud, or hacking operations that target credit and debit cards, and (3) acts of fraud that target the federal government or the interests of the federal government.[30]

ETHICS CHALLENGE

As noted earlier in this section, child pornography is illegal, both online and in the real world. Pornography involving adults, however, is legal for adult consumption, and has a massive presence on the Internet. What might be some ethical problems with the easy availability of pornography online? What are the arguments for and against legislation that would make it more difficult to view pornography on the Internet?

CAREER PREP

Computer Forensic Specialist

Job Description:

- Investigate misbehavior on computer systems by collecting and analyzing computer-related evidence. Retrieve data that have been encrypted or electronically stored on a commercial or personal computer.
- Work for a law enforcement or homeland security agency to investigate crimes or terrorists' activities, or for a private company to protect commercial data and defend against worms, viruses, and other malware.

What Kind of Training Is Required?

- An extensive knowledge of computers, computer programming, and data retrieval is essential. A number of colleges, universities, and online educational organizations offer computer forensic courses that provide the skills necessary for this career.
- A complete understanding of the rules of evidence in criminal courts and the ability to establish a proper chain of custody for all evidence retrieved from targeted computer databases.

debra hughes, 2010/Used under license from Shutterstock.com

Annual Salary Range?

- $52,000–$85,000

GETTING LINKEDIN

Most of the postings on LinkedIn for forensic computer specialists have been posted by banks and other financial institutions. A internship offered by a bank in Medford, Massachusetts, for example, promises the opportunity to gain experience in the field of "incident response"—that is, security breaches and bank robberies.

14-2 HOW IMPORTANT IS PRIVACY IN THE AGE OF TERRORISM?

How far should a government go in hacking its own citizens for purposes of national security? That question was at the forefront of the national political conversation in March 2017, when WikiLeaks—an international nonprofit organization that publishes secret information—released nine thousand pages of documents describing the inner workings of the Central Intelligence Agency (CIA).

The leaked documents described dozens of sophisticated hacking techniques that the CIA has developed to, for example, compromise Skype conversations, Wi-Fi networks, and personal passwords. One program, codenamed Weeping Angel, purportedly allows CIA agents to use Samsung "smart" televisions as "bugs" to record nearby conversations, even when the television is turned off.[31]

The technological range of the CIA's spying capabilities may have come as a shock, but the agency's spying efforts should have been no surprise. Since the attacks of September 11, 2001, homeland security officials have placed paramount importance on tracking communications among suspected terrorists. To do so, the federal government has greatly enhanced the capabilities of law enforcement and intelligence agencies to collect and store information on these suspects.

At the same time, the federal government has angered many Americans, who feel that their privacy rights have been ignored or discarded for the sake of national security. "We need a government that protects our civil liberties and privacy rights and protects our families from evil terrorists," says Washington, D.C., lawyer Lanny Davis, succinctly summarizing an ongoing balancing act that goes to the heart of American ideals of fairness and justice. "We must have both."[32]

Jewel Samad/AFP/Getty Images

A white rose is placed on the name of one of the victims of the September 11, 2001, terrorist attacks at a memorial in New York City. **What strategies do you think the federal government should implement to prevent similar large-scale terrorist attacks in the future?**

14-2a National Security and Privacy

As has been noted several times in this textbook, our Constitution upholds the premise that Americans should not be subjected to the unreasonable use of government power. As we have also pointed out, reasonableness is a highly subjective concept, and Americans are often willing to give their government more leeway in times of national crisis.

When it comes to antiterrorism efforts and homeland security, this flexibility has manifested itself in the form of federal legislation that expands the government's ability to locate, observe, prosecute, and punish suspected terrorists. The first legislative step in this direction, however, took place decades before September 11, 2001, and was designed primarily to weaken the office of the presidency.

LO**14-3** Summarize the three federal laws that have been particularly influential on our nation's counterterrorism strategies.

FOREIGN SURVEILLANCE Until the 1970s, policies regarding governmental **surveillance,** or monitoring, of individuals or groups that posed national security threats to the United States were primarily the domain of the executive branch. That is, the president and his advisers decided whom the federal government would target for its spy operations. Following President Richard Nixon's abuse of this discretion to eavesdrop on political opponents during the 1974 presidential campaign, in 1978 Congress passed the Foreign Intelligence Surveillance Act (FISA).[33] This legislation provided a legal framework for the government's electronic monitoring of suspected criminals and national security threats.

Surveillance The close observation of a person or group by government agents, in particular to uncover evidence of criminal or terrorist activities.

Under FISA, federal agents are able to eavesdrop on the communications of foreign persons or foreign entities, without a court order, for up to a year, as long as the purpose of the surveillance is national security and not law enforcement. If this surveillance uncovers wrongdoing by an American citizen, the government has seventy hours to gain judicial authorization to continue to monitor the suspect's activities.[34]

If the target is a "foreign agent" operating within the United States, FISA requires permission from a special court to engage in surveillance. This court, known as the Foreign Intelligence Surveillance Court, or FISA Court, is made up of eleven federal judges assigned by the chief justice of the Supreme Court. The FISA warrant application must identify the target of the surveillance, the nature of the information sought, and the monitoring method. The government agency must also certify that the goal of the surveillance is to "obtain foreign intelligence information."[35]

MATERIAL SUPPORT Another crucial piece of counterterrorism legislation was passed in response to the 1995 truck bombing of the Alfred P. Murrah Federal Building in Oklahoma City, Oklahoma, which killed 168 people. The primary goal of this legislation, the

Antiterrorism and Effective Death Penalty Act (AEDPA), is to hamper terrorist organizations by cutting off their funding. The law prohibits persons from "knowingly providing *material support* or resources" to any group that the United States has designated a "foreign terrorist organization."[36]

Material support is defined very broadly in the legislation, covering funding, financial services, lodging, training, expert advice or assistance, communications equipment, transportation, and other physical assets.[37] Because it covers such a wide range of activities, the material support statute has frequently been the basis for charges against domestic defendants linked with the terrorist group ISIS. The "support" does not have to be substantial. In 2016, Washington, D.C., Metro Transit Officer Nick Young was charged with providing material support to ISIS in the form of $245 worth of Google Play gift cards.

FIGURE 14.3 THE PATRIOT ACT AND ELECTRONIC SURVEILLANCE

- **Section 201:** Enables government agents to wiretap the communications of any persons suspected of terrorism or the dissemination of chemical weapons.
- **Section 204:** Makes it easier for government agents to get a warrant to search stored e-mail communications held by Internet service providers (ISPs).
- **Section 206:** The "roving wiretap" provision removes the requirement that government agents specify the particular places or things to be searched when obtaining warrants for surveillance of suspected terrorists.
- **Section 210:** Gives government agents enhanced authority to access the duration and timing of phone calls, along with phone numbers and credit cards used to pay for cell phone service.
- **Section 213:** The "sneak and peek" provision removes the requirement that government agents give notice to a target when they have searched her or his property.*
- **Section 214:** Removes the requirement that government agents prove that the subject of a FISA search is actually the "agent of a foreign power."
- **Section 215:** The "business records" provision permits government agents to access "business records, medical records, educational records and library records" without showing probable cause of wrongdoing if the investigation is related to terrorist activities.

Under Title II of the Patriot Act, the sections listed here greatly expanded the ability of federal intelligence operatives and law enforcement agents to conduct electronic surveillance operations on suspected terrorists.

*In 2012, this rule was revised to require notice within thirty days of the search in most circumstances.

THE PATRIOT ACT Enacted six weeks after the September 11, 2001, terrorist attacks, the **Patriot Act**[38] greatly strengthened the ability of federal law enforcement agents to investigate and incarcerate terrorist suspects. At 342 pages, the Patriot Act covered numerous areas related to homeland security, including immigration law and border protection, grants to local police departments, and compensation for the victims of the September 11 attacks.

Here, we focus on the legislation's rules regarding surveillance, summarized in Figure 14.3. Critics of the Patriot Act have been especially concerned with Sections 213 and 215, which allow government agents to conduct searches and seizures without many of the Fourth Amendment protections discussed in Chapter 6.

Specifically, Section 215 provides the National Security Agency (NSA), a federal agency that focuses on foreign intelligence operations, with the authority to collect the telephone billing records of Americans who have made calls to other countries, as those records are considered reasonably "relevant" to the agency's counterterrorism investigations.[39]

Furthermore, the Patriot Act requires third parties such as telephone companies and Internet providers to turn over records of stored electronic communications to the federal government without notice to the persons who made those communications. Government agents do not need judicial permission to issue **national security letters,** as such requests are called. The agents only need to show, after the fact, that the targeted communications are relevant to a terrorism investigation.[40] National security letters can be used to collect:

1. Credit information from banks and loan companies.
2. Telephone and Internet data, including names, call times, physical addresses, and e-mail addresses.
3. Financial records, such as money transfers and bank accounts.
4. Travel records held by "any commercial entity."[41]

As we will soon see, widespread use of such

Material Support The act of helping a terrorist organization by engaging in any of a wide range of activities, including providing financial support, training, and expert advice or assistance.

Patriot Act Legislation that has greatly expanded the ability of government agents to monitor and apprehend suspected terrorists.

National Security Letters Legal notices that compel the disclosure of customer records held by banks, telephone companies, Internet service providers, and other companies to the federal government.

surveillance tactics has led to a great deal of controversy over the federal government's information-gathering practices.

14-2b Mass Surveillance

Following a series of controversies concerning whether the NSA should be allowed to intercept telephone and e-mail communications of suspected terrorists, in 2008 Congress passed an amended version of FISA. This legislative action did not, however, place greater limits on the NSA, which had amassed a vast database by secretly keeping track of millions of phone calls made by Americans who were not under suspicion of any wrongdoing. Instead, it essentially legalized government surveillance tactics that had previously been illegal by giving the NSA more freedom to act without oversight by the FISA court.[42]

Rena Schild/Shutterstock.com

Do you agree with these protesters that the federal government should not be allowed to collect information about the telephone habits of U.S. citizens without first obtaining permission from a court? Why or why not?

FOURTH AMENDMENT AND HOMELAND SECURITY The problem with the original FISA, according to some observers, was that it required a lengthy review process before the FISA court would issue a warrant allowing government agents to monitor a terrorist suspect. In an environment where individuals can rapidly change their e-mail addresses and modes of Internet communication, or use multiple cell phone numbers, this procedure was, in the critics' view, too slow and cumbersome for effective intelligence gathering.[43] The NSA, FBI, and other government agencies argued that they needed more freedom to collect massive amounts of information quickly without judicial oversight.

This need, of course, must be tempered by the Fourth Amendment, which broadly requires that the government have probable cause of wrongdoing before intruding on a citizen's reasonable expectation of privacy. The amended FISA's authorization of large-scale warrantless electronic eavesdropping, in which hundreds of millions of phone and Internet records have been collected and stored in databases, created concerns that the federal government aimed to "write off the Fourth Amendment as technologically obsolete."[44]

METADATA COLLECTION In 2013, an NSA contractor named Edward Snowden revealed that, under the revised FISA, the NSA had monitored the cell phone and Internet activity of approximately 113 million Americans without probable cause or a warrant from the FISA court. Through a program known as Prism, the NSA gained access to the information by sending national security letters to several major telephone companies and ISPs, including Apple, Facebook, Google, Microsoft, Skype, Verizon, Yahoo, and YouTube.[45] The providers then allowed the NSA to access and store the information.

"Red Flagging" Agents of the federal government had not been listening to actual phone conversations or reading hundreds of millions of e-mails. Rather, they had been collecting *metadata*, which reveal such things as the time and duration of the communication and the sender and recipient.

The metadata collection—justified, according to the FISA court, under Section 215 of the Patriot Act (see Figure 14.3)[46]—had been designed to retroactively determine communications patterns that might raise a "red flag" of terrorist activity. If the NSA was able to uncover a pattern of communication that suggested such activity, it would apply for a FISA warrant and undertake further investigations of the individuals involved. Using this process, the FISA court was issuing about 1,800 orders each year for domestic surveillance.[47]

Revising the Patriot Act In 2015, following a firestorm of criticism in response to Snowden's revelations about "government spying," Congress ended the NSA's bulk collection of private phone data. Now, government agencies such as the NSA must petition the FISA Court for access to the metadata, which are stored by companies such as AT&T and Verizon.[48] In theory, a communications company could refuse to cooperate with an NSA

CAREER PREP

Customs and Border Protection Agent

Job Description:

- Ensure that laws are observed when goods and people enter the United States. Work at ports of entry and along the U.S. borders with Canada and Mexico to prevent smuggling and the entrance of illegal aliens.
- Conduct surveillance along the border using electronic sensors, infrared scopes, low-light television systems, and aircraft.

Jim Parkin/ShutterStock.com

What Kind of Training Is Required?

- Be fluent in Spanish or be able to learn the Spanish language.
- Pass a thorough background investigation, medical examination, fitness test, and drug test.

Annual Salary Range?

- $40,000–$110,000

SOCIAL MEDIA CAREER TIP

Consider setting up personal and career-oriented Facebook pages or Twitter accounts and keeping your posts separated. Remember, though, that material on your "personal" page or account may still be seen by others outside your network.

request for metadata, subject to the court's review. In practice, it remains to be seen how this partnership will impact federal antiterrorism investigations.

EXPECTATIONS OF PRIVACY According to a 2016 report by the news service *Reuters*, Yahoo, in compliance with a FISA Court order, recently created a special software program that scanned all incoming e-mail traffic for a particular digital signature provided by the FBI. Yahoo voluntarily agreed to turn over any e-mails containing this digital signature—presumably associated with a foreign terrorist organization—to U.S. intelligence officials.[49]

As Yahoo's cooperation with the FBI shows, in spite of revisions to the Patriot Act, the federal government still has access to large amounts of communications data. Thus, criticism of government metadata collection continues. Critics point out that while such tactics may contribute to a small number of homeland security investigations, there is no evidence that it has ever disrupted any major terrorist organizations or operations.[50] This limited impact, they argue, does not justify the significant *invasion of privacy* involved.

Privacy Precedents As you may recall from Chapter 6, an individual usually has no expectation of privacy with regard to information voluntarily disclosed to third parties. So, for example, a person does not have an expectation of privacy for something written on the outside of an envelope given to the U.S. Postal Service or garbage left on the curb for collection.[51] As a result, government agents can search and seize that information without a warrant.

Several federal appeals courts have held that defendants have no reasonable expectation of privacy over information "voluntarily" provided to a telephone company or an ISP. In 2013, a federal judge refused to grant a new trial to defendants convicted of providing material support in the form of funds to an African terrorist organization. Federal agents admitted that they had initially become interested in the defendants' behavior because of telephone records contained in the NSA database.

The judge ruled that the agents did not need a warrant to obtain such information from the telephone company because individuals have "no legitimate expectation of privacy" in phone call data.[52]

In general, these judicial decisions rely on the precedent set by the United States Supreme Court in its *Smith v. Maryland* (1979)[53] decision. That case involved the police's warrantless seizure of phone numbers dialed from the home of a robbery suspect. The Court ruled that the defendant had voluntarily turned over the phone numbers to a third party—the phone company—for billing purposes and therefore had no reasonable expectation of privacy in the matter.

Privacy and Technology One federal judge has gone against the tide with regard to metadata and expectations of privacy. In 2013, U.S. District Judge Richard Leon of the District of Columbia found that the NSA's phone-data collection program "almost certainly" violated the Fourth Amendment.[54] Judge Leon argued that the Supreme Court's *Maryland* case involved a "one-time" search of phone calls emanating from the home of a single criminal suspect. In contrast, the NSA metadata program was a "daily, all-encompassing indiscriminate dump" of information from "the phones of people who are not suspected of any wrongdoing."[55]

Judge Leon's opinion raises an interesting question: Have our reasonable expectations of privacy changed because of technological innovations? The judge referred to the Supreme Court's 2012 decision that it is unconstitutional for the police to use a GPS device to track a suspect's movement without a warrant, offering it as proof that such expectations have changed.[56] He noted that justices who made the *Maryland* ruling in 1979 could not "have ever imagined how the citizens of [today] would interact with their phones."[57]

FOREIGN SURVEILLANCE TARGETS Foreign citizens do not enjoy the same protections under the Fourth Amendment as U.S. citizens. This distinction is important to the operation of a separate NSA data-collection program—mandated under the revised FISA of 2008—that allows the government to monitor non-U.S. citizens believed to be located in another country. Section 702 of the FISA Amendment Act permits eavesdropping (not merely metadata collection) without a warrant of foreign persons to obtain information related to the following:

1. National security matters, such as details of an "actual or potential attack" or "other grave hostile acts [by a] foreign power or agent of a foreign power."
2. Foreign "intelligence activities."
3. "The conduct of the foreign affairs of the United States."[58]

In the event that the target comes to the United States, surveillance without a warrant can continue for seventy-two hours if a lapse would pose a threat of death or bodily harm to U.S. citizens. After this time period, a warrant must be obtained to continue the surveillance on American soil.[59] The broad language of this amended law allowed the NSA to target nearly 90,000 foreign people and organizations for surveillance in 2013.[60]

The law also permits warrantless eavesdropping on any person who communicates with the target of foreign surveillance, even if that person is an American citizen. According to a detailed analysis of the NSA's global surveillance practices, the agency intercepts communications of nine incidental "bystanders" for every single "legally targeted" foreigner.[61]

This loophole has allowed the NSA to gather highly personal information, such as baby pictures, medical records, and flirtatious Webcam chats, involving innocent persons, including Americans.[62] At the same time, it provides a valuable tool to uncover terrorist operations on U.S. soil, a growing concern that we will examine in the following section.

14-2c National Security and Speech

In the context of homeland security, former FBI director James Comey was careful to distinguish the "mouth runners"—those who merely talk about their anti-American or violent beliefs—from potential terrorists. "This is a great country with lots of traditions of protecting mouth-running," said Comey. "We should continue that. But those who are inclined to cross the line, I've got to focus on them."[63]

How do our federal intelligence and law enforcement agencies tell the "mouth runners," protected by the American tradition of free speech, from those who pose an actual threat? This question arises every time a "lone wolf," seemingly appearing out of nowhere and acting alone, carries out an act of violence on U.S. soil. Concern about such "small-scale attacks" by homegrown terrorists is "what keeps me up at night," says U.S. representative Michael McCaul, a Republican from Texas who chairs the House Homeland Security Committee.[64]

HIDDEN THREATS As a rule, individuals who intend to offer material support to terrorist organizations do not enjoy First Amendment protections. That is, they cannot claim to be harmless "mouth runners." Rather, by statute, many of the activities that constitute material support are considered true threats, as defined earlier in the chapter.[65]

Sometimes, the true threat is legally obvious. Several years ago, for example, six Bosnian immigrants living in

Illinois, Missouri, and New York were indicted for providing material support to terrorist organizations in Syria and Iraq after sending $8,000 worth of U.S. military uniforms, technical gear, and weapons to those countries. It would be difficult, if not impossible, to claim that such behavior was a protected form of free speech.

The vast majority of terrorist sympathizers online, however, behave like political supporters or sports fans, showing their enthusiasm by posting comments and videos to share with friends. Furthermore, being an ISIS advocate is not against the law. Neither is expressing hatred for the United States. Consequently, counterterrorism investigators are faced with the nearly impossible task of differentiating between those terrorism suspects who are fantasizing in public and those who are planning actual violence.

FOLLOWING "KNOWN WOLVES" In 2013, the FBI opened a preliminary investigation against Omar Mateen, who had been boasting of ties to the terrorist groups Hezbollah and Al Qaeda at his workplace in St. Lucie County, Florida. A year-long investigation followed, during which FBI agents monitored Mateen's movements and interviewed him twice. Finding no evidence to suggest that he was anything more than a "mouth runner," the FBI terminated the surveillance.

Two years later, early on the morning of June 12, 2016, Mateen fatally shot forty-nine people at the Pulse nightclub in Orlando before being killed by local police. (Recall that "lone wolves" are terrorists who are presumed to act alone, rather than as part of a terrorist group. Lone wolves like Mateen are sometimes called "known wolves," because authorities have reason to know that they post a threat.)

This example highlights two difficulties for America's homeland security efforts. First, "known wolves" such as Mateen are highly unpredictable. Second, thousands of people in the United States express support for ISIS and other terrorist groups, and law enforcement authorities do not have the resources to physically track each one. "We don't expect to eradicate crime, but we've made a political promise that we're going to stop every act of terrorism," said one observer. "It's ridiculous."[66]

14-3 WHAT IS THE DEBATE OVER GUN CONTROL?

According to the Bureau of Alcohol, Tobacco, Firearms and Explosives (ATF), 9 million firearms were manufactured in the United States in 2014, up from 5.4 million in 2010.[67] Based on the ATF's data, the *Washington Post* estimates that there are approximately 357 million firearms in the United States, not counting illegally owned guns and weapons on military bases.[68]

Supporters of stricter *gun control* would like to see this number significantly reduced. **Gun control** refers to the policies that federal and state governments implement to limit access to firearms in this country. Opponents of gun control counter that someone who is planning to commit a crime with a gun is probably going to obtain that firearm illegally. Consequently, stricter gun control "prevents only law abiding citizens from owning handguns."[69]

14-3a Regulating Gun Ownership

The Second Amendment to the U.S. Constitution states, "A well regulated Militia, being necessary to the security of a free State, the right of the people to keep and bear Arms, shall not be infringed." Because this language is somewhat archaic and vague, the United States Supreme Court has attempted to clarify the amendment's modern meaning. In two separate rulings, the Court stated that the Second Amendment provides individuals with a constitutional right to bear arms and that this right must be recognized at all levels of government—federal, state, and local.[70]

BACKGROUND CHECKS In both of its Second Amendment cases, the Supreme Court emphasized that, to promote public safety, the government could continue to prohibit certain persons—such as criminals and mentally ill individuals—from legally purchasing firearms. The primary method for doing so involves **background checks** of individuals who purchase firearms from federally licensed gun dealers. The mechanics of background checks are regulated by the Brady Handgun Violence Prevention Act, enacted in 1993.[71]

LO14-4 Explain how background checks, in theory, protect the public from firearm-related violence.

Known as the Brady Bill, this legislation requires a person wishing to purchase a gun from a licensed firearms dealer to complete an application. The application process includes a background check by a law enforcement agency, usually the FBI. The applicant can be prohibited from purchasing a firearm if his or her

Gun Control Efforts by a government to regulate or control the sale of guns.

Background Check An investigation of a person's history to determine whether that person should be, for example, allowed to legally purchase a firearm.

record contains one of a number of "red flags," including a previous felony conviction, evidence of illegal drug addiction, or wrongdoing associated with domestic violence.[72] From the passage of the Brady Bill until the end of 2014, about 2.8 million of 180 million applications for firearms purchases were denied because of federal and state background checks.[73]

CAREER TIP A number of states require individuals to undergo firearm training in a classroom and on a target range before purchasing a handgun. Experts called *certified handgun instructors* administer such training to those individuals who want a gun permit.

MENTAL HEALTH ISSUES Any person who has been involuntarily committed to a "mental institution" or "adjudicated as a mental defective" is barred from purchasing or possessing firearms. A person may be designated "mentally defective" when a court or other legal entity determines one of the following:

1. The person is a danger to herself or himself or others.
2. The person lacks the mental capacity to manage her or his own affairs.
3. The person has been found insane or incompetent to stand trial by a criminal or military court.[74]

In 2007, a student with mental health issues shot and killed thirty-two people on the Virginia Tech campus in Blacksburg. As a result, most states began providing the federal government with the names of residents who had been involuntary committed for psychiatric treatment. About 6,500 firearm purchase applications in this country are denied each year because of the applicant's mental health.[75]

14-3b Recent Legislative Efforts

Because of federal inaction, it has largely been left to the states to determine the direction of gun control in this country. Following a 2012 mass shooting at an elementary school in Newtown, Connecticut, thirteen states passed measures tightening the background check requirements for firearm purchases within their borders.

Seven of these states require such checks for private gun sales, which federal law does not. In addition, sixteen states made it more difficult for mentally ill individuals to buy firearms, and two dozen states passed legislation limiting the ability of domestic abusers to own guns.[76]

At the same time, in 2016 Texas became the fortieth state to permit "open carry"—the popular term for allowing people to carry firearms in plain sight.[77] That same year, Idaho, Mississippi, Oklahoma, and West Virginia enacted legislation that lessened restrictions on gun ownership and use.[78] The United States Supreme Court has declined to hear any new cases involving federal, state, or local firearms regulations since 2008, meaning that the fate of gun control will continue to be decided by the voters and their elected representatives.

14-4 WHAT IS WHITE-COLLAR CRIME?

Two New York men take $81 million from investors as part of a fraudulent scheme to buy and resell tickets for events such as the Broadway musical *Hamilton*. The scouting director for the St. Louis Cardinals illegally accesses the player personnel files of a rival professional baseball team. Operators at legitimate call centers in India pose as tax collectors from the Internal Revenue Service and other authority figures to extort $300 million from about 15,000 victims in the United States. A Santa Fe, New Mexico, luxury-home builder fails to complete projects for which he has already been paid.

These cases represent a variety of criminal behavior with different motives, different methods, and different victims. Yet they all fall into the category of *white-collar crime*, an umbrella term for wrongdoing marked by deceit and scandal rather than violence. As we mentioned in Chapter 1, white-collar crime has a broad impact on the global economy, costing American businesses alone hundreds of billions of dollars in losses each year. Despite its global and national importance, however, white-collar crime has consistently challenged a criminal justice system that has difficulty defining the problem, much less effectively combatting it.

14-4a Defining White-Collar Crime

White-collar crime is not an official category of criminal behavior measured by the federal government in the Uniform Crime Report. Rather, the term covers a broad range of illegal acts involving "lying, cheating, and stealing," according to the FBI's website on the subject.[79] To give a more technical definition, white-collar crimes are financial activities characterized by deceit and concealment that do not involve physical force or violence. Figure 14.4 lists and describes some common types of white-collar crime.

FIGURE 14.4 WHITE-COLLAR CRIMES

Embezzlement
Embezzlement is a form of employee fraud in which an individual uses his or her position within an organization to *embezzle*, or steal, the employer's funds, property, or other assets. Pilferage is a less serious form of employee fraud in which the individual steals items from the workplace.

Tax Evasion
Tax evasion occurs when taxpayers underreport (or do not report) their taxable income or otherwise purposely attempt to evade a tax liability.

iStock.com/Skodonnell

iStock.com/Oztasbc

Credit-Card Fraud
Credit-card fraud involves obtaining credit-card numbers through a variety of schemes (such as stealing them from the Internet) and using the numbers for personal gain.

Mail and Wire Fraud
This umbrella term covers all schemes that involve the use of mail, radio, television, the Internet, or a telephone to intentionally deceive in a business environment.

Securities Fraud
Securities fraud covers illegal activity in the stock market. Stockbrokers who steal funds from their clients are guilty of securities fraud, as are those who engage in *insider trading*, which involves buying or selling securities on the basis of information that has not been made available to the public.

Bribery
Also known as *influence peddling*, bribery occurs in the business world when somebody within a company or government sells influence, power, or information to a person outside the company or government who can benefit. A county official, for example, could give a construction company a lucrative county contract to build a new jail. In return, the construction company would give some of the proceeds, known as a *kickback*, to the official.

Consumer Fraud
This term covers a wide variety of activities designed to defraud consumers, from selling counterfeit art to offering "free" items, such as electronic devices or vacations, that include a number of hidden charges.

Insurance Fraud
Insurance fraud involves making false claims in order to collect insurance payments. Faking an injury in order to receive payments from a workers' compensation program, for example, is a form of insurance fraud.

iStock.com/DNY59

DIFFERENT TECHNIQUES To differentiate white-collar crime from "regular" crime, criminologists Michael L. Benson of the University of Cincinnati and Sally S. Simpson of the University of Maryland focus on technique. For example, in an ordinary burglary, a criminal uses physical means, such as picking a lock, to get somewhere he or she should not be—someone else's home—to do something that is clearly illegal. Furthermore, the victim is a specific identifiable individual—the homeowner. In contrast, white-collar criminals usually (1) have legal access to the place where the crime occurs; (2) are spatially separated from the victim, who is often unknown; and (3) behave in a manner that is at least superficially legitimate.[80]

LO14-5 Indicate some of the ways that white-collar crime is different from violent or property crime.

Benson and Simpson also identify three main techniques used by white-collar criminals to carry out their crimes:[81]

1. *Deception*. White-collar crime almost always involves a party who deceives and a party who is deceived. The nation's federal Medicare system, which provides health insurance for those sixty-five years of age and older, is a frequent target of deceptive practices. For example, over a period of fourteen years, the federal government allegedly paid $1 billion for unnecessary or even harmful treatments to Medicare patients at various health-care facilities in South Florida. The operator of those facilities, Philip Esformes, was charged with a host of crimes, including bribing state regulators to help cover up his schemes.[82]
2. *Abuse of trust*. A white-collar criminal often operates in a position of trust and misuses that trust for personal benefit. In 2017, for example, a Rhode Island financial adviser was sentenced to eighty-four months in prison for using $21 million of his investors' funds to cover up his own business losses and stealing an additional $2.5 million to purchase a waterfront home.
3. *Concealment and conspiracy*. To continue their illegal activities, white-collar criminals need to conceal those activities. In *odometer fraud*, for example, an automobile dealership "rolls back" the odometers of used cars so that a higher price can be charged for the vehicles. As soon as the fraud is discovered, the scheme can no longer succeed.

VICTIMS OF WHITE-COLLAR CRIME As the examples above show, sometimes the victim of a white-collar crime is obvious. A dishonest financial adviser is stealing directly from his or her clients, and odometer fraud denies consumers the actual value of their purchased automobiles. But who was victimized in the fraudulent Medicare scheme? In that instance, the "victims" were the U.S. taxpayers, who collectively had to cover the cost of the treatments. Such health-care scams defraud U.S. taxpayers out of at least $82 billion each year.[83] Often, white-collar crime does not target individuals but rather large groups or even abstract concepts such as "society" or "the environment."

14-4b Regulating and Policing White-Collar Crime

For legal purposes, a corporation can be treated as a person capable of forming the intent necessary to commit a crime. Thus, in March 2017, the German automobile company Volkswagen pleaded guilty to violating the Clean Air Act and and paid a $4.3 billion fine to the federal government. Volkswagen officials had knowingly equipped about 600,000 cars with software designed to evade American emissions tests.

Public health researchers at Harvard University and the Massachusetts Institute of Technology estimated that fifty-nine Americans will die prematurely because of the excess pollution caused by Volkswagen's deceitfulness.[84] The damage that resulted from Volkswagen's illegal activity is an example of *corporate violence*. In contrast to assaults committed by individual people, **corporate violence** results from policies or actions undertaken by a corporation. In the United States, parallel regulatory and criminal systems have evolved to prevent corporate violence and other forms of white-collar crime.

CAREER TIP Eighteen state governments completely or partially control the sale of alcoholic beverages. These states rely on *alcoholic beverage control officers* to enforce regulations on beer, wine, and distilled spirits within their borders.

Corporate Violence Physical harm to individuals or the environment that occurs as the result of corporate policies or decision making.

Regulation A governmental order or rule having the force of law that is usually implemented by an administrative agency.

Compliance The state of operating in accordance with governmental standards.

THE REGULATORY JUSTICE SYSTEM Although most white-collar crimes cause harm, these harms are not necessarily covered by criminal statutes. Indeed, more often they are covered by *administrative* laws, which we first encountered in Chapter 3. Such laws make up the backbone of the U.S. regulatory system, through which the government attempts to control the actions of individuals, corporations, and other institutions. The goal of **regulation** is not prevention or punishment as much as **compliance,** or the following of regulatory guidelines.[85]

For example, in 2012, the appliance manufacturer Gree sold thousands of defective humidifiers that were prone to overheating and catching fire. Incidents involving this malfunction caused nearly $4.5 million in property damage, yet Gree did not recall the products until September 2013. Furthermore, the company failed to report the defect to the U.S. Consumer Product Safety Commission (CPSC) as required by federal law, and its employees lied to CPSC staff members during the investigation that followed. In 2016, Gree agreed to pay $15.45 million in penalties stemming from its lack of compliance with federal product safety regulations.

The CPSC—which protects the public from unreasonable risks of injury or death associated with consumer products—is one of the federal administrative agencies whose compliance oversight brings them into contact with white-collar crime. Other important federal regulatory agencies with regard to white-collar crime include:

1. The *Environmental Protection Agency (EPA),* which regulates air quality, water quality, and toxic waste. The EPA was involved in the federal government's response to Volkswagen's emissions-testing evasion scheme, described earlier.
2. The *Food and Drug Administration (FDA),* which protects public health by regulating food products and a wide variety of drugs and medical practices.
3. The *Occupational Safety and Health Administration (OSHA),* which enforces workplace health and safety standards.
4. The *Securities and Exchange Commission (SEC),* which ensures that financial markets such as the New York Stock Exchange operate in a fair manner.

In 2015, the Federal Communications Commission voted to regulate the Internet as a *public utility* (a company that provides a public service, such as electricity or telephone communications). This move may eventually impact federal law enforcement efforts to combat the various forms of cyber crime we discussed earlier in the chapter.

LAW ENFORCEMENT AND WHITE-COLLAR CRIME In general, when officials at a regulatory agency find that criminal prosecution is needed to punish a particular violation, they will refer the matter to the U.S. Department of Justice. Either through such referrals or at their own discretion, federal officials prosecute white-collar crime using the investigatory powers of several different federal law enforcement agencies.

The FBI has become the lead agency when it comes to white-collar crime, particularly in response to financial scandals. The U.S. Postal Inspection Service is also active in such investigations, as fraudulent activities often involve the U.S. mail. In addition, the Internal Revenue Service's Criminal Investigative Division has jurisdiction over a wide variety of white-collar crimes, including tax fraud, and operates perhaps the most effective white-collar crime lab in the country.[86]

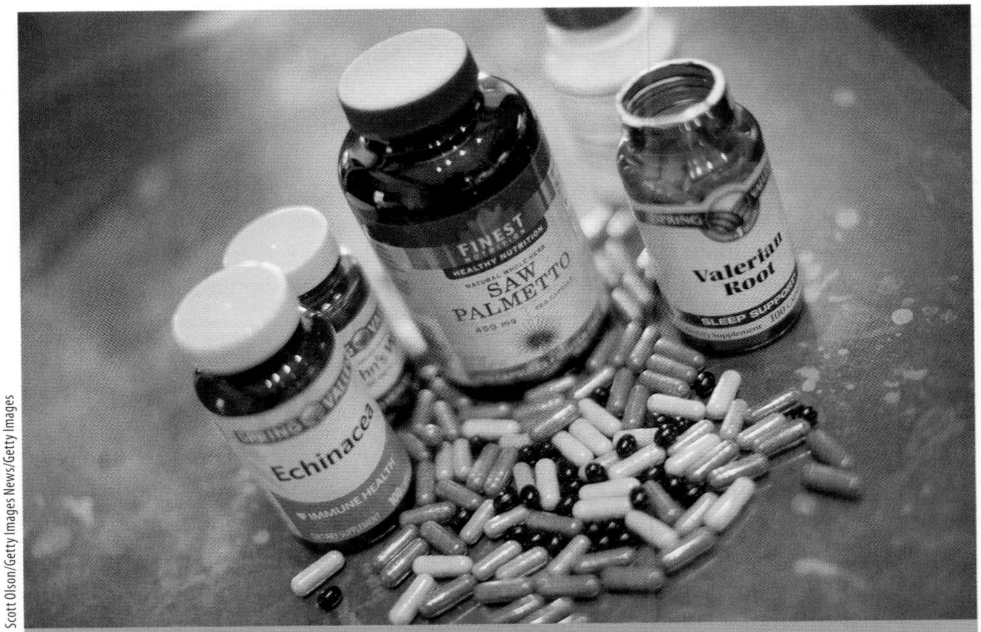

Scott Olson/Getty Images News/Getty Images

Suppose a drug manufacturer mislabels the ingredients of a particular supplement, and, as a result, a person who takes the supplement dies. **Has the drug manufacturer committed a white-collar crime? Does it matter if the mislabeling was accidental? Explain your answers.**

ETHICS CHALLENGE

Several years ago, General Motors Co. (GM) admitted criminal wrongdoing related to flawed ignition switches in its automobiles that have been linked to at least 124 deaths. GM employees were aware of the defect for nearly a decade before addressing the problem. Although the company paid a $900 million fine, no individual employees of GM were criminally charged in this matter. Do you think fines, civil lawsuits, and the financial ramifications of a damaged reputation are enough to ensure that corporations behave ethically? Or do you agree with the mother of one GM crash victim who said that "jail time" for executives is the only "serious deterrent" against corporate wrongdoing? Explain your answer.

STUDY TOOLS 14

LOCATED IN TEXTBOOK

- ☐ Rip out the Chapter Review Card.
- ☐ Review with the Chapter Quiz following this chapter.

LOCATED AT WWW.CENGAGEBRAIN.COM

- ☐ Review key terms flash cards.
- ☐ Read the chapter on all your favorite devices.
- ☐ Complete an Exam to test your knowledge.
- ☐ Check out Visual Summaries and You Decide activities to explore chapter concepts.

Quiz

1. Hackers sometimes employ ________________________, or networks of hijacked computers, to carry out various illegal online activities.

2. Web thieves have opportunities to practice ________________________theft because of the large amount of personal financial information that is stored on the Internet.

3. ________________________ ________________________such as films and music is vulnerable to being "pirated" by unauthorized users on the Internet.

4. Someone who makes a "true threat" that places a victim in fear of unlawful violence is not always protected by the First Amendment's guarantee of freedom of ________________________.

5. A person who contributes funds to a "foreign terrorist organization" runs the risk of being prosecuted for the federal crime of providing ________________________ ________________________ under federal law.

6. The controversy over whether federal agents need a warrant before collecting metadata concerning phone and Internet activity hinges on a person's ________________________ ________________________ of privacy when using her or his telephone or going online.

7. The Brady Bill requires a person who wants to purchase a firearm from a licensed dealer to undergo a ________________________ ________________________ to determine whether he or she is eligible for gun ownership.

8. The United States Supreme Court has ruled that a government body can prohibit gun ownership for those with a criminal record or a history of ________________________ ________________________.

9. White-collar criminals often use deception, concealment, and the abuse of ________________________ to perpetrate theft without violence.

10. Regulatory agencies require ________________________ with various guidelines to protect individuals from corporate violence.

Answers to the Chapter 14 Quiz can be found in the Answers section in the back of the book.

ENDNOTES

1

1. James Queally, "The Fine Line for Police between a 'Hate Crime' and a 'Hate Incident.'" *www.latimes.com. Los Angeles Times*: January 6, 2017, Web.

2. *Virginia v. Black*, 536 U.S. 343 (2003). Many United States Supreme Court cases will be cited in this book, and it is important to understand these citations. *Virginia v. Black* refers to the parties in the case that the Court is reviewing. "U.S." is the abbreviation for *United States Reports*, the official publication of United States Supreme Court decisions. "536" refers to the volume of the United States Reports in which the case appears, and "343" is the page number. The citation ends with the year the case was decided, in parentheses. Most, though not all, Supreme Court case citations in this book will follow this formula.

3. *Elonis v. United States*, 575 U.S. __________ (2015).

4. Ellen Barry, "Indian Cinemas Must Play the National Anthem, Supreme Court Rules." *www.nytimes.com. New York Times*: November 30, 2016, Web.

5. Herman Bianchi, *Justice as Sanctuary: Toward a New System of Crime Control* (Bloomington: Indiana University Press, 1994), 72.

6. "Justice for All?" *www.wholeads.us*. The Reflective Democracy Campaign: July 2015, Web.

7. Vindu Goel and Nicole Perlroth, "For Sale on the Dark Web: Yahoo Users' Stolen Records," *New York Times* (December 16, 2016), B1.

8. David E. Sanger and Nicole Perlroth, "Encrypted Messaging Apps Face New Scrutiny over Possible Role in Attacks," *New York Times* (November 17, 2015), A12.

9. Megan Kurlychek, "What Is My Left Hand Doing? The Need for Unifying Purpose and Policy in the Criminal Justice System," *Criminology & Public Policy* (November 2011), 909.

10. National Highway Traffic Safety Administration, *Early Estimate of Motor Vehicle Traffic Fatalities for the First Half (Jan–Jun) of 2016* (Washington, D.C.: U.S. Department of Transportation, October 2016), 1.

11. "Smartphone Use While Driving Grows beyond Texting to Social Media, Web Surfing, Selfies, Video Chatting." *www.about.att.com*. AT&T Newsroom: May 19, 2015, Web.

12. "State Laws." *www.distraction.gov*. Distraction.gov: visited January 3, 2017, Web.

13. Jay Winsten, quoted in Matt Richtel, "On Your Phone at the Wheel? Watch Out for the Textalyzer," *New York Times* (April 28, 2016), A1.

14. *Ibid.*

15. *Gonzales v. Oregon*, 546 U.S. 243 (2006).

16. Alison Smith and Richard M. Thompson II, "Criminal Offenses Enacted from 2008–2013," *Congressional Research Service* (June 23, 2014).

17. DEA Public Affairs, "DEA Announces Actions Related to Marijuana and Industrial Hemp." *www.dea.gov*. Drug Enforcement Administration: August 11, 2016, Web.

18. 545 U.S. 1, 15 (2005).

19. John Ingold, "*Obama: Feds Won't Arrest Marijuana Users in Colorado, Washington*." *www.denverpost.com. Denver Post:* December 14, 2012, Web.

20. James Q. Wilson, "What to Do about Crime: Blaming Crime on Root Causes," *Vital Speeches* (April 1, 1995), 373.

21. Herbert Packer, *The Limits of the Criminal Sanction* (Stanford, Calif.: Stanford University Press, 1968), 154–173.

22. *Ibid.*

23. Daniel Givelber, "Meaningless Acquittals, Meaningful Convictions: Do We Reliably Acquit the Innocent?" *Rutgers Law Review* 49 (Summer 1997), 1317.

24. Deborah L. Rhode, "Why Is Adultery Still a Crime?" *www.latimes.com. Los Angeles Times*: May 2, 2016, Web.

25. O.C.G.A. Section 40-6-241 (2010).

26. Alan Blinder, "A Cheeseburger, a Suburban Traffic Stop and a Ticket for Eating While Driving," *New York Times* (January 21, 2015), A10.

27. George P. Fletcher, "Some Unwise Reflections about Discretion," *Law & Contemporary Problems* (Autumn 1984), 279.

28. *Every 25 Seconds: The Human Toll of Criminalizing Drug Use in the United States* (New York: Human Rights Watch, October 2016), 6.

29. Antonin Scalia, "The Rule of Law as a Law of Rules," *University of Chicago Law Review* 56 (1989), 1178–1180.

30. John Kleinig, *Ethics and Criminal Justice: An Introduction* (New York: Cambridge University Press, 2008), 33–35.

31. Packer, *op. cit.*, 154–173.

32. Givelber, *op. cit.*, 1317.

33. Federal Bureau of Investigation, *Crime in the United States*, 2015, Table 1. *www.ucr.fbi.gov*. U.S. Department of Justice: 2016, Web.

34. Matt Zapotosky, Adam Goldman, and Scott Higham, "Police in Dallas: 'He Wanted to Kill White People, Especially White Officers.'" *www.washingtonpost.com. Washington Post:* July 8, 2016, Web.

35. Quoted in "Paralysed by YouTube," *The Economist* (October 31, 2015), 28.

36. Bureau of Justice Statistics, *Police Use of Nonfatal Force, 2002–11* (Washington, D.C.: U.S. Department of Justice, November 2015), 1.

37. Quoted in Pervaiz Shallwani, Ana Campoy, and Valerie Bauerlein, "Prevalence of Video Puts Police under the Lens." *www.wsj.com*. Wall Street Journal: April 10, 2015, Web.

38. Quoted in Michael Wilson and Michael Schwartz, "Officers Confront Dual Role: Villain and Victim," *New York Times* (July 10, 2016), A1.

39. Charles Kurzman and David Schanzer, *Law Enforcement Assessment of the Violent Extremism Threats* (Durham, NC: Triangle Center on Terrorism and Homeland Security, June 25, 2015), 3.

40. Quoted in Robin Wright, "After the Islamic State," *New Yorker* (December 12, 2016), 31.

41. Quoted in Scott Shane, Matt Apuzzo, and Eric Schmitt, "Online Embrace from ISIS, a Few Clicks Away," *New York Times* (December 9, 2015), A1.

42. Quoted in Philip Shishkin and Patrick O'Connor, "San Bernardino Shooting Shows How U.S. Terror Defenses Are Tested." *www.wsj.com. Wall Street Journal:* December 6, 2015, Web.

43. Bureau of Justice Statistics, *Prisoners in 2015* (Washington, D.C.: U.S. Department of Justice, December 2016), 1.

44. *Ibid.*, Table 1, page 3.

45. Bureau of Justice Statistics, *Correctional Populations in the United States, 2015* (Washington, D.C.: U.S. Department of Justice, December 2016), Table 1.

46. "One Nation, Behind Bars," *The Economist* (August 17, 2013), 12.

47. *Justice Reinvestment in Alabama: Analysis and Policy Framework* (Washington, D.C.: Bureau of Justice Assistance, March 2015), 1–2.

48. Quoted in Erica Goode, "U.S. Prison Populations Decline Reflecting New Approach to Crime," *New York Times* (July 26, 2013), A11.

49. "Office of Research: Population Reports." *www.cdcr.ca.gov*. California Department of Corrections and Rehabilitation: visited January 5, 2017, Web.

50. "Death Row Inmates by State and Size of Death Row by Year," *www.deathpenaltyinfo.org*. Death Penalty Information Center: visited January 6, 2017, Web.

51. *The Death Penalty in 2016: Year End Report* (Washington, D.C.: Death Penalty Information Center, 2016), 3.

52. "National Statistics on Death Penalty and Race," *www.deathpenaltyinfo.org*. Death Penalty Information Center: December 9, 2016, Web.

53. *Prisoners in 2015*, *op. cit.*, Table 3, page 6.

54. "Inmate Ethnicity." *www.bop.gov*. Federal Bureau of Prisons: November 26, 2016, Web.

2

1. Quoted in N. R. Kleinfield, et al., "Killers Fit a Profile, but So Do Many Others," *New York Times* (October 4, 2015), A1.

2. Scott E. Wolfe and David C. Pyrooz, "Rolling Back Prices and Raising Crime Rates? The Walmart Effect on Crime in the United States," *British Journal of Criminology* (March 2014), 199–221.

3. Matthew Larson and Gary Sweeten, "Breaking Up Is Hard to Do: Romantic Dissolution, Offending, and Substance Abuse during the Transition to Adulthood," *Criminology* (August 2012), 605–635.

4. James Q. Wilson and Richard J. Herrnstein, *Crime and Human Nature: The Definitive Study of the Causes of Crime* (New York: Simon & Schuster, 1985), 44.

5. David C. Rowe, *Biology and Crime* (Los Angeles: Roxbury, 2002), 2.

6. L. E. Kreuz and R. M. Rose, "Assessment of Aggressive Behavior and Plasma Testosterone in Young Criminal Population," *Psychosomatic Medicine* 34 (1972), 321–332.

7. H. Persky, K. Smith, and G. Basu, "Relation of Psychological Measures of Aggression and Hostility to Testosterone Production in Men," *Psychosomatic Medicine 33* (1971), 265, 276.

8. Cindy-Lee Dennis and Simone N. Vigod, "The Relationship between Postpartum Depression, Domestic Violence, Childhood Violence, and Substance Use: Epidemiologic Study of a Large Community Sample," *Violence against Women* (April 2013), 503–517.

9. Quoted in Pam Belluck, "'Thinking of Ways to Harm Her': New Findings on Timing and Range of Maternal Mental Illness," *New York Times* (June 16, 2014), A1.

10. Bureau of Justice Statistics, *Health Problems of Prison and Jail Inmates* (Washington, D.C.: U.S. Department of Justice, September 2006), 1.

11. Kleinfield, et al., *op. cit.*

12. Jeffrey W. Swanson, et al., "Mental Illness and Reduction of Gun Violence and Suicide: Bringing Epidemiologic Research to Policy," *Annals of Epidemiology* (May 2015), 366–376.

13. Jonathan M. Metzl and Kenneth T. MacLeish, "Mental Illness, Mass Shootings, and the Politics of American Firearms," *American Journal of Public Health* (February 2015), 240–249.

14. Philip Zimbardo, "Pathology of Imprisonment," *Society* (April 1972), 4–8.

15. Jean Marie McGloin and Kyle J. Thomas, "Incentive for Collective Deviance: Group Size and Changes in Perceived Risk, Cost, and Reward," *Criminology* (August 2016), 459–486.

16. Eric Chyn, "Moved to Opportunity: The Long-Run Effect of Public Housing Demolition on Labor Market Outcomes of Children." *www.ericchyn.com*. Eric Chyn, Department of Economics, University of Virginia: October 12, 2016, Web.

17. Clifford R. Shaw and Henry D. McKay, *Report on the Causes of Crime, Vol. 2: Social Factors in Juvenile Delinquency* (Washington, D.C.: National Commission on Law Observance and Enforcement, 1931).

18. Emile Durkheim, *The Rules of Sociological Method*, trans. Sarah A. Solovay and John H. Mueller (New York: Free Press, 1964).

19. Robert K. Merton, *Social Theory and Social Structure* (New York: Free Press, 1957). See the chapter on "Social Structure and *Anomie*."

20. Richard Quinney, *The Social Reality of Crime* (Boston: Little, Brown, 1970).

21. Philip G. Zimbardo, "The Human Choice: Individuation, Reason, and Order versus Deindividuation, Impulse, and Chaos," in *Nebraska Symposium on Motivation*, ed. William J. Arnold and David Levie (Lincoln, Neb.: University of Nebraska Press, 1969), 287–293.

22. Edwin H. Sutherland, *Criminology*, 4th ed. (Philadelphia: Lippincott, 1947).

23. Michael E. Roettger and Raymond Swisher, "Associations of Fathers' History of Incarceration with Sons' Delinquency and Arrest among Black, White, and Hispanic Males in the United States," *Criminology* (November 2011), 1109–1147.

24. Lindsay A. Robertson, Helena M. McAnally, and Robert J. Hancox, "Childhood and Adolescent Television Viewing and Antisocial Behavior in Early Adulthood," *Pediatrics* (March 2013), 439–446.

25. *Brown v. Entertainment Merchants Association* (EMA), 564 U.S. 786 (2011).

26. Travis Hirschi, *Causes of Delinquency* (Berkeley: University of California Press, 1969).

27. James Q. Wilson and George L. Kelling, "Broken Windows," *Atlantic Monthly* (March 1982), 29.

28. Jeremy Staff, et al., "Early Life Risks, Antisocial Tendencies, and Preteen Delinquency," *Criminology* (November 2015), 677–701.

29. Michael R. Gottfredson and Travis Hirschi, *A General Theory of Crime* (Stanford, Calif.: Stanford University Press, 1990).

30. *Ibid.*, 90.

31. *Ibid.*

32. Terrie Moffitt, "Adolescent-Limited and Life-Course-Persistent Antisocial Behavior: A Developmental Taxonomy," *Psychological Review 100* (1993), 679–680.

33. *Ibid.*, 674.

34. Howard S. Becker, *Outsiders: Studies in the Sociology of Deviance* (New York: Free Press, 1963).

35. David G. Myers, *Psychology*, 7th ed. (New York: Worth Publishers, 2004), 576–577.

36. National Survey on Drug Use and Health, "The NSDUH Report." *www.archive.samhsa*. Substance Abuse and Mental Health Services Administration, March 27, 2008: Web.

37. Bureau of Justice Statistics, *Fact Sheet: Drug Related Crimes* (Washington, D.C.: U.S. Department of Justice, September 1994), 1.

38. *ADAM II: 2013 Annual Report* (Washington, D.C.: Office of National Drug Policy, January 2014), xi.

39. Bureau of Justice Statistics, "Alcohol and Crime: Data from 2002 to 2008." *www.bjs. gov*. Bureau of Justice Statistics: September 3, 2010, Web.

40. Richard Friedman, "Why Can't Doctors Identify Killers?" *New York Times* (May 28, 2014), A21.

41. James A. Inciardi, *The War on Drugs: Heroin, Cocaine, and Public Policy* (Palo Alto, Calif.: Mayfield, 1986), 148.

42. "The Black Market." *www.havocscope.com. Havocscope:* visited January 10, 2017, Web.

43. *Crime in the United States, 2015, op. cit.*, "Persons Arrested," and Table 29.

44. Mark J. Pletcher, et al., "Association between Marijuana Exposure and Pulmonary Function over 20 Years," *JAMA* (January 2012), 173–181.

45. "Legalized Marijuana," *The Week* (November 25, 2016), 11.

46. Federal Bureau of Investigation, *Crime in the United States, 2015. www.ucr.fbi.gov*. U.S. Department of Justice: 2016, Web.

47. *Ibid.*, "About Crime in the U.S."

48. *Ibid.*, Table 1.

49. *Ibid.*, Expanded Homicide Data Table 10.

50. *Ibid.*, Table 1.

51. *Ibid.*, "Offense Definitions."

52. *Ibid.*, Table 29.

53. Marcus Felson, *Crime in Everyday Life* (Thousand Oaks, Calif.: Pine Forge Press, 1994), 3.

54. "FBI Releases 2015 Crime Statistics from the National Incident-Based Reporting System, Encourages Transition." *www.ucr.fbi.gov*. Federal Bureau of Investigation: December 12, 2016.

55. "National Incident-Based Reporting System: Tables with All Offenses." *www.ucr.fbi.gov*. Federal Bureau of Investigation, 2016: Web.

56. Victor E. Kappeler, Mark Blumberg, and Gary W. Potter, *The Mythology of Crime and Criminal Justice*, 2d ed. (Prospect Heights, Ill.: Waveland Press, *1993*), 31.

57. David Lisak and Paul M. Miller, "Repeat Rape and Multiple Offending among Undetected Rapists," *Violence & Victims* (2002), 73–84.

58. Lois H. Harrington, et al., *President's Task Force on Victims of Crime: Final Report* (Washington, D.C.: U.S. Department of Justice, December 1982), viii.

59. 18 U.S.C. Section 3771 (2006).

60. Susan Herman, *Parallel Justice for Victims of Crime* (Washington, D.C.: The National Center for Victims of Crime, 2010), 45–48.

61. Chris E. Kubrin, et al., "Does Fringe Banking Exacerbate Neighborhood Crime Rates?" *Criminology and Public Policy* (May 2011), 437–464.

62. Larry Cohen and Marcus Felson, "Social Change and Crime Rate Trends: A Routine Activity Approach," *American Sociological Review* (1979), 588–608.

63. Kubrin, et al., *op. cit.*, 441.

64. Cohen and Felson, *op. cit.*

65. Stefano Comino, Giovanni Mastrobuoni, and Antonio Nicolo, *Silence of the Innocents: Illegal Immigrants Underreporting of Crime and Their Victimization* (Bonn, Germany: IZA, October 2016).

66. Marre Lammers, et al., "Biting Once, Twice: The Influence of Prior on Subsequent Crime Location Choice,"*Criminology* (August 2015), 309–329.

67. R. Barry Ruback, Valerie A. Clark, and Cody Warner, "Why Are Crime Victims at Risk of Being Victimized Again? Substance Use, Depression, and Offending as Mediators of the Victimization-Revictimization Link," *Journal of Interpersonal Violence* (January 2014), 157–185.

68. Monica Davey, "Chicago Police Try to Predict Who May Shoot or Be Shot," *New York Times* (May 24, 2016), A11.

69. Quoted in Kevin Johnson, "Criminals Target Each Other, Trend Shows," *USA Today* (August 31, 2007), 1A.

70. Franklin E. Zimring, *The Great American Crime Decline* (New York: Oxford University Press, 2007), 45–72.

71. James Q. Wilson, "Concluding Essay in Crime," in James Q. Wilson and Joan Petersilia, eds., *Crime* (San Francisco: Institute for Contemporary Studies Press, 1995), 507.

72. John DiIulio, *How to Stop the Coming Crime Wave* (New York: Manhattan Institute, 1996), 4.

73. James Fox, *Trends in Juvenile Violence* (Boston: Northeastern University Press, 1996), 1.

74. Zimring, *op. cit.*, 6.

75. *Ibid.*, 197–198.

76. Federal Bureau of Investigation, *Crime in the United States*, 2010, Table 1. *www.ucr.fbi.gov*. U.S. Department of Justice, 2011, Web; and *Crime in the United States, 2015, op. cit.*, Table 1.

77. *Crime in the United States, 2015, op. cit.*, Table 1.

78. Scott Calvert and Pervaiz Shibani, "Homicide Rose in Most Big Cities This Year." *www.wsj.com. Wall Street Journal:* December 22, 2016, Web.

79. *Criminal Victimization, 2015, op. cit.*, 4.

80. Timothy Williams, "Whether Crime Is Up or Down Depends on Data Being Used," *New York Times* (September 28, 2016), A12.

81. Quoted in *ibid*.

82. Zusha Elinson and Pervaiz Shibani, "Cities Grapple with Rising Murder Rates." *www.wsj.com. WallStreetJournal*: March 12, 2016, Web.

83. *Crime in the United States, 2015, op. cit.*, Expanded Homicide Data Table 3.

84. Michael Planty and Jennifer L. Truman, *Firearm Violence, 1993–2011* (Washington, D.C: U.S. Department of Justice, May 2013), 5.

85. Justin Glawe, "America's Mass Shooting Capital Is Chicago." *www.thedailybeast.com. The Daily Beast*: October 8, 2015, Web.

86. *Crime in the United States, 2015, op. cit.*, Expanded Homicide Data Table 6.

87. Keith Humphreys, "Pot Legalization Hasn't Done Anything to Shrink the Racial Gap in Drug Arrest." *www.washingtonpost.com. Washington Post*: March 21, 2016, Web.

88. Julie Furdella and Charles Puzzanchera, *Delinquency Cases in Juvenile Court, 2013* (Washington, D.C.: Office of Juvenile Justice and Delinquency Prevention, October 2015), 2.

89. Ruth D. Peterson, "The Central Place of Race in Crime and Justice—The American Society of Criminology's 2011 Sutherland Address," *Criminology* (May 2012), 303–327.

90. Patricia Y. Warren, "Inequality by Design: The Connection between Race, Crime, Victimization, and Social Policy," *Criminology & Public Policy* (November 2010), 715.

91. Eric A. Stewart, Ronald L. Simons, and Rand D. Donger, "Assessing Neighborhood and Social Psychological Influence on Childhood Violence in an African American Sample," *Criminology* (November 2002), 801–829.

92. William Alex Pridemore, "A Methodological Addition to the Cross-National Empirical Literature on Social Structure and Homicide: A First Test of the Poverty-Homicide Thesis," *Criminology* (February 2008), 133.

93. Andrew Sum, Ishwar Khatiwada, and Joseph McLaughlin, *The Consequences of Dropping Out of High School* (Boston: Center for Labor Market Studies, October 2009), 10.

94. *Crime in the United States, 2015, op. cit.*, Expanded Homicide Data Table 6.

95. Bureau of Justice Statistics, *Correctional Populations in the United States, 2015* (Washington, D.C.: U.S. Department of Justice, December 2016), Appendix table 4, page 17; and *Crime in the United States, 2015, op. cit.*, Table 33.

96. Federal Bureau of Investigation, *Crime in the United States, 2000* (Washington, D.C.: U.S. Department of Justice, 2001), Table 33, page 221; and *Crime in the United States, 2015, op. cit.*, Table 33.

97. Bureau of Justice Statistics, *Prisoners in 2015* (Washington, D.C.: U.S. Department of Justice, December 2016), Table 1, page 3.

98. Jennifer Schwartz and Bryan D. Rookey, "The Narrowing Gender Gap in Arrests: Assessing Competing Explanations Using Self Report, Traffic Fatality, and Official Data on Drunk Driving, 1980–2004," *Criminology* (August 2008), 637–638.

99. Quoted in Barry Yoeman, "Violent Tendencies: Crime by Women Has Skyrocketed in Recent Years," *Chicago Tribune* (March 15, 2000), 3.

100. Elizabeth Swavola, Kristine Riley, and Ram Subramanian, *Overlooked: Women and Jails in an Era of Reform* (New York: Vera Institute of Justice, 2016), 23–24.

101. Schwarz and Rookey, *op. cit.*, 637–671.

102. Meda Chesney-Lind, "Patriarchy, Prisons, and Jails: A Critical Look at Trends in Women's Incarceration," *Prison Journal* (Spring/Summer 1991), 57.

103. *Criminal Victimization, 2015, op. cit.*, Table 7, page 9.

104. Erika Harrell, *Violent Victimization Committed by Strangers, 1993–2010* (Washington, D.C.: U.S. Department of Justice, December 2012), 2.

105. *Intimate Partner Violence in the United States* (Atlanta, Ga.: National Center for Injury Prevention and Control, February 2014), 1–2.

106. "Domestic Violence National Statistics." *www.ncadv.org*. National Coalition against Domestic Violence: visited January 15, 2017, Web.

107. Eve S. Buzawa, "Victims of Domestic Violence," in Robert C. Davis, Arthur Lurigio, and Susan Herman, eds., *Victims of Crime*, 4th ed. (Los Angeles: Sage, 2013), 36–37.

108. Shannan Catalano, *Stalking Victims in the United States–Revised* (Washington, D.C.: U.S. Department of Justice, September 2012), 1, 5.

3

1. Alison Smith and Richard M. Thompson II, "Criminal Offenses Enacted from 2008–2013," *Congressional Research Service* (June 23, 2014).

2. Erik Eckholm, "Legal Conflicts on Medical Marijuana Ensnare Hundreds as Courts Debate a New Provision," *New York Times* (April 9, 2015), A14.

3. Quoted in "Judge: Federal Law Trumps Montana's Medical Pot Law," *Associated Press* (January 23, 2012).

4. *Texas v. Johnson,* 491 U.S. 397 (1989).

5. Anita Hofschneider, "Federal Judge Strikes Down Maui County's GMO Moratorium." *www.civilbeat.org. Honolulu Civil Beat*: June 30, 2015, Web.

6. "Conagra Subsidiary Sentenced in Connection with Outbreak of Salmonella Poisoning Related to Peanut Butter." *www. fda.gov*. U.S. Food and Drug Administration: December 13, 2016, Web.

7. 478 U.S. 186 (1986)

8. 539 U.S. 558, 578 (2003).

9. Joel Feinberg, *The Moral Limits of the Criminal Law: Harm to Others* (New York: Oxford University Press, 1984), 221-232.

10. Henry M. Hart Jr., "The Aims of the Criminal Law," *Law & Contemporary Problems 23* (1958), 405-406.

11. John L. Diamond, "The Myth of Morality and Fault in Criminal Law Doctrine," *American Criminal Law Review 34* (Fall 1996), 111.

12. Kentucky Statutes Section 437.060; and New Hampshire Revised Statutes Section 207:61.

13. "Idaho Senate Bill 1332." *www.legiscan.com. LegiScan*: March 19, 2014, Web.

14. Lawrence M. Friedman, *Crime and Punishments in American History* (New York: Basic Books, 1993), 10.

15. Federal Criminal Rules Handbook, Section 2.1 (West 2008).

16. 625 Illinois Compiled Statutes Annotated Section 5/16–104 (West 2002).

17. Johannes Andenaes, "The Moral or Educative Influence of Criminal Law," *Journal of Social Issues* 27 (Spring 1971), 17, 26.

18. Thomas A. Mullen, "Rule without Reason: Requiring Independent Proof of the Corpus Delicti as a Condition of Admitting Extrajudicial Confession," *University of San Francisco Law Review 27* (1993), 385.

19. *Hawkins v. State,* 219 Ind. 116, 129, 37 N.E.2d 79 (1941).

20. David C. Biggs, " 'The Good Samaritan Is Packing': An Overview of the Broadened Duty to Aid Your Fellowman, with the Modern Desire to Possess Concealed Weapons," *University of Dayton Law Review 22* (Winter 1997), 225.

21. Le Trinh, "In Which States Do I Have a Duty to Help?" *www.blogs.findlaw.com*. FindLaw: May 20, 2015, Web.

22. Model Penal Code Section 2.02.

23. Model Penal Code Section 2.02(c).

24. "Strict Liability." *www.law.cornell.edu*. Legal Information Institute: visited January 20, 2017, Web.

25. *United States v. Dotterweich,* 320 U.S. 277 (1943).

26. Quoted in Clarence Walker, "The New War on Drug Dealers: Charging Them with Murder When Their Customers Die of Overdose." *www.alternet.org*. Alternet: May 31, 2015, Web.

27. *State v. Stiffler,* 763 P.2d 308, 311 (Idaho Ct.App. 1988).

28. *State v. Harrison,* 425 A.2d 111 (1979).

29. Richard G. Singer and John Q. LaFond, *Criminal Law: Examples and Explanations* (New York: Aspen Law & Business, 1997), 322.

30. *State v. Linscott,* 520 A.2d 1067 (1987).

31. *Morissette v. United States,* 342 U.S. 246, 251–252 (1952).

32. Federal Bank Robbery Act, 18 U.S.C.A. Section 2113.

33. *In re Winship,* 397 U.S. 358, 364, 368–369 (1970).

34. Federal Bureau of Investigation, *Hate Crime Statistics, 2015,* Table 1. *www.ucr.fbi.gov*. U.S. Department of Justice: 2016, Web.

35. *United States v. Jiminez Recio,* 537 U.S. 270 (2003).

36. Paul H. Robinson, *Criminal Law Defenses* (St. Paul, Minn.: West, 2008), Section 173, Ch. 5Bl.

37. *M'Naghten's Case,* 10 Cl.&F. 200, Eng.Rep. 718 (1843). Note that the name is also spelled M'Naughten and McNaughten.

38. Model Penal Code Section 401 (1952).

39. Joshua Dressler, *Cases and Materials on Criminal Law*, 2d ed. (St. Paul, Minn.: West Group, 1999), 599.

40. Danny Cevallos, "Don't Rely on Insanity Defense," *www.cnn.com*. CNN: July 17, 2015, Web.

41. Lawrence P. Tiffany and Mary Tiffany, "Nosologic Objections to the Criminal Defense of Pathological Intoxication: What Do the Doubters Doubt?" *International Journal of Law and Psychiatry* 13 (1990), 49.

42. Paul Walsh, "Rare Defense Wins Dismissal of Child Assault Case, but Jailed Falcon Heights Mom Lost Home, Job." *www.startribune.com. Star Tribune*: July 20, 2015, Web.

43. 518 U.S. 37 (1996).

44. Quoted in Gary Fields and John R. Emshwiller, "As Criminal Laws Proliferate, More Are Ensnared." *www.wsj.com. Wall Street Journal*: July 23, 2011, Web.

45. *Lambert v. California,* 335 U.S. 225 (1957).

46. Federal Bureau of Investigation, *Crime in the United States, 2015,* Expanded Homicide Tables 14 and 15. *www.ucr.fbi.gov*. U.S. Department of Justice: 2016, Web.

47. Craig L. Carr, "Duress and Criminal Responsibility," *Law and Philosophy 10* (1990), 161.

48. Arnold N. Enker, "In Supporting the Distinction between Justification and Excuse," *Texas Tech Law Review 42* (2009), 277.

49. *United States v. May,* 727 F.2d 764 (1984).

50. *People v. Murillo,* 587 N.E.2d 1199, 1204 (Ill. App.Ct. 1992).

51. Florida Statutes Section 776.03 (2005).

52. *Ibid.*

53. Michael Bloomberg, quoted in "A Lethal Right to Self-Defense," *The Week* (May 4, 2012), 13.

54. Ray Downs, "'Medical Necessity' Defense in Marijuana Cases Still a Battle in Florida, but More Victories Possible." *www.browardpalmbeach.com. Broward/Palm Beach New Times*: March 18, 2015, Web.

55. 287 U.S. 435 (1932).

56. Kenneth M. Lord, "Entrapment and Due Process: Moving toward a Dual System of Defenses," *Florida State University Law Review* 25 (Spring 1998), 463.

57. Henry J. Abraham, *Freedom and the Court: Civil Liberties in the United States*, 7th ed. (New York: Oxford University Press, 1998), 38-41.

58. Emily Yoffe, "A Campus Rape Ruling, Reversed." *www.slate.com. Slate*: September 15, 2015, Web.

59. *Skinner v. Oklahoma*, 316 U.S. 535, 546–547 (1942).

4

1. Quoted in Andrew Welsh-Huggins, "Fast-Acting Ohio State Officer Praised for Killing Attacker." *www.bigstory.ap.com*. Associated Press: November 28, 2016, Web.

2. Egon Bittner, *The Functions of Police in a Modern Society*, Public Health Service Publication No. 2059 (Chevy Chase, Md.: National Institute of Mental Health, 1970), 38–44.

3. Carl Klockars, "The Rhetoric of Community Policing," in *Community Policing: Rhetoric or Reality*, eds. Jack Greene and Stephen Mastrofski (New York: Praeger Publishers, 1991), 244.

4. Jack R. Greene and Carl B. Klockars, "What Do Police Do?" in *Thinking about Police*, 2d ed., ed. Carl B. Klockars and Stephen D. Mastrofski (New York: McGraw-Hill, 1991), 273–284.

5. Federal Bureau of Investigation, *Crime in the United States, 2015*, Table 29. *www.ucr.fbi.gov*. U.S. Department of Justice: 2016, Web.

6. Reprinted in *The Police Chief* (January 1990), 18.

7. Howard Sheppard, "Police Statewide Reverse over 600 Opioid Overdoses with Naloxone." *www.fox43.com. Fox43 News*: March 1, 2016, Web.

8. Libor Jany, "Minneapolis Police to Try Buddy System on Mental Health Calls." *www.startribune.com. Minneapolis Star Tribune*: September 6, 2016, Web.

9. Jerome H. Skolnick, "Police: The New Professionals," *New Society* (September 5, 1986), 9–11.

10. Quoted in Nancy Ritter, ed., "LAPD Chief Bratton Speaks Out: What's Wrong with Criminal Justice Research—and How to Make It Right," *National Institute of Justice Journal* 257 (2007), 29.

11. Gary Kleck and J. C. Barnes, "Do More Police Lead to More Crime Deterrence?" *Crime & Delinquency* (August 2014), 716–738.

12. Klockars, *op. cit.*, 250.

13. James Q. Wilson, *Varieties of Police Behavior: The Management of Law and Order in Eight Communities* (Cambridge, Mass.: Harvard University Press, 1968).

14. Craig D. Uchida and Marc L. Swatt, "Operation LASER and the Effectiveness of Hotspot Patrol: A Panel Analysis," *Police Quarterly* (September 2013), 287–304.

15. Quoted in Joel Rubin, "Stopping Crime before It Starts," *Los Angeles Times* (August 21, 2010), A17.

16. Quoted in Kimberly Kindy, "Creating Guardians, Calming Warriors." *www.washingtonpost.com. Washington Post*: December 10, 2015, Web.

17. Quoted in Mitch Smith and Timothy Williams, "'Bulletproof Warrior' Course Brings Scrutiny in Minnesota," *New York Times* (July 15, 2016), A17.

18. "Cops or Soldiers?" *The Economist* (March 22, 2014), 27.

19. Quoted in Kindy, *op. cit*.

20. Associated Press, "Militarized Police Forces Come Under Congressional Scrutiny" (September 9, 2014).

21. Matt Apuzzo and Eric Lichtblau, "After F.B.I.'s Inquiry, a Focus on What Else Could Be Done," *New York Times* (June 15, 2016), A1.

22. Bureau of Justice Statistics, *Local Police Departments, 2013: Equipment and Technology* (Washington, D.C.: U.S. Department of Justice, July 2015), 6.

23. James H. Chenoweth, "Situational Tests: A New Attempt at Assessing Police Candidates," *Journal of Criminal Law, Criminology and Police Science* 52 (1961), 232.

24. Yossef S. Ben-Porath et al., "Assessing the Psychological Suitability of Candidates for Law Enforcement Positions," *The Police Chief* (August 2011), 64–70.

25. Quoted in *How Are Innovations in Technology Transforming Policing?* (Washington, D.C.: Police Executive Research Forum, January 2012), 2.

26. Bureau of Justice Statistics, *Local Police Departments, 2013: Personnel, Policies, and Practices* (Washington, D.C.: U.S. Department of Justice, May 2015), 7.

27. *Ibid.*, Table 7, page 7.

28. D. P. Hinkle, "College Degree: An Impractical Prerequisite for Police Work," *Law and Order* (July 1991), 105.

29. *Local Police Departments, 2013: Personnel, Policies, and Practices, op. cit.*, 7.

30. Bureau of Justice Statistics, *State and Local Law Enforcement Training Academies* (Washington, D.C.: U.S. Department of Justice, July 2016), 1.

31. National Advisory Commission on Civil Disorder, *Report* (Washington, D.C.: U.S. Government Printing Office, 1968), Chapter 11.

32. *Local Police Departments, 2013: Personnel, Policies, and Practices, op. cit.*, Table 4, page 4.

33. Kevin Johnson, "Women Move into Law Enforcement's Highest Ranks." *www.usatoday.com. USA Today*: December 2, 2015, Web.

34. Gene L. Scaramella, Steven M. Cox, and William P. McCamey, *Introduction to Policing* (Thousand Oaks, Calif.: Sage Publications, 2011), 318.

35. Kenneth J. Novak, Robert A. Brown, and James Frank, *Women on Patrol: An Analysis of Differences in Officer Arrest Behavior* (Bingley, United Kingdom: Emerald Group Publishing Ltd., 2006), 21–27.

36. Quoted in Robin N. Haarr and Merry Morash, "The Effect of Rank on Police Women Coping with Discrimination and Harassment," *Police Quarterly* (December 2013), 403.

37. Quoted in *Talk of the Nation*, "What Changes as Women Rise through Law Enforcement's Ranks." *www.npr.org*. National Public Radio: April 2, 2013, Web.

38. Katherine Stuart van Wormer and Clemens Bartollas, *Women and the Criminal Justice System*, 3d ed. (Upper Saddle River, N.J.: Pearson Education, 2011), 318–319.

39. Quoted in Teresa Lynn Wertsch, "Walking the Thin Blue Line: Policewomen and Tokenism Today," *Women and Criminal Justice* (1998), 35–36.

40. Quoted in Kimberly A. Lonsway, Rebecca Paynich, and Jennifer N. Hall, "Sexual Harassment in Law Enforcement: Incidence, Impact, and Perception," *Police Quarterly* (June 2013), 196.

41. *Local Police Departments, 2013: Personnel, Policies, and Practices*, Figure 5, page 5.

42. *State and Local Law Enforcement Training Academies, op. cit.*, 1.

43. David Alan Sklansky, "Not Your Father's Police Department: Making Sense of the New Demographics of Law Enforcement," *Journal of Criminal Law and Criminology* (Spring 2006), 1209–1243.

44. Quoted in Libor Jany, "Minneapolis' Black Police Officers Walk a Cultural Tightrope." *www.startribune.com. Minneapolis Star Tribune:* March 5, 2016, Web.

45. John S. Dempsey and Linda S. Forst, *An Introduction to Policing*, 8th ed. (Boston: Cengage Learning, 2016), 196.

46. *Wygant v. Jackson Board of Education*, 476 U.S. 314 (1986).

47. Bureau of Justice Statistics, *Census of State and Local Law Enforcement Agencies, 2008* (Washington, D.C.: U.S. Department of Justice, July 2011), 1; and Bureau of Justice Statistics, *Federal Law Enforcement Officers, 2008* (Washington, D.C.: U.S. Department of Justice, June 2012), 1.

48. *Local Police Departments, 2013: Personnel, Policies, and Practices, op. cit.*, Table 3, page 3.

49. *Ibid.*, Table 2, page 3.

50. Bureau of Justice Statistics, *Sheriffs' Office Personnel, 1993–2013* (Washington, D.C.: U.S. Department of Justice, June 2016), Table 2, page 3.

51. Bureau of Justice Statistics, *Sheriffs' Offices, 2003* (Washington, D.C.: U.S. Department of Justice, May 2006), 15–18.

52. Bureau of Justice Statistics, *Sheriffs' Departments, 1997* (Washington, D.C.: U.S. Department of Justice, February 2000), 14.

53. *Budget-in-Brief: Fiscal Year 2017* (Washington, D.C.: U.S. Department of Homeland Security, 2016), 9.

54. "Sector Profile-Fiscal Year 2016 (October 1st through Sept. 30th)." *www.cbp.gov*. United States Border Patrol: 2016, Web.

55. "FY 2016 ICE Immigration Removals." *www.ice.gov*. U.S. Immigrations and Customs Enforcement: visited January 22, 2017, Web."

56. John Hudson, "FBI Drops Law Enforcement as 'Primary' Mission." *www.foreignpolicy.com. Foreign Policy*: January 5, 2014, Web.

57. Uniform Controlled Substances Act (1994), Section 201(h).

58. "Fact Sheet." *www.usmarshals.gov*. United States Marshals Service: March 11, 2016, Web.

59. "Statistical Data for Three Fiscal Years—Criminal Investigation (CI)." *www.irs.gov*. Internal Revenue Service: October 12, 2016, Web.

60. Michael Moran, "Security Market Growth Continues." *www.sm.asisonline.org*. ASIS International: May 15, 2015, Web.

61. Bureau of Justice Statistics, *Local Police Departments, 2007* (Washington, D.C.: U.S. Department of Justice, December 2010), Table 8, page 13.

62. Seattle Police Department, Seattle Police Manual, "5.120—Secondary Employment." *www.seattle.gov*. Seattle Police Department: March 19, 2014, Web.

63. Kelsey Seidler, "2016 National Retail Security Survey Results Released." *www.losspreventionmedia.com*. LPM Insider: August 8, 2016, Web.

64. Kevin Strom, et al., *The Private Security Industry: A Review of the Definitions, Available Data Sources, and Paths Moving Forward* (Research Triangle Park, N.C.: RTI International, December 2010), 4-11—4-15.

5

1. Kenneth Culp David, *Police Discretion* (St. Paul, Minn.: West Publishing Co., 1975).

2. C. E. Pratt, "Police Discretion," *Law and Order* (March 1992), 99–100.

3. "More than a Hunch," *Law Enforcement News* (September 2004), 1.

4. Herbert Jacob, *Urban Justice* (Boston: Little, Brown, 1973), 27.

5. Bureau of Justice Statistics, *Local Police Departments*, 2003 (Washington, D.C.: U.S. Department of Justice, May 2006), 24.

6. Albuquerque Police Department Procedural Orders, *Use of Force* (Albuquerque, N.M.: Albuquerque Police Department, May 1, 2016), 2–14.

7. Samuel Walker, *The Police in America: An Introduction*, 2d ed. (New York: McGraw-Hill, 1992), 16.

8. George L. Kelling and Mark H. Moore, "From Political to Reform to Community: The Evolving Strategy of Police," in *Community Policing: Rhetoric or Reality*, ed. Jack Greene and Stephen Mastrofski (New York: Praeger Publishers,1988), 13.

9. Michael White, *Controlling Officer Behavior in the Field* (New York: John Jay College of Criminal Justice, 2011), 19.

10. Henry M. Wrobleski and Karen M. Hess, *Introduction to Law Enforcement and Criminal Justice*, 7th ed. (Belmont, Calif.: Wadsworth/ Thomson Learning, 2003), 119.

11. Bureau of Justice Statistics, *Local Police Departments, 2013: Personnel, Policies, and Practices* (Washington, D.C.: U.S. Department of Justice, May 2015), 2.

12. Connie Fletcher, "What Cops Know," *On Patrol* (Summer 1996), 44–45.

13. Walker, *op. cit.*, 103.

14. Eric J. Scott, *Calls for Service: Citizens Demand an Initial Police Response* (Washington, D.C.: National Institute of Justice, 1981), 28–30.

15. Vivian B. Lord, et al., "Factors Influencing the Response of Crisis Intervention Team-Certified Law Enforcement Officers," *Police Quarterly* (December 2011), 388.

16. E. Fuller Torrey, *Justifiable Homicides by Law Enforcement Officers: What Is the Role of Mental Illness?* (Arlington, Va.: Treatment Advocacy Center, September 2013), 3.

17. Lord, et al., *op. cit.*, 390–391.

18. *Ibid.*, 391–392.

19. William G. Gay, Theodore H. Schell, and Stephen Schack, *Routine Patrol: Improving Patrol Productivity*, vol. 1 (Washington, D.C.: National Institute of Justice, 1977), 3–6.

20. Quoted in Ryan Boetel, "APD Chief, IRO Often at Odds over Lapel Video," *Albuquerque Journal* (December 27, 2014), A1.

21. Fletcher, *op. cit.*, 46.

22. Quoted in Eric Lichtblau, "Once Last Resort, F.B.I. Stings Become Common in ISIS Fight," *New York Times* (June 8, 2016), A1.

23. *Ibid.*

24. Quoted in Phil Fairbanks, "Feds Defend Arrest of Rochester Terror Suspect Amid Criticism from Family." *www.buffalonews.com. The Buffalo News*: January 6, 2016, Web.

25. Federal Bureau of Investigation, *Crime in the United States, 2015*, Table 25. *www.ucr.fbi.gov*. U.S. Department of Justice: 2016, Web.

26. James M. Cronin, Gerard R. Murphy, Lisa L. Spahr, Jessica I. Toliver, and Richard E. Weger, *Promoting Effective Homicide Investigations* (Washington, D.C.: Police Executive Research Forum, August 2007), 102–103.

27. Karen Matison Hess, Christine Hess Orthmann, and Henry Lim Cho, *Criminal Investigation*, 11th ed. (Boston: Cengage Learning, 2017), 119.

28. Joseph Peterson, Ira Sommers, Deborah Baskin, and Donald Johnson, *The Role and Impact of Forensic Evidence in the Criminal Justice Process* (Washington, D.C.: National Institute of Justice, September 2010), 8–9.

29. Igor Pacheco, Brian Cerchiai, and Stephanie Stoiloff, *Miami-Dade Research Study for the Reliability of ACE-V Process: Accuracy & Precision in Latent Fingerprint Examinations* (Miami, Fla.: Miami-Dade Police Department Forensic Services Bureau, December 2014), 5–12.

30. Simon A. Cole, "More Than Zero: Accounting for Error in Latent Fingerprinting Identification," *Journal of Criminal Law and Criminology* (Spring 2005), 985–1078.

31. Quoted in "New DNA Database Helps Crack 1979 N.Y. Murder Case," *Miami Herald* (March 14, 2000), 18A.

32. Judith E. Lewter, "The Use of Forensic DNA in Criminal Cases in Kentucky as Compared with Other Selected States," *Kentucky Law Journal* (1997–1998), 223.

33. "CODIS–NDIS Statistics." *www.fbi.gov*. Federal Bureau of Investigation: November 2016, Web.

34. *Maryland v. King*, 569 U.S. _____ (2013).

35. *Glendale Police Staffing Study* (Glendale, Ariz.: City of Glendale, 2010), 19.

36. Kark Vick, "What It's Like Being a Cop Now," *Time* (August 24, 2015), 35.

37. "911 Wireless Services." *www.fcc.gov*. Federal Communications Commission: visited January 27, 2017, Web.

38. *Future Trends in Policing* (Washington, D.C.: Police Executive Research Forum, 2014), 31.

39. Bureau of Justice Statistics, *Local Police Departments 2007*, (Washington, D.C.: U.S. Department of Justice, December 2010), Table 12, page 15.

40. Jerry H. Ratcliffe, et al., "The Philadelphia Foot Patrol Experiment: A Randomized Controlled Trial of Police Patrol Effectiveness in Violent Crime Hotspots," *Criminology* (August 2011), 795–830.

41. Quoted in Cory P. Haberman, "A View Inside the 'Black Box' of Hot Spot Policing from a Sample of Police Commanders," *Police Quarterly* (December 2016), 497.

42. Oliver Roeder, Lauren Brooke-Eisen, and Julia Bowling, *What Caused the Crime Decline?* (New York: Brennan Center for Justice, 2015)

43. Quoted in "New Model Police," *The Economist* (June 9, 2007), 29.

44. Lawrence W. Sherman, "Policing for Crime Prevention," in *Preventing Crime: What Works, What Doesn't, What's Promising*, ed. Lawrence W. Sherman, Denise C. Gottfredson, and Doris MacKenzie (Washington, D.C.: U.S. Office of Justice Programs, 1977), 229.

45. William Sousa and George L. Kelling, "Of 'Broken Windows,' Criminology, and Criminal Justice," in *Police Innovation: Contrasting Perspectives*, ed. David L. Weisburd and Anthony A. Braga (New York: Cambridge University Press, 2006), 77–97.

46. Dan McKay, "Overhaul at ADP Moves Cops into Neighborhoods," *Albuquerque Journal* (December 15, 2015), A1.

47. George Fachner and Steven Carter, *Collaborative Reform Model: Final Assessment Report of the Las Vegas Metropolitan Police Department* (Washington, D.C.: Community Oriented Policing Services, May 2014), Table 6, page 26.

48. Herman Goldstein, "Improving Policing: A Problem-Oriented Approach," *Crime and Delinquency* 25 (1979), 236–258.

49. Bureau of Justice Assistance, *Problem-Oriented Drug Enforcement: A Community-Based Approach for Effective Policing* (Washington, D.C.: Office of Justice Programs, 1993), 5.

50. Quoted in Vick, *op. cit.*, 34.

51. Quoted in Heather MacDonald, "The New Nationwide Crime Wave." *www.wsj.com*. Wall Street Journal: May 29, 2015, Web.

52. Rich Morin, et al., "Behind the Badge." *www.pewsocialtrends.org*. Pew Research Center: January 11, 2017, Web.

53. Harry J. Mullins, "Myth, Tradition, and Ritual," *Law and Order* (September 1995), 197.

54. William Westly, *Violence and the Police: A Sociological Study of Law, Custom, and Morality* (Cambridge, Mass.: MIT Press, 1970).

55. "Honoring Officers Killed in 2016." *www.odmp.org*. Officer Down Memorial Page: visited January 28, 2017, Web.

56. "FBI Releases 2015 Statistics on Law Enforcement Officers Killed and Assaulted." *www.fbi.gov*. Federal Bureau of Investigation: October 18, 2016, Web.

57. John S. Dempsey and Linda S. Forst, *An Introduction to Policing*, 8th ed. (Boston: Cengage Learning, 2016), 181.

58. Steven G. Brandl and Meghan S. Stroshine, "The Physical Hazards of Police Work Revisited," *Police Quarterly* (September 2012), 263.

59. "Causes of Law Enforcement Deaths." *www.nleomf.org*, National Law Enforcement Officers Memorial Fund: visited January 28, 2017, Web.

60. Gail A. Goolsakian, et al., *Coping with Police Stress* (Washington, D.C.: National Institute of Justice, 1985).

61. Kim S. Ménard and Michael L. Arter, "Stress, Coping, Alcohol Use, and Posttraumatic Stress Disorder among an International Sample of Police Officers: Does Gender Matter?" *Police Quarterly* (December 2014), 309–310.

62. University at Buffalo, "Impact of Stress on Police Officers' Physical and Mental Health." *www.sciencedaily.com*. Science Daily: September 29, 2008, Web.

63. Elizabeth A. Mumford, Bruce G. Taylor, and Bruce Kubu, "Law Enforcement Officer Safety and Wellness," *Police Quarterly* (June 2015), 122.

64. Daniel W. Clark, Elizabeth K. White, and John M. Violanti, "Law Enforcement Suicide: Current Knowledge and Future Directions," *The Police Chief* (May 2012), 48.

65. *Plakas v. Drinksi*, 19 F.3d 1143, 1150 (7th Cir.) (1994).

66. Bureau of Justice Statistics, *Police Use of Nonfatal Force, 2002–11* (Washington, D.C.: U.S. Department of Justice, November 2015), 1.

67. Bureau of Justice Statistics, *Arrest-Related Deaths Program Redesign Study, 2015–16: Preliminary Findings* (Washington, D.C.: U.S. Department of Justice, December 2016), Figure 1, page 1.

68. David J. Spotts, "Reviewing Use-of-Force Practices," *The Police Chief* (August 2012), 12.

69. H. Range Hutson, Deirdre Anglin, Phillip Rice, Demetrious N. Kyriacou, Michael Guirguis, and Jared Strote, "Excessive Use of Force by Police: A Survey of Academic Emergency Physicians," *Emergency Medicine Journal* (January 2009), 20–22.

70. *Scott v. Harris*, 127 S.Ct. 1779 (2007).

71. 471 U.S. 1 (1985).

72. 471 U.S. 1, 11 (1985).

73. 490 U.S. 386 (1989).

74. *Brosseau v. Haugen*, 543 U.S. 194 (2004).

75. Frank Newport, "Public Opinion Context: Americans, Race and Police." *www.gallup.com*. Gallup: July 8, 2016, Web.

76. Quoted in Richard Pérez-Peña and Timothy Williams, "Glare of Video Is Shifting Public's View of Police," *New York Times* (July 31,2015), A1.

77. Phillip Atiba Goff, et al., *The Science of Justice: Race, Arrests, and Police Use of Force* (New York: Center for Policing Equity, July 2016), 15.

78. Ronald G. Fryer, Jr., "An Empirical Analysis of Racial Differences in Police Use of Force." *www.nber.org*. National Bureau of Economic Research: July 2016, Web.

79. Bureau of Justice Statistics, *Police Behavior during Traffic and Street Stops, 2011* (Washington, D.C.: U.S. Department of Justice, September 2013), Table 5, page 7, and Table 7, page 9.

80. Dempsey and Forst, *op. cit.*, 252–253.

81. Quoted in Jeff Proctor and Fernanda Santos, "Two Former Albuquerque Officers Are on Trial in the Killing of a Homeless Man," *New York Times* (September 19, 2016), A11.

82. *Department of Justice Report Regarding the Criminal Investigation into the Shooting Death of Michael Brown by Ferguson, Missouri Police Officer Darren Wilson* (Washington, D.C.: U.S. Department of Justice, March 4, 2015), 11.

83. Jocelyn M. Pollock and Ronald F. Becker, "Ethics Training Using Officers' Dilemmas," *FBI Law Enforcement Bulletin* (November 1996), 20–28.

84. Quoted in Thomas J. Martinelli, "Dodging the Pitfalls of Noble Cause Corruption and the Intelligence Unit," *The Police Chief* (October 2009), 124.

85. Pollock and Becker, *op. cit.*, 20–28.

86. Brandon V. Zuidema and H. Wayne Duff, "Organizational Ethics through Effective Leadership," *Law Enforcement Bulletin* (March 2009), 8–9.

6

1. *Rodriguez v. United States*, 575 U.S. ________ (2015).

2. *Illinois v. Caballes*, 543 U.S. 405 (2005).

3. *Michigan v. Summers*, 452 U.S. 692 (1981).

4. *Brinegar v. United States*, 338 U.S. 160 (1949).

5. Rolando V. del Carmen, *Criminal Procedure for Law Enforcement Personnel* (Monterey, Calif.: Brooks/Cole Publishing Co., 1987), 63–64.

6. *Maryland v. Pringle*, 540 U.S. 366 (2003).

7. 500 U.S. 44 (1991).

8. *United States v. Leon*, 468 U.S. 897 (1984).

9. Milton Hirsh and David Oscar Markus, "Fourth Amendment Forum," *Champion* (December 2002), 42.

10. 430 U.S. 387 (1977).

11. 467 U.S. 431 (1984).

12. 468 U.S. 897 (1984).

13. 514 U.S. 1 (1995).

14. *California v. Greenwood*, 486 U.S. 35 (1988).

15. *Ibid.*

16. 389 U.S. 347 (1967).

17. *Ibid.*, 361.

18. 486 U.S. 35 (1988).

19. *Ibid.*

20. *United States v. Jacobsen*, 466 U.S. 109, 117 (1984).

21. *United States v. Blanton*, 479 F.2d 327 (5th Cir. 1973).

22. *Coolidge v. New Hampshire*, 403 U.S. 443, 467 (1971).

23. *Millender v. Messerschmidt*, 620 F.3d 1016 (9th Cir. 2010).

24. del Carmen, *op. cit.*, 158.

25. *Katz v. United States*, 389 U.S. 347, 357 (1967).

26. 547 U.S. 398 (2006).

27. 414 U.S. 234–235 (1973).

28. 395 U.S. 752 (1969).

29. *Ibid.*, 763.

30. Carl A. Benoit, "Questioning 'Authority': Fourth Amendment Consent Searches," *FBI Law Enforcement Bulletin* (July 2008), 24.

31. *Bumper v. North Carolina*, 391 U.S. 543 (1968).

32. *State v. Stone*, 362 N.C. 50, 653 S.E.2d 414 (2007).

33. 267 U.S. 132 (1925).

34. *United States v. Ross*, 456 U.S. 798, 804–809 (1982); and *Chambers v. Maroney*, 399 U.S. 42, 44, 52 (1970).

35. 453 U.S. 454 (1981).

36. *Arizona v. Gant*, 556 U.S. 332 (2009).

37. Adam Liptak, "Justices Significantly Cut Back Officers' Searches of Cars of People They Arrest," *New York Times* (April 22, 2009), A12.

38. Dale Anderson and Dave Cole, "Search and Seizure after *Arizona v. Gant*," *Arizona Attorney* (October 2009), 15.

39. *Whren v. United States*, 517 U.S. 806 (1996).

40. 403 U.S. 443 (1971).

41. *Kyollo v. United States*, 533 U.S. 27 (2001).

42. 388 U.S. 42 (1967).

43. 18 U.S.C. Sections 2510(7), 2518(1)(a), 2516 (1994).

44. Christopher K. Murphy, "Electronic Surveillance," in "Twenty-Sixth Annual Review of Criminal Procedure," *Georgetown Law Journal* (April 1997), 920.

45. *United States v. Nguyen*, 46 F.3d 781, 783 (8th Cir. 1995).

46. Joseph Siprut, "Privacy through Anonymity: An Economic Argument for Expanding the Right of Privacy in Public Places," *Pepperdine Law Review* 33 (2006), 311, 320.

47. *California v. Riley*, 134 S.Ct. 2473 (2014).

48. *Ibid.*, 2485.

49. *Ibid.*, 2473.

50. 392 U.S. 1 (1968).

51. *Ibid.*, 20.

52. *Ibid.*, 21.

53. See *United States v. Cortez*, 449 U.S. 411 (1981); and *United States v. Sokolow*, 490 U.S. 1 (1989).

54. *United States v. Arvizu*, 534 U.S. 266 (2002).

55. *Ibid.*, 270.

56. *United States v. Place*, 462 U.S. 696 (1983).

57. *Hibel v. Sixth Judicial District Court*, 542 U.S. 177 (2004).

58. *Ibid.*, 182.

59. *Minnesota v. Dickerson*, 508 U.S. 366 (1993).

60. *People v. Boswell*, Ill.App.1st 122275 (2014).

61. *Arizona v. Johnson*, 555 U.S. 328 (2009).

62. Rolando V. del Carmen and Jeffrey T. Walker, *Briefs of Leading Cases in Law Enforcement*, 2d ed. (Cincinnati, Ohio: Anderson, 1995), 38–40.

63. *Florida v. Royer*, 460 U.S. 491 (1983).

64. See also *United States v. Mendenhall*, 446 U.S. 544 (1980).

65. del Carmen, *op. cit.*, 97–98.

66. 514 U.S. 927 (1995).

67. Linda J. Collier and Deborah D. Rosenbloom, *American Jurisprudence*, 2d ed. (Rochester, N.Y.: Lawyers Cooperative Publishing, 1995), 122.

68. 547 U.S. 586 (2006).

69. *United States v. Banks*, 540 U.S. 31, 41 (2003).

70. *Hudson v. Michigan*, 547 U.S. 586, 593 (2006).

71. Tom Van Dorn, "Violation of Knock-and-Announce Rule Does Not Require Suppression of All Evidence Found in Search," *The Police Chief* (October 2006), 10.

72. *Utah v. Strieff*, 579 U.S. ____ . No. 14–373. Supreme Court of the United States (June 20, 2016).

73. *Ibid.*, 2.

74. *Ibid.*, 20.

75 "Warrantless Searches and Seizures" in *Georgetown Law Journal Annual Review of Criminal Procedure, 2011* (Washington, D.C.: Georgetown Law Journal, 2011), 955.

76. *Atwater v. City of Lago Vista*, 532 U.S. 318, 346–347 (2001).

77. *Brown v. Mississippi*, 297 U.S. 278 (1936).

78. *Miranda v. Arizona*, 384 U.S. 436 (1966).

79. H. Richard Uviller, *Tempered Zeal* (Chicago: Contemporary Books, 1988), 188–198.

80. *Orozco v. Texas*, 394 U.S. 324 (1969); *Oregon v. Mathiason*, 429 U.S. 492 (1977); and *California v. Beheler*, 463 U.S. 1121 (1983).

81. *Orozco, op. cit.*, 325.

82. *Pennsylvania v. Muniz*, 496 U.S. 582 (1990).

83. del Carmen, *op. cit.*, 267–268.

84. *New York v. Quarles*, 467 U.S. 649 (1984).

85. Ethan Bronner and Michael S. Schmidt, "In Questions at First, No Miranda for Suspect," *New York Times* (April 23, 2013), A13.

86. *Moran v. Burbine*, 475 U.S. 412 (1986).

87. *Michigan v. Mosley*, 423 U.S. 96 (1975).

88. *Fare v. Michael C.*, 442 U.S. 707, 723–724 (1979).

89. 512 U.S. 452 (1994).

90. 560 U.S. 370 (2010).

91. Richard A. Leo, "Inside the Interrogation Room," *Journal of Criminal Law and Criminology* (1996), 266.

92. Saul M. Kassin and Lawrence S. Wrightsman, "Prior Confessions and Mock Juror Verdicts," *Journal of Social Psychology* (1980), 133–146.

93. "False Admissions or Confessions." *www.innocenceproject.org*. The Innocence Project: visited February 3, 2017, Web.

94. Saul M. Kassin, "Internalized False Confessions," in Michael P. Toglia, et al., eds., *Handbook of Eyewitness Psychology*, Vol. 1 (New York: Psychology Press, 2007), 171.

95. Douglas Starr, "The Interview: Do Police Interrogation Techniques Produce False Confessions?" *The New Yorker* (December 9, 2013), 43–44.

96. *Ibid.*, 44.

97. "Christopher Abernathy." *www.law.umich.edu*. The National Registry of Exonerations: visited on February 3, 2017, Web.

98. Gregg McCrary, quoted in Starr, *op. cit.*, 46.

99. "Innocence Project, Wrongfully Convicted Floyd Bledsoe and Others Testify in Support of Kansas Bill That Would Require the Recording of Interrogations." *www.innocenceproject.org*. The Innocence Project: February 11, 2016.

100. Jennifer L. Mnookin, "Can a Jury Believe What It Sees?" *New York Times* (July 14, 2014), A19.

7

1. Quoted in "Teen Who Urged Suicide via Text Will Stand Trial, Court Rules." *www.cbsnews.com. Crime Insider*: July 1, 2016, Web.

2. Roscoe Pound, "The Administration of Justice in American Cities," *Harvard Law Review 12* (1912).

3. Russell Wheeler and Howard Whitcomb, *Judicial Administration: Text and Readings* (Englewood Cliffs, N.J.: Prentice Hall, 1977), 3.

4. Larry J. Siegel, *Criminology: Instructor's Manual*, 6th ed. (Belmont, Calif.: West/Wadsworth Publishing Co., 1998), 440.

5. Gerald F. Velman, "Federal Sentencing Guidelines: A Cure Worse Than the Disease," *American Criminal Law Review* 29 (Spring 1992), 904.

6. John Bacon, "Dylann Roof Pleads Guilty to State Murder Charges in Church Rampage." *www.usatoday.com. USA Today*: April 10, 2017, Web.

7. Wayne R. LaFave, "Section 4.6. Multiple Jurisdiction and Multiple Prosecution," *Substantive Criminal Law*, 2d ed. (C.J.S. Criminal Section 254), 2007.

8. 18 U.S.C. Section 3231; and *Solorio v. United States*, 483 U.S. 435 (1987).

9. 372 U.S. 335 (1963).

10. 384 U.S. 436 (1966).

11. 408 U.S. 238 (1972).

12. 428 U.S. 153 (1976).

13. *Birchfield v. North Dakota*, 579 U.S. ____. No. 14-1468. Supreme Court of the United States (June 23, 2016).

14. Public Law Number 103-322, Section 16001, 108 Statute 2036 (1994); codified as amended at 18 U.S.C. Section 2259.

15. *Paroline v. United States*, 134 S.Ct. 1710 (2014).

16. Stephen Labrecque, "'Virtual Certainty' in a Digital World: The Sixth Circuit's Application of the Private Search Doctrine to Digital Storage Devices in *United States v. Lichtenberger*." *www.lawdigitalcommons.bc.edu. Boston College Law Review*: April 29, 2016, Web.

17. David R. Stras and James F. Spriggs II, "Explaining Plurality Opinions," *Georgetown Law Journal* 99 (March 2010), 519.

18. Barry R. Schaller, *A Vision of American Law: Judging Law, Literature, and the Stories We Tell* (Westport, Conn.: Praeger, 1997).

19. Harlington Wood Jr., "Judiciary Reform: Recent Improvements in Federal Judicial Administration," *American University Law Review 44* (June 1995), 1557.

20. Pub. L. No. 76–299, 53 Stat. 1223, codified as amended at 28 U.S.C. Sections 601–610 (1988 & Supp. V 1993).

21. James E. Lozier, "The Missouri Plan a.k.a. Merit Selection Is the Best Solution for Selecting Michigan's Judges," *Michigan Bar Journal* 75 (September 1996), 918.

22. Ciara Torres-Spelliscy, Monique Chase, and Emma Greenman, *Improving Judicial Diversity*, 2d ed. (New York: Brennan Center for Justice, 2010), 1.

23. Tracey E. George and Albert H. Yoon, *The Gavel Gap: Who Sits in Judgment on State Courts?* (Washington, D.C.: American Constitution Society for Law and Policy, 2016), 7.

24. "Demographic Data Provided by Justices and Judges Relative to Gender, Race/Ethnicity, and Gender Identity/Sexual Orientation (Gov. Code, Section 12011.5(n))." *www.courts.ca.gov*. California Courts: December 31, 2015, Web.

25. "The Gavel Gap: Texas." *www.gavelgap.com*. American Constitution Society for Law and Policy: visited February 7, 2016, Web.

26. "Diversity on the Bench." *www.fjc.gov*. Federal Judicial Center: visited February 7, 2016, Web.

27. 295 U.S. 78 (1935).

28. *Brady v. Maryland*, 373 U.S. 83 (1963).

29. *Wearry v. Cain*, 577 U.S. ___, No. 14-10008. Supreme Court of the United States (March 7, 2016).

30. *Gideon v. Wainwright*, 372 U.S. 335 (1963); *Massiah v. United States*, 377 U.S. 201 (1964); *United States v. Wade*, 388 U.S. 218 (1967); *Argersinger v. Hamlin*, 407 U.S. 25 (1972); and *Brewer v. Williams*, 430 U.S. 387 (1977).

31. Larry Siegel, *Criminology*, 6th ed. (Belmont, Calif.: West/Wadsworth Publishing Co., 1998), 487–488.

32. Center for Professional Responsibility, *Model Rules of Professional Conduct* (Washington, D.C.: American Bar Association, 2003), Rules 1.6 and 3.1.

33. *United States v. Wade*, 388 U.S. 218, 256–258 (1967).

34. 372 U.S. 335 (1963).

35. 387 U.S. 1 (1967).

36. 407 U.S. 25 (1972).

37. Laurence A. Benner, "Eliminating Excessive Public Defender Workloads," *Criminal Justice* (Summer 2011), 25.

38. "Providing Defense Services: Standard 5-7.1. *www.americanbar.org*. American Bar Association: visited February 11, 2017, Web.

39. "The Court Decides, and Doesn't: A Big Victory for Public Defense in New York," *New York Times* (June 24, 2016), A26.

40. Bureau of Justice Statistics, *County-Based and Local Public Defender Offices, 2007* (Washington, D.C.: U.S. Department of Justice, September 2010), 3.

41. "State-by-State Court Fees." *www.npr.org. National Public Radio*: May 19, 2014, Web.

42. Mark Walker, "In S.D. Right to an Attorney Comes with a Price." *www.argusleader.com. Argus Leader*: March 4, 2016, Web.

43. Randolph Braccialarghe, "Why Were Perry Mason's Clients Always Innocent?" *Valparaiso University Law Review* (Fall 2004), 65.

44. John Kaplan, "Defending Guilty People," *University of Bridgeport Law Review* (1986), 223.

45. 491 U.S. 554 (1989).

8

1. Lawrence M. Friedman and Robert V. Percival, *The Roots of Justice* (Chapel Hill, N.C.: University of North Carolina Press, 1981).

2. *Riverside County, California v. McLaughlin*, 500 U.S. 44 (1991).

3. *Bail Fail: Why the U.S. Should End the Practice of Using Money for Bail* (Washington, D.C.: Justice Policy Institute, September 2012), 7.

4. Bureau of Justice Statistics, *Felony Defendants in Large Urban Counties, 2009—Statistical Tables* (Washington, D.C.: U.S. Department of Justice, December 2013), Table 18, page 21; and Table 19, page 21.

5. *Bail Fail*, *op. cit.*, 13.

6. Jeremy Ball and Lisa Bostaph, "He versus She: A Gender-Specific Analysis of Legal and Extralegal Effects on Pretrial Release for Felony Defendants," *Women & Criminal Justice* 19 (2009), 95–119.

7. Michael R. Jones, *Unsecured Bonds: The As Effective and Most Efficient Pretrial Release Option* (Washington, D.C.: Pretrial Justice Institute, October 2013).

8. New York Court of Appeals Judge Sol Wachtler, quoted in David Margolik, "Law Professor to Administer Courts in State," *New York Times* (February 1, 1985), B2.

9. Sam Skolnick, "Grand Juries: Power Shift?" *The Legal Times* (April 12, 1999), 1.

10. Bruce Frederick and Don Stemen, *The Anatomy of Discretion: An Analysis of Prosecutorial Decision Making—Summary Report* (New York: Vera Institute of Justice, December 2012), 4–16.

11. Carolyn C. Hartley and Lisa Frohmann, *Cook County Target Abuser Call (TAC): An Evaluation of a Specialized Domestic Violence Court* (Washington, D.C.: National Institute of Justice, August 2003).

12. 18 U.S.C. Section 3553(e) (2006).

13. 404 U.S. 257 (1971).

14. Fred C. Zacharias, "Justice in Plea Bargaining," *William and Mary Law Review* 39 (March 1998), 1121.

15. Bureau of Justice Statistics, *Prosecutors in State Courts, 2007—Statistical Tables* (Washington, D.C.: U.S. Department of Justice, December 2011), 2.

16. Milton Heumann, *Plea Bargaining: The Experiences of Prosecutors, Judges, and Defense Attorneys* (Chicago: University of Chicago Press, 1978), 58.

17. Albert W. Alschuler, "The Defense Attorney's Role in Plea Bargaining," *Yale Law Journal* 84 (1975), 1200.

18. Stephen J. Schulhofer, "Plea Bargaining as Disaster," *Yale Law Journal* 101 (1992), 1987.

19. North Carolina General Statutes Section 15A-832(f) (2003).

20. 18 U.S.C. Section 3771 (2004).

21. "Man Admits Abducting, Killing Jacob Wetterling," *Associated Press* (September 7, 2016).

22. 407 U.S. 514 (1972).

23. 391 U.S. 145 (1968).

24. *Blanton v. Las Vegas*, 489 U.S. 538 (1989).

25. *Apodaca v. Oregon*, 406 U.S. 404 (1972); and *Lee v. Louisiana*, No. 07-1523 (2008).

26. 332 U.S. 46 (1947).

27. *Salinas v. Texas*, 570 U.S. _____ (2013).

28. Quoted in James C. McKinley, Jr., "Jurors in Patz Case Fall a Vote Shy of a Conviction,"*New York Times* (May 9, 2015), A1.

29. 397 U.S. 358 (1970).

30. 380 U.S. 224 (1965).

31. 476 U.S. 79 (1986).

32. Eric L. Muller, "Solving the Batson Paradox: Harmless Error, Jury Representation, and the Sixth Amendment," *Yale Law Journal* 106 (October 1996), 93.

33. 499 U.S. 400 (1991).

34. 502 U.S. 1056 (1992).

35. 511 U.S. 127 (1994).

36. Harry Kalven and Hans Zeisel, *The American Jury* (Boston: Little, Brown, 1966), 163–167.

37. Maria Cramer, "Victim's Text Messages Tossed in Aaron Hernandez Case." *www.bostonglobe.com. Boston Globe*: December 12, 2014, Web.

38. Thomas J. Reed, "Trial by Propensity: Admission of Other Criminal Acts Evidenced in Federal Criminal Trials," *University of Cincinnati Law Review* 50 (1981), 713.

39. Quoted in Dan Wetzel, "Aaron Hernandez Avoids Major Defeat." *www.sports.yahoo.com. Yahoo Sports*: March 4, 2015, Web.

40. Reed, *op. cit.*, 713.

41. *People v. Zackowitz*, 254 N.Y. 192 (1930).

42. Federal Rules of Procedure, Rule 804(b)(2).

43. Arthur Best, *Evidence: Examples and Explanations*, 4th ed. (New York: Aspen Law & Business, 2001), 89–90.

44. David W. Broeder, "The University of Chicago Jury Project," *Nebraska Law Review* 38 (1959), 744–760.

45. 164 U.S. 492 (1896).

46. *United States v. Fioravanti*, 412 F.2d 407 (3d Cir. 1969).

47. Bureau of Justice Statistics, *Criminal Appeals in State Courts* (Washington, D.C.: U.S. Department of Justice, September 2015), 1.

48. Bill Rankin, "Ross Harris Launches Appeal of Murder Conviction." *www.myajc.com. Atlanta Journal-Constitution*: January 4, 2017, Web.

49. David W. Neubauer, *America's Courts and the Criminal Justice System*, 5th ed. (Belmont, Calif.: Wadsworth Publishing Co, 1996), 254.

50. "Exonerated by DNA." *www.innocenceproject.org. The Innocence Project*: visited February 14, 2017, Web.

51. "The National Registry of Exonerations." *www.law.umich.edu. Michigan Law School & Northwestern Law School*: visited February 14, 2017, Web.

52. "Eyewitness Misidentification." *www.innocenceproject.org. The Innocence Project*: visited February 14, 2017, Web.

53. Erik Eckholm, "Inmate Freed as Bite Marks Are Refuted," *New York Times* (April 9, 2016), A10.

54. *District Attorney's Office v. Osborne*, 557 U.S. 52 (2009).

55. Theresa Hsu Schriever, "In Our Own Backyard: Why California Should Care about *Habeas Corpus*," *McGeorge Law Review* 45 (2014), 764–798.

9

1. Herbert L. Packer, "Justification for Criminal Punishment," in *The Limits of Criminal Sanction* (Palo Alto, Calif.: Stanford University Press, 1968), 36–37.

2. Frank O. Bowman III, "Playing '21' with Narcotics Enforcement: A Response to Professor Carrington," *Washington and Lee Law Review* 52 (1995), 972.

3. James Q. Wilson, *Thinking about Crime* (New York: Basic Books, 1975), 235.

4. Ashley Nellis, *Life Goes On: The Historic Rise of Life Sentences in America* (Washington, D.C.: The Sentencing Project, September 2013), 1.

5. Isaac Ehrlich, "Participation in Illegitimate Activities: A Theoretical and Empirical Investigation," *Journal of Political Economy* 81 (May/June 1973), 521–564.

6. Avinash Singh Bhati, *An Information Theoretic Method for Estimating the Number of Crimes Averted by Incapacitation* (Washington, D.C.: Urban Institute, July 2007), 18–33.

7. Todd Clear, *Harm in Punishment* (Boston: Northeastern University Press, 1980).

8. Patricia M. Clark, "An Evidence-Based Intervention for Offenders," *Corrections Today* (February/March 2011), 62–64.

9. Kimberly S. Burke, *An Inventory and Examination of Restorative Justice Practices for Youth in Illinois* (Chicago: Illinois Criminal Justice Information Authority, April 2013), 6–7.

10. Gregory W. O'Reilly, "Truth-in-Sentencing: Illinois Adds Yet Another Layer of 'Reform' to Its Complicated Code of Corrections," *Loyola University of Chicago Law Journal* (Summer 1996), 986, 999–1000.

11. David E. Olson, et al., *Final Report: The Impact of Illinois' Truth-in-Sentencing Law on Sentence Lengths, Time to Serve and Disciplinary Incidents of Convicted Murderers and Sex Offenders* (Chicago: Illinois Criminal Justice Information Authority, June 2009), 4–5.

12. Paul W. Keve, *Crime Control and Justice in America: Searching for Facts and Answers* (Chicago: American Library Association, 1995), 77.

13. *Debtor's Prisons in New Hampshire* (Concord, N.H.: American Civil Liberties Union of New Hampshire, September 23, 2015).

14. *Bearden v. Georgia*, 462 U.S. 660 (1983).

15. Kate Stith and José A. Cabranes, "Judging under the Federal Sentencing Guidelines," *Northwestern University Law Review* 91 (Summer 1997), 1247.

16. Quoted in Jacqueline Lee, "Brock Turner Case: Probation Department's Report Spared Scrutiny." *www.mercurynews.com. Mercury News*: December 19, 2016, Web.

17. Mark M. Lanier and Claud H. Miller III, "Attitudes and Practices of Federal Probation Officers towards Pre-Plea/Trial Investigative Report Policy," *Crime & Delinquency* 41 (July 1995), 365–366.

18. Nancy J. King and Rosevelt L. Noble, "Felony Jury Sentencing in Practice: A Three-State Study," *Vanderbilt Law Review* (2004), 1986.

19. Julie R. O'Sullivan, "In Defense of the U.S. Sentencing Guidelines Modified Real-Offense System," *Northwestern University Law Review* 91 (1997), 1342.

20. "Aggravating Factors for Capital Punishment by State." *www.deathpenaltyinfo.org*. Death Penalty Information Center: visited February 16, 2017, Web.

21. John Paul Wilson and Nicholas O. Rule, "Facial Trustworthiness Predicts Extreme Criminal-Sentencing Outcomes," *Psychological Science* (August 2015), 1325–1331.

22. 18 U.S.C. Section 2113(a) (1994).

23. "Statistical Information Packet, Fiscal Year 2015, Washington," Table 7. *www.ussc.gov*. United States Sentencing Commission: 2016, Web; and "Statistical Information Packet, Fiscal Year 2015, Mississippi," Table 7. *www.ussc.gov*. United States Sentencing Commission: 2016, Web.

24. "Statistical Information Packet, Fiscal Year 2015, Fourth Circuit," Table 7. *www.ussc.gov*. United States Sentencing Commission: 2016, Web; and "Statistical Information Packet, Fiscal Year 2015, Ninth Circuit," Table 7. *www.ussc.gov*. United States Sentencing Commission: 2016, Web.

25. Keith Williams, "Practical Child Porn Defense: Fighting the Pitchfork Mentality," *Aspatore* (July 2012), 3911.

26. Cassia Spohn and David Holleran, "The Imprisonment Penalty Paid by Young, Unemployed Black and Hispanic Male Offenders," *Criminology* 35 (2000), 281.

27. "Key Findings and Recommendations." *www.illinoissenatedemocrats.com*. Illinois Disproportionate Justice Impact Study Commission: 2011, Web.

28. "Report on the Continued Impact of *United States v. Booker* on Federal Sentencing." *www.ussc.gov*. United States Sentencing Commission: December 2012, Web.

29. Xia Wang, et al., "Assessing the Differential Effects of Race and Ethnicity on Sentence Outcomes under Different Sentencing Systems," *Crime and Delinquency* (February 2013), 87–114.

30. David C. Baldus and George Woodworth, "Race Discrimination and the Legitimacy of Capital Punishment: Reflections on the Interaction of Fact and Perception," *DePaul Law Review* (2004), 1411.

31. Spohn and Holleran, *op. cit.*, 301.

32. 28 U.S.C. Section 991 (1994).

33. Bureau of Justice Statistics, *Felony Sentences in State Courts, 2006—Statistical Tables* (Washington, D.C.: U.S. Department of Justice, December 2009), Table 3.5, page 20.

34. Sonja B. Starr, "Estimating Gender Disparities in Federal Criminal Cases." *www.repository.law.umich.edu*. University of Michigan Law School: August 1, 2012, Web.

35. Clarice Feinman, *Women in the Criminal Justice System*, 3d ed. (Westport, Conn.: Praeger, 1994), 35.

36. Darrell Steffensmeier, John Kramer, and Cathy Streifel, "Gender and Imprisonment Decisions," *Criminology 31* (1993), 411.

37. Larry Hannah, "Lonzie Barton's Mother Sentenced to 7 Years in Baker Drug Case; Will Serve 12 Years Total." *www.jacksonville.com. Florida Times-Union*: March 22, 2016, Web.

38. Quoted in Kareem Fahim and Karen Zraick, "Seeing Failure of Mother as Factor in Sentencing," *New York Times* (November 17, 2008), A24.

39. John C. Coffee, "Repressed Issues of Sentencing," *Georgetown Law Journal* 66 (1978), 987.

40. Pub. L. No. 98–473, 98 Stat. 1987, codified as amended at 18 U.S.C. Sections 3551-3742 and 28 U.S.C. Sections 991–998 (1988).

41. Julia L. Black, "The Constitutionality of Federal Sentences Imposed under the Sentencing Reform Act of 1984 after *Mistretta v. United States*," *Iowa Law Review 75* (March 1990), 767.

42. *Fifteen Years of Guidelines Sentencing: An Assessment of How Well the Federal Criminal Justice System Is Achieving the Goals of Sentencing Reform* (Washington, D.C.: U.S. Sentencing Commission, November 2004), 46.

43. *Blakely v. Washington*, 542 U.S. 296 (2004); *United States v. Booker*, 543 U.S. 220 (2005); and *Gall v. United States*, 552 U.S. 38 (2007).

44. *Demographic Differences in Federal Sentencing Practices: An Update of the Booker Report's Multivariate Regression Analysis* (Washington, D.C.: U.S. Sentencing Commission, March 2010), C-3.

45. William Rhodes, et al., *Federal Sentencing Disparity: 2005–2012* (Washington, D.C.: Bureau of Justice Statistics, October 22, 2015), 38–43.

46. "Table N: National Comparison of Sentence Imposed and Position Relative to the Guideline Range, Fiscal Year 2013." *www.ussc.gov*. United States Sentencing Commission: 2013, Web.

47. Neal B. Kauder and Brian J. Ostrom, *State Sentencing Guidelines: Profiles and Continuum* (Williamsburg, Va.: National Center for State Courts, 2008), 15.

48. N.Y. Penal Law Sections 220.21, 60.5, 70.0(3) (1973).

49. Public Law Number 99–570 (1986).

50. 21 U.S.C. Section 859(b) (1986); 21 U.S.C. Section 861(a) (1986); and 18 U.S.C. Section 924(c)(1)(A)(i) (1998).

51. Todd R. Clear, George F. Cole, and Michael D. Reisig, *American Corrections*, 7th ed. (Belmont, Calif.: Thomson Wadsworth, 2006), 68–69.

52. Washington Revised Code Annotated Section 9.94A.030.

53. Nina Shapiro, "Should Washington Bring Back Parole?" *www.seattletimes.com. Seattle Times*: November 10, 2015, Web.

54. Matt Taibbi, "Cruel and Unusual Punishment: The Shame of Three Strikes Laws." *www.rollingstone.com. Rolling Stone*: March 27, 2013, Web.

55. *Lockyer v. Andrade*, 270 F.3d 743 (9th Cir. 2001).

56. *Ibid.*, 76.

57. Rob Kuznia, "An Unprecedented Experiment in Mass Forgiveness." *www.washingtonpost.com. Washington Post*: February 8, 2016, Web.

58. *United States Sentencing Commission, Report to Congress: Mandatory Minimum Penalties in the Federal Criminal Justice System* (Washington, D.C.: United States Sentencing Commission, October 2011), xxviii.

59. "Recent State-Level Reforms to Mandatory Minimums Laws." *www.famm.org*. Families against Mandatory Minimums: June 1, 2016, Web.

60. Kathy A. Bolton, "Branstad Signs Bill Allowing Early Release of Hundreds of Drug Felons," *www.desmoinesregister.com. Des Moines Register*: May 12, 2016, Web.

61. Nevada House Bill Number 239 (2009).

62. Jim Parsons, et al., *End of an Era? The Impact of Drug Reform in New York City* (New York: Vera Institute of Justice, 2015).

63. Scott Shackford, "Here's What to Expect from the Latest Attempt at Federal Sentencing Reform." *www.reason.com. Reason*: May 11, 2016, Web.

64. Justice for All Act of 2004, Pub. L. No. 108– 405, 118 Stat. 2260.

65. Paul G. Cassell, "In Defense of Victim Impact Statements," *Ohio State Journal of Criminal Law* (Spring 2009), 614.

66. Edna Erez, "Victim Voice, Impact Statements, and Sentencing: Integrating Restorative Justice and Therapeutic Jurisprudence Principles in Adversarial Proceedings," *Criminal Law Bulletin* (September/October 2004), 495.

67. Bryan Myers and Edith Greene, "Prejudicial Nature of Impact Statements," *Psychology, Public Policy, and Law* (December 2004), 493.

68. Bryan Myers and Jack Arbuthnot, "The Effects of Victim Impact Evidence on the Verdicts and Sentencing Judgments of Mock Jurors," *Journal of Offender Rehabilitation* (1999), 95–112.

69. *Payne v. Tennessee*, 501 U.S. 808 (1991).

70. Comments made at the Georgetown Law Center, "The Modern View of Capital Punishment," *American Criminal Law Review 34* (Summer 1997), 1353.

71. "America and Its Fellow Executioners," *New York Times* (January 10, 2016), SR10.

72. David Bruck, quoted in Bill Rankin, "Fairness of the Death Penalty Is Still on Trial," *Atlanta Journal-Constitution* (July 29, 1997), A13.

73. "Methods by State." *www.deathpenaltyinfo.org*. Death Penalty Information Center: visited February 17, 2017, Web.

74. *In re Kemmler*, 136 U.S. 447 (1890).

75. 217 U.S. 349 (1910).

76. Pamela S. Nagy, "Hang by the Neck until Dead: The Resurgence of Cruel and Unusual Punishment in the 1990s," *Pacific Law Journal 26* (October 1994), 85.

77. 553 U.S. 35 (2008).

78. Rose Carmen Goldberg, "Safe and Effective for Human Executions?" *www.stanfordlawreview.com. Stanford Law Review*: May 2015, Web.

79. *Glossip v. Gross*, 576 U.S. ____ (2015).

80. *Ibid.*, No. 14–7955. Supreme Court of the United States (June 29, 2015), 28.

81. 408 U.S. 238 (1972).

82. 408 U.S. 309 (1972) (Stewart, concurring).

83. 536 U.S. 584 (2002).

84. *Hurst v. Florida*, 577 U.S. ____ (2016).

85. *Ford v. Wainwright*, 477 U.S. 399, 422 (1986).

86. 536 U.S. 304 (2002).

87. *Penry v. Lynaugh*, 492 U.S. 302 (1989).

88. 543 U.S. 551 (2005).

89. *The Death Penalty in 2016 Year End Report* (Washington, D.C.: Death Penalty Information Center, December 2016), 1.

90. *Ibid.*, 3.

91. Craig Haney, "Floridians Pefer Life without Parole over Capital Punishment for Murderers." *www.tampabay.com. Tampa Bay Times*: August 16, 2016, Web.

92. Federal Bureau of Investigation, *Crime in the United States, 2015*, Table 1. *www.ucr.fbi.gov*. U.S. Department of Justice: 2016, Web.

93. Legislative Auditor, *Performance Audit: Fiscal Costs of the Death Penalty* (Carson City, Nev.: State of Nevada, 2014), 1.

94. Jessica M. Reyes, "Top Court: Delaware's Death Penalty Law Unconstitutional." *www.delawareonline.com. The News Journal*: August 3, 2016, Web.

95. *Tucker v. Louisiana*, 578 U.S. ____ (2016), No. 15-946. Supreme Court of the United States (May 31, 2016), 1.

96. Mark Berman, "Justices Breyer and Ginsburg: 'It Is Highly Likely' the Death Penalty Is Unconstitutional." *www.washingtonpost.com. Washington Post*: June 29, 2015, Web.

97. *Tucker v. Louisiana*, *op. cit.*

98. Dan Boyd, "65% Support Bringing Back Death Penalty," *Albuquerque Journal* (October 3, 2016), A1.

10

1. "Brooklyn Judge Attempts to Rewrite Laws with an Outrageous Wrist-Slap for Felon." *www.nypost.com. New York Post*: May 25, 2016, Web.

2. Bureau of Justice Statistics, *Probation and Parole in the United States, 2015* (Washington, D.C.: U.S. Department of Justice, December 2016), 1.

3. Michael Tonry, *Sentencing Matters* (New York: Oxford Press, 1996), 28.

4. *Probation and Parole in the United States, 2015, op. cit.*, 1.

5. Corrections Task Force of the President's Commission on Law Enforcement and Administration of Justice (1967).

6. Shaila Dewan and Andrew W. Lehren, "Spared from a Criminal Record, as Long as You Can Pay," *New York Times* (December 12, 2016), A1.

7. Paul H. Hahn, *Emerging Criminal Justice: Three Pillars for a Proactive Justice System* (Thousand Oaks, Calif.: Sage Publications, 1998), 106–108.

8. Bureau of Justice Statistics, *Correctional Populations in the United States, 2015* (Washington, D.C.: U.S. Department of Justice, December 2016), Table 1, page 2.

9. Bureau of Justice Statistics, *State Corrections Expenditures, FY 1982–2010* (Washington, D.C.: U.S. Department of Justice, April 2014), 1.

10. "Supervision Costs Significantly Less Than Incarceration in Federal System." *www.news.uscourts.gov*. United States Courts: July 18, 2013, Web.

11. "Cost of Corrections." *www.ncdps.gov*. North Carolina Public Department of Public Safety: June 30, 2016, Web.

12. Dewan and Lehren, *op. cit.*

13. Paul W. Keve, *Crime Control and Justice in America* (Chicago: American Library Association, 1995), 183.

14. Gerald Bayens and John Ortiz Smykla, *Probation, Parole, & Community-Based Corrections* (New York: McGraw-Hill, 2013), 186–217.

15. *Alternative Sentencing in the Federal Criminal Justice System* (Washington, D.C.: United States Sentencing Commission, May 2015), 4.

16. Joan Petersilia and Susan Turner, *Prison versus Probation in California: Implications for Crime and Offender Recidivism* (Santa Monica, Calif.: RAND Corporation, 1986).

17. *Probation and Parole in the United States, 2015, op. cit.*, Table 4, page 5.

18. Quoted in Marisa Gerber, "Under a Plea Deal, the Wife of Slain Bell Gardens Mayor Gets 90 Days in Jail for His Killing." *www.latimes.com. Los Angeles Times*: November 30, 2016, Web.

19. Debra C. Weiss, "Judge Makes Celibacy Outside of Marriage a Condition of Probation." *www.abajournal.com. ABA Journal*: February 7, 2017, Web; and Milton J. Valencia, "Judge Calls Ex-Lobbyist a Liar, Prepares Strict Probation Terms." *www.bostonglobe.com. Boston Globe*: January 6, 2017, Web.

20. 705 So.2d 172 (La. 1997).

21. Neil P. Cohen and James J. Gobert, *The Law of Probation and Parole* (Colorado Springs, Colo.: Shepard's/McGraw-Hill, 1983), Section 5.01, 183–184; Section 5.03, 191–192.

22. 534 U.S. 112 (2001).

23. Bureau of Justice Statistics, *Felony Defendants in Large Urban Counties, 2009—Statistical Tables* (Washington, D.C.: U.S. Department of Justice, December 2013), Table 28, page 32.

24. Carl B. Klockars, Jr., "A Theory of Probation Supervision," *Journal of Criminal Law, Criminology, and Police Science 63* (1972), 550–557.

25. *Probation and Parole in the United States, 2015, op. cit.*, Table 3, page 4.

26. Todd R. Clear, George F. Cole, and Michael D. Reisig, *American Corrections*, 11th ed. (Belmont, Calif.: Wadsworth Cengage Learning, 2016), 206.

27. Klockars, *op. cit.*, 551.

28. Quoted in Gary Fields, "Changes in Sentencing Policy Raise Pressure on Probation Officers." *www.wsj.com. Wall Street Journal*: July 5, 2016, Web.

29. 389 U.S. 12.

30. *Morrissey v. Brewer (1972)* and *Gagnon v. Scarpelli* (1973).

31. 465 U.S. 420.

32. *Felony Defendants in Large Urban Counties, 2009—Statistical Tables, op. cit.*, Table 6, page 10.

33. Jennifer L. Skeem and Sarah Manchak, "Back to the Future: From Klockars' Model of Effective Supervision to Evidence-Based Practice in Probation," *Journal of Offender Rehabilitation 47* (2008), 231.

34. *Probation and Parole, 2015, op. cit.*, Table 3, page 4.

35. Pamela M. Casey, Roger K. Warren, and Jennifer K. Elek, *Using Offender Risk and Needs Assessment Information at Sentencing* (Williamsburg, Va.: National Center for State Courts, 2011), Table 1, page 5.

36. James Q. Wilson, "Making Justice Swifter," *City Journal 7* (1997), 4.

37. Graeme Wood, "Prison without Walls," *The Atlantic* (September 2010), 92–93.

38. Angela Hawken, et al., *HOPE II: A Follow-Up to Hawaii's HOPE Evaluation* (Washington, D.C.: National Institute of Justice, May 2016).

39. *Clear, Cole, and Reisig, op. cit.*, 413.

40. *Probation and Parole in the United States, 2015, op cit.*, Table 5, page 6.

41. Bureau of Justice Statistics, *Probation and Parole in the United States, 2012* (Washington, D.C.: U.S. Department of Justice, December 2013), Table 7, page 9.

42. Nicole D. Porter, *The State of Sentencing 2015: Developments in Policy and Practice* (Washington, D.C.: The Sentencing Project, 2015), 5.

43. *Morrissey v. Brewer, op. cit.*

44. Todd R. Clear and Edward Latessa, "Probation Officer Roles in Intensive Supervision: Surveillance versus Treatment," *Justice Quarterly* 10 (1993), 441–462.

45. 442 U.S. 1 (1979).

46. American Civil Liberties Union, *A Living Death: Life without Parole for Nonviolent Offenses* (November 2013), 2.

47. Marie Gottschalk, "Days without End: Life Sentences and Penal Reform." *www.prisonlegalnews.org*. Prison Legal News: April 11, 2013, Web.

48. William Parker, *Parole: Origins, Development, Current Practices, and Statutes* (College Park, Md.: American Correctional Association, 1972), 26.

49. Clear, Cole, and Reisig, *op. cit.*, 387.

50. Quoted in Michael Winerip, Michael Schwartz, and Robert Gebeloff, "For Blacks Facing Parole, Signs of Broken System in New York," *New York Times* (December 5, 2016), A1.

51. *Ibid.*

52. Clear, Cole, and Reisig, *op. cit.*, 393.

53. Peter Holley, "Sirhan Sirhan Denied Parole Despite a Kennedy Confidant's Call for the Assassin's Release." *www.washingtonpost.com*. *Washington Post*: February 11, 2016.

54. Quoted in Jonathan J. Cooper, "California Governor Denies Parole for Manson Follower." *www.bigstory.ap.org*. *Associated Press*: July 22, 2016, Web.

55. Mark P. Rankin, Mark H. Allenbaugh, and Carlton Fields, "Parole's Essential Role in Bailing Out Our Nation's Criminal Justice Systems," *Champion* (January 2009), 47–48.

56. 18 U.S.C. Sections 1961–1968.

57. 516 U.S. 442 (1996).

58. "Fact Sheet: Asset Forfeiture 2016." *www.usmarshals.gov*. U.S. Marshals Service: March 11, 2016, Web.

59. *ISP Fact Sheet: Intensive Supervision Program* (Trenton, N.J.: Administrative Office of the Courts, February 2015), 1–2.

60. *Probation and Parole in the United States, 2010* (Washington, D.C.: U.S. Department of Justice, November 2011), Appendix table 3, page 31.

61. Clear, Cole, and Reisig, *op. cit.*, 238.

62. Paul Stageberg and Bonnie Wilson, *Recidivism among Iowa Probationers* (Des Moines, Iowa: *The Iowa Divisi*, July 2005); and Paul Koniceck, *Five Year Recidivism Follow-Up Offender Releases* (Columbus, Ohio: Ohio Department of Rehabilitation and Correction, August 1996).

63. Stephanie Fahy, et al., "Use of Electronic Offender-Tracking Devices Expands Sharply." *www.pewtrusts.org*. The Pew Charitable Trusts: September 7, 2016, Web.

64. Anita Raghavanjan, "Rajat Gupta to Finish Insider Trading Sentence at His Home," *New York Times* (January 21, 2016), B3.

65. Josh Kurtz, "New Growth in a Captive Market," *New York Times* (December 31, 1989), 12.

66. Michael Tonry and Mary Lynch, "Intermediate Sanctions," in *Crime and Justice*, vol. 20, ed. Michael Tonry (Chicago: University of Chicago Press, 1996), 99.

67. Dennis Palumbo, Mary Clifford, and Zoann K. Snyder-Joy, "From Net Widening to Intermediate Sanctions: The Transformation of Alternatives to Incarceration from Benevolence to Malevolence," in *Smart Sentencing: The Emergence of Intermediate Sanctions*, eds. James M. Byrne, Arthur Lurigio, and Joan Petersilia (Newbury Park, Calif.: Sage, 1992), 231.

11

1. James M. Beattie, *Crime and the Courts in England, 1660–1800* (Princeton, N.J.: Princeton University Press, 1986), 506–507.

2. Samuel Walker, *Popular Justice* (New York: Oxford University Press, 1980), 11.

3. Michael Meranze, *Laboratories of Virtue: Punishment, Revolution, and Authority in Philadelphia, 1760–1835* (Chapel Hill: University of North Carolina Press, 1996), 55.

4. Negley K. Teeters, *The Cradle of the Penitentiary: The Walnut Street Jail at Philadelphia, 1773–1835* (Philadelphia: Pennsylvania Prison Society, 1955), 30.

5. Negley K. Teeters and John D. Shearer, *The Prison at Philadelphia's Cherry Hill* (New York: Columbia University Press, 1957), 142–143.

6. Henry Calvin Mohler, "Convict Labor Policies," *Journal of the American Institute of Criminal Law and Criminology* 15 (1925), 556–557.

7. Zebulon Brockway, *Fifty Years of Prison Service* (Montclair, N.J.: Patterson Smith, 1969), 400–401.

8. Robert Martinson, "What Works? Questions and Answers about Prison Reform," *Public Interest* 35 (Spring 1974), 22.

9. See Ted Palmer, "Martinson Revisited," *Journal of Research on Crime and Delinquency* (1975), 133; and Paul Gendreau and Bob Ross, "Effective Correctional Treatment: Bibliotherapy for Cynics," *Crime & Delinquency* 25 (1979), 499.

10. Robert Martinson, "New Findings, New Views: A Note of Caution Regarding Sentencing Reform," *Hofstra Law Review* 7 (1979), 243.

11. Byron Eugene Price and John Charles Morris, eds., *Prison Privatization: The Many Facets of a Controversial Industry*, Volume 1 (Santa Barbara, Calif.: Praeger, 2012), 58.

12. Charles H. Logan, *Criminal Justice Performance Measures in Prisons* (Washington, D.C.: U.S. Department of Justice, 1993), 5.

13. Todd R. Clear and George F. Cole, *American Corrections*, 4th ed. (Belmont, Calif.: Wadsworth Publishing Co., 1997), 245–246.

14. Alfred Blumstein, "Prisons," in *Crime*, eds. James Q. Wilson and Joan Petersilia (San Francisco: ICS Press, 1995), 392.

15. Cassia Spohn and David Holleran, "The Effect of Imprisonment on Recidivism Rates of Felony Offenders: A Focus on Drug Offenders," *Criminology* (May 1, 2002), 329–357.

16. Bureau of Justice Statistics, *Census of State and Federal Correctional Facilities, 2005* (Washington, D.C.: U.S. Department of Justice, October 2008), 2.

17. *Ibid.*

18. Charles H. Logan, "Well Kept: Comparing Quality of Confinement in a Public and Private Prison," *Journal of Criminal Law and Criminology* 83 (1992), 580.

19. Bert Useem and Peter Kimball, *Stages of Siege: U.S. Prison Riots, 1971–1986* (New York: Oxford University Press, 1989).

20. Bert Useem, "Disorganization and the New Mexico Prison Riot of 1980," *American Sociology Review* 50 (1985), 685.

21. Peter M. Carlson and John J. DiIulio, Jr., "Organization and the Management of the Prison," in *Prison and Jail Administration: Practice and Theory*, 3rd ed., ed. Peter M. Carlson (Burlington, Mass.: Jones & Bartlett Learning, 2015), 272.

22. John J. DiIulio, *Governing Prisons* (New York: Free Press, 1987), 12.

23. *Ibid.*

24. Todd R. Clear, George F. Cole, and Michael D. Reisig, *American Corrections*, 11th ed. (Boston: Wadsworth Cengage Learning, 2016), 155–156.

25. Peter M. Carlson, "Inmate Classification," in *Prison and Jail Administration: Practice and Theory*, 3rd ed., *op. cit.*, 53–57.

26. Douglas Page, "The Prison of the Future," *Law Enforcement Technology* (January 2012), 11–13.

27. Daniel P. Mears, "Supermax Prisons: The Policy and the Evidence," *Criminology and Public Policy* (November 2013), 684.

28. "Facts about Pelican Bay's SHU," *California Prisoner* (December 1991).

29. David Brooks, "The Prison Problem," *New York Times* (September 29, 2015), A27.

30. Bureau of Justice Statistics, *Prisoners in 2015* (Washington, D.C.: U.S. Department of Justice, December 2016), Table 9, page 14; and Table 10, page 15.

31. Allen J. Beck, "Growth, Change, and Stability in the U.S. Prison Population, 1980–1995," *Corrections Management Quarterly* (Spring 1997), 9–10.

32. John Pfaff, "The Micro and Macro Causes of Prison Growth," *Georgia State Law Review* (Summer 2012), 1237–1271.

33. "Table D-5: U.S. District Courts—Criminal Defendants Sentenced after Conviction, by Offense, during the 12-Month Period Ending September 30, 2015." *www.uscourts.gov*. U.S. District Courts: 2016, Web.

34. Joan Petersilia, "Beyond the Prison Bubble," *Wilson Quarterly* (Winter 2011), 27.

35. *Time Served: The High Cost, Low Return of Longer Prison Terms* (Washington, D.C.: The Pew Center on the States, June 2012), 2.

36. *Fifteen Years of Guidelines Sentencing: An Assessment of How Well the Federal Criminal Justice System Is Achieving the Goals of Sentencing Reform* (Washington, D.C.: U.S. Sentencing Commission, November 2004), 46.

37. *Prisoners in 2015, op. cit.*, Table 1, page 3.

38. *Ibid.*

39. Julie Samuels, Nancy La Vigne, and Samuel Taxy, *Stemming the Tide: Strategies to Reduce the Growth and Cut the Cost of the Federal Prison System* (Washington, D.C.: Urban Institute, November 2013), 1.

40. Comprehensive Crime Control Act of 1984, Public Law Number 98–473.

41. *Prisoners in 2015, op. cit.*, Appendix table 6, page 31.

42. "Inmate Gender." *www.bop.gov*. Federal Bureau of Prisons: January 28, 2017, Web.

43. Bureau of Justice Statistics, *Prisoners in 2012: Trends in Admissions and Releases, 1991–2012* (Washington, D.C.: U.S. Department of Justice, December 2013), Appendix table 10, page 43; and Bureau of Justice Statistics, *Prison and Jail Inmates 1995* (Washington, D.C.: U.S. Department of Justice, August 1996), Table 6, page 6.

44. Quoted in Jeremy Travis, "Assessing the State of Mass Incarceration: Tipping Point or the New Normal?" *Criminology & Public Policy* (November 2014), 571.

45. Rosemary Gartner, Anthony N. Doob, and Franklin E. Zimring, "The Past as Prologue? Decarceration in California Then and Now," *Criminology & Public Policy* (May 2011), 294–296.

46. Samantha Harvell, Jeremy Welsh-Loveman, and Hanna Love, *Reforming Sentencing and Corrections Policy* (Washington, D.C.: Urban Institute, December 2016), 6.

47. "What You Need to Know about the New Federal Prison Release." *www.themarshallproject.org*. The Marshall Project: October 29, 2015, Web.

48. "The Right Choices," *The Economist* (June 20, 2015), 26.

49. "Prison Population Trends 1999–2014: Broad Variation among States in Recent Years," *www.sentencingproject.org*. The Sentencing Project: February 16, 2016, Web.

50. Bureau of Justice Statistics, *Parents in Prison and Their Minor Children* (Washington, D.C.: U.S. Department of Justice, March 2010), 1.

51. John Tierney, "Prison and the Poverty Trap," *New York Times* (February 19, 2013), D1.

52. *Ibid.*

53. *Rethinking the Blues: How We Police in the U.S. and at What Cost* (Washington, D.C.: Justice Policy Institute, May 2012), 34.

54. *Prisoners in 2015, op. cit.*, Table 5, page 8.

55. Bryan L. Sikes and Michelle Morato, "A Wealth of Inequalities: Mass Incarceration, Employment, and Racial Disparities in U.S. Household Wealth, 1996 to 2011," *The Russell Sage Foundation Journal of the Social Sciences* (October 2016), 129–152.

56. Quoted in Scott Cohn, "Private Prison Industry Grows despite Critics." *www.nbcnews.com. CNBC.com*: October 18, 2011, Web.

57. *Prisoners in 2015, op. cit.*, Appendix table 2, page 28.

58. "A Tale of Two Systems: Cost, Quality, and Accountability in Private Prisons," *Harvard Law Review* (May 2002), 1872.

59. "Federal Prison System per Capita Costs." *www.bop.gov*. Bureau of Prisons: 2015, Web.

60. Simon Hakin and Erwin A. Blackstone, *Prison Break: A New Approach to Public Cost and Safety* (Oakland, Calif.: The Independent Institute, June 2014), 4.

61. Jennifer Palmer, "Adding Beds Isn't Enough to Address Oklahoma Prison Overcrowding, Experts Say." *www.newsok.com. The Oklahoman:* October 25, 2015, Web.

62. Jennifer Sullivan, "Overcrowding to Force State to Export Prisoners to Michigan." *www.seattletimes.com. Seattle Times:* June 2, 2015, Web.

63. Gerald G. Gaes, "The Current Status of Prison Privatization Research on American Prisons." *www.works.bepress.com.* Selected Works: 2012, Web.

64. Gregory Geisler, *CIIC: Lake Erie Correctional Institution* (Columbus, Ohio: Correctional Institution Inspection Committee, January 2013), 16.

65. Curtis R. Blakely and Vic W. Bumphus, "Private and Public Sector Prisons," *Federal Probation* (June 2004), 27.

66. John DiIulio, "Prisons, Profits, and the Public Good: The Privatization of Corrections," in *Criminal Justice Center Bulletin* (Huntsville, Tex.: Sam Houston State University, 1986).

67. David M. Siegel, "Internalizing Private Prison Externalities: Let's Start with the GED," *New England Law* (February 4, 2016), 4–5.

68. Quoted in Cohn, *op. cit.*

69. Brian Bennett, "U.S. Rethinks Immigrant Holding Sites," *Los Angeles Times* (September 6, 2016), A1.

70. Fredreka Schouten, "Private Prisons Bank on Trump," *USA Today* (February 24, 2017), 1A.

71. Bureau of Justice Statistics, *Jail Inmates in 2015* (Washington, D.C.: U.S. Department of Justice, December 2016), 1.

72. Arthur Wallenstein, "Jail Crowding: Bringing the Issue to the Corrections Center Stage," *Corrections Today* (December 1996), 76–81.

73. Quoted in Fox Butterfield, "'Defying Gravity,' Inmate Population Climbs," *New York Times* (January 19, 1998), A10.

74. *Jail Inmates in 2015, op. cit.*, Table 3, page 4.

75. *Ibid.*

76. 441 U.S. 520 (1979).

77. *Ibid.*, at 546.

78. *Jail Inmates in 2015, op. cit.*, Table 3, page 4. Bureau of Justice Statistics, *Census of Jails: Population Changes, 1993–2013* (Washington, D.C.: U.S. Department of Justice, December 2015), 3.

79. Bureau of Justice Statistics, *Census of Jails: Population Changes, 1993–2013* (Washington, D.C.: U.S. Department of Justice, December 2015), 3.

80. Doris J. James and Lauren E. Glaze, *Bureau of Justice Statistics Special Report: Mental Health Problems of Prison and Jail Inmates* (Washington, D.C.: U.S. Department of Justice, September 2006), 1.

81. Bureau of Justice Statistics, *Medical Problems of State and Federal Prison and Jail Inmates, 2011–2012* (Washington, D.C.: U.S. Department of Justice, October 2016), 11.

82. Bureau of Justice Statistics, *Disabilities among Prison and Jail Inmates, 2011–12* (Washington, D.C.: U.S. Department of Justice, December 2015), 1.

83. Jennifer C. Karberg and Doris J. James, *Bureau of Justice Statistics Special Report: Substance Dependence, Abuse, and Treatment of Jail Inmates, 2002* (Washington, D.C.: U.S. Department of Justice, July 2005), 1.

84. Quoted in Michael Schwirtz, "Rikers Island Struggles with a Surge in Violence and Mental Illness," *New York Times* (March 19, 2014), A1.

85. Quoted in Sara Scullin, "Building to a Better Blueprint," *Law Enforcement Technology* (June 1015), 21.

86. Heather L. Peters, "Tour of New Muskegon County Jail Brings Out Hundreds of Curious Citizens," *www.mlive.com*. Mlive.com: August 22, 2015, Web.

87. R. L. Miller, "New Generation Justice Facilities: The Case for Direct Supervision," *Architectural Technology* 12 (1985), 6–7.

88. David Bogard, Virginia A. Hutchinson, and Vicci Persons, *Direct Supervision Jails: The Role of the Administrator* (Washington, D.C.: National Institute of Corrections, February 2010), 1–2.

12

1. Erving Goffman, "On the Characteristics of Total Institutions," in *Asylums: Essays on the Social Situation of Mental Patients and Other Inmates* (New York: Doubleday, 1961), 6.

2. Donald Clemmer, *The Prison Community* (Boston: Christopher, 1940).

3. John Irwin, *Prisons in Turmoil* (Boston: Little, Brown, 1980), 67.

4. Jeremy Luallen and Ryan Kling, "A Method for Analyzing Changing Prison Populations: Explaining the Growth of the Elderly in Prison," *Evaluation Review* (December 2014), 459–486.

5. Bureau of Justice Statistics, *Medical Problems of State and Federal Prisoners and Jail Inmates, 2011–12* (Washington, D.C.: U.S. Department of Justice, February 2015), 1.

6. Bureau of Justice Statistics, *Mortality in Local Jails and State Prisons, 2000–2013—Statistical Tables* (Washington, D.C.: U.S. Department of Justice, August 2015), Table 16, page 20.

7. *Ibid.*, Table 23, page 23.

8. Michael E. Horowitz, "Top Management and Performance Challenges Facing the Department of Justice—2014." *www.oig.justice.gov*. Office of the Inspector General, 2014, Web.

9. Michael Ollove, "Elderly Inmates Burden State Prisons." *www.pewtrusts.org*. The Pew Charitable Trusts: March 17, 2016, Web.

10. Michael Vitiello, "Addressing the Special Problems of Mentally Ill Prisoners: A Small Piece of the Solution to Our Nation's Prison Crisis," *Denver University Law Review* (Fall 2010), 57–62.

11. Katherine Stuart van Wormer and Clemens Bartollas, *Women and the Criminal Justice System*, 3d ed. (Upper Saddle River, N.J.: Pearson Education, 2011), 143.

12. Bureau of Justice Statistics, *Mental Health Problems of Prison and Jail Inmates* (Washington, D.C.: U.S. Department of Justice, December 2006), Table 1, page 3.

13. William Kanapaux, "Guilty of Mental Illness." *www.psychiatrictimes.com. Psychiatric Times*: January 1, 2004, Web.

14. Bureau of Justice Statistics, *Census of State and Federal Correctional Facilities, 2005* (Washington, D.C.: U.S. Department of Justice, October 2008), 6.

15. *Behind Bars II: Substance Abuse and America's Prison Population* (New York: The National Center on Addiction and Substance Abuse at Columbia University, February 2010), 4.

16. *Ibid.*, 83–84.

17. Devah Pager and Bruce Western, *Investigating Prisoner Reentry: The Impact of Conviction Status on the Employment Prospects of Young Men* (Washington, D.C.: National Institute of Justice, October 2009), 6.

18. *Census of State and Federal Correctional Facilities, 2005, op. cit.*, 6.

19. Lois M. Davis, et al., *Evaluating the Effectiveness of Correctional Education* (Santa Monica, Calif.: The Rand Corporation, 2013), xvi.

20. *Ibid.*, xvii.

21. Robert Johnson, *Hard Time: Understanding and Reforming the Prison*, 2d ed. (Belmont, Calif.: Wadsworth, 1996), 133.

22. Srinivas Konda, et al., "U.S. Correctional Officers Killed or Injured on the Job," *Corrections Today* (November/December 2013), 122–123.

23. Benjamin Steiner and Calli M. Cain, "The Relationship between Inmate Misconduct, Institutional Violence, and Administrative Segregation: A Systematic Review of the Evidence," in *Restrictive Housing in the U.S.: Issues, Challenges, and Future Directions* (Washington, D.C.: National Institute of Justice, 2016), 166–167.

24. Daniel P. Mears, et al., "The Code of the Street and Inmate Violence: Investigating the Salience of Imported Belief Systems," *Criminology* (August 2013), 695–728.

25. Lee H. Bowker, *Prison Victimization* (New York: Elsevier, 1981), 31–33.

26. Stephen C. Light, "The Severity of Assaults on Prison Officers: A Contextual Analysis," *Social Science Quarterly* 71 (1990), 267–284.

27. Frank Tannenbaum, *Crime and Community* (Boston: Ginn & Co., 1938).

28. Randy Martin and Sherwood Zimmerman, "A Typology of the Causes of Prison Riots and an Analytical Extension to the 1986 Virginia Riot," *Justice Quarterly* 7 (1990), 711–737.

29. Bert Useem, "Disorganization and the New Mexico Prison Riot of 1980," *American Sociological Review* 50 (1985), 677–688.

30. Quoted in Christopher Harress, "Brutal Murder Underlines Increasingly Dangerous Conditions in Alabama Prison System." *www.al.com. AL.com:* October 7, 2016, Web.

31. James E. Robertson, "The Prison Rape Elimination Act of 2003: A Primer," *Criminal Law Bulletin* (May/June 2004), 270–273.

32. Deborah Sontag, "Push to End Prison Rape Loses Earlier Momentum," *New York Times* (May 13, 2015), A1.

33. Quoted in Larissa MacFarquhar, "Out and Up," *New Yorker* (December 12, 2016), 60.

34. Irwin, *op. cit.*, 47.

35. Leo Carroll, "Race, Ethnicity, and the Social Order of the Prison," in *The Pains of Imprisonment*, eds. R. Johnson and H. Toch (Beverly Hills, Calif.: Sage, 1982).

36. Craig Haney, "Psychology and the Limits of Prison Pain," *Psychology, Public Policy, and Law* (December 1977), 499.

37. Alan J. Drury and Matt DeLisi, "Gangkill: An Exploratory Empirical Assessment of Gang Membership, Homicide Offending, and Prison Misconduct," *Crime & Delinquency* (January 2011), 130–146.

38. George W. Knox, "The Problem of Gangs and Security Threat Groups (STGs) in American Prisons and Jails Today: Recent Findings from the 2012 NGCRC National Gang/STG Survey." *www.ngcrc.com*. National Gang Crime Research Center: 2012, Web.

39. George W. Knox, "The Problem of Gangs and Security Threat Groups (STGs) in American Prisons Today: Recent Research Findings from the 2004 Prison Gang Survey." *www.ngcrc.com*. National Gang Crime Research Center: 2006, Web.

40. John Winterdyk and Rick Ruddell, "Managing Prison Gangs: Results from a Survey of U.S. Prison Systems," *Journal of Criminal Justice* 38 (2010), 733–734.

41. Quoted in John J. DiIulio, Jr., *No Escape: The Future of American Corrections* (New York: Basic Books, 1991), 268.

42. Jack Henry Abbott, *In the Belly of the Beast* (New York: Vintage Books, 1991), 54.

43. Michel Foucault, *Discipline and Punish: The Birth of the Prison* (New York: Pantheon Books, 1977), 128.

44. Lucien X. Lombardo, *Guards Imprisoned: Correctional Officers at Work* (Cincinnati, Ohio: Anderson Publishing Co., 1989), 51–71.

45. Clair A. Crip, "Inmate Disciplinary Procedures," in *Prison and Jail Administration: Practice and Theory*, 3d ed. Peter M. Carlson (Burlington, Mass.: Jones & Bartlett Learning, 2015), 344.

46. Goffman, *op. cit.*, 7.

47. Todd R. Clear, George F. Cole, and Michael D. Reisig, *American Corrections*, 11th ed. (Boston: Wadsworth Cengage Learning, 2016), 340.

48. *Wolff v. McDonnell*, 418 U.S. 539 (1974).

49. Liman Program & Association of State Correctional Administrators, *Time-In-Cell: ASCA-Liman 2014 National Survey of Administrative Segregation in Prison* (New Haven, Conn.: Yale Law School, 2015).

50. 475 U.S. 312 (1986).

51. *Stanley v. Hejirika*, 134 F.3d 629 (4th Cir. 1998).

52. Christopher R. Smith, *Law and Contemporary Corrections* (Belmont, Calif.: Wadsworth, 1999), Chapter 6.

53. 503 U.S. 1 (1992).

54. Van Wormer and Bartollas, *op. cit.*, 387.

55. Cristina Rathbone, *A World Apart: Women, Prison, and a Life behind Bars* (New York: Random House, 2006), 46.

56. "Labor Force Statistics from the Current Population Survey: Employed Persons by Detailed Occupation, Sex, Race, and Hispanic or Latino Ethnicity," *www.bls.gov*. Bureau of Labor Statistics: 2016, Web.

57. Kelly A. Cheeseman, Janet L. Mullings, and James W. Marquart, "Inmate Perceptions of Security Staff across Various Custody Levels," *Corrections Management Quarterly* (Spring 2001), 44.

58. Michael H. Jaime and Armand R. Burruel, "Labor Relations in Corrections," in *Prison and Jail Administration: Practice and Theory*, 3d ed., *op. cit.*, 264.

59. *Wolff v. McDonnell*, *op. cit.*

60. *Hudson v. Palmer*, 468 U.S. 517 (1984).

61. 429 U.S. 97 (1976).

62. Juan A. Lozano, "Judge: Texas Prison's Water Violates Standards of Decency." *www.bigstory.ap.org*. *Associated Press*: June 22, 2016, Web.

63. 501 U.S. 294 (1991).

64. *Wilson v. Seiter*, 501 U.S. 294, 304 (1991).

65. *Woodall v. Foti*, 648 F.2d, 268, 272 (5th Cir. 1981).

66. Paige St. John, "In a First, California Agrees to Pay for Transgender Inmate's Sex Reassignment." *www.latimes.com*. *Los Angeles Times*: August 10, 2015, Web.

67. *Brown v. Plata*, 563 U.S. _____ (2011).

68. Quoted in Alexandra Marks, "Martha Checks in Today," *Seattle Times* (October 8, 2004), A8.

69. Bureau of Justice Statistics, *Sourcebook of Criminal Justice*, 3d ed. (Washington, D.C.: U.S. Department of Justice, 2003), Table 6.56, page 519; and Bureau of Justice Statistics, *Prisoners in 2015* (Washington, D.C.: U.S. Department of Justice, December 2016), Table 9, page 14.

70. Bureau of Justice Statistics, *Profile of Jail Inmates 2002*, (Washington, D.C.: U.S. Department of Justice, July 2004), 10.

71. Bureau of Justice Statistics, *Prior Abuse Reported by Inmates and Probationers* (Washington, D.C.: U.S. Department of Justice, April 1999), 2.

72. *Caught in the Net: The Impact of Drug Policies on Women and Families* (Washington, D.C.: American Civil Liberties Union, 2004), 18–19.

73. Bureau of Justice Statistics, *Parents in Prison and Their Minor Children* (Washington, D.C.: U.S. Department of Justice, March 2010), 2.

74. Kelly Bedard and Eric Helland, "Location of Women's Prisons and the Deterrent Effect of 'Harder' Time," *International Review of Law and Economics* (June 2004), 152.

75. *Ibid.*

76. Sarah Schirmer, Ashley Nellis, and Marc Mauer, *Incarcerated Parents and Their Children: Trends 1991–2007* (Washington, D.C.: The Sentencing Project, February 2009), 5.

77. Joseph R. Carlson, "Prison Nurseries: A Pathway to Crime-Free Futures," *Corrections Compendium* (Spring 2009), 17–24.

78. Quoted in Sarah Yager, "Prison Born." *www.theatlantic.com*. *The Atlantic*: July/August 2015, Web.

79. Rathbone, *op. cit.*, 4.

80. *Ibid.*, 158.

81. Van Wormer and Bartollas, *op. cit.*, 137–138.

82. Barbara Bloom and Meda Chesney-Lind, "Women in Prison," in *It's a Crime: Women and Justice*, 4th ed., ed. Roslyn Muraskin (Upper Saddle River, N.J.: Prentice Hall, 2007), 542–563.

83. Piper Kerman, *Orange Is the New Black: My Year in a Women's Prison* (New York: Spiegal and Grau, 2011), 131.

84. Barbara Owen, et al., "Gendered Violence and Safety: A Contextual Approach to Improving Security in Women's Facilities." *www.ncjrs.gov*. National Criminal Justice Reference Service: December 2008, Web.

85. Nancy Wolff, Cynthia Blitz, Jing Shi, Jane Siegel, and Ronet Bachman, "Physical Violence inside Prisons: Rates of Victimization," *Criminal Justice and Behavior* 34 (2007), 588–604.

86. Van Wormer and Bartollas, *op. cit.*, 146–148.

87. Cited in Bloom, Owen, and Covington, *op. cit.*, 26.

88. Quoted in S. P. Sullivan, "Obama Tells N.J. Inmate's Recovery Story during Newark Stop." *www.nj.com*. NJ.com: November 3, 2015, Web.

89. *Prisoners in 2015*, *op. cit.*, Table 7, page 11.

90. Joan Petersilia, *When Prisoners Come Home:Parole and Prisoner Reentry* (New York: Oxford University Press, 2003), 39.

91. Victor Hassine, *Life without Parole: Living in Prison Today*, eds. Thomas J. Bernard and Richard McCleary (Los Angeles: Roxbury Publishing Co., 1996), 12.

92. Bruce Western, et al., "Stress and Hardship after Prison," *American Journal of Sociology* (March 2015), 1526.

93. Quoted in Jon Mooallem, "You Just Got Out of Prison. Now What?" *New York Times Sunday Magazine* (July 29, 2015), 38.

94. "Public Housing for People with Criminal Histories." *www.archive.vera.org*. Vera Institute of Justice: 2015, Web.

95. "National Inventory of the Collateral Consequences of Conviction." *www.niccc.csgjusticecenter.org*. The Council of State Governments: visited March 4, 2017, Web.

96. Saneta deVuono-Powell, et al., *Who Pays? The True Cost of Incarceration on Families* (Oakland, Calif.: Ella Baker Center, 2015), 20.

97. *Ill Equipped: U.S. Prisons and Offenders with Mental Illness* (New York: Human Rights Watch, 2003).

98. Quoted in Kevin Johnson, "After Years of Solitary, Freedom Is Hard to Grasp," *USA Today* (June 9, 2005), 2A.

99. *Census of State and Federal Correctional Facilities, 2005*, *op. cit.*, Table 6, page 5.

100. Quoted in MaryEllen Resendez, "Neighbors Continue Battle against Sex Offender Halfway House in Mesa." *www.abc15.com*. *ABC15 Arizona*: February 8, 2016, Web.

101. Belinda Brooks Gordon and Charlotte Bilby, "Psychological Interventions for Treatment of Adult Sex Offenders," *British Medical Journal* (July 2006), 5–6.

102. Bureau of Justice Statistics, *Recidivism of Prisoners Released in 1994* (Washington, D.C.: U.S. Department of Justice, June 2002), Table 9, page 8.

103. R. Karl Hanson and Kelly Morton-Bourgon, "The Characteristics of Persistent Sexual Offenders: A Meta-Analysis of Recidivism Studies, *Journal of Consulting and Clinical Psychology* 73 (2005), 1154–1163.

104. New Jersey Revised Statute Section 2C:7–8(c) (1995).

105. Georgia Code Annotated Section 42-9-44.1(b)(1).

106. Public Law Number 109–248, Section 116, 120 Statute 595 (2006).

107. Abby Goodnough, "After Two Cases in Florida, Crackdown on Molesters," *Law Enforcement News* (May 2004), 12.

108. *United States v. Comstock*, 560 U.S. 126 (2010).

13

1. Jennifer M. O'Connor and Lucinda K. Treat, "Getting Smart about Getting Tough: Juvenile Justice and the Possibility of Progressive Reform," *American Criminal Law Review* 33 (Summer 1996), 1299.

2. *In re Gault*, 387 U.S. 1, 15 (1967).

3. Samuel Davis, *The Rights of Juveniles: The Juvenile Justice System*, 2d ed. (New York: C. Boardman Co., 1995), Section 1.2.

4. Quoted in Anthony Platt, *The Child Savers* (Chicago: University of Chicago Press, 1969), 119.

5. 383 U.S. 541 (1966).

6. *Ibid.*, 556.

7. 387 U.S. 1 (1967).

8. 397 U.S. 358 (1970).

9. 421 U.S. 519 (1975).

10. 403 U.S. 528 (1971).

11. Rebecca Santana, "At What Age an Adult? Many in Louisiana Say 17 Is Too Young." *www.bigstory.ap.org*. *Associated Press*: May 7, 2016, Web.

12. Research Network on Adolescent Development and Juvenile Justice, *Youth on Trial: A Developmental Perspective on Juvenile Justice* (Chicago: John D. & Catherine T. MacArthur Foundation, 2003), 1.

13. Richard E. Redding, "Juveniles Transferred to Criminal Court: Legal Reform Proposals Based on Social Science Research," *Utah Law Review* (1997), 709.

14. Kyle J. Thomas, "Delinquent Peer Influence on Offending Versatility: Can Peers Promote Specialized Delinquency?" *Criminology* (May 2015), 280–307.

15. Bureau of Justice Statistics, *Co-Offending among Adolescents in Violent Victimizations, 2004-13* (Washington, D.C.: U.S. Department of Justice, July 2016), 1.

16. Martha Grace Duncan, "'So Young and So Untender': Remorseless Children and the Expectations of the Law," *Columbia Law Review* (October 2002), 1469.

17. 543 U.S. 551 (2005).

18. *Ibid.*, 567.

19. 560 U.S. 48 (2010).

20. *Ibid.*, 50.

21. 132 S. Ct. 2455 (2012).

22. *Ibid.*, 2463.

23. *Surveillance Summaries: Youth Risk Behavior Surveillance—United States, 2015* (Washington, D.C.: Centers for Disease Control and Prevention, June 10, 2016).

24. Federal Bureau of Investigation, *Crime in the United States, 2015*, Table 38. *ucr.fbi.gov.* U.S. Department of Justice: 2016, Web.

25. Sarah Hockenberry and Charles Puzzanchera, *Juvenile Court Statistics 2013* (Washington, D.C.: National Center for Juvenile Justice, July 2015), 7.

26. "One Day Count of Juveniles in Residential Placement Facilities, 1997-2013." *www.ojjdp.gov*. Office of Juvenile Justice and Delinquency Prevention: visited March 22, 2017, Web.

27. David McDowell, "Juvenile Curfew Laws and Their Influence on Crime," *Federal Probation* (December 2006), 58.

28. *Crime in the United States, 2015, op. cit.*, Table 29.

29. Office of Juvenile Justice and Delinquency Prevention, "Community Prevention Grants Program." *www.ojjdp.gov.* Office of Juvenile Justice and Delinquency Prevention: visited March 24, 2017, Web.

30. *Juvenile Court Statistics, 2013, op. cit.*, 20.

31. Melissa Sickmund and Charles Puzzancherra, eds., *Juvenile Offenders and Victims: 2014 National Report* (Pittsburgh: National Center for Juvenile Justice, December 2014), 158, 196.

32. *Juvenile Court Statistics, 2013, op. cit.*, 12.

33. Sara Goodkind, et al., "Are Girls Really Becoming More Delinquent? Testing the Gender Convergence Hypothesis by Race and Ethnicity, 1976–2005," *Children and Youth Services Review* (August 2009), 885–889.

34. "Girls and the Juvenile Justice System." *www.ojjdp.gov*. Office of Juvenile Justice and Delinquency Prevention: 2015, Web.

35. *Ibid.*

36. Meda Chesney-Lind, *The Female Offender: Girls, Women, and Crime* (Thousand Oaks, Calif.: Sage Publications, 1997).

37. Margaret A. Zahn, et al., "The Girls Study Group—Charting the Way to Delinquency Prevention for Girls," *Girls Study Group: Understanding and Responding to Girls' Delinquency* (Washington, D.C.: Office of Juvenile Justice and Delinquency Prevention, October 2008), 3.

38. *Crime in the United States, 2015, op. cit.*, Table 38 and Table 40.

39. National Center for Education Statistics and Bureau of Justice Statistics, *Indicators of School Crime and Safety: 2015* (Washington, D.C.: U.S. Department of Justice, May 2016), 42.

40. Heather L. Schwartz, et al, *The Role of Technology in Improving K–12 School Safety* (Santa Monica, Calif.: RAND Corporation, 2016), x.

41. *Juvenile Offenders and Victims: 2014 National Report, op. cit.*, 47.

42. *Indicators of School Crime and Safety, 2015, op. cit.*, 24.

43. *Ibid.*, 108.

44. Jacob Kang-Brown, et al., *A Generation Later: What We've Learned about Zero-Tolerance in Schools* (New York: Vera Institute of Justice, December 2013), 2.

45. *Indicators of School Crime and Safety: 2015, op. cit.*, 100.

46. "The Perils of Peanut Tossing," *The Economist* (December 21, 2013), 35.

47. Kathryn C. Monahan, et al., "From the School Yard to the Squad Car: School Discipline, Truancy, and Arrest," *Journal of Youth and Adolescence* (July 2014), 1110–1122.

48. Lana Shapiro and Andrew Adesman, "Exponential, Not Additive, Increase in Risk of Weapons Carrying by Adolescents Who Themselves Are Frequent and Recurrent Victims of Bullying," *Developmental & Behavioral Pediatrics* (May 2014), 165–171.

49. Young-Shin Kim and Bennett Leventhal, "Bullying and Suicide: A Review," *International Journal of Adolescent Medicine and Health* (April-June 2008), 133–154.

50. Marvin E. Wolfgang, *From Boy to Man, from Delinquency to Crime* (Chicago: University of Chicago Press, 1987).

51. Quoted in John H. Laub and Robert J. Sampson, "Understanding Desistance from Crime," in *Crime and Justice: A Review of Research* (Chicago: University of Chicago Press, 2001), 6.

52. Travis Hirschi and Michael Gottfredson, "Age and the Explanation of Crime," *American Journal of Sociology* 89 (1982), 552–584.

53. Robert J. Sampson and John H. Laub, "A Life-Course View on the Development of Crime," *Annals of the American Academy of Political and Social Science* (November 2005), 12.

54. David P. Farrington, "Offending from 10 to 25 Years of Age," in *Prospective Studies of Crime and Delinquency*, ed. Katherine Teilmann Van Dusen and Sarnoff A. Mednick (Boston: Kluwer-Nijhoff Publishers, 1983), 17.

55. Office of Juvenile Justice and Delinquency Prevention, *Juveniles in Court* (Washington, D.C.: U.S. Department of Justice, June 2003), 29.

56. Carl McCurley and Howard Snyder, *Cooccurrence of Substance Abuse Behaviors in Youth* (Washington, D.C.: Office of Juvenile Justice and Delinquency Prevention, 2008).

57. Gary McClelland, Linda Teplin, and Karen Abram, "Detection and Prevalence of Substance Abuse among Juvenile Detainees," *Juvenile Justice Bulletin* (Washington, D.C.: Office of Juvenile Justice and Delinquency Prevention, June 2004), 10.

58. Arrestee Drug Abuse Monitoring Program, *Preliminary Data on Drug Use and Related Matters among Adult Arrestees and Juvenile Detainees* (Washington, D.C.: National Institute of Justice, 2003).

59. Bonita M. Veysey, "Adolescent Girls with Mental Health Disorders Involved with the Juvenile Justice System." *www.ncmhjj.com.* National Center for Mental Health and Juvenile Justice: July 2003, Web.

60. Larry J. Siegel and Brandon C. Welsh, *Juvenile Delinquency: The Core*, 4th ed. (Belmont, Calif.: Wadsworth Cengage Learning, 2011), 268.

61. Edward P. Mulvey, *Highlights from Pathways to Desistance: A Longitudinal Study of Serious Adolescent Offenders* (Washington, D.C.: Office of Juvenile Justice and Delinquency Prevention, March 2011), 1–3.

62. David Finkelhor, et al., *Juvenile Justice Bulletin: Children's Exposure to Violence, Crime, and Abuse: An Update* (Washington, D.C.: Office of Juvenile Justice and Delinquency Prevention, September 2015), 7.

63. Kimberly A. Tyler and Katherine A. Johnson, "A Longitudinal Study of the Effects of Early Abuse on Later Victimization among High-Risk Adolescents," *Violence and Victims* (June 2006), 287–291.

64. Grover Trask, "Defusing the Teenage Time Bombs," *Prosecutor* (March/April 1997), 29.

65. Ashley Nellis, *The Lives of Juvenile Lifers: Findings from a National Survey* (Washington, D.C.: The Sentencing Project, March 2012), 2.

66. Cathy Spatz Widom, *The Cycle of Violence* (Washington, D.C.: National Institute of Justice, October 1992).

67. Janet Currie and Erdal Tekin, *Does Child Abuse Cause Crime?* (Atlanta: Andrew Young School of Policy Studies, April 2006), 27–28.

68. David C. Pyrooz and Gary Sweeten, "Gang Membership between Ages 5 and 17 Years in the United States," *Journal of Adolescent Health* (April 2015), 414.

69. Karl G. Hill, Christina Lui, and J. David Hawkins, *Early Precursors of Gang Membership: A Study of Seattle Youth* (Washington, D.C.: Office of Juvenile Justice and Delinquency Prevention, December 2001).

70. Amanda B. Gilman, Karl G. Hill, and J. David Hawkins, "Long-Term Consequences of Adolescent Gang Membership for Adult Functioning," *American Journal of Public Health* (May 2014), 938–945.

71. *Juvenile Offenders and Victims: 2014 National Report, op. cit.*, 69.

72. Los Angeles Police Department, "Why Young People Join Gangs." *www.lapdonline.org*. Los Angeles Police Department: visited March 24, 2017, Web.

73. Michelle Arciaga Young and Victor Gonzalez, "Getting Out of Gangs, Staying Out of Gangs: Gang Intervention and Desistance Strategies," *National Gang Center Bulletin* (January 2013).

74. *Crime in the United States, 2015, op. cit.*, Table 32.

75. *Juvenile Court Statistics, 2013, op. cit.*, 31.

76. *Ibid.*, 53.

77. 42 U.S.C. Sections 5601–5778 (1974).

78. S'Lee Arthur Hinshaw II, "Juvenile Diversion: An Alternative to Juvenile Court," *Journal of Dispute Resolution* (1993), 305.

79. *Juvenile Court Statistics, 2013, op. cit.*, 38.

80. Office of Juvenile Justice and Delinquency Prevention, *Delinquency Cases Waived to Criminal Court, 2011* (Washington, D.C.: U.S. Department of Justice, December 2014), 2.

81. Rhode Island General Laws Section 14-1-7.1 (1994 and Supp. 1996).

82. 467 U.S. 253 (1984).

83. *Juvenile Court Statistics, 2013, op. cit.*, 32.

84. Julie Furdella and Charles Puzzanchera, *Delinquency Cases in Juvenile Court, 2013* (Washington, D.C.: Office of Juvenile Justice and Delinquency Prevention, October 2015), 3.

85. Barry C. Feld, "Criminalizing the American Juvenile Court," *Crime and Justice* 17 (1993), 227–254.

86. *Delinquency Cases in Juvenile Court, 2013, op. cit.*, 3.

87. Sarah Hockenberry, *Juveniles in Residential Placement, 2013* (Washington, D.C.: Office of Juvenile Justice and Delinquency Prevention, May 2016), 1.

88. *Ibid.*, 4.

89. Thomas Grisso, *Double Jeopardy: Adolescent Offenders with Mental Disorders* (Chicago: University of Chicago Press, 2004), 2–3.

90. Howard N. Snyder and Melissa Sickmund, *Juvenile Offenders and Victims: 2006 National Report* (Washington, D.C.: National Center for Juvenile Justice, March 2006), 235.

14

1. "Porn Sites Get More Visitors Each Month than Netflix, Amazon, and Twitter Combined," *www.huffingtonpost.com*. Huffington Post: May 4, 2013, Web.

2. "Senate Bill 188." *https://olis.leg.state.or.us*. 78th Oregon Legislative Assembly—2015 Regular Session: visited March 27, 2017, Web.

3. Thomas J. Holt, Adam M. Bossler, and Kathryn C. Seigfried-Spellar, *Cybercrime and Digital Forensics: An Introduction* (New York: Routledge, 2015), 11.

4. Quoted in "Special Report Cyber-Security: Hackers Inc.," *The Economist* (July 12, 2014), 5.

5. William R. Graham, Jr., "Uncovering and Eliminating Child Pornography Rings on the Internet," *Law Review of Michigan State University Detroit College of Law* (Summer 2000), 466.

6. Richard Wortley and Stephen Smallbone, "The Problem of Internet Child Pornography." *www.popcenter.org*. Center for Problem Oriented Policing: 2006, Web.

7. David Wall, "Cybercrimes and the Internet," in *Crime and the Internet*, ed. David Wall (New York: Routledge, 2001), 1–17.

8. Janet Gilmore, "Campus Alerting 80,000 Individuals to Cyberattack." *news.berkeley.edu. Berkeley News:* February 26, 2016, Web.

9. Rosalie L. Donlon, "Hacked! The Cost of a Cyber Breach, in 5 Different Industries." *www.propertycasualty360.com*. Property Casualty 360: October 16, 2015, Web.

10. Internet Crime Complaint Center, *IC3 2015 Internet Crime Report* (Glen Allen, Va.: National White Collar Crime Center, 2016), 16.

11. Bureau of Justice Statistics, *Victims of Identity Theft, 2014* (Washington, D.C.: U.S. Department of Justice, September 2015), 1.

12. *Ibid.*

13. Jordan Robertson, "E-Mail Spam Goes Artisanal." *www.bloomberg.com. Bloomberg Technology*: January 19, 2016, Web.

14. *Social Media Brand Fraud Report* (Sunnyvale, Calif.: Proofpoint, 2016), 7.

15. David E. Sanger and Nicole Perloth, "Bank Hackers Steal Millions via Malware," *New York Times* (February 14, 2015), A1.

16. *Seizing Opportunity through License Compliance: BSA Global Software Survey* (Washington, D.C.: Business Software Alliance, May 2016), 2, 5.

17. Holt, Bossler, and Seigfried-Spellar, *op. cit.*, 24.

18. Quoted in Stephanie Chen, "In a Wired World, Children Unable to Escape Cyberbullying." *www.cnn.com. CNN*: October 5, 2010, Web.

19. Sameer Hinduja and Justin W. Patchin, "2016 Cyberbullying Data." *www.cyberbullying.org*. Cyberbullying Research Center: November 26, 2016, Web.

20. Bureau of Justice Statistics, *Stalking Victimization in the United States* (Washington, D.C.: U.S. Department of Justice, January 2009), 1.

21. Holt, Bossler, and Seigfried-Spellar, *op. cit.*, 229–230.

22. *United States v. Alkhabaz*, 104 F.3d 1492 (1997).

23. Quoted in Jack Moore, "ISIS Hit List of Arkansas Civilians Leaves Targets, Authorities Unmoved." *www.newsweek.com. Newsweek*: June 6, 2016, Web.

24. Derek Harp, quoted in Erin Kelly, "As Cyberthreats Rise, Push for Intelligence Heightened," *USA Today* (December 24, 2014), 3A.

25. Eduard Kovacs, "Cyberterrorist Attacks Unsophisticated but Effective: Former FBI Agent." *www.securityweek.com. Security Week*: March 14, 2016, Web.

26. "Welcome All Bug Bounty Hunters." *newsroom.uber.com*. Uber Newsroom: March 22, 2016, Web.

27. Quoted in Marc Santora, "In Hours, Thieves Took $45 Million in A.T.M. Scheme," *New York Times* (May 10, 2013), A1.

28. *2016 Internet Security Threat Report* (Mountain View, Calif.: Symantec, April 2016), 5.

29. Holt, Bossler, and Seigfried-Spellar, *op. cit.*, 17–20.

30. *Ibid.*, 68.

31. Scott Shane, Matthew Rosenberg, and Andrew W. Lehren, "WikiLeaks Releases Trove of Alleged C.I.A. Hacking Documents," *New York Times* (March 8, 2017), A1.

32. Lanny J. Davis, "Protection from Terrorism and Intrusion on Privacy Rights—We Can, We Must Have Both." *www.thehill.com. The Hill*: June 7, 2013, Web.

33. 50 U.S.C. Sections 1801–1811.

34. 50 U.S.C. Sections 1801(a)(1)-(3).

35. 50 U.S.C. Section 1804(a)(6).

36. 18 U.S.C. Section 2339B(a)(1) (1996).

37. 18 U.S.C. Section 2339A(b) (Supp. I 2001).

38. Uniting and Strengthening America by Providing Appropriate Tools Required to Intercept and Obstruct Terrorism (USA PATRIOT) Act of 2001, Pub. L. No. 107–56, 115 Stat. 272 (2001).

39. 50 U.S.C. Section 1861(b)(2)(A) (2006).

40. 18 U.S.C. Section 2709 (2012).

41. John S. Dempsey and Linda S. Forst, *An Introduction to Policing*, 7th ed. (Clifton Park, N.Y.: Delmar Cengage Learning, 2014), 537.

42. FISA Amendment Act of 2008, Pub. L. No. 110–261, 122 Stat. 2436 (2008).

43. John Yoo, "The Legality of the National Security Agency's Bulk Data Surveillance Programs." *scholarship.law.berkeley.edu*. Berkeley Law Scholarship Repository: 2014, Web.

44. Jay Bookman, "Which Do You Value? Privacy, or the Illusion of Security." *www.ajc.com*. AJC.com: December 17, 2013, Web.

45. Timothy B. Lee, "Here's Everything We Know about PRISM to Date." *www.washingtonpost.com. Washington Post Wonkblog*: June 12, 2013, Web.

46. Steven G. Bradbury, "Understanding the NSA Programs: Bulk Acquisition of Telephone Metadata under Section 215 and Foreign-Targeted Collection under Section 702," *Lawfare Research Paper Series* (September 1, 2013), 2.

47. Charlie Savage and Matt Apuzzo, "U.S. Spied on 5 American Muslims, a Report Says," *New York Times* (July 10, 2014), A17.

48. Jennifer Steinhauer and Jonathan Weisman, "U.S. Surveillance in Place since 9/11 Is Sharply Limited," *New York Times* (June 2, 2015), A1.

49. Joseph Menn, "Yahoo Secretly Scanned Customer Emails for U.S. Intelligence Sources." *www.reuters.com. Reuters*: October 4, 2016, Web.

50. Steinhauer and Weisman, *op. cit.*

51. *Katz v. United States*, 389 U.S. 347, 351 (1967); and *California v. Greenwood*, 486 U.S. 35 (1988).

52. *United States v. Moalin et al.*, Case No. 10cr4246 JM (S.D. Cal. November 18, 2013).

53. 442 U.S. 735 (1979).

54. *Klayman v. Obama*, 957 F.Supp.2d 825 (D.D.C. December 16, 2013).

55. Quoted in "A Powerful Rebuke of Mass Surveillance," *New York Times* (December 17, 2013).

56. *United States v. Jones*, 565 U.S. ____ (2012).

57. Quoted in "A Powerful Rebuke of Mass Surveillance," *op. cit.*

58. 50 U.S.C. Section 1881a (2011).

59. Edward C. Liu, *Surveillance of Foreigners outside the United States under Section 702 of the Foreign Intelligence Surveillance Act (FISA)*

(Washington, D.C.: Congressional Research Service, April 13, 2016), 1.

60. Ellen Nakashima, "Feds Report 90,000 Foreign Surveillance Targets," *Dallas Morning News* (June 28, 2014), 11A.

61. David E. Sanger and Matt Apuzzo, "Officials Defend N.S.A. after New Privacy Details Are Reported," *New York Times* (July 7, 2014), A9.

62. *Ibid.*

63. Quoted in "Colorado Teen Shannon Conley's Support of ISIS Raises Alarm about American Jihadists," *Associated Press* (September 10, 2014).

64. Quoted in Stephen Collinson, "Paris Attack: The New Terror." *www.cnn.com*. CNN.com: January 8, 2015, Web.

65. 18 U.S.C. Section 2339A(b)(1).

66. Quoted in Matt Apuzzo and Michael S. Schmidt, "F.B.I. Emphasizes Speed as ISIS Exhorts Individuals to Attack," *New York Times* (July 28, 2015), A11.

67. Bureau of Alcohol, Tobacco, *Firearms and Explosives, Annual Statistical Update 2016* (Washington, D.C.: U.S. Department of Justice, August 2016), Exhibit 1, page 1.

68. Christopher Ingraham, "There Are Now More Guns than People in the United States." *www.washingtonpost.com*. *Washington Post*: October 5, 2015, Web.

69. Lawrence H. Silberman, quoted in David Nakamura and Robert Barnes, "Appeals Court Rules D.C. Handgun Ban Unconstitutional," *Washington Post* (March 10, 2007), A1.

70. *District of Columbia v. Heller*, 554 U.S. 570 (2008); and *McDonald v. Chicago*, 561 U.S. 3025 (2010).

71. 18 U.S.C. 922(t).

72. Ronald J. Frandsen et al., *Background Checks for Firearm Transfers, 2010—Statistical Tables* (Washington, D.C.: U.S. Department of Justice, February 2013), 1.

73. Jennifer C. Karberg et al., *Background Checks for Firearm Transfers, 2013–2014—Statistical Tables* (Washington, D.C.: U.S. Department of Justice, June 2016), 1.

74. 27 C.F.R. Section 478.11 (2010).

75. Karberg, et al., *op. cit.*, Appendix Table 5, page 21.

76. "Gun Laws," *The Economist* (May 3, 2014), 28.

77. "New Laws for Handgun Licensing Program (Formerly Known as Concealed Handgun Licensing): Effective January 1, 2016," *www.dps.texas.gov*. Texas Department of Public Safety: visited January 5, 2017, Web.

78. Campbell Robertson and Timothy Williams, "As States Expand Gun Rights, the Police Object," *New York Times* (May 4, 2016), A10.

79. The Federal Bureau of Investigation, "White-Collar Crime." *www.fbi.gov*. Federal Bureau of Investigation: visited March 31, 2017, Web.

80. Michael L. Benson and Sally S. Simpson, *White-Collar Crime: An Opportunity Perspective* (New York: Routledge, 2009), 79–80.

81. *Ibid.*, 81–87.

82. Jay Weaver, "Wealthy Miami Beach Executive Charged Anew with Bribing State Healthcare Regulators." *www.miamiherald.com*. *Miami Herald*: February 13, 2017, Web.

83. "That's Where the Money Is," *The Economist* (May 31, 2014), 13.

84. Steven R. H. Barrett, "Impact of the Volkswagen Emissions Control Defeat Device on US Public Health." *http://iopscience.iop.org*. *IOP Science*: 2015, Web.

85. Benson and Simpson, *op. cit.*, 189.

86. David O. Friedrichs, *Trusted Criminals: White Collar Crime in Contemporary Society*, 4th ed. (Belmont, Calif.: Wadsworth Cengage Learning, 2010), 278–283.

DISCRETION IN ACTION CASE STUDIES

1.1 In 2015, prosecutor Thom LeDoux decided that no charges would be filed in a "sexting" scandal that involved about one hundred Cañon City High School students. Because nobody had been coerced to share or view the inappropriate images, LeDoux decided that the students were merely "doing stupid things" and did not deserve to be punished under Colorado criminal law.

On a practical level, it would be unreasonable for the criminal justice system to resolve the issue of sexting in the United States. According to one study, about 30 percent of American teenagers have shared a nude photo of themselves with another teenager. As one expert puts it, the child pornography laws under which this behavior often falls "are not meant to deal with a privacy violation but a really horrific form of abuse." Most prosecutors agree with Peter Weir, a district attorney in Jefferson County, Colorado, who believes that the goal in most teen sexting cases should be to "educate" rather than "prosecute."

Exceptions do, however, occur. Recently, two sixteen-year-old sweethearts who traded nude photos were charged with the felony of "exploiting a minor" by authorities in Fayetteville, North Carolina. The charges, which could have resulted in lengthy prison sentences, caused such a community outcry that the penalty was eventually reduced to a year's probation. Because of the possibility that prosecutors will use their discretion to severely punish young "sexters," approximately twenty states have passed laws mandating a softer approach to the problem in cases involving willing participants.

2.1 Several years ago, prosecutors in Mecklenburg County, North Carolina, dropped all domestic violence charges against professional football player Greg Hardy, citing lack of victim cooperation. The victim, despite assisting the police following Hardy's arrest, made it known that she would not testify against Hardy in court, and in fact left North Carolina so that she could not be compelled to do so.

As noted in the text, faced with uncooperative victims, prosecutors will consistently "drop" domestic violence cases. To remedy this situation, many jurisdictions in the United States have implemented "no-drop" policies. Such policies require prosecutors to carry through with a domestic violence case once an arrest has been made, even if this goes against the wishes of the victim. There is little question that no-drop policies increase the prosecution and conviction rates of domestic violence offenders. Critics contend, however, that such policies are unethical because they ignore the wishes of domestic violence victims.

3.1 After University of Virginia senior George Huguely was arrested for the death of his twenty-two-year-old ex-girlfriend Yeardley Love in 2010, prosecutors charged him with first degree murder, punishable by life in prison. The prosecutors asserted that Huguely was enraged because Love was dating someone else, and that he intended to kill her in a premeditated act. Huguely's lawyers insisted that, at worst, their client was guilty of involuntary manslaughter. At the time of the crime, they pointed out, he was drunk and had no intent to harm Love, much less kill her. Furthermore, they argued, Love died from suffocation well after Huguely left her apartment.

In 2012, a Charlottesville, Virginia, jury found Huguely guilty of second degree murder, reasoning that although he did not intend to kill Love, he did act with malice aforethought and his violent behavior was the cause of her death. A judge later sentenced Huguely to twenty-three years in prison.

4.1 The two officers, Holder and Reynolds, believing that the matter required their "immediate attention," forced their way back into Teresa Sheehan's room. When Sheehan continued to wave the knife in a threatening manner, Officer Reynolds pepper-sprayed her in the face. Sheehan still refused to drop the knife. Then, Holder shot her twice.

Sheehan survived her gunshot injuries, and eventually brought a lawsuit against the city of San Francisco. In the suit, she alleged that the police officers, acting on behalf of the city government, had violated her rights under the Americans with Disability Act by subduing her in a way that did not take into account her mental illness. The case eventually made its way to the United States Supreme Court, where the justices ruled against Sheehan. The use of force by Officers Holder and Reynolds, the Court ruled, was reasonable under the circumstances, regardless of whether Sheehan suffered from a mental illness or not.

5.1 In December 2015, Cuyahoga County prosecutor Timothy J. McGinty recommended that the grand jury not bring any criminal charges against Cleveland police officer Timothy Loehmann for the death of twelve-year-old Tamir Rice. When the grand jury followed McGinty's recommendation, its decision was met with outrage, particularly in the city's African American community. Many of Cleveland's black residents believed that Loehmann, who is white, fired without hesitation on Rice because the boy was African American.

For his part, McGinty called the incident a "perfect storm of human error, mistakes, and miscommunications." He argued that Loehmann did not deserve to be charged because there was no way the officer could have known that Tamir was holding a pellet gun instead of a real one. Under those circumstances, McGinty felt, a police officer could reasonably have feared for his own life or the lives of those nearby.

6.1 In 1996, two Washington, D.C., police officers pulled over Michael J. Wren—a young African American male who was driving a truck with temporary plates in a high-crime neighborhood—for failing to signal while making a right turn. They found two large bags of crack cocaine in Wren's possession, and arrested him. The United States Supreme Court upheld Wren's conviction, ruling that as long as police officers have probable cause to believe that a traffic violation has occurred, the "real" reason for making the stop is irrelevant.

As Justice Antonin Scalia put it, "Subjective intentions play no role in ordinary, probable-cause, Fourth Amendment analysis." In practical terms, this ruling gives law enforcement agents the ability to confirm "hunches" about serious illegal behavior as long as the target of these hunches commits even the most minor traffic violation. Such violations could include failing to properly signal during a turn, making a rolling stop at a stop sign, or driving five miles over the posted speed limit.

7.1 Gerard Marrone decided that his conscience prevented him from representing Levi Aron, and he withdrew from the case. His replacement, Jennifer McCann, criticized Marrone's actions. "To sit there and say, 'This is a hard case, I don't want to take it.'" McCann said. "That's for somebody else, that's not who I am." She added, "It's not about defending [Aron's] actions. It's about defending his rights." In 2012, Aron pleaded guilty to charges of second degree murder and kidnapping, and was sentenced to forty years to life in prison.

8.1 During a trial that was decided by a judge rather than a jury, defense attorney Norman Seigel insisted that the prosecution had failed to prove beyond a reasonable doubt that Oral "Nick" Hillary killed Garrett Phillips. "What evidence do they have?" Siegel asked during his opening statement. "Not one person will say, 'I saw Nick Hillary kill Garrett Phillips.' Why? Because it didn't happen."

Siegel also suggested that shoddy police work had let the real killer escape. Perhaps, he suggested, the culprit was the man in the hoodie, who could have fled the crime scene in the direction suggested by the police dog. In any event, Siegel created enough reasonable doubt that, on September 29, 2016, Judge Felix J. Catena acquitted the defendant, noting that the prosecution's entire case was circumstantial.

9.1 Pledge Chun "Michael" Deng died from injuries he suffered during a hazing ritual carried out by members of Baruch College's Pi Delta Psi fraternity in 2013. In all, thirty-eight members of the fraternity were charged in connection with Deng's death, including five who faced murder charges.

As of May 2017, only one of these defendants had gone to trial. In January 2017, twenty-five-year-old Ka-Wing Yuen pleaded guilty to conspiracy to hinder apprehension and conspiracy to haze for helping cover up Deng's death. A Monroe County, Pennsylvania, judge placed Yuen on five years' probation and ordered him to perform one hundred hours of community service and pay a $1,000 fine. "We have one down and thirty-seven to go," said Assistant District Attorney Kimberly Metzger after Yuen's plea bargain.

10.1 Susan Atkins was a disciple of cult leader Charles Manson and, in the summer of 1969, participated in one of the most sensationalized mass murders in American history. The woman Atkins stabbed sixteen times was Sharon Tate, an actress and the wife of film director Roman Polanski. On September 2, 2009, the California Board of Parole unanimously denied compassionate release for Atkins, marking the eighteenth time she had been refused parole. Three months later, Atkins died of brain cancer. Her case highlights the extent to which parole boards are often swayed by the nature of the crime above all other considerations.

12.1 The example given here is loosely taken from an online account of an inmate describing how he "downed a duck." After the correctional officer delivered the sympathy card with the funds, the inmate eventually turned the officer into a "golden goose" who helped with an escape attempt. Although this account is impossible to verify, there have been real-life examples of prison employees being duped into conspiring with inmates.

In the summer of 2015, for example, prisoners Richard Matt and David Sweat escaped the Clinton Correctional Facility in upstate New York with the help of correctional officer Gene Palmer and a civilian prison employee named Joyce Mitchell. Matt gave Palmer a series of paintings the inmate had finished while behind bars, and in return Palmer apparently smuggled tools into the prison that Matt and Sweat used to escape.

For her part, Mitchell told investigators that she talked with Matt "every day and he treated me with respect and was nice to me. He made me feel special." Mitchell eventually procured two pairs of spectacles equipped with lights for the inmates, so that they could work on their escape route at night. (After a three-week manhunt, Matt was shot and killed, and Sweat was shot and captured. Both Palmer and Mitchell received prison sentences for their misconduct.)

13.1 In 2008, a Denver, Colorado, prosecutor chose to charge seventeen-year-old James Stewart as an adult for vehicular homicide. After Stewart was moved to an adult jail, he tightened several bed sheets around his neck and hung himself. Stewart's suicide led to a change in state law that requires judges to review prosecutorial waivers in certain situations and makes it much less likely that a juvenile offender awaiting trial will be held in an adult jail.

In the first year after this law was passed, the number of juvenile offenders waived to state adult court dropped by nearly 85 percent. Nonetheless, Colorado prosecutors dislike the new law. One claims that he and his colleagues are in a better position than judges to decide whether a juvenile should be tried in adult court, due to a prosecutor's "experience" and "years and years of weighing one case against similarly situated cases."

14.1 After lower courts upheld the conviction of Anthony Elonis for threatening to commit an act of violence against his wife, he appealed to the U.S. Supreme Court. There, Elonis's attorneys argued that the prosecution should have been required to prove that their client intended to harm his wife, *not* that she reasonably feared he would do so. In other words, the Court was asked to decide which point of view matters most in such cases—the speaker's or the listener's.

In 2015, the justices decided in Elonis's favor by a 7-2 margin. Ordering a retrial, the Court ruled that the trial court had been wrong to convict Elonis without proving that he had intended for his violent online postings to be taken as threats by his wife. "Wrongdoing," explained Chief Justice John Roberts, Jr., "must be conscious to be criminal."

The decision in *Elonis v. United States* poses a difficult challenge for American courts—to establish the true motives of defendants such as Elonis who make online threats. "How does one prove what's in somebody else's mind?" asked Supreme Court Justice Ruth Bader Ginsberg. Along those same lines, Cindy Southworth of the National Network to End Domestic Violence points out that "Every abuser says, 'I didn't mean for her to think I would kill her.'" On the other side, free speech advocates worry that "words are slippery things" and argue that laws disregarding the speaker's intent run the risk of punishing speech simply because it is "crudely" expressed.

ANSWERS TO CHAPTER QUIZ QUESTIONS

1

1. Violent
2. Property
3. Federalism
4. State
5. Discretion
6. Ethics
7. Crime control
8. Due process
9. Terrorism
10. Recidivism

2

1. Criminologists
2. Theory
3. Rational choice
4. Psychology
5. Disorganization
6. Learning
7. Abuse
8. Uniform Crime Reports
9. Victim
10. Self-reported

3

1. Constitution
2. Case
3. Civil
4. Felony
5. Misdemeanor
6. Intent
7. Insanity
8. Self-defense
9. Entrapment
10. Due process

4

1. Enforce
2. Services
3. Intelligence
4. Probationary
5. Double
6. Sheriffs'
7. Highway
8. FBI (Federal Bureau of Investigation)
9. ATF (Bureau of Alcohol, Tobacco, Firearms and Explosives)
10. Deter

5

1. Policy
2. Deter/prevent
3. Forensics
4. DNA
5. Incident
6. Random
7. Community
8. Stress
9. Reasonable
10. Noble cause

6

1. Probable cause
2. Exclusionary
3. Privacy
4. Consent
5. Reasonable
6. Frisk
7. Custody
8. Warrant
9. Before
10. Waive

7

1. Defendants
2. Crime control
3. Jurisdiction
4. Federal
5. *Certiorari*
6. Concurring
7. Governor
8. Prosecutors
9. Counsel
10. Public

8

1. Bail
2. Grand jury
3. Plea bargain
4. Bench
5. Reasonable doubt
6. *Voir dire*
7. Prejudice
8. Direct
9. Cross
10. Appeal

9

1. Deterrence
2. Rehabilitation
3. Indeterminate
4. Good time
5. Mitigating
6. Disparity
7. Discrimination
8. Guidelines
9. Lethal injection
10. Juveniles

10

1. Diverting
2. Probation
3. Recidivism
4. Parole
5. Technical
6. Parole board
7. Mandatory
8. Forfeiture
9. Shock
10. Electronic monitoring

11

1. Medical
2. Warden
3. Classification
4. Maximum
5. Supermax
6. Drug
7. Decarceration
8. Overcrowding
9. Pretrial detainees
10. Sheriff

12

1. Total institution
2. Health-care
3. Relative deprivation
4. Legitimate
5. Malicious
6. Deliberate
7. Correctional officers
8. Reentry
9. Halfway
10. Notification

13

1. Government/state
2. Status offense
3. Death penalty
4. Aging out
5. Gangs
6. Arrest
7. Refer
8. Waiver
9. Adjudicatory
10. Disposition

14

1. Botnets
2. Identity
3. Intellectual property
4. Speech
5. Material support
6. Reasonable expectation
7. Background check
8. Mental illness
9. Trust
10. Compliance

INDEX

C

D

E

F

G

H

I

J

K

L

M

N

O

P

Q

R

S

T

U

V

W

Y

Z

STEPS OF THE CRIMINAL JUSTICE SYSTEM

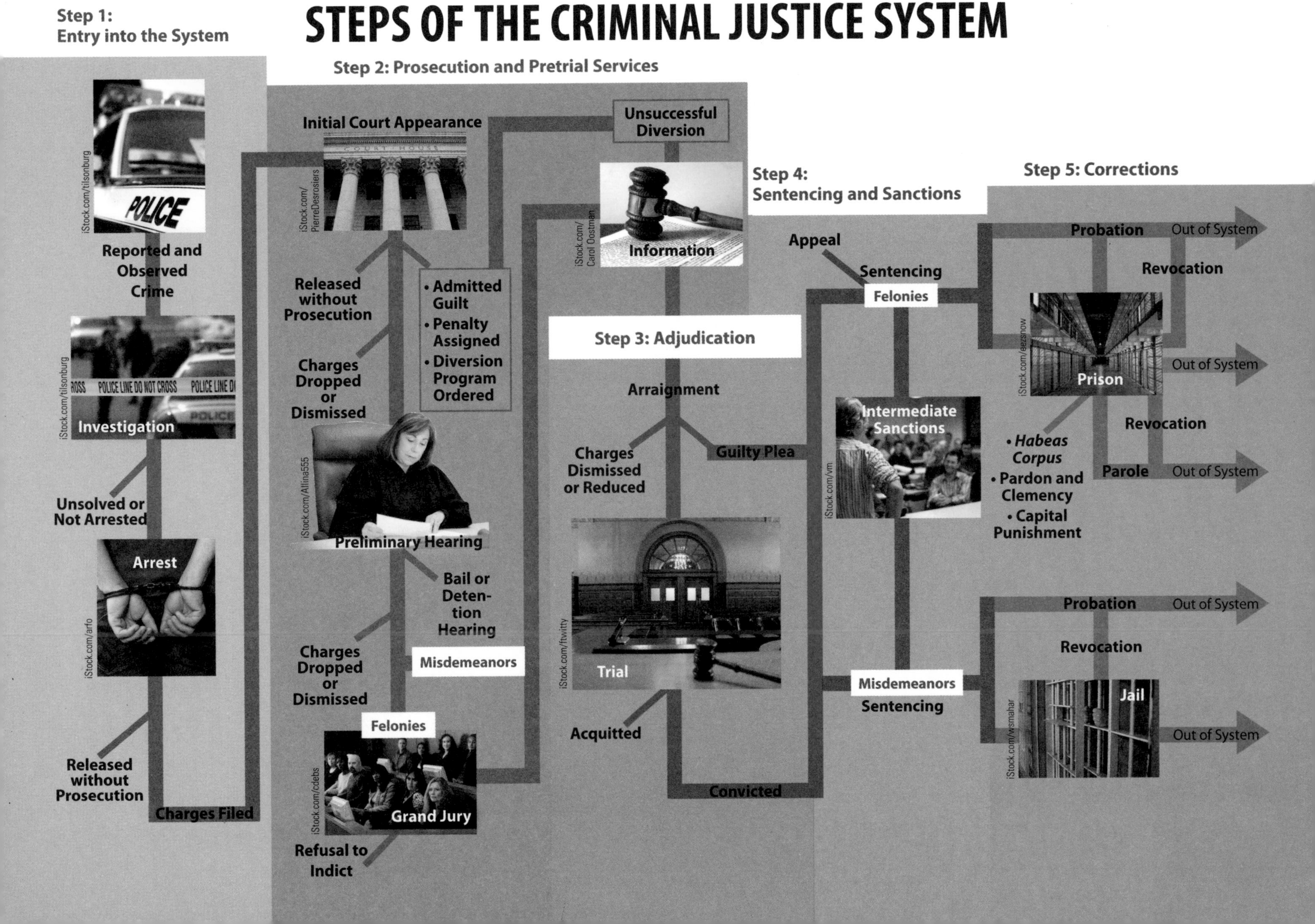

STEPS OF THE CRIMINAL JUSTICE SYSTEM

Step 1: Entry into the System

- Once a law enforcement agency has established that a crime has been committed, a suspect must be identified and apprehended for the case to proceed through the system.
- Sometimes a suspect is apprehended at the scene of the crime; at other times, however, identification of a suspect requires an extensive investigation.
- Often, no one is identified or apprehended. In some instances, a suspect is arrested, and later the police determine that no crime was committed and the suspect is released.

Step 2: Prosecution and Pretrial Services

- After an arrest, law enforcement agencies present information about the case and about the accused to the prosecutor, who will decide if formal charges will be filed with the court.
- A suspect charged with a crime must be taken before a judge without unnecessary delay.
- At the initial appearance, the judge informs the accused of the charges and decides whether there is probable cause to detain the accused person.
- If the offense is not serious, the determination of guilt and an assessment of a penalty may also occur at this stage.
- Often, the defense counsel is assigned at the initial appearance. All suspects charged with serious crimes have a right to be represented by an attorney. If the suspect cannot afford a defense attorney, the court will provide one for him or her at the public's expense.
- A pretrial release decision may also be made at the initial appearance. The court may decide that the suspect poses a threat to society and place him or her in jail until the trial.
- The court may decide to release the suspect with the understanding that he or she will return for the trial, or release the suspect on bail (meaning he or she must provide the court with monetary payment [bail], which will be returned when the suspect appears for the trial).
- In many jurisdictions, the initial appearance may be followed by a preliminary hearing. The main function of this hearing is to discover if there is probable cause to believe that the accused committed a known crime within the jurisdiction of the court. If the judge does find probable cause or the accused waives his or her right to the preliminary hearing, the case may be sent to a grand jury.
- A grand jury hears evidence against the accused presented by the prosecutor and decides if there is sufficient evidence to cause the accused to be brought to trial. If the grand jury finds sufficient evidence, it submits to the court an indictment, a written statement of the essential facts of the offense charged against the accused.
- Misdemeanor cases and some felony cases proceed by the issuance of an information, a formal, written accusation submitted to the court by a prosecutor.
- In some jurisdictions, defendants—often those without prior criminal records—may be eligible for diversion programs. In these programs, the suspect does not go to trial and instead must complete a rehabilitation program, such as drug treatment. If he or she is successful, the charges may be dropped, and his or her criminal record may remain clear.

Step 3: Adjudication

- Once an indictment or information has been filed with the trial court, the accused is scheduled for an arraignment.
- At the arraignment, the accused is informed of the charges, advised of his or her rights, and asked to enter a plea to the charges.
- Sometimes a plea of guilty is the result of negotiations between the prosecutor and the defendant. If the defendant pleads guilty and this plea is accepted by the judge, no trial is held and the defendant is sentenced.
- If the accused pleads not guilty, a date is set for the trial. A person accused of a serious crime is guaranteed a trial by jury.
- During the trial, the prosecution and defense present evidence, and the judge decides issues of law. The jury then decides whether the defendant will be acquitted (found not guilty) or convicted (found guilty of the initial charges or of other offenses).
- If the defendant is found guilty, he or she may request that the trial be reviewed by a higher court to assure that the rules of trial procedure were followed.

Step 4: Sentencing and Sanctions

- After a conviction, a sentence is imposed. In most cases, the judge decides the sentence, though sometimes the jury makes this decision.
- Some of the sentencing choices available to judges and juries include: the death penalty, incarceration in prison or jail, probation (allowing the convicted person to remain in the community as long as he or she follows certain rules), and fines. In many jurisdictions, persons convicted of certain types of offenses must serve a prison term.

Step 5: Corrections

- Offenders sentenced to incarceration usually serve time in a local jail or a prison. Offenders sentenced to less than one year usually go to jail, while those sentenced to more than one year go to prison.
- A prisoner may become eligible for parole after serving part of his or her sentence. Parole is the release of a prisoner before the full sentence has been served. If released under parole, the convict will be supervised in the community for the balance of his or her sentence.

CRIMINAL JUSTICE TIMELINE

	Supreme Court Criminal Justice Decisions	Legal Events
1900s	1903 Lottery ticket ban upheld	
1910s	1914 ***Weeks v. U.S.:*** Exclusionary rule adopted for federal courts 1919 ***Schenck v. U.S.:*** Socialist found guilty of obstructing war effort	1914 Harrison Narcotics Act passed 1919 Prohibition begins
1920s	1923 ***Frye v. U.S.:*** Scientific evidence admissible if it has gained general acceptance 1927 ***Tumey v. Ohio:*** Paying a judge only if defendant is found guilty is unconstitutional 1928 ***Olmstead v. U.S.:*** Wiretaps legal if no trespass	1921 William Taft becomes Chief Justice 1925 Federal Probation Act
1930s	1932 ***Powell v. Alabama:*** Limited right to counsel in capital cases established 1939 ***U.S. v. Miller:*** Right to bear arms limited to militia	1930 Charles Evans Hughes becomes Chief Justice 1931 National Commission on Law Observance and Enforcement—Wickersham Commission 1933 Prohibition ends 1935 199 executions in U.S.; highest rate in 20th century 1937 FDR's court packing plan defeated 1939 Administrative Office of U.S. Courts created
1940s		1941 Harlan Stone becomes Chief Justice 1946 Fred Vinson becomes Chief Justice
1950s	1956 ***Griffin v. Illinois:*** Indigents entitled to court-appointed attorney for first appeal	1953 Earl Warren becomes Chief Justice
1960s	1961 ***Mapp v. Ohio:*** Exclusionary rule required in state courts 1963 ***Fay v. Noia:*** Right to *habeas corpus* expanded ***Brady v. Maryland:*** Prosecutors must turn over evidence favorable to defense ***Gideon v. Wainwright:*** Indigents have right to counsel 1966 ***Sheppard v. Maxwell:*** Conviction reversed based on prejudicial pretrial publicity ***Miranda v. Arizona:*** Suspects must be advised of rights before interrogation 1967 ***In re Gault:*** Requires counsel for juveniles	1966 Bail Reform Act favors pretrial release 1967 President's Commission on Law Enforcement and Administration of Justice 1969 Warren Burger becomes Chief Justice
1970s	1972 ***Furman v. Georgia:*** Declares state death penalty laws unconstitutional ***Barker v. Wingo:*** Adopts flexible approach to speedy trial 1975 ***Gerstein v. Pugh:*** Arrestee entitled to a prompt hearing 1976 ***Gregg v. Georgia:*** Upholds death penalty ***North v. Russell:*** Upholds non-lawyer judges 1979 ***Burch v. Louisiana:*** Six-member juries must be unanimous	1970 Organized Crime Control Act 1971 Prison riot in Attica, New York 1972 Break-in at Watergate 1973 National Advisory Commission on Criminal Justice Standards and Goals Nixon declares war on drugs 1977 Determinate sentencing enacted in 4 states
1980s	1986 ***Batson v. Kentucky:*** Jurors cannot be excluded because of race 1987 ***U.S. v. Salerno:*** Preventive detention upheld 1989 ***Mistretta v. U.S.:*** U.S. sentencing guidelines upheld	1982 Victim and Witness Protection Act 1984 Bail Reform Act: judge may consider if defendant is a danger to the community 1985 DNA first used in criminal case 1986 William Rehnquist becomes Chief Justice 1987 U.S. Sentencing Guidelines begin
1990s	1991 ***Payne v. Tennessee:*** Victim impact statements admissible during sentencing ***Burns v. Reed:*** Prosecutors have qualified immunity in civil lawsuits ***Chisom v. Roemer:*** Voting Rights Act applies to elected judges 1995 ***U.S. v. Lopez:*** Federal law barring guns in school unconstitutional	1993 Three-strikes laws gain currency 1994 New Jersey passes Megan's Law 1995 U.S. prison population tops one million 1996 Antiterrorism and Effective Death Penalty Act limits *habeas* petitions in federal court
2000s	2004 ***Hamdi v. Rumsfeld:*** U.S. citizens seized overseas during antiterror military operations must be given access to U.S. courts 2005 ***Roper v. Simmons:*** Capital punishment for crimes committed when the offender was under eighteen years of age is unconstitutional 2009 ***Arizona v. Gant:*** After arresting a driver, police can only search areas of the car within driver's reach or to preserve crime evidence	2002 The Patriot Act enacted into law; Department of Homeland Security established 2005 John Roberts, Jr., becomes Chief Justice
2010s	2011 ***Brown v. Plata:*** Severe prison overcrowding limits inmates' access to health care in violation of the U.S. Constitution 2012 ***U.S. v. Jones:*** Lengthy police surveillance of a suspect using a GPS tracking device requires a search warrant ***Miller v. Alabama:*** Mandatory life-without-parole sentences for juvenile murderers are unconstitutional 2013 ***Maryland v. King:*** As part of the normal booking process, law enforcement officers may take DNA samples of those suspects arrested for serious crimes	2010 The federal Fair Sentencing Act reduces the sentencing disparity between penalties for crack and powder cocaine 2012 California voters modify the state's "three-strikes" law to allow for a life sentence only when the new felony conviction is "serious or violent" 2013 The U.S. prison and jail population levels off at approximately 2.3 million 2016 Four states legalize recreational use of marijuana, bringing the total to eight, plus the District of Columbia

CRIMINAL JUSTICE TIMELINE CONTINUED

	Famous Trials		Leading Crimes	
1900s			1901	President McKinley assassinated by anarchist
			1908	Butch Cassidy and the Sundance Kid killed in Bolivia
1910s			1915	Anti-Semitic lynching of Leo Frank in Atlanta
			1919	Black Sox scandal in baseball
1920s	1921	Sacco and Vanzetti sentenced to death for murder	1921	Charles Ponzi sentenced to prison for pyramid scheme
	1925	Scopes "Monkey Trial"	1924	Leopold and Loeb plead guilty to thrill murder
	1927	Teapot Dome trials become symbol of government corruption	1929	St. Valentine's Day massacre ordered by Al Capone in Chicago
1930s	1931	Chicago mobster Al Capone found guilty of income tax evasion	1934	Bonnie and Clyde killed
	1935	Bruno Hauptman convicted of kidnapping Charles Lindbergh's young son		"Baby Face" Nelson and "Pretty Boy" Floyd killed
	1939	Crime boss "Lucky" Luciano found guilty of compulsory prostitution		
1940s	1941	Murder, Inc. trials	1945	Bank robber Willie Sutton escapes from prison
	1948	Caryl Chessman sentenced to death for kidnapping and robbery	1947	Hollywood hopeful Black Dahlia's mutilated body found
	1949	Alger Hiss found guilty of perjury in the onset of the Cold War		
1950s	1951	Julius and Ethel Rosenberg sentenced to death for espionage	1950	Brinks armored car robbery in Boston
	1954	Dr. Samuel Sheppard convicted of murder	1957	George Metesky confesses to a string of New York City bombings
	1958	Daughter of movie actress Lana Turner found not guilty of killing mom's gangster lover	1959	Murder of Kansas farm couple becomes basis of *In Cold Blood*
1960s	1964	Teamster president Jimmy Hoffa found guilty	1962	French Connection drug bust
	1966	Dr. Sam Sheppard acquitted in second trial	1963	President Kennedy assassinated
	1968	Black Panther Huey Newton found guilty of voluntary manslaughter	1964	Boston Strangler arrested
	1969	Chicago 7 found guilty of incitement to riot and conspiracy	1966	Richard Speck kills eight Chicago nurses
			1968	Martin Luther King, Jr., and Robert Kennedy assassinated
			1969	Manson family commits Helter Skelter murders
1970s	1971	Lt. William Calley found guilty of murder in My Lai massacre	1971	Skyjacker D.B. Cooper disappears
	1976	Heiress Patty Hearst found guilty of bank robbery	1974	Heiress Patty Hearst kidnapped by terrorists
	1977	Maryland governor Marvin Mandel found guilty of mail fraud	1974–1978	Ted Bundy confesses to killing thirty women between these years; he also confesses to rape, kidnapping, and necrophilia; he dies by electric chair in 1989
			1975	Jimmy Hoffa disappears
			1977	Serial murderer Son of Sam arrested in New York
			1978	Jonestown massacre
			1978–1991	Jeffrey Dahmer's killing and cannibalism spree; he is imprisoned in 1992, and is murdered while incarcerated in 1994
1980s	1980	John Wayne Gacy convicted of killing 33 boys	1980	Headmistress Jean Harris kills Scarsdale Diet Doctor
	1982	Automaker John DeLorean acquitted of cocaine trafficking	1981	President Ronald Reagan survives assassination attempt by John Hinckley
	1984	Mayflower Madam pleads guilty to misdemeanor of promoting prostitution	1984	21 killed at San Diego McDonald's
	1987	Subway vigilante Bernhard Goetz acquitted of attempted murder	1987	Savings and loan mogul Charles Keating accused of fraud
	1989	Televangelist Jim Bakker found guilty of fraud	1989	Junk bond king Michael Milken pays $600 million fine
1990s	1993	L.A. police officers found guilty in federal court of civil rights violations against Rodney King	1992	Boxer Mike Tyson charged with rape
	1995	O. J. Simpson found not guilty of murdering his ex-wife Nicole and her friend, Ronald Goldman	1994	Fire in Waco kills Branch Davidians
	1996	During second trial, Menendez brothers found guilty of killing wealthy parents	1995	Oklahoma City bombing
	1997	Timothy McVeigh sentenced to death for Oklahoma City bombing	1997	Nanny in Boston charged with child murder
2000s	2000	NYPD officers acquitted for killing Amadou Diallo	2001	Terrorists strike targets in New York City and the Washington, D.C., area, including Flight 93, which crashes in a Pennsylvania field
	2003	Washington State's Gary Ridgway sentenced as worst serial killer in U.S. history	2007	Student Cho Seung Hui murders five faculty members and twenty-seven students on the campus of Virginia Tech in Blacksburg, Virginia
	2006	Zacarias Moussaoui convicted for conspiring to kill U.S. citizens as part of the September 11, 2001, terrorist attacks	2009	Bernard Madoff pleads guilty to running a $65 billion Ponzi scheme
2010s	2013	George Zimmerman found not guilty of second degree murder by reason of self-defense for killing teenager Trayvon Martin during an altercation in Sanford, Florida	2012	Adam Lanza kills twenty children and six adult staff members during a shooting spree at Sandy Hook Elementary School in Newtown, Connecticut
	2017	Minnesota police officer acquitted for killing Philando Castile	2016	Gunman with ties to terrorist organization ISIS fatally shoots forty-nine people at a gay nightclub in Orlando
				"Internet of Things" DDoS attack disrupts Amazon, Twitter, and Netflix website traffic

CHAPTER REVIEW

CHAPTER 1 LEARNING OBJECTIVES / OUTLINE / KEY TERMS

1-1 **Define *crime*.** Crime is any action punishable under criminal statutes. Because a crime is considered an offense against society, alleged criminals are prosecuted by the state rather than by victims. Crimes are punishable by sanctions that bring about a loss of personal freedom or, in some cases, life.

1-2 **Outline the three levels of law enforcement.** Because we have a federal system of government, law enforcement occurs (a) at the federal (national) level, (b) at the state level, and (c) at the local level. Because crime is mostly a local concern, most employees in the criminal justice system work for local governments. Agencies at the federal level include the FBI, the DEA, and the U.S. Secret Service, among others.

1-3 **List the essential elements of the corrections system.** Criminal offenders are placed on probation, incarcerated in a jail or prison, transferred to community-based corrections facilities, or released on parole.

1-4 **Define *ethics*, and describe the role that it plays in discretionary decision making.** Ethics consist of the moral principles that guide a person's perception of right and wrong. Most criminal justice professionals have a great deal of discretionary leeway in their day-to-day decision making, and their ethical beliefs can help ensure that they make such decisions in keeping with society's established values.

1-5 **Describe the defining aspects of a terrorist act, and identify one common misperception concerning domestic terrorism.** A terrorist act can be broadly defined as the use or threat of violence to achieve political goals. Domestic terrorism, despite a common public perception, does not include only extremist acts by radical Muslims in the United States.

1-1 WHAT IS CRIME?

Assault A threat or an attempt to do violence to another person that causes that person to fear immediate physical harm. (p. 5)

Battery The act of physically contacting another person with the intent to do harm, even if the resulting injury is insubstantial. (p. 5)

Burglary The act of breaking into or entering a structure (such as a home or office) without permission for the purpose of committing a felony. (p. 5)

Conflict Model A criminal justice model in which the content of criminal law is determined by the groups that hold economic, political, and social power in a community. (p. 4)

Consensus Model A criminal justice model in which the majority of citizens in a society share the same values and beliefs. (p. 4)

Crime An act that violates criminal law and is punishable by criminal sanctions. (p. 3)

Deviance Behavior that is considered to go against the norms established by society. (p. 5)

Larceny The act of taking property from another person without the use of force with the intent of keeping that property. (p. 5)

Morals Principles of right and wrong behavior, as practiced by individuals or by society. (p. 4)

Murder The unlawful killing of one human being by another. (p. 5)

Public Order Crime Behavior that has been labeled criminal because it is contrary to shared social values, customs, and norms. (p. 6)

Robbery The act of taking property from another person through force, threat of force, or intimidation. (p. 5)

Sexual Assault Forced or coerced sexual intercourse (or other sexual acts). (p. 5)

White-Collar Crimes Nonviolent crimes committed by business entities or individuals to gain a personal or business advantage. (p. 6)

1-2 WHAT IS THE PURPOSE OF CRIMINAL JUSTICE?

Criminal Justice System The interlocking network of law enforcement agencies, courts, and corrections institutions designed to enforce criminal laws and protect society from criminal behavior. (p. 7)

Justice The quality of fairness that must exist in the processes designed to determine whether individuals are guilty of criminal wrongdoing. (p. 7)

1-3 HOW DOES THE CRIMINAL JUSTICE SYSTEM WORK?

Federalism A form of government in which a written constitution provides for a division of powers between a central government and several regional governments. (p. 8)

Formal Criminal Justice Process The model of the criminal justice process in which participants follow formal rules to create a smoothly functioning disposition of cases from arrest to punishment. (p. 12)

System A set of interacting parts that, when functioning properly, achieve a desired result. (p. 12)

1-4 HOW DO CRIMINAL JUSTICE PROFESSIONALS MAKE DECISIONS?

Discretion The ability of individuals in the criminal justice system to make operational decisions based on personal judgment instead of formal rules or official information. (p. 12)

Ethics The moral principles that govern a person's perception of right and wrong. (p. 14)

Informal Criminal Justice Process A model of the criminal justice system that recognizes the informal authority exercised by individuals at each step of the criminal justice process. (p. 12)

1-5 WHAT'S HAPPENING IN CRIMINAL JUSTICE TODAY?

Biometrics Methods to identify a person based on unique physical characteristics, such as fingerprints or facial configuration. (p. 16)

Capital Crime A criminal act that makes the offender eligible to receive the death penalty. (p. 19)

Civil Liberties The basic rights and freedoms for American citizens guaranteed by the U.S. Constitution, particularly in the Bill of Rights. (p. 18)

Crime Control Model A criminal justice model that places primary emphasis on the right of society to be protected from crime and violent criminals. (p. 15)

Domestic Terrorism Acts of terrorism that take place on U.S. soil without direct foreign involvement. (p. 17)

Due Process Model A criminal justice model that places primacy on the right of the individual to be protected from the power of the government. (p. 15)

Evidence-Based Practices Approaches or strategies that have been extensively researched and shown consistently to produce the desired outcomes. (p. 15)

Homeland Security A concerted national effort to prevent terrorist attacks within the United States and reduce the country's vulnerability to terrorism. (p. 17)

FIGURE 1.1 MARIJUANA AND CRIMINAL LAW

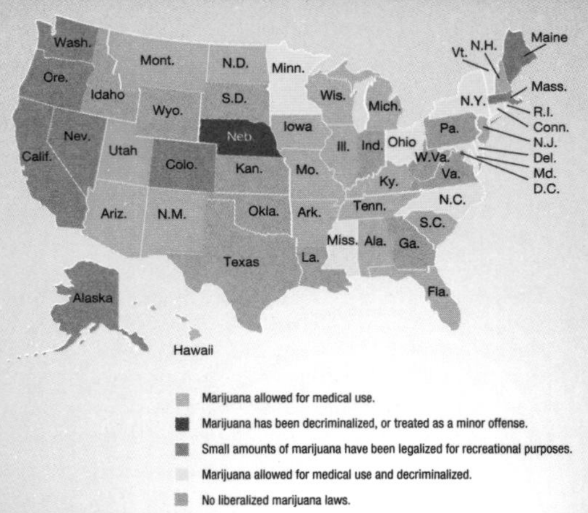

As this map shows, at the beginning of 2017 most states—representing about three-fourths of the population of the United States—allow for the use of marijuana under certain circumstances. Remember that *any* use of the drug is outlawed under federal law.

FIGURE 1.3 FEDERAL PRISONS: ADMISSIONS AND RELEASES

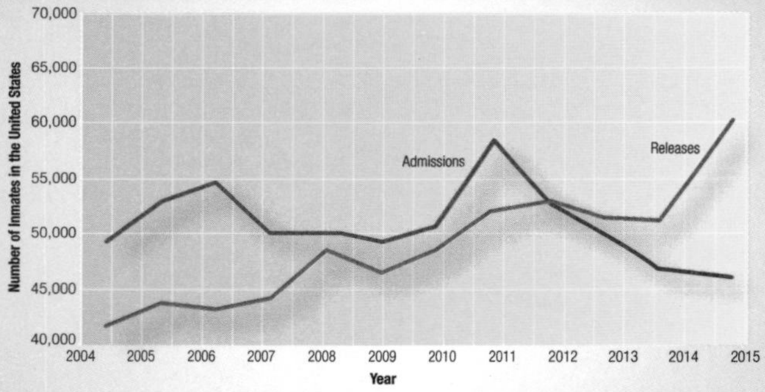

From 2012 to 2015, the number of inmates released from federal prisons has been greater than the number of inmates admitted to federal prisons, an important factor in the overall reduction of federal inmates in the United States.

Source: Bureau of Justice Statistics, *Prisoners in 2014* (Washington, D.C.: U.S. Department of Justice, September 2015), Appendix table 2, page 29; and Bureau of Justice Statistics, *Prisoners in 2015* (Washington, D.C.: U.S. Department of Justice, December 2016), Table 7, page 11.

Justice Reinvestment A corrections policy that promotes (a) a reduction in spending on prisons and jails and (b) reinvestment of the resulting savings in programs that decrease crime and reduce reoffending. (p. 18)

Recidivism The act of committing a new crime after having been punished for a previous crime by being convicted and sent to jail or prison. (p. 19)

Terrorism The use or threat of violence to achieve political objectives. (p. 17)

CHAPTER 2 LEARNING OBJECTIVES / OUTLINE / KEY TERMS

2-1 Discuss the difference between a hypothesis and a theory in the context of criminology. A hypothesis is a proposition, usually presented in an "If . . ., then . . ." format, that can be tested by researchers. If enough different authorities are able to test and verify a hypothesis, it will usually be accepted as a theory. Because theories can offer explanations for behavior, criminologists often rely on them when trying to determine the causes of criminal behavior.

2-2 Contrast the medical model of addiction with the criminal model of addiction. Those who support the medical model believe that addicts are not criminals, but mentally or physically ill individuals who are forced into acts of petty crime to "feed their habit." Those in favor of the criminal model believe that abusers and addicts endanger society with their behavior and should be treated like any other criminals.

2-3 Identify the publication in which the FBI reports crime data and list the two main ways in which the data are reported. Every year the FBI releases the Uniform Crime Reports (UCR), in which it presents different crimes as (a) a rate per 100,000 people and (b) a percentage change from the previous year.

2-4 Describe the three ways that victims' rights legislation increases the ability of crime victims to participate in the criminal justice system. (a) The right to be informed of victims' rights in general and of specific information relating to the relevant criminal case; (b) the right to be present at court proceedings involving the victim; and (c) the right to be heard on matters involving the prosecution, punishment, and release of the offender.

2-5 Explain why income level appears to be more important than race when it comes to crime trends. Criminologists have found that the most consistent indicators of criminal behavior are circumstances such as low family earning power and the absence of a parent. In addition, failure to obtain a high school diploma appears to have a positive correlation with criminal activity, regardless of the race or ethnicity of the individual.

2-1 WHAT IS A THEORY?

Causation The relationship in which a change in one measurement or behavior creates a recognizable change in another measurement or behavior. (p. 24)

Correlation The relationship between two measurements or behaviors that tend to move in the same direction. (p. 24)

Criminology The scientific study of crime and the causes of criminal behavior. (p. 23)

Hypothesis A possible explanation for an observed occurrence that can be tested by further investigation. (p. 24)

Theory An explanation of a happening or circumstance that is based on observation, experimentation, and reasoning. (p. 24)

2-2 WHICH THEORIES OF CRIME ARE MOST WIDELY ACCEPTED?

Anomie A condition in which the individual feels a disconnect from society due to the breakdown or absence of social norms. (p. 29)

Biology The science of living organisms, including their structure, function, growth, and origin. (p. 25)

Control Theory A series of theories that assume that all individuals have the potential for criminal behavior, but are restrained by the damage that such actions would do to their relationships with family, friends, and members of the community. (p. 30)

Genetics The study of how certain traits or qualities are transmitted from parents to their offspring. (p. 25)

Hormone A chemical substance, produced in tissue and conveyed in the bloodstream, that controls certain cellular and body functions, such as growth and reproduction. (p. 26)

Learning Theory The theory that delinquents and criminals must be taught both the practical and the emotional skills necessary to participate in illegal activity. (p. 30)

Life Course Criminology The study of crime based on the belief that behavioral patterns developed in childhood can predict delinquent and criminal behavior later in life. (p. 30)

Psychology The scientific study of mental processes and behavior. (p. 25)

Rational Choice Theory A school of criminology that holds that wrongdoers act as if they weigh the possible benefits of criminal or delinquent activity against the expected costs of being apprehended. (p. 24)

Social Conflict Theories Theories that view criminal behavior as the result of class conflict. (p. 29)

Social Disorganization Theory The theory that deviant behavior is more likely in communities where social institutions such as the family, schools, and the criminal justice system fail to exert control over the population. (p. 28)

Social Process Theories Theories that consider criminal behavior to be the predictable result of a person's interaction with his or her environment. (p. 30)

Social Psychology The study of how individual behavior is influenced by the behavior of groups in social situations. (p. 27)

Sociology The study of the development and functioning of groups of people who live together within a society. (p. 27)

Strain Theory The assumption that crime is the result of frustration felt by individuals who cannot reach their financial and personal goals through legitimate means. (p. 28)

Testosterone The hormone primarily responsible for the production of sperm and the development of male secondary sex characteristics. (p. 26)

2-3 WHAT IS THE CONNECTION BETWEEN DRUG USE AND CRIME?

Criminal Model of Addiction An approach to drug abuse that holds that drug offenders harm society by their actions to the same extent as other criminals and should face the same punitive sanctions. (p. 34)

Drug Any substance that modifies biological, psychological, or social behavior; in particular, an illegal substance with those properties. (p. 31)

Drug Abuse The use of drugs that results in physical or psychological problems for the user, as well as disruption of personal relationships and employment. (p. 33)

Legalization Making a formerly illegal product or action lawful. In the context of marijuana, the process includes strict regulation, including a ban on sale to or use by minors. (p. 34)

Medical Model of Addiction An approach to drug addiction that treats drug abuse as a mental illness and focuses on treating and rehabilitating offenders rather than punishing them. (p. 33)

Psychoactive Drug A chemical that affects the brain, causing changes in emotions, perceptions, and behavior. (p. 32)

2-4 HOW IS CRIME MEASURED?

Dark Figure of Crime A term used to describe the actual amount of crime that takes place. The "figure" is "dark," or impossible to detect, because a great number of crimes are never reported to the police. (p. 37)

Part I Offenses The most serious crimes recorded by the FBI in its Uniform Crime Reports. (p. 35)

Part II Offenses All crimes recorded by the FBI that do not fall into the category of Part I offenses. (p. 35)

Self-Reported Surveys Methods of gathering crime data that rely on participants to reveal and detail their own criminal or delinquent behavior. (p. 37)

Uniform Crime Reports (UCR) An annual report compiled by the FBI to give an indication of criminal activity in the United States. (p. 34)

Victim Survey A method of gathering crime data that directly surveys participants to determine their experiences as victims of crime. (p. 37)

2-5 WHAT ROLE DO VICTIMS PLAY IN CRIMINAL JUSTICE?

Repeat Victimization The theory that certain people and places are more likely to be subject to repeated criminal activity and that past victimization is a strong indicator of future victimization. (p. 39)

Victim Any person who suffers physical, emotional, or financial harm as the result of a criminal act. (p. 38)

2-6 WHAT ARE SOME IMPORTANT CRIME TRENDS IN THE UNITED STATES?

Domestic Violence An act of willful neglect or physical violence that occurs within a familial or other intimate relationship. (p. 44)

Stalking The criminal act of causing fear in a person by repeatedly subjecting that person to unwanted or threatening attention. (p. 44)

FIGURE 2.7 VIOLENT CRIME IN THE UNITED STATES, 1990–2015

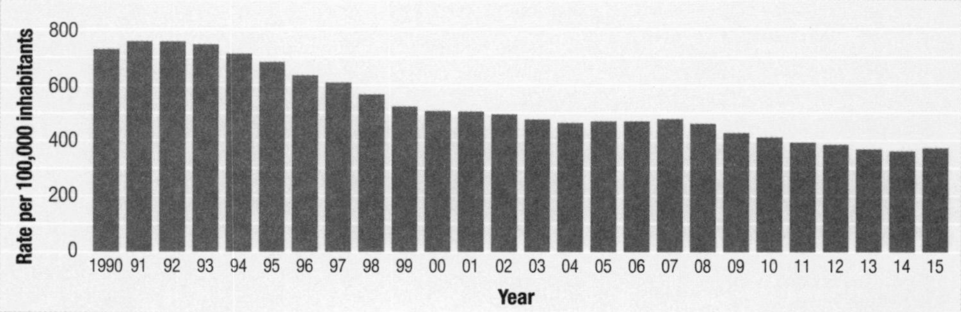

According to statistics gathered each year by the FBI, American violent crime rates dropped steadily in the second half of the 1990s, leveled off for several years, and then decreased steadily until a slight rise in 2015.

Source: Federal Bureau of Investigation.

CHAPTER 3 LEARNING OBJECTIVES / OUTLINE / KEY TERMS

3-1 **List the four written sources of American criminal law.** (a) The U.S. Constitution and state constitutions, (b) statutes passed by Congress and state legislatures (plus local ordinances), (c) administrative agency regulations, and (d) case law.

3-2 **Discuss the primary goals of civil law and criminal law and explain how these goals are realized.** Civil law is designed to resolve disputes between private individuals and other entities such as corporations. In these disputes, one party, called the plaintiff, tries to gain monetary damages by proving that the accused party, or defendant, is to blame for a tort, or wrongful act. In contrast, criminal law exists to protect society from criminal behavior. To that end, the government prosecutes defendants, or persons who have been charged with committing a crime.

3-3 **List and briefly define the most important excuse defenses for crimes. Insanity**—different tests of insanity can be used, including (a) the *M'Naghten* rule (right-wrong test); (b) the ALI/MPC test, also known as the substantial-capacity test; and (c) the irresistible-impulse test. **Intoxication**—can be voluntary or involuntary, with the latter being a possible criminal defense. **Mistake**—sometimes valid if the law was not published or reasonably known or if the alleged offender relied on an official statement of the law that was erroneous. Also, a mistake of fact may negate the mental state necessary to commit a crime.

3-4 **Describe the four most important justification criminal defenses. Duress**—requires that (a) the threat is of serious bodily harm or death, (b) the harm is greater than that caused by the crime, (c) the threat is immediate and inescapable, and (d) the defendant became involved in the situation through no fault of his or her own. **Justifiable use of force**—use of force in the defense of one's person, dwelling, or property or the prevention of a crime. **Necessity**—may apply if the harm caused by the crime actually committed is less than the harm that would have been caused by the criminal act avoided. **Entrapment**—can be used when the criminal action was induced by governmental persuasion or trickery.

3-5 **Explain the importance of the due process clause in the criminal justice system.** The due process clause acts to limit the power of government. In the criminal justice system, the due process clause requires that certain procedures be followed to ensure that criminal proceedings are fair and that all criminal laws are reasonable and in the interest of the public good.

3-1 WHAT ARE THE WRITTEN SOURCES OF AMERICAN CRIMINAL LAW?

Administrative Law The body of law created by administrative agencies (in the form of rules, regulations, orders, and decisions) in order to carry out their duties and responsibilities. (p. 49)

Ballot Initiative A procedure in which the citizens of a state, by collecting enough signatures, can force a public vote on a proposed change to state law. (p. 49)

Case Law The rules of law announced in court decisions. (p. 49)

Constitutional Law Law based on the U.S. Constitution and the constitutions of the various states. (p. 48)

Precedent A court decision that furnishes an example or authority for deciding subsequent cases involving similar facts. (p. 49)

Rule of Law The principle that the rules of a legal system apply equally to all persons, institutions, and entities—public or private—that make up a society. (p. 47)

Stare Decisis (pronounced *ster-ay dih-si-ses*). A legal doctrine under which judges are obligated to follow the precedents established in prior decisions. (p. 50)

Statutory Law The body of law enacted by legislative bodies. (p. 48)

Supremacy Clause A clause in the U.S. Constitution establishing that federal law is the "supreme law of the land" and shall prevail when in conflict with state constitutions or statutes. (p. 48)

3-2 WHY DO SOCIETIES NEED LAWS?

3-3 WHAT IS THE DIFFERENCE BETWEEN CIVIL AND CRIMINAL LAW?

Beyond a Reasonable Doubt The degree of proof required to find the defendant in a criminal trial guilty of committing the crime. The defendant's guilt must be the only reasonable explanation for the criminal act before the court. (p. 53)

Civil Law The branch of law dealing with the definition and enforcement of all private or public rights, as opposed to criminal matters. (p. 52)

Defendant In a civil court, the person or institution against whom an action is brought. In a criminal court, the person or entity who has been formally accused of violating a criminal law. (p. 52)

Liable In a civil court, legal responsibility for one's own or another's actions. (p. 52)

Plaintiff The person or institution that initiates a lawsuit in civil court proceedings by filing a complaint. (p. 52)

Preponderance of the Evidence The degree of proof required in a civil case. In general, this requirement is met when a plaintiff proves that a fact more likely than not is true. (p. 53)

3-4 WHAT ARE THE DIFFERENT CATEGORIES OF CRIMES?

Felony A serious crime, usually punishable by death or imprisonment for a year or longer. (p. 53)

Infraction In most jurisdictions, a noncriminal offense for which the penalty is a fine rather than incarceration. (p. 53)

Mala In Se A descriptive term for acts that are inherently wrong, regardless of whether they are prohibited by law. (p. 54)

Mala Prohibita A descriptive term for acts that are made illegal by criminal statute and are not necessarily wrong in and of themselves. (p. 54)

Misdemeanor A criminal offense that is not a felony; usually punishable by a fine and/or a jail term of less than one year. (p. 53)

3-5 WHAT ARE THE ELEMENTS OF A CRIME?

Actus Reus (pronounced *ak-tus ray-uhs*). A guilty (prohibited) act. (p. 58)

Attempt The act of taking substantial steps toward committing a crime while having the ability and the intent to commit the crime, even if the crime never takes place. (p. 55)

Attendant Circumstances The facts surrounding a criminal event that must be proved to convict the defendant of the underlying crime. (p. 59)

Conspiracy A plot by two or more people to carry out an illegal or harmful act. (p. 60)

Corpus Delicti The body of circumstances that must exist for a criminal act to have occurred. (p. 54)

Felony-Murder An unlawful homicide that occurs during the attempted commission of a felony. (p. 59)

Hate Crime Laws Statutes that provide for greater sanctions against those who commit crimes motivated by bias against an individual or a group based on race, ethnicity, religion, gender, sexual orientation, disability, or age. (p. 60)

Inchoate Offenses Conduct deemed criminal without actual harm being done, provided that the harm that would have occurred is one the law tries to prevent. (p. 60)

Involuntary Manslaughter A homicide in which the offender had no intent to kill the victim. (p. 57)

Mens Rea (pronounced *mehns ray-uh*). Mental state, or intent. A wrongful mental state is usually as necessary as a wrongful act to establish criminal liability. (p. 55)

Negligence A failure to exercise the standard of care that a reasonable person would exercise in similar circumstances. (p. 56)

Recklessness The state of being aware that a risk does or will exist and nevertheless acting in a way that consciously disregards this risk. (p. 56)

Statutory Rape A strict liability crime in which an adult engages in a sexual act with a minor. (p. 58)

Strict Liability Crimes Certain crimes, such as traffic violations, in which the defendant is guilty regardless of her or his state of mind at the time of the act. (p. 57)

Voluntary Manslaughter A homicide in which the intent to kill was present in the mind of the offender, but malice was lacking. (p. 57)

3-6 WHICH DEFENSES ARE AVAILABLE UNDER CRIMINAL LAW?

Alibi Proof that a suspect was somewhere other than the scene of the crime at the time of the crime, typically offered to demonstrate that the suspect was not guilty of the crime. (p. 61)

Competency Hearing A court proceeding to determine mental competency (p. 62)

Duress Unlawful pressure brought to bear on a person, causing the person to perform an act that he or she would not otherwise perform. (p. 64)

Duty to Retreat The requirement that a person claiming self-defense prove that she or he first took reasonable steps to avoid the conflict that resulted in the use of deadly force. (p. 65)

Entrapment A defense in which the defendant claims that he or she was induced by a public official—usually an undercover agent or police officer—to commit a crime that he or she would otherwise not have committed. (p. 66)

Infancy The status of a person who is below the legal age of majority. Under early American law, infancy excused young wrongdoers of criminal behavior because presumably they could not understand the consequences of their actions. (p. 61)

Insanity A defense for criminal liability that asserts a lack of criminal responsibility due to mental instability. (p. 61)

Intoxication A defense for criminal liability in which the defendant claims that the taking of intoxicants rendered him or her unable to form the requisite intent to commit a criminal act. (p. 63)

Irresistible-Impulse Test A test for the insanity defense under which a defendant who knew his or her action was wrong may still be found insane if he or she was unable, as a result of a mental deficiency, to control the urge to complete the act. (p. 62)

***M'Naghten* Rule** A test of criminal responsibility, derived from M'Naghten's Case in 1843, that relies on the defendant's inability to distinguish right from wrong. (p. 61)

Necessity A defense against criminal liability in which the defendant asserts that circumstances required her or him to commit an illegal act. (p. 65)

Self-Defense The legally recognized privilege to protect one's self or property from injury by another. (p. 64)

Substantial-Capacity Test (ALI-MPC Test) A test for the insanity defense that states that a person is not responsible for criminal behavior when he or she "lacks substantial capacity" to understand that the behavior is wrong or to know how to behave properly. (p. 62)

3-7 HOW DO CRIMINAL PROCEDURES PROTECT OUR CONSTITUTIONAL RIGHTS?

Bill of Rights The first ten amendments to the U.S. Constitution. (p. 66)

Due Process Clause The provisions of the Fifth and Fourteenth Amendments to the Constitution that guarantee that no person shall be deprived of life, liberty, or property without due process of law. (p. 67)

Procedural Criminal Law Law that governs procedures for investigating and prosecuting crimes. (p. 66)

Procedural Due Process A provision in the Constitution that states that the law must be carried out in a fair and orderly manner. (p. 67)

Substantive Criminal Law Law that defines crimes and punishments. (p. 66)

Substantive Due Process The constitutional requirement that laws must be fair and reasonable in content and must further a legitimate governmental objective. (p. 67)

CHAPTER 4 LEARNING OBJECTIVES / OUTLINE / KEY TERMS

4-1 **List the four basic responsibilities of the police.** (a) To enforce laws, (b) to provide services, (c) to prevent crime, and (d) to preserve the peace.

4-2 **Identify the differences between the police academy and field training as learning tools for recruits.** The police academy is a controlled environment where police recruits learn the basics of policing from instructors in classrooms. In contrast, field training takes place in the "real world": the recruit goes on patrol with an experienced police officer.

4-3 **Describe the challenges facing women who choose law enforcement as a career.** Many male officers believe that their female counterparts are not physically or mentally strong enough for police work, which puts pressure on women officers to continually prove themselves. Female officers must also deal with tokenism, or the stigma that they were hired only to fulfill diversity requirements, and sexual harassment in the form of unwanted advances or obscene remarks.

4-4 **Indicate some of the most important law enforcement agencies under the control of the Department of Homeland Security.** (a) U.S. Customs and Border Protection, which polices the flow of goods and people across U.S. international borders and oversees the U.S. Border Patrol; (b) U.S. Immigration and Customs Enforcement, which investigates and enforces our nation's immigration and customs laws; and (c) the U.S. Secret Service, which protects high-ranking federal government officials and federal property.

4-5 **Analyze the importance of private security today.** In the United States, businesses and citizens spend billions of dollars each year on private security. Increased crime in the workplace, along with concerns about terrorism, have fueled the growth in spending on private security.

4-1 WHAT DO POLICE DO?

Intelligence-Led Policing (ILP) An approach that measures the risk of criminal behavior associated with certain individuals or locations so as to predict when and where such criminal behavior is most likely to occur in the future. (p. 74)

Militarism The use of military training, tactics, and weaponry in policing. (p. 75)

4-2 HOW DOES SOMEONE BECOME A POLICE OFFICER?

Field Training The segment of a police recruit's training in which he or she is removed from the classroom and placed on the beat, under the supervision of a senior officer. (p. 77)

Probationary Period A period of time at the beginning of a police officer's career during which she or he may be fired without cause. (p. 77)

Recruitment The process by which law enforcement agencies develop a pool of qualified applicants from which to select new employees. (p. 76)

FIGURE 4.1 THE MAIN ELEMENTS OF A LAW ENFORCEMENT ACADEMY CURRICULUM

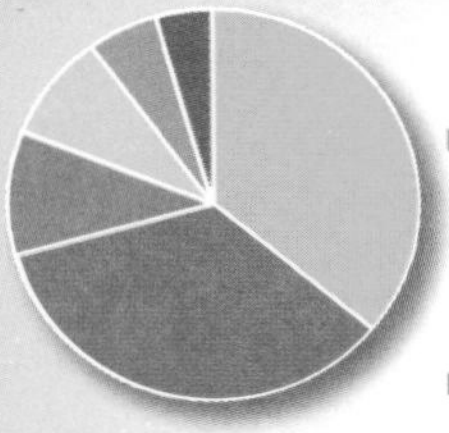

* This title refers to training in leadership and crisis management skills.

As this figure shows, a typical police academy cadet spends most of her or his time learning about the basic necessities of police work, such as defensive tactics, firearms, and patrol procedures.

Source: Adapted from Sue Rahr and Stephen K. Rice, *New Perspectives in Policing* (Washington, D.C.: National Institute of Justice, April 2015), Figure 1, page 8.

4-3 WHAT IS THE STATUS OF WOMEN AND MINORITIES IN POLICING?

Double Marginality The situation in which minority law enforcement officers face suspicion both from their white colleagues and from members of the minority community to which they belong. (p. 79)

Sexual Harassment A repeated pattern of unwelcome sexual advances and/or obscene remarks. Under certain circumstances, sexual harassment is illegal and can be the basis for a civil lawsuit. (p. 79)

FIGURE 4.2 POLICE DIVERSITY IN AMERICAN CITIES

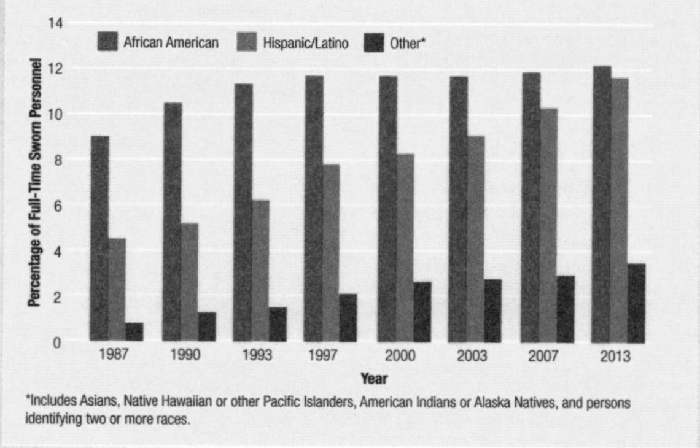

This graph shows that the percentage of members of some minority groups that make up local police department forces in the United States has been steadily growing since the late 1980s.

Source: Bureau of Justice Statistics, *Local Police Departments, 2013: Personnel, Policies, and Practices* (Washington, D.C.: U.S. Department of Justice, May 2015), Figure 5, page 5

4-4 WHAT ARE THE DIFFERENT KINDS OF LAW ENFORCEMENT AGENCIES?

Coroner The medical examiner of a county, usually elected by popular vote. (p. 81)

Drug Enforcement Administration (DEA) The federal agency responsible for enforcing the nation's laws and regulations regarding narcotics and other controlled substances. (p. 86)

Federal Bureau of Investigation (FBI) The branch of the Department of Justice responsible for investigating violations of federal law. (p. 85)

Human Trafficking The practice of illegally transporting a person from one country to another for the purpose of forced labor or sexual exploitation. (p. 84)

Infrastructure The services and facilities that support the day-to-day needs of modern life, such as electricity, food, transportation, and water. (p. 84)

Private Security The provision of policing services by private companies or individuals. (p. 87)

Secondary Policing The situation in which a police officer accepts off-duty employment from a private company or government agency. (p. 87)

Sheriff The primary law enforcement officer in a county, usually elected to the post by a popular vote. (p. 81)

U.S. Customs and Border Protection (CBP) The federal agency responsible for protecting U.S. borders and facilitating legal trade and travel across those borders. (p. 82)

U.S. Immigration and Customs Enforcement (ICE) The federal agency that enforces the nation's immigration and customs laws. (p. 83)

U.S. Secret Service A federal law enforcement organization with the primary responsibility of protecting the president, the president's family, the vice president, and other important political figures. (p. 84)

CHAPTER REVIEW

CHAPTER 5 LEARNING OBJECTIVES / OUTLINE / KEY TERMS

5-1 Explain why police officers are allowed discretionary powers. Police officers are considered trustworthy and able to make honest decisions. They have experience and training. They are knowledgeable in criminal behavior. Finally, they must be able to take reasonable steps to protect themselves.

5-2 List the three primary purposes of police patrol. (a) The deterrence of crime, (b) the maintenance of public order, and (c) the provision of certain services that are not related to crime.

5-3 Describe how forensic experts use DNA fingerprinting to solve crimes. Law enforcement agents gather trace evidence such as blood, semen, skin, and hair from the crime scene. Because these items are rich in DNA, which provides a unique genetic blueprint for every living organism, crime labs can create a DNA profile of the suspect and test it against other such profiles stored in databases. If the profiles match, then law enforcement agents have found a strong suspect for the crime.

5-4 Clarify the concepts of nondeadly force, deadly force, and reasonable force in the context of police use of force. Nondeadly force is force that is not likely to cause death or great bodily harm. Deadly force is force that a police officer is aware will place a subject in direct threat of serious injury or death. In either case, police use of force is legally justified only if it is reasonable—that is, if a reasonable person would find the degree of force necessary under the circumstances.

5-5 Explain what an ethical dilemma is and name four categories of ethical dilemmas that a police officer typically may face. An ethical dilemma is a situation in which police officers (a) do not know the right course of action, (b) have difficulty doing what they consider to be right, and/or (c) find the wrong choice very tempting. The four types of ethical dilemmas involve (a) discretion, (b) duty, (c) honesty, and (d) loyalty.

5-1 HOW DO LAW ENFORCEMENT AGENTS USE DISCRETION?

Policy A set of guiding principles designed to influence the behavior and decision making of police officers. (p. 92)

5-2 HOW DO POLICE OFFICERS FIGHT CRIME?

Ballistics The study of firearms, including the firing of the weapon and the flight of the bullet. (p. 98)

Broken Windows Theory The theory that, by cracking down on quality-of-life crimes, law enforcement convinces both criminals and law-abiding citizens that lawlessness will no longer be tolerated in a particular area. (p. 102)

Bureaucracy A hierarchically-structured administrative organization that carries out specific functions. (p. 93)

Clearance Rates A comparison of the number of crimes cleared by arrest and prosecution with the number of crimes reported during any given time period. (p. 97)

Cold Case A criminal investigation that has not been solved after a certain amount of time. (p. 97)

Cold Hit The establishment of a connection between a suspect and a crime, often through the use of DNA evidence, in the absence of an ongoing criminal investigation. (p. 99)

Community Policing A policing philosophy that emphasizes community support for and cooperation with the police in preventing crime. (p. 102)

Computer-Aided Dispatch (CAD) A method of dispatching police patrol units to the site of 911 emergencies with the assistance of a computer program. (p. 100)

Confidential Informant (CI) A human source for police who provides information concerning illegal activity in which he or she is involved. (p. 96)

Crime Mapping Technology that allows crime analysts to identify trends and patterns of criminal behavior within a given area. (p. 101)

Delegation of Authority A principle of command in which personnel take orders from and are responsible to those in positions of power directly above them. (p. 94)

Detective The primary police investigator of crimes. (p. 95)

Directed Patrol A patrol strategy designed to focus on a specific type of criminal activity in a specific geographic area. (p. 101)

FIGURE 5.1 A TYPICAL POLICE DEPARTMENT CHAIN OF COMMAND

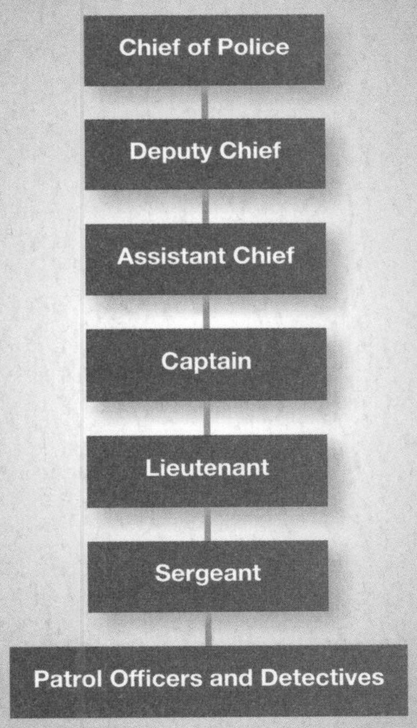

Most American police departments follow this model of the chain of command, though smaller departments with fewer employees often eliminate several of these categories.

5-2 HOW DO POLICE OFFICERS FIGHT CRIME? (CONTINUED)

DNA Fingerprinting The identification of a person based on a sample of her or his DNA, the genetic material found in the cells of all living things. (p. 98)

Forensics The application of science to establish facts and evidence during the investigation of crimes. (p. 97)

Hot Spots Concentrated areas of high criminal activity that draw a directed police response. (p. 101)

Incident-Driven Policing A reactive approach to policing that emphasizes a speedy response to calls for service. (p. 100)

Proactive Arrests Arrests that occur because of concerted efforts by law enforcement agencies to respond to a particular type of offender or criminal behavior. (p. 101)

Problem-Oriented Policing A policing philosophy that requires police to identify potential criminal activity and develop strategies to prevent or respond to that activity. (p. 103)

Random Patrol A patrol strategy that relies on police officers monitoring a certain area with the goal of detecting crimes in progress or preventing crime due to their presence. (p. 101)

Reactive Arrests Arrests that come about as part of the ordinary routine of police patrol and responses to calls for service. (p. 101)

Trace Evidence Evidence such as a fingerprint, blood, or hair found in small amounts at a crime scene. (p. 97)

5-3 WHAT ARE THE CHALLENGES OF BEING A POLICE OFFICER?

Blue Curtain A metaphorical term used to refer to the value placed on secrecy and the general mistrust of the outside world shared by many police officers. (p. 104)

Burnout A mental state that occurs when a person suffers from exhaustion and has difficulty functioning normally as a result of overwork and stress. (p. 105)

Civil Rights Violation Any interference with a citizen's constitutional rights by a civil servant such as a police officer. (p. 108)

Deadly Force Force applied by a police officer that is likely or intended to cause death. (p. 106)

Police Subculture The values and perceptions that are shared by members of a police department and, to a certain extent, by all law enforcement agents. (p. 104)

Racial Profiling The practice of targeting people for police action based solely on their race, ethnicity, or national origin. (p. 107)

Reasonable Force The degree of force that is appropriate to protect the police officer or other citizens and is not excessive. (p. 106)

Socialization The process through which a police officer is taught the values and expected behavior of the police subculture. (p. 104)

Stressors The aspects of police work and life that lead to feelings of stress. (p. 105)

FIGURE 5.3 THE ORLANDO (FLORIDA) POLICE DEPARTMENT'S USE-OF-FORCE MATRIX

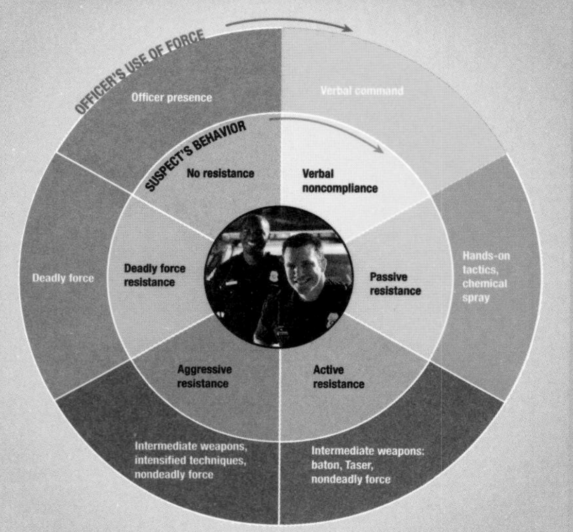

iStock.com/kali9

Like most local law enforcement agencies, the Orlando Police Department has a policy to guide its officers' use of force. Such policies instruct an officer on how to react to an escalating series of confrontations with a civilian and are often expressed visually, as shown here.

Source: Michael E. Miller, "Taser Use and the Use-of-Force Continuum," *Police Chief* (September 2010), 72.

5-4 HOW IMPORTANT IS ETHICS IN POLICING?

Duty A police officer's moral sense that she or he should behave in a certain manner. (p. 110)

Noble Cause Corruption Knowing misconduct by a police officer with the goal of attaining what the officer believes is a "just" result. (p. 109)

Police Corruption The abuse of authority by a law enforcement officer for personal gain. (p. 108)

6-1 **Outline the four major sources that may provide probable cause.** (a) Personal observation, usually based on an officer's personal training, experience, and expertise; (b) information gathered from informants, eyewitnesses, victims, police bulletins, and other sources; (c) evidence, which often has to be in plain view; and (d) association, which generally must involve a person with a known criminal background who is seen in a place where criminal activity is openly taking place.

6-2 **Explain when searches can be made without a warrant.** Searches and seizures can be made without a warrant if they are incidental to an arrest (but they must be reasonable); when they are made with voluntary consent; when they involve the "movable vehicle" exception; when property has been abandoned; and when items are in plain view, under certain restricted circumstances (see *Coolidge v. New Hampshire*).

6-3 **Distinguish between a stop and a frisk, and indicate the importance of the case *Terry v. Ohio*.** Though the terms *stop* and *frisk* are often used in concert, they describe separate acts. A stop occurs when an officer briefly detains a person he or she reasonably believes to be suspicious. A frisk is the physical "pat-down" of a suspect. In *Terry v. Ohio*, the Supreme Court ruled that an officer must have "specific and articulable facts" before making a stop, but those facts may be "taken together with rational inferences."

6-4 **List the four elements that must be present for an arrest to take place.** (a) Intent, (b) authority, (c) seizure or detention, and (d) the understanding of the person that he or she has been arrested.

6-5 **Indicate situations in which a *Miranda* warning is unnecessary.** (a) When no questions that are testimonial in nature are asked of the suspect; (b) when there is no suspect and witnesses in general are being questioned at the scene of a crime; (c) when a person volunteers information before the police ask anything; (d) when a suspect has given a private statement to a friend without the government orchestrating it; (e) during a stop and frisk when no arrests have been made; (f) during a traffic stop; and (g) when a threat to public safety exists.

6-1 HOW DOES THE FOURTH AMENDMENT RESTRICT POLICE DISCRETION?

Exclusionary Rule A rule under which any evidence that is obtained in violation of the accused's rights, as well as any evidence derived from illegally obtained evidence, will not be admissible in criminal court. (p. 115)

Fruit of the Poisoned Tree Evidence that is acquired through the use of illegally obtained evidence and is therefore inadmissible in court. (p. 115)

"Good Faith" Exception The legal principle that evidence obtained with the use of a technically invalid search warrant is admissible during trial if the police acted in good faith. (p. 116)

"Inevitable Discovery" Exception The legal principle that illegally obtained evidence can be admissible in court if police using lawful means would inevitably have discovered it. (p. 116)

Probable Cause Reasonable grounds to believe the existence of facts warranting certain actions, such as the search or arrest of a person. (p. 114)

Search and Seizure A legal term, as found in the Fourth Amendment to the U.S. Constitution, that generally refers to the search for and confiscation of evidence by law enforcement agents. (p. 114)

6-2 WHAT ARE THE RULES FOR SEARCHES AND SEIZURES?

Affidavit A written statement of facts, confirmed by the oath or affirmation of the party making it and made before a person having the authority to administer the oath or affirmation. (p. 118)

Consent Searches Searches by police that are made after the subject of the search has agreed to the action. (p. 119)

Electronic Surveillance The use of electronic equipment by law enforcement agents to record private conversations or observe conduct that is meant to be private. (p. 122)

Plain View Doctrine The legal principle that objects in plain view of a law enforcement agent who has the right to be in a position to have that view may be seized without a warrant and introduced as evidence. (p. 121)

Private Search Doctrine The legal principle that a private search eliminates an owner's reasonable expectation of privacy regarding the object searched. (p. 117)

Search The process by which police examine a person or property to find evidence that will be used to prove guilt in a criminal trial. (p. 117)

Searches Incidental to Arrests Searches for weapons and evidence that are conducted on persons who have just been arrested. (p. 119)

Search Warrant A written order, based on probable cause and issued by a court, commanding that police officers or criminal investigators search a specific person, place, or property to obtain evidence. (p. 118)

Seizure The forcible taking of a person or property in response to a violation of the law. (p. 118)

6 Police and the Constitution: The Rules of Law Enforcement

6-3 WHEN CAN POLICE STOP AND FRISK A SUSPECT?

Frisk A pat-down or minimal search by police to discover weapons. (p. 125)

Stop A brief detention of a person by law enforcement agents for questioning. (p. 124)

6-4 WHAT ARE THE RULES FOR MAKING AN ARREST?

Arrest The act of depriving a person suspected of criminal activity of his or her liberty. (p. 125)

Arrest Warrant A written order, based on probable cause and issued by a judge or magistrate, commanding that the person named on the warrant be arrested by the police. (p. 126)

Exigent Circumstances Situations that require extralegal or exceptional actions by the police. (p. 127)

Warrantless Arrest An arrest made without a warrant for the action. (p. 128)

FIGURE 6.3 THE DIFFERENCE BETWEEN A STOP AND AN ARREST

Both stops and arrests are considered seizures because both police actions restrict an individual's freedom to "walk away." Both must be justified by a showing of reasonableness. You should be aware, however, of the differences between a stop and an arrest. During a stop, police can interrogate the person and make a limited search of his or her outer clothing. If certain events occur during the stop, such as the discovery of an illegal weapon, then officers may arrest the person. If an arrest is made, the suspect comes under police control and is protected by the U.S. Constitution in a number of ways that will be discussed later in the chapter.

PhotoDisc / Getty Images

	Stop	Arrest
Justification	Reasonable suspicion	Probable cause
Warrant	None	Required in some, but not all, situations
Intent of Officer	To investigate suspicious activity	To make a formal charge against the suspect
Search	May frisk, or "pat down," for weapons	May conduct a full search for weapons or evidence
Scope of Search	Outer clothing only	Area within the suspect's immediate control or "reach"

6-5 WHAT ARE THE *MIRANDA* RIGHTS?

Admission A statement acknowledging that certain facts concerning a crime are true but falling short of a confession. (p. 128)

Coercion The use of physical force or mental intimidation to compel a person to do something—such as confess to committing a crime—against her or his will. (p. 128)

Confession A statement acknowledging that the suspect participated in some aspect of a crime. (p. 128)

Custodial Interrogation The questioning of a suspect after that person has been taken into custody. (p. 129)

Custody The forceful detention of a person or the person's perception that he or she is not free to leave the immediate vicinity. (p. 129)

False Confession A confession of guilt when the confessor did not, in fact, commit the crime. (p. 131)

Interrogation The direct questioning of a suspect to gather evidence of criminal activity and to try to gain a confession. (p. 128)

***Miranda* Rights** The constitutional rights of accused persons taken into custody by law enforcement officials, including the right to remain silent and the right to counsel. (p. 128)

CHAPTER 7 LEARNING OBJECTIVES / OUTLINE / KEY TERMS

7-1 Define *jurisdiction* and contrast geographic and subject-matter jurisdiction. Jurisdiction relates to the power of a court to hear a particular case. Courts are typically limited in geographic jurisdiction— for example, to a particular state. Some courts are restricted in subject matter, such as a small claims court, which can hear only cases involving civil matters under a certain monetary limit.

7-2 Explain the difference between trial and appellate courts. Trial courts are courts of the first instance, where a case is first heard. Appellate courts review the proceedings of lower courts. Appellate courts do not have juries.

7-3 Explain briefly how a case is brought to the United States Supreme Court. Cases decided in U.S. courts of appeals, as well as cases decided in the highest state courts (when federal questions arise), can be appealed to the Supreme Court. If at least four justices approve of a case filed with the Supreme Court, the Court will issue a writ of *certiorari,* ordering the lower court to send the Supreme Court the record of the case for review.

7-4 List the different names given to public prosecutors and indicate the general powers that they have. At the federal level, the prosecutor is called the U.S. attorney. In state and local courts, the prosecutor may be referred to as the prosecuting attorney, state attorney, district attorney, county attorney, or city attorney. Prosecutors in general have the power to decide when and how the state will pursue an individual suspected of criminal wrongdoing. In some jurisdictions, the district attorney is also the chief law enforcement officer, holding broad powers over police operations.

7-5 Explain why defense attorneys must often defend clients they know to be guilty. In our criminal justice system, the most important responsibility of a defense attorney is to be an advocate for her or his client. This means ensuring that the client's constitutional rights are protected during criminal justice proceedings, regardless of whether the client is guilty or innocent.

7-1 WHAT ROLE DO COURTS PLAY IN SOCIETY?

7-2 HOW DO AMERICAN COURTS OPERATE?

Appellate Courts Courts that review decisions made by lower courts, such as trial courts; also known as courts of appeals. (p. 139)

Concurrent Jurisdiction The situation that occurs when two or more courts have the authority to preside over the same criminal case. (p. 137)

Dual Court System The separate but interrelated court system of the United States, made up of the courts on the national level and the courts on the state level. (p. 139)

Extradition The process by which one jurisdiction surrenders a person accused or convicted of violating another jurisdiction's criminal law to the second jurisdiction. (p. 138)

Jurisdiction The authority of a court to hear and decide cases within an area of the law or a geographic territory. (p. 137)

Opinions Written statements by appellate judges expressing the reasons for the court's decision in a case. (p. 139)

Trial Courts Courts in which most cases begin and in which questions of fact are examined. (p. 139)

7-3 HOW DO STATES ORGANIZE THEIR COURTS?

Magistrate A public civil officer or official with limited judicial authority within a particular geographic area, such as the authority to issue an arrest warrant. (p. 140)

Problem-Solving Courts Lower courts that have jurisdiction over one specific area of criminal activity, such as illegal drugs or domestic violence. (p. 140)

FIGURE 7.1 THE DUAL COURT SYSTEM

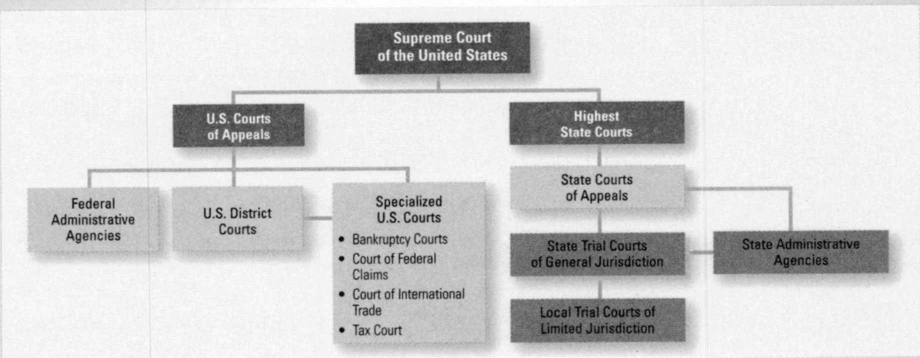

7-4 HOW DOES THE FEDERAL GOVERNMENT ORGANIZE ITS COURTS?

Concurring Opinions Separate opinions prepared by judges who support the decision of the majority but who want to make a particular point or to voice disapproval of the grounds on which the decision was made. (p. 144)

Dissenting Opinions Separate opinions in which judges disagree with the conclusion reached by the majority of the court and expand on their own views about the case. (p. 144)

Judicial Review The power of a court to review the actions of the executive and legislative branches and, if necessary, declare those actions unconstitutional. (p. 142)

Oral Arguments The verbal arguments presented in person by attorneys to an appellate court. (p. 144)

Rule of Four A rule of the United States Supreme Court that the Court will not issue a writ of *certiorari* unless at least four justices approve of the decision to hear the case. (p. 143)

Writ of *certiorari* A request from a higher court asking a lower court for the record of a case. (p. 143)

FIGURE 7.3 GEOGRAPHIC BOUNDARIES OF THE FEDERAL CIRCUIT COURTS OF APPEALS

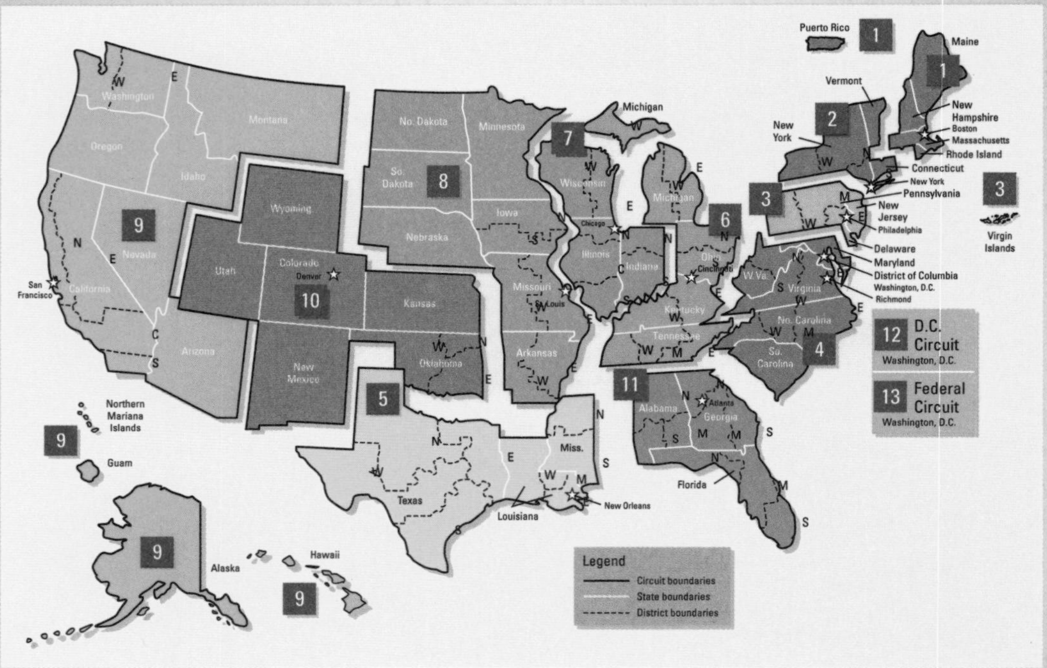

Source: Administrative Office of the United States Courts.

7-5 HOW DO JUDGES FUNCTION IN THE COURT SYSTEM?

Docket The list of cases entered on a court's calendar and thus scheduled to be heard by the court. (p. 146)

Missouri Plan A method of selecting judges that combines appointment and election. (p. 146)

Nonpartisan Elections Elections in which candidates are presented on the ballot without any party affiliation. (p. 146)

Partisan Elections Elections in which candidates are affiliated with and receive support from political parties. (p. 146)

7-6 WHAT IS THE COURTROOM WORK GROUP?

Attorney-Client Privilege A rule of evidence requiring that communications between a client and his or her attorney be kept confidential, unless the client consents to disclosure. (p. 152)

Attorney General The chief law officer of a state; also, the chief law officer of the nation. (p. 149)

Courtroom Work Group The social organization consisting of the judge, prosecutor, defense attorney, and other court workers. (p. 147)

Defense Attorney The lawyer representing the defendant. (p. 150)

Public Defenders Court-appointed attorneys who are paid by the state to represent defendants who cannot afford private counsel. (p. 150)

Public Prosecutor Individuals, acting as trial lawyers, who initiate and conduct cases in the government's name and on behalf of the people. (p. 148)

CHAPTER 8 LEARNING OBJECTIVES / OUTLINE / KEY TERMS

8-1 **Identify the steps involved in the pretrial criminal process.** (a) Suspect taken into custody or arrested; (b) initial appearance before a magistrate, at which time the defendant is informed of his or her constitutional rights and a public defender may be appointed or private counsel may be hired by the state to represent the defendant; (c) the posting of bail or release on recognizance; (d) preventive detention, if deemed necessary to ensure the safety of other persons or the community, or regular detention, if the defendant is unable to post bail; (e) preliminary hearing (mini-trial), at which the judge rules on whether there is probable cause and the prosecutor issues an information, or in the alternative (f) grand jury hearings, after which an indictment is issued against the defendant if the grand jury finds probable cause; (g) arraignment, in which the defendant is informed of the charges and must respond by pleading not guilty or guilty (or in some cases *nolo contendere*); and (h) plea bargaining.

8-2 **Indicate why prosecutors, defense attorneys, and defendants often agree to plea bargains.** For prosecutors, a plea bargain removes the risk of losing the case at trial, particularly if the evidence against the defendant is weak. For defense attorneys, the plea bargain may be the best deal possible for a potentially guilty client. For defendants, plea bargains give a measure of control over a highly uncertain future.

8-3 **Identify the basic protections enjoyed by criminal defendants in the United States.** According to the Sixth Amendment, a criminal defendant has the right to a speedy and public trial by an impartial jury in the community where the crime was committed. Additionally, a person accused of a crime must be informed of the nature of the crime and be confronted with the witnesses against him or her. Further, the accused must be able to summon witnesses in her or his favor and have the assistance of counsel.

8-4 **Contrast challenges for cause and peremptory challenges during *voir dire*.** A challenge for cause occurs when an attorney provides the court with a legally justifiable reason why a potential juror should be excluded—for example, the juror does not understand English. In contrast, peremptory challenges do not require any justification by the attorney and are usually limited to a small number. They cannot, however, be based, even implicitly, on race or gender.

8-5 **List the standard steps in a criminal jury trial.** (a) Opening statements by the prosecutor and the defense attorney; (b) presentation of evidence, usually in the form of questioning by the prosecutor, known as direct examination; (c) cross-examination by the defense attorney of the same witnesses; (d) presentation of the defendant's case, which may include putting the defendant on the stand and direct examination of the defense's witnesses; (e) cross-examination by the prosecutor; (f) after the defense closes its case, rebuttal by the prosecution, which may involve new evidence; (g) cross-examination of any new prosecution witnesses by the defense and possible introduction of new defense witnesses, called the surrebuttal; (h) closing arguments by both the defense and the prosecution; (i) the charging of the jury by the judge, during which the judge sums up the case and instructs the jurors on the rules of law that apply; (j) jury deliberations; and (k) presentation of the verdict.

8-1 WHAT HAPPENS AFTER ARREST?

Bail The dollar amount or conditions set by the court to ensure that an individual accused of a crime will appear for further criminal proceedings. (p. 158)

Bail Bond Agent A businessperson who agrees, for a fee, to pay the bail amount if the accused fails to appear in court as ordered. (p. 159)

Initial Appearance An accused's first appearance before a judge or magistrate following arrest. (p. 158)

Preventive Detention The retention of an accused person in custody due to fears that she or he will commit a crime if released before trial. (p. 159)

Property Bond An alternative to posting bail in cash, in which the defendant gains pretrial release by providing the court with property as assurance that he or she will return for trial. (p. 159)

Release on Recognizance (ROR) A judge's order that releases an accused person from jail with the understanding that he or she will return of his or her own will for further proceedings. (p. 159)

Risk Assessment A method for determining the likelihood that an offender will be involved in future wrongdoing. (p. 159)

8-2 HOW DOES A PROSECUTOR LINK A DEFENDANT TO A CRIME?

Case Attrition The process through which prosecutors, by deciding whether to prosecute each person arrested, effect an overall reduction in the number of persons prosecuted. (p. 161)

Deferred Prosecution When a prosecutor agrees to delay criminal proceedings against a defendant as long as the defendant meets certain requirements. (p. 161)

Discovery Formal investigation by each side prior to trial. (p. 160)

Grand Jury A group of citizens called to decide if there is probable cause to believe that the defendant committed a crime. (p. 160)

Indictment A charge or written accusation, issued by a grand jury, that probable cause exists to believe that a named person has committed a crime. (p. 160)

Information The formal charge against the accused issued by the prosecutor after a preliminary hearing has found probable cause. (p. 160)

Preliminary Hearing An initial hearing in which a magistrate decides if there is probable cause to believe that the defendant committed the crime with which he or she is charged. (p. 160)

8 Pretrial Procedures and the Criminal Trial

8-3 WHY DO SO MANY DEFENDANTS PLEAD GUILTY?

Arraignment A court proceeding in which the suspect is formally charged with the criminal offense stated in the indictment. (p. 163)

Nolo Contendere Latin for "I will not contest it." A plea in which a criminal defendant chooses not to challenge, or contest, the charges brought by the government. (p. 163)

Plea Bargaining The process by which the accused and the prosecutor work out a mutually satisfactory conclusion to the case. (p. 163)

8-4 WHAT ARE THE SPECIAL FEATURES OF CRIMINAL TRIALS?

Acquittal A declaration following a trial that the individual accused of the crime is innocent in the eyes of the law and thus is absolved from the charges. (p. 166)

Bench Trial A trial conducted without a jury, in which a judge makes the determination of the defendant's guilt or innocence. (p. 165)

Jury Trial A trial before a judge and a jury. (p. 165)

Statutes of Limitations Laws limiting the amount of time prosecutors have to bring criminal charges against a suspect after the crime has occurred. (p. 165)

8-5 HOW IS THE JURY SELECTED?

Challenge for Cause A *voir dire* challenge for which an attorney states the reason why a prospective juror should not be included on the jury. (p. 168)

Master Jury List The list of citizens in a court's district from which a jury can be selected. (p. 167)

Peremptory Challenges *Voir dire* challenges to exclude potential jurors from serving on the jury without any supporting reason or cause. (p. 168)

Venire The group of citizens from which the jury is selected. (p. 167)

Voir Dire The preliminary questions that the trial attorneys ask prospective jurors to determine whether they fit to serve on the jury. (p. 167)

8-6 WHAT HAPPENS DURING A CRIMINAL TRIAL?

Circumstantial Evidence Indirect evidence that is offered to establish, by inference, the likelihood of a fact that is in question. (p. 171)

Closing Arguments Arguments made by each side's attorney after the cases for the plaintiff and defendant have been presented. (p. 175)

Confrontation Clause The part of the Sixth Amendment that guarantee all defendants the right to confront witnesses testifying against them during the criminal trial. (p. 173)

Cross-Examination The questioning of an opposing witness during trial. (p. 173)

Direct Evidence Evidence that establishes the existence of a fact that is in question without relying on inference. (p. 171)

Direct Examination The examination of a witness by the attorney who calls the witness to the stand to testify. (p. 173)

Evidence Anything that is used to prove the existence or nonexistence of a fact. (p. 170)

Expert Witness A witness with professional training or substantial experience qualifying her or him to testify on a certain subject. (p. 170)

Hearsay A statement made by an out-of-court speaker that is later offered in court by a witness (not the speaker) concerning a matter before the court. (p. 173)

Lay Witness A witness who can truthfully and accurately testify on a fact in question without having specialized training or knowledge. (p. 170)

Opening Statements The attorneys' statements to the jury at the beginning of the trial. (p. 170)

Real Evidence Evidence that is brought into court and seen by the jury, as opposed to evidence that is described for a jury. (p. 170)

Rebuttal Evidence given to counteract or disprove evidence presented by the opposing party. (p. 175)

Relevant Evidence Evidence tending to make a fact in question more or less probable than it would be without the evidence. (p. 172)

Testimony Verbal evidence given by witnesses under oath. (p. 170)

8-7 WHAT HAPPENS AT THE END OF A CRIMINAL TRIAL?

***Allen* Charge** An instruction by a judge to a deadlocked jury that asks the jurors in the minority to reconsider the majority opinion. (p. 176)

Appeal The process of seeking a higher court's review of a lower court's decision for the purpose of correcting or changing this decision. (p. 176)

Charge The judge's instructions to the jury following the attorneys' closing arguments. (p. 176)

Double Jeopardy To twice place at risk (jeopardize) a person's life or liberty. (p. 177)

Habeas Corpus An order that requires corrections officials to bring an inmate before a court and explain why he or she is being held in prison. (p. 179)

Hung Jury A jury whose members are so irreconcilably divided in their opinions that they cannot reach a verdict. (p. 176)

Sequestration The isolation of jury members during a trial to ensure that their judgment is not tainted by outside information. (p. 176)

Verdict A formal decision made by the jury. (p. 176)

Wrongful Conviction The conviction, either by verdict or by guilty plea, of a person who is factually innocent of the charges. (p. 178)

CHAPTER 9 LEARNING OBJECTIVES / OUTLINE / KEY TERMS

9-1 **List and contrast the four basic philosophical reasons for sentencing criminals.** (a) Retribution, (b) deterrence, (c) incapacitation, and (d) rehabilitation. Under the principle of retributive justice, the severity of the punishment is proportional to the severity of the crime. Punishment is an end in itself. In contrast, the deterrence approach seeks to prevent future crimes by setting an example. Punishment is based on its deterrent value and not necessarily on the severity of the crime. The incapacitation theory of punishment simply argues that a criminal in prison cannot inflict further harm on society. In contrast, the rehabilitation theory asserts that criminals can be rehabilitated in the appropriate prison environment.

9-2 **Contrast indeterminate with determinate sentencing.** Indeterminate sentencing policies set a minimum and maximum amount of time that an offender must spend in prison. Within these limits, a judge may prescribe a specific term. Determinate sentencing requires the offender to serve a fixed amount of time, although this may be reduced for "good time."

9-3 **Explain some of the reasons why sentencing reform has occurred.** One reason for reform is sentencing disparity, a situation in which those convicted of similar crimes receive dissimilar sentences (often due to a particular judge's sentencing philosophy). Sentencing discrimination has also occurred on the basis of defendants' gender, race, or economic standing.

9-4 **Describe the goal of mandatory minimum sentencing guidelines and explain why these laws have become unpopular in recent years.** Mandatory minimum sentencing guidelines set fixed punishments for certain crimes. For the most part, these sentences are immune from judicial discretion. For that reason, they are unpopular with judges, who feel the laws do not recognize the individual aspects of each case. The guidelines also are believed to contribute to America's immense prison population and the racial imbalance of those behind bars.

9-5 **Identify the two stages that make up the bifurcated process of death penalty sentencing.** The first stage of the bifurcated process requires a jury to find the defendant guilty or not guilty of a crime that is punishable by execution. If the defendant is found guilty, then, in the second stage, the jury reconvenes to decide whether the death sentence is warranted.

9-1 WHY DO WE PUNISH CRIMINALS?

Deterrence The strategy of preventing crime through the threat of punishment. (p. 184)

Incapacitation A strategy for preventing crime by detaining wrongdoers in prison, thereby separating them from the community and reducing criminal opportunities. (p. 184)

Just Deserts A sanctioning philosophy based on the assertion that criminal punishment should be proportionate to the severity of the crime. (p. 184)

Rehabilitation The philosophy that society is best served when wrongdoers are provided the resources needed to eliminate their criminal behavior. (p. 185)

Restitution Monetary compensation for damages done to the victim by the offender's criminal act. (p. 185)

Restorative Justice An approach to punishment designed to repair the harm done to the victim and the community by the offender's criminal act. (p. 185)

Retribution The philosophy that those who commit criminal acts should be punished for breaking society's rules to the extent required by just deserts. (p. 184)

9-2 WHAT IS THE STRUCTURE OF THE SENTENCING PROCESS?

Aggravating Circumstances Any circumstances accompanying the commission of a crime that may justify a harsher sentence. (p. 190)

Determinate Sentencing Imposition of a sentence that is fixed by a sentencing authority and cannot be reduced by judges or other corrections officials. (p. 187)

"Good Time" A reduction in time served by prisoners based on good behavior, conformity to rules, and other positive behavior. (p. 187)

Indeterminate Sentencing Imposition of a sentence that prescribes a range of years rather than a specified number of years to be served. (p. 187)

FIGURE 9.1 AVERAGE SENTENCE LENGTH AND ESTIMATED TIME TO BE SERVED IN STATE PRISON

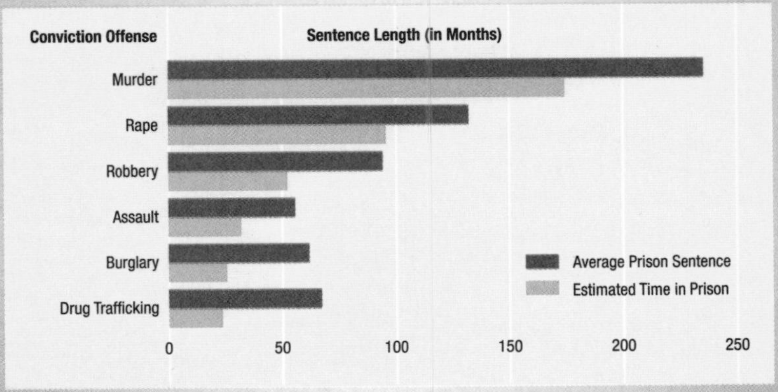

Source: *National Corrections Reporting Program: Sentence Length of State Prisoners, by Offense, Admission Type, Sex, and Race,* "Table 9: First Releases from State Prison, 2009." *www.bjs.gov*. Bureau of Justice Statistics: May 5, 2011, Web.

9 Punishment and Sentencing

9-2 WHAT IS THE STRUCTURE OF THE SENTENCING PROCESS? (CONTINUED)

Mitigating Circumstances Any circumstances accompanying the commission of a crime that may justify a lighter sentence. (p. 190)

Presentence Investigative Report An investigative report on an offender's background that assists a judge in determining the proper sentence. (p. 189)

"Real Offense" The actual offense committed, as opposed to the charge levied by a prosecutor as the result of a plea bargain. (p. 190)

Truth-In-Sentencing Law Legislative attempts to ensure that convicts will serve approximately the terms to which they were initially sentenced. (p. 187)

9-3 WHAT ARE SOME PROBLEMS WITH SENTENCING?

Sentencing Discrimination A situation in which the length of a sentence appears to be influenced by a defendant's race, gender, economic status, or other non-relevant factor. (p. 192)

Sentencing Disparity A situation in which those convicted of similar crimes do not receive similar sentences. (p. 192)

FIGURE 9.2 AVERAGE MAXIMUM SENTENCES FOR SELECTED CRIMES IN STATE AND FEDERAL COURTS

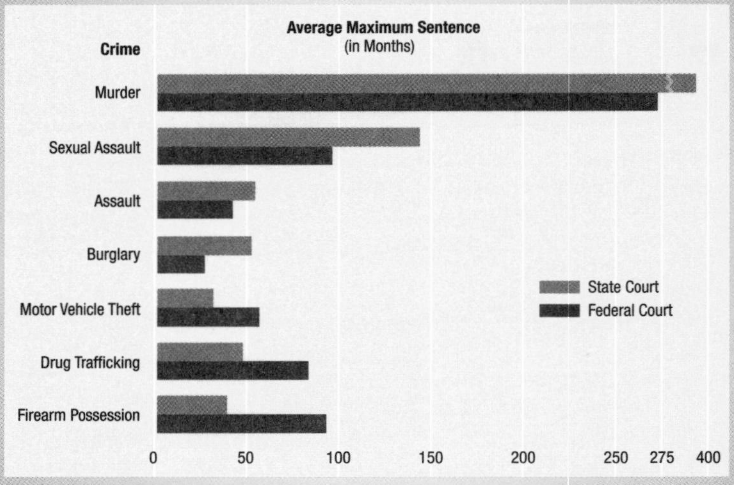

Source: Bureau of Justice Statistics, *Felony Defendants in Large Urban Counties, 2009–Statistical Tables* (Washington, D.C.: U.S. Department of Justice, December 2013), Table 25, page 30; and "Statistical Information Packet, Fiscal Year 2009, First Circuit," Table 7. *www.ussc.gov*. United States Sentencing Commission: 2010, Web.

9-4 HOW HAVE POLITICIANS TRIED TO "FIX" SENTENCING?

Departure A stipulation in sentencing guidelines that allows a judge to adjust his or her sentencing decision based on the special circumstances of a particular case. (p. 195)

Habitual Offender Laws Statutes that require lengthy prison sentences for those who are convicted of repeated felonies. (p. 196)

Mandatory (Minimum) Sentencing Guidelines Statutorily determined punishments that must be applied to those who are convicted of specific crimes. (p. 196)

Sentencing Guidelines Legislatively determined guidelines that judges are required to follow when sentencing those convicted of specific crimes. (p. 194)

Victim Impact Statement (VIS) A statement to the sentencing body in which the victim is given the opportunity to describe how the crime has affected her or him. (p. 197)

9-5 WHAT IS THE STATUS OF CAPITAL PUNISHMENT IN THE UNITED STATES?

Capital Punishment The use of the death penalty to punish wrongdoers for certain crimes. (p. 198)

FIGURE 9.5 THE BIFURCATED DEATH PENALTY PROCESS

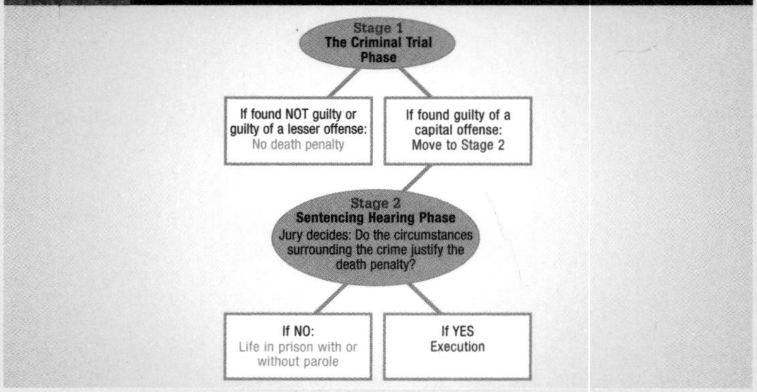

CHAPTER 10 LEARNING OBJECTIVES / OUTLINE / KEY TERMS

10-1 **Explain the justifications for community-based corrections programs.** One justification involves reintegration of the offender into society. Reintegration restores family ties, encourages employment and education, and secures a place for the offender in the routine functioning of society. Other justifications involve diversion and cost savings. By diverting criminals to alternative modes of punishment, further overcrowding of jail and prison facilities can be avoided, as can the costs of incarcerating the offenders.

10-2 **Describe the three general categories of conditions placed on a probationer.** (a) Standard conditions, such as requiring that the probationer notify the agency of a change of address, not leave the jurisdiction without permission, and remain employed; (b) punitive conditions, such as restitution, community service, and home confinement; and (c) treatment conditions, such as required drug or alcohol treatment.

10-3 **Identify the main differences between probation and parole.** Probation is a sentence handed down by a judge that generally acts as an alternative to incarceration. Parole is a form of early release from prison determined by a parole authority, often a parole board. Probationers are usually first-time offenders who have committed nonviolent crimes, while parolees have often spent significant time in prison.

10-4 **Explain which factors influence the decision to grant parole.** In deciding whether to grant parole, parole board members primarily consider the severity of the underlying crime and the threat the offender will pose to the community if released. Other factors include the offender's level of remorse and his or her behavior while incarcerated.

10-5 **List the three levels of home monitoring.** (a) Curfew, which requires that the offender be at home during specified hours; (b) home detention, which requires that the offender be at home except for education, employment, and counseling; and (c) home incarceration, which requires that the offender be at home at all times except for medical emergencies.

10-1 WHY DO WE NEED COMMUNITY CORRECTIONS?

Community Corrections The correctional supervision of offenders in the community as an alternative to sending them to prison or jail. (p. 205)

Diversion An effort to keep offenders out of prison or jail by diverting them into programs that promote treatment and rehabilitation rather than punishment. (p. 206)

Reintegration A goal of corrections that focuses on preparing the offender for a return to the community unmarred by further criminal behavior. (p. 206)

10-2 HOW DOES PROBATION WORK?

Authority The power conferred on an agent of the law to enforce obedience. (p. 211)

Caseload The number of individual probationers or parolees under the supervision of a probation or parole officer. (p. 211)

Probation A criminal sanction in which a convict is allowed to remain in the community rather than be imprisoned. (p. 207)

Revocation The formal process that follows the failure of a probationer or parolee to comply with the terms of his or her probation or parole. (p. 208)

Split Sentence Probation A sentence that consists of incarceration in a prison or jail, followed by a probationary period in the community. (p. 208)

Suspended Sentence A judicially imposed condition in which an offender is not required to begin serving her or his prison term immediately after being sentenced. (p. 208)

Technical Violation An action taken by a probationer or parolee that, although not criminal, breaks the terms of probation or parole as designated by the court. (p. 211)

FIGURE 10.1 PROBATION IN AMERICAN CORRECTIONS

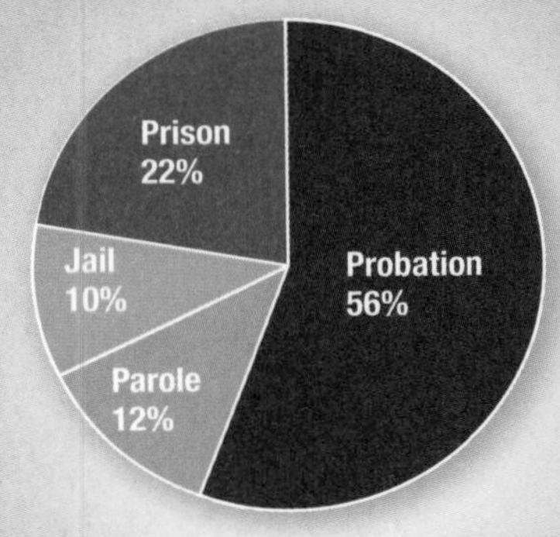

As this pie graph shows, the majority of convicts under the control of the American corrections system are on probation.

Source: Bureau of Justice Statistics, *Correctional Populations in the United States, 2015* (Washington, D.C.: U.S. Department of Justice, December 2016), Table 1, page 2.

10-3 HOW DOES PAROLE WORK?

Discretionary Release The release of an inmate into a community supervision program at the discretion of the parole board within limits set by law. (p. 214)

Mandatory Release Release from prison that occurs when an offender has served the full length of the sentence, minus adjustments for good time. (p. 216)

Parole The conditional release of an inmate before his or her sentence has expired. (p. 213)

Parole Board A body of appointed civilians that decides whether a convict should be granted conditional release before the end of his or her sentence. (p. 215)

Parole Contract An agreement between the state and the offender that establishes the conditions of parole. (p. 213)

Parole Grant Hearing A hearing in which the entire parole board or a subcommittee determines whether to grant parole. (p. 215)

Parole Guidelines Standards that are used in the parole process to measure the risk that a potential parolee will recidivate. (p. 217)

FIGURE 10.3 PROBATION VERSUS PAROLE

	Probation	Parole
Basic Definition	An **alternative to imprisonment** in which a person who has been convicted of a crime is allowed to serve his or her sentence in the community subject to certain conditions and supervision by a probation officer.	An **early release** from a correctional facility, in which the convicted offender is given the chance to spend the remainder of her or his sentence under supervision in the community.
Timing	The offender is sentenced to a probationary term in place of a prison or jail term. If the offender breaks the conditions of probation, he or she is sent to prison or jail. Therefore, **probation generally occurs *before* imprisonment**.	Parole is a form of early release. Therefore, **parole occurs *after* an offender has spent time behind bars.**
Authority	**Probation is under the domain of the judiciary.** A judge decides whether to sentence a convict to probation, and a judge determines whether a probation violation warrants revocation and incarceration.	**Parole often falls under the domain of the parole board.** This administrative body determines whether the prisoner qualifies for early release and the conditions under which the parole must be served.
Characteristics of Offenders	As a number of studies have shown, probationers are normally less involved in the criminal lifestyle. Most of them are **first-time offenders who have committed nonviolent crimes.**	Many parolees have **spent months or even years in prison** and, besides abiding by conditions of parole, must make the difficult transition to "life on the outside."

Probation and parole have many aspects in common. In fact, probation and parole are so similar that many jurisdictions combine them into a single agency. There are, however, some important distinctions between the two systems, as noted above.

10-4 WHAT ARE SOME TYPES OF INTERMEDIATE SANCTIONS?

Day Reporting Center (DRC) A community-based corrections center to which offenders report on a daily basis for treatment, education, and rehabilitation. (p. 218)

Electronic Monitoring A supervision technique in which the offender's whereabouts are kept under surveillance by an electronic device. (p. 220)

Forfeiture The process by which the government seizes private property attached to criminal activity. (p. 218)

Home Confinement A community-based sanction in which offenders serve their terms of incarceration in their homes. (p. 220)

Intensive Supervision Probation (ISP) A form of probation in which the offender is placed under stricter and more frequent surveillance and control than in conventional probation. (p. 219)

Intermediate Sanctions Sanctions that are more restrictive than probation and less restrictive than imprisonment. (p. 217)

Pretrial Diversion Program An alternative to trial in which the offender agrees to participate in a specified counseling or treatment program in return for withdrawal of the charges. (p. 217)

Shock Incarceration A short period of incarceration that is designed to deter further criminal activity by "shocking" the offender with the hardships of imprisonment. (p. 219)

Widen the Net To increase the number of citizens who are under the control and surveillance of the American corrections system. (p. 222)

CHAPTER 11 LEARNING OBJECTIVES / OUTLINE / KEY TERMS

11-1 **Contrast the Pennsylvania and the New York penitentiary theories of the 1800s.** Basically, the Pennsylvania system imposed total silence on its prisoners. Based on the concept of separate confinement, penitentiaries were constructed with back-to-back cells facing both outward and inward. Prisoners worked, slept, and ate alone in their cells. In contrast, New York used the congregate system: Silence was imposed, but inmates worked and ate together.

11-2 **List and briefly explain the four types of prisons.** (a) Maximum-security prisons, which are designed mainly with security and surveillance in mind. Such prisons are usually large and consist of cell blocks, each of which is set off by a series of gates and bars. (b) Medium-security prisons, which offer considerably more educational and treatment programs and allow more contact between inmates. Such prisons are usually surrounded by high fences rather than by walls. (c) Minimum-security prisons, which permit prisoners to have televisions and computers and often allow them to leave the grounds for educational and employment purposes. (d) Supermaximum-security (supermax) prisons, in which prisoners are confined to one-person cells for up to twenty-three hours per day under constant video camera surveillance.

11-3 **Identify some factors that have caused the prison population to grow dramatically in the last several decades.** Factors include the willingness of prosecutors to bring felony rather than misdemeanor charges, the enhancement and stricter enforcement of drug laws, the increased probability of incarceration, the increase in time served for each crime, and the expansion of the federal prison system.

11-4 **Describe the arguments for and against private prisons.** Proponents of private prisons contend that they can be run more cheaply and efficiently than public ones. Opponents of prison privatization dispute such claims. They also argue that private prisons are financially motivated to deny inmates the same protections and rights they receive in public correctional facilities.

11-5 **Summarize the distinction between jails and prisons, and indicate the importance of jails in the American corrections system.** Generally, a prison is for those convicted of felonies who will serve lengthy periods of incarceration, whereas a jail is for those who have been convicted of misdemeanors and will serve less than a year of incarceration. Jails also hold individuals awaiting trial, juveniles awaiting transfer to juvenile authorities, probation and parole violators, and mentally ill inmates. In any given year, almost 12 million people are admitted to jails. It is at this point that treatment and counseling have the best chance to deter future criminal behavior on the part of these low-level offenders.

11-1 HOW HAVE AMERICAN PRISONS EVOLVED?

Congregate System A nineteenth-century penitentiary system developed in New York in which inmates were kept in separate cells during the night but worked together in the daytime in silence. (p. 227)

Medical Model A model of corrections in which the psychological and biological roots of an inmate's criminal behavior are identified and treated. (p. 227)

Penitentiary An early form of correctional facility that emphasized separating inmates from society and from each other. (p. 226)

Separate Confinement A nineteenth-century penitentiary system developed in Pennsylvania in which inmates were kept separate from each other at all times, with daily activities taking place in individual cells. (p. 226)

11-2 HOW ARE PRISONS ORGANIZED AND MANAGED?

Classification The process through which prison officials screen each incoming inmate to best determine that inmate's security and treatment needs. (p. 231)

Custody Level The security designation given to new inmates. (p. 231)

Lockdown A disciplinary action taken by prison officials in which all inmates are ordered to their quarters and nonessential prison activities are suspended. (p. 233)

Maximum-Security Prison A correctional institution designed and organized to control and discipline dangerous felons, as well as prevent escape. (p. 232)

Medium-Security Prison A correctional institution that houses less dangerous inmates and therefore uses less restrictive measures to prevent violence and escapes. (p. 233)

Minimum-Security Prison A correctional institution designed to allow inmates, most of whom pose low security risks, a great deal of freedom of movement and contact with the outside world. (p. 234)

Supermax Prison A highly secure correctional facility that manages offenders who would pose a threat to the security and safety of other inmates and staff members if housed in the general inmate population. (p. 233)

Warden The prison official who is ultimately responsible for the organization and performance of a correctional facility. (p. 230)

11-3 WHAT TRENDS ARE DRIVING THE AMERICAN PRISON POPULATION?

11-4 WHAT ARE PRIVATE PRISONS?

Private Prisons Correctional facilities operated by private corporations instead of the government and, therefore, reliant on profits for survival. (p. 236)

11-5 WHAT ROLE DO JAILS PLAY IN THE CORRECTIONS SYSTEM?

Direct Supervision Approach A process of prison and jail administration in which correctional officers are in continuous visual contact with inmates during the day. (p. 242)

Fee System A system in which the sheriff's department is reimbursed by a government agency for the costs of housing jail inmates. (p. 240)

Jail A facility, usually operated by the county government, used to hold persons awaiting trial or those who have been found guilty of minor crimes (mostly misdemeanors). (p. 238)

New-Generation Jail A type of jail designed to encourage interaction between inmates and jailers and offering greater opportunities for treatment. (p. 242)

Pretrial Detainees Individuals who cannot post bail after arrest and are therefore forced to spend the time prior to their trial incarcerated in jail. (p. 239)

Time Served The period of time a person denied bail (or unable to pay it) has spent in jail prior to his or her trial. (p. 239)

FIGURE 11.2 TYPES OF OFFENSES OF FEDERAL AND STATE PRISON INMATES

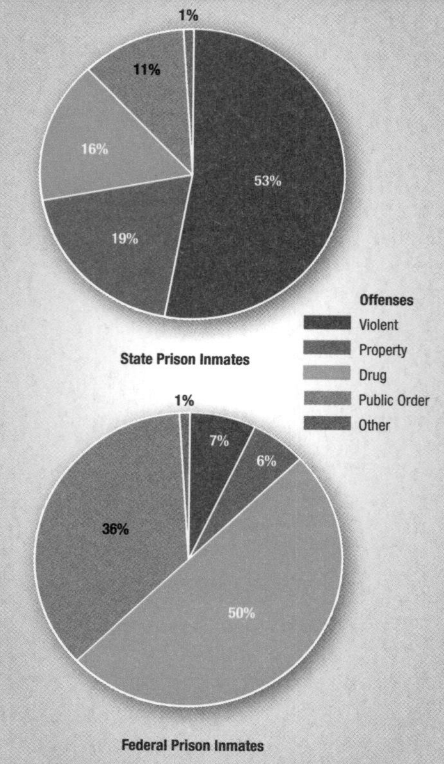

As the comparison above shows, state prisoners are most likely to have been convicted of violent crimes, while federal prisoners are most likely to have been convicted of drug and public order offenses.

Source: Bureau of Justice Statistics, *Prisoners in 2015* (Washington, D.C.: U.S. Department of Justice, December 2016), Table 9, page 14; and Table 10, page 15.

FIGURE 11.4 THE INMATE POPULATION OF THE UNITED STATES

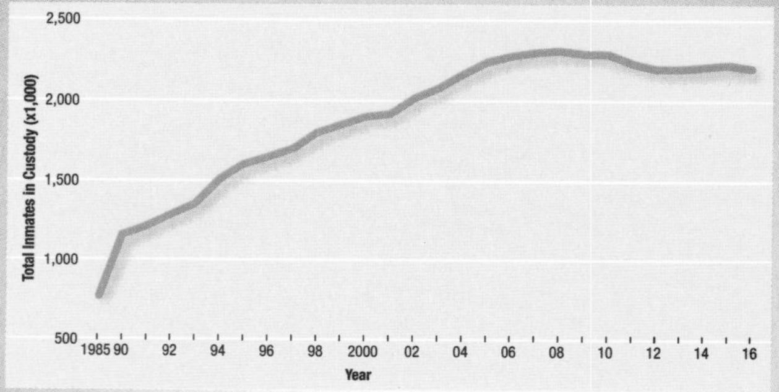

The total number of inmates in the United States has risen from 744,208 in 1985 to about 2.2 million in 2016.

Source: U.S. Department of Justice.

FIGURE 11.5 THE MAIN DIFFERENCES BETWEEN PRISONS AND JAILS

	Prisons	Jails
1.	. . . are operated by the federal and state governments.	. . . are operated by county and city governments.
2.	. . . hold inmates who may have lived quite far away before being arrested.	. . . hold mostly inmates from the local community.
3.	. . . house only those who have been convicted of a crime.	. . . house those who are awaiting trial or have recently been arrested, in addition to convicts.
4.	. . . generally hold inmates who have been found guilty of serious crimes and received sentences of longer than one year.	. . . generally hold inmates who have been found guilty of minor crimes and are serving sentences of less than a year.
5.	. . . often offer a wide variety of rehabilitation and educational programs for long-term prisoners.	. . . due to smaller budgets, tend to focus only on the necessities of safety, food, and clothing.

CHAPTER 12 LEARNING OBJECTIVES / OUTLINE / KEY TERMS

12-1 **Explain the concept of prison as a total institution.** Though many people spend time in partial institutions—schools, companies where they work, and religious organizations—only in prison is every aspect of an inmate's life controlled, and that is why prisons are called total institutions. Every detail for every prisoner is fully prescribed and managed.

12-2 **Indicate some of the reasons for violent behavior in prisons.** (a) To separate the powerful from the weak and establish a prisoner hierarchy; (b) to minimize one's own probability of being a target of assault; (c) to enhance one's self-image; (d) to obtain sexual relief; and (e) to obtain material goods through extortion or robbery.

12-3 **Describe the hands-off doctrine of prisoner law and indicate two standards used to determine if prisoners' rights have been violated.** The hands-off doctrine assumes that the care of prisoners should be left to prison officials and that it is not the place of judges to intervene. Nonetheless, the Supreme Court has created two standards to be used by the courts in determining whether a prisoner's Eighth Amendment protections against cruel and unusual punishment have been violated. Under the "deliberate indifference" standard, prisoners must show that prison officials were aware of harmful conditions at the facility and failed to remedy them. Under the "identifiable human needs" standard, prisoners must show that they were denied a basic need such as food, warmth, or exercise.

12-4 **Contrast parole, expiration release, pardon, and furlough.** Parole is an early release program for those incarcerated. Expiration release occurs when the inmate has served the maximum time for her or his initial sentence minus good-time credits. A pardon can be given only by the president or by one of the fifty governors. Furlough is a temporary release while in jail or prison.

12-5 **Explain the goal of prisoner reentry programs.** Based on the ideals of promoting desistance, these programs have two main objectives: (a) to prepare a prisoner for a successful return to the community, and (b) to protect the community by reducing the chances that the ex-convict will continue her or his criminal activity after release from prison.

12-1 HOW DO INMATES ADJUST TO LIFE IN PRISON?

Prisonization The socialization process through which a new inmate learns the accepted norms and values of the prison culture. (p. 246)

Prison Programs Organized activities for inmates that are designed to improve their physical and mental health and/or provide them with vocational skills. (p. 248)

Total Institution An institution, such as a prison, that provides all of the necessities for existence to those who live within its boundaries. (p. 245)

12-2 HOW VIOLENT IS LIFE BEHIND BARS?

Deprivation Model A theory that inmate aggression is the result of the frustration inmates feel at being deprived of freedom, consumer goods, and other staples of life outside the institution. (p. 249)

Prison Gang A group of inmates who band together within the corrections system to engage in social and criminal activities. (p. 250)

Relative Deprivation The theory that inmate aggression is caused when freedoms and services that the inmate has come to accept as normal are decreased or eliminated. (p. 249)

Security Threat Group (STG) A group of three or more inmates who engage in activity that poses a threat to the safety of other inmates or the prison staff. (p. 251)

12-3 HOW DO CORRECTIONAL OFFICERS MAINTAIN DISCIPLINE?

"Deliberate Indifference" The standard for establishing a violation of an inmate's Eighth Amendment rights, requiring that prison officials were aware of harmful conditions in a correctional institution and failed to take steps to remedy those conditions. (p. 256)

"Hands-Off" Doctrine The unwritten judicial policy that favors noninterference by the courts in the administration of prisons and jails. (p. 255)

"Identifiable Human Needs" The basic human necessities that correctional facilities are required by the Constitution to provide to inmates. (p. 256)

Solitary Confinement A disciplinary practice that involves placing the punished inmate in a separate cell to isolate him or her from human contact. (p. 254)

12-4 ARE WOMEN'S PRISONS DIFFERENT?

12-5 WHAT HAPPENS TO EX-INMATES?

Civil Confinement The practice of confining individuals against their will if they present a danger to the community. (p. 264)

Desistance The process through which criminal activity decreases and reintegration into society increases over a period of time. (p. 260)

Expiration Release The release of an inmate from prison at the end of his or her sentence without any further correctional supervision. (p. 259)

Furlough Temporary release from a prison for purposes of vocational or educational training, to ease the shock of release, or for personal reasons. (p. 259)

FIGURE 12.2 FEMALE PRISONERS IN THE UNITED STATES BY RACE, ETHNICITY, AND AGE

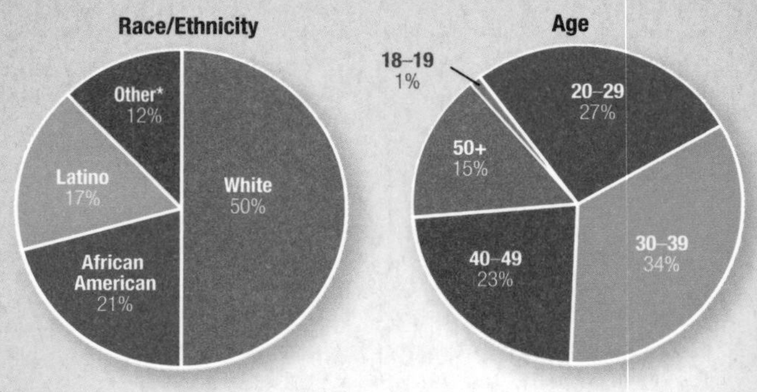

*Includes American Indians, Alaska Natives, Native Hawaiians, other Pacific Islanders, and persons identifying two or more races.

Source: Bureau of Justice Statistics, *Prisoners in 2015* (Washington, D.C.: U.S. Department of Justice, December 2016), Table 8, page 13.

Halfway Houses A community-based form of early release that places inmates in residential centers and allows them to reintegrate with society (p. 261)

Pardon An act of executive clemency that overturns a conviction and erases mention of the crime from the person's criminal record. (p. 259)

Prisoner Reentry A corrections strategy designed to prepare inmates for a successful return to the community and to reduce recidivism. (p. 259)

Sex Offender Notification Law Legislation that requires law enforcement authorities to provide notice when convicted sex offenders are released into the community. (p. 263)

Work Release Programs Temporary release of convicts from prison for purposes of employment. (p. 261)

FIGURE 12.3 PRISONER REENTRY ISSUES

1. **Housing.** Nearly two-thirds of the men were living with family members, and about half considered their housing situation "temporary." Many were concerned about their living environment: Half said that drug dealing was a major problem in their neighborhoods, and almost 25 percent were living with drug and alcohol abusers.
2. **Employment.** After one year, only about one-third of the former inmates had a full-time job, and another 11 percent were working part time.
3. **Family and friends.** One in four of the men identified family support as the most important thing keeping them from returning to criminality. Another 16 percent said that avoiding certain people and situations was the most crucial factor in their continued good behavior.
4. **Programs and services.** About two-thirds of the former inmates had taken part in programs and services such as drug treatment and continuing education.
5. **Health.** More than half of the men reported suffering from a chronic health condition, and 29 percent showed symptoms of depression.
6. **Substance use.** About half of the men admitted to weekly drug use or alcohol intoxication. Men who had strong family ties and those who were required to maintain telephone contact with their parole officers were less likely to engage in frequent substance use.
7. **Parole violation and recidivism.** More than half of the former inmates reported that they had violated the conditions of their parole, usually by drug use or having contact with other parolees. Fifteen percent of the men returned to prison in the year after release. Four out of five of the returns were the result of a new crime.

Researchers from the Urban Institute in Washington, D.C., asked nearly three hundred former prisoners (all male) in the Cleveland, Ohio, area about the most pressing issues they faced in their first year after release. The answers provide a useful snapshot of the many challenges of reentry.

Source: Christy A. Visher and Shannon M. E. Courtney, *One Year Out: Experience of Prisoners Returning to Cleveland* (Washington, D.C.: Urban Institute, April 2007), 2.

13-1 **List the four major differences between juvenile courts and adult courts.** (a) No juries, (b) different terminology, (c) limited adversarial relationship, and (d) confidentiality.

13-2 **Identify and briefly describe the single most important U.S. Supreme Court case with respect to juvenile justice.** The case was *In re Gault*, decided by the Supreme Court in 1967. In this case, a minor had been arrested for allegedly making an obscene phone call. His parents had not been notified and had not been present during the juvenile court judge's decision-making process. The Supreme Court held that juveniles are entitled to many of the same due process rights granted to adult offenders, including notice of charges, the right to counsel, the privilege against self-incrimination, and the right to confront and cross-examine witnesses.

13-3 **Describe the reasoning behind recent U.S. Supreme Court decisions that have lessened the harshness of sentencing outcomes for violent juvenile offenders.** In banning capital punishment and limiting the availability of life sentences without parole for offenders who committed their crimes as juveniles, the Supreme Court has focused on the concept of "diminished culpability." This concept is based on the notion that violent juvenile offenders cannot fully comprehend the consequences of their actions and have a greater capacity for rehabilitation than adult violent offenders.

13-4 **Describe the one variable that always correlates highly with juvenile crime rates.** The older a person is, the less likely he or she will exhibit criminal behavior. This process is known as aging out. Thus, persons in any at-risk group will commit fewer crimes as they get older.

13-5 **Describe the four primary components of pretrial juvenile justice procedure.** (a) Intake, in which an official of the juvenile court engages in a screening process to determine what to do with the youthful offender; (b) pretrial diversion, which may consist of probation, treatment and aid, and/or restitution; (c) jurisdictional waiver to an adult court, in which case the youth leaves the juvenile justice system; and (d) some type of detention, in which the youth is held until the disposition process begins.

13-1 WHY DO WE HAVE A SEPARATE JUSTICE SYSTEM FOR JUVENILES?

Juvenile Delinquency Illegal behavior committed by a person who is under an age limit specified by statute. (p. 269)

Parens Patriae A doctrine that holds that the state has a responsibility to look after the well-being of children and to assume the role of parent if necessary. (p. 267)

Status Offender A juvenile who has engaged in behavior deemed unacceptable for those under a certain statutorily determined age. (p. 268)

FIGURE 13.1 STATUS OFFENSES

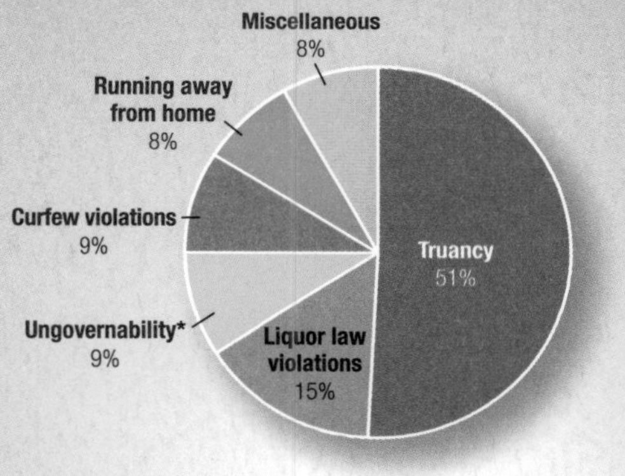

* Being beyond the control of parents, teachers, or other adult authority figures.

About 109,000 status offenses are processed by juvenile courts in the United States each year. The most common, as this graph shows, are truancy (skipping school) and liquor-related offenses.

Source: Sarah Hockenberry and Charles Puzzanchera, *Juvenile Court Statistics, 2013* (Pittsburgh, Pa.: National Center for Juvenile Justice, July 2015), 66.

13-2 HOW IS DELINQUENCY DETERMINED?

13-3 HOW MUCH JUVENILE DELINQUENCY IS THERE IN THE UNITED STATES?

Bullying Overt acts taken by students with the goal of intimidating, harassing, or humiliating other students. (p. 275)

13-4 WHY DO JUVENILES COMMIT CRIMES?

Age of Onset The age at which a juvenile first exhibits delinquent behavior. (p. 277)

Aging Out A term used to explain the fact that criminal activity declines with age. (p. 277)

Child Abuse Mistreatment of children involving physical, emotional, and/or sexual damage. (p. 277)

Child Neglect A form of child abuse in which the child is denied certain necessities such as shelter, food, care, and love. (p. 277)

Youth Gang A self-formed group of youths with several identifiable characteristics, including a gang name and other recognizable symbols, a geographic territory, and participation in illegal activities. (p. 278)

13-5 WHAT HAPPENS AFTER A JUVENILE IS ARRESTED?

Automatic Transfer The process by which a juvenile is transferred to adult court as a matter of state law. (p. 281)

Detention The temporary custody of a juvenile in a secure facility after a petition has been filed and before the adjudicatory process begins. (p. 281)

Detention Hearing A hearing to determine whether a juvenile should be detained, or remain detained, while waiting for the adjudicatory process to begin. (p. 281)

Intake The process by which an official of the court must decide whether to file a petition, release the juvenile, or place the juvenile under some other form of supervision. (p. 280)

Judicial Waiver The process in which the juvenile judge, based on the facts of the case at hand, decides that the alleged offender should be transferred to adult court. (p. 281)

Low-Visibility Decision Making A term used to describe the discretionary power police have in determining what to do with misbehaving juveniles. (p. 279)

Petition The document filed with a juvenile court alleging that the juvenile is a delinquent or a status offender and requesting that the court either hear the case or transfer it to an adult court. (p. 280)

Prosecutorial Waiver A procedure by which the prosecutor has discretion to decide whether a case will be heard by a juvenile court or an adult court. (p. 281)

Referral The notification process through which a law enforcement officer or other concerned citizen makes the juvenile court aware of a juvenile's unlawful or unruly conduct. (p. 280)

FIGURE 13.5 THE JUVENILE JUSTICE PROCESS

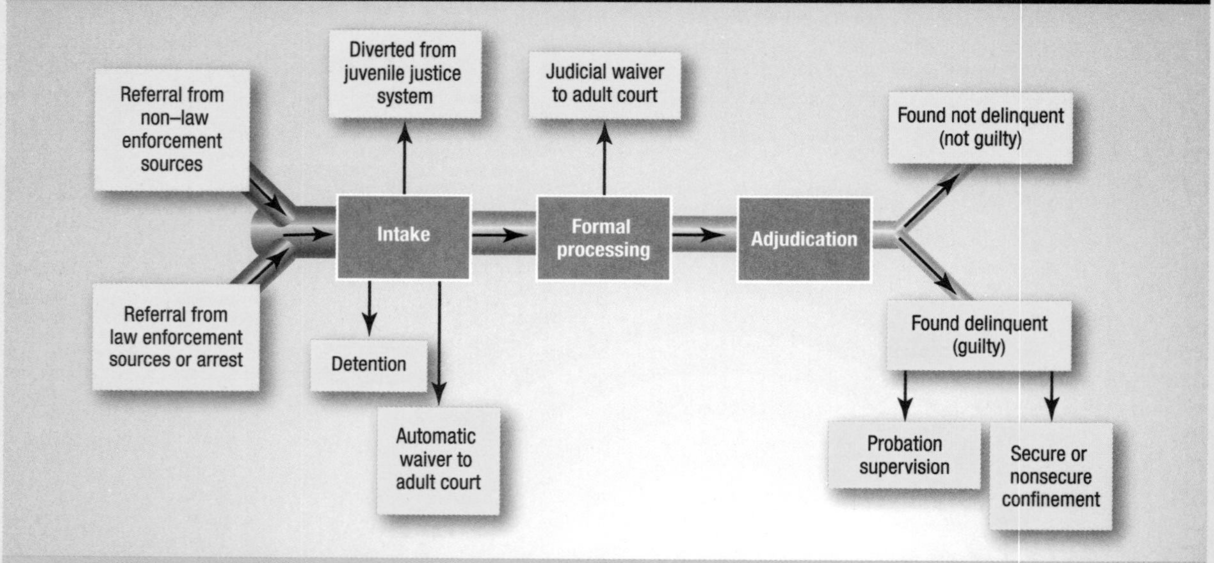

This diagram shows the possible tracks that a young person may take after her or his first contact with the juvenile justice system (usually a police officer).

Source: Office of Juvenile Justice and Delinquency Prevention.

13-6 HOW ARE JUVENILES TRIED AND PUNISHED?

Adjudicatory Hearing The process through which a juvenile court determines whether there is sufficient evidence to support the initial petition. (p. 282)

Aftercare The variety of therapeutic, educational, and counseling programs made available to juvenile delinquents after they have been released from a correctional facility. (p. 286)

Boot Camp A variation on traditional shock incarceration in which juveniles (and some adults) are sent to secure confinement facilities modeled on military basic training camps. (p. 285)

Disposition Hearing A hearing in which the juvenile judge or officer decides the appropriate punishment for a youth found to be delinquent or a status offender. (p. 282)

Graduated Sanctions A continuum of disposition options used in juvenile corrections with the goal of ensuring that the juvenile's punishment matches the wrongdoing in severity. (p. 283)

Predisposition Report A report prepared during the disposition process that provides the judge with relevant background material to aid in the disposition decision. (p. 283)

Residential Treatment Program A government-run facility for juveniles whose offenses are not deemed serious enough to warrant incarceration in a training school. (p. 284)

Training Schools A correctional institution for juveniles found to be delinquent or status offenders. (p. 285)

14-1 **Outline the three major reasons why the Internet is conducive to the dissemination of child pornography.** The Internet provides (a) a quick way to transmit child pornography from providers to consumers; (b) security, such as untraceable e-mails and password-protected websites and chat rooms; and (c) anonymity for buyers and sellers of child pornography.

14-2 **Define *malware*, and identify the main way in which worms differ from viruses and Trojans.** *Malware* is a general term that describes any program or file that is harmful to a computer or a computer user. Worms can spread autonomously—that is, they do not require a human act to move from computer to computer. Viruses and Trojans require user intervention, such as a user's clicking on a corrupted file, to be installed on a target computer.

14-3 **Summarize the three federal laws that have been particularly influential on our nation's counter-terrorism strategies.** (a) The Foreign Intelligence Surveillance Act (FISA) laid the groundwork for electronically monitoring national security threats. (b) The Antiterrorism and Effective Death Penalty Act (AEDPA) prohibited the provision of material support to foreign terrorist organizations. (c) The Patriot Act greatly strengthened the ability of law enforcement agents to investigate and prosecute suspected terrorists.

14-4 **Explain how background checks, in theory, protect the public from firearm-related violence.** Any person who wants to buy a firearm from a federally licensed dealer must go through an application process that includes a background check. This process is designed to keep firearms out of the hands of individuals who are deemed safety risks. Consequently, a person will fail the background check—and have the gun purchase denied—if he or she exhibits any one of a number of dangerous tendencies, including showing signs of mental illness, having a felony conviction, being addicted to illegal drugs, or engaging in domestic violence.

14-5 **Indicate some of the ways that white-collar crime is different from violent or property crime.** A wrongdoer committing a "regular" crime usually uses physical means to get somewhere he or she should not be in order to do something clearly illegal. Also, the victims of violent and property crimes are usually easily identifiable. In contrast, a white-collar criminal generally has legal access to the crime scene, where he or she is doing something seemingly legitimate. Furthermore, victims of white-collar crimes are often unknown or unidentifiable.

14-1 WHAT IS CYBER CRIME?

Botnet A network of computers that have been appropriated without the knowledge of their owners and used to spread harmful programs via the Internet. (p. 291)

Cyber Crime A crime that occurs online, in the virtual community of the Internet, as opposed to in the physical world. (p. 289)

Cyber Fraud Any misrepresentation knowingly made over the Internet with the intention of deceiving another and on which a reasonable person would and does rely to his or her detriment. (p. 292)

Cyberattack An attempt to damage or disrupt computer systems or electronic networks operated by computers. (p. 295)

Cyberbullying To bully electronically by sending repeated, hurtful messages via texting or the enternet (p. 294)

Cyberstalking The crime of stalking committed in cyberspace through the use of e-mail, text messages, or other forms of electronic communication. (p. 294)

Data Breach The illegal appropriation of protected or confidential information. (p. 292)

FIGURE 14.1 FRAUDULENT ACTIVITY ON THE INTERNET

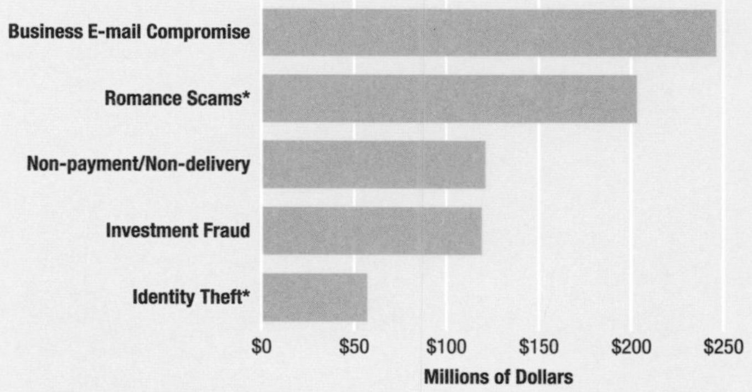

Business E-mail Compromise: Victims, mostly businesses, are instructed via e-mail to redirect invoice payments to nonexistent suppliers.

Non-payment/Non-delivery: Victims are scammed at e-commerce websites; either (1) goods and services are shipped, and payment is never rendered, or (2) payment is sent, and goods and services are never received.

Investment Fraud: Deceptive practices that convince victims to make investments or purchases (such as for real estate) on the basis of false information, usually promising a large return with minimal financial risk.

*Described in the text.

In its most recent annual report on cyber crime, the Internet Crime Complaint Center highlighted five "frequently reported Internet crimes." These crimes, along with the annual total losses reported by their victims, are detailed above.

Source: Internet Crime Complaint Center, *IC3 2015 Internet Crime Report* (Glen Allen, Va.: National White Collar Crime Center, 2016), 16, 226–230.

14 Today's Challenges in Criminal Justice

14-1 WHAT IS CYBER CRIME? (CONTINUED)

Encryption The translation of computer data into a secret code with the goal of protecting that data from unauthorized parties. (p. 296)

Hack The illegal use of one computer system to gain access to another computer system and steal or manipulate the data in the targeted system. (p. 291)

Identity Theft The theft of personal information, such as a person's name, driver's license number, or Social Security number. (p. 292)

Intellectual Property Property resulting from intellectual, creative processes. (p. 293)

Phishing Sending an unsolicited e-mail that falsely claims to be from a legitimate organization in an attempt to acquire sensitive information from the recipient. (p. 293)

Spam Bulk e-mails, particularly of commercial advertising, sent in large quantities without the consent of the recipient. (p. 293)

Trojan Malware that appears to be beneficial to a computer user, but causes damage to the computer when it is installed and activated. (p. 291)

True Threat An act of speech or expression that is not protected by the First Amendment because it is done with the intention of placing a specific victim or group of victims in fear of unlawful violence. (p. 294)

Virus A computer program that can replicate itself and interfere with the normal use of a computer. A virus cannot exist as a separate entity and must attach itself to another program to move through a network. (p. 291)

Worm A computer program that can automatically replicate itself and interfere with the normal use of a computer. A worm does not need to be attached to an existing file to move from one network to another. (p. 291)

14-2 HOW IMPORTANT IS PRIVACY IN THE AGE OF TERRORISM?

Material Support The act of helping a terrorist organization by engaging in any of a wide range of activities, including providing financial support, training, and expert advice or assistance. (p. 299)

National Security Letters Legal notices that compel the disclosure of customer records held by banks, telephone companies, Internet service providers, and other companies to the federal government. (p. 299)

Patriot Act Legislation that has greatly expanded the ability of government agents to monitor and apprehend suspected terrorists. (p. 299)

Surveillance The close observation of a person or group by government agents, in particular to uncover evidence of criminal or terrorist activities. (p. 298)

14-3 WHAT IS THE DEBATE OVER GUN CONTROL?

Background Check An investigation of a person's history to determine whether that person should be, for example, allowed to legally purchase a firearm. (p. 303)

Gun Control Efforts by a government to regulate or control the sale of guns. (p. 303)

14-4 WHAT IS WHITE-COLLAR CRIME?

Compliance The state of operating in accordance with governmental standards. (p. 306)

Corporate Violence Physical harm to individuals or the environment that occurs as the result of corporate policies or decision making. (p. 306)

Regulation A governmental order or rule having the force of law that is usually implemented by an administrative agency. (p. 306)

FIGURE 14.4 WHITE-COLLAR CRIMES

Embezzlement
Embezzlement is a form of employee fraud in which an individual uses his or her position within an organization to *embezzle*, or steal, the employer's funds, property, or other assets. Pilferage is a less serious form of employee fraud in which the individual steals items from the workplace.

Tax Evasion
Tax evasion occurs when taxpayers underreport (or do not report) their taxable income or otherwise purposely attempt to evade a tax liability.

Credit-Card Fraud
Credit-card fraud involves obtaining credit-card numbers through a variety of schemes (such as stealing them from the Internet) and using the numbers for personal gain.

Mail and Wire Fraud
This umbrella term covers all schemes that involve the use of mail, radio, television, the Internet, or a telephone to intentionally deceive in a business environment.

Securities Fraud
Securities fraud covers illegal activity in the stock market. Stockbrokers who steal funds from their clients are guilty of securities fraud, as are those who engage in *insider trading*, which involves buying or selling securities on the basis of information that has not been made available to the public.

Bribery
Also known as *influence peddling*, bribery occurs in the business world when somebody within a company or government sells influence, power, or information to a person outside the company or government who can benefit. A county official, for example, could give a construction company a lucrative county contract to build a new jail. In return, the construction company would give some of the proceeds, known as a *kickback*, to the official.

Consumer Fraud
This term covers a wide variety of activities designed to defraud consumers, from selling counterfeit art to offering "free" items, such as electronic devices or vacations, that include a number of hidden charges.

Insurance Fraud
Insurance fraud involves making false claims in order to collect insurance payments. Faking an injury in order to receive payments from a workers' compensation program, for example, is a form of insurance fraud.